Lecture Notes in Computer Science 16055

Founding Editors

Gerhard Goos
Juris Hartmanis

Editorial Board Members

Elisa Bertino, *Purdue University, West Lafayette, IN, USA*
Wen Gao, *Peking University, Beijing, China*
Bernhard Steffen, *TU Dortmund University, Dortmund, Germany*
Moti Yung, *Columbia University, New York, NY, USA*

The series Lecture Notes in Computer Science (LNCS), including its subseries Lecture Notes in Artificial Intelligence (LNAI) and Lecture Notes in Bioinformatics (LNBI), has established itself as a medium for the publication of new developments in computer science and information technology research, teaching, and education.

LNCS enjoys close cooperation with the computer science R & D community, the series counts many renowned academics among its volume editors and paper authors, and collaborates with prestigious societies. Its mission is to serve this international community by providing an invaluable service, mainly focused on the publication of conference and workshop proceedings and postproceedings. LNCS commenced publication in 1973.

Vincent Nicomette · Abdelmalek Benzekri ·
Nora Boulahia-Cuppens · Jaideep Vaidya
Editors

Computer Security – ESORICS 2025

30th European Symposium
on Research in Computer Security
Toulouse, France, September 22–24, 2025
Proceedings, Part III

 Springer

Editors
Vincent Nicomette
INSA Toulouse
Toulouse, France

Abdelmalek Benzekri
Université Toulouse- Paul Sabatier
Toulouse, France

Nora Boulahia-Cuppens
Polytechnique Montreal
Montreal, QC, Canada

Jaideep Vaidya
Rutgers University
Newark, NJ, USA

ISSN 0302-9743 ISSN 1611-3349 (electronic)
Lecture Notes in Computer Science
ISBN 978-3-032-07893-3 ISBN 978-3-032-07894-0 (eBook)
https://doi.org/10.1007/978-3-032-07894-0

© The Editor(s) (if applicable) and The Author(s), under exclusive license to Springer Nature Switzerland AG 2026

This work is subject to copyright. All rights are solely and exclusively licensed by the Publisher, whether the whole or part of the material is concerned, specifically the rights of translation, reprinting, reuse of illustrations, recitation, broadcasting, reproduction on microfilms or in any other physical way, and transmission or information storage and retrieval, electronic adaptation, computer software, or by similar or dissimilar methodology now known or hereafter developed.

The use of general descriptive names, registered names, trademarks, service marks, etc. in this publication does not imply, even in the absence of a specific statement, that such names are exempt from the relevant protective laws and regulations and therefore free for general use.

The publisher, the authors and the editors are safe to assume that the advice and information in this book are believed to be true and accurate at the date of publication. Neither the publisher nor the authors or the editors give a warranty, expressed or implied, with respect to the material contained herein or for any errors or omissions that may have been made. The publisher remains neutral with regard to jurisdictional claims in published maps and institutional affiliations.

This Springer imprint is published by the registered company Springer Nature Switzerland AG
The registered company address is: Gewerbestrasse 11, 6330 Cham, Switzerland

If disposing of this product, please recycle the paper.

Preface

It is our great pleasure to welcome you to the thirtieth edition of the European Symposium on Research in Computer Security (ESORICS 2025). This symposium was founded to further the progress of research in computer, information and cyber security and in privacy, by establishing a European forum for bringing together researchers in this area, by promoting the exchange of ideas with system developers and by encouraging links with researchers in related areas.

Since its inception in 1990, ESORICS has been hosted in a series of European countries and has established itself as the premiere European research event in computer security. Starting biannually in 1990 in Toulouse, the symposium has been held annually since 2002. We are delighted to welcome you to the 30th edition of the symposium in Toulouse, where it was first held.

As one of the longest-running reputable conferences focused on security research, ESORICS 2025 attracted numerous high-quality submissions from all over the world, with authors affiliated with diverse academic, non-profit, governmental, and industrial entities. After two rounds of submissions, each followed by an extensive reviewing period, we wound up with an excellent program, covering a broad range of timely and interesting topics. A total of 605 unique submissions were received: 150 in the first round and 475 in the second (of which 20 were invited resubmissions). Three to four reviewers per submission in a single-blind review driven by selfless and dedicated PC members (and external reviewers) collectively did an amazing job providing thorough and insightful reviews. Some PC members even "went the extra mile" by reviewing more than their share. The end result was 100 accepted submissions: 10 and 90, in the first and second rounds, respectively – giving an overall acceptance rate of 16.52%.

The ESORICS 2025 technical program was organized into 27 tracks held in 3 parallel sessions as well as 3 impressive keynote talks by internationally prominent and active researchers across academia and industry: Carlos Aguilar, Pierangela Samarati, and V. S. Subrahmanian. The program testifies to the level of excellence and stature of ESORICS.

Putting together ESORICS 2025 was a team effort. We would like to express our sincere gratitude to:

- Authors and contributors: without high-quality submissions from the authors, the success of the conference would not have been possible.
- PC members and additional reviewers: for the effort they put into the evaluation and high-quality in-depth reviews.
- Organization Chairs: Denise Gross from ICO, Justine Praneuf from LAAS-CNRS, Charlotte Sébastien from Université de Toulouse, and Tifanny Vest from Université de Toulouse for all of their efforts in organizing the conference and managing all of the logistics.
- Publicity Chairs: Paria Shirani from the University of Ottawa, Canada, Wenjuan Li from Hong Kong Polytechnic University, China, and Sebastien Bardin from Software

Safety and Security Lab, CEA, France, for their efforts in spreading the word about ESORICS 2025.
- Web Chairs: Charlotte Sébastien from Université de Toulouse and Tifanny Vest from Université de Toulouse for their efforts and continuous and quick updates of the website.
- Workshops Chair Romain Laborde from IRIT, Université de Toulouse for handling the workshops organization and being involved in other organizational aspects.
- Sponsor Chair Giorgia Macilotti from Airbus Protect for helping to arrange sponsorship for the symposium.
- The ESORICS Steering Committee and in particular, the Steering Committee Chair Joaquin Garcia-Alfaro for providing advice with numerous organizational issues.
- Easychair for providing an excellent conference management system.

In closing, we believe that ESORICS 2025 was an overall success and we hope that all attendees enjoyed the symposium and their stay in Toulouse, France.

July 2025

Vincent Nicomette
Abdelmalek Benzekri
Nora Boulahia-Cuppens
Jaideep Vaidya

Organization

General Chairs

Vincent Nicomette — LAAS-CNRS, INSA de Toulouse, France
Abdelmalek Benzekri — IRIT, Université de Toulouse, France

Program Chairs

Nora Boulahia-Cuppens — Polytechnique Montréal, Canada
Jaideep Vaidya — Rutgers University, USA

Publicity Chairs

Paria Shirani — University of Ottawa, Canada
Wenjuan Li — Education University of Hong Kong, China
Sebastien Bardin — CEA, France

Organization Chairs

Denise Gross — ICO, France
Justine Praneuf — LAAS-CNRS, France
Charlotte Sébastien — Université de Toulouse, France
Tifanny Vest — Université de Toulouse, France

Workshops Chair

Romain Laborde — IRIT, Université de Toulouse, France

Sponsor Chair

Giorgia Macilotti — Airbus Protect, France

Web Chairs

Charlotte Sébastien   Université de Toulouse, France
Tifanny Vest   Université de Toulouse, France

Steering Committee

Joachim Biskup   University of Dortmund, Germany
Frédéric Cuppens   Polytechnique Montréal, Canada
Sabrina De Capitani di Vimercati   Università degli Studi di Milano, Italy
Joaquin Garcia-Alfaro (Chair)   Institut Polytechnique de Paris, France
Dieter Gollmann   Hamburg University of Technology, Germany
Sushil Jajodia   George Mason University, USA
Sokratis Katsikas   Norwegian University of Science and Technology, Norway
Mirek Kutyłowski   Wrocław University of Technology, Poland
Javier Lopez   Universidad de Málaga, Spain
Jean-Jacques Quisquater   Université catholique de Louvain, Belgium
Peter Y. A. Ryan   University of Luxembourg, Luxembourg
Pierangela Samarati   Università degli Studi di Milano, Italy
Einar Snekkenes   Norwegian University of Science and Technology, Norway
Michael Waidner   Technische Universität Darmstadt, Germany
Edgar Weippl   University of Vienna & SBA Research, Austria

Program Committee

Andrea Agiollo (Round 2)   TU Delft, The Netherlands
Massimiliano Albanese   George Mason University, USA
Cristina Alcaraz   University of Málaga, Spain
Abdelrahaman Aly   Technology Innovation Institute, United Arab Emirates
Shengwei An (Round 2)   Virginia Tech, USA
Hafiz Asif (Round 2)   Hofstra University, Rutgers University, USA
Mikael Asplund   Linköping University, Sweden
Vijay Atluri   Rutgers University, USA
Daniel Augot (Round 1)   Inria Saclay, France
Samiha Ayed (Round 2)   Université de technologie de Troyes, France
Sebastien Bardin   CEA LIST, France
Alessandro Barenghi   Politecnico di Milano, Italy

Ken Barker (Round 1)	University of Calgary, Canada
Giampaolo Bella (Round 2)	University of Catania, Italy
Abdelmalek Benzekri	Université de Toulouse, France
Elisa Bertino	Purdue University, USA
Clara Bertolissi (Round 2)	Aix-Marseille University, France
Bruhadeshwar Bezawada (Round 2)	Southern Arkansas University, USA
Smriti Bhatt (Round 2)	Purdue University, USA
Giuseppe Bianchi (Round 2)	University of Rome "Tor Vergata", Italy
Alex Biryukov	University of Luxembourg, Luxembourg
Jorge Blasco (Round 1)	Universidad Politécnica de Madrid, Spain
Carlo Blundo	Università degli Studi di Salerno, Italy
Tamara Bonaci (Round 2)	Northeastern University, USA
Rainer Böhme (Round 2)	University of Innsbruck, Austria
Pino Caballero-Gil	University of La Laguna, Spain
Maurantonio Caprolu (Round 2)	King Abdullah University of Science and Technology, Saudi Arabia
Xavier Carpent	University of Nottingham, UK
Aldar C.-F. Chan (Round 2)	University of Hong Kong, China
Bo Chen (Round 2)	Michigan Technological University, USA
Rongmao Chen (Round 2)	National University of Defense Technology, China
Xiaofeng Chen (Round 2)	Xidian University, China
Yuan Cheng (Round 2)	University of Nottingham Ningbo China, China
Sherman S. M. Chow (Round 2)	Chinese University of Hong Kong, China
Pietro Colombo (Round 2)	Università dell'Insubria, Italy
Michal Choras (Round 1)	Bydgoszcz University of Science and Technology, Poland
Mauro Conti	University of Padua, Italy
Bruno Crispo (Round 2)	University of Trento, Italy
Michel Cukier (Round 2)	University of Maryland, USA
Frédéric Cuppens	Polytechnique Montréal, Canada
Tooska Dargahi	Manchester Metropolitan University, UK
Saptarshi Das (Round 2)	Pennsylvania State University, USA
Sabrina De Capitani di Vimercati	Universita' degli Studi di Milano, Italy
Hervé Debar	Télécom SudParis, France
Jose Maria De Fuentes (Round 1)	Universidad Carlos III de Madrid, Spain
Soumyadeep Dey (Round 2)	IIT Kharagpur, India
Roberto Di Pietro (Round 2)	King Abdullah University of Science and Technology, Saudi Arabia
Tassos Dimitriou (Round 2)	Kuwait University, Kuwait
Xuhua Ding (Round 1)	Singapore Management University, Singapore

Josep Domingo-Ferrer — Universitat Rovira i Virgili, Spain
Andreas Ekelhart (Round 1) — Secure Business Austria, Austria
Santiago Escobar (Round 2) — Universitat Politècnica de València, Spain
David Espes (Round 2) — Université de Bretagne Ouest, France
Shuya Feng (Round 2) — University of Connecticut, USA
Anna Lisa Ferrara — Università degli studi del Molise, Italy
Josep Lluís Ferrer Gomila (Round 2) — Universitat de les Illes Balears, Spain
Philip W. L. Fong (Round 2) — University of Calgary, Canada
Olga Gadyatskaya — University of Leiden, The Netherlands
Debin Gao — Singapore Management University, Singapore
Joaquin Garcia-Alfaro — Institut Polytechnique de Paris, France
Essam Ghadafi — Newcastle University, UK
Giorgio Giacinto — University of Cagliari, Italy
Alberto Giaretta (Round 1) — Örebro Universitet, Sweden
Dieter Gollmann — Hamburg University of Technology, Germany
Lorena González Manzano — Universidad Carlos III de Madrid, Spain
Dimitris Gritzalis (Round 1) — Athens University of Economics & Business, Greece
Stefanos Gritzalis (Round 2) — University of Piraeus, Greece
Maanak Gupta (Round 2) — Tennessee Tech University, USA
M. Emre Gursoy (Round 2) — Koç University, Turkey
Gregory Gutin (Round 2) — Royal Holloway, University of London, UK
Hannes Hartenstein (Round 2) — Karlsruhe Institute of Technology, Germany
Hongxin Hu (Round 2) — University at Buffalo, SUNY, USA
Xinyi Huang (Round 2) — Fujian Normal University, China
Hugo Jonker — Open University of the Netherlands, The Netherlands
Sokratis Katsikas — Norwegian University of Science and Technology, Norway
Stefan Katzenbeisser — University of Passau, Germany
Jörg Keller — FernUniversität in Hagen, Germany
Latifur Khan (Round 2) — University of Texas at Dallas, USA
Hiroaki Kikuchi — Meiji University, Japan
Hyoungshick Kim (Round 2) — Sungkyunkwan University, South Korea
Ram Krishnan (Round 2) — University of Texas at San Antonio, USA
Marina Krotofil — Maersk, Switzerland
Christopher Kruegel (Round 2) — University of California Santa Barbara, USA
Alptekin Küpçü — Koç University, Turkey
Romain Laborde — Université de Toulouse, France
Peeter Laud — Cybernetica AS, Estonia
Maryline Laurent — Télécom SudParis, France

Zeyu Lei (Round 2) — Purdue University, USA
Shujun Li (Round 2) — University of Kent, UK
Wenting Li (Round 2) — Peking University, China
Jun Li (Round 2) — University of Oregon, USA
Kaitai Liang — Delft University of Technology, The Netherlands
Hoon Wei Lim (Round 2) — NCS Group, Singapore
Dan Lin (Round 2) — Vanderbilt University, USA
Peng Liu (Round 2) — Pennsylvania State University, USA
Giovanni Livraga — University of Milan, Italy
Valeria Loscri — Inria, France
Wenjing Lou (Round 2) — Virginia Tech, USA
Rongxing Lu (Round 2) — Queen's University, Canada
Haibing Lu (Round 2) — Santa Clara University, USA
Xiapu Luo (Round 2) — Hong Kong Polytechnic University, China
Eduard Marin — Telefónica Research, Spain
Jean-Yves Marion — Université de Lorraine, France
Fabio Martinelli (Round 2) — IIT-CNR, Italy
Amir Masoumzadeh (Round 2) — University at Albany - SUNY, USA
Barbara Masucci — University of Salerno, Italy
Wojciech Mazurczyk — Warsaw University of Technology, Poland
David Megías — Universitat Oberta de Catalunya, Spain
Weizhi Meng — Lancaster University, UK
Donika Mirdita (Round 2) — Fraunhofer Secure Information Technology, Germany
Chris Mitchell (Round 2) — Royal Holloway, University of London, UK
Barsha Mitra (Round 2) — BITS Pilani Hyderabad Campus, India
Sudip Mittal (Round 2) — Mississippi State University, USA
Meisam Mohammady (Round 2) — Iowa State University, USA
Haralambos Mouratidis (Round 2) — University of Essex, UK
Guillermo Navarro-Arribas — Autonomous University of Barcelona, Spain
Jianting Ning (Round 2) — Singapore Management University, Singapore
Antonino Nocera — University of Pavia, Italy
Gabriele Oligeri — Hamad Bin Khalifa University, Qatar
Melek Önen (Round 2) — EURECOM, France
Philippe Owezarski — LAAS-CNRS, France
Balaji Palanisamy (Round 2) — University of Pittsburgh, USA
Stefano Paraboschi (Round 2) — Università di Bergamo, Italy
Sikhar Patranabis (Round 2) — IBM Research India, India
Günther Pernul (Round 2) — Universität Regensburg, Germany
Josef Pieprzyk — CSIRO/Data61, Australia
Joachim Posegga — University of Passau, Germany
Mir Mehedi Pritom (Round 2) — Tennessee Tech University, USA

Megha Quamara (Round 2) — King's College London, UK
Silvio Ranise (Round 2) — University of Trento, Italy
Kai Rannenberg (Round 2) — Goethe University Frankfurt, Germany
Siddharth Prakash Rao (Round 2) — Nokia Bell Labs, Finland
Danda B. Rawat (Round 2) — Howard University, USA
Indrakshi Ray (Round 1) — Colorado State University, USA
Indrajit Ray (Round 2) — Colorado State University, USA
Peter Rønne — University of Luxembourg, Luxembourg
Carlos Rubio Medrano (Round 2) — Texas A&M University, USA
Peter Y. A. Ryan — University of Luxembourg, Luxembourg
Reihaneh Safavi-Naini — University of Calgary, Canada
Pierangela Samarati — Università degli Studi di Milano, Italy
Neetesh Saxena — Cardiff University, UK
Neta Rozen-Schiff (Round 2) — Hebrew University of Jerusalem, Israel
Dominique Schröder — Universität Erlangen-Nürnberg, Germany
Jörg Schwenk — Ruhr-Universität Bochum, Germany
Savio Sciancalepore — Eindhoven University of Technology, The Netherlands
R. Sekar (Round 2) — Stony Brook University, USA
Basit Shafiq (Round 2) — Lahore University of Management Sciences, Pakistan
Ankit Shah (Round 2) — Indiana University, USA
Siamak Shahandashti — University of York, UK
Alessandro Sorniotti (Round 1) — IBM Research Europe, Switzerland
Shantanu Sharma (Round 2) — New Jersey Institute of Technology, USA
Wenbo Shen (Round 2) — Zhejiang University, China
Weidong Shi (Round 2) — University of Houston, USA
Arunesh Sinha (Round 2) — Rutgers University, USA
Jayesh Soni (Round 2) — Florida International University, USA
Angelo Spognardi — Sapienza Università di Roma, Italy
Riccardo Spolaor — Shandong University, China
Natalia Stakhanova (Round 2) — University of Saskatchewan, Canada
Thorsten Strufe (Round 2) — Karlsruhe Institute of Technology, Germany
Wenhai Sun (Round 2) — Purdue University, USA
Shamik Sural (Round 2) — Indian Institute of Technology Kharagpur, India
Luis Suárez (Round 2) — Ericsson, Canada
Qiang Tang (Round 2) — University of Sydney, Australia
Nadia Tawbi — Laval University, Canada
Vicenc Torra — Umeå University, Sweden
Jacob Torrey (Round 2) — Thinkst Applied Research, USA
Ari Trachtenberg (Round 2) — Boston University, USA
Stacey Truex (Round 2) — Denison University, USA

Jalaj Upadhyay (Round 2) — Johns Hopkins University, USA
Tobias Urban (Round 2) — Westphalian University of Applied Sciences, Germany
Daniele Venturi — Sapienza University of Rome, Italy
Rakesh Verma (Round 2) — University of Houston, USA
Tran Viet Xuan Phuong (Round 2) — University of Arkansas at Little Rock, USA
Joao P. Vilela (Round 2) — University of Porto, Portugal
Di Wang (Round 2) — State University of New York at Buffalo, USA
Haining Wang (Round 2) — Virginia Tech, USA
Cong Wang (Round 2) — City University of Hong Kong, China
Xinyue Wang (Round 2) — Renmin University of China, China
Lingyu Wang (Round 2) — Concordia University, Canada
Han Wang (Round 2) — University of Kansas, USA
Wenqi Wei (Round 2) — Fordham University, USA
Edgar Weippl — University of Vienna, Austria
Avishai Wool (Round 1) — Tel Aviv University, Israel
Christos Xenakis (Round 2) — University of Piraeus, Greece
Yang Xiang (Round 2) — Swinburne University of Technology, Australia
Yue Xiao (Round 2) — IBM Research, USA
Shouhuai Xu (Round 2) — University of Colorado Colorado Springs, USA
Runhua Xu (Round 2) — Beihang University, China
Peng Xu (Round 2) — Huazhong University of Science and Technology, China

Guomin Yang (Round 2) — Singapore Management University, Singapore
Zhihao Yao (Round 2) — New Jersey Institute of Technology, USA
Roland Yap (Round 2) — National University of Singapore, Singapore
Miuyin Yong Wong (Round 2) — Georgia Institute of Technology, USA
Chuan Yue (Round 2) — Colorado School of Mines, USA
Stefano Zanero (Round 1) — Politecnico di Milano, Italy
Yuan Zhang (Round 2) — Fudan University, China
Zhikun Zhang (Round 2) — Zhejiang University, China
Kehuan Zhang (Round 2) — Chinese University of Hong Kong, China
Liang Zhao (Round 2) — Emory University, USA
Ziming Zhao (Round 2) — Northeastern University, USA
Yunlei Zhao (Round 2) — Fudan University, China
Jianying Zhou (Round 2) — Singapore University of Technology and Design, Singapore
Sencun Zhu (Round 2) — Pennsylvania State University, USA
Rui Zhu (Round 2) — Indiana University, USA

Additional Reviewers

Abbadini, Marco
Abdelgawad, Mahmoud
Abdullahi, Ahmed
Abu Jabal, Amani
Afzal, Zeeshan
Aghayarzadeh, Hamed
Agrawal, Anand
Ahmed, Basharat
Ahmed, Faisal
Akbar, Khandakar Ashrafi
Akbarzadeh, Aida
Al Kadri, Mhd Omar
Al Mahmud, Tamim
Alborch Escobar, Ferran
Alhaidari, Abdulrahman
Allami, Ali
Almani, Dimah
Almasan, Paul
Almutaitri, Abeer
Amaral Simões, Sancho
Arazzi, Marco
Armanuzzaman, Md
Arriaga, Afonso
Arrus, Aurora
Aryal, Kshitiz
Aung, Yan Lin
Avizheh, Sepideh
Azizli, Elmaddin
Bacho, Renas
Baecker, Ruben
Bashir, Shadaab Kawnain
Belguith, Sana
Benaloh, Josh
Beneš, Martin
Beretta, Michele
Berlato, Stefano
Bertrand, Léo
Bertrand, Simon
Bezawada, Bruhadeshwar
Bianchi, Federica
Binosi, Lorenzo
Binte Haq, Hina
Birashk, Amin
Biswas, Chinmoy
Bisways, Chinmoy
Boyapally, Harishma
Carlson, Trevor E.
Carminati, Michele
Carvalho, Tânia
Casagrande, Marco
Castiglione, Arcangelo
Castiglione, Gianpietro
Catuogno, Luigi
Cecconello, Stefano
Charlès, Alex
Chaturvedi, Bhuvnesh
Chawla, Abhimanyu
Chekole, Eyasu Getahun
Chen, Depeng
Chen, Juntao
Chen, Yumin
Chen, Zeyu
Chong, Chun Jie
Chouchoulis, Ioannis
Chu, Hien Thi Thu
Cihangiroglu, Mert
Cimato, Stelvio
Collu, Matteo Gioele
Cui, Hui
Cunha, Mariana
Dai, Jiongyu
Dai, Xushu
Daneshmand, Arash
Dang, Hai-Van
Das, Debayan
Das, Prajit Kumar
Das Chowdhury, Partha
Daudén-Esmel, Cristòfol
Deidda, Nicola
Demetrio, Luca
Demir, Nurullah
Demirkiran, Ferhat
Dey, Kunal
Di Gennaro, Marco
Di Paolo, Edoardo
Ding, Weikang

Dipta, Debopriya Roy
Dolati, Mahdi
Donadel, Denis
Droll, Jan
Du, Linkang
Du, Minxin
Duck, Gregory
Dunbar, Arthur
Eichhammer, Philipp
Erinola, Nurullah
Esposito, Sergio
Facchinetti, Dario
Fadavi, Mojtaba
Falanji, Reyhane
Falebita, Oluwatosin
Faraj, Omair
Farasat, Talaya
Feng, Hanwen
Ferrari, Stefano
Ferré-Queralt, Joan
Flamini, Andrea
Fotiadis, Georgios
Fouotsa, Tako Boris
Galeazzi, Alessandro
Gao, Yang
Garbelini, Matheus
García Díaz, Jorge Francisco
García Fernández, Pablo
George, Aleena Elsa
Ghorbel, Bassem
Ghosh, Soumyadyuti
Giannakopoulos, Thrasyvoulos
Giapantzis, Konstantinos
Gimenez, Pierre-François
Glas, Magdalena
Golinelli, Matteo
Gomes, Catarina
Gowdanakatte, Shwetha
Grill, Johannes
Grisafi, Michele
Groszschaedl, Johann
Grundmann, Matthias
Guiot, Miquel
Guo, Jinduo
Gupta, Deepti

Haefner, Kyle
Haffar, Rami
Haffey, Preston
Hamm, Peter
Hamm And Lieberknecht, Two Subreviewers Peter And Ann-Kristin
Han, Qiang
Han, Yanni
Haque, Md Shahedul
Hassanpour, Seyedeh Bahereh
Herranz, Javier
Hopkins, Jacob
Hore, Soumyadeep
Hosseini, Henry
Hou, Chenxi
Howard, Samuel
Hu, Chengcong
Huang, Mengdie
Huang, Qiqing
Huang, Zhicheng
Huso, Ingrid
Ibarrondo, Alberto
In, Junbeom
Ioannidis, Thodoris
Irfan, Muhammad
Jacob, Florian
Jacqmin, Quentin
Jiang, Shan
Jiang, Yuning
Jin, Heng
Jorba, Josep
Kaaniche, Nesrine
Kammueller, Florian
Kanpak, Halil Ibrahim
Karim Imtiaz
Katsis Charalampos
Kei, Andes Y. L.
Kembu, Vignesh Kumar
Kermabon-Bobinnec, Hugo
Kern, Sascha
Khan, Younas
Kimm, Hanke
Koffas, Stefanos
Koohpayeh Araghi, Tanya
Korichi, Youcef

Kouko, Gildas
Kumar, Gulshan
Kumari, Komal
Kunwar, Pradip
Lalande, Jean-Francois
Lara, Carlos
Laura Madison, Axel Durbet
Le Mouel, Florian
Leinweber, Marc
Lerch-Hostalot, Daniel
Li, Adrian Shuai
Li, Fagen
Li, Xiang
Li, Xiaoguo
Li, Yamin
Li Calsi, Davide
Liang, Yu
Ligier, Damien
Lin, Chao
Litzinger, Sebastian
Liu, Gaoxiang
Liu, Jiahao
Liu, Jianghua
Loh, Jia-Chng
Lombard-Platet, Marius
Longo, Riccardo
Lopez Morales, Efren
Lotto, Alessandro
Luchini, Chiara
Luo, Nanqing
Lybarger, Kevin
Löbner, Sascha
Ma, Jack P. K.
Ma, Jinhua
Ma, Wanlun
Ma, Zheyuan
Maehren, Marcel
Maffei, Ivo
Maitra, Sudip
Makropodis, Ioannis
Maldonado, Mark
Manzanares-Salor, Benet
Martins, Óscar
Marty, Pierre
Massidda, Emmanuele

McCarthy, Andrew
Meadows, Catherine
Meng, Qiaoran
Mercer, Rebekah
Merzdovnik, Georg
Michaud, Quentin
Mishra, Nimish
Mishra, Sagar
Mitra, Shaswata
Mohammadi, Sareh
Mondragon, Jennifer
Mostafiz, Mir Imtiaz
Mura, Raffaele
Müller, Mathis
Nagasubramaniam, Piyush
Nath, Souradip
Nelson, Jonathan
Neudert, Raphael
Nguyen, Hieu
Nicolazzo, Serena
Niknia, Ahad
Niow, Choon Hock
Noble, Daniel
P., Vinod
Palihawadana, Chamath
Pan, Ying-Yu
Panebianco, Francesco
Panja, Somnath
Patel, Raj
Paudel, Diwas
Persiano, Giuseppe
Pimpinella, Giovanni
Podder, Rakesh
Praharaj, Lopamudra
Preatoni, Riccardo
Psychogyiou, Aikaterini
Pucher, Michael
Puchta, Alexander
Pérez-Ramos, Edgar
Qiu, Tian Qu, Jiashu
Quadrio, Giacomo
Quinci, Arianna
Qureshi, Amna
Raciti, Mario
Rasul, Md Fazle

Regano, Leonardo
Reijsbergen, Daniel
Rizzi, Matteo
Rosenblattl, Jakob
Rossi, Matthew
Roy, Shovan
Russo, Luigi
Saadi Dadmarzi, Hamidreza
Sacchetta, Juri
Saha, Rahul
Samdaliri, Mahya
Sanna, Alessandro
Saqlain, Sabbir Ahmed
Sato, Shingo
Sauger, Gabriel
Senn, Judith
Serra-Ruiz, Jordi
Sha, Kailun
Shafir, Lior
Shahriar, Md Hasan
Sharif, Amir
Shen, Zilin
Shepherd, Carlton
Shi, Shanghao
Siemer, Jan Niklas
Singh, Animesh
Singh, Gurjot
Sinha, Sayani
Skandylas, Charilaos
Skrobot, Marjan
Song, Yongcheng
Song, Zirui
Soria-Comas, Jordi
Spadafora, Chiara
Spiesberger, Patrick
Srivastava, Gautam
Stifter, Nicholas
Streicher, Klaus
Stylianou, Ioannis
Sun, Shihua
Sözen Esen, Derya
Thomas, Julian
Thomas, Tony
Tian, Guohua
Tian, Jianwen

Tippe, Pascal
Todd, James
Torabi, Sadegh
Tripathi, Himanshu
Trombetta, Alberto
Tsado, Yakubu
Tuck, Bryan
Tureček, Philip
Udovenko, Aleksei
Valeriani, Lorenzo
Vasilopoulos, Dimitrios
Wan, Guoan
Wang, Cheng-Long
Wang, Hongxiao
Wang, Jingzhe
Wang, Lulu
Wang, Shuo
Wang, Wenli
Wang, Xinhai
Wang, Yuyu
Wazan, Ahmad Samer
Wen, Tian
Wong, Harry W. H.
Wu, Jiaojiao
Wu, Pengfei
Xie, Xinhong
Xu, Chenming
Xu, Difei
Xu, Peng
Xu, Shengmin
Xue, Haiyang
Yan, Yingfei
Yang, Fan
Yang, Yang
Yang, Zeyu
Yin, Zihao
Younas, Affan
Yu, Chia-Mu
Yu, Hexuan
Yu, Tianchi
Yuan, Quan
Yuan, Wei
Yuan, Yijun
Zari, Oualid
Zhang, Bokang

Zhang, Chaoyu
Zhang, Ke
Zhang, Zicheng
Zhao, Rui

Zhou, Ming
Zhu, Rui
Zhu, Xiaogang
Özfatura, Kerem

Contents – Part III

QUIC-Fuzz: An Effective Greybox Fuzzer For The QUIC Protocol 1
  Kian Kai Ang and Damith C. Ranasinghe

Systematic Assessment of Cache Timing Vulnerabilities on RISC-V
Processors 23
  Cédrick Austa, Jan Tobias Mühlberg, and Jean-Michel Dricot

No Root, No Problem: Automating Linux Least Privilege and Securing
Ansible Deployments 43
  *Eddie Billoir, Romain Laborde, Daniele Canavese, Yves Rütschlé,
  Ahmad Samer Wazan, and Abdelmalek Benzekri*

NICraft: Malicious NIC Firmware-Based Cache Side-Channel Attack 64
  Amit Choudhari, Shorya Kumar, and Christian Rossow

Identifying Potential Timing Leakages from Hardware Design
with Precondition Synthesis 84
  Minu Chung and Hyungon Moon

LibAFLStar: Fast and State-Aware Protocol Fuzzing 105
  *Cristian Daniele, Timme Bethe, Marcello Maugeri, Andrea Continella,
  and Erik Poll*

PUSH for Security: A PUF-Based Protocol to Prevent Session Hijacking 124
  Emiliia Geloczi, Nico Mexis, and Stefan Katzenbeisser

Hardening HSM Clusters: Resolving Key Sync Vulnerabilities for Robust
CU Isolation 144
  Sarat Chandra Prasad Gingupalli

AcouListener: An Inaudible Acoustic Side-Channel Attack on AR/VR
Systems 164
  Fengliang He, Hong-Ning Dai, Hanyang Guo, Xiapu Luo, and Jiadi Yu

Verifying DRAM Addressing in Software 184
  *Martin Heckel, Florian Adamsky, Jonas Juffinger, Fabian Rauscher,
  and Daniel Gruss*

Epistemology of Rowhammer Attacks: Threats to Rowhammer Research Validity 204
  Martin Heckel, Hannes Weissteiner, Florian Adamsky, and Daniel Gruss

Personalized Password Guessing via Modeling Multiple Leaked Credentials of the Same User 224
  Fugeng Huang, Jiahong Yang, Haibo Cheng, Wenting Li, and Ping Wang

WelkIR: Flow-Sensitive Pre-trained Embeddings from Compiler IR for Vulnerability Detection 243
  Hao Huang, Xiuwei Shang, Junqi Zhang, Shaoyin Cheng, Weiming Zhang, and Nenghai Yu

Edge Coverage Feedback of Embedded Systems Fuzzing Based on Debugging Interfaces 263
  Weihua Jiao, Qingbao Li, Xilong Li, Zhifeng Chen, Weiping Yao, Guimin Zhang, and Fei Cao

Cache Demote for Fast Eviction Set Construction and Page Table Attribute Leakage 283
  Taehun Kim, Hyerean Jang, and Youngjoo Shin

WaitWatcher and WaitGuard: Detecting Flush-Based Cache Side-Channels Through Spurious Wakeups 303
  Lukas Lamster, Fabian Rauscher, Martin Unterguggenberger, and Stefan Mangard

T-Time: A Fine-Grained Timing-Based Controlled-Channel Attack Against Intel TDX 323
  Woomin Lee, Taehun Kim, Seunghee Shin, Junbeom Hur, and Youngjoo Shin

Unraveling DoH Traces: Padding-Resilient Website Fingerprinting via HTTP/2 Key Frame Sequences 342
  Baiyang Li, Yujia Zhu, Yuedong Zhang, Qingyun Liu, and Li Guo

NLSaber: Enhancing Netlink Family Fuzzing via Automated Syscall Description Generation 361
  Lin Ma, Xingwei Lin, Ziming Zhang, and Yajin Zhou

The Hidden Dangers of Public Serverless Repositories: An Empirical Security Assessment 382
  Eduard Marin, Jinwoo Kim, Alessio Pavoni, Mauro Conti, and Roberto Di Pietro

CapMan: Detecting and Mitigating Linux Capability Abuses at Runtime to Secure Privileged Containers 402
Alireza Moghaddas Borhan, Hugo Kermabon-Bobinnec, Lingyu Wang, Yosr Jarraya, and Suryadipta Majumdar

Digital Twin for Adaptive Adversary Emulation in IIoT Control Networks 423
Javier Parada, Cristina Alcaraz, Javier Lopez, Juan Caubet, and Rodrigo Román

Formal Security Analysis of ss2DNS 443
Ali Sadeghi Jahromi, AbdelRahman Abdou, and Paul C. van Oorschot

High-Efficiency Fuzzing Technique Using Hooked I/O System Calls for Targeted Input Analysis 464
Wenju Sun, Xi Xiao, Qiben Yan, Guangwu Hu, Qing Li, and Chuan Chen

VeriFLo: Verifiable Provenance with Fault Localization for Inter-Domain Routing 484
Utku Tefek, Ertem Esiner, Felix Kottmann, and Deming Chen

The Polymorphism Maze: Understanding Diversities and Similarities in Malware Families 505
Antonino Vitale, Simone Aonzo, Savino Dambra, Nanda Rani, Lorenzo Ippolito, Platon Kotzias, Juan Caballero, and Davide Balzarotti

End-to-End Non-profiled Side-Channel Analysis on Long Raw Traces 526
Jintong Yu, Yuxuan Wang, Shipei Qu, Yubo Zhao, Yipeng Shi, Pei Cao, Xiangjun Lu, Chi Zhang, Dawu Gu, and Cheng Hong

Author Index 545

QUIC-Fuzz: An Effective Greybox Fuzzer For The QUIC Protocol

Kian Kai Ang[✉] and Damith C. Ranasinghe[✉]

University of Adelaide, Adelaide, Australia
{kiankai.ang,damith.ranasinghe}@adelaide.edu.au

Abstract. Network applications are routinely under attack. We consider the problem of developing an effective and efficient fuzzer for the recently ratified QUIC network protocol to uncover security vulnerabilities. QUIC offers a *unified* transport layer for low latency, reliable transport *streams* that is *inherently* secure, ultimately representing a complex protocol design characterised by new features and capabilities for the Internet. Fuzzing a *secure transport layer* protocol is not trivial. The interactive, strict, rule-based, asynchronous nature of communications with a target, the stateful nature of interactions, security mechanisms to protect communications (such as integrity checks and encryption), and inherent overheads (such as target initialisation) challenge *generic* network protocol fuzzers. We discuss and address the challenges pertinent to fuzzing transport layer protocols (like QUIC), developing mechanisms that enable fast, effective fuzz testing of QUIC implementations to build a prototype *grey-box* mutation-based fuzzer—QUIC-Fuzz. We test 6, *well-maintained* server-side implementations, including from Google and Alibaba with QUIC-Fuzz. The results demonstrate the fuzzer is both highly effective and generalisable. Our testing uncovered **10 new** security vulnerabilities, precipitating 2 CVE assignments thus far. In code coverage, QUIC-Fuzz outperforms other existing state-of-the-art network protocol fuzzers—Fuzztruction-Net, ChatAFL, and ALFNet—with up to an 84% increase in code coverage where QUIC-Fuzz outperformed *statistically significantly* across all targets and with *a majority of bugs* only discoverable by QUIC-Fuzz. We open-source QUIC-Fuzz on GitHub https://github.com/QUICTester/QUIC-Fuzz.

Keywords: QUIC · Network Protocol Fuzzing · Network Security

1 Introduction

QUIC is a *secure* transport layer protocol *optimised* for performance. It currently provides transport layer services for HTTP/3. QUIC establishes *inherently* secure communication channels, ensuring message confidentiality, integrity, and availability for Internet applications over UDP while also providing a reliable transport layer service. Effectively, the protocol design aims to reduce the latency and connection overheads associated with the use of TLS [10] over TCP for secure transport [28]. However, the services provided by QUIC differ from TCP and TLS over TCP and include the ability to have data available before a secure handshake is completed, the possibility of multiple simultaneous streams, and the provision of five different security levels for connections. Importantly, network applications provide external facing interfaces to the world, making them a common attack vector for adversaries to exploit. Given QUIC's role in various Internet applications—driven largely by its use in HTTP/3—implementation bugs within QUIC can severely affect the security and quality of Internet applications.

Despite research to advance fuzzing and its proven effectiveness at uncovering vulnerabilities by automatically generating and injecting inputs to test software systems, adopting fuzzing techniques to test network protocols is not straightforward. Recent efforts have led to methods to address inherent challenges facing fuzz testing network protocols [6,25,27], including the investigation of LLMs to automate fuzzing processes, such as generating test sequences [24]. However, many of these techniques and tools have been developed to test application-layer protocols, leaving transport layer protocols (such as QUIC), which provide reliable and secure services, relatively under-explored. This is because testing secure transport layer protocols such as QUIC poses unique challenges.

Challenges.

C1 Input Integrity and Interpretability. First, secure services in QUIC are built with features to support five different security levels. Cryptographic operations and checksums support security services, such as authentication and message confidentiality. Consequently, a fuzzer must account for the negotiated encryption secrets and cryptographic techniques when generating mutated inputs to exercise deeper functionality, code, and states. Current state-of-the-art replay-based fuzzers [6,27,29] apply direct mutations to recorded messages, corrupting encrypted messages and compromising message integrity. Such inputs fail integrity checks and are not meaningfully interpreted at a target; instead, are simply discarded without further processing. This impacts the *effectiveness* of the fuzzer.

C2 Non-determinism. Second, QUIC is *complex* and *unique*. It provides secure and reliable services with a holistic protocol. QUIC implementations optimise performance to manage reliable and secure service paths while servicing multiple clients setting up multiple streams with endpoints—and fuzzing such a protocol introduces non-deterministic behaviours at a target that can hinder making incremental fuzzing progress. For instance, when a target receives the same input at different time intervals influenced by factors—such as the resource scheduling and timeouts used in reliable data transfer—the target may exercise a different code path. Therefore, fuzzers may not be able to reliably use the same test case to reach a previously observed, interesting state that would allow mutation-guided input generation methods to make incremental progress. This can impact the *effectiveness* of the fuzzer by impeding its ability to explore deeper code and new protocol states.

C3 Test Execution Overhead. Third, in fuzz testing, the need to spawn a new target instance for every fuzz test introduces a significant initialisation overhead when dealing with network protocol implementations. These overheads can include loading the shared libraries, loading and parsing configuration files, and initialising cryptographic primitives. The overhead significantly impacts testing *efficiency*; the test case executions per second.

Our Work. QUIC's growing prominence motivates us to address these challenges to build an *effective* and *efficient* fuzzer for testing the IETF-ratified QUIC implementations capable of uncovering software bugs and potential security vulnerabilities. To this end, we design and build QUIC-FUZZ—a grey-box mutation-based fuzzer that: i) performs mutations on recorded encrypted QUIC messages without breaking their integrity, ii) enables fast synchronous communication with the target to address barriers to fuzzing progress from non-deterministic behaviours, and iii) mitigates the target initialisation overhead.

In particular, we developed a QUIC-specific cryptographic module to strategically decrypt and re-encrypt messages within the fuzzer's workflow, allowing the fuzzer to modify the actual message content while preserving message integrity. To minimise non-deterministic behaviour at the target, we integrate a synchronisation protocol to serialise communication between the fuzzer and the target. Effectively ensuring every event triggered by the same test case occurs in the same order at the target. Then, we integrate a snapshot protocol to determine when to capture a pre-initialised target state, which can be restored at the start of each fuzzing iteration to remove the initialisation overhead. In this study, we focus on fuzz testing the more impactful server-side implementations of QUIC because the same protocol library is used by clients and servers while server failures affect multiple active connections, as in DoS attacks.

Contributions. We summarise the contributions made in this work as follows:

- We propose QUIC-FUZZ, a grey-box fuzzer for QUIC.
- To enable effective mutations on encrypted and integrity-protected QUIC messages, we develop a QUIC-specific cryptographic module. To increase fuzzing efficiency: i) we integrate a synchronisation protocol to allow fast synchronous communication between the fuzzer and the target, then ii) a snapshot protocol, to determine strategic locations to save server state to reduce target initialisation overheads.
- We open-source QUIC-FUZZ at https://github.com/QUICTester/QUIC-Fuzz.

Findings. We have used QUIC-FUZZ to test 6 publicly available, well-maintained QUIC servers—including Google and Alibaba (as listed in Table 4)—to assess the fuzzer's effectiveness and help contribute to improving the security and robustness of QUIC implementations as well as the safety of end-users.

- Thus far, QUIC-FUZZ has uncovered 10 bugs with a *bug bounty award* and two CVE assignments.

– Importantly, the state-of-the-art baseline fuzzers discovered only four of the bugs found by QUIC-FUZZ in ten executions over the course of 48-hour-long fuzzing campaigns.

Responsible Disclosure. Following the practice of responsible disclosure, we shared our findings with corresponding development teams by sending bug reports to either vendors or developers in accordance with their reporting policies. We summarise the current state of disclosures and vendor responses in Table 1.

2 Network Protocol Fuzzing Primer

We provide a brief overview of the QUIC protocol handshake to understand the process of secure connection establishment (our focus) and recent optimisations for ALFNET, Snapfuzz, and then delve into our framework in Sect. 3.

2.1 QUIC

An entity using QUIC must complete a handshake with its endpoints before it can communicate. Unlike TLS over TCP, where the negotiation of transport and cryptographic parameters is performed separately, QUIC combines transport and cryptographic parameter negotiations into a single handshake using *packets*, *frames* and *messages* defined in [17, Section 12.4] carrying different data types. To simplify our explanations, we refer to the frames and messages encapsulated within the frames—such as CRYPTO frames—as simply *messages*.

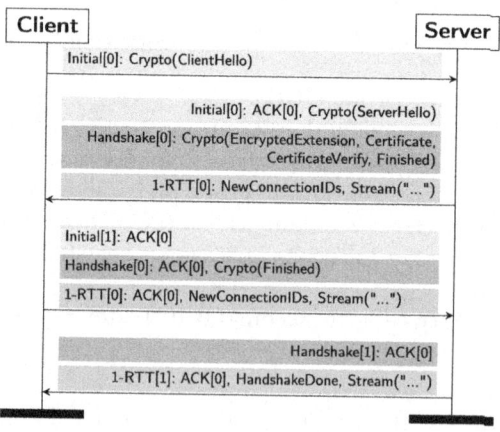

Fig. 1. QUIC *Basic* handshake with Initial, Handshake and 1-RTT packets. Packet numbers for are inside the square brackets.

QUIC Handshake. QUIC provides **five** different security configurations, namely: i) Basic (illustrated in Fig. 1); ii) Client address validation without client authentication; iii) Client authentication without address validation ; iv) Client address validation and authentication; and v) Handshake with a pre-shared key. We illustrate the Basic handshake in Fig. 1. At the beginning, a client sends the server an Initial packet with a ClientHello message containing application protocol negotiation, transport parameters, and the cryptographic information required to perform the key exchange. The server continues the handshake with an Initial packet and a Handshake packet. The Initial packet contains a ServerHello message containing the cryptographic information needed to complete the secret exchange. The Handshake packet carries an EncryptedExtensions message that contains transport parameters and the negotiated application protocol version, a Certificate message that contains the server's certificate, a CertificateVerify message that is used to request that the client verify the server's certificate, and a Finished message that carries verify_data, a keyed hash computed using the handshake secret combined with the *transcript hash* of all the previous TLS messages exchanged. For example, in Fig. 1, the server uses the *transcript hash* comprising ClientHello, ServerHello, EncryptedExtensions, the server's Certificate, and the server's CertificateVerify messages.

Once a server sends the Finished message, it can transmit application data using the Stream frame in 1-RTT packets. The client continues the handshake by verifying the server's certificate and the verify_data in the server's Finished message for authentication, key confirmation, and handshake integrity. The client then computes its verify_data using the handshake secret combined with the *transcript hash* that includes all TLS messages exchanged until the server's Finished message. The client includes the verify_data in its Finished message and sends it to the server. Similarly, the server verifies the verify_data in the client's Finished message for authentication, key confirmation, and handshake integrity. Following the successful verification of the verify_data, the server sends the client a 1-RTT packet with a HandshakeDone message to indicate that the handshake is confirmed and the QUIC connection established. Notably, in contrast to TLS over TCP relying on IP addresses and port numbers, a QUIC connection is identified by a set of connection ID s. Further connection ID s for use post-handshake are exchanged through the NewConnectionID messages.

2.2 Snapfuzz for ALFNet

Snapfuzz [3] proposes an optimisation framework for ALFNET [27]. ALFNET is a grey-box mutation-based fuzzer specifically designed for stateful network protocols. Effectively, ALFNET operates as the client application and directs its generated inputs in a sequence through network sockets (e.g. TCP/IP, UDP/IP) to the target. The inputs are generated by mutating a seed (sequences of recorded message exchanges between a client and server). In contrast to traditional fuzzers, ALFNET introduces the concept of using the SUT's state feedback to guide the fuzzing process. It uses a modified form of edge coverage combined with state awareness to efficiently identify interesting inputs that alter the control flow of the target application to help explore new code and states.

Snapfuzz framework features two important components: i) transforming slow asynchronous network communications between a fuzzer and a target into fast synchronous communication to eliminate synchronisation delays and ii) automatically deferring the creation of the Forkserver (responsible for spawning a new target instance for fuzzing) until the latest possible safe point. Snapfuzz implements these ideas with binary re-writing techniques to intercept `read()` and `write()` type syscalls to redirect them to custom system call handlers.

We adopt the Snapfuzz-ALFNET framework to address the pertinent challenges associated with fuzzing QUIC. Importantly, we address the limitations of current frameworks to build an *efficient* and *effective* fuzzer for QUIC targets.

3 QUIC-FUZZ Design

Our mutation-based grey box fuzzer, QUIC-FUZZ, integrates three key components to address the challenges discussed in Sect. 1:

1. QUIC-specific Cryptographic Module to generate integrity-protected inputs.
2. Synchronisation Protocol to reduce delays and synchronise communication between the fuzzer and the target.
3. Snapshot Protocol to automate saving server state at strategic locations to reduce server initialisation overhead.

In this section, we discuss how the design addresses fuzzing challenges **C1**-**C3**; Fig. 2 presents an overview of QUIC-FUZZ and the fuzzing loop.

C1 **Input Integrity and Interpretability.** A Basic QUIC connection involves three different encryption levels for secure communication. At each encryption level, the client and server use the respective keys for encryption, encoding, and checksums. If either peer fails to validate an incoming protected message, the message is discarded without further processing.

The same principle applies to fuzzing: If the generated input cannot be recognised as an integrity-protected message, it is discarded before exercising interesting functionality. However, replay-based fuzzers (e.g. ALFNET) apply direct mutations to the seed (encrypted messages recorded during normal communication), do not alter actual content, and consequently invalidate the integrity of the generated input. In addition, fuzzers like ALFNET rely on the target's responses as feedback to guide state exploration. Because the responses from the QUT (QUIC Under Test) are also encrypted, the fuzzer cannot effectively extract detailed state information. The only information the fuzzer can collect and use as state feedback is the packet type, an unprotected field in the packet header. However, the packet type alone is insufficient for accurately inferring the QUT's state. This is because packets of the same type can carry different content. For example, an Initial packet can carry either a PING, a CRYPTO, or a CONNECTION_CLOSE frame. These roadblocks limit the effectiveness of a replay-based fuzzer, including inhibiting its ability to exercise deeper protocol codes and states.

Methods for Resolving C1. We design a QUIC-specific Cryptographic Module to manage all cryptographic operations on the inputs and responses. Recall that the seed contains sequences of messages exchanged in a previous QUIC session. Before entering the fuzzing loop, the module decrypts the seed the user

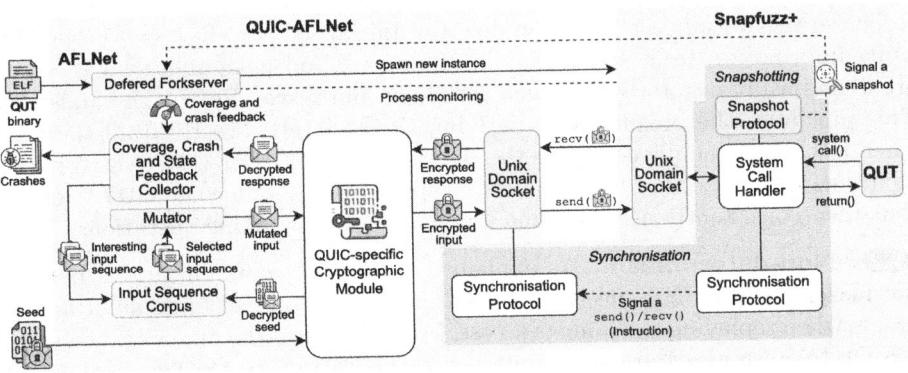

Fig. 2. An overview of QUIC-FUZZ. The QUIC-specific Cryptographic Module enables the fuzzer (in our prototype, ALFNet) to generate integrity-protected inputs. The Synchronisation Protocol allows synchronous communication between the fuzzer and the target (QUT) to address issues arising from non-determinism and delays impacting fuzzing throughput. The Snapshot Protocol determines a strategic location to save state to reduce server initialisation overhead.

provides. The fuzzer then stores the decrypted input sequence as plain text in the Input Sequence Corpus. Because the input is now in plaintext, the fuzzer can safely mutate it without compromising the seed's integrity.

To ensure the QUT receives integrity-protected inputs, the module attempts to encrypt the input before sending it to the QUT. Notably, the encryption process may fail, particularly when the mutated packet structure is malformed. In such cases, the fuzzer opts to send the mutated input without encryption. This action is acceptable because unencrypted inputs are unlikely to be favoured in subsequent input scheduling if they do not contribute to uncovering new state or coverage. Consequently, it provides useful feedback to guide the fuzzer. In addition, the module decrypts all responses from the QUT, allowing the fuzzer to extract valuable state information to accurately infer the QUT's state.

However, to decrypt a seed, the cryptographic module requires the same secrets from the previous connection because the seed contains sequences of messages exchanged in a previous QUIC session. Further, the QUIC-specific Cryptographic Module and the QUT must use the same secret for encryption. If they do not share the same secret, the encrypted inputs sent by the fuzzer would be rejected by the QUT as invalid, and the fuzzer would be unable to decrypt and analyse the QUT's responses. We employ the following methods to ensure that the cryptographic module and the QUT maintain the same secrets as those used during seed generation for Initial, Handshake, and 1-RTT encryption levels.

As mentioned in [33, Section 5.2], any QUIC peer (including the QUT) can derive the Initial secret using `HKDF-Extract` with a default salt value and the Destination Connection ID (DCID) from the client's first Initial packet header. Therefore, we have designed the cryptographic module to perform the same operation as the QUT, extracting the DCID from the first packet in the seed to derive the Initial secret. But, unlike the Initial secret, which can be derived using information from the packet header, the Handshake and 1-RTT secrets are dynamically negotiated between the client and server during the handshake. This precludes the possibility of deriving these secrets directly from the seed. Therefore, we manually configure the Handshake and 1-RTT secrets used during seed generation into the QUIC-specific Cryptographic module and QUT to ensure that they consistently use the same secrets for cryptographic operations.

C2 Non-determinism. As explained in Sect. 1, communications between the fuzzer and the QUT need to be synchronised to prevent non-deterministic events when replaying the same test case. For example, if the fuzzer acknowledges the QUT's response too early while the response remains in flight or fails to acknowledge the QUT's response in time, the QUT executes a different path to re-transmit the response. This is expected, especially in protocols that provide reliable data transfer, such as QUIC.

A simple mitigation is setting a user-specified timeout to wait for the QUT's response before sending the next input. But, the response may still arrive after the timeout expires. Further, such a solution sees each fuzzing iteration send a sequence of inputs and wait for a timeout after each input, with the delays significantly reducing the fuzzing throughput. In our ablation studies (see Sect. 5.5), we demonstrate the impact of eliminating these delays in QUIC-FUZZ.

Methods for Resolving C2. We adopt a Synchronisation Protocol to coordinate communication between QUIC-FUZZ and the QUT. Specifically, the protocol monitors the send-and-receive operations on the QUT and signals appropriate instructions to the fuzzer. For example, when the QUT begins to receive data, the Synchronisation Protocol signals the fuzzer to send an input. Similarly, when the QUT performs a send operation, the protocol signals the fuzzer to receive the QUT's response. Notably, applying the Synchronisation Protocol eliminates the need for manual timeout settings.

C3 Test Execution Overhead. QUIC servers often require a long initialisation phase—we observed $\sim$ 1 to 30 ms periods across the QUTs we tested—before a target is ready to accept a connection. The initialisation process includes time for parsing configuration files, loading shared libraries, configuring security features, setting transport parameters, and binding to a network socket. Repeating this process in each iteration introduces significant overheads to fuzz testing a target and reduces the fuzzing throughput, that is, the fuzzer's *efficiency*.

Methods for Resolving C3. When initialising the Forkserver, we integrate a Snapshot Protocol to monitor the QUT initialisation process via its system calls. Effectively, we determine when the QUT is ready to accept a connection and signal the Forkserver to capture a snapshot of the QUT. Subsequently, the Forkserver can spawn new QUT instances directly from the snapshot in each fuzzing iteration to remove the initialisation overhead.

4 Implementation

The QUIC-FUZZ prototype features two key components: QUIC-AFLNet and Snapfuzz+. QUIC-AFLNet extends ALFNET (commit ver 6d86ca0c) with the integration of our QUIC-Specific Cryptography Module. Snapfuzz+ implements our modifications to Snapfuzz (commit ver ef005157), to realise the Synchronisation and Snapshot Protocols. Table 5 in the Appendix summarises the implementation effort. Here, we describe key aspects of our implementation.

4.1 QUIC-AFLNet

We follow ALFNET guidelines to implement the functions required to parse QUIC input and response sequences. These functions are used to: i) identify the offset of each input in an input sequence stored in an array and ii) extract state feedback from the QUT response. Notably, these functions can handle both encrypted and decrypted message sequences depending on whether the QUIC-specific Cryptographic Module is enabled. In the following, we discuss implementing the QUIC-specific Cryptographic Module.

QUIC-Specific Cryptographic Module. The module's encryption and decryption process follows the description in [33, Section 5], with its implementation using helper functions from the OpenSSL-3.0.2 [1] library. It supports testing the QUT with TLS1.3 mandatory cipher suite, `TLS_AES_128_GCM_SHA256`.

Seed Corpus. Notably, as with ALFNET, QUIC-FUZZ saves interesting seeds with a minor modification. When the QUIC-AFLNet identifies an interesting input that leads to a crash, new coverage, or state, it saves *both* the unencrypted input and the respective secrets used for encryption in the results folder. This is important for future mutations of the seed and also enables users to reproduce QUT execution using the saved input for further analysis.

4.2 Snapfuzz+

We adopt the Snapfuzz framework (see Sect. 2.2) and its implementation. We extend Snapfuzz's binary re-writing support with our System Call Handle module by implementing the system call handling necessary for QUIC server implementations. Minimising initialisation overhead requires identifying the latest safe point at which to signal the deferred Forkserver to snapshot a target. Our synchronisation protocol extension support the server implementation paradigms employed by QUIC developers. In the following, we briefly detail the modifications made to Snapfuzz to support fuzzing QUIC servers.

System Call Handler. The QUIC implementations we test rely on an extended set of system calls. In particular, we add support for the following system calls families: `epoll_create()`, `epoll_ctl()`, `epoll_wait()` `recvmsg()`, `recvmmsg()`, `sendmsg()`, and `sendmmsg()`.

```
1  static int run_server(int fd){
2    while(1){
3      // ...
4      struct msghdr mess = {
5        // allocate buffers to store
6        // incoming datagram
7      };
8      ssize_t ret = recvmsg(fd, &mess, 0);
9      if(ret > 0){
10       // process datagram
11     }
12     for (i = 0; i != num_conns; ++i){
13       // send datagram
14     }
15   }
16 }
```

Listing 1. Example of a QUIC *receive-send* server main loop.

```
1  static int run_server(int fd){
2    while(1){
3      // ...
4      while(1){
5        struct msghdr mess = {
6          //allocate buffers to store
7          //incoming datagrams
8        };
9        ssize_t ret = recvmsg(fd, &mess, 0);
10       if(ret == -1)
11         break;
12       //process datagram
13     }
14     for(i = 0; i != num_conns; ++i){
15       //send datagram
16     }
17   }
18 }
```

Listing 2. Example of a QUIC *receive-break-send* server main loop.

Synchronisation Protocol. We extended the synchronisation protocol in Snapfuzz to support the implementation paradigms in QUIC server implementations.

In general, we identified two QUIC server implementation methods. We illustrate these methods in code Listings 1 and 2. QUIC implementations employing Listing 1 will always check whether there is data to transmit (line 12–14) after calling a `recvmsg()` (line 8). The existing synchronisation protocol in Snapfuzz assumes such a design—the server consistently operates in a sequential receive and send order. In contrast, the implementation logic abstracted in code Listing 2 repeatedly calls `recvmsg()` (lines 4–13) until it encounters an error (-1) in the last `recvmsg()` (line 11). This design choice ensures that the server fully processes all incoming data from the kernel receive buffer. When there is no more data to read, the kernel returns an error (-1) to inform the server that the receive operation will be blocked. At this point, the server enters the sending loop (line 14–16) to transmit its response. However, the existing synchronisation protocol always notifies the fuzzer to deliver input whenever the server invokes a `recvmsg()`. Consequently, such a server target always has fuzzing input to process and never has a chance to enter the sending loop (lines 14–16).

To support both paradigms, we extend the synchronisation protocol logic to account for the two design choices observed.

5 Evaluation

In this section, we conduct a series of extensive experiments to evaluate QUIC-FUZZ with other state-of-the-art grey-box network protocol fuzzers. These experiments aim to answer the following research questions:

1. How does QUIC-FUZZ perform compared to previous state-of-the-art network protocol fuzzers? (Branch coverage experiments in Sect. 5.2)
2. How does QUIC-FUZZ compare in bug-finding capability to previous state-of-the-art network protocol fuzzers? (Sect. 5.3 and 5.4)
3. How effective are the components and techniques? (Sect. 5.5)

To answer these questions, we benchmark the performance of the fuzzers based on coverage (we use branch coverage as in [7]). Next, we assess the bug-finding capabilities of the fuzzers by analysing the crashes identified in the first experiment to manually triage all unique bugs. Then, we assess the impact of the modules we develop on fuzzing performance using a branch coverage metric.

5.1 Experimental Setup

All of the experiments are run on an AMD Ryzen Threadripper 3990X CPU with 256 GB of RAM where one core is allocated per fuzzing instance.

We compare QUIC-FUZZ with three[1] state-of-the-art, open-source, grey-box fuzzers: FUZZTRUCTION-NET [7], CHATAFL [24], and ALFNET [27] (baseline). These are selected for the following reasons: i) FUZZTRUCTION-NET outperformed other grey-box fuzzers (SGFUZZ [6] and STATEALF [25]) in fuzzing secure protocols; ii) CHATAFL is a concurrent work not included in the FUZZTRUCTION-NET benchmark and represents the first fuzzer to employ an LLM in network protocol fuzzing; iii) ALFNET serves as a baseline since ours is built on top of ALFNET whilst also serving to support our ablations study; and iv) they are all open-sourced. All fuzzers are run with Address Sanitiser enabled to detect bugs that do not result in a crash (all configuration settings are in Appendix A.1).

QUIC Server Targets (QUTs). We select *publicly* available and *well-maintained* QUIC servers for our evaluations. We summarise the servers we selected in Table 4. We test 6 QUIC implementations written in C/C++. These include Google-quiche from Google, XQUIC from Alibaba, and LSQUIC from Lite Speed Technologies. For replay-based fuzzers (QUIC-FUZZ, CHATAFL, ALFNET), we patch static values for secrets, verification data, connection IDs, and packet numbers in the QUTs to eliminate non-determinism caused by ephemeral values.

5.2 Coverage Experiments

Coverage results are reported in Figure 3. In summary, QUIC-FUZZ outperforms all others and we can observe an increase in branch coverage of up to 84%. Further, Table 6 (in Appendix) shows that QUIC-FUZZ achieves *median* code coverage improvements that are statistically significant across

---

[1] We also considered Bleem [22], which is not publicly available, and contacted the authors to request source code for benchmarking, we have not received a reply.

all targets compared to the ALFNET and CHATAFL. We observe significant improvements in 5 out of 6 targets compared to FUZZTRUCTION-NET.

To evaluate the effectiveness of a fuzzer, we use code coverage metrics to provide a quantitative comparison. We conduct a fuzzing campaign that involves running each fuzzer for 48 h for each of the 6 targets shown in Table 4. To remove randomness, we conduct ten trials [20] of each experiment.

Generally, we observe that both ALFNET and CHATAFL saturate coverage early and fail to explore new code to achieve higher coverage. As discussed in **C1** of Sect. 3, because CHATAFL and ALFNET apply mutations directly to the seed, most of the mutated inputs cannot pass integrity checks and are discarded without further processing. Consequently, these fuzzers are limited to exploring the functions that deal with unencrypted components of a packet and those with the correct integrity (the initial seed to the fuzzer). Further, CHATAFL and ALFNET do not synchronise fuzzing events, hence, performance is impacted by the non-determinism issues discussed in **C2**. As a result, the fuzzers cannot reliably re-use an interesting test cases to make incremental progress.

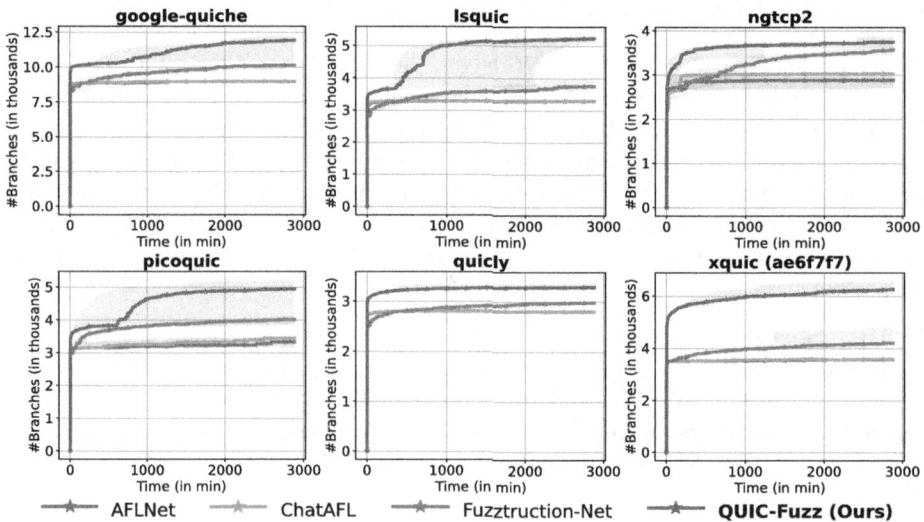

Fig. 3. The median branch coverage (in thousands) achieved by fuzzers in ten trials of 48-hour executions. The coloured area represents the best/worst coverage achieved by a fuzzer. Notably, we fuzzed two versions of Xquic (Alibaba), with the coverage reported here corresponding to the version we fuzzed before identifying the bugs we reported. The subsequent version (released with the fixes for the bug we identified) was found to contain a new bug, as Table 1 shows.

In contrast, FUZZTRUCTION-NET uses a QUIC client harness that can account for the negotiated encryption secrets when generating fuzz inputs. This harness effectively provides a built-in secure and liable transport layer with the QUT, mitigating the need to inject delays that characterises the poor performance of ALFNET and ChatALF while avoiding problems with non-determinism.

However, QUIC-FUZZ performs better than FUZZTRUCTION-NET in terms of coverage. During the experiment, the throughput of FUZZTRUCTION-NET was observed to be significantly lower (~ 0.20 executions per second) than that of QUIC-FUZZ (~ 25 executions per second). We attribute the performance difference to: i) the time needed to perform dynamic fault injection on the client harness, ii) the initialisation overhead of the QUT—which QUIC-FUZZ mitigates by employing a Snapshot Protocol—as well as the additional overhead of initialising the client harness (see **C3**), and iii) because the harness is effectively a complete client application and therefore expends time processing packets and their payloads, unlike QUIC-FUZZ, which is purpose-built for fuzzing.

Table 1. Overview of the software bugs discovered in the fuzzing campaign with QUIC-FUZZ. M11 is a known bug that is not addressed at the time of testing.

Server	Fault Description	Bug ID	Disclosed	Status
Picoquic	CVE-2024-45402: Double Free in Picotls when processing an unexpected public key length	M1	✓	Fixed
	NULL pointer dereference when copying data from a STREAM frame	M2	✓	Fixed
	Heap OOB read on a zero-sized heap when parsing a QPACK header	M3	✓	Fixed
	Null pointer dereference after failing to match a stream ID with an existing stream context	M4	✓	Fixed
Quicly	CVE-2024-45396: Assertion failure when processing an ACK frame in the draining stage	M5	✓	Fixed
Xquic (ae6f7f7)	NULL pointer dereference when handling a Stateless Reset packet on a destroyed connection	M6	✓	Fixed
	Stack OOB read when copying a string for logs	M7	✓	Fixed
	NULL pointer dereference when checking whether application data is available for reading or when handling the FIN bit in the byte stream	M8	✓	Fixed
	Heap OOB read when comparing an HTTP/3 header	M9	✓	Fixed
Xquic (6803065)	NULL pointer dereference when logging a Version Negotiation event	M10	✓	Fixed
Ngtcp2	Assertion failure when writing a CONNECTION_CLOSE frame using an unsupported cipher suite by the TLS library (known bug)	M11	✓	Fixed

5.3 Bug-Finding Capability and Case Studies

QUIC-FUZZ discovered 10 new security vulnerabilities (as summarised in Table 1). These discoveries have resulted in a bug bounty award and 2 CVE assignments thus far. We responsibly disclosed all vulnerabilities to the respective developers. We detail Proofs of Concept (PoCs) for reproducing bugs and bug *case studies* with bug *impact* discussions at our GitHub repo https://github.com/QUICTester/QUIC-Fuzz.

5.4 Bug Benchmark

As shown in Table 2, 6 out of 10 bugs can only be discovered by QUIC-FUZZ. In addition, QUIC-FUZZ triggers those bugs that can be found by at least two fuzzers more reliably and with significantly less time (see Figure 4).

Table 2. Unique bug benchmark study results from a fuzzing campaign of ten trials of 48-hour fuzzing runs.

Bug ID	AFLNet	ChatAFL	Fuzztruction-Net	QUIC-Fuzz
M1	0/10	0/10	6/10	5/10
M2	0/10	0/10	0/10	3/10
M3	0/10	0/10	0/10	2/10
M4	0/10	0/10	0/10	1/10
M5	0/10	0/10	10/10	10/10
M6	0/10	0/10	0/10	1/10
M7	0/10	0/10	3/10	10/10
M8	0/10	0/10	0/10	10/10
M9	0/10	0/10	0/10	2/10
M10	10/10	10/10	3/10	10/10
M11	0/10	0/10	2/10	9/10

To measure the bug-finding capability of QUIC-FUZZ with other fuzzers, we consider a bug-based benchmark and conduct two experiments. We manually triaged the crashes identified by all of the fuzzers during the coverage experiments in Sect. 5.2 and spent efforts to identify the unique bugs (new and known bugs) uncovered by each fuzzer. First, we use data to compare the probability of a unique bug being triggered within ten fuzzing trials. We summarise the results in Table 2. Second, to assess the efficiency of each fuzzer and the reliability of its bug-discovering capability, we adopt [34]'s approach, using the Kaplan-Meier estimator [19] to model the *survival function* of those bugs that are discovered by at least *two* of the fuzzers. We report the results in Fig. 4. We discuss the results in detail in the following sections.

Unique Bug Benchmark. As shown in Table 2, the second-best fuzzer, FUZZTRUCTION-NET, detected only 5 out of 11 of the bugs uncovered by QUIC-FUZZ. Overall, for three of the five common bugs uncovered by both QUIC-FUZZ and FUZZTRUCTION-NET, we can observe the probability of the bugs being discovered by QUIC-FUZZ to be significantly higher than FUZZTRUCTION-NET.

As expected, both ALFNet and CHATAFL perform poorly, indicating the need to address the challenges we described as well as the need for a protocol-specific fuzzer that is effective at discovering bugs. Interestingly, CHATAFL and ALFNET are able to discover one bug, **M10**. This particular bug can be triggered by mutating the version field in the Initial packet header. Notably, the version field starts at the second byte of the Initial packet and is unprotected. When a server observes a version it does not support, it immediately sends a Version Negotiation packet without further processing the remaining packet. Consequently, a mutation to a seed—as performed in ALFNET—can trigger **M10**, as we explain in Sect. 5.3.

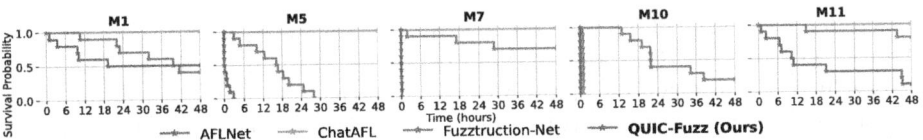

Fig. 4. Survival probability plots for the four bugs (M1, M5, M7, M10, M11 described in Table 1) found by at least two of the benchmark fuzzers within 48 h, as shown in Table 2. Only M10 is found by all of the fuzzers.

Survival Probability. Overall, QUIC-FUZZ can detect bugs more quickly and consistently than other fuzzers: it identifies three out of the five common bugs (**M5**, **M7**, and **M10**) with a 100% success rate within 4 h of fuzzing. In contrast, the second-best fuzzer, FUZZTRUCTION-NET, is guaranteed (100%) to find only one bug (**M5**) within 29 h of fuzzing.

Interestingly, QUIC-FUZZ, CHATAFL, and ALFNET can detect **M10** within 5 min in all ten trials (100% success). By comparison, FUZZTRUCTION-NET demonstrates only a 80% chance of triggering the bug within 48 h of fuzzing. We attribute this to i) the overheads impacting fuzzing throughput as we discussed in Sect. 5.2 and ii) the FUZZTRUCTION-NET scheduling algorithm, as explained in [7], also not favouring inputs that covers less code. This may prevent FUZZTRUCTION-NET from exercising code paths that do *not* involve cryptographic operations or deep functionality, where bugs like **M10** can reside.

Table 3. Median branch coverage after ten 48-hour runs with different modules enabled in QUIC-FUZZ. The modules are added from the left (AFLNet as the baseline) to the right (+Snapshot Protocol: the *full* version of QUIC-FUZZ). The percentages show the change in coverage compared to the previous configuration. Changes <0.1% are not displayed and statistically significant changes are marked in bold (based on a Mann-Whitney U test at a 0.05 significance level).

QUIC server	AFLNet (baseline)	+QUIC-specific Cryptographic Module	p-value	+Synchronisation Protocol	p-value	+Snapshot Protocol (QUIC-FUZZ)	p-value
Google-quiche	8984	10354 (**+15%**)	0.0002	11545 (**+12%**)	0.0058	11915 (+3%)	0.4405
Lsquic	3294	3584 (**+9%**)	0.0002	4724 (**+32%**)	0.0002	5238 (**+11%**)	0.0003
Ngtcp2	2881	3779 (**+31%**)	0.0002	3711 (-2%)	0.3447	3744 (+1%)	0.3447
Picoquic	3328	3805 (**+14%**)	0.0002	4891 (**+29%**)	0.0009	4940 (+1%)	0.6232
Quicly	2807	3260 (**+16%**)	0.0002	3291 (+1%)	0.0046	3291	0.7831
Xquic	3568	5784 (**+62%**)	0.0002	6211 (**+7%**)	0.0002	6262 (+1%)	0.3075

5.5 Effectiveness of QUIC-FUZZ Modules

We report the ablation study results in Table 3. We can observe each technique applied in QUIC-FUZZ is effective and contributes to improving performance, often the improvement is statistically significant.

To evaluate the effectiveness of the techniques within the three modules that we investigate using QUIC-FUZZ, we conduct three additional series of experiments, one for each module. Specifically, we run QUIC-FUZZ on all of the targets with different subsets of modules enabled and collect the resulting code coverage. We use ALFNET as our baseline. We begin with the configuration where only the QUIC-specific Cryptographic Module is activated. Then, we sequentially enable the Synchronisation Protocol and Snapshot Protocol. Notably, we evaluate whether each addition has a statistically significant impact on the branch coverage achieved by the fuzzer in ten trials. We report our results in Table 3 and defer the discussing the effectiveness of each module to Appendix A.3.

6 Discussion

In this section, we discuss the potential limitations of our design and provide insights for future research on fuzzing secure protocols.

Ephemeral Values. Manual configuration is needed in QUIC-FUZZ to address non-determinism that can emerge from ephemeral values, such as Connection IDs used in connections in QUIC over a UDP data stream. As explained in Sect. 5.1, these fields are patched with static values to ensure the QUT always uses the same values in each fuzzing iteration. Notably, FUZZTRUCTION-NET can remove this effort because the fault injection method employs a complete client application able to establish a secure connection with a target.

System Call Handler. QUIC-FUZZ does not currently support Rust servers (Neqo, Quiche, Quinn, S2n-quic). Fuzzing these additional servers—while meeting our selection criteria of being well maintained and publicly available—requires extending binary re-writing support for system calls within the System Call Handler to those used in the target list of servers. We leave this for future studies.

Grammar Aware Mutations. QUIC-FUZZ performs random mutations on decrypted packet content without considering packet structure and grammar. This suggests that one avenue for improving QUIC-FUZZ would involve enabling grammar-based mutations. Notably, CHATAFL demonstrates the effectiveness of such an approach for *non-secure* application layer protocols. However, in our adaptation of CHATAFL to fuzz QUIC, we observed that LLMs—specifically GPT3.5, which is used by CHATAFL—lack the ability to extract grammar when interpreting complex transport layer protocol messages, undermining their effectiveness for the task. This provides avenues for further exploration of the use of LLMs for fuzzing transport layer protocols.

7 Related Work

Our work investigates fuzzing for security testing QUIC. Here, we discuss related approaches for fuzzing QUIC and network protocol fuzzing, more generally.

QUIC Testing. Researchers have explored and developed testing methods to check the adherence of a QUIC implementation to its specification, for versions *before* [9,14,16,23,30] and after [4] its ratification by the IETF.

Protocol Fuzzing. In general, grey-box fuzzers for network protocols and applications [3,6,21,25,27,29,31] operate in a feedback-driven loop to generate fuzz input by mutating packets captured from previous network sessions. Recent CHATAFL [24], leverages pre-trained LLMs to perform grammar-aware mutations and predict the next input when testing *application layer* protocols to generate more effective inputs. Other than grey-box fuzzing, there are approaches to fuzz test network protocols, such as black-box fuzzing [12,13,15,18,22,36], symbolic executions [8,26,32] and grammar-based fuzzing [5,24,35]. By contrast, QUIC-FUZZ focuses on generating mutated yet integrity-protected packets.

Fuzzing QUIC. While we are *unaware* of an effective grey-box fuzzer for the *IETF-ratified QUIC*, fuzzing techniques and tools [7,22,25,27] capable of fuzz-testing QUIC exist. STATEAFL, an extension of ALFNET [27], infers the SUT states by observing the content of SUT's memory allocations to eliminate the need to write a custom message parser. BLEEM [22] introduces a Man-in-the-Middle approach that fuzzes both the client and the server simultaneously by actively intercepting and modifying packets exchanged. However, ALFNET, STATEAFL, and BLEEM does not account for packet protections (such as encryption) in secure protocols like QUIC; rather, they perform direct mutations on encrypted packets (seeds) and suffer from the problems discussed in Sect. 3.

A concurrent study, FUZZTRUCTION-NET [7], leverages a network peer (client or server) as a harness to generate fuzzing inputs. It dynamically injects faults into the harness to: i) modify variable values for targeted field mutations, and ii) alter the harness's execution trace (e.g., changing the function call destination) to achieve sequence mutation. As discussed in Sect. 6, FUZZTRUCTION-NET does not require protocol-specific crypto modules and deals with ephemeral values without manual patching. But, the approach requires identifying the optimal fault insertion location to ensure the peer remains operational while testing. Further, the number of variables available for mutation in a harness can exceed the number of fields in a QUIC packet. Hence, FUZZTRUCTION-NET has a larger exploration space during mutation compared to a replay-based fuzzer like QUIC-FUZZ and must carefully select impactful variables for mutation. Consequently, QUIC-FUZZ's execution speed is 125% faster than FUZZTRUCTION-NET (25 exec/s vs 0.2 exec/s on our execution hardware).

Optimising the Fuzzing Loop. Previous works [2,38] have also intercept network system calls to synchronise fuzzing events. In addition, snapshot techniques [11,21,31,37] have been applied to fuzzing to mitigate initialisation overhead, especially on stateful targets that require reset [27]. Because Snapfuzz [3] adopts both of these methods—synchronisation and snapshotting—for ALFNET, we adopted and extended it in our work.

8 Conclusions and Future Work

In this study, we have developed and implemented a grey-box mutation-based fuzzer—QUIC-FUZZ—to discover vulnerabilities beyond specification bugs in QUIC server-side implementations. We have evaluated QUIC-FUZZ on six QUIC servers and compared the fuzzer developed against three state-of-the-art network protocol fuzzers. Extensive evaluations demonstrate that QUIC-FUZZ is both efficient and effective for fuzzing QUIC targets. In particular, QUIC-FUZZ outperforms all other fuzzers—with up to an 84% increase in code coverage—and uncovers 10 security vulnerabilities, with two CVEs assigned from developers and a bug bounty reward received. Extending QUIC-FUZZ to leverage LLMs to perform grammar-aware mutations and predict the next message during fuzzing represent potentially fruitful avenues for future research.

A Appendix

A.1 Configurations Used in Benchmarks and Implementation Effort

ALFNET (commit `6d86ca0c`). We follow their description to enable state-aware mode and the region-level mutation operators. As in QUIC-FUZZ, we include the required functions for parsing QUIC input and response sequences.

CHATAFL (commit `1ea603eb`). Because CHATAFL is built on top of ALFNET, we include the same functions we added to ALFNET and enable the same fuzzing configurations. To ensure that the LLM understands the QUIC protocol contexts, we modify the LLM prompt templates in CHATAFL by replacing all the "request" keywords with "packet" because QUIC does not operate under the concept of requests.

FUZZTRUCTION-NET (commit `9e981022`). FUZZTRUCTION-NET generates fuzz inputs by injecting faults into clients. As such, we use the `Ngtcp2` QUIC client (commit version `f3f15b6`) as the harness because it was the chosen client in the benchmark with QUIC servers tested in FUZZTRUCTION-NET.

We detail the QUIC server implementations tested in our experiments in Table 4 and summarise the implementation effort in Table 5.

Table 4. QUIC server implementations tested.

Name	Commit Version	Language	URL
Google-Quiche	149b7e6	C++	https://github.com/google/quiche
Lsquic	c4f359f	C	https://github.com/litespeedtech/lsquic
Ngtcp2	e2372a8	C/C++	https://github.com/ngtcp2/ngtcp2
Picoquic	8f4f77f	C	https://github.com/private-octopus/picoquic
Quicly	6a90372	C	https://github.com/h2o/quicly
Xquic	ae6f7f7, 6803065	C	https://github.com/alibaba/xquic

Table 5. Implementation effort.

Component	Library	Lines of Code
QUIC-AFLNet	AFLNet, OpenSSL-3.0.2	3530
Snapfuzz+	Snapfuzz	724

A.2 Statistical Significance Testing of Branch Coverage

Coverage results are reported in Fig. 3. In summary, QUIC-FUZZ outperforms all others fuzzers and we can observe an increase in code coverage of up to 84%. Table 6 reports that QUIC-FUZZ achieves *median* code coverage improvements that are statistically significant across all targets compared to the ALFNET and CHATAFL. We observe significant improvements in 5 out of 6 targets compared to FUZZTRUCTION-NET.

Table 6. The median branch coverage achieved by our QUIC-FUZZ compared to ALFNET, CHATAFL and FUZZTRUCTION-NET in ten trials of 48-hour executions. The percentage shows the improvement of QUIC-FUZZ in branch coverage compared to the SToA fuzzer. The statistically significant changes are marked in bold (based on a Mann-Whitney U test with a 0.05 significance threshold).

QUIC server	QUIC-FUZZ (Ours)	ALFNET		p-value	CHATAFL		p-value	FUZZTRUCTION-NET		p-value
Google-Quiche	11915	8984	**33%**	0.0002	8987	**33%**	0.0002	10136	**18%**	0.0002
Lsquic	5238	3294	**59%**	0.0002	3302	**59%**	0.0002	3759	**39%**	0.0002
Ngtcp2	3744	2882	**30%**	0.0002	3034	**23%**	0.0002	3570	**5%**	0.0006
Picoquic	4940	3329	**48%**	0.0002	3450	**43%**	0.0002	4014	23%	0.1404
Quicly	3291	2807	**17%**	0.0002	2808	**17%**	0.0002	2985	**10%**	0.0002
Xquic	6262	3569	**75%**	0.0002	3593	**74%**	0.0002	4205	**49%**	0.0002

A.3 Ablation Study Discussion

We report the ablation study results in Table 3 in Sect. 5.5. We can observe each technique applied in QUIC-FUZZ is effective and contributes to improving performance in a manner that is statistically significant. We discuss the results and observations further here.

+QUIC-specific Cryptographic Module—addressing C1. The crypto module for handling QUIC-specific security functions described in Sect. 3 leads to statistically significant improvements across all targets. As a result of the addition, QUIC-FUZZ achieves an increase of up to 62% increase in branch coverage compared to the ALFNET (baseline). The crypto module we developed for QUIC aids the fuzzer in generating inputs with the correct integrity while ensuring the interpretability of decrypted data. This allows the fuzzer to reliably re-use the same test case to make incremental progress. This increases the likelihood of the fuzzer reaching deeper functionality in the target.

+Synchronisation Protocol—addressing C2. Next, we activate the Synchronisation Protocol in addition to the previous configuration. As discussed in Sect. 3, this module incorporates techniques to ensure that the fuzzing events are synchronised without manual interventions for timeout settings while mitigating delays impacting testing efficiency, which would otherwise reduce the fuzzer's throughput. Overall, the addition of the synchronisation protocol is seen to be effective at significantly improving median coverage metrics above those possible by adding cryptographic support.

Interestingly, Ngtcp2 does not show a statistically significant improvement in the median coverage metric. Although, in terms of the best coverage metrics for each configuration in the 10 trial, the +Synchronisation Protocol achieves higher coverage than the +QUIC-specific Cryptographic Module (3835 vs 3823), both configurations achieve similar median code coverage. In the previous configuration (+QUIC-specific Cryptographic Module), the manual timeout is empirically determined during a dry run phase for use during the fuzz testing phase. In the case of Ngtcp2 implementation, the server implementation leads to more consistent behaviour in terms of processing various inputs; the empirically determined minimum timeout set to synchronise the fuzzing events in the dry run phase appears nearly to be optimal in this case. This consistency allows the fuzzer to re-use the same test case to reach its target state and explore further.

Overall, these results highlight that the performance impact which can arise from non-determinism, as discussed in **C3**, is mitigated by the synchronisation protocol.

+Snapshot Protocol—addressing C3. This configuration represents the full version of QUIC-FUZZ. With the addition of the Snapshot protocol discussed in Sect. 3, the fuzzer mitigates the target initialisation overhead by spawning an initialised target instance from the snapshot captured during the initialisation of the Forkserver. Consequently, we can observe improvements in performance for targets that require long initialisation, such as Lsquic, where the difference is statistically significant.

References

1. Openssl. https://github.com/openssl/openssl. Accessed 15 Oct 2024
2. Preeny. https://github.com/zardus/preeny. Accessed 7 Nov 2024
3. Andronidis, A., Cadar, C.: SnapFuzz: high-throughput fuzzing of network applications. In: International Symposium on Software Testing and Analysis (ISSTA), pp. 340–351 (2022)
4. Ang, K.K., Farrelly, G., Pope, C., Ranasinghe, D.C.: An automated blackbox non-compliance checker for QUIC server implementations. In: Asia Conference on Computer and Communications Security (AsiaCCS) (2025)
5. Aschermann, C., Frassetto, T., Holz, T., Jauernig, P., Sadeghi, A.R., Teuchert, D.: Nautilus: fishing for deep bugs with grammars. In: Network and Distributed System Security (NDSS) (2019)
6. Ba, J., Böhme, M., Mirzamomen, Z., Roychoudhury, A.: Stateful greybox fuzzing. In: USENIX Security Symposium (USENIX Security), pp. 3255–3272 (2022)
7. Bars, N., Schloegel, M., Schiller, N., Bernhard, L., Holz, T.: No peer, no cry: network application fuzzing via fault injection (2024)
8. Chen, Y., et al.: Savior: towards bug-driven hybrid testing. In: Symposium on Security and Privacy (S&P), pp. 1580–1596 (2020)

9. Crochet, C., Rousseaux, T., Piraux, M., Sambon, J.F., Legay, A.: Verifying quic implementations using ivy. In: Workshop on Evolution, Performance and Interoperability of QUIC (EPIQ), pp. 35–41 (2021)
10. Dierks, T., Rescorla, E.: The transport layer security (tls) protocol version 1.2. RFC 5246 (2008)
11. Dong, Z., Böhme, M., Cojocaru, L., Roychoudhury, A.: Time-travel testing of android apps. In: International Conference on Software Engineering (ICSE), pp. 481–492 (2020)
12. Eddington, M.: Peach fuzzing platform. https://gitlab.com/gitlab-org/security-products/protocol-fuzzer-ce. Accessed 2 Aug 2024
13. Feng, X., et al.: Snipuzz: black-box fuzzing of iot firmware via message snippet inference. In: Conference on Computer and Communications Security (CCS), pp. 337–350 (2021)
14. Ferreira, T., Brewton, H., D'Antoni, L., Silva, A.: Prognosis: closed-box analysis of network protocol implementations. In: Special Interest Group on Data Communication (SIGCOMM), pp. 762–774 (2021)
15. Gascon, H., Wressnegger, C., Yamaguchi, F., Arp, D., Rieck, K.: Pulsar: stateful black-box fuzzing of proprietary network protocols. In: Security and Privacy in Communication Networks, pp. 330–347 (2015)
16. Goel, V., Paulo, R., Paasch, C.: Testing quic with packetdrill. In: Workshop on Evolution, Performance and Interoperability of QUIC (EPIQ), pp. 1–7 (2020)
17. Iyengar, J., Thomson, M.: QUIC: a UDP-based multiplexed and secure transport. RFC 9000 (2021)
18. jtpereyda: Boofuzz: Network protocol fuzzing for humans
19. Kaplan, E.L., Meier, P.: Nonparametric estimation from incomplete observations. J. Am. Stat. Assoc. **53**(282), 457–481 (1958)
20. Klees, G., Ruef, A., Cooper, B., Wei, S., Hicks, M.: Evaluating fuzz testing. In: Conference on Computer and Communications Security (CCS), pp. 2123–2138 (2018)
21. Li, J., Li, S., Sun, G., Chen, T., Yu, H.: Snpsfuzzer: a fast greybox fuzzer for stateful network protocols using snapshots. Inf. Forensics Secur. **17**, 2673–2687 (2022)
22. Luo, Z., et al.: Bleem: packet sequence oriented fuzzing for protocol implementations. In: USENIX Security Symposium (USENIX Security), pp. 4481–4498 (2023)
23. McMillan, K.L., Zuck, L.D.: Formal specification and testing of quic. In: Special Interest Group on Data Communication (SIGCOMM), pp. 227–240 (2019)
24. Meng, R., Mirchev, M., Böhme, M., Roychoudhury, A.: Large language model guided protocol fuzzing. In: Network and Distributed System Security (NDSS) (2024)
25. Natella, R.: Stateafl: greybox fuzzing for stateful network servers. Empir. Softw. Eng. **27**(7), 191 (2022)
26. Ognawala, S., Hutzelmann, T., Psallida, E., Pretschner, A.: Improving function coverage with munch: a hybrid fuzzing and directed symbolic execution approach. In: Symposium on Applied Computing, pp. 1475–1482 (2018)
27. Pham, V.T., B hme, M., Roychoudhury, A.: Aflnet: a greybox fuzzer for network protocols. In: International Conference on Software Testing, Validation and Verification (ICST), pp. 460–465 (2020)
28. Postel, J.: Transmission control protocol. RFC 793 (1981)
29. Qin, S., Hu, F., Ma, Z., Zhao, B., Yin, T., Zhang, C.: Nsfuzz: towards efficient and state-aware network service fuzzing. Trans. Softw. Eng. Methodol. **32**(6), 1–26 (2023)

30. Rath, F., Schemmel, D., Wehrle, K.: Interoperability-guided testing of quic implementations using symbolic execution. In: Workshop on Evolution, Performance and Interoperability of QUIC (EPIQ), pp. 15–21 (2018)
31. Schumilo, S., Aschermann, C., Jemmett, A., Abbasi, A., Holz, T.: Nyx-Net: network fuzzing with incremental snapshots. In: European Conference on Computer Systems (EuroSys) (2022)
32. Stephens, N., et al.: Driller: augmenting fuzzing through selective symbolic execution. In: Network and Distributed System Security (NDSS) (2016)
33. Thomson, M., Turner, S.: Using TLS to secure QUIC. RFC 9001 (2021)
34. Wagner, J.B.: Elastic program transformations automatically optimizing the reliability/performance trade-off in systems software (2017), 149 (2017)
35. Wang, J., Chen, B., Wei, L., Liu, Y.: Superion: grammar-aware greybox fuzzing. In: International Conference on Software Engineering (ICSE), pp. 724–735 (2019)
36. Wu, F., et a.: Logos: log guided fuzzing for protocol implementations. In: International Symposium on Software Testing and Analysis (ISSTA), pp. 1720–1732 (2024)
37. Xu, W., Kashyap, S., Min, C., Kim, T.: Designing new operating primitives to improve fuzzing performance. In: Conference on Computer and Communications Security (CCS) (2017)
38. Zeng, Y., et al.: Multifuzz: a coverage-based multiparty-protocol fuzzer for iot publish/subscribe protocols. Sensors **20**(18), 5194 (2020)

Systematic Assessment of Cache Timing Vulnerabilities on RISC-V Processors

Cédrick Austa[(⊠)], Jan Tobias Mühlberg, and Jean-Michel Dricot

Université Libre de Bruxelles, Avenue Roosevelt 50, 1050 Bruxelles, Belgium
{cedrick.austa,jan.tobias.muehlberg,jean-michel.dricot}@ulb.be

Abstract. While interest in the open RISC-V instruction set architecture is growing, tools to assess the security of concrete processor implementations are lacking. There are dedicated tools and benchmarks for common microarchitectural side-channel vulnerabilities for popular processor families such as Intel x86-64 or ARM, but not for RISC-V. In this paper we describe our efforts in porting an Intel x86-64 benchmark suite for cache-based timing vulnerabilities to RISC-V. We then use this benchmark to evaluate the security of three commercially available RISC-V processors, the T-Head C910 and the SiFive U54 and U74 cores. We observe that the C910 processor exhibits more distinct timing types than the other processors, leading to the assumption that code running on the C910 would be exposed to more microarchitectural vulnerability sources. In addition, our evaluation reveals that 37.5% of the vulnerabilities covered by the benchmark exist in all processors, while only 6.8% are absent from all cores. Our work, in particular the ported benchmark, aims to support RISC-V processor designers to identify leakage sources early in their designs and to support the development of countermeasures.

Keywords: RISC-V architecture · Cache timing side channel · Microarchitectural vulnerability · Security · Benchmark

1 Introduction

Modern processors include many performance-enhancing features, such as caching, paging, out-of-order execution and speculative executions, which improve computer system performances. However, these features can be exploited to create side channels.

A *side channel* is an unintended communication channel between two entities, where one party observes information that is inadvertently leaked by the functioning of the other party's system [1]. This communication channel can be exploited either actively, by interacting with the system and observing how it reacts, or passively, by observing behavioral changes. A processor microarchitecture is a processor-specific logic implementation of an instruction set architecture (ISA) [2]. While the latter is the definition of the instruction set requirements, e.g., the supported instruction set and data types, the registers, and the privilege modes, the microarchitecture describes the specifics of an ISA implementation, e.g., the instruction pipeline stages, the implementation of the cache and other optimization features. Microarchitectural side-channel vulnerabilities stem from and exploit effects of operations performed on a specific processor microarchitecture, which are not documented in the ISA. Examples of such vulnerabilities are cache-based side-channels which are used to extract information by observing operations on the cache or to build more sophisticated attacks, e.g., Meltdown vulnerability [3]. This category of vulnerabilities has been extensively studied for Intel processors [4–6], AMD processors [6–9], and ARM processors [10,11], and tools have been made available to evaluate their security.

The recent and open-source RISC-V ISA, which has gained a lot of popularity amongst industry and researchers, did not receive that much attention. Though, we now that RISC-V implementations are not exempt from microarchitectural vulnerabilities [12,13]. E.g., Gerlach et al. [12] already demonstrated that some differences may be observed between vulnerabilities on the Intel x86-64 architecture and the RISC-V architecture. Moreover, since RISC-V is an open-source ISA, different RISC-V hardware implementations are made available by CPU vendors, which leads to processor-specific vulnerabilities. As a result, the RISC-V architecture needs its own security toolkit to evaluate existing and future RISC-V processors. Recently, Thomas et al. [14] provides automatic detection of architectural vulnerabilities but benchmarks or test suites to assess the microarchitectural attack surface of a given RISC-V implementation are currently missing. In this paper we address this shortcoming. With a focus on cache-based timing vulnerabilities, we ported a benchmark [4,15] to target RISC-V and evaluate it on three commercially available processors.

Contributions. We ported and extended a benchmark from Intel x86-64 [4] to detect cache-based side-channel vulnerabilities for the RISC-V ISA. The original benchmark is based on a theoretical three-step model proposed in Deng et al. [15] and is made of two software components: the first allows to observe the different cache timing types on a processor, while the second allows to determine cache-based timing vulnerabilities on the L1 data cache of this processor. By allowing for different cache hierarchies, different cache set associativities, and different cache eviction strategy parameters, our ported benchmark is more flexible and easier to adapt to new RISC-V implementations. Our contributions are:

- porting and translating original work from Deng et al. [4] to RISC-V processors;
- refactoring the benchmark to support new RISC-V processor configurations;
- evaluating cache-based vulnerabilities on the three commercially available RISC-V processors, the T-Head C910, and the SiFive U74 and U54;
- identifying and interpreting timing differences between memory operations;
- identifying L1 data cache-based vulnerabilities across all implementations.

With our evaluation, we show that the translated benchmark can be used to successfully identify cache timing leakage sources and potential vulnerabilities on RISC-V processors. By doing so, we demonstrate the utility of such a benchmark for RISC-V chip designers to identify vulnerabilities in their designs for which countermeasures should be implemented. Our results show that 39 out of the 88 cache-based timing vulnerabilities highlighted in Deng et al. [4] are present in all implementations. We make our benchmark available under an open-source license: https://github.com/ReSP-Lab/risc-v-sidechannel-benchmark.

Even though such an evaluation was never performed on RISC-V implementations, we do not consider that following confidential disclosure procedures with the manufacturers are warranted: (i) most of the implementations we evaluate are used in development boards that are mainly dedicated to hobbyists and researchers, (ii) the benchmark on which we based our work as well as the covered vulnerabilities are not new, (iii) the vulnerabilities are rather involved and not easily exploitable in practice, and (iv) subsets of these vulnerabilities have already been reported by Gerlach et al. [12] for the same or similar processors.

2 Background

Below we provide background on caches and caching behavior in modern processors, we outline how caches can be abused in side-channel attacks, and we summarize Deng et al. [4]'s work as the foundation of our research.

2.1 System Caches and Caching

To optimize performance, when a processor requires data from (slow) main memory it first checks the (fast) caches if this data is already available. If the data is in the cache, the cache *hits*; otherwise, the cache *misses* and data is fetched from main memory and placed into the cache. *Caching* exploits *temporal locality* and *spatial locality* [2]: As a consequence of temporal locality, data is loaded into the cache from main memory when a cache miss occurs. This happens in *cache blocks* that include data from adjacent addresses, thus exploiting spatial locality.

Cache Hierarchy. To decrease the *miss penalty*, i.e., the latency overhead due to cache misses, a *multi-level cache hierarchy* is often used. The highest level and the lowest level in the hierarchy respectively are the L1 cache and the *last-level cache (LLC) cache*. The lower the cache level in the hierarchy, the larger are both the cache size and the latency to access data in this cache.

Cache Specifications. The performance impact of a cache depends on cache capacity C, block size b, and the degree of associativity N [2]. Let $B = C/b$ be the number of cache blocks in a cache. The cache is N-*way set associative* when these blocks are grouped into S sets of N ways, i.e., block locations in the set, with $S = B/N$ and $1 \leq N \leq B$. The number of ways per set determines how memory addresses in main memory are mapped to cache locations: If $N = 1$, any memory address is mapped to only one block; such a cache is called a *direct mapped* cache. If $N = B$, any memory address can be mapped to every blocks in the cache; such a cache is called a *fully associative* cache.

Cache Replacement Policy. When a miss occurs while the cache is fully populated, a cache block needs to be evicted to load the target block into the cache set. For a N-way set associative cache with $N > 1$, a *cache replacement policy* is necessary to select which block to evict. Examples of cache replacement policies are the *random* replacement policy (evicting a random block), the first-in first-out (FIFO) replacement policy (evicting the oldest block), or the least recently used (LRU) policy. In LRU, to avoid tracking the last use of each way in a set, approximations of this policy, so-called pseudo-LRU (PLRU) policies, are used.

Cache Coherence Protocol. In multicore processors, cache coherence protocols are used to track cache block states among private and shared caches. By doing so, each core reads the same content from a cache block at any time between two write operations. The two main categories of cache coherence protocols are *directory-based* protocols and *snooping* protocols. The former track cache block states using a directory, in a centralized way where the state of a cache block is known by accessing the directory. The latter track cache block states using a snooping bus and the state of a cache block is stored locally in the cache and each cache block state alteration is broadcasted on the bus for other listeners. Examples of states are the followings: M(odified), O(wned), E(xclusive), S(hared), or I(nvalid). The choice of a cache coherence protocol has impact on performance and scalability.

2.2 Cache-Based Timing Vulnerabilities

Cache-based microarchitectural attacks exploit the cache status as a leaking information source. Information is collected either by observing timing differences on cache block accesses [3,16] or by measuring power consumption differences on cache block content change [17,18]. *Cache-based timing* attacks exploit the observed latency between cache hits and cache misses, e.g. the access time increases whenever cache blocks to load are lower in the cache hierarchy. Attackers can interact with the cache using a specific memory operation and measure the operation time or latency to infer the victim's cache state. According to Su et al. [19], a succeeding cache attack depends on the following three conditions:

1. a relation should exist between a change in the cache state and target sensitive information;
2. at least one cache in the cache hierarchy is shared between both the attacker program and the victim program;
3. both programs sharing the cache can infer changes to each other's cache state by monitoring their own cache state.

To illustrate how the cache state may be exploited, we describe selected well-known cache-based timing attacks below.

Prime+Probe [20]. This first cache-based timing attack works on cache sets as follows: (i) the attacker fills one or more sets with its own cache blocks (*prime*), (ii) victim cache blocks are accessed, and (iii) the attacker reloads its own cache blocks in each set and measures timing (*probe*). In this attack, the cache probing is longer if attacker cache blocks were evicted by victim cache blocks.

Evict+Time [20]. This attack, which was introduced with Prime+Probe, consists in the following steps: (i) the attacker runs the victim program and measures timing, (ii) the attacker evicts a victim cache block (*evict*), and (iii) the attacker runs the victim program again and measures timing (*time*). If the evicted cache block was accessed by the victim, the execution time is longer to load the victim cache block.

Flush+Reload [21]. To perform this attack, (i) the attacker flushes a victim cache block (*flush*), (ii) the victim program eventually accesses the victim cache block, and (iii) the attacker reloads the victim cache block and measures timing (*reload*). If the victim accessed the flushed cache block, the reload operation time is shorter for the attacker. A variant of this attack, *Evict+Reload*, was proposed by Gruss et al. [22] to avoid the flush instruction requirement.

Flush+Flush [23]. This attack uses steps (i) and (ii) from the Flush+Reload attack. For step (iii) the attacker flushes the victim cache block again and measures timing. If the victim accessed their cache block, the flush operation takes longer than if they did not.

Table 1. L1 cache timing-based vulnerabilities [4]. The *No.* column assigns each type of vulnerability a number range. The *Attack Strategy* column gives a common name for each set of vulnerabilities and each vulnerability types that would be exploited in an attack in a similar manner. Inv. means invalidation.

No.	Attack Strategy	No.	Attack Strategy
1-4	Cache Collision	45-46	Cache Collision Inv.
5-8	Flush + Reload	47-50	Flush + Flush
9-10	Reload + Time	51-52	Flush + Reload Inv.
11-14	Flush + Probe	53-54	Reload + Time Inv.
15-16	Flush + Time	55-58	Flush + Probe Inv.
17-20	Cache Coherence Flush + Reload	59-60	Flush + Time Inv.
21-28	Cache Coherence Prime + Probe	61-64	Cache Coherence Flush + Reload Inv.
29-32	Cache Coherence Evict + Time	73-76	Cache Coherence Evict + Time Inv.
33-36	Bernstein's Attack	77-80	Bernstein's Inv. Attack
37-38	Evict + Probe	81-82	Evict + Probe Inv.
39-40	Prime + Time	83-84	Prime + Time Inv.
41-42	Evict + Time	85-86	Evict + Time Inv.
43-44	Prime + Probe	87-88	Prime + Probe Inv.

(a) Third step as memory access operation.   (b) Third step as invalidation operation.

Table 2. Test configurations for the L1-D cache benchmarks. For memory accesses: read and write operations. For invalidations: flush and write operations.

Test config.	Step 1	Step 2	Step 3	Run
RF_RF_RF_TS	read/flush	read/flush	read/flush	time-slicing
RF_RF_RF_SMT	read/flush	read/flush	read/flush	SMT
RF_RF_W_TS	read/flush	read/flush	write	time-slicing
RF_RF_W_SMT	read/flush	read/flush	write	SMT
RF_W_RF_TS	read/flush	write	read/flush	time-slicing
RF_W_RF_SMT	read/flush	write	read/flush	SMT
RF_W_W_TS	read/flush	write	write	time-slicing
RF_W_W__SMT	read/flush	write	write	SMT
W_RF_RF_TS	write	read/flush	read/flush	time-slicing
W_RF_RF_SMT	write	read/flush	read/flush	SMT
W_RF_W_TS	write	read/flush	write	time-slicing
W_RF_W_SMT	write	read/flush	write	SMT
W_W_RF_TS	write	write	read/flush	time-slicing
W_W_RF_SMT	write	write	read/flush	SMT
W_W_W_TS	write	write	write	time-slicing
W_W_W_SMT	write	write	write	SMT

2.3 Deng et al. [4] Benchmark Suite

Observable Timing Types. In their work, Deng et al. [4] study timing differences between memory operations depending on the cache level in which data is located, depending on the cache block data state (i.e., *dirty* or *clean*) and whether the attacker is running their program on the same core as the victim. As a result, 66 different timing types are considered instead of only the two traditional timing types for cache-based timing vulnerabilities (i.e., *fast* or *slow*). Even though some of these timing types were already exploited in the literature, e.g., both Flush+Reload [21] and Flush+Flush [23] rely on at least two of these 66 timing types, their work emphasizes the existence of such distinct timing types. To obtain the 66 timing types (i.e., 22 timing types per operation) the following cases are considered:

- either a read, write or flush operation is used to access data (3 operations);
- data is present either on the local L1/L2/L3 cache or on a remote L1/L2/L3 cache and the cache block in which data is present is either in dirty or clean state (6 × 2 = 12 cases), **or** data is present both in either the local L1, L2 or L3 cache and either the remote L1, L2 or L3 cache in clean state (3 × 3 = 9 cases), **or** data is only present in the DRAM (1 case).

A first part of their benchmark suite implementation generates histograms to identify the different timing types existing on a target. Each timing type which may be distinguished from the others in this histogram corresponds to a timing leakage source which can be exploited by an adversary to monitor cache usage.

Three-Step Model. Deng et al. [4] propose an improvement for a theoretical model [15] describing cache timing vulnerabilities as sequences of three steps (i.e., three memory-related operations), each modifying the state of a target cache block: state initialization, state alteration, and timing observation. From each step, one of 17 possible cache block states should be reached for the target cache block. The memory-related operations which can be used for each step correspond to the read, write and flush operations, depending on the resulting cache block state.

To validate their three-step model and detect all possible L1-D cache-based timing vulnerabilities on concrete processors, a subset of the previous timing types are used in a benchmark suite. In particular, benchmarks are automatically generated to evaluate the 88 vulnerabilities Deng et al. [4] identified as "strong" out of 4913 possible vulnerabilities. These 88 vulnerabilities are summarized in Table 1. For more details, the reader is re-oriented towards Deng et al. [4].

Moreover, to evaluate the existence of each vulnerability on a processor, their benchmark suite considers 16 test configurations for each vulnerability. These configurations aim to reach the same three cache block states for a vulnerability by applying different memory-related operation; cache block access can be performed with read or write operations, while cache block invalidation can be performed with flush or write. These configurations also compare timing differences observed whenever a victim and an adversary are located on the same physical core and whenever either *time-slicing* or *simultaneous multithreading (SMT)* is used. With some of these configurations, Deng et al. [4] identified vulnerabilities relying on cache coherence. Table 2 lists these test configurations.

3 Threat Model, Benchmark Suite, Experimental Setup

The goal of our work is to develop and evaluate a benchmark to assess the security of RISC-V implementations regarding cache-based timing vulnerabilities. Below we define our attacker model, and present the ported benchmark suite and our experimental setup.

3.1 Threat Model

We assume an attacker model where the adversary is able to gain unprivileged access to a system of interest and execute code on that system, and that this code can access hardware performance counters of the system, in particular clock cycle counters to measure memory operation latencies. Moreover, we only consider vulnerabilities which are evaluated in the benchmark (cf. Sect. 2.3, Table 1). We also make the assumptions that the conditions listed in Sect. 2.2 are satisfied: the existence of a link between cache states and victim secrets, and a shared and mutually observable cache state between victim and attacker code.

Under these conditions, we can rely on measurements from hardware performance counters to determine if the system is vulnerable or not. If no vulnerability is found that way—i.e., by relying on accurate clock cycle counters—the chances for an adversary to find vulnerabilities by relying on less accurate timers, such as POSIX timers, would be null. However, vulnerabilities found that way may not always result in exploitable vulnerabilities in practice. Verifying exploitability would typically be specific to a victim program and goes beyond the scope of this work. Also the inclusion of additional sources of information leakage, hardware side channels or microarchitectural side channels other than caches, is beyond the scope of this work.

3.2 Benchmark Suite Implementation and Porting

Regarding the porting to RISC-V, we decided (i) to segment the source code into smaller dedicated header and source files to ease for the code maintenance; (ii) to move all inline assembly snippets into inline assembly functions in a dedicated file to reduce the number of redundant code lines and, hence, to ease source code maintenance and corrections; (iii) to dedicate a header file for each target which defines all target specifications, related parameters (e.g., for Gruss et al. [24] eviction algorithm), and the (optional) related inline assembly `flush` function, to ease the support implementation for a new target; (iv) to allow the user to define which cache levels are exist on the target so that we can use the benchmark more constrained or developed targets.

In order to facilitate the evaluation of cache-based timing vulnerabilities, huge pages of 2MB are used to find conflicting addresses. Since most processors use virtually indexed physically tagged caches, this allows us to avoid taking virtual address translation into account. While this approach is relevant for embedded systems, it is less realistic for scenarios involving a fully-fledged operating system. Yet, since the goal of this work is not to evaluate the difficulty to build eviction sets on the targets, we consider this a minor limitation. In this context, eviction is not performed by building conflict sets, as it is the case in the original benchmark suite [4], but by using the eviction algorithm presented by Gruss et al. [24]. Deng et al. [4] only covered processors that use an LRU policy on L1 and L2 caches, which means that only sequential access to N cache blocks is required to evict a cache set. The authors built conflict sets only to evict the L3 cache of their targets. When considering targets that use different cache replacement policies per cache level, this method would require us to build a specific conflict set for each of these cache levels. Instead, the eviction algorithm proposed by Gruss et al. [24] allows us to deal with different replacement policies than the LRU policy by adapting the algorithm parameters, and conflicting addresses are easy to list since the set index is straightforward to obtain using huge pages on our targets, which has performance benefits. Nevertheless, this approach requires to define adequate algorithm parameters. For our study we manually explored different sets of parameters and settled on parameters that produce stable results with small error margins in our evaluation.

3.3 Evaluation Targets and Experimental Setup

For the experiments, three single-board computer (SBCs) with RISC-V application cores were used. These SBCs are the BeagleV-Ahead [25] (SoC: TH1520, core: C910), the BeagleV-Fire [26] (SoC: U54-MC, app. core: U54) and the HiFive Unmatched [27] (SoC: FU740, app. core: U74). Their cache specifications are given in Table 3. Note that since the cache replacement policy for the L2 cache from U54 is not documented, we made the assumption it was a PLRU policy. Experiments were performed with the Ubuntu images available for these SBCs (images from the SBC provider or from Ubuntu Boards).

Table 3. Evaluated system-on-chip cache specifications. Both SiFive cores use a directory-based cache coherence protocol, while the C910 core uses a snooping cache coherence protocol.

Core	L1-D cache			L2 cache		
	Size	Ways	Replacement	Size	Ways	Replacement
C910	64kB	2	FIFO	1MB	16	FIFO
U54	32kB	8	random	2MB	16	PLRU
U74	32kB	8	random	2MB	16	random

First, none of the selected SBCs benefits from an L3 cache. Thus, 27 timing types are not considered during the evaluation of memory operations, resulting to the measurement of only 39 out of the 66 timing types proposed by Deng et al. [4]. Moreover, previously selected images allow the user-mode to use the `rdcycle` instruction which are used to obtain high accuracy timings for the benchmarks. Unfortunately, by using these images, flush instructions are not available except for the C910 processor which leaves it available to user-mode programs. As a result, only 26 timing types can be measured for the evaluations of the U54 and U74 processors. However, to be able to measure DRAM latency for each operation, flush instruction is replaced by L2 eviction when necessary.

Finally, as proposed by Deng et al. [4], we measure latencies on 8 cache lines from distinct cache sets at a time, in order to minimize false negatives. Regarding false positives, [4] proposed to isolate cores to reduce software noise. We decided to not isolate cores to have a more realistic situation, since our configuration is not running anything else than the operating system and our benchmarks. Moreover, we only observe a small differences when isolating cores; we still observe differences between distinct evaluations with isolation, probably due to last level cache conflicts with the operating system and our process, and due to random cache policies.

4 Results

4.1 Timing Types

Measurements. The observed timing types from our tests on the three evaluated cores are given in Fig. 1. The most frequent clock cycle latency from all tests is presented as a bar plot and a percentile interval of 95% is superposed to the plot as an error bar. Timing type labels refer to a subset of the 22 timing types per operation described in Sect. 2.3. Obviously, timing types related to L3 cache are not considered.

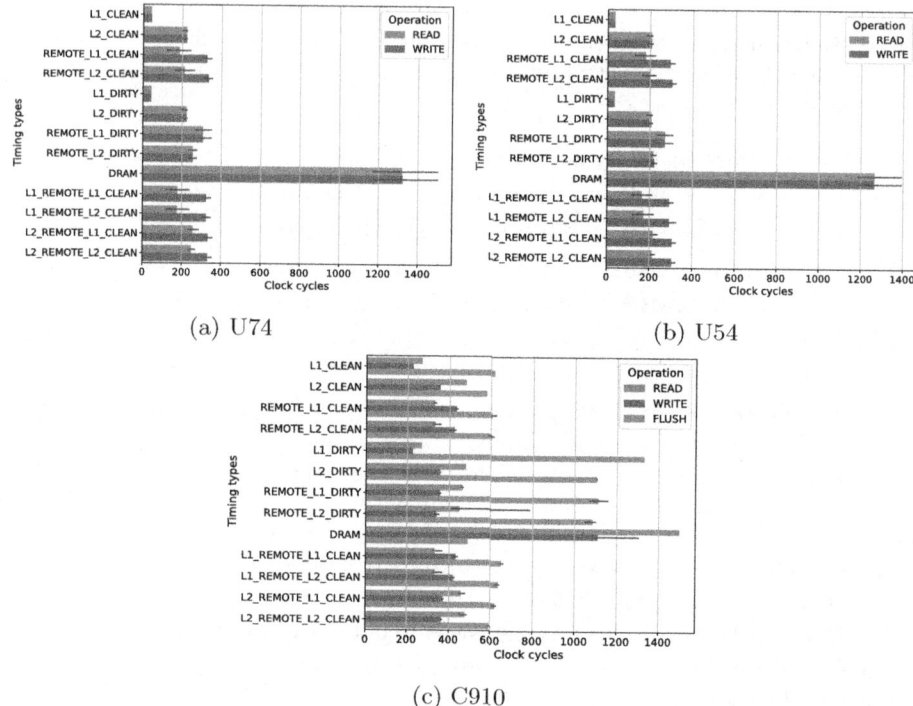

Fig. 1. Most frequent clock cycle latencies over 10000 tests, per timing type and per target. Label prefixes `Lx_` or `REMOTE_Lx`, refer to the cache block location in the cache level x on local or remote core. Label suffixes `_CLEAN` or `_DIRTY`, refer to the cache block state before the memory operation, respectively.

Observations and Preliminary Discussion. From Fig. 1, the observed clock cycle latencies differ between most of the evaluated timing types, for all cores. For both SiFive cores, we see four groups of timing types which seem to show to observable different latencies for the write operation, while five groups show observable differences for the read operation. We assume the observed latency overheads appearing for the write operation come from the directory-based cache coherence protocol which ensures that other existing cache block copies are invalidated on remote caches. Regarding the T-Head core, four groups of timing types can be observed, both for the write and read operations. Nevertheless, we see differences between the read and write operations due to the use of a snooping cache coherence protocol. In particular, a MESI protocol is used between L1-D caches with a bypassing mechanism and a MOESI protocol is used to ensure coherence between L1-D caches and the L2 cache. Our interpretation is that overheads appear either due to the cache coherence, to the snoop buffer, to store (or write) buffers, or to the load-store unit present between cores and their L1 cache. However, timing type latencies observed for the flush operation are more heterogeneous than for the read and write operations. In particular, latencies are larger when cache block has to be written back into main memory (cache block is dirty), and latencies decrease when cache block is located in lower levels of the cache hierarchy. The minimum latency observed for this operation is when cache block is already written back into main memory.

From the previous observations, we learn that the read operation is the main leakage source on both SiFive cores, while the dominant leakage source on the T-Head is the flush operation. We also learn that the C910 core exposes more potentially vulnerable behavior than the SiFive cores: first due to the differences observed between all memory operations and, second, due to the availability of the flush instruction.

4.2 L1 Data Cache Vulnerabilities

Measurements. The evaluation of the three targets for the 88 strong vulnerabilities identified by Deng et al. [4] is provided by Fig. 2. On Fig. 2, the presence of a vulnerability for a specific test configuration, as described in Table 2, for a given target is indicated by a marker. In addition, two categories indicate whether the vulnerability is present in all evaluated CPUs or absent from all of them.

Cache timing vulnerability scores (CTVSs) [4] are used to quantify how a target is vulnerable by providing the ratio of vulnerabilities which are observable on a target. These CTVSs are given in Table 4. In addition, the ratio of vulnerabilities successfully observed on a target (i.e., a success ratio), only taking into account all valid test configurations for the latter, is provided too in Tables 5 and 6. Valid test configurations depend on the support of flush instruction in user mode or on the support of SMT, which leads to different maximum number of cases per target. Thus, for each table, the success ratio for test configurations shared between all targets or exclusive to some targets (e.g., depending on the flush instruction support) is given. This success ratio is obtained by dividing the number of successfully observed vulnerabilities for the target with the total number of cases for the considered category.

Observations and Preliminary Discussion. A first observation that can be made from Fig. 2 is regarding the vulnerabilities which are absent from all

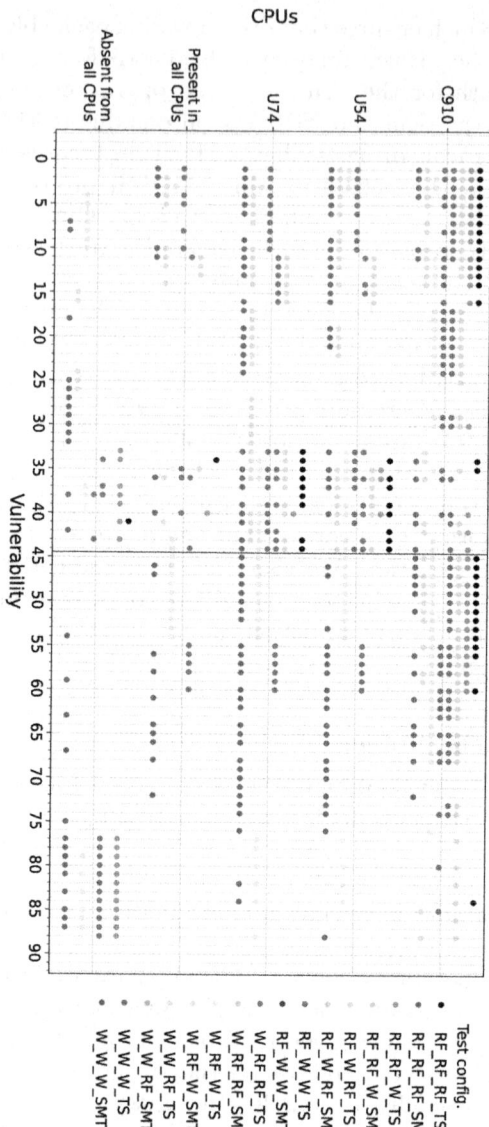

Fig. 2. Evaluated timing types per vulnerability on target RISC-V SoCs: vulnerabilities on the left part have a read or write access as a third step, while vulnerabilities on the right have an invalidation as a third step. To read this plot, choose a target on the vertical axis. Then, for a vulnerability located on the horizontal axis, determine which test configuration allows to detect the vulnerability for the target. Example: vulnerability #1 uses an invalidation as a first step. From all targets, markers from the top half dedicated to this vulnerability are only present for the C910 core. The top half corresponds to test configurations starting with RF_; they are test configurations where the first step is performed either with a read operation (memory access) or with a flush operation (invalidation). As a result, we deduce that since the flush operation is only accessible from U-mode on the C910, vulnerability #1 will only be marked on the C910 for this set of test configurations. We can also note, for example, that the W_RF_RF_TS test configuration, allows to observe vulnerability #1 on all targets.

Table 4. cache timing vulnerability.

	C910	U54	U74	All	None
CTVS	70/88	64/88	77/88	39/88	6/88

Table 5. Ratio of vulnerabilities successfully observed for different running configurations: whether an attacker is present or not and whether the victim and the attacker run on the same core (time-slicing or hyper-threading) or not. Note that none of the targets support SMT.

Core	Victim, attacker Same core		Victim, attacker Different cores	Victim only
	Time-slicing	SMT		
C910	36/157	0	17/38	34/93
U54	70/157	0	24/38	54/93
U74	89/157	0	26/38	62/93
All	23/157	0	14/38	28/93
None	52/157	0	8/38	24/93

(a) Shared test configurations.

Core	Victim, attacker Same core		Victim, attacker Different cores	Victim only
	Time-slicing	SMT		
C910	122/233	0	31/52	65/131

(b) Exclusive test configurations.

boards. In particular, absent vulnerabilities relate to observable timing differences by evicting or invalidating addresses out of the sensitive memory locations, which conflict with addresses in the sensitive memory locations of interest. This result can be interpreted as follows: (i) most of the vulnerabilities relying on invalidation are on the C910 core and SiFive cores only rely on remote `write` operations to invalidate cache blocks, in our implementation; (ii) no significant timing difference is observed for the `write` operation on SiFive cores between `REMOTE_L1_CLEAN` and `REMOTE_L2_CLEAN`, making vulnerabilities #79, #81, and #83, which rely on the eviction of remote-only memory location, less effective.

Then, from Table 4, it also appears that the U74 core exhibits more vulnerabilities than the U54. We could interpret this as the former being more vulnerable or less secure than the latter. However, from the more detailed view provided by Fig. 2, we learn that the presence of these vulnerabilities on one of these cores is a result of the specific benchmark run as the vulnerabilities are only observed for one or two test configurations. This is supported by the similarities between both microarchitectures, in particular for the L1 cache, and Fig. 1 which does not highlight any significant difference between observable timing types. Thus, we

Table 6. Ratio of vulnerabilities successfully observed for different test configurations and memory operations. *Inv.* means invalidation.

Core	Local Read	Local Write	Remote Write Inv.	Flush Inv.
C910	34/96	24/96	29/96	0
U54	62/96	45/96	41/96	0
U74	75/96	52/96	50/96	0
All	24/96	16/96	25/96	0
None	8/96	32/96	44/96	0

(a) Shared test configurations.

Core	Local Read	Local Write	Remote Write Inv.	Flush Inv.
C910	51/80	49/80	48/80	70/176

(b) Exclusive test configurations.

assume that if some vulnerabilities identified on the U74 core are false positives, the number of vulnerabilities absent from all evaluated targets should increase. Depending on the previous assumption, the U74 would be either more or less (in case previous assumption is correct) vulnerable than the C910, but further research is needed to assess this.

Even though the C910 might present more vulnerabilities than both SiFive cores, it appears from Tables 5 and 6 that, on shared test configurations, less configurations led to observable timing differences on the C910. It seems that, if the C910 presents more vulnerabilities, both SiFive cores present more ways to exploit each of their vulnerabilities. Finally, it also clearly appears that allowing the flush instruction provides ways to exploit these vulnerabilities which are not present on SiFive cores, from user mode.

4.3 Discussion

From our results in Sect. 4.1 and Fig. 2 we learn that the T-Head C910, featuring a U-mode flush instruction, has more observable latency differences than the other cores. These differences provide additional attack surface and potentially more exploitable vulnerabilities. An effective way to improve the security the C910 would be to restrict access to flush to the M-mode (cf. [12]).

Following our interpretation of cycle latencies and CTVS, both SiFive cores, the U54 and U74, expose the same set of vulnerabilities which is smaller than that of the T-Head core. The absence of the flush instruction in U-mode definitively plays an important role for test configurations relying on a local invalidation step. An attacker who gains control over the kernel or firmware may still be able to invoke flush in M-mode. However, these attacks are beyond the scope of our threat model and we therefore did not study timing of flush instructions on these cores. Yet, on shared test configurations (cf. Tables 5 and 6) both SiFive cores score substantially higher numbers vulnerabilities than the T-Head core. This may be due to the difference of cache coherence protocols or other microarchitectural design differences.

Both parts of the benchmark suite, the evaluation of timing types and the evaluation of L1-D cache vulnerabilities, provide valuable information about timing types an adversary may exploit a RISC-V processor. The histograms should help the designer to identify leakage sources in their design and to make choices to improve its resilience against cache-based timing vulnerabilities. Then, identifying the test configurations for which an implementation present a given vulnerability help to assess the security of their design and to determine which implemented countermeasures and design choices really have an impact on their design security, e.g., restricting the access to flush instructions.

Limitations. Our benchmark does not consider virtual addresses and S-mode executions in general. Thus, our results are representative for embedded systems but are incomplete regarding scenarios that involve an operating system. Depending on how virtual addresses are managed, finding conflicting addresses in a cache set may be more difficult in these scenarios. Moreover, we did not study systems with an L3 cache yet, which may, depending on the availability of flush, present even more timing differences than the cores studied. Our benchmark is also dependent on knowledge of the target cache specifications (cf. Table 3). Evaluating implementations with missing specifications may lead to poor results. Finally, we only use the eviction algorithm from Gruss et al. [24], which may be limited depending on cache replacement policies or the supported access pattern detection features.

5 Related Work

Kelsey et al. [28] first introduced the idea of using the cache hit ratio to perform attacks on substitution box (S-boxes) from symmetric encryption algorithms. Based on this idea, [29] implements a first example of cache attack on DES. Bernstein [16] reported the extraction of an AES key from a remote computer by observing larger timings on S-boxes due to cache block eviction, and Percival [30] describes how memory between threads could be used both as a covert channel and as a side channel to attack RSA.

New ways to leverage cache timing differences are still being proposed. Gruss et al. [22] introduce cache template attacks which consist on a phase dedicated to the cache profiling with respect to an event of interest, followed by an exploitation phase which infers event occurrences by monitoring the cache. Yan et al. [31] illustrates that cache coherence protocols, more specifically directory-based protocols, can be considered an exploitable source of timing leakage. Briongos et al. [32] introduces Reload+Refresh which exploits the cache replacement policies and determines if a cache block is accessed by the victim.

For eviction-based attacks, different approaches to perform eviction or to build eviction sets exist, including eviction-based remote Rowhammer [33] and a parameterizable eviction strategy by Gruss et al. [24]. The latter strategy is the one used in our work. Similarly, Liu et al. [34], Song et al. [35] and Vila et al. [36] present formal definitions and methods to build minimal eviction sets. These approaches could be incorporated in our work by relying on conflict sets to perform the eviction, as an alternative to our method (see Sect. 3.2) and as originally performed by Deng et al. [4].

More recently, Lipp et al. [37,38] and Kogler et al. [18] propose a software-based power side-channel attacks which measure power consumption due to operations on the cache or to the bit flips occurring on cache replacement to extract keys or to break address space randomization. If similar software interfaces allowing to monitor the power consumption would be available on RISC-V processors, timing measurement could be replaced in our benchmark with power consumption monitoring operations as an attempt to detect cache misses, similarly to what Bertoni et al. [17] proposed.

Lyu et al. [39], Su et al. [19] and Shen et al. [40] survey cache-based side channel attacks and countermeasures. Purnal et al. [41] analyze the effectiveness of randomization to protect caches and Deng et al. [11] analyze the effectiveness of secure caches on ARM processors. Our benchmark can be used to validate hardened RISC-V designs that incorporate these countermeasures.

Le [13] study the security of the RISC-V architecture and Gerlach et al. [12] propose benchmarks and cases to evaluate and demonstrate vulnerabilities in selected RISC-V boards, including some of the 88 vulnerabilities from Deng et al. [4]. Thomas et al. [14] provide a fuzzing tool to detect architectural vulnerabilities in RISC-V implementations. Work in this direction is complementary to our approach, providing additional points of evidence for the presence or absence of vulnerabilities and building confidence in existing designs.

Finally, Oleksenko et al. [42] propose a model-based black-box approach to detect speculative leakage sources in CPUs by observing traces. Fabian et al. [43] propose a framework, supporting formal models for composite speculation mechanisms, which is used inside a program analysis tool to detect speculative vulnerabilities in code snippets. Barthe et al. [44] present a testing framework to assess given program security based on a description language dedicated to leakage models of microarchitectural optimizations. In comparison, our work is a model-based white-box approach focusing on the identification of vulnerabilities, which could inform leakage models of formal approaches to program security. Since we use a white-box approach, implementation specifications help to obtain accurate results by adequately adapting the benchmark parameters to the target. However, our work is predominantly useful for processor developers, enabling early evaluation of a processor implementation for cache-based timing leakage.

6 Conclusion

In this paper we reported on porting a comprehensive benchmark suite for cache-based timing vulnerabilities to RISC-V. We evaluate the benchmark on three commercially available RISC-V cores and present our findings, showing diverging leakage profiles across the processors with 37.5% of vulnerabilities present across all three processors and 6.8% of vulnerabilities being absent from all cores. Our benchmark and evaluation artifacts are available under an open-source license.

We anticipate that the ported benchmark will be useful for researchers as well as commercial developers of RISC-V implementations to evaluate leakage patterns of processors, to inform developers of potentially diverging security risks across different implementations, and to guide the development of strong testing and verification tools for RISC-V processors as well as for software compiled for RISC-V. As our benchmark suite helps to identify the different timing types and leakage patterns, our work can also support the development of concrete and formal leakage models. We have taken care and refactored the benchmark specifically to allow for easy re-configuration towards microarchitectures with different cache hierarchies, different cache set associativies, and different cache eviction strategies, which should greatly improve reusability of our artifacts.

In future work, we will evaluate the security of processors from other vendors and the exploitability of our findings for S-mode and U-mode. Regarding exploitability, we will provide proofs of concept based on the benchmark for specific applications with different risk profiles. Furthermore, we will evaluate countermeasures against cache timing vulnerabilities, e.g., cache partitioning and secure caches. We will also investigate the impact of different cache-coherence models on the security of open-source RISC-V cores with our benchmark. The security of implementations of Trusted Execution Environments against cache-based timing vulnerabilities could be another target of future work. Finally, we seek to extend the benchmark towards similar vulnerabilities, e.g., translation-lookaside buffer or transient execution vulnerabilities.

Acknowledgements. This research is supported by the CyberExcellence program of the Wallon region of Belgium under GA #2110186.

References

1. Szefer, J.: Principles of Secure Processor Architecture Design. Springer International Publishing (2019). https://doi.org/10.1007/978-3-031-01760-5
2. Harris, S.L.: Digital Design and Computer Architecture: RISC-V edition. Morgan Kaufmann, Cambridge (2022). Includes index
3. Lipp, M., et al.: Meltdown: reading kernel memory from user space. In: 27th USENIX Security Symposium (USENIX Security 18) (2018)
4. Deng, S., Xiong, W., Szefer, J.: A benchmark suite for evaluating caches vulnerability to timing attacks. In: Proceedings of the 25th International Conference on Architectural Support for Programming Languages and Operating Systems, ASPLOS 20. ACM (2020). https://doi.org/10.1145/3373376.3378510
5. Rauscher, F., Fiedler, C., Kogler, A., Gruss, D.: A systematic evaluation of novel and existing cache side channels. In: Network and Distributed System Security Symposium (NDSS) 2025 (2025). https://doi.org/10.14722/ndss.2025.23253, https://www.ndss-symposium.org/ndss2025/. Network and Distributed System Security Symposium 2025 : NDSS 2025
6. Purnal, A., Verbauwhede, I.: Cache side-channel attacks on existing and emerging computing platforms. Ph. D. thesis (2023)
7. Ren, X., Moody, L., Taram, M., Jordan, M., Tullsen, D.M., Venkat, A.: I see dead ops: leaking secrets via Intel/AMD micro-op caches. In: 2021 ACM/IEEE 48th Annual International Symposium on Computer Architecture (ISCA), pp. 361–374 (2021). https://doi.org/10.1109/ISCA52012.2021.00036
8. Irazoqui, G., Eisenbarth, T., Sunar, B.: Cross processor cache attacks. In: Proceedings of the 11th ACM on Asia Conference on Computer and Communications Security, ASIA CCS 16. ACM (2016). https://doi.org/10.1145/2897845.2897867
9. Lipp, M., Hadžić, V., Schwarz, M., Perais, A., Maurice, C., Gruss, D.: Take a way: exploring the security implications of AMD's cache way predictors. In: Proceedings of the 15th ACM Asia Conference on Computer and Communications Security, ASIA CCS 2020, pp. 813–825. Association for Computing Machinery, New York, NY, USA, (2020). https://doi.org/10.1145/3320269.3384746
10. Lipp, M., Gruss, D., Spreitzer, R., Maurice, C., Mangard, S.: ARMageddon: cache attacks on mobile devices. In: 25th USENIX Security Symposium, pp. 549–564. USENIX Association (2016). https://www.usenix.org/conference/usenixsecurity16/technical-sessions/presentation/lipp
11. Deng, S., Matyunin, N., Xiong, W., Katzenbeisser, S., Szefer, J.: Evaluation of cache attacks on arm processors and secure caches (2021)

12. Gerlach, L., Weber, D., Zhang, R., Schwarz, M.: A security risc: microarchitectural attacks on hardware RISC-V CPUs. In: 2023 IEEE Symposium on Security and Privacy (SP), pp. 2321–2338 (2023). https://doi.org/10.1109/SP46215.2023.10179399
13. Le, A.-T.: Research of RISC-V out-of-order processor cache-based side-channel attacks-systematic analysis, security models and countermeasures. Ph. D. thesis (2023)
14. Thomas, F., Hetterich, L., Zhang, R., Weber, D., Gerlach, L., Schwarz, M.: Discovering architectural CPU vulnerabilities via differential hardware fuzzing, RISCVuzz (2024)
15. Shuwen Deng, Wenjie Xiong, and Jakub Szefer. Analysis of secure caches using a three-step model for timing-based attacks. *Journal of Hardware and Systems Security*, 3 (4): 397–425, November 2019. ISSN 2509-3436https://doi.org/10.1007/s41635-019-00075-9
16. Bernstein, D.J.: Cache-timing attacks on AES (2005). https://cr.yp.to/antiforgery/cachetiming-20050414.pdf
17. Bertoni, G., Zaccaria, V., Breveglieri, L., Monchiero, M., Palermo, G.: AES power attack based on induced cache miss and countermeasure. In: International Conference on Information Technology: Coding and Computing (ITCC 05) - Volume II, vol. 1, pp. 586–591. IEEE (2005). https://doi.org/10.1109/itcc.2005.62
18. Kogler, A., et al.: Collide+power: leaking inaccessible data with software-based power side channels. In: USENIX Security (2023)
19. Chao, S., Zeng, Q.: Survey of CPU cache-based side-channel attacks: systematic analysis, security models, and countermeasures. Secur. Commun. Netw. 1–15 (2021). https://doi.org/10.1155/2021/5559552. ISSN 1939-0114
20. Osvik, D.A., Shamir, A., Tromer, E.: Cache Attacks and Countermeasures: The Case of AES, pp. 1–20. Springer Berlin Heidelberg (2006). https://doi.org/10.1007/11605805_1
21. Yarom, Y., Falkner, K.: FLUSH+RELOAD: a high resolution, low noise, l3 cache side-channel attack. In: 23rd USENIX Security Symposium (USENIX Security 14), pp. 719–732. USENIX Association, San Diego, CA (2014). https://www.usenix.org/conference/usenixsecurity14/technical-sessions/presentation/yarom
22. Gruss, D., Spreitzer, R., Mangard, S.: Cache template attacks: automating attacks on inclusive last-level caches. In: 24th USENIX Security Symposium (USENIX Security 15), pp. 897–912. USENIX Association, Washington, D.C. (2015). https://www.usenix.org/conference/usenixsecurity15/technical-sessions/presentation/gruss
23. Gruss, D., Maurice, C., Wagner, K., Mangard, S.: Flush+Flush: A Fast and Stealthy Cache Attack, pp. 279–299. Springer International Publishing (2016). https://doi.org/10.1007/978-3-319-40667-1_14
24. Gruss, D., Maurice, C., Mangard, S.: Rowhammer.js: a remote software-induced fault attack in javascript 300–321 (2016). https://doi.org/10.1007/978-3-319-40667-1_15
25. BeagleBoard.org Foundation: BeagleV-Ahead. https://www.beagleboard.org/boards/beaglev-ahead. Accessed 21 Feb 2025
26. BeagleBoard.org Foundation: BeagleV-Fire. https://www.beagleboard.org/boards/beaglev-fire. Accessed 21 Feb 2025
27. SiFive: HiFive Unmatched. https://www.sifive.com/boards/hifive-unmatched. Accessed 21 Feb 2025

28. Kelsey, J., Schneier, B., Wagner, D., Hall, C.: Side Channel Cryptanalysis of Product Ciphers, pp. 97–110. Springer Berlin Heidelberg (1998). https://doi.org/10.1007/bfb0055858
29. Page, D.: Theoretical use of cache memory as a cryptanalytic side-channel. Cryptology ePrint Archive, Paper 2002/169 (2002). https://eprint.iacr.org/2002/169
30. Percival, C.: Cache missing for fun and profit (2005). https://www.daemonology.net/hyperthreading-considered-harmful/
31. Yan, M., Sprabery, R., Gopireddy, B., Fletcher, C., Campbell, R., Torrellas, J.: Attack directories, not caches: side channel attacks in a non-inclusive world. In: 2019 IEEE Symposium on Security and Privacy (SP). IEEE (2019). https://doi.org/10.1109/sp.2019.00004
32. Briongos, S., Malagon, P., Moya, J.M., Eisenbarth, T.: RELOAD+REFRESH: abusing cache replacement policies to perform stealthy cache attacks. In: 29th USENIX Security Symposium (USENIX Security 20), pp. 1967–1984. USENIX Association (2020). https://www.usenix.org/conference/usenixsecurity20/presentation/briongos
33. Kim, Y., et al.: Flipping bits in memory without accessing them: an experimental study of dram disturbance errors. In: 2014 ACM/IEEE 41st International Symposium on Computer Architecture (ISCA), pp. 361–372 (2014). https://doi.org/10.1109/ISCA.2014.6853210
34. Liu, F., Yarom, Y., Ge, Q., Heiser, G., Lee, R.B.: Last-level cache side-channel attacks are practical. In: 2015 IEEE Symposium on Security and Privacy, pp. 605–622 (2015). https://doi.org/10.1109/SP.2015.43
35. Song, W., Liu, P.: Dynamically finding minimal eviction sets can be quicker than you think for side-channel attacks against the LLC. In: 22nd International Symposium on Research in Attacks, Intrusions and Defenses (RAID 2019), pp. 427–442. USENIX Association, Beijing (2019). https://www.usenix.org/conference/raid2019/presentation/song
36. Vila, P., Kopf, B., Morales, J.F.: Theory and practice of finding eviction sets. In: 2019 IEEE Symposium on Security and Privacy (SP), pp. 39–54. IEEE (2019). https://doi.org/10.1109/sp.2019.00042
37. Lipp, M., et al.: Platypus: software-based power side-channel attacks on x86. In: 2021 IEEE Symposium on Security and Privacy (SP), pp. 355–371 (2021). https://doi.org/10.1109/SP40001.2021.00063
38. Lipp, M., Gruss, D., Schwarz, M.: AMD prefetch attacks through power and time. In: 31st USENIX Security Symposium (USENIX Security 22), pp. 643–660. USENIX Association, Boston, MA (2022). https://www.usenix.org/conference/usenixsecurity22/presentation/lipp
39. Lyu, Y., Mishra, P.: A survey of side-channel attacks on caches and countermeasures. J. Hardware Syst. Secur. 2(1), 33–50 (2017). https://doi.org/10.1007/s41635-017-0025-y
40. Shen, C., Chen, C., Zhang, J.: Micro-architectural cache side-channel attacks and countermeasures. In: Proceedings of the 26th Asia and South Pacific Design Automation Conference, ASPDAC 21, pp. 441–448. ACM (2021). https://doi.org/10.1145/3394885.3431638
41. Purnal, A., Giner, L., Gruss, D., Verbauwhede, I.: Systematic analysis of randomization-based protected cache architectures. In: 2021 IEEE Symposium on Security and Privacy (SP), pp. 987–1002. IEEE (2021). https://doi.org/10.1109/sp40001.2021.00011

42. Oleksenko, O., Guarnieri, M., Köpf, B., Silberstein, M.: Hide and seek with spectres: efficient discovery of speculative information leaks with random testing. In: 2023 IEEE Symposium on Security and Privacy (SP), pp. 1737–1752. IEEE (2023)
43. Fabian, X., Guarnieri, M., Patrignani, M.: Automatic detection of speculative execution combinations. In: Proceedings of the 2022 ACM SIGSAC Conference on Computer and Communications Security, pp. 965–978 (2022)
44. Barthe, G., et al.: Testing side-channel security of cryptographic implementations against future microarchitectures. In: Proceedings of the 2024 on ACM SIGSAC Conference on Computer and Communications Security, pp. 1076–1090 (2024)

No Root, No Problem: Automating Linux Least Privilege and Securing Ansible Deployments

Eddie Billoir[1,2(✉)], Romain Laborde[1], Daniele Canavese[1],
Yves Rütschlé[2], Ahmad Samer Wazan[3], and Abdelmalek Benzekri[1]

[1] IRIT, Université de Toulouse, CNRS, Toulouse INP, Toulouse, France
{eddie.billoir,laborde,daniele.canavese,benzekri}@irit.fr
[2] Airbus Protect, Blagnac, France
yves.rutschle@airbus.com
[3] Zayed University, Abu-Dhabi, UAE
ahmad.wazan@zu.ac.ae

Abstract. This article addresses the challenges of enforcing the Principle of Least Administrative Privilege (PoLAP) in Linux systems. We present an innovative approach that orchestrates multiple Linux low-level security mechanisms to provide fine-grained control over the privileges of system administrators. We implemented a completely open-source framework to monitor, analyze, and grant the minimum set of privileges required to perform specific administrative tasks. To demonstrate its practicality in modern deployment approaches, we integrated our framework with the Ansible automation platform towards a zero-trust strategy in Infrastructure-as-Code environments. Our solution reduces the risk of supply chain and internal attacks associated with administrative privilege management while maintaining operational efficiency.

Keywords: Operating system · Access Control · Least Privilege · Linux · Zero-Trust Strategy · Ansible

1 Introduction

Cybersecurity threats are no longer just from outside. The 2024 Data Breach Investigations Report [51] by Verizon states that "35% of breaches were caused by insiders" (e.g.,, employees, contractors, and other trusted individuals). Financial motives are frequently the root cause of these incidents, revealing that even those granted substantial trust and access within an organization can abuse their privileges for personal reasons [3]. This clearly emphasizes the significant role of internal threats in modern cyberattacks and the need to monitor and control privileged access to a system properly. Managing user privileges is particularly challenging due to modern networks and software components' growing complexity and technological heterogeneity.

Recent incidents illustrate the scale of these threats. For example, a former Ubiquiti cybersecurity engineer exploited administrative access to steal confidential data, extort money from the company, and significantly damage its reputation [4]. Similarly, a former Chief Information Security Officer (CISO) of the Hospi Grand Ouest healthcare group in France orchestrated a cyber attack that compromised sensitive healthcare data [52]. These cases highlight the need for a targeted approach to securing administrative privileges, particularly in environments where the risk of abuse is high.

The concept of *privileged access*, mainly used by system administrators, is one of the most fertile avenue for internal exploitation. These users often have unrestricted control over critical systems, making the latter prime targets for malicious actions. Recent software supply-chain attacks demonstrates it as well [2,7,14]. The *Principle of Least Privilege* (PoLP) is an engineering process that involves understanding users' responsibilities to grant them only the minimum permissions required to accomplish their tasks using computer systems [45]. This principle applies to all users but is paramount for system administrators, who often possess elevated privileges essential for system maintenance but can also present substantial risks when misused.

Many organizations implement PoLP via *Privileged Account/Access Management*(PAM) [30], which is the practice of controlling and monitoring elevated access rights to critical resources, ensuring that only authorized users can perform high-risk operations. By enforcing PoLP and providing robust auditing capabilities, organizations can significantly reduce the attack surface and mitigate potential threats from both external and internal actors [17]. In this paper, we focus on the *Principle of Least Administrative Privilege* (PoLAP) as a specific case where we consider applying the PoLP principle to the IT infrastructure administrators. PoLAP, part of PAM, addresses a specific focus on administrators who can modify system configurations and require special access.

Managing the minimum administrative privileges for even the simplest operations in the current Linux ecosystems is daunting for two reasons. First, many access control systems exist (e.g., POSIX file permissions, ACLs, D-Bus, polkit, Linux capabilities, SELinux, and AppArmor access control mechanisms). Second, the interaction of these systems is convoluted and non-trivial to manage. Commonly, Linux solutions suggest creating a new Linux Security Module (LSM). However, introducing an additional LSM increases complexity without addressing the configuration burden of the other mechanisms since all security mechanisms policies must still be aligned with the policy of the new LSM. Instead, we propose an innovative approach: a methodology and an extensible framework that coordinates as many existing Linux access control mechanisms as possible to enable coherent, contextualized access control featuring Just-in-Time (JIT) privilege elevation for administrative tasks.

Our approach follows the MAPE-K (Monitor, Analyse, Plan, Execute – Knowledge) methodology [21]. First, during the *Monitor phase*, we observe the privileges needed to perform an administrative operation. Secondly, in the *Analyze phase*, we examine them and generate a global policy (the *Knowledge*) restricting an administrator to the minimum necessary privileges to fulfill the operation. Optionally, the *Plan phase* audits the system to verify policy compliance before enforcement. Finally, the *Execute phase* enforces the policy to secure the deployment. We implemented a proof-of-concept tool, gensr, which automates the entire workflow. The gensr source code is freely available online [24]. In order to test the practicality of our approach, we also developed a plugin for Ansible, a well-known tool used to automate system configurations and software deployment in IT infrastructures. This plugin automatically generates the global policy of Ansible playbooks, showing that we can avoid potential privilege abuse in large network deployments without increasing the system's complexity. Finally, we propose a zero-trust process for Ansible-based deployments.

This paper is structured as follows: In Sect. 2, we present a short discussion on how administrative privileges are currently managed and why PoLAP is important. In Sects. 3 and 4, we introduce RootAsRole (RaR), present the design of our solution in an Ansible environment and an associated zero-trust process. Section 6 discusses related work. Finally, Sect. 7 contains our conclusions, while Sect. 8 lists the documents in annex.

2 Why Do We Need the Principle of Least Administrative Privilege?

2.1 Applying PoLAP Is Mandatory ...

Initially, most operating systems designed their administrative model around a single superuser, commonly referred to as *root*. This design was suitable for minimal infrastructures, where a single administrator could manage all the system features. In stark contrast, the modern trend is to multiply the number of system administrators.

Firstly, organisations are increasingly implementing IT service management models that develop co-administration. Small and medium companies usually outsource the management of their IT infrastructures to external service providers. Bigger organizations often integrate an IT infrastructure team, each member can operate administration tasks on the managed systems. Finally, some organizations adopt an admin-by-request approach to grant users administrative privileges for a limited time when they have an occasional need to install or update software for instance.

Many companies are adopting new hybrid usage of IT devices, either Personally Owned/Company-enabled or Corporate- Owned/Personally Enabled. A trade-off between organizations' data security and employees personal data privacy is mandatory. Accordingly, co-administration of such devices between administrators of organizations and employees is required, especially there is a need for preventing unlawful access to personal data by administrators.

This situation is also exacerbated by new deployment approaches such as Infrastructure-as-Code (IaC), which aim to simplify the management of (virtual) data center resources by leveraging human-readable configuration and script files instead of hardware or interactive tools. This methodology has many advantages, such as allowing faster and more system provisioning and reducing human errors. On the other hand, it also can massively distribute administrative authority. This approach replaces the traditional single-administrator with a collaborative framework where developers, DevOps engineers, and sometimes third-party configuration repositories hold administrative responsibilities on an entire infrastructure.

Not only do IT service management and technological trends demand a multiple administrative system, but several regulations also require or suggest it. For instance, Regulation (EU) 2016/679 [37], more commonly known as GDPR (General Data Protection Regulation), in Recital 78, suggests "minimising the processing of personal data [...] as soon as possible". Other European regulations either mandate or encourage it, including the Cyber Resilience Act (Regulation (EU) 2024/2847) [39], Export Control (Regulation (EU) 2021/821) [38] or NIS 2 [33] (e.g., Directive 49). In France, military regulation such as II901 [19] enforces it too. Furthermore, some domain-specific regulations like ESA [10] (e.g., ESA_REG_004), or EASA Part-IS [40] (Article 11, Regulation 2021/2223) establish additional requirements in the spatial and aeronautics sectors.

2.2 ...but Applying PoLAP on Linux Systems Is Challenging

The traditional model of relying on a single superuser with unrestricted privileges shared across multiple stakeholders poses significant risks and is no longer sustainable from IT service management and legal perspectives. However, implementing PoLAP on Linux system is complex and challenging.

In a general-purpose Linux distribution, such as Debian or Red Hat, access control to the resources (e.g., files, main memory, sockets) is fragmented into a variety of mechanisms, which usually include, but are not limited to:

- *POSIX File Access Control*, that is the foundational model built on file ownership (user, group, and others) and basic permission rights (read, write, and execute);
- *Discretionary Access Control Lists (ACLs)*, which extends the POSIX model, allowing more fine-grained permissions by enabling specific rules for individual users or groups beyond the traditional owner-group-other scheme;
- *Inter-Process Communication (IPC) access control mechanisms*, like D-Bus [13] and polkit [41], which govern how processes communicate with each other—these frameworks provide centralized control and define permissions for privileged software operations initiated by unprivileged users and services;
- *Linux capabilities* [28], which is implemented by the kernel since version 2.2, breaks down the traditional 'all-or-nothing' root powers initially associated to UID 0 into distinct rights known as capabilities (e.g., `CAP_NET_BIND_SERVICE` to bind a port less than 1024 or `CAP_DAC_OVERRIDE` to bypass POSIX and ACL access control mechanisms). There are different capabilities management solutions [6] that allow basic control such as command `setcap` or more fine-grained control such as `sr` [54];

- *Namespaces* [29], which allow isolation of system resources (e.g., containerization) such as process IDs, network interfaces, mount points, and more. However, namespaces do not, by themselves, enforce access control on shared resources—they are primarily isolation primitives. Their security properties emerge only when considering the principle of *least common mechanism* [45];
- *cgroups*, which complements Linux namespaces to provide administrative limits on the usage of shared resources;
- *Linux Security Modules (LSMs)* which provides an interface for security checks to be hooked by new kernel extensions. This component allows new security mechanisms such as SELinux [46] and AppArmor [50], which provide Mandatory Access Control (MAC) to Linux.

Furthermore, ensuring complete mediation—every access to every object must be checked for authority [45]—is difficult in Linux due to its fragmented security model. While these mechanisms together create a strong layered security approach, combining them in a consistent way is challenging. Each security technology has distinct security models and configuration languages, and their interactions introduce non-trivial implications. Additionally, the Linux kernel itself does not always provide full fine-grained granularity for its Linux capabilities [6]. Even LSMs cannot enforce complete mediation because they cannot make decisions on access requests that are denied by other security mechanisms. For example, Fig. 1 depicts the complex access control workflow enforced by Linux OS when a user tries to read a file. First, the POSIX and ACL rules are sequentially checked. If access is refused, the kernel checks if the process has either capability CAP_DAC_OVERRIDE or CAP_DAC_READ_SEARCH. If this is not the case, the access is refused. If either POSIX, ACL or capabilities allow the access, the system will call all the LSMs installed on the system to verify if they all grant the access. Configuring PoLAP requires fine grained configuration for each security mechanisms, which have each their own configuration language and security concepts.

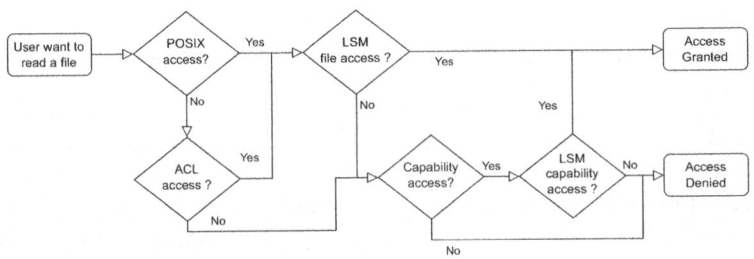

Fig. 1. Access control workflow implemented in Linux systems to control file accesses.

The second challenge is that there may be several ways of performing the same system action, and therefore several access control workflows to manage. Let us consider rebooting the system. According to the kernel documentation, the only requirement for rebooting a system is to own the `CAP_SYS_BOOT` capability. However, several Linux distributions use systemd [48] as the system and service manager (i.e., systemd runs as PID 1 and starts the rest of the system). In such systems, executing the `reboot` command calls a D-Bus method called `org.freedesktop.login1.Manager.Reboot`. D-Bus relies on its own access control system as well as Polkit, and both security mechanisms have different configuration formats. But, if the `reboot` command is used with the `--force` option, it directly calls the `reboot` system call, bypassing D-Bus. To make even more confusing, the `--force` parameter explicitly requires the user to be the root user.

These two examples showcase how complex managing administrative privileges is, even for simplistic operations like rebooting the operating system.

3 Orchestrating Linux Security Mechanisms to Enforce PoLAP Using RootAsRole

RootAsRole (RaR) is an open-source project [24] which we developed originally to provide a simple command, called `sr` (Switch-Role), as an alternative to the traditional `sudo` tool [53]. Its use is similar, but implements a role-based access control model [11] to support Linux capabilities. In order to help in configuring a RaR policy, we developed the `capable` tool, which monitors the specific Linux capabilities required to execute common commands [54]. This tool allowed us to uncover potential kernel design issues and challenges [6].

However, as discussed in Sect. 2.2, Linux capabilities alone are insufficient for applying PoLAP correctly and handling every administrative task. In this paper, we aim to leverage a wide range of available access control mechanisms to broaden the addressed use cases, better understand the administrator's needs, and minimize their system privileges in alignment with the PoLAP definition.

In the following paragraphs, we first present an overview of our approach; then, we detail its two main phases, i.e., the privilege monitoring and the deployment.

3.1 General Approach

Enforcing PoLAP, even for a single Linux administrative task, requires configuring a complex chain of heterogeneous security mechanisms. Building a new LSM simply adds complexity and does not solve this problem. We therefore propose an alternative approach, which consists in orchestrating the existing security mechanisms in a consistent and unified way to control the security chain globally (see Fig. 2).

Our approach follows the MAPE-K methodology [21]. It consists in monitoring the different privileges (e.g., access to files, requested capabilities, or D-Bus services calls) required to perform a specific administrative task (Monitor). The second step is to find the minimum set of necessary privileges based on the previous result (Analysis). These two steps are implemented by the command `gensr generate`, which produces a RaR policy containing the monitored privileges and with minimal filtering rules. The next step involves an auditing phase (Plan), like the SELinux "permissive" phase, but for the compliance of RaR general policy, this still needs to be implemented in our proof-of-concept. This step is optional for small infrastructures, but important for complex industrial ones. Finally calling the `gensr deploy` command enforces the configuration to the system (e.g., the ACLs and D-Bus). From then on, the `sr` command can be used as a `sudo` alternative to execute commands in a safer environment, granting only minimal rights and with additional security features [24] (Deploy).

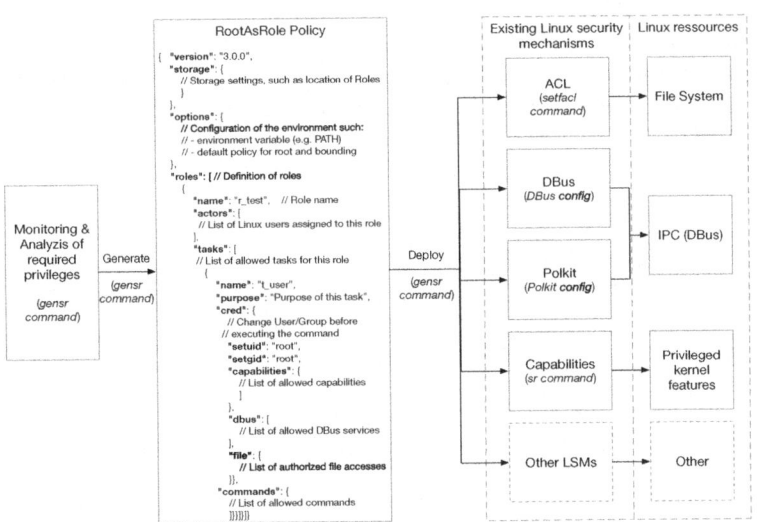

Fig. 2. General approach overview.

3.2 Monitoring and Analysis of Privileges

The first objective is to monitor the system in order to obtain a full set of privileges requested by a generic command. Doing this manually is cumbersome; thus we developed a tool to monitor privileges. The first version of this tool was limited to examine Linux capabilities [54]. In line with our MAPE-K methodology, this article extends these features and introduces an automated approach.

Two approaches can be employed [8] to determine the minimal set of permissions. The *record-then-replace* strategy starts by granting all the privileges to the studied process and captures the permissions used during its execution. In the *fail-then-add* approach, the process under study starts with no permissions. When it fails due to missing authorization, the absent permissions are suggested incrementally; this procedure is repeated until the process under study can run to completion. *Record-then-replace* is faster. However, this strategy can only capture the first way of performing a program under study. In the case of `reboot`, it will only detect the dbus access control workflow, while *fail-then-add* can identify both dbus and syscall methods. This behaviour can also introduce security issues when the Linux kernel does not correctly implement the access control workflow [5,15,55] (see Sect. 8.1 for more details). *Fail-then-add* is safer because it doesn't grant initially any privileges to the command under study. Nevertheless, this strategy cannot handle commands that depends on the system state (e.g., apt install somepackage) because partial failures may set the system in an unstable state (e.g., the package can be in broken state). Therefore, we implemented both *fail-then-add* and *record-then-replace* strategies to provide a comprehensive approach.

Our `gensr` implementation process consists of the following phases: 1) initialization, 2) monitoring, and 3) analysis. Figure 3 depicts the different steps of each phase. In the *record-then-replace* strategy, the program under study starts as root with all the capabilities. On the other hand, the process to be monitored is executed using a new user with no capabilities in the *fail-then-add* strategy and repeated until it can terminate.

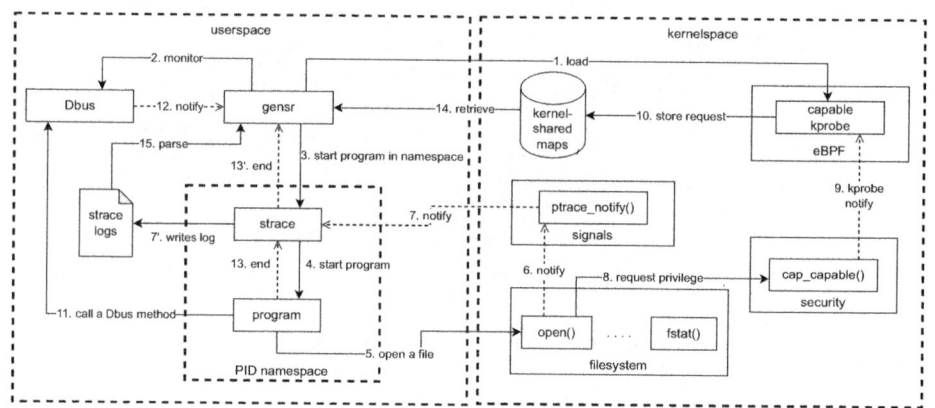

Fig. 3. Our monitoring and analysis process implemented by `gensr`.

Figure 3 depicts the monitoring workflow[1]. The initialization phase consists of:

1. Loading and attaching [42] an eBPF program to the `cap_capable` kprobe function call [32] to monitor capabilities requests. An eBPF program is a kernel-based virtual machine that allows the execution of user-defined bytecode in a secure and high-performance manner. Kprobe is a kernel debugging mechanism that enables the attachment of our eBPF program to the `cap_capable` kernel function entry point, which allows us to provide a dynamic way to trace and monitor Linux capabilities requests.

---

[1] For the sake of readability, the numbers in the arrow labels match the numbers in the following lists.

2. Connecting to the D-Bus system socket and invoking the org.freedesktop.DBus.Monitoring.BecomeMonitor D-Bus method, enabling us to intercept all D-Bus methods invoked on the system bus instance.
3. Starting a new PID namespace [27] to limit the collected information on the program under study.

Then, the monitoring stage dynamically supervises the process under study. It consists of:

4. Launching the program under study for monitoring its file-system syscalls via strace, a Linux utility for monitoring and debugging interactions between user-space processes and the kernel [47] based on ptrace.
5. The program under study performs some filesystem operations (e.g., an *open* syscall).
6. Since syscalls are monitored by ptrace, calling them triggers a notification to the strace process via the ptrace_notify kernel call.
7. The ptrace_notify call informs the strace process, which translates the syscall into a human-readable format using its static call database and logs the monitored data.
8. During the syscall, the program may request Linux capabilities (e.g., CAP_DAC_OVERRIDE to bypass the ACLs).
9. Here, when the kernel enters into cap_capable function, kprobes is notified.
10. Our eBPF program then collect all the process information, such as the PID namespace identifier and the requested capabilities. It then stores the gathered data in eBPF maps which allows user-space processes to access it.
11. The program under study opens a D-Bus socket to invoke a method call (e.g., to reboot the system).
12. The D-Bus system notifies all monitoring processes, hence gensr collect the data based on the PID namespace identifier.
13. After the program under study terminates, strace also ends its execution.

Finally, gensr can start its analysis stage:

14. It retrieves all stored data from eBPF maps, filtering out information unrelated to the monitored program.
15. It parses the strace log file to extract file paths and verifies the corresponding file permissions in the current filesystem.
16. gensr compiles all the information based on PID identifiers, generating a comprehensive report detailing the monitored activities.

The whole monitoring process is implemented by executing gensr generate -- mode [manual | automatic] -- <program-to-monitor> <options> <args>. The manual mode generates only the capabilities, D-Bus, and file sections of the RaR policy, letting administrators choose the roles, tasks, actors, setuid, and setgid sections to their context. The automatic mode generates a full RaR policy where roles, tasks, actors, setuid, and setgid are set to values based on the hash of the monitored program name and its arguments, although this procedure may change as new organisational features are introduced.

3.3 Deployment of RootAsRole Policies

Our deployment approach aligns with the principles of Just-In-Time (JIT) privileged access by ensuring that privileges—both static and dynamic—are granted only during the execution of specific administrative tasks [16]. Static permissions, such as ACLs and D-Bus/Polkit access control, are predefined and remain fixed within the system. In contrast, Linux capabilities are granted on the fly and activated only during the execution of authorized processes or tasks.

To further enforce secure privilege management, our RaR `gensr` dynamically creates and manages users to ensure enforcement of both ACLs and D-Bus permissions. This design is nearly aligned with the principles of *JIT account creation and deletion* and *JIT disabled administrative accounts*, as these users are generated and activated only during the deployment of the policy. However, users and ACLs are not deleted immediately after the task is completed; instead, they remain in the system until the RaR policy is uninstalled.

Additionally, our `sr` tool implements the *JIT privilege* technique by leveraging the Linux capabilities bounding set, a mechanism placing an upper limit on the capabilities a process (and its descendants) can acquire, to provide stricter control over privilege assignment. In addition, it also implements the *JIT impersonation* technique, that is, by dynamically switching users, privileges are granted just-in-time for specific tasks, aligning with the elevated operations required for administrative execution.

The deployment of the RaR policy is automatically done by executing `gensr deploy -c <policy-file>`. This command creates the users/groups, the ACLs, the D-Bus/Polkit policies and copies the RaR policy in `/etc./security/rootasrole.json` for our `sr` command. It is also possible to uninstall the policy by executing `gensr undeploy -c <policy-file>`. It removes the users/groups, the ACLs, the D-Bus/Polkit policies previously created, and the `rootasrole.json` file. Our `gensr` command is freely available online[2].

4 Enforcing PoLAP in Ansible Deployments

Ansible [1] is a well-known open-source technology for automating IT management tasks such as software provisioning, configuration management, and application deployment. System administrators can define repeatable IT management tasks in script files known as *playbooks*, which list the actions to be performed on the managed hosts. A key playbook feature is its idempotency, which enhances the predictability of IT tasks. Executing a playbook any number of times will always yield the same state for the target-managed hosts.

Ansible provides an extensive collection of ready-to-use content (plugins, modules, roles, and playbooks) that simplifies the automation of common server tasks such as installing packages, creating and managing users, manipulating files and permissions, and managing services. Ansible Galaxy[3] is a freely accessible website where anyone from the community can create and share resources

---

[2] https://github.com/LeChatP/RootAsRole-gensr
[3] https://galaxy.ansible.com/.

for Ansible, fostering a collaborative ecosystem that continuously expands its capabilities and speed up deployment process implementation.

However, the Ansible approach to administration has two main drawbacks. First, it multiplies the number of administrators (see Sect. 2). Second, Ansible has an all-or-nothing approach to privileges since the only implemented solution to acquire administrative rights is to use a single boolean value `become: true`, which will give all privileges to any Ansible task specifying it.

4.1 Practical Example

Let's consider Alice, Dorine, and Mallory. Alice is a system administrator responsible for deploying an Apache2 web server that hosts a website developed by Dorine. Instead, Mallory is an Ansible Galaxy contributor who created the Ansible role[4] `mallory_net_input` to simplify the firewall policy configuration on Linux systems. To deploy the website, Alice writes the playbook presented in Fig. 4. As she does not develop the website and is not a network administrator, she uses Dorine's playbook to deploy the website content and Mallory's Ansible role to open TCP port 80 on the firewall to access the web server.

```
1.  ---
2.  - name: Ansible Playbook to Install and Setup Apache on Ubuntu
3.    hosts: webserver
4.    become: true
5.    gather_facts: false
6.    tasks:
7.      - name: Install latest version of Apache
8.        ansible.builtin.apt: name=apache2 update_cache=true state=fixed force=true
9.        [...]
10.     - name: Deploy website source code
11.       ansible.builtin.import_tasks: tasks/deploy-website.yml
12.       [...]
13.     - name: Open port 80
14.       ansible.builtin.import_role: name=mallory_net_input
15.       vars:
16.         mallory_net_input_protocol: tcp
17.         mallory_net_input_port: 80
18.         mallory_net_input_state: accepting
```

Fig. 4. Example of a playbook to install and configure an Apache2 server.

The playbook is described below:

1. Lines 2–6 define the metadata of the playbook, such as the name and the managed hosts where the tasks will be executed. An important statement is line 4, which declares that every task will be executed with administrative privileges on the managed hosts. By default, Ansible will use `sudo` to elevate the privileges to root.
2. The first task (lines 7–8) ensures that the last version of Apache2 is installed on the managed host.
3. The next tasks (line 9) ensure website's directory exists (omitted for brevity).

---

[4] For the sake of clarity, an Ansible role is not the same as an RBAC role. An *Ansible role* is essentially a parametric script that can be reused in playbooks and tasks.

4. In lines 10–11, Alice calls Dorine's playbook (`deploy-website.yml`) to install her website on the web server.
5. Next tasks (line 12) are in charge of deploying the Apache2 configuration, to enable the website (omitted for brevity).
6. The last task (lines 13–18) calls the `mallory_net_input` role to ensure the firewall accepts incoming HTTP requests.

It is important to note that Ansible will execute the `mallory_net_input` community role and the `deploy-website.yml` playbook on the managed host with all administrative privileges (due to the line `become: true`); Consequently, Alice, Dorine, and Mallory should be considered administrators since they have root privileges over the managed host through the execution of their playbook or role. In addition, although using the Mallory's role and Dorine's playbook simplifies Alice's playbook implementation, many tasks are not directly visible to her, which can lead to potential supply chain attacks. For instance, if Mallory's role maliciously installs a reverse shell in addition to configuring the firewall, she can surreptitiously gain full root privileges for the system. The same risk may exist with insiders, i.e., Dorine and even Alice. A deep review of the playbooks and roles is thus mandatory before applying them in a strictly controlled way in the production environment. In the following paragraphs, we will show how our approach can be used to tackle these issues.

4.2 Deploying Ansible Playbooks with RootAsRole

The deployment of Ansible playbooks within the RaR framework introduces a structured and secure workflow that strengthens privilege management during configuration automation. The global view, shown in Fig. 5, illustrates a multi-stage process that starts from the control host and ends with a secure deployment on the target infrastructure.

The process begins on the Ansible control host (ideally, a VM or a container), where an initial playbook and inventory are defined. These are passed as input (Step 1) during the `gensr` pipeline by invoking the `ansible-playbook` command with the command line option `--become-method gensr` (Step 2). A testing infrastructure must be available prior to this step—ideally, and its provisioning should also be automated. The testing environment is defined using the initial inventory and serves as a safe environment for `gensr` to analyze the playbook and gather the information necessary to automatically generate the policy (Step 3).

Following this analysis phase, `gensr` produces a modified version of the playbook (Step 4) and the corresponding RaR policy (Step 5). The generated playbook uses `sr` instead of `sudo` and applies the RaR policy thanks to our new Ansible plugin. These outputs are then deployed via Ansible: first the RaR policy is installed on the remote hosts using a predefined playbook (Step 6), then the modified playbook containing critical administrative tasks is executed (Step 7). This ensures that privilege escalations are tightly controlled and occur only within the boundaries defined by the generated policy. The main interest of this process is to avoid supply-chain attacks during the update of an Ansible role

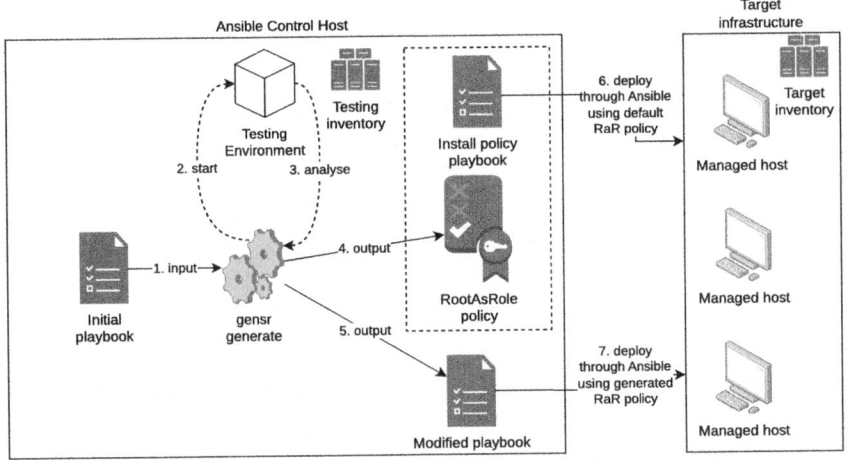

Fig. 5. Global Ansible automated deployment process view.

or module. The initial and modified playbooks as well as the RaR policy are available on the companion website [23].

Future developments of gensr will rely on eBPF in place of strace. This will allow to audit the system before enforcing the RaR policy, which will implement the Plan part of the MAPE-K methodology.

4.3 Towards a Zero-Trust Ansible Deployment Process

Using RaR allows Alice to verify and control the privileges of the roles and playbooks that she imported into her Ansible playbook. This eliminates the need to trust Dorine or Mallory. However, the organization still relies on Alice, who can abuse her position. In this section, we thus explore a deployment process that complies with a zero-trust strategy.

Let's consider Alice, Bob, and Charlie, who are responsible for deploying Ansible playbooks. Alice develops and tests the playbook within her personal development environment. As the deployment tester, Bob validates the playbook in a production-representative infrastructure, ensuring its reliability and compatibility. Finally, Charlie deploys the playbook to the real production infrastructure if Bob confirms its verification. This sequence is illustrated in Fig. 6.

The integration of RaR policy generation enhances this workflow by allowing each participant to verify the playbook and its associated RaR policy independently. For instance:

1. Alice generates the initial RaR policy and verifies its conformity to the tasks in her playbook. She then transmits the playbook to Bob and the policy to Bob and Charlie.
2. Bob validates the Ansible playbook and the RaR policy. He may generate a RaR policy using gensr to compare it to Alices' one to check if Alice did

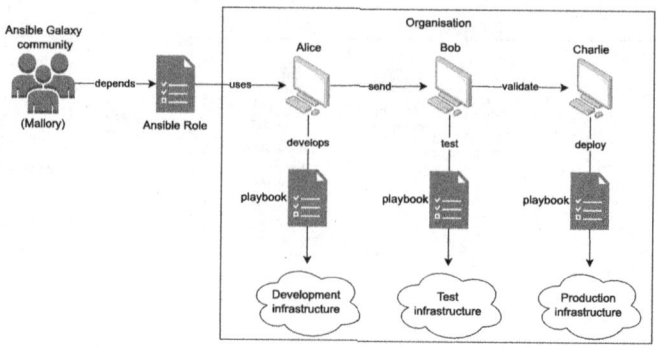

Fig. 6. Project process to deploy in production example.

not add supplementary privileges for a future attack. Bob then transmits the playbook and the policy to Charlie.
3. Charlie, who received the RaR policy from both Alice and Charlie, can compare them. If they differ, it means that Bob has modified Alice's policy, thus indicating a potential attack.

This layered approach creates a chain of verification, reducing the organization's need for implicit trust in the stakeholders because:

- Input from Mallory (i.e., people outside the organization) or Dorine are verified by Alice;
- Input from Alice is verified by Bob and Charlie;
- Input from Bob is verified by Charlie.

This verification process mitigates the need to trust Mallory, Alice, and Bob. However, it also puts Charlie in a privileged position since nobody can verify his activities. This poses a significant risk, as he has the final word over deployments. The deployment environment such as versioning tools (e.g., Git) can address this issue by preventing the edition of the playbook by Charlie. Charlie's deployment can include an automatic verification step by requiring Alice and Bob to sign the policy with their respective credentials during the development and testing phases.

This solution is easy to implement because the same organization employs Alice, Bob, and Charlie; thus, all the actors belong to the same authority. This approach is a step towards a future zero-trust procedure for Ansible playbook deployments where no involved entity needs to be fully trusted.

5 Discussion

5.1 Security Analysis

The gensr generate tool introduces significant risks that must be considered. To grant privileges to a program under analysis, gensr generate requires full system privileges in the worst case. Therefore, its usage must be strictly limited to authorized administrators. We recommend using a dedicated initial RaR policy to ensure granular control.

Additionally, `gensr generate` executes the commands of the analyzed program directly on the system, albeit within a PID namespace. If the program being analyzed is malicious, it will still execute on the system. At the end of the monitoring process, `gensr generate` grants the program all necessary privileges to function properly. Thus, the generated RaR policy must also be reviewed to evaluate the granted privileges. Furthermore, `gensr generate` should only be used in a controlled test environment that mirrors the production setup to avoid unintended impacts on live data or operations. This approach aligns with invoking the program within a testing environment, as detailed in Sect. 4.2. Finally, since Ansible playbooks can execute commands directly on the Ansible Control Host, it must also be isolated. Containerization solutions, like Docker, can test program behavior but are not foolproof, as they require privileged containers (i.e., containers with extra Linux capabilities), reducing isolation. Standard Docker containers lack all Linux capabilities required by `gensr generate` (currently, 6 additional are needed). Consequently, we recommend using virtual machines to ensure better isolation and security.

We also do not support use cases that alter the kernel source code, such as loading kernel modules (e.g., installing the VirtualBox hypervisor).

5.2 Usability and Performance

Regarding usability, RaR incorporates features inspired by prior research [5]. These design choices help in preventing common misconfigurations and improve the overall RaR adminstrators' experience. Furthermore, RaR supports interchangeable policy formats, allowing RaR administrators to switch from JSON format for better readability or CBOR format for better performance. Nevertheless, a comprehensive usability evaluation remains an open task and is planned as future work.

RaR version 3.1.0 `sr` tool introduces significant optimisations and outperforms the original `sudo` implementation by up to 66% when using the CBOR policy format. A complete performance analysis is available on our github project [22]. While we acknowledge that the Rust reimplementation of `sudo` [12] may achieve better raw performance, RaR supports more security features aligned with the PoLAP. However, improving the performance of RaR is still an ongoing work. For instance, switching to the SQLite [25] format or using a DBMS could further improve the performance.

6 Related Work

SELinux and AppArmor are the main LSMs to enforce fine-grained access control in Linux systems. They come with `audit2allow` [43] and `aa-genprof` [49] respectively to help security administrators to create security policies. However, as mentioned in Sect. 2, both solutions only operate at the end of the security mechanisms workflow, shadowing previous access-denied decisions. This means that any system administrator needs to configure the previous access control systems two times. Landlock [26] is another LSM which allows a process to restrict its own privileges regarding file system operations, thus allowing the software developers to apply their access control policy. While this approach may mitigate external attacks, it does not address internal threats. Our approach is different because we do not intend to build a new security mechanism but instead offer a system for orchestrating existing low-level mechanisms in Linux systems.

Other approaches were proposed for Linux systems. Markus Lorch et al. [31] developed a privilege access management framework called PRIMA based on POSIX DAC and the Slashgrid kernel module. This work was only meant to manage file access mechanisms without working on privileged program execution. Open policy agent [35] is an open-source, general-purpose policy engine that unifies policy enforcement across various systems. It can be integrated with sudo to verify whether a privileged command is allowed. While it supports many systems, it does not manage low-level access control mechanisms such as ACLs, capabilities, or D-Bus, which must be already configured. BPF Compiler Collection [20] is another framework designed to facilitate the development and deployment of eBPF programs in the Linux kernel. Among its features, it includes the capable tool, which logs every privilege request in real-time. However, this tool is limited to monitoring activities only.

Regarding Ansible deployment controls, Ansible Automation Platform [44] is a web-based interface and enterprise solution for managing Ansible, developed by Red Hat. Its main feature is to organise and control permissions to edit Ansible resources (playbook, roles, inventory, etc.) based on the RBAC model. However, this solution does not prevent supply chain attacks (e.g., Mallory's role), nor insiders' attacks (Alice creates a malicious playbook).

Finally, many proprietary Privileged Access/Account Management solutions are available such as SUSE Manager [36], IBM IGI [18], CyberArk [9] or Okta [34]. Although they propose just-in-time access control (e.g., creation of users for a task), these proprietary solutions apparently only rely on user access, file access, and command access management. We were unable to precisely determine the level of control on the privileges (e.g., capabilities, D-Bus) offered by these solutions based solely on the available documentation.

7 Conclusion and Future Work

Following the zero-trust strategy and recent surge of threats, we argue that Principle of Least Administrative Privileges shall be carefully considered. However, granting the minimum set of administrative privileges for even the simplest administrative operations in the current Linux ecosystems is challenging. We therefore enhanced RootAsRole, an open-source project, to allow fine-grained control over Linux system administrators privileges. Instead of building yet another Linux security module, thus further increasing the already complex

Linux security management ecosystem, our innovative approach aims at coordinating the currently available low-level Linux access control mechanisms in a unified way. We designed a solution to obtain the minimum necessary privileges needed to perform administrative tasks and generate and enforce the respective RootAsRole policy restricting administrators. We integrated RootAsRole with Ansible by implementing different plugins to test its practicability in Infrastructure-as-Code environments. We demonstrated that our solution initiates another practical step for organizations to enforce a zero-trust strategy in administrative roles.

For future work, we plan to make RootAsRole extensible by the community by providing interfaces to easily create plugins to integrate more security mechanisms managed (e.g., LSMs, namespaces, cgroups). and thus to adhere to the principle of complete mediation. We also plan to create a role engineering methodology to facilitate the elicitation of administrative roles in order to address the organizational dimension of PoLAP, particularly considering the challenges of carefully managing manual processes and mitigating the risk of colluding malicious administrators. Finally, our long-term objective is to prove that a RootAsRole policy enforces the Principle of Least Administrative Privileges with the least impact on operational performance.

Acknowledgements. This work has been partially funded by Institut Cybersécurité Occitanie and projects CNRS EU-CHECK and Horizon Europe DUCA (GA 101086308).

Disclosure of Interests. There are no competing interests.

8 Annexes

```
1.  {"roles": [{
2.     "name": "rar_e4cea3cea6e87ab64741a2282121b087c777f877075c0455e830f7c0",
3.     "tasks": [{"name": 5,
4.        "purpose": "Open port 80",
5.        "cred": {
6.           "setuid": "rar_10db069b8c9c596fd8653ee3f40f4496e67c4fdb19e72d3e932f4183",
7.           "setgid": "rar_10db069b8c9c596fd8653ee3f40f4496e67c4fdb19e72d3e932f4183",
8.           "capabilities": { "default": "none", "add": ["CAP_NET_ADMIN", "CAP_NET_RAW"] },
9.        "dbus": [],
10.       "files": {
11.          "/run": "WX",
12.          "/run/xtables.lock": "RW"
13.       },
14.       "commands": { "default": "all" }}}]}]}
15.
```

Fig. 7. Sample of the policy generated by gensr based on the Ansible playbook.

8.1 Privilege Validation Ordering Mistake Example

In Sect. 3.2, we explained that the *fail-then-add* strategy gives more assurance on the final set of privileges than the *record-then-replace* strategy. We provide here a concrete example. Figure 8 displays a sample of the Linux kernel source

```
1. if (capable(CAP_SYS_ADMIN) || uid_eq(key->uid, current_fsuid())) {
2.
```

Fig. 8. Privilege validation ordering mistake in security/keys/keyctl.c file.

```
1. if (uid_eq(key->uid, current_fsuid()) || capable(CAP_SYS_ADMIN)) {
2.
```

Fig. 9. Privilege validation ordering in security/keys/keyctl.c after being fixed by Christian Göttsche (kernel version > 6.5).

code related to the modification of the linux keyring permissions[5]. This condition verifies that the current process has the `CAP_SYS_ADMIN` capability, if not, it checks that the owner of the process is also the keyring owner in order to allow it to modify the keyring access permissions. The order in which conditions are written is important. Indeed, the *record-then-replace* approach will detect that the process needs the `CAP_SYS_ADMIN` capability to execute the code because this privilege was used by the fully privileged process. In the *fail-then-add* approach, the process has no privilege but will be able to execute the code because the second condition statement related to the UID is valid. As a consequence, this approach will detect that no privileges are required to execute the code, which is the good result. Hopefully, this ordering issue was fixed in July 2023 in kernel version 6.5 (see Fig. 9). Now, the *record-then-replace* approach provides the same output as the *fail-then-add*.

8.2 Report Generated by Gensr for the Malicious Version of Mallory's Role

```
1.  { "capabilities": [
2.      "CAP_NET_ADMIN",
3.      "CAP_NET_RAW"
4.    ],
5.    "files": {
6.      "/run/xtables.lock": "RW",
7.      "/etc/shadow": "R",
8.      "/home/ansible": "R",
9.      "/run": "WX"
10.   },
11.   "dbus": []}
12.
```

Fig. 10. Report generated by gensr when there is a hidden reverse shell in Mallory's role.

Figure 10 shows a sample of the report generated when the Mallory's role installs a hidden reverse shell using netcat and tries to print `/etc./shadow` to obtain the list of passwords. This malicious role needs two additional read access permissions (on `/etc./ansible` used by netcat and `/etc./shadow` to print the content of the file). Therefore, this attack is blocked by the RootAsRole policy (Fig. 7).

---
[5] https://github.com/torvalds/linux/commit/2d7f105edbb3b2be5ffa4d833abbf9b6965 e9ce7#diff-ef5441b5221c8fb580169c2d83b7db9e82344ebbd4751f523a8fe5b63a976c11 L1091.

References

1. Ansible project: Homepage | Ansible Collaborative (2024). https://www.ansible.com/
2. Assaraf, A.: 1/6 | How We Hacked Multi-Billion Dollar Companies in 30 Minutes Using a Fake VSCode Extension (Oct 2024). https://medium.com/extensiontotal/the-story-of-extensiontotal-how-we-hacked-the-vscode-marketplace-5c6e66a0e9d7
3. Ball, D.G.V., Deborah: mass leak of client data rattles swiss banking. Wall Street J. (2010)
4. Belanger, A.: Ex-Ubiquiti engineer behind "breathtaking" data theft gets 6-year prison term (May 2023). https://arstechnica.com/tech-policy/2023/05/ex-ubiquiti-engineer-behind-breathtaking-data-theft-gets-6-year-prison-term/
5. Billoir, E.e.a.: Implementing the principle of least privilege using linux capabilities: challenges and perspectives. In: 2023 7th Cyber Security in Networking Conference (CSNet), pp. 130–136. IEEE, Montreal, QC, Canada (Oct 2023). https://doi.org/10.1109/CSNet59123.2023.10339753, https://ieeexplore.ieee.org/document/10339753/
6. Billoir, E., et al.: Implementing the principle of least administrative privilege on operating systems: challenges and perspectives. Annals Telecommun. **79**(11), 857–880 (2024). https://doi.org/10.1007/s12243-024-01033-5
7. Boehs, E.: Everything I know about the XZ backdoor. https://boehs.org/node/everything-i-know-about-the-xz-backdoor
8. Carter, M.K.: Techniques to approach least privilege. IDPro Body of Knowledge **1**(9) (2022)
9. Homepage. https://www.cyberark.com/
10. Highlights of ESA rules and regulations. https://www.esa.int/About_Us/Law_at_ESA/Highlights_of_ESA_rules_and_regulations
11. Ferraiolo, D.F., et al.: Proposed nist standard for role-based access control. ACM Trans. Inf. Syst. Secur. **4**(3), 224 274 (2001).https://doi.org/10.1145/501978.501980, https://doi.org/10.1145/501978.501980
12. Foundation, T.T.: trifectatechfoundation/sudo-rs, https://github.com/trifectatechfoundation/sudo-rs, original-date: 2022-12-12T16:40:01Z
13. Dbus. https://www.freedesktop.org/wiki/Software/dbus/
14. Goldman, I., Kadkoda, Y.: Can You Trust Your VSCode Extensions? - Aqua Security. https://www.aquasec.com/blog/can-you-trust-your-vscode-extensions/ (Jan 2023)
15. Göttsche, C.: Security: Keys: Perform capable check only on privileged operations · torvalds/linux@2d7f105. https://github.com/torvalds/linux/commit/2d7f105edbb3b2be5ffa4d833abbf9b69-65e9ce7
16. Haber, M.J.: Just in time. In: Privileged Attack Vectors, pp. 285–294. Apress, Berkeley, CA (2020). https://doi.org/10.1007/978-1-4842-5914-6_21
17. Haber, M.J.: Privileged Attack Vectors: Building Effective Cyber-Defense Strategies to Protect Organizations. Apress, Berkeley, CA (2020). https://doi.org/10.1007/978-1-4842-5914-6, http://link.springer.com/10.1007/978-1-4842-5914-6
18. Technical overview - IBM Documentation. https://www.ibm.com/docs/en/sig-and-i/5.2.3?topic=overview-technical
19. Instruction interminist rielle relative la protection des syst mes d'informations sensibles - l gifrance
20. iovisor: Github project: Iovisor/bcc (Jan 2025). https://github.com/iovisor/bcc

21. Kephart, J., Chess, D.: The vision of autonomic computing. Computer **36**(1), 41–50 (2003). https://doi.org/10.1109/MC.2003.1160055
22. LeChatP: LeChatP/RaR-perf. https://github.com/LeChatP/RaR-perf
23. LeChatP: LeChatP/rootasansible. https://github.com/LeChatP/RootAsAnsible
24. LeChatP: Github project: LeChatP/RootAsRole (Jan 2025). https://github.com/LeChatP/RootAsRole
25. tursodatabase/limbo (Apr 2025). https://github.com/tursodatabase/limbo
26. Landlock(7) - Linux manual page. https://www.man7.org/linux/man-pages/man7/landlock.7.html
27. Namespaces(7) - Linux manual page. https://www.man7.org/linux/man-pages/man7/namespaces.7.html
28. capabilities(7). https://man7.org/linux/man-pages/man7/capabilities.7.html
29. namespaces(7) - linux manual page. https://www.man7.org/linux/man-pages/man7/namespaces.7.html
30. Lopriore, L.: Access privilege management in protection systems. Inf. Softw. Technol. **44**(9), 541–549 (2002). https://doi.org/10.1016/S0950-5849(02)00067-8
31. Lorch, M.e.a.: The prima system for privilege management, authorization and enforcement in grid environments. In: Proceedings. First Latin American Web Congress, pp. 109–116 (Nov 2003). https://doi.org/10.1109/GRID.2003.1261705
32. Nakamura, Y.: Writing eBPF Kprobe Program with Rust Aya (Sep 2024)
33. Directive (EU) 2022/2555 of the European Parliament and of the Council (Dec 2022). http://data.europa.eu/eli/dir/2022/2555/oj/eng
34. Okta Privileged Access | Okta. https://www.okta.com/products/privileged-access/
35. Open Policy Agent. https://www.openpolicyagent.org/
36. SUSE Manager Documentation : : SUSE Manager Documentation. https://documentation.suse.com/suma/4.3/en/suse-manager/index.html#_what_is_suse_manager
37. PARLIAMENT T.E. UNION, T.C.O.T.E: Regulation (EU) 2016/679 of the European Parliament and of the Council (Apr 2016). http://data.europa.eu/eli/reg/2016/679/oj/eng, legislative Body: EP, CONSIL
38. PARLIAMENT, T.E, UNION, T.C.O.T.E: Regulation (EU) 2021/821 of the European Parliament and of the Council (May 2021). http://data.europa.eu/eli/reg/2021/821/oj/eng, legislative Body: CONSIL, EP
39. PARLIAMENT, T.E, UNION, T.C.O.T.E: Regulation (eu) 2024/2847 of the european parliament and of the council (Nov 2024). https://eur-lex.europa.eu/eli/reg/2024/2847/oj
40. Commission Delegated Regulation (EU) 2021/2223 (Sep 2021). http://data.europa.eu/eli/reg_del/2021/2223/oj/eng, legislative Body: COM, HOME
41. Polkit-org/polkit (Jan 2025). https://github.com/polkit-org/polkit
42. Qeole: Answer to "eBPF - difference between loading, attaching, and linking?" (Jul 2021)
43. 8.3.8. Allowing Access: Audit2allow | Red Hat Product Documentation. https://docs.redhat.com/en/documentation/red_hat_enterprise_linux/6/html/-security-enhanced_linux/sect-security-enhanced_linux-fixing_problems-allowing_access_audit2allow
44. Red Hat Ansible Automation Platform. https://www.redhat.com/en/technologies/management/ansible
45. Saltzer, J., Schroeder, M.: The protection of information in computer systems. Proc. IEEE **63**(9), 1278–1308 (1975). https://doi.org/10.1109/PROC.1975.9939

46. SELinux Wiki. https://selinuxproject.org/page/Main_Page
47. Strace. https://strace.io/
48. System and Service Manager. https://systemd.io/
49. aa-genprof - profile generation utility for AppArmor. https://manpages.ubuntu.com/manpages/oracular/en/man8/aa-genprof.8.html
50. Apparmor [Wiki ubuntu-fr]. https://doc.ubuntu-fr.org/apparmor
51. 2024 Data Breach Investigations Report, https://www.verizon.com/business/resources/reports/dbir/
52. Vitard, A.: Un ancien RSSI suspecté d'être à l'origine de la cyberattaque du groupe de santé Hospi Grand Ouest. Digitale, Usine (Dec (2024)
53. Wazan, A.S., Chadwick, D.W., Venant, R., Laborde, R., Benzekri, A.: RootAsRole: towards a secure alternative to sudo/su commands for home users and SME administrators. In: Jøsang, A., Futcher, L., Hagen, J. (eds.) SEC 2021. IAICT, vol. 625, pp. 196–209. Springer, Cham (2021). https://doi.org/10.1007/978-3-030-78120-0_13
54. Wazan, A.S., et al.: RootAsRole: a security module to manage the administrative privileges for Linux. Comput. Sec., 102983 (2022). https://doi.org/10.1016/j.cose.2022.102983, https://linkinghub.elsevier.com/retrieve/pii/S0167404822003753
55. Zhou, J., et al.: Automatic permission check analysis for linux kernel. IEEE Trans. Dependable Sec. Comput. **20**(3), 1849–1866 (2023). https://doi.org/10.1109/TDSC.2022.3165368

NICraft: Malicious NIC Firmware-Based Cache Side-Channel Attack

Amit Choudhari[(✉)], Shorya Kumar, and Christian Rossow

CISPA Helmholtz Center for Information Security, Saarbrücken, Germany
{amit.choudhari,rossow}@cispa.de

Abstract. Being in the central position for network communication, Network Interface Card (NICs) can intercept, modify, and generate network packets. But little is known about how NICs can launch attacks that go beyond simple traffic sniffing and manipulation.

In this work, we demonstrate how a malicious NIC can leverage a stock operating system to leak memory access patterns of user-space processes via a cache side-channel attack. Specifically, we uncover an exploitable gadget in the TCP/IP stack's IP reassembly process that enables a Prime+Probe cache side-channel attack. Our approach achieves fine-grained control, targeting individual cache sets. We validate its practicality by establishing a high-accuracy bi-directional covert channel between a user application and the NIC that bypasses firewalls, achieving transmission rates of 0.1 bits/sec upstream and 0.76 bits/sec downstream. In addition, we demonstrate its application in monitoring system activity by detecting periods of keystroke activity of 20 users across multiple sessions with a precision of over 96%, highlighting the potential privacy risks.

1 Introduction

Internal hardware devices are often overlooked as potential attack vectors, despite the inherent risks of malicious firmware. As Network Interface Card (NICs), Graphics Processing Unit (GPUs) and other peripheral devices typically prioritize performance and time to market over security, they are often found vulnerable to compromise. Numerous examples show how attackers can exploit these weaknesses: injecting malware to eavesdrop on network traffic [38], abusing firmware vulnerabilities [10], and exploiting buggy update tools [7]. Similarly, supply chain attacks or untrusted vendors can compromise firmware, as demonstrated by NIC backdoors that provide a shell on the GPU [37].

NICs are prime attack targets due to their Direct Memory Access (DMA) capabilities and role in mediating network traffic. Malicious firmware can enable eavesdropping [4] and traffic manipulation [11,19,25]. Furthermore, researchers have explored how malicious NICs can also directly exfiltrate sensitive system-level information [34]. However, countermeasures such as Input-Output Memory Management Unit (IOMMU) protections [3,13] constrain DMA access to specific memory regions, effectively defending against direct memory attacks.

Timing-based cache side-channel vulnerabilities present a unique threat as they operate without memory access authorization. IOMMU protections block memory attacks but not side channels. Traditionally, NICs interact with the CPU cache indirectly, transferring data to main memory using DMA, which is only fetched into the cache later by the driver. This latency limits direct control over Last-Level Cache (LLC) loads, making cache side-channel attacks challenging.

To accelerate packet processing, Intel introduced the Data Direct I/O (DDIO) hardware extension, enabling the NIC to directly transfer packets to the processor's LLC. This allows the NIC to directly manipulate and observe the LLC, simplifying cache side-channel attacks. Another extension, Remote Direct Memory Access (RDMA), allows remote machines to access pre-allocated memory regions directly. The combination of RDMA and DDIO facilitates network-based cache attacks [18]. However, these approaches rely on specialized hardware extensions that may be unavailable or disabled for security reasons, particularly in commodity systems. This raises a critical research question: *Can a malicious NIC orchestrate cache side-channel attacks without relying on these extensions?*

In this work, we introduce NICraft[1], a cache side-channel attack orchestrated by a malicious NIC, based on PRIME+PROBE(P+P) (Sect. 2.2) at cache set granularity. We exploit fragmented IP packet reassembly, a predictable mechanism in the Linux kernel's TCP/IP stack, to control memory access patterns and induce observable cache interference in (almost) arbitrary cache sets. NICraft leverages two kernel-level gadgets: one for priming, triggered upon receiving an IP fragment and another for probing, activated during final IP reassembly. The final packet's response delay reveals target address access via eviction in the target cache set. This enables NICraft to leak fine-grained system activity such as user keypresses, while bypassing traditional host- and network-based defenses.

Previous research has exploited predictable Operating System (OS) mechanisms, such as task scheduling in real-time systems [6] or file system synchronization [14], to mount timing-based side-channel attacks. However, these methods neither control cache access patterns nor involve cache interference. In contrast, NICraft uniquely exploits IP reassembly, a key operation in the TCP/IP stack, to construct cache interference gadgets and orchestrate side-channel attacks. By relying solely on standard NIC functionality, we show that a NIC can perform cache side-channel attacks without specialized hardware extensions. To the best of our knowledge, this is the first work to leverage predictable OS-level operations in the network stack for cache-based side-channel attacks. Thus, broadening the applicability of such NIC-based attacks to commodity systems.

Our experimental results demonstrate the impact of NICraft. We establish a high-accuracy covert channel between a user application and the NIC, achieving a data transmission rate of 0.1 bits/sec upstream and 0.76 bits/sec downstream. Furthermore, we use this side-channel capability to monitor system activity by detecting periods of keystroke activity across multiple users with a precision of over 96%. This highlights a previously unexplored threat model.

---

[1] https://github.com/amit-choudhari/NICraft.

As part of NICraft, this work makes the following key contributions:

1. We identify an exploitable gadget in the Linux TCP/IP stack, enabling a malicious NIC firmware to execute a P+P attack at cache set granularity, without specialized hardware like DDIO or RDMA.
2. We develop signal amplification techniques (the *Aging* and *Domino effect*) and maximize cache set coverage through DHCP manipulation.
3. We demonstrate practical attacks bypassing on-system firewalls: a covert channel between the NIC and a user-space application, and an attack that detects system activity (such as keystroke activity) from the NIC.

2 Background

2.1 Network Interface Card (NIC)

A NIC facilitates communication between a computer and a network by transmitting data packets as signals over mediums like Ethernet or Wi-Fi. NICs can intercept, modify, and create packets while managing DMA operations, allowing direct data transfer between the NIC and main memory without CPU involvement. During initialization, the NIC driver allocates circular linked lists of buffers: RX ring buffers for incoming packets and TX ring buffers for outgoing packets. These buffers, shared between the NIC and the driver, match the NIC's Maximum Transmission Unit (MTU)–typically 1500 bytes for Ethernet. The driver also allocates descriptors specifying buffer sizes and physical addresses, enabling the NIC to perform DMA transfers. At any point, DMA is restricted to the RX/TX rings, i.e., a NIC cannot access memory globally.

To transmit data, an application creates a socket buffer (skb). The NIC driver retrieves the data from the skb and prepares it for transmission, fragmenting larger message into MTU-compliant packets. These packets are placed in the TX ring for processing and will be transmitted over the network eventually.

To receive data, the NIC processes incoming packets and transfers them to main memory via DMA. It then interrupts the driver, which maps RX buffers to socket buffers (skb) for TCP/IP stack processing. This avoids an additional memory copy. If an IP packet is fragmented during transmission, its fragments are validated within the TCP/IP stack of the OS, including header checksum verification. Once the final IP fragment arrives, the kernel reassembles them into the original packet respecting the offsets to ensure proper order.

2.2 Cache Organization and Side-Channel Attacks

Cache Hierarchy. Modern processors use hierarchical caches (Level 1 (L1), Level 2 (L2), and LLC) to reduce memory latency. These hierarchies often follow inclusivity, ensuring that data in lower-level caches (L1/L2) also resides in the LLC, shared across cores. While this simplifies cache management, it also makes the LLC vulnerable to side-channel attacks due to its shared and predictable structure. The LLC is structured into sets and slices for efficient storage. Sets are logical groups of cache lines, with memory addresses mapped to sets based on specific bits. Slices are physical divisions enabling parallel access to different LLC parts, improving efficiency and reducing contention.

Replacement Policies. Cache replacement policies determine which cache line to evict when inserting new data into a full cache set. The Least Recently Used (LRU) policies, most commonly found in LLC, evict the longest-unused cache line, leveraging temporal locality for efficiency but adding hardware complexity. Pseudo-LRU policies mitigate this complexity by approximating LRU behavior with lower overhead and comparable performance.

Cache Side Channel Attacks. Side-channel attacks monitor state changes in shared resources like the LLC to infer a victim's activity. PRIME+PROBE (P+P) is a popular timing side-channel technique to uncover memory access patterns. In P+P, the attacker primes a specific cache set by initializing it to a known state. After the victim executes operations that may evict attacker's cache lines, the attacker probes the same set, measuring access times. Longer access times indicate cache miss, revealing the victim's memory access patterns.

3 Threat Model

Our threat model targets standard computers, including server and non-server CPUs, that use NICs for network communication. We consider a scenario where the attacker controls the NIC firmware to monitor and inject packets, to control Interrupt Requests (IRQs) and thus influence kernel packet processing.

Using these capabilities, the attacker orchestrates a cache side-channel attack through the malicious NIC. The NIC crafts packets to exploit predictable TCP/IP stack operations, causing timing variations and allowing the attacker to infer memory access patterns on specific cache sets with precision. The attacker knows (or can deduce) the cache sets used by the victim process [29]. Strategically, the attacker places packets in the NIC's RX queue to induce interference in targeted cache sets. The attacker's firmware uses a reliable timing source or an equivalent mechanism, such as counter threads.

The model assumes an unmodified Linux OS and does not require DDIO or RDMA extensions, enabling the attack on commodity systems. No other microarchitectural behaviors such as speculative execution are exploited, relying instead on standard NIC capabilities and TCP/IP stack cache side-channel leakage.

4 Methodology

This section explains NICraft, beginning with an overview and an analysis of exploitable gadgets in the TCP/IP stack. It then addresses practical challenges in achieving fine-grained observations of single cache line evictions.

4.1 Attack Overview

Figure 1 illustrates the general idea of NICraft in which the attacker uses malicious NIC firmware to orchestrate a cache side-channel attack, leaking memory access patterns of a victim process on the host CPU. NICraft operates in two

```
1   static int ip_frag_queue(
        struct ipq *qp, struct
        sk_buff *skb)
2   {
3       err = pskb_trim_rcsum(skb,
            end - offset);
4       if (LAST_FRAGMENT)) {
5           ...
6           err = ip_frag_reasm(qp,
                skb, prev_tail, dev)
            ;
7           ...
8           return err;
9       }
10      ...
11  }
```

Listing 1.1. IP fragmentation method invoked on receiving each fragment. Blue: priming checksum function. Red: final fragment's reassembly function.

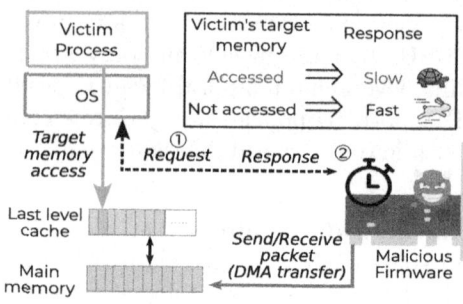

Fig. 1. Attack overview: Black arrow shows TX-RX flow, green blocks represent LLC ring buffer data, and the red block indicates secret-dependent memory access evicting packet data. (Color figure online)

steps: (1) The NIC sends a crafted request to the host, triggering a side-channel gadget in the TCP/IP stack to process the request and generate a response. (2) The NIC measures the response delay to infer the victim's access to the target memory. These crafted packets leverage standard TCP/IP mechanisms without requiring user-space services. For example, a TCP SYN sent to an unbound TCP port triggers a TCP RST—the timing of which depends on the cache state. During packet processing by the kernel and driver, headers and data are loaded into the cache. The NIC firmware maps packet data to the same cache set as the victim's memory to observe access patterns. By managing Interrupt Request (IRQs), the NIC aligns the timing of packet processing with the victim's memory access, inducing observable timing variations due to cache collisions.

The NIC extracts access patterns from user-space using the P+P technique, based on the observation that the TCP/IP stack (i.e., the kernel) accesses some packets *twice*. For priming, the NIC enqueues packets to occupy the target cache set X. Next, the NIC either triggers the victim application or waits for the victim to access the target memory within the same cache set X. When the victim accesses this memory, at least one of the NIC's packet cache lines is evicted based on the cache replacement policy. For probing, the NIC sends a packet to *reload* previously cached packets. A processing delay indicates victim evictions and is incorporated into the packet response time. The NIC measures delays with an internal timer, where longer delays indicate evictions in cache set X.

Leveraging IP Reassembly. A critical insight of NICraft is that it can provoke the OS kernel to access the same packet twice. Typically, a single memory access suffices to process a packet. The NIC transfers a packet into main memory via DMA and raises a hardware interrupt to notify the driver. The driver, followed by the network stack, consumes these packets in ring buffer order. During

```
1   bool skb_try_coalesce(struct
         sk_buff *to, struct
         sk_buff *from, ...)
2   {
3     if (len <= skb_tailroom(to))
         {
4       BUG_ON(skb_copy_bits(from,
             0,
5           skb_put(to, len), len));
6     }
7   }
```

Listing 1.2. Function to coalesce fragmented data into the tail of the first fragment, red higlights data copying function.

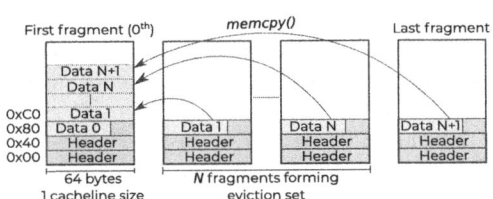

Fig. 2. reassembly_load gadget: Loads data block of N fragments into cache to copy them to the tail of first (0th).

processing, the packet is loaded into the cache. Afterward, the memory is freed and not accessed again. Without additional measures, the NIC cannot trigger a second access to the same memory location.

However, we identified two gadgets in the TCP/IP stack that load packet data into the cache at *two distinct times*. The Internet Protocol (IP) fragments packets into smaller pieces if their size exceeds the MTU. These fragments are accessed again when the kernel reassembles the original IP packet before passing it to higher layers. NICraft leverages IP reassembly for P+P as follows:

$P + P$ *Priming:* When a host receives a fragmented packet, it maps the packet's fields into the *sk_buff* struct. As shown in Listing 1.1 (line 3), the host verifies the checksum of the IP header and stores the fragments in a queue until all fragments of an IP packet have been received. If the header and associated data share a cache line, they are together loaded into the cache. This partial processing creates the *checksum_load* gadget that we leverage for P+P priming.

$P + P$ *Probing:* To verify if the victim's memory access evicted fragments from the cache, the NIC triggers reaccess of the primed cache lines. As shown in line 6 in Listing 1.1, upon receiving the final fragment, the host coalesces all fragments before passing the complete packet to the transport layer. As shown in Listing 1.2, fragments smaller than the RX buffer are coalesced by copying their data into the tail of the first fragment before being freed (overcoming side-effects of *fast_string* operation Appendix A). This copying reaccesses the primed fragments, creating the *reassembly_load* gadget for P+P probing.

Controlling a Cache Set. NICraft creates an eviction set for an N-way cache. The NIC uses DMA-based physical addresses to map packets to cache sets and slices [28]. As shown in Fig. 2, the first fragment (*Data 0*) is not reloaded into the cache, making it unusable for the attack. Likewise, the last fragment, which triggers *reassembly_load* during the probe phase, is not suitable for priming. To address these exceptions, the NIC creates $N + 2$ fragments, excluding the first and last fragments from the target cache set. The middle N fragments are accessed twice: first during checksum validation (*checksum_load*) and again during reassembly when the final fragment completes the IP packet (*reassembly_load*).

The host processes packets sequentially, forcing the NIC to copy them in RX ring order. To align N fragments in RX buffers and cache them in the same set, the NIC interleaves malformed packets (we refer to as *dummy_packets*) between fragments. The driver drops these *dummy_packets*, reducing work and noise.

However, the NIC faces an additional challenge to target cache sets beyond the memory ranges allocated for RX buffers. The MTU-constrained buffer size initially limits the NIC to a couple hundred cache sets. Varying the MTU size enables access to additional unique cache sets. We broaden NICraft's scope to target more cache sets by dynamically adjusting the MTU without OS-level modifications. We leverage the DHCP renewal process with Option 26 to dynamically modify the MTU size. Adjusting the MTU size triggers a corresponding resizing of the ring buffers, enabling the NIC to target a wider range of cache sets.

Furthermore, we scan the targetable eviction sets for MTU sizes between 1000B and 9216B. Note that smaller MTUs that could not accommodate $N+2$ fragments' data were excluded, as that is the prerequisite for NICraft. The scan identifies 78% of all cache sets (6400 out of 8192) on the Intel Skylake CPU, as shown in Fig. 7 on page 11. These results highlight NICraft's scalability, as MTU adjustments efficiently target most cache sets.

Synchronization and Noise Reduction. To leak the victim's access patterns, NICraft requires the NIC to synchronize with minimal noise. The attacker faces three key synchronization challenges: (1) Minimize noise during the priming phase. (2) Control the interval between priming and probing, with minimum noise. (3) Trigger victim to access memory associated with sensitive operations.

Minimizing Noise During Priming: Sending $N+2$ fragments and hundreds of *dummy_packets* often triggers multiple IRQs due to network processing constraints. Multiple Interrupt Service Routine (ISRs) and delayed packet consumption disrupt the priming phase by polluting the cache. NICraft mitigates this by ensuring all crafted packets are processed in a single IRQ. The NIC disables interrupts until all packets are copied to main memory, forming a 'tape' of packets. The NIC then raises a single interrupt to ensure all packets are consumed sequentially.

P + P Timing: The attacker controls the interval between prime (*checksum_load*) and probe (*reassembly_load*) phases by introducing delay before the last fragment. Delaying the last fragment via a new IRQ pollutes the cache. To mitigate this, NICraft inserts *dummy_packets* into the RX queue before the last fragment and raises a single IRQ afterward (see Fig. 3). The driver processes these packets sequentially, delaying the probe phase. The *dummy_packets* packets, discarded early, cause minimal cache pollution while delaying the probe.

Triggering the Victim: In NICraft, the attacker triggers the victim to access target data by sending crafted TCP/IP packets, timing attacks with legitimate requests like TLS handshakes, or aligning with periodic tasks. For instance, logging into a service may load sensitive data into the cache during encrypted

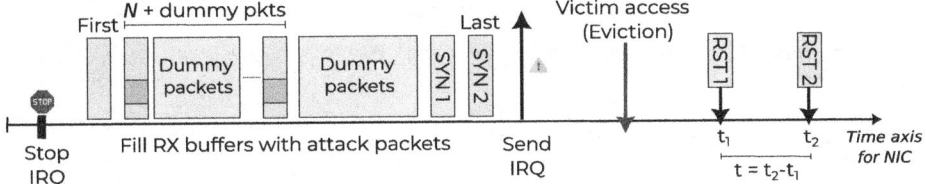

Fig. 3. The NIC inserts N IP fragments with data colliding in the target set. In the prime phase, TCP/IP stack computes checksum of these fragments. In the probe phase, a final fragment ("SYN2") triggers the reassembly. The interval t between two RSTs reflects reassembly speed, indicating if the victim evicted a fragment.

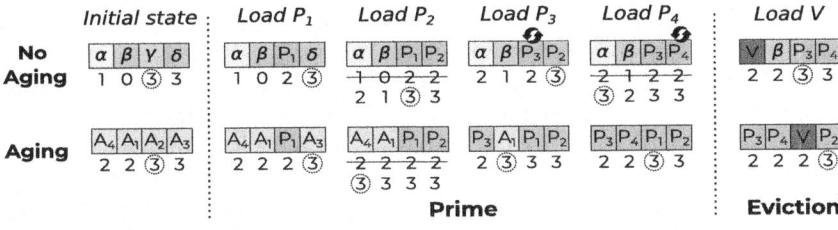

Fig. 4. Impact of *Aging* on cache priming: Top shows *without Aging*, bottom shows *with Aging*, ensuring victim evicts attacker-controlled fragments. Dotted circle on age: next eviction candidate, recycle arrows: *Self eviction*.

session handling. Alternatively, by repeatedly performing P+P, the attacker monitors non-periodic activities and detects specific events. This approach allows the attacker to infer system activity, user activity, or specific access patterns.

Time Measurement. The host processes all packets (TCP fragments and *dummy_packets*) during a single ISR, and the NIC receives an acknowledgment (RST) only after the last TCP fragment is processed. This time frame includes scheduling and processing hundreds of packets, introducing noise and weakening the eviction signal. As shown in Fig. 3, NICraft extracts reassembly time by adding a new SYN segment ($SYN1$) just before $SYN2$ in the RX ring buffer, generating $RST1$ and $RST2$. As packets are consumed sequentially, $RST2$ timing (t_2) depends on the cache eviction event. The NIC measures the timing variation (t) between these two RSTs to infer the victim's access patterns accurately.

4.2 Towards Cache-Set Granularity Attacks

Building on NICraft's fundamentals, we explore two challenges of measuring single cache line evictions from a NIC in practical settings. First, the priming fragments must fully occupy the target cache set. If the cache set is not fully dominated by the attacker's data, the victim may fail to evict attacker's data, compromising the accuracy of the attack. Second, amplifying the weak signal from a single cache line miss is essential, as it may go undetected by the NIC.

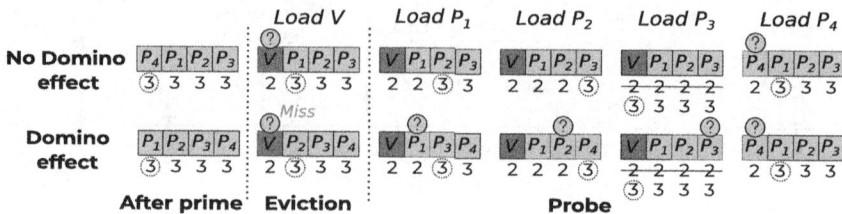

Fig. 5. Eviction comparison: Top (*without Domino effect*): Only P_4 is evicted; Bottom (*with Domino effect*): Sequentially evicting all fragments during probing.

Cache Set Aging. Loading a new cache line into a fully occupied N-way cache set requires evicting an existing line. This eviction decision is governed by the cache replacement policy, which tracks the age of each cache line. For example, Intel Skylake processor's LLC follows the Quad-Age LRU (QRLU) replacement policy [2], where each cache line is assigned two bit age (ranging from 0 to 3). New cache lines are assigned an age of 2, which decrements with each access until reaching 0. When no free slots are available, the oldest cache line (age 3) is evicted. If no line has an age of 3, all ages increment until one reaches age 3.

Variability in initial cache line ages and complex replacement policies, such as adaptive and QLRU, makes it challenging to prime the cache set with a single access. This unreliability increases the risk of the attacker missing the victim's eviction. The top half of Fig. 4 (*No Aging*) shows a 4-way cache where initial line ages are 1 (α), 0 (β), 3 (γ), and 3 (δ). In this case, γ—being the leftmost cache line with age 3—is the next eviction candidate. The attacker attempts to fill the cache set (from left to right) by sequentially loading P_1, P_2, P_3, and P_4 (four fragments of a packet P). However, due to *Self eviction* (new cache load (P_3) evicts earlier fragment (P_1)), α and β remain in cache. This prevents the set from being fully primed by P and causes the attacker to miss the eviction.

A more practical approach, referred to as *Aging* (Appendix B), creates an eviction set larger than N to increment cache line ages to 2 or 3. The bottom half of Fig. 4 (*Aging* case) shows a cache set after *Aging*, with ages set to 2 (A_4), 2 (A_3), 3 (A_2), and 3 (A_1). A_2, the leftmost cache line with age 3, is replaced by P_1. This process continues until P_4 fills the entire cache set. In the *No Aging* case, α and β have lower initial ages, making them harder to evict. In contrast, A_{1-4} have higher ages, preventing *Self eviction*. Age disparity primarily causes *Self eviction*. Cache lines aged in pattern (2^*3^+) (i.e., consist of zero or more lines with age 2, followed by at least one line with age 3) act as an empty cache set, enabling the next N cache misses to fully occupy it.

Having assessed the impact of the preparatory step, we examine the process of reaching it. Due to the likelihood of *Self eviction*, filling an N-way cache set with an eviction set of exactly N cache lines is difficult. However, the LRU cache replacement policy mitigates this issue as the eviction set grows, which gradually reduces the disparity in the ages of cache lines. Increasing the eviction set size increments the ages of lower-aged cache lines, resulting in uniform aging.

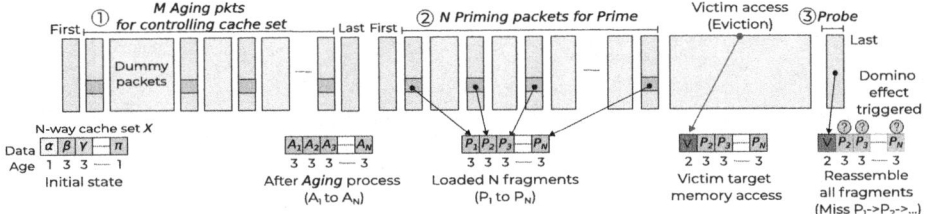

Fig. 6. End-to-end attack: (1) send M *aging* packets to prepare the cache set X, (2) send N priming packets to prime the cache set and enable the victim to evict one cache line P_n, and (3) send Last packet to trigger *Domino effect*

Domino Effect. The NIC, connected via the PCIe bus, operates at a lower frequency than the host CPU–e.g., 1 GHz for a Netronome Agilio CX SmartNIC versus 3.4 GHz for an Intel Skylake CPU. A single LLC miss on the host incurs 250 cycles of latency, but the NIC perceives this delay indirectly via TX events. The periodic polling of the TX ring by the NIC adds further delays. These factors make it challenging for the NIC to detect individual cache line misses.

In NICraft, we introduce a novel technique, *Domino effect*, which amplifies the eviction signal by leveraging *Aging* as a preparatory step. This enhances timing differences from cache evictions, allowing the NIC to distinguish cache hits from misses. We leverage the QRLU replacement policy to amplify a single cache miss into multiple misses, making them detectable by the NIC. The key idea is to evict the next fragment to be probed, triggering a cascading chain of cache misses during IP reassembly. Figure 5 compares the impact of two scenarios on a 4-way cache: one without (top) and one with *Domino effect* (bottom), respectively. P_1–P_4 represent the four fragments of a packet P used for priming.

Without the *Domino effect* (top), after the priming, let P_4 be the next eviction candidate as it has age 3 and is on the leftmost side. When the victim accesses its sensitive data, it replaces this cache line (P_4) with its own data (V), assigning the new line an insertion age of 2. During the probe phase, all the fragments are accessed sequentially, with only a single cache miss occurring. Specifically, P_1, P_2, and P_3 are hits, while P_4 is a miss.

In contrast, triggering the *Domino effect* (bottom), forces the QLRU policy to amplify a single eviction's impact. Unlike the previous case, after the prime phase, P_1 becomes the next eviction candidate, and when the victim accesses its data (V), it evicts P_1 and assigns its cache line an insertion age of 2. In probe phase, sequentially accessing the fragments triggers a cascading chain of cache misses—the 'domino' effect. Loading P_1 evicts P_2, loading P_2 evicts P_3, and so on. This *Domino effect* occurs because priming arranges packets in sequential eviction order. Furthermore, both priming and probing phases access the cache lines in the same order. A single victim access disrupts the LRU pattern. In this 4-way cache, the *Domino effect* amplifies a single cache line miss into four.

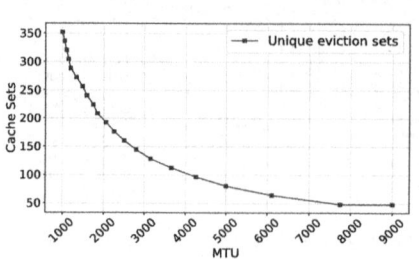
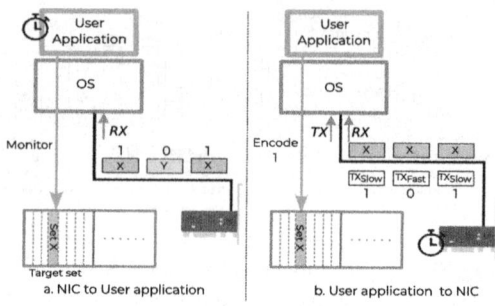

Fig. 7. Targetable cache sets for corresponding MTUs.

Fig. 8. Covert channel attack: NIC to App (left) and App to NIC (right).

End-to-End Attack Design. As shown in Fig. 6, NICraft begins with the NIC sending *Aging* packets, A, to prime the cache. These packets mimic fragmented TCP segments, with the number of fragments (M) exceeding the cache's associativity (N), i.e., $M > N$. The *Aging* phase overfills the cache set, ensuring that it is fully primed for eviction in the subsequent phase. The NIC ignores responses from *Aging* packets. Next, the attacker initiates the PRIME+PROBE attack by sending N priming fragments, P. These P packets target the same cache set used during the aging phase. The NIC organizes A and P packets in its ring buffer: the first M packets for *Aging* and the next N for priming. By carefully crafting both A and P to match an eviction set of size $M + N$, the attacker triggers the *Domino effect*, amplifying a single cache miss into multiple observable misses, enabling NICraft to reliably detect the side-channel signal.

5 Attack Use Cases

5.1 Experimental Setup

We evaluate NICraft on an Intel Skylake i7-6700 CPU with stock Linux 6.2.16, using a Netronome Agilio CX 2x10GbE NIC with programmable firmware to install malicious code. Notably, attackers are not limited to reprogrammable NICs; malicious code can be introduced via proprietary firmware updates or compromises. The firmware handles packet modification, DMA transfers, IRQ control, and the timer. For simplicity, a remote server crafts fragmented TCP SYN packets and transmits them to the victim server. The NIC intercepts, modifies, and utilizes these packets to perform the attack. Alternatively, the NIC could generate these packets directly, reducing external dependencies.

5.2 Bi-directional Covert Channel

While a malicious NIC could communicate through hidden packet modifications or through collaborating user-space processes opening listening ports, such channels can be readily blocked by firewalls or network policies, and they fail when applications have no network access. In contrast, cache-based covert channels avoid network visibility altogether, enabling stealthy communication through microarchitectural interference. NICraft establishes a bidirectional covert channel between the NIC and a user-space application, focusing on reliability over raw throughput. By exploiting cache interference rather than IP traffic, the NIC and a user-space application exchange data even under strict network restrictions.

The NIC and the user-space app communicate over the N-way LLC by priming and probing two agreed-upon cache sets: U for upstream (app to NIC) and D for downstream (NIC to app). A 1 is encoded as eviction, and a 0 as no eviction.

For downstream transfers (Fig. 8 left), the app monitors cache set D in three steps. It first primes D by loading one or more cache lines. Next, to send a 1, the NIC fragments a TCP SYN into $N+2$ IP packets targeting D, evicting the app's data. To send a 0, packets are crafted without evicting D. Finally, the app probes D; data absence indicates 1, presence indicates 0.

For upstream transfers (Fig. 8 right), the NIC primes U using two fragmented TCP SYNs, S_1 and S_2. Fragments in S_1 perform *Aging* on U, while $N+2$ IP fragments in S_2 prime U. Next, the app encodes 1 by evicting cache lines from U, or skips eviction to encode 0. Finally, the NIC exploits *reassembly_load* to trigger the *Domino effect*, delaying fragment reassembly and the TCP RST response. A delayed RST indicates 1, and a timely RST indicates 0.

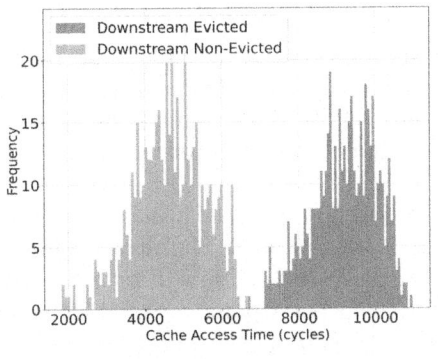
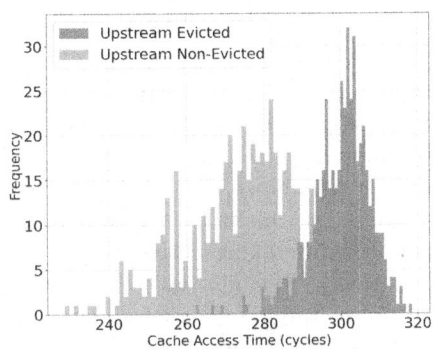

(a) Downstream Eviction Histogram   (b) Upstream Eviction Histogram

Fig. 9. Cache Timing Analysis of the Covert Channel.

We evaluate the covert channel's reliability, efficiency, and timing characteristics using a 1000-bit stream for both communication directions. Each bit is transmitted 15 times for downstream and 75 times for upstream, with each transmission lasting 0.1 ms and 0.3 ms, respectively. The counts (15 and 75) were heuristically chosen to balance throughput and error rate.

We measure the covert channel's reliability using the Bit Error Rate (BER). Downstream achieves a BER below 0.9%, demonstrating robustness. In contrast, upstream has higher BER of 10% due to the NIC's clock challenges. These differences are also reflected in the timing histograms in Figs. 9a and 9b. For the downstream channel, Fig. 9a reveals a clear separation between evicted and non-evicted cache access times, with negligible overlap. The upstream channel's timing overlap, as shown in Fig. 9b, is due to the noisy channel, contributing to higher BER. Error correction codes can mitigate this higher BER.

We evaluate the channel efficiency by measuring the throughput. Upstream achieves about 0.1 bit/s, while downstream maintains a consistent 0.76 bit/s. The upstream transmission time is slower due to two factors. First, higher noise in the channel leads to retransmission. The NIC's slower clock limits precise time variation measurements, while polling mechanisms delay RST packet notifications. Furthermore, indirect processing adds latency via the NIC, main memory, and cache. Second, the NIC has to search for the ring buffers in the target cache set; failure to find the target eviction set leads to flushing the buffers.

5.3 Run-Time Detection of System Activity

Systems exhibit privacy leaking activities such as typing, active processes, peripheral usage, or cryptographic operations (e.g., YubiKey encryption). A malicious NIC could infer *some* of these activities by monitoring network traffic. However, this approach fails for local (i.e., non-networked) activities, or in scenarios like offline systems (e.g., military deployments) and systems with multiple interfaces (e.g., Wi-Fi vs. LAN vs. 5G). In such cases, a NIC can leverage our P+P attack to infer system activity without relying on network traffic.

To demonstrate this using NICraft, we use detection of periods of keystroke activity as a concrete example. Typing activity triggers kernel routines, leaving measurable traces in the LLC. By leveraging P+P, the NIC detects these traces and infers keystroke activity timing without direct access to the keyboard or OS input subsystem.

Our experiment targets the popular *libinput* library, which manages input events and remains active unless the compositor restarts. The attack detects execution of the *libinput_event_get_keyboard_event* function. First, the NIC primes the target cache set aligned to the function's entry point. Next, it waits for a keypress to trigger the target function. Finally, it probes the cache set. When no keypress occurs, the packet reassembly completes quickly as all fragments are cached. A keypress evicts a fragment, potentially triggering a *Domino effect*, delaying packet reassembly and the corresponding RST.

To distinguish keypress events from idle states, the attacker collects response time samples t_{kp} and t_{idle}, and calibrates the threshold t_{thr} as their midpoint. In real-time, the attacker collects W response time samples using a sliding window. The samples above the 80th percentile are averaged, and the mean is compared to t_{thr}. If it exceeds t_{thr}, a keypress event is detected. Both W and the 80th percentile threshold were heuristically chosen to balance accuracy and noise.

Evaluation. We evaluate NICraft using a widely adopted typing activity dataset [15] containing data from 20 subjects typing free and transcribed text.

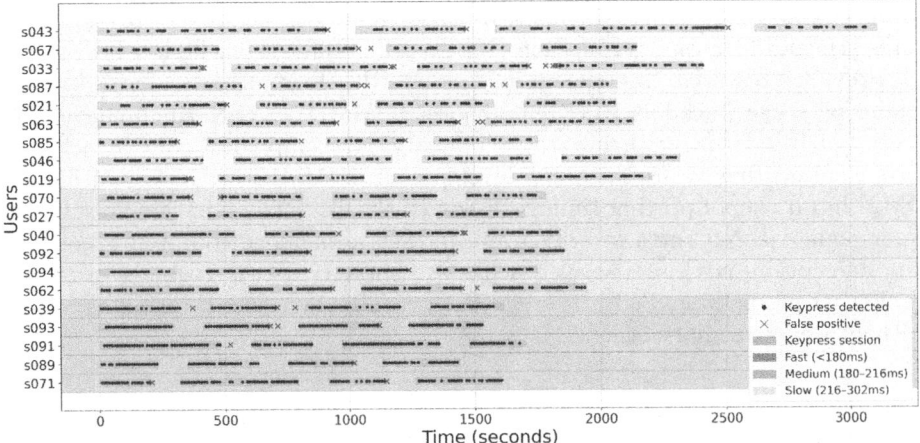

Fig. 10. Illustrates the keystroke experiment for 20 users. Valid detections (blue dots), actual typing activity (yellow highlights) and FP (red crosses). (Color figure online)

Table 1. Summarizes the key performance metrics for different typing speeds.

Typing Speed	TP	FP	FN	TN	Precision	Recall	Specificity
Fast	0.78	0.05	0.22	0.94	0.981	0.780	0.947
Medium	0.70	0.06	0.29	0.93	0.979	0.707	0.938
Slow	0.52	0.09	0.48	0.90	0.967	0.518	0.906

We group subjects by typing speed based on their keystroke intervals: fast typists average 127–177 ms (σ: 108–115 ms), while medium typists range from 180–216 ms (σ: 127–158 ms) and slow typists range from 216–302 ms (σ: 144–168 ms). We introduce idle periods between the typing sessions to evaluate the attack's specificity. Figure 10 shows a visual representation of the experiment.

Table 1 summarizes performance metrics, including True Positive (TP), False Positive (FP), precision, recall, and specificity for different typing speeds. The attack achieves over 96% detection precision consistently. Most FPs were attributed to windowing effects, such as overlaps with idle phases or delayed detections during transitions. For example, in the *Fast* scenario, 6 out of 10 FPs occurred immediately after activity. Longer pauses during typing–more common among slower typists–contributed to increased False Negative (FN), lowering recall. To ensure high detection confidence, NICraft's design intentionally prioritized reducing FP over FN, striking a balance between sensitivity and reliability.

6 Related Work

DMA, and NIC-Based Attacks. NICs use DMA for efficient data transfer. Despite protections like the IOMMU, attacks such as Thunderclap [26] and others [27,34] show how misconfigurations or bypasses enable malicious peripherals to inject code or overwrite memory. Defense techniques such as secure architectures [41] and firmware verification [20] exist but suffer from high overhead.

Previous research has shown malicious NIC firmware can eavesdrop on traffic or stage backdoors [37,38], bypass IOMMU to perform unauthorized access [9,10]. Growing firmware complexity [4] compounds the attack surface, complicating secure firmware development. IOMMU restricts unauthorized DMA, but it cannot prevent timing-based attacks like cache side-channels. Unlike prior malicious NIC attacks which aim for active memory compromise or traffic interception, NICraft passively leaks system activity via cache interference, exploiting predictable TCP/IP stack behaviors to bypass IOMMU protections without direct memory access.

Microarchitectural Attacks. Early works [24,30] demonstrated P+P's effectiveness in cryptographic key extraction and cross-VM attacks, later extending to browser-based attacks [21,29], speculative execution [16], and prefetcher-based side channels [31].

A critical enabler for P+P is constructing eviction sets—groups of memory addresses mapping to the same cache set [28,40]. Our approach uses kernel-allocated NIC ring buffers to build these sets, following the method by Maurice et al. [28]. Tools such as CacheQuery [39], nanoBench [2], and other studies [5] identify cache replacement policies. Building on prior research, NICraft introduces novel kernel gadgets for P+P, innovative signal-amplification techniques (*Domino effect, Aging*) and dynamic MTU variation (via DHCP Option 26) to expand the range of targeted cache sets.

Network Side-Channel Attacks. Prior attacks exploit shared resources or timing variations caused by network interfaces and traffic processing to infer sensitive information. NetCAT [18] leverages Intel's DDIO to establish covert channels between remote clients and sandboxed processes or isolated clients on a victim machine. By exploiting the shared cache state between the NIC and CPU enabled by DDIO, NetCAT can perform attacks like keystroke timing inference over an SSH connection. However, the attack depends entirely on DDIO, which is absent in consumer-grade NICs and can be disabled, limiting its practicality. In contrast, NICraft operates without relying on DDIO, broadening the attack surface to commodity systems.

Unlike NICraft, Packet Chasing [35] assumes an attacker on the host CPU. The attack primarily leaks downstream data. By mapping cache sets to NIC ring descriptors, it reveals details of inbound traffic, such as packet size and timing. The host-based attacker can directly observe cache interference, easing downstream data leakage without relying on DDIO. The attack depends on stable descriptor reuse and becomes noisier with frequent changes in driver configurations, ring buffer allocations, and particularly when DDIO is disabled. NICraft differs by mounting the attack from the NIC itself, without requiring host-side software execution.

Other works, such as NetSpectre [32] exploit speculative execution vulnerabilities to leak data remotely but requires hard-to-identify Spectre gadgets. NetHammer [22], on the other hand, targets DRAM Rowhammer vulnerabilities by crafting network packets, inducing bit flips in memory. NICraft instead exploits predictable OS-level behaviors to induce microarchitectural cache contention without speculative execution or memory corruption.

NICraft broadens network side-channel threats by showing that a malicious NIC can leak host activity purely through cache interference, without relying on DDIO, speculative execution, or privileged code.

7 Discussion and Mitigation

Limitations and Improvements. Our current method focuses on detecting local (non-networked) activities—a stricter scenario often overlooked by traffic-based inference (e.g., in offline or multi-interface environments). By not relying on any network-layer cues, we demonstrate the inherent power of a malicious NIC to infer system activities solely via side-channels. Integrating network knowledge (e.g., synchronizing with packet flows) would make such attacks more potent.

The attack is limited to cache sets at fixed offsets in ring buffers, hindering optimal eviction set construction. It targets one cache set at a time because identifying multiple sets within the current RX buffers is challenging. Overcoming this limitation might enable simultaneous attacks on multiple cache sets; e.g., AES T-tables require monitoring 16 cache sets simultaneously.

Our implementation is fine-tuned for an Intel Skylake platform, overcoming microarchitectural behaviors such as fast-string optimizations and leveraging the observed QLRU-based cache replacement policy. Broader applicability to other platforms was not evaluated and may require calibration.

Generalizability. Although NICraft was evaluated on a specific platform, its core techniques remain broadly applicable within x86 systems. The Domino and Aging strategies exploit fundamental cache behaviors—specifically, that recently accessed cache lines are prioritized over older ones. Such aging effects are common across x86 processors, which employ QLRU approximations in LLC replacement policies [12], as confirmed by empirical studies [1,2].

While the overall attack protocol remains unchanged, adapting NICraft to other environments would require two categories of adjustments. First, porting to different operating systems would involve selecting alternative kernel-level gadgets that exhibit predictable cache access patterns, depending on how IP reassembly or similar functionality is implemented. Second, adapting to different CPU architectures would require recalibrating system-specific parameters such as cache set mappings, fragment sizing relative to cache line size, and buffer layouts. These parameters influence eviction timing, Aging and Domino amplification, and cache interference visibility. We leave exploring these adaptations to future work.

Mitigation. To mitigate our attack, one approach is to statically or dynamically partition the LLC [23]. For example, Intel CAT [12] partitions cache access by *Class of Service* per core. Isolating the kernel from user caches can effectively prevent memory access pattern leaks across privilege levels. However, unless we also isolate different kernel threads, access patterns *within* the kernel would still leak. Hardware-based PMU performance counters may detect unusual cache activity dynamically and terminate the attack at runtime [8]. Nevertheless, such detection mechanisms are vulnerable to camouflage techniques [17], where the attacker mimics legitimate activity to evade detection.

NIC-driven anomalies, such as excessive small fragmented packets or unusual offsets, also reveal malicious behavior. In the driver, especially when unjustified by normal conditions, provides another detection mechanism. Similarly, techniques like CloudRadar [42], which detect side-channel attacks by correlating multiple cache anomalies, demonstrate the feasibility of anomaly-based approaches to flag malicious NIC-driven fragmentation patterns.

Beyond detection, proactive software defenses can further disrupt the attacker's ability to mount a reliable side-channel. Randomizing network buffer allocations and introducing jitter in fragment handling disrupt cache set predictability, degrading the attack's success rate with minimal performance overhead. It is non-trivial to avoid priming since the kernel must access packet headers (e.g., sequence numbers). Similarly, probing remains unavoidable because, even if data copying is deferred during reassembly, the data must eventually be combined before delivery to userspace. This issue likely extends to other kernel-based TCP/IP stacks, as it arises from fundamental operations inherent to their design. For fragmented packets, we propose a software-based mitigation to flush the header cache line after processing the header. This ensures that any data sharing the same cache line as the header is accessed directly from main memory.

8 Conclusion

In this work, we introduced NICraft, a malicious NIC-orchestrated P+P cache side-channel attack that exploits IP reassembly in the kernel's TCP/IP stack. Relying solely on standard NIC functionality, NICraft is applicable to commodity systems. By establishing a covert channel that bypasses on-system firewalls and detecting system activity like keystroke events, we highlight the feasibility and breadth of this threat—including local or offline scenarios. These findings underscore the need to reevaluate firmware-level security, especially as NICs becomes increasingly sophisticated. Future research should explore robust defenses, including methods to detect malicious firmware activity and stricter peripheral-OS isolation, to protect against this evolving class of side-channel attacks.

Acknowledgments. We thank Yepeng Pan, Till Schlüter, Manoj Gudi, and the anonymous reviewers for their valuable feedback and insightful suggestions.

A Fast-String Optimization on X86 CPU

A technical challenge arises when aligning packets in the buffer. During the probe phase (via the *reassembly_load* gadget), the *skb_copy_bits()* API copies data between fragment using *memcpy()*. When the source data is not cached, the CPU triggers a cache line miss, loading only the specific cache line needed. However, Intel's fast-strings optimization [33,36]causes the CPU to prefetch the next cache line, even if not needed. Consequently, a cache line miss also occurs when both the source and destination are cached, complicating PRIME+PROBE attacks.

Reverse-engineering on Intel Skylake CPUs reveals that this optimization is suppressed when $((dst < src) \land (src < 16))$, where src and dst are offsets within their respective cache lines during *memcpy()*. To meet this condition, we vary the IP header size using options fields, allowing header to share the cache line with the data. During priming (*checksum_load* gadget), the CPU loads the header for checksum computation, ensuring the data is loaded into the target cache set.

B Aging with Reaccess

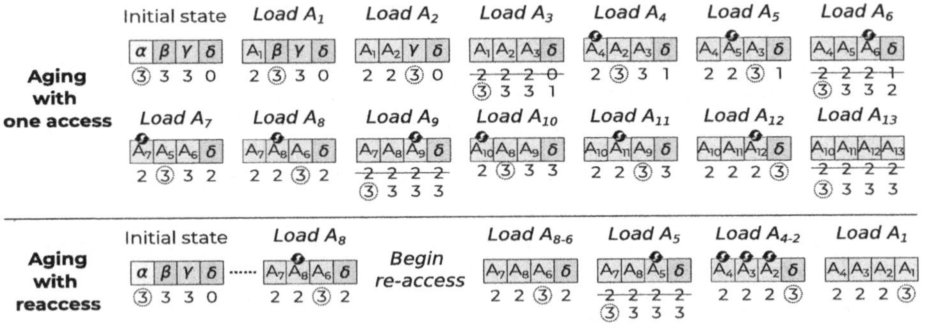

Fig. 11. *aging* techniques: single access per packet (top) vs. re-accessing the same packet (bottom), where A_x denotes the *Aging* packet number x.

Figure 11 demonstrates the *Aging* process in a 4-way cache set. Initially, the cache holds lines with ages 3 (α), 3 (β), 3 (γ), and 0 (δ), with α as the next eviction candidate. In the single-access scenario (top), the attacker loads fragments sequentially: A_1, A_2, A_3, and so forth, until the cache is filled. α is replaced by A_1 (inserted at age 2), followed by A_{2-6}, progressively evicting older lines. Eventually, δ ages to 3 and becomes evictable. Loading A_{13} evicts δ, completing the *Aging* phase. Thirteen packets are needed—over three times the associativity—making eviction set construction non-trivial.

Re-accessing fragments significantly reduces this overhead. As shown in the bottom of Fig. 11, the attacker loads eight fragments (A_{1-8}) via *checksum_load*, then re-accesses them during *reassembly_load* in reverse order. After re-accessing A_1, the set is fully aged. Thus, reaccess reduces the eviction set requirement to at most twice the associativity ($2N$), improving practicality.

References

1. Abel, A.: Cache replacement policy empirical study
2. Abel, A., Reineke, J.: nanoBench: a low-overhead tool for running microbenchmarks on x86 systems. In: ISPASS (2020)
3. AMD Inc.: AMD IOMMU Architectural Specification, Rev 2.00 (2011)
4. Blanco, A., Eissler, M.: One Firmware to Monitor 'Em All. In: Hack.Lu 2012. Core Security Technologies (2012)
5. Briongos, S., Malagón, P., Moya, J.M., Eisenbarth, T.: RELOAD+REFRESH: abusing cache replacement policies to perform stealthy cache attacks. In: USENIX Security (2020)
6. Chen, C.Y., et al.: Schedule-based side-channel attack in fixed-priority real-time systems (2015)
7. Chen, K.: Reversing and exploiting an Apple firmware update. Black Hat **69** (2009)
8. Choudhari, A., Guilley, S., Karray, K.: SpecDefender: transient execution attack defender using performance counters. In: ASHES (2022)
9. Duflot, L., Perez, Y., Morin, B.: What If You Can't Trust Your Network Card? In: RAID (2011)
10. Duflot, L., Perez, Y.A., Valadon, G., Levillain, O.: Can you still trust your network card. CanSecWest/core10 (2010)
11. Eran, H., Zeno, L., Tork, M., Malka, G., Silberstein, M.: NICA: an infrastructure for inline acceleration of network applications. In: USENIX ATC (2019)
12. Intel Corporation: Intel Resource Director Technology (Intel RDT) for 2nd Generation Intel Xeon Scalable Processors: Reference Manual
13. Intel Corporation: Intel Virtualization Technology for Directed I/O, Architecture Specification - Rev. 2.3 (2014)
14. Jiang, Q., Wang, C.: Sync+Sync: a covert channel built on fsync with storage. In: USENIX Security (2024)
15. Killourhy, K.S., Maxion, R.A.: Free vs. transcribed text for keystroke-dynamics evaluations. In: Proceedings of the LASER Workshop on Learning from Authoritative Security Experiment Results (2012)
16. Kocher, P., et al.: Spectre attacks: exploiting speculative execution. In: (S&P'19) (2019)
17. Kosasih, W., Feng, Y., Chuengsatiansup, C., Yarom, Y., Zhu, Z.: SoK: can we really detect cache side-channel attacks by monitoring performance counters? In: ACM Asia CCS (2024)
18. Kurth, M., Gras, B., Andriesse, D., Giuffrida, C., Bos, H., Razavi, K.: NetCAT: practical cache attacks from the network. In: IEEE (SP) (2020)
19. Le, Y., et al.: UNO: uniflying host and smart NIC offload for flexible packet processing. In: Symposium on Cloud Computing (2017)
20. Li, Y., McCune, J.M., Perrig, A.: VIPER: verifying the integrity of PERipherals' firmware. In: CCS (2011)
21. Lipp, M., Gruss, D., Schwarz, M., Bidner, D., Maurice, C., Mangard, S.: Practical keystroke timing attacks in sandboxed javascript. In: ESORICS (2017)
22. Lipp, M., et al.: Nethammer: inducing rowhammer faults through network requests. In: IEEE Euro S&P Workshops (2020)
23. Liu, F., et al.: CATalyst: defeating last-level cache side channel attacks in cloud computing. In: IEEE HPCA (2016)
24. Liu, F., Yarom, Y., Ge, Q., Heiser, G., Lee, R.B.: Last-level cache side-channel attacks are practical. In: IEEE Symposium on Security and Privacy (2015)

25. Liu, M., Peter, S., Krishnamurthy, A., Phothilimthana, P.M.: E3:energy-efficient microservices on SmartNIC-accelerated servers. In: USENIX ATC (2019)
26. Markettos, A.T., et al.: Thunderclap: exploring vulnerabilities in operating system IOMMU protection via DMA from untrustworthy peripherals. In: NDSS (2019)
27. Markuze, A., et al.: Characterizing, exploiting, and detecting DMA code injection vulnerabilities in the presence of an IOMMU. In: EuroSys (2021)
28. Maurice, C., Le Scouarnec, N., Neumann, C., Heen, O., Francillon, A.: Reverse engineering intel last-level cache complex addressing using performance counters. In: RAID (2015)
29. Oren, Y., Kemerlis, V.P., Sethumadhavan, S., Keromytis, A.D.: The spy in the sandbox: practical cache attacks in javascript and their implications. In: ACM CCS (2015)
30. Osvik, D.A., Shamir, A., Tromer, E.: Cache attacks and countermeasures: the case of AES. In: Topics in Cryptology - CT-RSA (2006)
31. Schlüter, T., et al.: Fetchbench: systematic identification and characterization of proprietary prefetchers. In: ACM CCS (2023)
32. Schwarz, M., Schwarzl, M., Lipp, M., Masters, J., Gruss, D.: NetSpectre: read arbitrary memory over network. In: ESORICS (2019)
33. Stack Overflow: Enhanced rep movsb for memcpy (2017). https://stackoverflow.com/questions/43343231/enhanced-rep-movsb-for-memcpy
34. Stewin, P., Bystrov, I.: Understanding DMA malware. In: DIMVA (2013)
35. Taram, M., Venkat, A., Tullsen, D.M.: Packet chasing: spying on network packets over a cache side-channel. In: ACM/IEEE ISCA (2020)
36. Techarp: Cpu fast string bios option (2018). https://www.techarp.com/bios-guide/cpu-fast-string/
37. Triulzi, A.: Project Maux Mk.II: I Own the NIC, Now I Want a Shell. In: The 8th Annual PacSec Conference (2008)
38. Triulzi, A.: The jedi packet takes over the Deathstar: taking NIC backdoor to the next level. In: CanSecWest Conference (2010)
39. Vila, P., Ganty, P., Guarnieri, M., Köpf, B.: CacheQuery: learning replacement policies from hardware caches. In: ACM SIGPLAN (2020)
40. Vila, P., Köpf, B., Morales, J.F.: Theory and practice of finding eviction sets. In: IEEE (SP) (2019)
41. Wang, X., Shen, W., Bu, Y., Zhou, J., Zhou, Y.: DMAAUTH: a lightweight pointer integrity-based secure architecture to defeat DMA attacks. In: USENIX Security (2024)
42. Zhang, T., Zhang, Y., Lee, R.B.: Cloudradar: a real-time side-channel attack detection system in clouds (2016)

Identifying Potential Timing Leakages from Hardware Design with Precondition Synthesis

Minu Chung and Hyungon Moon(✉)

UNIST (Ulsan National Institute of Science and Technology),
Ulsan, Republic of Korea
{minu0122,hyungon}@unist.ac.kr

Abstract. Computer systems operate on hardware that does not execute in constant time. Timing leakage, which refers to information leakage through this timing variability, enables even remote attackers to steal secrets from production systems. The significance of timing leakage necessitates mechanisms to identify, understand, and prevent potential timing leakage at design time for hardware modules. This work proposes a mechanism that automatically identifies potential timing leakages from hardware design by synthesizing the precondition that confines the timing channel. Our mechanism, LeakSynth, obtains this precondition by gathering examples of initial states exhibiting variable or constant execution times. Specifically, LeakSynth synthesizes the predicate that distinguishes these examples and interprets it to produce a precondition under which the hardware module's timing leakage is confined to a subset of its internal registers. Our evaluation using nine hardware modules, including four processors, demonstrates that LeakSynth can quickly synthesize the preconditions. We also show that the preconditions can be used to automatically produce annotations for existing constant-time verification tools. Not to mention that such annotations must be written manually without the help of LeakSynth, the automatically generated annotations are more relaxed, i.e., encompass more initial states.

Keywords: Program Synthesis · Model Checking · Hardware Analysis

1 Introduction

Computer systems operate on hardware that does not execute in constant time. Memory access latency is influenced by cache metadata, and the execution time of a branch instruction depends on the state of the branch predictor. This timing variability creates a timing side-channel, resulting in *timing leakage*. An attacker exploiting this side-channel can infer sensitive information by observing the latency of specific operations (e.g., data load). Previous studies have demonstrated that an attacker can uncover a wide range of confidential information through this timing side-channel, such as cryptographic keys [2,3,32,51], memory layout [23,30,37], or user behaviors [31,33,55].

The timing variability of hardware modules is inevitable. A cryptographic accelerator requires more time to encrypt or decrypt larger amounts of data, and most processors employ caches to opportunistically improve performance. The performance gain resulting from this timing variability is so crucial that eliminating it to eradicate timing leakages is considered impractical. As a result, security-sensitive systems implement selective, attack- or domain-specific defenses against timing leakages.

Efforts to mitigate these timing leakages are classified into run-time and design-time mechanisms. Run-time mechanisms usually target specific side channels, preventing the attacker from inferring the secrets by either cleansing the secrets or disturbing the attacker's timing measurement. On the other hand, design-time mechanisms either enable leakage-free hardware design through language extensions [8,9,19,63] or formally prove the constant-time (CT) execution of hardware [26,27] under the assumption that the hardware is initialized to one of the predefined states. Hardware designers using the former mechanisms can control the timing channel so that the security-sensitive partition (i.e., high) does not affect the timing of the other partitions (i.e., low). The latter mechanism approaches the problem differently by verifying the absence of timing leakage with module abstraction and constraint solving. Iodine [26] verifies the absence of timing leakage under the assumptions specified by the developer, and Xenon [27] recommends potential assumptions to help the developer derive them. Conjunct [21] also follows a similar direction and focuses on verifying the safety of constant-time instructions for processors.

A common observation among the latter approaches is that system builders, who often use and augment hardware designs, typically *cleanse* the hardware's microarchitectural state before utilizing it for computation. Cleansing the microarchitectural state is often required and considered a means to prevent timing leakage because it breaks the relationship between timing behavior and the secret. Existing studies examine if the cleansing achieves the goal by verifying that executions beginning after the cleanse exhibit constant-time behavior.

What is still missing is a mechanism to inform the system builder how the microarchitectural states must be cleansed and the consequences of such cleansing, i.e., which states could still leak through the timing channel after the proposed cleansing. We refer to this consequence as the *potential timing leakage*.

This paper presents LEAKSYNTH, a system that fills out this gap by automatically identifying potential timing leakages from hardware design. Behind the design of LEAKSYNTH is the observation that attackers infer some secrets by measuring the latency of some executions. The set of executions whose latency the attacker can measure, referred to as *attacker-observable* execution, is limited. An attacker-observable execution ends when the hardware module reaches a state that satisfies a certain condition. This is because an attacker measures the latency of the module's operations, such as the execution of an instruction or the computation of a hash value, and there exists a well-defined condition indicating the end of operations. From the latency, what an attacker learns is usually related to the content of the module's registers at the beginning of the attacker's latency measurement; in other words, the hardware module's state when an attacker-observable execution begins.

On top of this observation, we first formulate the problem of identifying the potential timing leakage as the problem of learning a set of hardware module's states such that if the hardware module is always initialized to one of these states at the beginning of an attacker-observable execution, the attacker can infer the content of some, not all registers of the module. §4 provides further details.

To solve this problem, LEAKSYNTH takes the hardware design and the condition indicating the end of executions as inputs and leverages recent advances in the field of programming by examples [34]. It synthesizes a set of states in which a hardware module can be cleansed for confining the timing leakage. While synthesizing the states, LEAKSYNTH leaves a set of module's registers vulnerable to timing leakage if it helps and is required to find a useful set of states. Roughly speaking, LEAKSYNTH automatically collects the examples of initial states likely to belong to the set it is synthesizing and those that are unlikely to. These two sets, each containing likely and unlikely examples, are fed to a commodity program synthesis engine to synthesize a predicate over the hardware module's states. LEAKSYNTH then interprets this predicate into the precondition and the set of vulnerable registers.

We empirically show the performance and effectiveness of LEAKSYNTH by producing the precondition and the corresponding vulnerable registers for nine hardware modules written in Verilog or Chisel, including the seven used to evaluate previous works [26, 27]. Experimental results show that LEAKSYNTH quickly verifies whether a hardware module's execution is in constant time or not, obtains the first constant-time precondition in most benchmarks and continues to refine its precision to identify as many results as possible. We also found that LEAKSYNTH can automatically produce the annotations that the existing constant-time verification tools need, which should otherwise be written manually. The automatically produced annotations are often more desirable than the manually written ones by confining fewer bits. LEAKSYNTH also produced the constant-time precondition for a hardware module, Divider, that the existing tools could not prove constant-time due to their restricted completeness.

2 Backgrounds and Motivation

Timing-Based Attacks in Hardware. Timing-based side-channel attacks [49,59] exploit execution latency to infer otherwise inaccessible data. Prime and probe attacks [49], for instance, enable attackers to infer memory access patterns in victim processes. The attacker first sets the cache tag to a specific value by filling out the cache sets, lets the victim run to evict some of the cache lines, and then measures the access latency to each set to determine if the victim evicted any line. The attacker can determine cache metadata based on latency, making these registers or memory locations vulnerable to timing-based attacks.

Program Synthesis. Program synthesis is a technique that generates programs satisfying high-level specifications. Its practical applications have spurred significant advances [5,6,35,40,44,45,56]. A standard for formulating a program synthesis problem is called *syntax-guided synthesis* (SyGuS), in which the search space is defined as a context-free grammar. A program synthesizer generates candidate programs satisfying the specifications. LEAKSYNTH follows the *programming by example* (PBE) paradigm, where a specification is composed of a set of input-output pairs. As the input-output pairs, LEAKSYNTH uses the concrete initial states and a Boolean value indicating whether the initial state is variable-time or not.

Model Checking. Model checking [18] is a widely used technique to verify the properties of hardware modules. Advances in incremental induction have helped maintain its viability for property testing [13,14,22]. Model checkers take transition system specifications written in languages such as Verilog [39], Btor2 [48], or AIGER [11]. We use AVR [28] for LEAKSYNTH, as it supports Verilog and is optimized for source-level model checking. LEAKSYNTH uses AVR as an example generator to collect the examples for precondition synthesis and to check the soundness of the constant-time preconditions.

3 Assumption and Threat Model

We consider the attackers who aim to extract secrets through timing-based side channels but cannot obtain them otherwise. To this end, the attackers send requests to a victim hardware module and measure response times, inferring the module's initial state as a bridge to the targeted secrets.

LEAKSYNTH is designed for developers who wish to identify the potential sources of timing leakages in their hardware modules at design time. The developer understands the behavior of the hardware design and how the module communicates with the other modules. With this knowledge, they are capable of specifying the terminating condition for the states in which the hardware module responds to the requester (e.g., responding with the computation results or finishing to execute an instruction). LEAKSYNTH uses this terminating condition to synthesize the constant-time preconditions.

4 Preliminary

This section formulates the problem that we address with LEAKSYNTH. Table 1 summarizes the terms and symbols that we define in this section.

4.1 Attacker-Observable Executions

State and Hardware Design. We represent a state of a hardware design as a store $\sigma \in \Sigma = \mathcal{R} \to \mathbb{Z}$. A store σ maps a module's internal registers to their

Table 1. Glossary

Symbol	Description
σ	A state of a hardware module
Σ	The set of possible states a hardware module may have
$\mathcal{R}$	The set of register names in a hardware module
τ	The transition system representing a hardware module
$Input$	The set of input names in a hardware module
$Output$	The set of output names in a hardware module
$\mathcal{I}$	The set of all possible inputs
P_{term}	Terminating predicate of a hardware module
M	Base hardware module under test
PM	Product module composed of two base hardware modules
P_{CT}^{PM}	CT precondition of a product module
P_{CT}	CT precondition of a hardware module
R_{vul}	The set of vulnerable registers
CTE	Constant-time Examples
VTE	Variable-time Examples

values. The input and output of the hardware design are formalized similarly, $\iota \in \mathcal{I} = Input \to \mathbb{Z}$ and $o \in \mathcal{O} = Output \to \mathbb{Z}$. $\mathcal{R}$, $Input$, and $Output$ refer to the set of register names, input names, and output names that a hardware module has, respectively. A hardware design in Verilog specifies transitions between these states and the corresponding outputs under the input at each execution step (i.e., clock cycle). More formally, a hardware module is represented as a transition system $\tau : (\Sigma, \mathcal{I}) \to \Sigma$ and a mapping $\tau_{out} : (\Sigma, \mathcal{I}) \to \mathcal{O}$. For example, if a hardware module's state is σ_t and the input is ι_t at cycle t, the module's state on the next cycle σ_{t+1} is $\tau(\sigma_t, \iota_t)$. The outputs at the next cycle is $\tau_{out}(\sigma_{t+1}, \iota_{t+1})$ where σ_{t+1} and ι_{t+1} are the state and input at cycle $t+1$.

Execution. We formalize an execution of a hardware module as a sequence of the module's states $(\sigma_0, \sigma_1, ..., \sigma_n)$. Such an execution is uniquely determined by the initial state σ_0 and the sequence of inputs, because a verilog module specifies a transition system (τ) that satisfies $\sigma_k = \tau(\sigma_{k-1}, \iota_{k-1})$.

Execution Time. In this formalization, we reinterpret the attacker's capability of measuring the execution time as the capability to measure the execution length corresponding to a particular operation. Specifically, an attacker uses this capability to measure the length of a state sequence, i.e., learns the length n of an execution $(\sigma_0, \sigma_1, ..., \sigma_n)$. From n, the attacker's goal is to infer some secrets engraved in the first state of this execution, σ_0, which is the state at the moment when the attacker gains control of the module. The state may contain some secret in one of the registers because the module has arrived at the state as a result of prior executions before the attacker is granted control of the module.

Terminating States and Predicate. To identify potential timing leakages, we assume that there are certain states at which an operation terminates. Such states can be specified as a predicate over the module's states, where the predicate evaluates to True when the operation terminates. We call such a predicate the *terminating predicate* (P_{term}). Formally, P_{term} is a predicate $P : \Sigma \rightarrow \{\text{true}, \text{false}\}$ that evaluates to True when and only when an operation terminates.

Attacker-Observable Executions. Using the terminating predicate, we introduce the notion of *attacker-observable executions*, which are sequences of states for which an attacker can measure the execution time, i.e., the length. We make no assumptions about when an attacker may issue a command to the hardware module under test. Instead, we assume the attacker is notified when the module's state and inputs satisfy P_{term}. Formally, the attacker can only measure the length of executions ending with a state $\sigma_n \in \Sigma$ that satisfies P_{term}. These executions may begin from any state, unless the hardware module is initialized to specific states before the attacker gains control.

4.2 Potential Leakage Identification Problem

To define the problem of identifying potential timing leakages in hardware modules, we begin with a simple variant of the problem. The problem can be called the *constant-time precondition synthesis* problem, which is defined as the task of finding the set of initial states that lead to the same execution length under the terminating predicate P_{term} and the same input sequence. We define the problem in this way because such initial states leading to timing-safe executions is what the users of LEAKSYNTH, the system builders are interested in. Similar to the terminating states, such a set of initial states leading to the constant-time execution can be specified as a predicate $P_{init} : \Sigma \rightarrow \{\text{true}, \text{false}\}$ over the module's states where P_{init} evaluates to True when the module is initialized to a state that leads to a constant execution length under P_{term}. The system builders can use the set of initial states specified as predicates P_{init} to ensure the lack of timing leakages by initializing the hardware module before the attacker gains control.

On top of this definition, we define the problem of identifying potential timing leakages as the task of finding the set of initial states (P_{init}) and the set of vulnerable registers (R_{vul}) such that if an execution begins from a state satisfying P_{init}, the length of the execution depends only on the content of the registers in R_{vul}. This definition can be considered as a generalization of the constant-time precondition synthesis problem, where the set of vulnerable registers R_{vul} is empty. We take this generalization from the observation introduced earlier; the hardware modules do not execute in constant time because many performance optimizations come with opportunistic behaviors that may lead to timing leakages. The best we could have under these circumstances is to work with a relaxed definition of constant-time execution, where the execution length depends only on the content of a subset of registers. Formally, the problem of identifying potential timing leakages is to find a tuple (P_{init}, R_{vul}) such that the execution length is constant under P_{term} when the hardware module is initialized to a state satisfying P_{init} and the content of the registers in R_{vul}. To give the solution a specific name, we call the predicate satisfying the definition above a *constant-time precondition* and denote it as P_{CT}. By solving the problem, LEAKSYNTH is designed to produce the tuple (P_{CT}, R_{vul}) for a hardware module with terminating predicate P_{term}.

5 LEAKSYNTH Design

5.1 Approach Overview

LEAKSYNTH collects many pairs of *timing indistinguishable* states with a model checker and synthesizes preconditions using these pairs from a hardware module with the developer annotations for the terminating predicate P_{term} (detailed in §6) to derive the constant-time precondition and vulnerable register tuples (P_{CT}, R_{vul}). We call a pair of states, σ_1 and σ_2, as timing indistinguishable if all possible executions, E_1 and E_2, originating from σ_1 and σ_2, respectively, have the same length when provided with the same sequence of inputs. Using such pairs, LEAKSYNTH first synthesizes constant-time preconditions that only the tuples of timing indistinguishable states (σ_1, σ_2) satisfy. We denote such a precondition as a *constant-time precondition from product module* (P_{CT}^{PM}) for the reason we explain in the next paragraph. As detailed later in this section, the synthesis flow ensures that the P_{CT}^{PM}s can be post-processed to produce the constant-time precondition and vulnerable register tuples (P_{CT}, R_{vul}) that LEAKSYNTH aims to find. As described earlier in §4, the constant-time precondition P_{CT} is a predicate over the states of the module with the guarantee that if an execution begins with a state that satisfies P_{CT}, its execution time depends only on the input sequence and the states of registers that are classified as vulnerable (R_{vul}) with P_{CT}.

LEAKSYNTH uses the *product module*, which is analogous to the well-known technique called the *product program* [26,27], to collect the pairs of timing indistinguishable states. For a hardware module $M = (\Sigma, \mathcal{R}, Input, Output, \tau, \tau^{out})$, LEAKSYNTH constructs a product module PM as follows

$$PM = (\Sigma \times \Sigma, \mathcal{R}_{PM}, Input, Output_{PM}, \tau_{PM}, \tau_{PM}^{out})$$

and call the original hardware design the *base module* if we need to relate a hardware design to the corresponding product module. The product module has two instances of the base module. The two instances take the same inputs, making the input names of the product module the same as the base module because LEAKSYNTH intends to find pairs of states whose execution times are the same when given the same input sequence.

5.2 P_{CT} Synthesis Flow

Figure 1a illustrates the flow by which LEAKSYNTH generates P_{CT}^{PM}s from a hardware module described in Verilog. It first constructs a product module PM that we introduced in §5.1 (①), from a hardware design with the developer annotations for termination. Using the PM, LEAKSYNTH synthesizes a new P_{CT}^{PM} as a result, using one of the three heuristics (②) that we designed (see §5.4). To synthesize a P_{CT}^{PM}, each heuristic first collects the positive and negative examples (③) for predicate synthesis (see §5.3). We call the positive examples the *constant-time examples (CTEs)* because each example corresponds to a tuple of timing indistinguishable states, where executions from them terminate simultaneously. The negative examples are called the *variable-time examples (VTEs)*. The collected examples are then fed to a program synthesis engine (④) as detailed in §5.5. The engine synthesizes a predicate that the CTEs satisfy but the VTEs do not. LEAKSYNTH refines PM (⑤) using the synthesized predicate to find new VTEs and more predicates until AVR cannot find more VTEs (⑥). If the iteration (⑥) is finished, the conjunction of synthesized predicates is collected as a P_{CT}^{PM} because the synthesis flow guarantees that for all (σ_0, σ_1) satisfying P_{CT}^{PM}, σ_0 and σ_1 are timing indistinguishable. This P_{CT}^{PM} is used to refine PM (⑦) for new CTEs, resulting in new P_{CT}^{PM}s. The synthesis process terminates after reaching the target number of iterations the developer asks, or when no

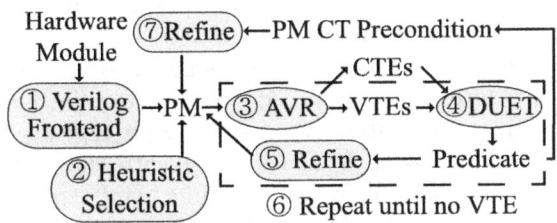

(a) The product module CT precondition synthesis flow (see §5.2 and Algorithm 1).

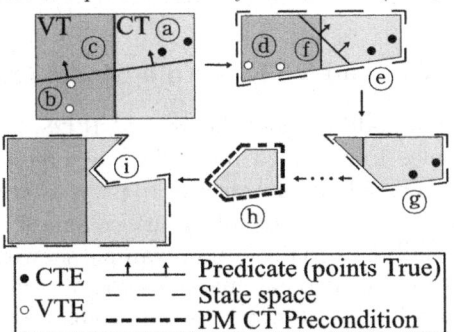

(b) The overview of state space refinement flow using harvested CTEs and VTEs until a product module CT precondition is found.

Fig. 1. Product module CT precondition synthesis flow and state space refinement

Algorithm 1. (P_{CT}, R_{vul}) Synthesis Procedure (Bottom-Up Heuristic §5.4)

1: **Input:** M // Hardware Module
2: **Output:** (P_{CT}, R_{vul}) tuples
3:   PM ← Verilog Frontend(M)
4: **for** Target iterations **do**
5:     CTE, VTE ← AVR(PM)
6:     Predicates ← ∅
7:     **while** VTE is found **do**
8:         Predicate ← Duet(CTE, VTE)
9:         And(Predicates, Predicate)
10:        Refine(PM, +Predicate)
11:        _, VTE ← AVR(PM)
12:     P_{CT}^{PM} ← Predicates
13:     Refine(PM, -P_{CT}^{PM})
14: (P_{CT}, R_{vul}) tuples ← Post process(P_{CT}^{PM}s)

further CTEs are produced. Algorithm 1 presents this synthesis procedure in pseudocode. After synthesizing P_{CT}^{PM}s, LEAKSYNTH post-processes (§5.6) the resulting P_{CT}^{PM} to produce (P_{CT}, R_{vul}).

Figure 1b illustrates the examples and predicates LEAKSYNTH generates to obtain a P_{CT}^{PM} during the internal iteration represented as ⑥ in Fig. 1a. Each iteration starts (③) by harvesting CTEs (black dots around ⓐ) and VTEs (white dots around ⓑ). With these examples, DUET (④) synthesizes a predicate (ⓒ), which LEAKSYNTH uses to refine PM (⑤). Using the refined PM, LEAKSYNTH finds more VTEs (white dots around ⓓ) from the refined state space (ⓔ), and synthesizes a new predicate (ⓕ). LEAKSYNTH repeats this iteration by further refining the state space from ⓔ to ⓖ with the new predicate. This internal iteration terminates (⑥) when the refined state space is found to have no more VTEs which is a P_{CT}^{PM} (ⓗ). For the subsequent iteration to find more CT preconditions, this P_{CT}^{PM} is used to refine the initial state space (ⓘ).

5.3   Harvesting CTEs and VTEs with a Model Checker

LEAKSYNTH uses a commodity model checker (AVR [28] in our implementation) to harvest the examples from which it synthesizes predicates. To harvest the VTEs, LEAKSYNTH queries its model checker to prove that the two base modules of PM terminate simultaneously for all input sequences regardless of the first state. Such a query usually returns a counterexample showing that there exists an execution of PM in which the two base modules do not terminate simultaneously. LEAKSYNTH harvests the tuple of states for the two base modules, corresponding to the PM's first state of the counterexample as the negative example, VTE.

To harvest the positive examples or CTEs, LEAKSYNTH queries its model checker to prove that the two base modules of PM never terminate simultaneously for all input sequences regardless of the first state. A failure to this attempt gives a counterexample showing an input sequence and a tuple of states such that the two executions of base modules terminate simultaneously. Unfortunately, the example LEAKSYNTH harvests by this procedure could be a spurious CTE. This is because the existence of an input sequence that produces executions of equal length from a pair of states (σ_1, σ_2) does not guarantee that all input sequences will yield executions of identical length when initiated from these states. To address this, LEAKSYNTH filters out such spurious examples, leveraging that a spurious CTE is always a VTE by definition. We also introduce several heuristics that LEAKSYNTH uses in §5.4 for this problem.

5.4 Three Heuristics to Harvest CTEs

As mentioned in §5.2, LEAKSYNTH uses three heuristics to harvest CTEs. The three heuristics differ in how LEAKSYNTH constrains the PM before running AVR. LEAKSYNTH starts three workers in parallel to gain different advantages from each heuristic simultaneously.

Top-Down. In this heuristic, LEAKSYNTH begins by constraining PM with the *trivial* P_{CT}^{PM}, which is a conjunction of primitive constructed such that every register in the base module becomes a vulnerable register defined in §4.2. Subsequently, LEAKSYNTH removes one primitive expression from the trivial P_{CT}^{PM} to create a more permissive variation and examines if this variation still excludes VTEs. If this is the case, the variation is a more general P_{CT}^{PM} encompassing more CTEs than the earlier one, and LEAKSYNTH repeats the same procedure using this new variation. Otherwise, LEAKSYNTH collects a VTE as a result of the failed examination and uses the previous variation to collect a CTE. It then uses these CTE and VTE to synthesize a predicate that augments the variation to obtain another P_{CT}^{PM}. LEAKSYNTH repeats this procedure until all the expressions in the original trivial P_{CT}^{PM} have been tested and takes the generalized P_{CT}^{PM}.

Bottom-Up. In this heuristic, LEAKSYNTH does not begin with any constraint to PM, unlike the top-down heuristic. Instead, it collects synthesized predicates to construct P_{CT}^{PM}, ensuring it is free of VTEs. This heuristic has the advantage of widening the search space and improving speed, but it has a weakness in LEAKSYNTH's CTE harvesting procedure. While harvesting CTEs, the bottom-up search potentially harvests spurious CTEs which could turn out to be VTEs.

Mutation. In addition to the top-down and bottom-up heuristics, LEAKSYNTH mutates P_{CT}^{PM}s to efficiently synthesize more P_{CT}^{PM}s. Since a P_{CT}^{PM} is a conjunctive form of primitive expressions that make registers vulnerable or bound, mutation enables LEAKSYNTH to find a new value to which an already bound register can be bound. LEAKSYNTH constrains PM with a mutated P_{CT}^{PM} and uses the bottom-up heuristic to augment it. In this procedure, LEAKSYNTH rarely suffers from spurious CTEs because PM is already constrained with a relatively precise candidate of P_{CT}^{PM}. When the mutation heuristic terminates, LEAKSYNTH gains a new P_{CT} that is similar to the previous P_{CT}^{PM}. This heuristic has the advantage of being the fastest but produces the least broadening P_{CT}^{PM} as an output.

$\langle Predicate \rangle ::= \langle PrimExpr \rangle$
$\quad | \quad \langle Predicate \rangle \land \langle PrimExpr \rangle$

$\langle PrimExpr \rangle ::= \langle AExpr \rangle \mid \langle BExpr \rangle$

$\langle AExpr \rangle ::= \langle LeftA \rangle = \langle RightA \rangle$	(Vulnerable)
$\quad \mid \quad \langle LeftA \rangle = \langle Const \rangle$	(Bounded)
$\quad \mid \quad \langle RightA \rangle = \langle Const \rangle$	(Bounded)
$\langle BExpr \rangle ::= \langle LeftB \rangle = \langle RightB \rangle$	(Vulnerable)
$\quad \mid \quad \langle LeftB \rangle = \langle Const \rangle$	(Bounded)
$\quad \mid \quad \langle RightB \rangle = \langle Const \rangle$	(Bounded)

Fig. 2. The grammar used by LEAKSYNTH to synthesize predicates from examples with two base modules named `Left` and `Right`, containing registers A and B.

5.5 Synthesizing P_{CT}^{PM}

LEAKSYNTH uses a commodity program synthesis engine implementing programming by examples. Among others, we choose DUET [44], a recently developed tool synthesizing a predicate from examples and grammar. A challenge in this synthesis is choosing the proper grammar to synthesize P_{CT}^{PM} that can easily be post-processed to produce (P_{CT}, R_{vul}). We address this challenge by using the grammar under which a predicate becomes a conjunction of primitive expressions.

The grammar that LEAKSYNTH uses for predicate synthesis is designed to ensure that the primitive expressions have one of the two forms. For post-processing into (P_{CT}, R_{vul}) tuples over states of the base module M, each primitive expression should either *bound* a register in M to a constant or constrain that one register from the two base modules must have the same value. The equality between a constant and a register (e.g., $r = c$) in one of the two base modules fulfills the former of these two constraints. The equality between the same registers (e.g., $r_1 = r_2$) in the two base modules satisfies the latter. Having this equality as a primitive expression in a P_{CT}^{PM} implies that the execution time of two executions becomes indistinguishable only if the two executions start from initial states where the value of the register matches. Because of this direct relationship, such registers indeed become vulnerable registers with respect to a P_{CT}. On top of these observations, LEAKSYNTH generates the grammar for each DUET run using the VTEs and CTEs it uses for synthesis. Figure 2 shows an example of grammar that LEAKSYNTH generates for the examples with two base modules `Left` and `Right` that both contain registers A and B.

5.6 Post-processing P_{CT}^{PM} to Produce the Tuple (P_{CT}, R_{vul})

LeakSynth post-processes P_{CT}^{PM} that it synthesizes using the flow described in §5.2. The grammar shown in Fig. 2 does not constrain P_{CT}^{PM} to bound one register in the two base module instances to the same constant. For example, a P_{CT}^{PM} may bound a register of one instance, namely the left one r_left, to a constant c while bounding the other one, namely the right one r_right, to a different constant d. As one register cannot be bound to two different constants, such a P_{CT}^{PM} cannot be used to produce a valid P_{CT}.

To handle such registers, LeakSynth generates two variations P_{CT}^1 and P_{CT}^2 where the register r is bound to c in P_{CT}^1 and d in P_{CT}^2. It then uses the model checker to examine if each variation is a constant-time precondition and continues to the subsequent step only if it satisfies the definition. As a result, LeakSynth may produce more tuples (P_{CT}, R_{vul}) than P_{CT}^{PM}s. LeakSynth may not produce a new tuple (P_{CT}, R_{vul}) from a P_{CT}^{PM}, as we noticed that the result of post-processing sometimes leads to a P_{CT} that it found from post-processing a previously found P_{CT}^{PM}.

5.7 Producing Annotations for Existing Tools from (P_{CT}, R_{vul})

As mentioned earlier, the result of LeakSynth can also be used to automatically produce the annotations for existing constant-time verification tools such as Iodine [26] and Xenon [27]. Due to their reliance on abstract interpretation, they are incapable of reasoning with P_{CT}s that bound some registers to constants. That is, only the tuples having no bounded registers can be used to create annotations for Iodine and Xenon because they are not complete enough to prove the constant-time property of the hardware modules beginning executions from states where some registers are bound to constants. For the annotations, Iodine and Xenon require two sets of port names and two sets of register or port names to be specified. The two sets of port names are the sources and sinks, indicating where the input flows in and output flows out, respectively. Following our assumption, we consider all inputs as sources and all outputs as sinks. The two sets of register or port names are called the initially equivalent set and the always equivalent set. By definition (§4), executions starting from states where the vulnerable registers have the same values should have the same execution time, given a tuple (P_{CT}, R_{vul}). This definition matches the definition of the initially equivalent set in Iodine and Xenon, which try to prove the constant-time property under the assumption that the values of the registers in the initially equivalent set are the same. For the always equivalent set, we place all input port names because LeakSynth assumes the same input sequence in all executions. §7.2 presents the evaluation of the effectiveness of LeakSynth in producing the annotations for Iodine and Xenon.

6 Implementation Details

The core of LeakSynth is written in 5106 lines of Python code that drives open-source components such as Icarus Verilog [39], AVR [28], and DUET [44].

LEAKSYNTH also uses Antlr [7] to handle P_{CT}s. One design parameter of LEAKSYNTH is the number of VTEs and CTEs it uses for one DUET invocation. Using too many examples makes predicate synthesis slow, but some benchmarks could produce more general predicates from a few additional examples at an early stage. We choose ten as this parameter empirically, and it is automatically reduced if LEAKSYNTH experiences time out while synthesizing a predicate using DUET.

LEAKSYNTH takes as the input a hardware module with developer annotations specifying the terminating predicate P_{term}. To be specific, LEAKSYNTH reserves a keyword `end_` for a 1-bit register used to indicate if the hardware module's execution is finished. The developer can specify P_{term} by setting `end_` to 1 when the hardware module's state satisfies it. Our experiences from annotating the nine benchmarks used for evaluation suggest that this task would be

Table 2. The table presents the overall evaluation results of LEAKSYNTH. From left to right, the columns represent the following: the hardware module name; the number of P_{CT}^{PM}s synthesized; the number of (P_{CT}, R_{vul})s interpreted; the targeted number of P_{CT}^{PM}s sent to LEAKSYNTH; the time taken to synthesize the first P_{CT}^{PM}; the time taken to synthesize the last P_{CT}^{PM}; the time spent post-processing P_{CT}^{PM}s into (P_{CT}, R_{vul})s; the number of registers in a hardware module; the total number of register bits in a hardware module; the lines of code for PM; the input bits constrained by LEAKSYNTH (**LS**), Iodine (I), and Xenon (X); and finally, the register bits constrained by LEAKSYNTH, Iodine, and Xenon.

Benchmark		P_{CT}^{PM}	(P_{CT}, R_{vul})	Tgt	Synth. P_{CT}^{PM} First	Last	Post-process	Num. Reg.	Total Bits	LOC	Input LS	I	X	Register LS	I	X
MIPS [47]	ADD	100	136	100	1.1 m	23.1 m	15.0 m	63	772	1,852	1	1	1	2–21	142	240
	LW	100	133	100	1.1 m	19.5 m	13.1 m									
	BEQ	100	143	100	1.1 m	24.9 m	15.5 m									
Yarvi [60]	ADD	100	192	100	1.7 m	59.3 h	11.5 h	78	1,464	1,946	0	1	34	1–329	354	398
	LW	100	176	100	1.7 m	67.1 h	8.1 h									
	SW	100	195	100	1.7 m	100.0 h	9.0 h									
	BEQ	100	184	100	1.7 m	10.0 h	6.7 h									
PicoRV32 [61]	ADD	10	17	10	1.0 h	10.8 h	71.6 h	159	1,350	3,360	1	–	–	2–382	–	–
	LW	10	12	10	9.8 m	3.0 h	15.2 h									
	SW	10	15	10	9.3 m	9.6 h	58.9 h									
	BEQ	10	18	10	1.2 h	9.5 h	42.3 h									
Rocket [4]	ADD	10	10	10	49.5 m	10.7 h	7.8 h	189	1,829	12,664	2	–	–	1826	–	–
	LW	10	10	10	1.0 h	10.7 h	7.4 h									
	SW	10	10	10	42.3 m	8.5 h	6.8 h									
	BEQ	10	10	10	25.1 m	9.0 h	7.0 h									
FPU [24]		3	3	10	26.3 s	1.8 m	13.9 s	107	821	2,954	0	0	3	1–3	0	9
ALU [58]		1	1	10	23.0 s	23.0 s	2.1 s	7	203	2,136	1	14	14	6	6	6
Divider [25]		11	13	100	43.2 s	9.6 m	25.6 m	25	453	744	1	4	4	5–384	453	449
SHA-256 [54]		100	101	100	2.0 m	29.1 m	7.6 m	39	1,135	1,364	1	5	5	7	15	15
AES-256 [1]		14	14	100	19.9 m	4.4 h	2.5 h	634	13,358	532,332	0	–	0	1–14	–	0

straightforward for developers, as they are familiar with the input and output signals of the hardware module and can identify where the output is generated. For instance, the processor benchmarks we used have valid signals for stages such as instruction fetch, and instruction decode. We were able to annotate processor benchmarks using the write-back valid signal. Modules like the FPU, Divider, SHA-256, and AES-256 generate outputs at distinct stages within their finite state machine, allowing clear annotation at those stages. In the case of the ALU, we could easily locate a dedicated register indicating if the computation is finished and use it to determine when `end_` should be set to 1.

7 Evaluation

We evaluate the effectiveness and performance of LEAKSYNTH by synthesizing the P_{CT}^{PM} and interpret to (P_{CT}, R_{vul}) for the nine hardware modules using a machine running Ubuntu 18.04.6 with a Xeon Gold 6136 CPU and 128 GB of RAM. Table 2 shows the results.

7.1 Performance

From column 2 to 4 in Table 2 (P_{CT}^{PM}, (P_{CT}, R_{vul}), and Tgt) show the statistics of 20 LEAKSYNTH runs for the nine hardware designs. For each benchmark, LEAKSYNTH was requested to synthesize 10 to 100 P_{CT}^{PM}s, as the target column shows, before the post-processing (see §5.6). The table demonstrates that LEAKSYNTH succeeds in synthesizing a non-trivial number of P_{CT}^{PM}s and deriving (P_{CT}, R_{vul}) tuples from them. All P_{CT}s that LEAKSYNTH derived are non-empty, and we prove effectiveness of some (P_{CT}, R_{vul}) tuples by deriving Iodine annotations leading to successful constant-time verification. The number of P_{CT}^{PM}s and (P_{CT}, R_{vul}) are not the same for the reasons explained in §5.6.

From column 5 to 10 in Table 2 (Synth. P_{CT}^{PM} First, Last, Post-process, Num. Reg., Total Bits, and LOC) show the latency of LEAKSYNTH's P_{CT}^{PM} synthesis and post-processing, along with the complexity of each benchmark in several metrics. We report latencies for the first and the last P_{CT}^{PM} synthesized. The first P_{CT}^{PM} synthesis latency indicates LEAKSYNTH's ability to quickly obtain an P_{CT}^{PM} from most benchmarks. The latency of the last P_{CT}^{PM} highlights LEAKSYNTH's capabilities and limitations. LEAKSYNTH continues to find more P_{CT}^{PM}s after 9 h for some benchmarks, after finding some, suggesting that LEAKSYNTH can improve precision as long as it runs.

7.2 Comparison with Iodine and Xenon

The last six columns in Table 2 (Input and Register) shows that LEAKSYNTH generates (P_{CT}, R_{vul})s requiring the initialization of only a few bits, making them more relaxed (i.e., general) than those found by Iodine or Xenon. For instance, while Iodine proves MIPS's constant-time execution with a human-engineered precondition constraining 1 and 142 bits respectively for inputs and internal registers, LEAKSYNTH only constrains 1 and up to 21 bits for inputs and internal registers. This pattern recurs in other benchmarks, such as Divider and SHA-256. In these cases, the set of registers found by LEAKSYNTH is often a subset of the human-engineered preconditions for Iodine and Xenon, implying that LEAKSYNTH identifies correct, yet more relaxed, (P_{CT}, R_{vul})s. This also shows that a human-engineered precondition can mark several registers as vulnerable, while only one register is the actual cause and is responsible for timing variance. Note that we translated constraints from Iodine and Xenon, which cover inputs, registers, and wires, into constraints over inputs and registers for comparison.

Producing Annotations for Iodine and Xenon. From the (P_{CT}, R_{vul})s, LEAKSYNTH automatically produced annotations for FPU, ALU, AES-256, and Divider to run Iodine and Xenon. The annotations for FPU, ALU, and AES-256 were enough to lead the two tools to conclude that the modules execute in constant-time under the annotated assumptions, indicating the R_{vul}s synthesized from LEAKSYNTH is analogous to their initially equivalent set as expected, and showcasing the use case of LEAKSYNTH. However, LEAKSYNTH was unable to produce annotations for SHA-256, MIPS and Yarvi as they always included a bounded register, which cannot be processed by the two tools.

Imprecision of Iodine and Xenon Identified by LEAKSYNTH. We also observed an example showing the imprecision of Iodine and Xenon. They are sound in proving the constant-time property, suggesting that they are not complete, and may conclude a combination of module and annotation as timing unsafe when it is actually safe. The annotation that LEAKSYNTH produced for Divider was such an example. When running for the Divider with a LEAKSYNTH-produced annotation, Iodine and Xenon conclude that the module is unsafe. Upon thorough inspection of the code and the annotation, we found that the register `sticky` needs to be included in the initially equivalent set to lead Iodine and Xenon conclude that the module is safe, but the register in fact does not affect the timing behavior. `sticky` bit is used to track whether the result should be rounded or not, and thus does not affect the execution time of Divider. We also checked that R_{vul} without `sticky` is sound with AVR.

8 Related Work

Proving a Hardware Module Constant-Time. Iodine [26] and Xenon [27] are the closest to this work in that they prove a hardware module to be constant-time if the module satisfies the constant-time property. LEAKSYNTH is different from these in two folds. Firstly, LEAKSYNTH automatically identifies the (P_{CT}, R_{vul})s, whereas Iodine requires developers to find the necessary registers for creating R_{vul}s. Xenon recommends some registers called *public* but not the actual R_{vul}s, and does not recommend the *bound* registers, which the developers still have to find manually. Secondly, our focus lies in identifying potential timing leakage for specific attacker-observable executions. In other words, a non-constant-time hardware module could still have the tuple of (P_{CT}, R_{vul}) that cover a subset of the hardware module's possible executions. For instance, a processor might have such tuples for only a few instructions, leaving the remaining instructions vulnerable to leakage.

Conjunct [21] focuses on proving the safety of (constant-time) instructions, which can help study the safety of data-oblivious instructions [20,62]. Conjunct checks whether an instruction under test is safe for a bounded number of cycles by symbolic execution and tries to construct an invariant to check the instruction is safe for an unbounded number of cycles. Conjunct is similar to Iodine and Xenon in that it tries to find an invariant as a proof for constant-time with annotations and assumptions provided manually.

Hardware Analysis for Security. The emergence of hardware bugs [41,46] motivated research on hardware analysis to find security bugs [38,64]. Coppelia [64] generates code snippets that reveal vulnerabilities given a processor implementation and interface, using KLEE [15] for reachability analysis. Similarly, LEAKSYNTH collects the initial states that cause a PM to reach a particular state (i.e., constant-time or variable-time). However, the mechanism for obtaining such initial states is not a contribution of LEAKSYNTH, as it relies on an existing push-button model checker, AVR, for this purpose. Köpf et al. [42] utilizes SMV solver to create a PM and compare execution times, similar to LEAKSYNTH. RTL fuzzing [12,16,17,29,38,43,52,53] is another technique for detecting hardware vulnerabilities, but they are not designed for deriving constant-time preconditions as fuzzers cannot prove the absence of behavioral inconsistency.

Data-Driven Precondition Inference. LEAKSYNTH is inspired from techniques like precondition inference from examples [50]. It shares a similar strategy with PIE [50], using AVR-collected examples for precondition inference. The main difference lies in the application domain; PIE focuses on software's weakest preconditions, while LEAKSYNTH synthesizes preconditions of hardware modules. Halo [36] applies several techniques similar to LEAKSYNTH to enhance the reachable input generation rate for fuzzing. Halo collects a sufficient amount of reachable and unreachable inputs and draws invariants that hopefully contain reachable inputs that lead to unknown bugs in the software. Such an approach is similar to LEAKSYNTH narrowing down to find P_{CT}^{PM} containing only CTEs.

Software-Level Timing Leakage Control. Timing side channels exist in both software and hardware, motivating research on mechanisms for identifying potential software-level timing leakage. Backes et al. [10] introduced a method to discover and quantify information leaks using input partitions, with a core idea resembling LEAKSYNTH's approach. However, LEAKSYNTH focuses on timing leakage in hardware description rather than software. Vaughan and Chong [57] also employed a similar strategy, using developer-annotated Java programs to infer information-flow policies. These policies indicate revealable variables and conditions analogous to LeakSynth's R_{vul}. However, LeakSynth is designed for hardware and focuses on finding (P_{CT}, R_{vul})s, not inferring information flows.

9 Conclusion

This paper introduced LeakSynth, an end-to-end system that identifies the potential timing leakage by synthesizing CT preconditions and vulnerable registers for hardware modules. The system integrates a model checker and a program synthesis engine to create and incrementally improve preconditions. LeakSynth also automatically generates grammars from example sets for fast, interpretable precondition synthesis. Our empirical evaluation using nine hardware modules shows LeakSynth's efficiency, effectiveness, and use cases. It quickly finds the first product module CT precondition (<120 s), gradually enhances its precision, and produces annotations, which should otherwise be written manually, for existing tools.

Acknowledgement. This work was supported by the Institute of Information & Communications Technology Planning & Evaluation (IITP) grant funded by the Korea government (MSIT) (No. RS-2024-00437306, Development of Integrated Platform for Expanding and Safely Applying Memory-Safe Languages, 34%), IITP grant funded by the Korea government (MSIT) (No. RS-2024-00438729, Development of Full Lifecycle Privacy-Preserving Techniques using Anonymized Confidential Computing, 33%), IITP grant funded by the Korea government (MSIT) (No. RS-2024-00337414, Binary Micro-Security Patch Technology Applicable with Limited Reverse Engineering Capability under SW Supply Chain Environments, 33%).

References

1. Opencores - AES. https://opencores.org/projects/tiny_aes
2. Aldaya, A.C., Brumley, B.B., ul Hassan, S., Pereida Garc a, C., Tuveri, N.: Port contention for fun and profit. In: 2019 IEEE Symposium on Security and Privacy (SP), pp. 870–887 (2019)
3. Aldaya, A.C., Garc a, C.P., Tapia, L.M.A., Brumley, B.B.: Cache-timing attacks on RSA key generation. Cryptology ePrint Archive, Paper 2018/367 (2018). https://eprint.iacr.org/2018/367
4. Alliance, C.: Github - rocket-chip. https://github.com/chipsalliance/rocket-chip
5. Alur, R., et al.: Syntax-guided synthesis. In: 2013 Formal Methods in Computer-Aided Design, pp. 1–8 (2013)
6. Alur, R., Radhakrishna, A., Udupa, A.: Scaling enumerative program synthesis via divide and conquer. In: International Conference on Tools and Algorithms for the Construction and Analysis of Systems, pp. 319–336. Springer (2017)
7. Another tool for language recognition. https://www.antlr.org/
8. Ardeshiricham, A., Hu, W., Kastner, R.: Clepsydra: modeling timing flows in hardware designs. In: 2017 IEEE/ACM International Conference on Computer-Aided Design (ICCAD), pp. 147–154 (2017)

9. Ardeshiricham, A., Takashima, Y., Gao, S., Kastner, R.: Verisketch: synthesizing secure hardware designs with timing-sensitive information flow properties. In: CCS 2019, Proceedings of the 2019 ACM SIGSAC Conference on Computer and Communications Security, pp. 1623–1638. Association for Computing Machinery, New York, NY, USA (2019)
10. Backes, M., K pf, B., Rybalchenko, A.: Automatic discovery and quantification of information leaks. In: 2009 30th IEEE Symposium on Security and Privacy, pp. 141–153 (May 2009)
11. Biere, A., Heljanko, K., Wieringa, S.: AIGER 1.9 and beyond (2011). https://fmv.jku.at/papers/BiereHeljankoWieringa-FMV-TR-11-2.pdf
12. Borkar, P., et al.: Whisperfuzz: white-box fuzzing for detecting and locating timing vulnerabilities in processors (2024)
13. Bradley, A.R.: Sat-based model checking without unrolling. In: Jhala, R., Schmidt, D. (eds.) Verification, Model Checking, and Abstract Interpretation, pp. 70–87. Springer, Berlin Heidelberg, Berlin, Heidelberg (2011)
14. Cabodi, G., et al.: Hardware model checking competition 2014: an analysis and comparison of model checkers and benchmarks. J. Satisfiability Boolean Model. Comput. **9**(1), 135–172 (2014)
15. Cadar, C., Dunbar, D., Engler, D.: Klee: unassisted and automatic generation of high-coverage tests for complex systems programs. In: OSDI 2008, Proceedings of the 8th USENIX Conference on Operating Systems Design and Implementation, pp. 209–224. USENIX Association, USA (2008)
16. Chen, C., Gohil, V., Kande, R., Sadeghi, A.R., Rajendran, J.: Psofuzz: fuzzing processors with particle swarm optimization. In: 2023 IEEE/ACM International Conference on Computer Aided Design (ICCAD), pp. 1–9 (2023)
17. Chen, C., et al.: HyPFuzz: formal-assisted processor fuzzing. In: 32nd USENIX Security Symposium (USENIX Security 23), pp. 1361–1378. USENIX Association, Anaheim, CA (2023)
18. Clarke, E.M., Emerson, E.A., Sifakis, J.: Model checking: algorithmic verification and debugging. Commun. ACM **52**(11), 74–84 (2009)
19. Deng, S., et al.: Secchisel framework for security verification of secure processor architectures. In: HASP 2019, Proceedings of the 8th International Workshop on Hardware and Architectural Support for Security and Privacy. Association for Computing Machinery, New York, NY, USA (2019)
20. Deutschmann, L., Müller, J., Fadiheh, M.R., Stoffel, D., Kunz, W.: A scalable formal verification methodology for data-oblivious hardware. IEEE Trans. Comput. Aided Des. Integr. Circuits Syst. (2024)
21. Dinesh, S., Parthasarathy, M., Fletcher, C.: Conjunct: learning inductive invariants to prove unbounded instruction safety against microarchitectural timing attacks. In: 2024 IEEE Symposium on Security and Privacy (SP), p. 177. IEEE Computer Society (2024)
22. Een, N., Mishchenko, A., Brayton, R.: Efficient implementation of property directed reachability. In: 2011 Formal Methods in Computer-Aided Design (FMCAD), pp. 125–134 (2011)
23. Evtyushkin, D., Ponomarev, D., Abu-Ghazaleh, N.: Jump over ASLR: attacking branch predictors to bypass ASLR. In: 2016 49th Annual IEEE/ACM International Symposium on Microarchitecture (MICRO), pp. 1–13 (2016)
24. Github - fpu_mc/fpu (2022). https://github.com/monajalal/fpga_mc/tree/master/fpu
25. Github - dawsonjon/fpu: synthesiseable ieee 754 floating point library in verilog. https://github.com/dawsonjon/fpu

26. Gleissenthall, K., Kıcı, R.G., Stefan, D., Jhala, R.: IODINE: verifying constant-time execution of hardware. In: 28th USENIX Security Symposium (USENIX Security 19), pp. 1411–1428. USENIX Association, Santa Clara, CA (2019)
27. v. Gleissenthall, K., Kıcı, R.G., Stefan, D., Jhala, R.: Solver-aided constant-time hardware verification. In: CCS 2021, Proceedings of the 2021 ACM SIGSAC Conference on Computer and Communications Security, pp. 429–444. Association for Computing Machinery, New York, NY, USA (2021)
28. Goel, A., Sakallah, K.: Avr: abstractly verifying reachability. In: International Conference on Tools and Algorithms for the Construction and Analysis of Systems, pp. 413–422. Springer (2020)
29. Gohil, V., Kande, R., Chen, C., Sadeghi, A.R., Rajendran, J.: Mabfuzz: multi-armed bandit algorithms for fuzzing processors (2023)
30. Gruss, D., Maurice, C., Fogh, A., Lipp, M., Mangard, S.: Prefetch side-channel attacks: bypassing SMAP and kernel ASLR. In: CCS 2016, Proceedings of the 2016 ACM SIGSAC Conference on Computer and Communications Security, pp. 368–379. Association for Computing Machinery, New York, NY, USA (2016)
31. Gruss, D., Spreitzer, R., Mangard, S.: Cache template attacks: automating attacks on inclusive last-level caches. In: 24th USENIX Security Symposium (USENIX Security 15), pp. 897–912. USENIX Association, Washington, DC (2015)
32. Gullasch, D., Bangerter, E., Krenn, S.: Cache games – bringing access-based cache attacks on AES to practice. In: 2011 IEEE Symposium on Security and Privacy, pp. 490–505 (2011)
33. Gulmezoglu, B., Zankl, A., Tol, M.C., Islam, S., Eisenbarth, T., Sunar, B.: Undermining user privacy on mobile devices using AI. In: Asia CCS 2019, Proceedings of the 2019 ACM Asia Conference on Computer and Communications Security, pp. 214–227. Association for Computing Machinery, New York, NY, USA (2019)
34. Gulwani, S.: Programming by examples. Dependable Softw. Syst. Eng. **45**(137), 3–15 (2016)
35. Gulwani, S., Jha, S., Tiwari, A., Venkatesan, R.: Synthesis of loop-free programs. In: PLDI 2011, Proceedings of the 32nd ACM SIGPLAN Conference on Programming Language Design and Implementation, pp. 62–73. Association for Computing Machinery, New York, NY, USA (2011)
36. Huang, H., Zhou, A., Payer, M., Zhang, C.: Everything is good for something: counterexample-guided directed fuzzing via likely invariant inference. In: 2024 IEEE Symposium on Security and Privacy (SP), p. 141. IEEE Computer Society, Los Alamitos, CA, USA (2024)
37. Hund, R., Willems, C., Holz, T.: Practical timing side channel attacks against kernel space ASLR. In: 2013 IEEE Symposium on Security and Privacy, pp. 191–205 (2013)
38. Hur, J., Song, S., Kwon, D., Baek, E., Kim, J., Lee, B.: Difuzzrtl: differential fuzz testing to find CPU bugs. In: 2021 IEEE Symposium on Security and Privacy (SP), pp. 1286–1303 (2021)
39. Icarus verilog. http://iverilog.icarus.com/home
40. Jha, S., Gulwani, S., Seshia, S.A., Tiwari, A.: Oracle-guided component-based program synthesis. In: 2010 ACM/IEEE 32nd International Conference on Software Engineering, vol. 1, pp. 215–224. IEEE (2010)
41. Kocher, P., et al.: Spectre attacks: exploiting speculative execution. In: 2019 IEEE Symposium on Security and Privacy (SP), pp. 1–19 (2019)
42. Köpf, B., Basin, D.: Timing-sensitive information flow analysis for synchronous systems. In: European Symposium on Research in Computer Security, pp. 243–262. Springer (2006)

43. Laeufer, K., Koenig, J., Kim, D., Bachrach, J., Sen, K.: RFUZZ: coverage-directed fuzz testing of RTL on FPGAs. In: 2018 IEEE/ACM International Conference on Computer-Aided Design (ICCAD), pp. 1–8. IEEE (2018)
44. Lee, W.: Combining the top-down propagation and bottom-up enumeration for inductive program synthesis. Proc. ACM Program. Lang. **5**(POPL) (2021)
45. Lee, W., Heo, K., Alur, R., Naik, M.: Accelerating search-based program synthesis using learned probabilistic models. In: PLDI 2018, Proceedings of the 39th ACM SIGPLAN Conference on Programming Language Design and Implementation, pp. 436–449. Association for Computing Machinery, New York, NY, USA (2018)
46. Lipp, M., et al.: Meltdown: reading kernel memory from user space. Commun. ACM **63**(6), 46–56 (2020)
47. Github - iodine benchmark. https://github.com/gokhankici/iodine/tree/master/benchmarks/472-mips-pipelined
48. Niemetz, A., Preiner, M., Wolf, C., Biere, A.: Btor2, btormc and boolector 3.0. In: International Conference on Computer Aided Verification, pp. 587–595. Springer (2018)
49. Osvik, D.A., Shamir, A., Tromer, E.: Cache attacks and countermeasures: the case of AES. Cryptology ePrint Archive, Paper 2005/271 (2005). https://eprint.iacr.org/2005/271
50. Padhi, S., Sharma, R., Millstein, T.: Data-driven precondition inference with learned features. SIGPLAN Not. **51**(6), 42–56 (2016)
51. Ronen, E., Gillham, R., Genkin, D., Shamir, A., Wong, D., Yarom, Y.: The 9 lives of bleichenbacher's cat: new cache attacks on TLS implementations. In: 2019 IEEE Symposium on Security and Privacy (SP), pp. 435–452 (2019)
52. Rostami, M., Chilese, M., Zeitouni, S., Kande, R., Rajendran, J., Sadeghi, A.R.: Beyond random inputs: a novel ml-based hardware fuzzing (2024)
53. Schwarz, M., et al.: Automated detection, exploitation, and elimination of double-fetch bugs using modern CPU features. In: Proceedings of the 2018 on Asia Conference on Computer and Communications Security, pp. 587–600 (2018)
54. Opencores – sha_core. https://opencores.org/projects/sha_core
55. Shusterman, A., et al.: Robust website fingerprinting through the cache occupancy channel. In: 28th USENIX Security Symposium (USENIX Security 19), pp. 639–656. USENIX Association, Santa Clara, CA (2019)
56. Udupa, A., Raghavan, A., Deshmukh, J.V., Mador-Haim, S., Martin, M.M., Alur, R.: Transit: specifying protocols with concolic snippets. In: PLDI 2013, Proceedings of the 34th ACM SIGPLAN Conference on Programming Language Design and Implementation, pp. 287–296. Association for Computing Machinery, New York, NY, USA (2013)
57. Vaughan, J.A., Chong, S.: Inference of expressive declassification policies. In: 2011 IEEE Symposium on Security and Privacy, pp. 180–195. IEEE (2011)
58. Github - scarv/xcrypto: Xcrypto: a cryptographic ise for risc-v. https://github.com/scarv/xcrypto-ref
59. Yarom, Y., Falkner, K.: FLUSH+RELOAD: a high resolution, low noise, l3 cache Side-Channel attack. In: 23rd USENIX Security Symposium (USENIX Security 14), pp. 719–732. USENIX Association, San Diego, CA (2014)
60. Github - yarvi. https://github.com/tommythorn/yarvi
61. YosysHQ: Github - picorv32 project. https://github.com/YosysHQ/picorv32
62. Yu, J., Hsiung, L., El Hajj, M., Fletcher, C.W.: Data oblivious ISA extensions for side channel-resistant and high performance computing. In: Proceedings 2019 Network and Distributed System Security Symposium. NDSS 2019, Internet Society (2019)

63. Zhang, D., Wang, Y., Suh, G.E., Myers, A.C.: A hardware design language for timing-sensitive information-flow security. In: ASPLOS 2015, Proceedings of the Twentieth International Conference on Architectural Support for Programming Languages and Operating Systems, pp. 503–516. Association for Computing Machinery, New York, NY, USA (2015)
64. Zhang, R., Deutschbein, C., Huang, P., Sturton, C.: End-to-end automated exploit generation for validating the security of processor designs. In: 2018 51st Annual IEEE/ACM International Symposium on Microarchitecture (MICRO), pp. 815–827 (2018)

LibAFLstar: Fast and State-Aware Protocol Fuzzing

Cristian Daniele[1](✉), Timme Bethe[2], Marcello Maugeri[3],
Andrea Continella[2], and Erik Poll[1]

[1] Radboud University, Nijmegen, The Netherlands
{cristian.daniele,erik.poll}@ru.nl
[2] University of Twente, Enschede, The Netherlands
a.continella@utwente.nl, timme@timmebethe.nl
[3] University of Catania, Catania, Italy
marcello.maugeri@phd.unict.it

Abstract. Fuzzing is arguably one of the most effective software vulnerability discovery techniques. However, despite recent advances, fuzzing stateful software suffers from severe inefficiencies and scalability limitations. This hinders automated testing for software that relies on state models, such as protocol implementations. Unlike stateless approaches, efficient stateful fuzzers need to i) explore the state model of the target system, ii) focus on the most interesting states, iii) track which messages are interesting for each state, and iv) handle expensive restarts and synchronizations of the system. In this paper, we present LibAFLstar, a fast and state-aware protocol fuzzer that addresses the aforementioned challenges leveraging i) partial message sequences, ii) a novel state scheduler, iii) state-aware queues and bitmaps, and iv) persistent mode. We fine-tune our approach by running an extensive ablation study with more than 20 configurations over six protocol implementations. Then, we evaluate LibAFLstar on the same protocol implementations (FTP, RTSP and HTTP) for 24 hours. We compare LibAFLstar's performance with two state-of-the-art fuzzers: AFLNet and ChatAFL. Our experiments show that LibAFLstar is more than 30× faster than competitors and achieves, on average, 1.4× more coverage.

Keywords: Software Security · Software Testing · Fuzzing · Stateful Systems · Network Protocols

1 Introduction

Fuzzing is a well-known technique for finding bugs in systems. The idea behind fuzzing is simple: sending unexpected (e.g., malformed) messages to a System Under Test (SUT) to trigger unexpected behaviour. Despite being introduced more than 30 years ago, fuzzing has become very popular with the advent of AFL [36] (and its re-implementation AFL++ [16]), a *smart mutation-based* fuzzer highly effective at finding vulnerabilities in modern systems. In recent years, a plethora of fuzzers have been devised to target a variety of systems [8, 15,19,30], as surveyed in recent work [13,21,23,38]. Nevertheless, AFL++ and its descendant LIBAFL [17] remain the best choice when it comes to fuzzing *stateless* targets because of their speed and effectiveness.

Unfortunately, the effectiveness of AFL++ and generic smart mutation-based fuzzers are often confined to *stateless systems*—systems that do not require the implementation of a state model to function properly. Classical examples of stateless systems are PDF readers, MP3 players, or image libraries.

When dealing with *stateful systems*, existing smart mutation-based fuzzers are, unfortunately, not as effective. Stateful systems are characterized by a state model. Typical examples include any client or server implementing network protocols, such as FTP, SSH, TLS, and 5G. In these systems, message sequences (often called traces) play a crucial role, as unexpected traces may also expose vulnerabilities. Stateful fuzzing is much more challenging because of the difficulty in tracking states and dealing with dependencies between messages, adding a further layer of complexity to the typical fuzzing challenges [7]. In fact, stateful fuzzers need to understand and explore the state model of the target system (challenge C1), focus on the most interesting states (challenge C2), consider relations between states and interesting messages (challenge C3), and deal with expensive SUT restarts and synchronization (challenge C4).

Several stateful fuzzers have been proposed in recent years [9,10,37], however, none has fully addressed the aforementioned challenges. In fact, most approaches [4,27,35] require shutting down and restarting the SUT and require snapshotting to provide a new trace (i.e., a new sequence of messages) [31]. Also, all the above-mentioned tools do not use the actual state model of the SUT, implementing only a shallow notion of statefulness.

In this paper, we present LIBAFLSTAR, a fast and state-aware protocol fuzzer that solves the four above-mentioned challenges by combining:

1. **knowledge about the state model** — solving C1;
2. **state schedulers** to focus on the most interesting states — solving C2;
3. **state-aware queues** to group relevant messages by state — solving C3;
4. **persistent mode** to avoid resets of the SUT after every trace and expensive snapshotting, allowing for fast synchronization between the fuzzer and the SUT — solving C4.

We implement LIBAFLSTAR on top of LIBAFL and evaluate it on six targets from ProFuzzBench [26], comparing the performance of our tool with the state-of-the-art stateful fuzzers AFLNET [27] and CHATAFL [25].

In our experiments, we show that LIBAFLSTAR is, on average, 20× faster and achieves up to 3× the code coverage[1] of AFLNET and CHATAFL.

---

[1] In the paper, we use the term code coverage instead of *edge coverage* to avoid confusion with the edge coverage in the state model.

2 Background on Fuzzing

Stateless Fuzzing. According to the technique used to generate messages, fuzzers are divided into *grammar-based* and *mutation-based*. Grammar-based fuzzers leverage the grammar of the inputs (given by the analyst or automatically inferred) to generate inputs that slightly differ from the grammar [34], or to generate grammar-compliant inputs that pass specific checks or constraints in the code [24]. *Mutation-based* fuzzers do not require grammar; instead, they take sample messages as input (often called *seeds*) to start the mutations. *Smart* mutation-based fuzzers like AFL++ (often called *grey-box*) do not perform blind mutations, as brute-force or simple mutation-based tools do, but instead use heuristics (e.g., code coverage) to steer the generation of the messages towards the most promising ones. Specifically, smart mutation-based fuzzers store code coverage information in a matrix (a *bitmap*) and use a *queue* to store messages that trigger new code coverage, allowing for further mutations later.

Stateless fuzzers require little else: input grammar or a few seeds are often sufficient to find numerous bugs as proven by OSS-Fuzz [32], a Google initiative that found 36.000 bugs in 1.000 projects[2] thanks to three stateless fuzzers (AFL++ [16], libFuzzer[3] and Honggfuzz[4]).

Stateful Fuzzing. Although the boundary between stateful and stateless systems can sometimes be vague [10], it is clear that for efficient fuzzing of certain systems, the grammar of the messages or seed files alone is insufficient. In fact, stateful systems — i.e. systems that require a state model to enforce specific behaviours — require specific components or heuristics to manage their statefulness. For example, Daniele et al. [10] identified seven different categories of stateful fuzzers that implement such ad-hoc components to deal with the stateful nature of the SUT. Among others, they describe the *evolutionary grammar-based* fuzzers. These fuzzers combine a feedback mechanism (similar to AFL++) with the SUT's state model specification. In fact, they use the feedback information to steer the generation of the messages toward the most interesting ones and the knowledge of the state model to explore different states. LIBAFLSTAR falls in this category.

On a higher level, the main problem with stateful fuzzing is the need to deal with two different layers of inputs. In fact, while stateless systems only have to fuzz the messages; stateful systems need to fuzz both the messages and their order. Mutating the message order introduces additional complexity, as the same messages can be sent from any state.

---

[2] https://google.github.io/oss-fuzz/.
[3] https://llvm.org/docs/LibFuzzer.html.
[4] https://github.com/google/honggfuzz.

3 Challenges in Stateful Fuzzing

Stateful fuzzing is generally more challenging than stateless fuzzing, and using a stateless fuzzer to fuzz stateful systems is often not the best choice [10]. Specifically, four main challenges arise when fuzzing stateful systems:

C1 — State Model Exploration. Any well-designed stateful fuzzer must be able to explore the state space. In other words, the fuzzer needs to move from one state to another. This ability requires either i) the actual state model that the SUT implements or ii) the ability of the fuzzer to infer the state model of the SUT during the fuzzing campaign. Unfortunately, protocol specifications usually contain scattered information about the state model through different pages of prose, and stateful fuzzers struggle to infer a good approximation of the SUT state model. For example, AFLNET [27] infers the state model of the SUT at run time by observing *only* the response of the server. Despite this approach giving a good understanding of the state model the SUT implements, it might result in an inaccurate understanding. Different server responses might not trigger any transition state, and two identical server responses can instead cause a state transition.

C2 — States Prioritization. Given the large number of states that certain programs implement and the limited time availability, efficient stateful fuzzers need to prioritize the most interesting states to fuzz. While a naive approach that prioritizes states that trigger new coverage may work for some systems, it may perform poorly for others, potentially overlooking interesting states. Advanced stateful fuzzers should be able to schedule states according to their probability of covering a big portion of code, i.e., finding more bugs. For example, during the testing of an FTP implementation, it is not ideal to spend much time fuzzing the first state, as many commands are only available after a successful authentication.

C3 — Dependencies Between Messages and States. Stateless systems have no notion of previous executions: they just take in input one message at a time. For this reason, stateless fuzzers use a *global queue* to store messages that are interesting for the system as a whole. On the contrary, when fuzzing stateful systems, certain messages are interesting only in some states, i.e., after other messages. Despite fuzzers like AFLNET or CHATAFL [25] partially solving this problem by concatenating multiple messages in a single trace, this approach requires the restart of the SUT after every trace. This causes serious performance limitations, as explained in the next paragraph.

C4 — SUT Restarts and Synchronizations. SUT restarts represent a challenge for both stateless and stateful fuzzing. The time spent to restart the target system significantly reduces the number of inputs that can be processed in a given time budget. This makes fuzzers less efficient. Moreover, stateful systems often implement more complex behaviours, making the restart overhead even more expensive. Worse, when fuzzing stateful protocols that require communication between a client and a server, the synchronization between the two sides also plays a crucial role. When fuzzing a server, stateful fuzzers cannot send millions of messages sequentially; they must allow the server to process and acknowledge each message.

In Sect. 4, we address these challenges and propose a set of new techniques to design a fast and state-aware fuzzer for protocol implementations.

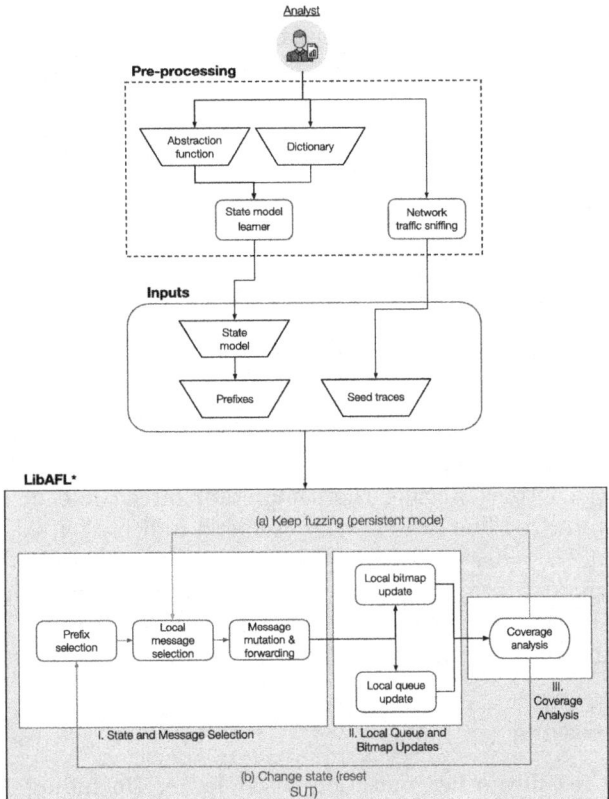

Fig. 1. LibAFLstar workflow. The approach takes in input the state model of the SUT and some seed traces. It then selects a state and keeps fuzzing it by sending malformed messages. It switches state when no more coverage is triggered.

4 LibAFLstar: Methodology and Design

In this section, we introduce LibAFLstar, a state-aware fuzzer that addresses the four challenges presented in Sect. 3.

Our fuzzer takes in input seed traces for the generation of the inputs and the state model of the SUT to create the *prefixes*, i.e., a set of partial sequences of messages.[5]

LIBAFLSTAR first sends a prefix to reach a target state, then appends a mutated message — derived from the sample traces — deemed interesting for that state. For our experiments, we obtain the sample traces by sniffing network traffic (like AFLNET and CHATAFL do) and the prefixes using a black-box state learning technique [28], since the official FTP specification does not provide an exhaustive state model description. More in detail, we leverage the learning techniques to infer the state model of the SUT and then determine prefixes for reaching each state.

The overview of the framework (presented in Fig. 1) consists of the following steps:

I. State and Message Selection. The state scheduler chooses a state to fuzz (*prefix selection* in Fig. 1), and a message scheduler selects the message to mutate from the *local queue* of the selected state (*local message selection* in Fig. 1). In fact, unlike other approaches that keep only one global queue of interesting messages [20,31], LIBAFLSTAR stores a queue of relevant messages for *each* state. This allows the fuzzer to select messages that are interesting for specific states, as detailed in Sect. 4.2.

II. Local Queue and Bitmap Updates. While fuzzing the chosen state, the code coverage is collected in the local bitmap, and inputs deemed interesting are inserted in the local message queue, as explained in Sect. 4.3.

III. Coverage Analysis. LIBAFLSTAR observes the coverage and decides whether to (a) continue fuzzing the same state (green line in Fig. 1) or (b) select a new state (red line in Fig. 1), as detailed in Sect. 4.4.

In the next sections, we expand on each of these phases with a running example that simulates the steps that LIBAFLSTAR performs to fuzz LightFTP, an FTP server commonly used to benchmark stateful fuzzers. In Sect. 5, we describe the implementation details of our prototype.

4.1 Preprocessing

Our approach, as any other mutation-based fuzzer (including AFLNET and CHATAFL), needs seed traces to bootstrap the fuzzing campaign. We collect these traces beforehand by sniffing the communication between the server and a client during legitimate protocol usage. As shown in prior work, the quality of the sniffed traffic strongly influences the generation of the seed traces and, therefore, the fuzzing performance [29]. We limit the risk of collecting incomplete or inaccurate network traffic by monitoring the network traffic between a client (executed by three different analysts) and the server for one hour in total. LIBAFLSTAR also needs the *prefixes* to be able to explore the state model. For

---

[5] Every prefix unambiguously identifies a certain state since stateful systems are usually deterministic.

instance, when fuzzing LightFTP (state model in Fig. 2), the prefixes required to reach all the states are:

- P_1: *USER ubuntu* (to reach the state S_1 – allowing the user to insert the password)
- P_2: *USER ubuntu, PASS ubuntu* (to reach the state S_2 – allowing the user to login)
- P_3: *USER ubuntu, PASS ubuntu, list* (to reach the state S_3 – allowing the user to show the repositories in the server)
- P_4: *USER ubuntu, PASS ubuntu, epsv* (to reach the state S_4 – allowing the user to enter in passive mode)

Retrieving the prefixes to reach each state is challenging, as the FTP specification lacks a defined state model. In addition, the actual implementation might adopt a slightly different version of the state model presented in the specification.

For our experiments, we infer the state model of live555 and Lighttpd from the specification and the state models of the different FTP implementations using the active learner tool LearnLib [33]. Other active learner tools are available and actively maintained[6] Interestingly, the four FTP implementations implement slightly different state models.

Active learning tools [33] use an *initial alphabet* to *actively* query the SUT with all the possible combinations of the *commands* in the initial alphabet. They observe (in a black-box fashion) requests and responses and infer the state model by improving their knowledge of the state model via counterexamples. Every time the tool finds an example that does not fit its assumption, it improves its knowledge of the state model. The approach is methodical and precise, although sometimes slow.

Since active learning tools struggle with non-deterministic behaviours, we developed an ad-hoc harness to address them. For example, by handling all the requests that triggered a timeout.

Additionally, LearnLib requires *abstraction functions* (one for requests and one for responses) to map raw messages into learner-compatible inputs. For example, the raw messages "*USER wrong_user1*" and "*USER wrong_user2*" are mapped to the same input "*USER wrong_user*" to limit the state explosion.

Writing the harness and the abstraction functions required around two hours of work.

Figure 2 shows the state model produced by LearnLib, which we use to extract the prefixes to reach every state.

It is worth it to mention that active learning provides the *best* possible list of prefixes. In fact, it provides all the prefixes to reach all the states. Simpler (and faster) approaches may involve extracting prefixes directly from network traffic or manually inferring the state model from the protocol specification. For example, the seed file used by AFLNET[7] {*USER ubuntu, PASS ubuntu,*

---

[6] https://des-lab.github.io/AALpy/
[7] https://github.com/aflnet/aflnet/blob/master/tutorials/lightftp/in-ftp/ftp_requests_full_normal.raw.

SYST, PWD, PORT 127,0,0,1,132,209, LIST, MKD test, QUIT} — obtained by sniffing the network traffic — would already cover 80% of the states. In fact, it would cover all the states but the state *S4* in Fig. 2, reachable only by sending the message *PASV* or *EPSV* from the states *S2* or *S3*.

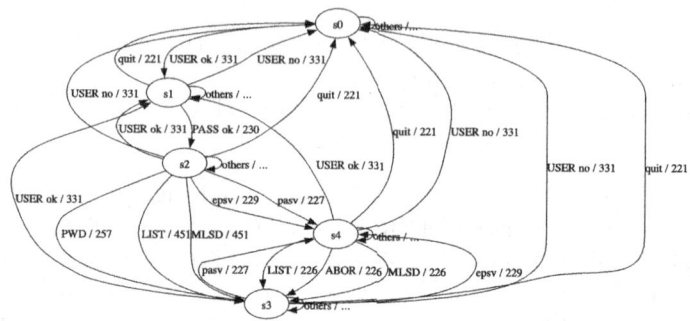

Fig. 2. LightFTP state model, inferred via LearnLib.

Using a state model in input allows LIBAFLSTAR to extract the prefixes used to effectively explore the state model of the SUT, addressing the challenge C1.

4.2 State and Message Selection

State Selection. LIBAFLSTAR selects promising states – in the sense of having a high probability of covering large portions of code – using the Outgoing Edges (OE) state scheduler. The scheduler prioritizes states with a higher number of outgoing edges. The logic behind this heuristic is that these states likely implement complex functionality, making them ideal fuzzing candidates. For the sake of comparison, we also implement a naive state scheduler, Round Robin (RR), which simply selects the target states in turn. The ability to focus on the most promising states addresses the challenge C2.

Message Selection. LIBAFLSTAR inherits LIBAFL's message selection strategy. More in detail, LIBAFLSTAR saves the messages that trigger new code coverage in the state's local queue and mutates them until no more coverage is discovered. It is worth mentioning that the queue is never empty, as the messages that do not discover new coverage are not removed from the queue but just moved to the end.

4.3 Local/Global Queues and Bitmaps

As already mentioned in Sect. 3, a message can be interesting for one state but not interesting for others. Thus, when fuzzing stateful systems, using a global queue for every state is not the best choice, as it fails to capture input-state dependencies.

For instance, while fuzzing LightFTP, sending commands that require prior authentication before the user is authenticated triggers an uninteresting error message. Similarly, when fuzzing stateful systems, the feedback information (recorded in bitmaps) should be associated with individual states rather than the system as a whole. For these reasons, LIBAFLSTAR can also work with local message queues and bitmaps for each state.

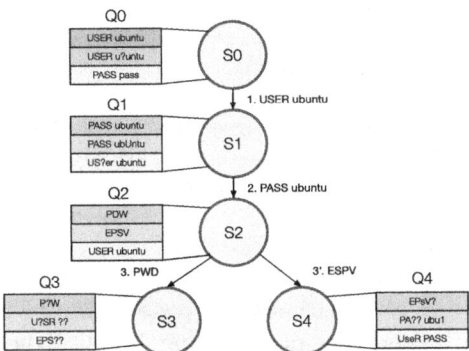

Fig. 3. LibAFLstar implements different queues for different states to be able to mutate only the messages deemed interesting for that specific state.

Figure 3 shows LIBAFLSTAR knowledge (state model and queues) while fuzzing LightFTP. In this example, the messages *PWD* and *EPSV* are interesting only when sent from state $S2$ and not from state $S0$. On the other hand, the message *USER ubuntu* is interesting in the states $S0$ and $S2$. In fact, despite messages that are interesting in one state might not be in another, a few inputs might be interesting for multiple states. Having the same message in multiple queues is not possible while sharing bitmap information, as, after the first time, interesting messages are not recognized as new. We solved this issue by allowing LIBAFLSTAR to have a bitmap for each state. This approach enables more fine-grained coverage tracking, allowing for precise queue management.

The ability of the fuzzer to keep state-related queues and bitmaps addresses challenge C3.

4.4 Coverage Analysis

After sending a message, LIBAFLSTAR can either (1) continue fuzzing without restarting the SUT (green arrow in Fig. 1) or (2) select a new state to fuzz (red arrow in Fig. 1).

We efficiently implement these two mechanisms by using the *AFL++ persistent mode*, which allows LIBAFLSTAR to send many messages to the SUT without restarting it. It is worth highlighting that the persistent mode was developed to fuzz state**less** systems exclusively — since there is no point in restarting the SUT if the behaviour does not change after restarts. On the contrary, LIBAFLSTAR uses the persistent mode to fuzz state**ful** systems efficiently.

```
1.  int state=0;
2.  //while (client\_connected()){
3.  while (AFL_LOOP<UINT_MAX}{
4.     command=receive_command();
5.     response=execute_command(command);
6.     send_response(response);
7.  }
```

Fig. 4. Modification on the SUT code to enable the persistent mode. The example presents the pseudo-code and not the actual LightFTP code. The original code is commented out, the code needed to run LIBAFLSTAR is in blue.

The persistent mode consists of a special loop that allows the fuzzer to cycle a specific portion of the code without any restart. LIBAFLSTAR leverages this mechanism to cycle the portion of code that handles the commands to send multiple messages to the same instance of the SUT. To enable the persistent mode, it is necessary to modify the code of the SUT to add this loop. For example, patching the LightFTP server requires the modification shown in Fig. 4.

Moreover, the persistent mode solves the synchronization overhead. Using the persistent mode allows our fuzzer to know when the SUT has finished its computation — thanks to a pipe message sent by the SUT to the fuzzer. This allows the fuzzer to send hundreds of messages per second, without worrying about overloading the SUT. As we discuss more extensively in Sect. 8, sending multiple messages without restarting the SUT might cause unexpected state transitions. In fact, some messages sent from a certain state might trigger a transition from the current state to a new one.

The persistent mode addresses challenge C4.

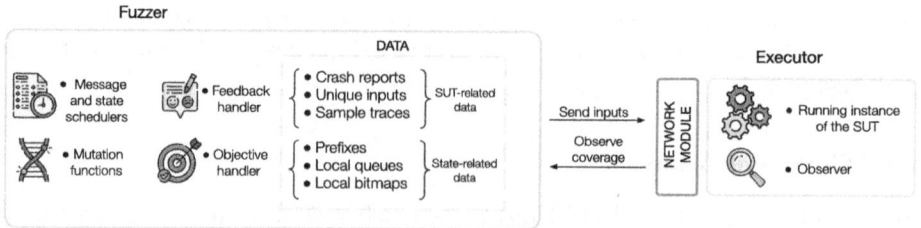

Fig. 5. LibAFLstar architecture.

5 Implementation Details

LIBAFLSTAR is written in Rust and built on top of LIBAFL. As shown in Fig. 5, it consists of three components:

1. the *Fuzzer*: it is the core of LIBAFLSTAR as it incorporates LIBAFLSTAR logic. It contains the standard LIBAFL scheduler algorithms for the messages and the new scheduler algorithms for the states (Round Robin and Outgoing Edges), introduced in Sect. 4.2. Additionally, it supports standard AFL++ mutation functions, such as havoc mutations. Moreover, it implements the standard *feedback handler*, i.e., a function that determines when an input is interesting and the standard *objective handler*, i.e., a function that determines if an input achieved the pre-determined goal — in our case, the crash of the system. All the non-volatile data used during the fuzzing campaign are stored in the Fuzzer. It stores data about crashes found, input that triggered the crashes, and the sample traces. Moreover, it stores all the data that are state-related, i.e., prefixes, local queues and local bitmaps;
2. the *Executor*: it manages everything regarding the SUT execution. More in detail, it handles the SUT initialization and restart, and contains the *Observer*, which monitors the SUT execution by tracking the code coverage and system behaviour.
3. the *Network Module*: it allows LIBAFLSTAR to communicate over network sockets. This module allows LIBAFLSTAR to operate in both client and server modes, enabling it to fuzz either side as needed.

The main modification we made in LIBAFL was to add a loop to the actual LIBAFL one. This loop enables LIBAFLSTAR to select a state via the state schedulers, reset the SUT to its initial state, and send the prefix to reach the target state. Once the prefix (and thus the state) is selected, LIBAFLSTAR fetches a message from the local queue of the selected state, mutates and forwards it to the SUT, and observes the coverage.

6 Experimental Results

We evaluated our approach on six real-world protocol implementations, namely LightFTP, BFTPD, ProFTPD, Pure-FTPd, Lighttpd, and live555. Our experiments are divided into two parts: an ablation study to assess the impact of different configuration settings (Sect. 6.1) and a comparative evaluation against other state-of-the-art stateful fuzzers (Sect. 6.2). We ran our experiments on a VPS equipped with an Intel Xeon (Ice Lake) processor (16 cores at 2.6 GHz) and 64 GB of DDR4 RAM.

6.1 Ablation Study

To investigate how different configurations affect performance and effectiveness, we conducted 24 experiments for each case study, with each run lasting one hour. To remove any randomness involved, we re-ran all the experiments three times and observed the average. LIBAFLSTAR can be configured with:

Table 1. Ablation study for one hour. SS = State Scheduler; LL = loop length (* with 1 meaning no persistent mode enabled) B = Bitmap; Q = Queue; EC = Edge Coverage (in %); E = Number of executions (in thousands); G = Global; L = Local.

	SS	LL	B	Q	BFTPD		LightFTP		lighttpd		live555		ProFTPD		PureFTPD	
					EC	E	EC	E	EC	E	EC	E	EC	E	EC	E
Round robin		1*	G	G	13.64	47	28.79	132	3.86	239	4.61	201	9.46	39	7.44	4.92
		10	G	G	16.62	66	32.81	459	4.62	1k	4.72	316	10.66	75	**8.29**	2.58
		100	G	G	17.19	365	34.38	2k	5.37	4k	4.85	329	11.65	465	7.47	2.28
		1000	G	G	–	–	34.38	4k	5.12	9k	4.61	303	12.01	3k	7.47	2.28
		1*	G	L	13.92	46	28.35	155	3.85	234	4.53	237	–	–	7.44	4.92
		10	G	L	16.62	84	32.59	557	4.64	1k	4.87	361	–	–	7.47	2.58
		100	G	L	17.19	316	34.38	3k	4.67	4k	4.79	572	–	–	7.54	2.28
		1000	G	L	18.47	2k	34.38	5k	4.87	10k	4.70	390	–	–	7.47	2.24
		1*	L	L	14.06	47	28.91	155	4.26	234	4.41	221	9.73	40	7.44	4.92
		10	L	L	16.12	71	33.04	554	4.69	1k	4.71	437	10.93	77	7.57	2.57
		100	L	L	16.69	429	34.38	2k	5.39	4k	4.85	538	11.44	455	7.57	2.30
		1000	L	L	**21.16**	3k	34.38	5k	5.18	9k	4.71	498	12.12	3k	7.64	2.24
Outgoing edges		1*	G	G	13.64	46	28.91	143	4.00	240	4.41	207	10.39	40	7.54	**5.20**
		10	G	G	16.69	71	33.26	466	4.51	1k	4.70	290	10.64	77	7.47	2.59
		100	G	G	16.83	379	34.49	2k	5.49	4k	4.81	417	11.62	427	7.57	2.30
		1000	G	G	18.96	2k	34.49	5k	5.09	8k	4.87	435	12.07	3k	7.47	2.26
		1*	G	L	14.20	46	30.13	169	4.06	235	4.41	237	9.22	1	7.44	5.11
		10	G	L	16.48	71	32.70	565	4.48	1k	4.85	413	9.26	1	7.57	2.59
		100	G	L	16.76	286	34.49	3k	4.71	4k	4.82	591	–	–	7.47	2.30
		1000	G	L	17.97	2k	34.38	5k	5.01	9k	4.84	384	–	–	7.87	2.22
		1*	L	L	14.06	46	29.69	169	4.24	236	4.48	229	10.27	41	7.44	5.21
		10	L	L	16.69	71	33.04	560	4.71	1k	4.77	435	10.90	77	7.57	2.56
		100	L	L	16.83	379	34.38	3k	5.45	4k	4.83	489	11.45	444	**7.87**	2.32
		1000	L	L	18.96	2k	**34.38**	4k	**5.60**	9k	**4.87**	464	**12.17**	3k	7.57	2.26

1. A state scheduling algorithm: round-robin (RR) or outgoing-edge-based (OE);
2. Either global or local queues and bitmaps;
3. A persistent loop of configurable length, where a length of 1 disables persistent mode.

The corresponding results are shown in Table 1.

State Schedulers Evaluation. As mentioned in Sect. 4.2, LIBAFLSTAR implements two state scheduler algorithms: RR and OE. Although the experiments do not show much difference between the two approaches, this may be due to the low complexity of the state model implemented by the protocols. Nevertheless, a closer look at the code coverage suggests *OE* to perform slightly better.

Global and Local Queues Evaluation. As mentioned in Sect. 3, local queues give more information about the quality of the messages for a certain state. The experiments show that local queues and local bitmaps, on average, give the best results in terms of coverage.

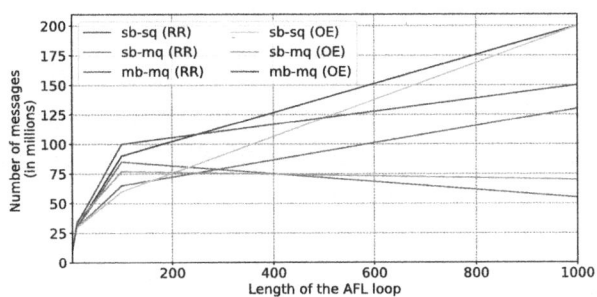

Fig. 6. Relation between the length of the AFL loop and the number of messages sent.

Persistent Loop Length Evaluation. As mentioned in Sect. 4.4, the length of the persistent loop tells the fuzzer how many messages to send before restarting the SUT. As shown in Fig. 6, longer persistent loops result in a higher number of messages sent. The results show that the length of the persistent loop is proportional to the number of executions, as bigger loops imply less time wasted in restarting the SUT. In fact, as explained in [2], resets are one of the biggest overheads when fuzzing stateful systems. Further experiments were conducted to determine whether bigger loops would have improved the quality of the fuzzing campaign. However, we did not notice any improvement for a length bigger than 1000.

Network Overhead Evaluation. Network protocols can add significant overhead due to network system calls [2]. We analyzed the network overhead by monitoring the user and system CPU usage during the fuzzing campaign and noted that the system calls overhead is about 50%, as shown in Fig. 7. We decided to fuzz the SUTs without replacing the network calls to be fair to AFLNET and CHATAFL.

6.2 Comparison with AFLNET and CHATAFL

For the benchmark, we compare LIBAFLSTAR (using local bitmaps and queues, the persistent loop length of 1000 and the outgoing edge state scheduler

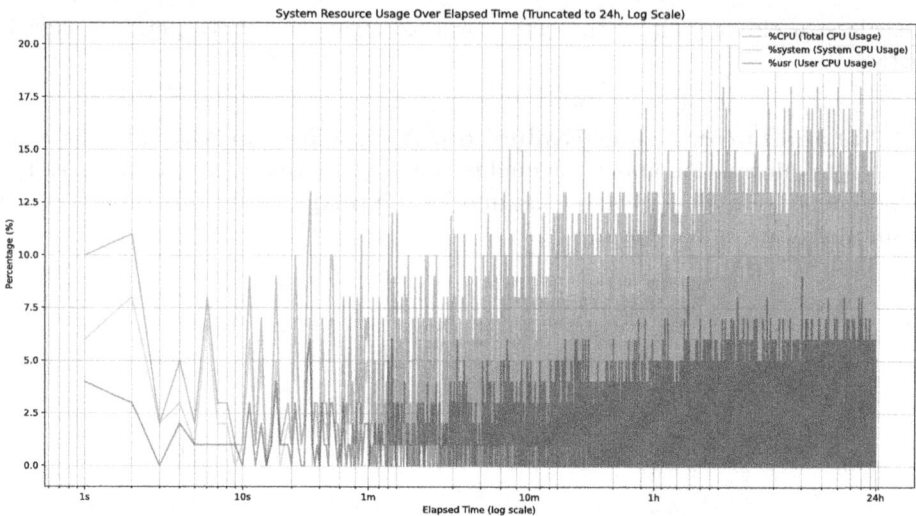

Fig. 7. CPU usage of LIBAFL* testing LightFTP.

algorithm) with two state-of-the-art stateful fuzzers, against AFLNET and CHATAFL. Due to fuzzing nondeterminism, this comparison was averaged across three runs of 24 hours. We selected AFLNET [27] since it is one of the most popular mutation-based open-source protocol fuzzers and CHATAFL [25] as it is one of the most recent stateful fuzzers published in a top conference. In the future, we plan to extend our benchmarking to SGPFuzzer [35] and Stateful Greybox Fuzzing [4].

Number of Messages per Second. Table 2 shows how LIBAFLSTAR sends many more messages than AFLNET and CHATAFL. This is due to the fact that LIBAFLSTAR drastically reduces the number of resets thanks to the persistent loop. Also, we attribute the huge improvement in terms of the number of messages to the very low impact on the performance of the synchronization between the fuzzer and the client (as explained in Sect. 4.4). While LIBAFLSTAR uses the persistent mode mechanism to synchronize the SUT and the fuzzer, the other fuzzers wait for the responses to be received. It is worth highlighting that AFLNET and CHATAFL record the number of traces, not the single messages sent. A fair comparison with LIBAFL* requires multiplying the *number of traces* and *number of traces per second* by the length of the trace — typically five or six messages. However, this adjustment does not take away the fact that LIBAFLSTAR is an order of magnitude faster than its competitors.

Total Coverage. LIBAFLSTAR achieves higher coverage on all the case studies, except ProFTPD (−1%). In all the other case studies, LIBAFLSTAR shows a significant improvement in terms of code coverage. More in detail, LIBAFLSTAR

Table 2. Results of 24 hours of fuzzing. We highlighted in bold the best results. Na means we used the specification to infer the state model of the SUT.

Subject	AFLNet			ChatAFL			LibAFLstar					
	code coverage (%)	No. Traces (k)	No. Traces/sec.	code coverage (%)	No. Traces (k)	No. Traces/sec.	code coverage (%)	No. Messages (kk)	No. Mess./sec.(~)	Setup persistent mode	Setup LearnLib (minutes)	LearnLib learning time (minutes)
LightFTP	32.4	305	3.5	34.7	250	2.8	**38.1**	67	775	1h	30	30
BFTPD	17.5	233	2.7	20.4	239	2.7	**25.4**	56	648	1h	30	30
ProFTPD	15.3	162	3.4	**17.4**	164	1.8	17.2	44	509	1h	30	45
PureFTPd	4.8	297	3.4	4.7	138	1.6	**14.1**	85	983	1h	30	30
Lighttpd	5.4	209	2.4	5.3	241	2.8	**5.9**	22	254	30m	Na	Na
live555	5.1	839	10.14	5.2	667	8.6	**5.8**	7	103	2h	Na	Na

achieves, on average, 48.6% more coverage than AFLNet and 42.7% more coverage than ChatAFL.

7 Related Work

State Awareness. A few papers have already explored the correlation between fuzzing and state learning. For example, De Ruiter et al. [11] used LearnLib to find logical bugs in TLS implementations; Bastani et al, [5] devised their active learner to synthesize a grammar to give to the fuzzer; Van-Thuan et al. [27], Yingchao Yu et al.[35] and Doupé et al.[12] developed algorithms to infer the state model of the SUT run-time by observing the responses of the (web) servers. Nevertheless, despite all the approaches dealing with the statefulness of the systems and partially solving Challenge C1 (Sect. 3), they do not implement schedulers to prioritize the most interesting states. Moreover, all stateful fuzzers (except those using snapshotting) rely on expensive resets to send fresh traces (challenge C2) and use timeouts to synchronize the server and client (challenge C3), which leads to poor performance.

State Schedulers. Fuzzers like AFLNet prioritize states based on the number of newly discovered edges; however, to the best of our knowledge, no stateful fuzzer employs an Outgoing Edges (OE) heuristic to prioritize interesting states. Nevertheless, the approach is related to PageRank [6], the search algorithm Google uses to measure the importance of web pages. PageRank scores the web pages according to the number of external websites that point to that page (ingoing edges). The heuristic is that *good* websites are likely to be linked more often from external websites. A similar heuristic applies to our OE algorithm: "states with many outgoing edges likely implement many features and therefore contain a lot of lines of code. This makes these states honeypots for fuzzers."

Persistent Mode for Stateful Fuzzing. LIBAFLSTAR is the first fuzzer that leverages the persistent mode to mitigate the overhead of shutting down and restarting the SUT.

Snapshotting is another technique that tries to solve the same challenge differently. Some stateful fuzzers [18,20,31] copy the memory of the SUT in a certain state to be able to go back to the same state later. This allows the fuzzer to reach one specific state more quickly in the future — via the snapshot previously created — and fuzz it. In the same way, the persistent mode allows the fuzzer to reach one specific state — just by sending the correct prefix — and fuzz it. Unfortunately, snapshotting often introduces considerable overhead that often makes sending the whole trace again less expensive.

8 Limitations and Future Work

LIBAFLSTAR requires the source code to be patched to enable the persistent mode. We noticed that the majority of the stateful protocols contain a single send-receive loop that processes the commands. In this scenario, the main loop is easy to spot and patch to enable the persistent mode. Moreover, the patch usually involves a few lines of code: 7 changes in the best scenario (ProFTPD) and 35 changes in the worst one (live555). However, in other cases, identifying such a loop can be more challenging and might require a deeper knowledge of the protocol logic. For example, OpenVPN [14], a widely used VPN implementation, is event-driven. This makes identifying the command loop much more challenging. Also, when triggering a new code coverage in a certain state (that we reached thanks to a specific prefix), we do not know whether the new coverage is triggered in that particular state. In fact, *unexpected* state transitions might have occurred before, as mentioned in Sect. 4.4. The persistent mode can also limit the reproducibility of detected bugs. To solve this problem, we save all the messages sent during the persistent mode loop that triggered a bug.

Future research could explore alternative scheduling algorithms to prioritize interesting states. For example, the technique devised by Liyanage et al. [22] can be used to predict how likely a certain state would lead to new edge discovery. Eventually, we plan to extend our validation to other case studies to assess the effectiveness of our approach. One solution can be to implement LIBAFLSTAR within ProFuzzBench [26], a widely used benchmark for stateful fuzzers, to have a more systematic and wide understanding of the effectiveness of our fuzzer. As already mentioned in Sect. 6.1, network calls might slow down the fuzzer's performance. Libraries like PREENY [8], Green-Fuzz [1], or Sabre [3] might help here to reduce the network overhead and additionally enhance the fuzzer performance.

9 Conclusion

In this paper, we presented LIBAFLSTAR, a fast and state-aware protocol fuzzer designed to address the challenges of fuzzing stateful systems. LIBAFLSTAR uses the notion of prefixes to navigate the state model, implements the outgoing edge state scheduler to prioritize states that most likely cover big portions of code, implements different queues and bitmaps for different states, and uses the persistent mode (i.e., the ability to keep the SUT running between traces) to reduce the number of restarts of the SUT. The ablation study confirms that all the above-mentioned strategies enhance the fuzzer performance. In fact, LIBAFLSTAR has the best results by using the outgoing edge scheduler algorithm, local queues, local bitmaps and the persistent mode. Also, the ablation study shows that the biggest improvement is given by the use of the persistent mode and that longer persistent loops positively affect the fuzzer speed.

We evaluated LIBAFLSTAR on six protocol implementations (LightFTP, BFTPD, ProFTPD, Pure-FTPd, Lighttpd and live555) and compared the results with AFLNET and CHATAFL. The results show that LIBAFLSTAR is over 30× faster than its competitors while achieving, on average, 1.4× more coverage.

Acknowledgments. We would like to thank our reviewers for their valuable inputs. We would also like to express our gratitude to the GARR Consortium for providing us with the cloud infrastructure necessary for the execution of the large-scale experiments. In addition, gratitude is extended to Leonardo Cantarella for his contribution to the setup of the Lighttpd case study. This work has been supported by the INTERSECT project (NWA.1160.18.301), funded by the Dutch Research Council (NWO), by the P6 project (Open Technology Programme No. 20475) funded by the Dutch Research Council (NWO), and by the Dutch Ministry of Economic Affairs and Climate Policy (EZK) through the AVR project "FirmPatch".

Data Availability. In the spirit of open science, we release the code for this project: https://github.com/LibAFLstar/LibAFLstar.

References

1. Andarzian, S.B., Daniele, C., Poll, E.: Green-fuzz: efficient fuzzing for network protocol implementations. In: International Symposium on Foundations and Practice of Security, Springer, pp. 253–268 (2023)
2. Andarzian, S.B., Daniele, C., Poll, E.: On the (in) efficiency of fuzzing network protocols

---

[8] https://github.com/zardus/preeny.

3. Arras, P.-A., et al.: SaBRe: load-time selective binary rewriting. Int. J. Softw. Tools Technol. Transfer **24**(2), 205–223 (2022)
4. Ba, J., Böhme, M., Mirzamomen, Z., Roychoudhury, A.: Stateful greybox fuzzing. In: 31st USENIX Security Symposium (USENIX Security 22) (2022)
5. Bastani, O., Sharma, R., Aiken, A., Liang, P.: Synthesizing program input grammars. In: ACM SIGPLAN Notices (2017)
6. Bianchini, M., Gori, M., Scarselli, F.: Inside pagerank. ACM Transactions on Internet Technology (TOIT) (2005)
7. Böhme, M., Cadar, C., Roychoudhury, A.: Fuzzing: Challenges and reflections. IEEE Software (2020)
8. Chen, J., et al.: Discovering memory corruptions in IoT through app-based fuzzing. In: NDSS, Iotfuzzer (2018)
9. Chen, Y., Lan, T., Venkataramani, G.: Exploring effective fuzzing strategies to analyze communication protocols. In: ACM Workshop on Forming an Ecosystem Around Software Transformation (2019)
10. Daniele, C., Andarzian, S.B., Poll, E.: Fuzzers for stateful systems: survey and research directions. ACM Computing Surveys (2024)
11. De Ruiter, J., Poll, E.: Protocol state fuzzing of TLS implementations. In: 24th USENIX Security Symposium (2015)
12. Doupé, A., Cavedon, L., Kruegel, C., Vigna, G.: Enemy of the state: a state-aware black-box web vulnerability scanner. In: 21st USENIX Security Symposium (2012)
13. Eisele, M., Maugeri, M., Shriwas, R., Huth, C., Bella, G.: Embedded fuzzing: a review of challenges, tools, and solutions. Cybersecurity (2022)
14. Feilner, M.: OpenVPN: Building and integrating virtual private networks. Packt Publishing Ltd (2006)
15. Feng, X., et al.: Snipuzz: black-box fuzzing of IoT firmware via message snippet inference. In: ACM SIGSAC Conference on Computer and Communications Security (2021)
16. Fioraldi, A., Maier, D., Eißfeldt, H., Heuse, M.: AFL++: combining incremental steps of fuzzing research. In: 14th USENIX Workshop on Offensive Technologies (WOOT 20) (2020)
17. Fioraldi, A., Maier, D.C., Zhang, D., Balzarotti, D.: LibAFL: a framework to build modular and reusable fuzzers. In: ACM SIGSAC Conference on Computer and Communications Security (2022)
18. Geretto, E., Giuffrida, C., Bos, H., Van Der Kouwe, E.: Snappy: efficient fuzzing with adaptive and mutable snapshots. In: Computer Security Applications Conference (2022)
19. Kim, K., Jeong, D.R., Kim, C.H., Jang, Y., Shin, I., Lee, B.: Hybrid fuzzing on the linux kernel. In NDSS, HFL (2020)
20. Li, J., Li, S., Sun, G., Chen, T., Yu, H.: SNPSFuzzer: a fast greybox fuzzer for stateful network protocols using snapshots. IEEE Transactions on Information Forensics and Security (2022)
21. Li, J., Zhao, B., Zhang, C.: Fuzzing: a survey. Cybersecurity **1**(1), 1–13 (2018). https://doi.org/10.1186/s42400-018-0002-y
22. Liyanage, D., Lee, S., Tantithamthavorn, C., Böhme, M.: Extrapolating coverage rate in greybox fuzzing. In: IEEE/ACM International Conference on Software Engineering (2024)
23. Manès, V.J., et al.: The art, science, and engineering of fuzzing: a survey. IEEE Transactions on Software Engineering (2019)

24. Mathis, B., Gopinath, R., Mera, M., Kampmann, A., Höschele, M., Zeller, A.: Parser-directed fuzzing. In: ACM SIGPLAN Conference on Programming Language Design and Implementation (2019)
25. Meng, R., Mirchev, M., Böhme, M., Roychoudhury, A.: Large language model guided protocol fuzzing. In: Proceedings of the 31st Annual Network and Distributed System Security Symposium (NDSS) (2024)
26. Natella, R., Pham, V.-T.: ProFuzzBench: a benchmark for stateful protocol fuzzing. In: ACM SIGSOFT International Symposium on Software Testing and Analysis (2021)
27. Pham, V.-T., Böhme, M., Roychoudhury, A.: AFLNET: a greybox fuzzer for network protocols. In: International Conference on Software Testing, Validation and Verification (ICST). IEEE (2020)
28. Raffelt, H., Steffen, B., Berg, T.: LearnLib: a library for automata learning and experimentation. In: Proceedings of the 10th International Workshop on Formal Methods for Industrial Critical Systems (2005)
29. Rebert, A., et al.: Optimizing seed selection for fuzzing. In: 23rd USENIX Security Symposium (2014)
30. Schumilo, S., Aschermann, C., Gawlik, R., Schinzel, S., Holz, T.: kAFL: hardware-assisted feedback fuzzing for OS kernels. In: 26th USENIX Security Symposium (2017)
31. Schumilo, S., Aschermann, C., Jemmett, A., Abbasi, A., Holz, T.: Nyx-Net: network fuzzing with incremental snapshots. In: European Conference on Computer Systems (2022)
32. Serebryany, K.: OSS-Fuzz: Google's continuous fuzzing service for open source software
33. Settles, B.: Active learning literature survey
34. Srivastava, P., Payer, M.: Gramatron: effective grammar-aware fuzzing. In: ACM SIGSOFT International Symposium on Software Testing and Analysis (2021)
35. Yu, Y., Chen, Z., Gan, S., Wang, X.: SGPFuzzer: a state-driven smart graybox protocol fuzzer for network protocol implementations. IEEE Access (2020)
36. Zalewski, M.: American Fuzzy Lop - Whitepaper. https://lcamtuf.coredump.cx/afl/technical_details.txt (2016)
37. Zhang, Z., Zhang, H., Zhao, J., Yin, Y.: A survey on the development of network protocol fuzzing techniques. Electronics (2023)
38. Zhu, X., Wen, S., Camtepe, S., Xiang, Y.: Fuzzing: a survey for roadmap. ACM Computing Surveys (CSUR) (2022)

PUSH for Security: A PUF-Based Protocol to Prevent Session Hijacking

Emiliia Geloczi[✉][ID], Nico Mexis[ID], and Stefan Katzenbeisser[ID]

Chair of Computer Engineering, University of Passau, Innstr. 41, Passau, Germany
{emiliia.geloczi,nico.mexis,stefan.katzenbeisser}@uni-passau.de

Abstract. Session hijacking attacks still affect thousands of users of web services every year. In this paper, we propose a novel lightweight hardware-binding protocol that associates a web session with a device using a unique fingerprint derived from an SRAM-based Physical Unclonable Function (PUF). The hardware/software co-design of the proposed protocol ensures continuous verification of the session's legitimacy without introducing additional latency. Furthermore, it enables the timely termination of a hijacked session, thereby mitigating the impact of session hijacking attacks.

Keywords: Session Hijacking · PUF · SRAM PUF · Hardware Binding

1 Introduction

According to Statista.com, approximately 67% of the global population use web services for different purposes [40] and have user accounts that store their sensitive data, such as bank card details. Despite many technical measures for account security [39], users still routinely become victims of attacks that lead to account loss and data compromise [19,23,41]. Moreover, they often unintentionally assist adversaries by opening seemingly legitimate but malicious files or links, thereby infecting their devices with malware. Such malware is often designed to obtain session identifiers (IDs) stored in session cookies. Using these session IDs, adversaries can access accounts that are active during the session without further authentication. This process is called a session hijacking [22].

Although it is unlikely to completely prevent session hijacking attacks, their impact can be mitigated, for example, by encrypting cookies [31]. Recent proposals introduce solutions based on the use of temporary cookies [13], sessions [35], or tokens [37], which require re-authentication and increase the load on the server. Some approaches bind the session to a virtual or physical asset, such as a browser [15] or a device [33], hence requiring adversaries not only to possess an active session ID but also to gain control over the associated asset. However, approaches that bind sessions to devices typically require additional hardware, such as a Trusted Platform Module (TPM) [33], which may introduce performance overhead, restrict the range of compatible devices, and enable vendor-imposed limitations, therefore transferring control over the device away from the user. In addition, all existing approaches rely on the persistent storage of cryptographic keys, introducing further security risks.

Contribution. In this paper, we propose a novel lightweight protocol that associates a web session with a physical device by utilising an SRAM Physical Unclonable Function (PUF). It serves as a natural fingerprint of a device, can be derived from existing hardware components, exhibits properties of uniqueness and unclonability, and eliminates the need to store cryptographic keys [20]. Our protocol, called **PUSH** (**PU**F against **S**ession **H**ijacking), mitigates session hijacking attacks by preventing an adversary from using a session ID without having access to the associated device. PUSH can be seamlessly integrated into existing client/server architectures, provides continuous verification of the session's legitimacy without introducing additional latency, and enables the timely termination of hijacked sessions. Furthermore, to the best of our knowledge, PUSH is the first PUF-based protocol to address the problem of session hijacking in web communication.

Paper Organisation. Section 2 provides the background information on PUFs. Section 3 describes the proposed PUSH protocol, its proof-of-concept implementation, and the potential challenges. The security analysis of PUSH is presented in Sect. 4. Section 5 provides an overview of related work, followed by their comparison with PUSH in Sect. 6. Finally, Sect. 7 concludes the paper and outlines directions for future research.

2 Background: Physical Unclonable Functions

During the manufacturing process of electronic devices, small differences in the characteristics of their components (e.g., transistors) may occur. As a result, even devices from the same product line may have slight variations in their physical characteristics [27]. While these differences are not significant in terms of functionality, they can form the basis of a unique device fingerprint, also known as a Physical Unclonable Function (PUF). As a function embedded in a physical object, PUF produces a response y upon receiving a challenge x [20]. The pair (x, y) is called the challenge-response pair (CRP). To serve as the fingerprint, PUF should be robust, unclonable, unpredictable and tamper-proof [26].

In our protocol, a start-up Static Random Access Memory (SRAM) PUF [16] is used, which is an integral part of almost all devices, not easily accessible externally, provides high entropy [11,12] and stable [43,45]. SRAM cells are initialised with different bit values due to slight variations in transistor characteristics. This bit pattern is unique to each SRAM module and can be considered as its fingerprint, however, it must be observed during module startup. Thus, the challenge is the set of memory addresses ($C := \{a_1, a_2, \ldots, a_n\}$), and the response is the set of corresponding bit values ($R := \{b_1, b_2, \ldots, b_n\}$). Together, C and R form CRP associated with SRAM PUF. CRP can contain any required number n of address-bit value pairs (a, b) (or (c, r) pairs: $(a, b) \rightarrow (c, r)$). In the remainder of this paper, when referring to PUF initialisation, we specifically mean the identification of the corresponding CRP.

3 Description of the PUSH Protocol

PUSH is a PUF-based protocol that binds a web session to a physical device (dongle) and continuously verifies the session's legitimacy. In this section, we present the system model in which PUSH operates, describe its operational workflow, detail the proof-of-concept implementation, evaluate its performance, and discuss potential challenges.

3.1 System Model

We consider a setting involving the following four legitimate parties in the PUSH protocol (see Fig. 1):

- *Dongle* is a Universal Serial Bus (USB) device to which a session is bound. It contains a PUF SRAM module and a crypto module.
  - *Crypto Module* performs initialisation of PUF, generation of cryptographic keys, and digital signing.
- *User's Device* is a device used to access web services, which hosts the following components:
  - *PUFMAN* (PUF MANager) is a service that communicates with the dongle via a USB port and provides an Application Programming Interface (API) for the browser.
  - *Browser* is a software application that allows a user to send requests to web servers and receive responses.
- *Server* is a system that processes user requests and provides responses.

The dongle, the user's device, PUFMAN, and the server are assumed to be trusted; however, the browser can be exposed to potential malicious extensions during the operation.

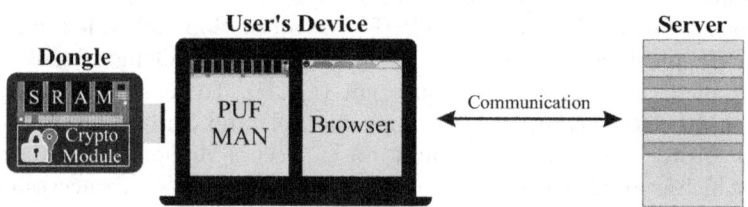

Fig. 1. PUSH Protocol Parties.

PUSH operates at the application layer and runs on top of the Hypertext Transfer Protocol Secure (HTTPS), ensuring secure communication between the browser, the server, and PUFMAN. Moreover, since PUSH is designed to integrate with existing web communication, it is assumed that session cookies are encrypted and stored securely using the default existing mechanisms, such as the Data Protection API (DPAPI) [31], which are not detailed in this paper.

In the protocol description, we use the abstract cryptographic building blocks such as $KeyGen(\cdot)$ and $Fuzzy(\cdot)$ to represent key generation and fuzzy extractor algorithms, respectively.

3.2 Operation Workflow

PUSH consists of three phases. The first phase (I) is dedicated to the initialisation of PUF on the dongle. During the second phase (II), the browser initiates its first communication with the server, performing enrolment. During the third phase (III), communication between the browser and the server takes place. The generalised workflow of the PUSH operation is illustrated in Fig. 2, and each phase is described in detail in the following sections.

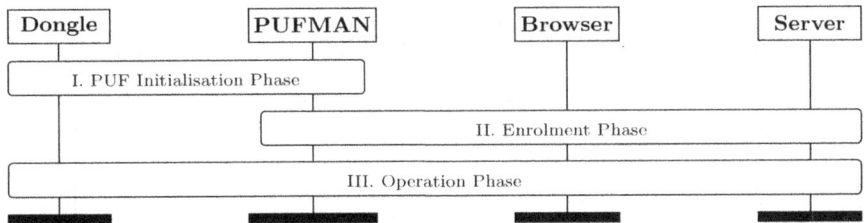

Fig. 2. Operation workflow of the PUSH protocol.

In hardware binding, it is critical that protocol parties can verify the existence of a dongle and confirm that it is not being simulated at the very first contact. For this purpose, our protocol includes a manufacturer-issued cryptographic key pair: a secret key SK_D, embedded in the dongle, and a corresponding public key PK_D, provided to the user. This key pair is used exclusively during the enrolment phase (II) to confirm the dongle's authenticity.

I. PUF Initialisation Phase. In this phase, a unique fingerprint of the dongle is identified and used to generate a pair of cryptographic keys: a secret key SK and a public key PK. This process is performed only once, unless the user explicitly requests re-initialisation. During this phase, PUSH operates according to the following algorithm (see Fig. 3):

First, PUFMAN sends a request to the Dongle to start the PUF initialisation phase (1). Inside the Dongle, the Crypto Module triggers the power-cycling of the SRAM module (2,3) and subsequently reads its content, obtaining a set of n memory values $MV_r := \{b_i \mid i = 0, \ldots, n\}$, where r is the reading iteration number, and b_i is a bit value in the memory cell at address i (4). Steps 2–4 are repeated k times to collect data for an analysis. Next, the Crypto Module computes the average Hamming Distance and Hamming Weight for each memory cell to identify a set of memory addresses (challenge) $C := \{c_i\}$ and their corresponding bit values (response) $R := \{r_i\}$, where $i = 0, \ldots, m$, forming $CRP := (C, R)$, which serves as a unique fingerprint of the Dongle (5). The response R is then processed using a fuzzy extractor $Fuzzy()$, and the result is used as a seed for a key generation function $KeyGen()$, producing a key pair (SK, PK) (6). Finally, the Crypto Module signs both C and PK using the manufacturer-issued secret key SK_D (7), and sends the challenge C, the public key PK, and their corresponding digital signatures $((C)_{SK_D}, (PK)_{SK_D})$ to PUFMAN (8).

After this phase is completed, the SRAM module is powered off, and the keys SK and PK are deleted. PUFMAN keeps C, PK, $(C)_{SK_D}$, and $(PK)_{SK_D}$.

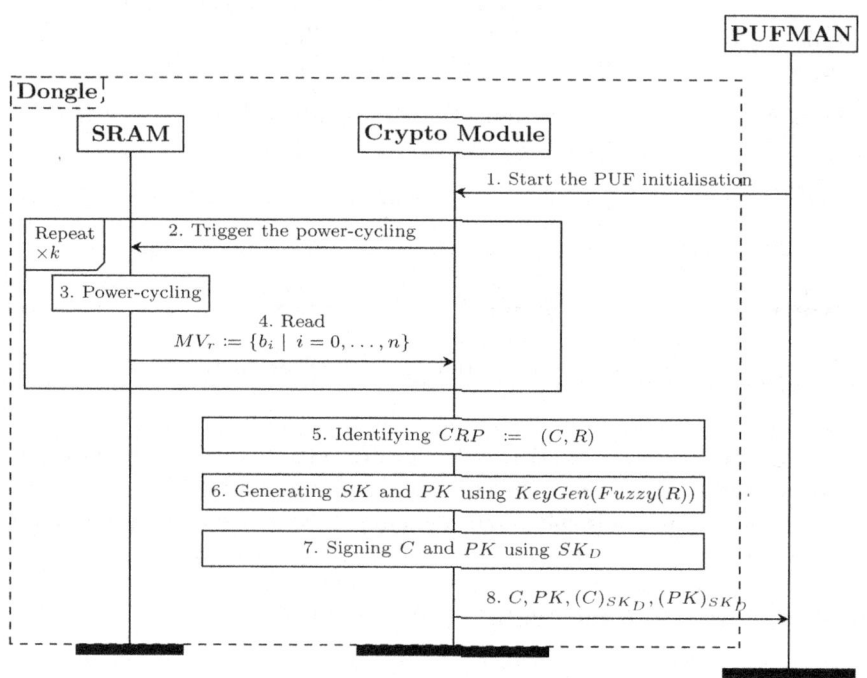

Fig. 3. Workflow of PUSH during the PUF Initialisation Phase (I).

II. Enrolment Phase. During this phase, the browser initiates its first connection with the server to perform enrolment. This process is executed only once unless the user explicitly requests re-enrolment. The phase follows the steps outlined in the algorithm presented in Fig. 4:

First, the User provides the Browser with the public key PK_D (1). The Browser then requests from PUFMAN the enrolment data associated with the Dongle $(C, PK, (C)_{SK_D}$ and $(PK)_{SK_D})$ (2), and receives the corresponding response (3). The Browser validates the received signatures $(C)_{SK_D}$ and $(PK)_{SK_D}$, using previously obtained from the User PK_D (4). If the validation is successful, the enrolment is continued (5); otherwise, it is terminated. Subsequently, the Server performs the enrolment procedure for the User: creates a session, assigns a *SessionID*, and stores it in the session *Cookies* (6). Finally, the Server sends *Cookies* to the Browser (7).

At the end of this phase, the User's session is established, and the Browser holds *Cookies* containing *SessionID*.

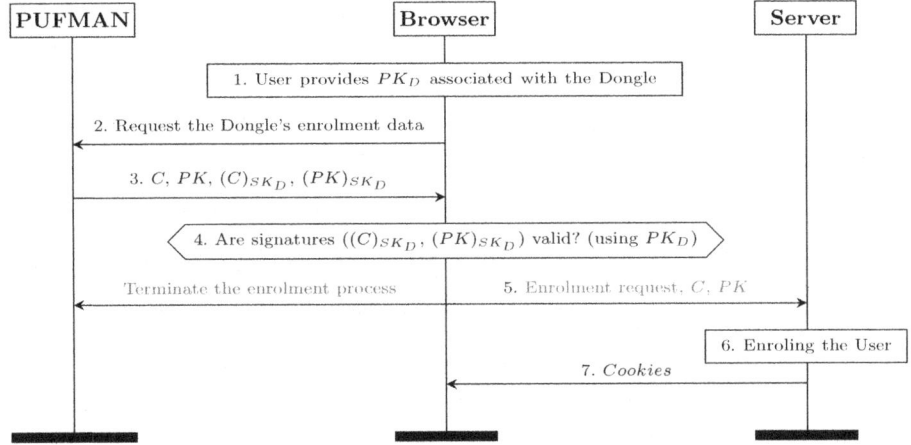

Fig. 4. Workflow of PUSH during the Enrolment Phase (II).

III. Operation Phase. After the enrolment phase is completed, PUSH proceeds to the operation phase, during which subsequent communication between the protocol parties is carried out according to the algorithm presented in Fig. 5:

The Browser requests a service from the Server and sends *Cookies* (1). The Server responds with the challenge C, a random nonce N and a request to sign C, N, and *Cookies* (2). This request is then forwarded to the Dongle via the Browser and PUFMAN (3).

Upon receiving the request, the Dongle initiates the signing process (4) (see Fig. 6): the Crypto Module triggers the power-up of the SRAM module, and reads values r_i for each address $c_i \in C$, forming the response $R := \{r_i\}$, where $i = 0, \ldots, m$ (4.1-4.2); then, it generates SK using $KeyGen(Fuzzy(R))$ (4.3) and signs N and *Cookies* with this SK (4.4).

After signing, the Dongle sends N, *Cookies*, and the signatures, $(N)_{SK}$ and $(Cookies)_{SK}$, to the Server via PUFMAN and the Browser (5). The Server then validates N and the signatures (using PK). If all items are valid, the session is continued; otherwise, it is terminated (6).

The signing procedure can be requested by the server on every interaction. However, this may introduce additional latency (see Sect. 3.5). To mitigate this, PUSH can be configured so that the server includes the signing request in one of its responses to the browser, and then receives the updated signature in one of the browser's subsequent requests. In the meantime, routine request-response operations continue uninterrupted (see Fig. 5 (- ->)).

Phases I–III describe the operation of PUSH under normal conditions. However, exceptions may arise that require special handling by the protocol. These exceptions and the corresponding PUSH behaviour are discussed in Sect. E.

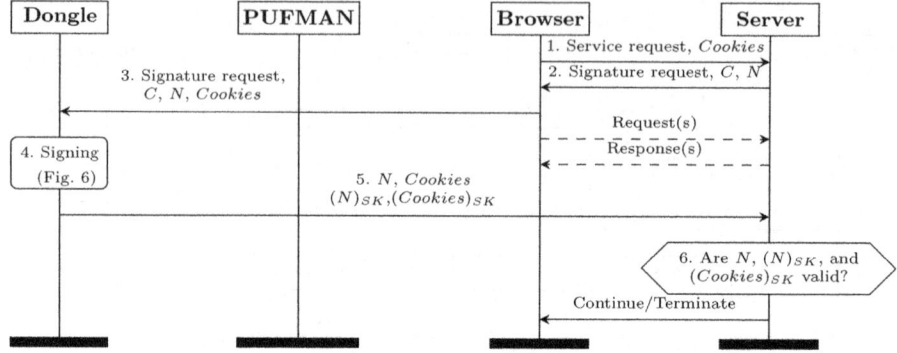

Fig. 5. Workflow of PUSH during the Operation Phase (III).

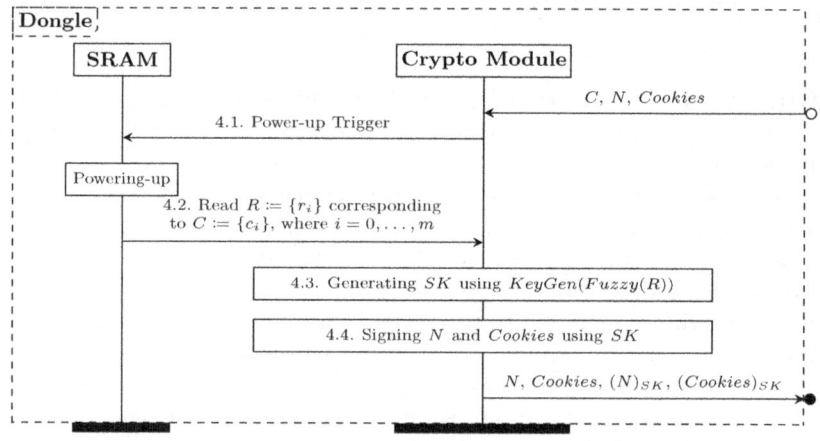

Fig. 6. Workflow of the PUSH protocol during the Signing Sub-phase.

E. Exception Cases Handling. Consider two scenarios where a user needs to replace a dongle or associate an additional dongle with the same account. In both cases, PUSH performs two steps: a common *preparation* phase, followed by either a dongle *replacement* or *association*.

Preparation: The user requests the server to generate a set of recovery keys $RKeys := (RK_1, \ldots, RK_n)$ and stores it securely. The dongle replacement or new association can only be completed if the user provides RK_i to the server, thereby preventing a potential unauthorised process initiated by an adversary. This step should be completed before the need for a replacement or new association, ideally, immediately after the initial enrolment with the server.

Dongle Replacement: The user requests PUFMAN to initiate the dongle replacement procedure. First, the PUF initialisation (I) for the new dongle is performed. Then, PUSH proceeds with the enrolment phase (II), but instead of the enrolment request (II.5), the browser sends a replacement request to the server. This request contains the user's recovery key RK_i and the new dongle's data obtained during the PUF initialisation phase. This allows the server to authenticate the user and associate the session with the new dongle.

Association of an Additional Dongle with an Existing Account: The user requests PUFMAN to associate an additional dongle with the existing account. First, the PUF initialisation (I) for the new dongle is performed, during which PUFMAN receives a challenge C_{new}, a public key PK_{new}, and their signed values $(C_{new})_{SK_{new_D}}$ and $(PK_{new})_{SK_{new_D}}$, where the secret key SK_{new_D} and the public key PK_{new_D} are issued by the manufacturer of the new dongle. Next, PUFMAN requests the old dongle to sign C_{new} and PK_{new}, receiving $(C_{new})_{SK_{old}}$ and $(PK_{new})_{SK_{old}}$. PUFMAN then passes all the data it has collected to the browser. The browser asks the user to enter PK_{new_D} and verifies items signed with SK_{new_D} to confirm the existence of the new dongle. Upon successful verification, the browser forms an additional association request to the server, including RK_i, C_{new}, PK_{new}, $(C_{new})_{SK_{old}}$ and $(PK_{new})_{SK_{old}}$, allowing the server to verify the source of the request, confirm the presence of both dongles, and associate the new dongle with the account.

3.3 Proof-of-Concept Implementation

Protocol Parties: For the implementation of the dongle, the Arduino Nano 33 BLE board [5], equipped with the external 512 Kb SRAM module [30], was selected (see Fig. 7a). The external SRAM can be power-cycled independently of the dongle, enabling PUF extraction at module startup without the need to reboot the dongle itself, simplifying implementation. PUFMAN is implemented as a service using the Microsoft ASP.NET Core Web Service Framework and provides the browser with an API to interact with the USB dongle (see Fig. 7b). To simulate web communication, we developed a demo browser (see Fig. 7c) and a demo server (see Fig. 7d) using the Microsoft .NET WPF and Microsoft ASP.NET Core 8.0 frameworks, respectively. Communication between the dongle and PUFMAN was carried out via the USB port, while all others are done via HTTPS. Alternatively, a memory pipe [32] could have been used for data transfer between PUFMAN and the browser.

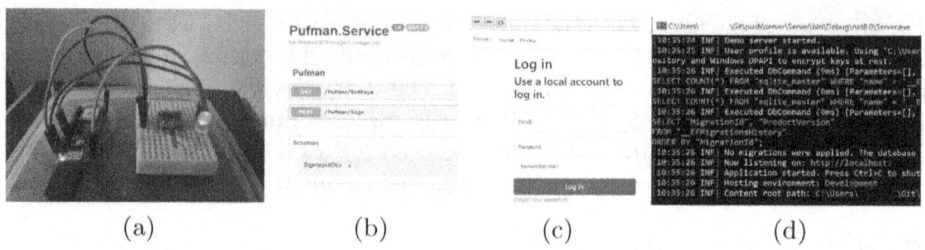

Fig. 7. PUSH prototype: (a) the dongle, (b) PUFMAN, (c) the browser, (d) the server.

PUF Handling and Key Generation: During PUF initialisation (I), the SRAM was power-cycled three times ($k = 3$) and its response sets MV_1, MV_2, MV_3 were analysed to identify CRP (16 B), consisting of values closest to the ideal in terms of both Hamming Distance ($= 0$) and Hamming Weight ($= 0.5$). Then, the response R was processed using the fuzzy extractor [29] and passed to the cryptographic algorithm for key generation. Any suitable asymmetric cryptosystem supporting key generation and digital signing can be selected. In our prototype, Curve25519 elliptic curve cryptography was used, which is well-suited to Arduino boards due to its lightweight nature. Implementation was performed using the Ed25519 class from the Arduino Cryptography Library [44].

3.4 Performance Evaluation

To evaluate the overhead introduced by PUSH, the following aspects were measured: execution time, RAM usage, required persistent storage, network payload, and power consumption (see Table 1). The protocol involves several data contributing to this overhead, including memory values MV (48 B); the challenge C and response R (16 B); cryptographic keys SK, PK, SK_D, PK_D, and signatures $(X)_Y$ (each 32 B); a nonce N (8 B). Furthermore, the following fine-consuming operations are performed: power-cycling, CRP identification, $KeyGen(Fuzzy(R))$, digital signing, and signature validation.

Table 1. Resource overhead introduced by the PUSH protocol.

Phase	Time	RAM (KB)			Storage (B)			Network			Power (mW)		
		D	UD	S	D	UD	S	D↔P	P↔Br	Br↔S	D	UD	S
I. PUF Initialisation	11 s	160	–		36	176	–	176 B	–		154	–	–
II. Enrolment	2 ms	–	2	–	–	32	48	–	176 B	48 B	154	–	–
III. Operation	419 ms	4	–	3	–	16 B	2.16 KB		176 B	154	–	–

D: Dongle; UD: User's Device (hosts Browser **Br** and PUFMAN **P**); S: Server;
↔: communication between protocol parties; –: no overhead introduced.

Based on Table 1, the PUF initialisation (I) is the most resource-intensive phase in terms of execution time and memory requirements. On average, this phase took 11 s (s), with around 9 s consumed by three power-cycling operations of the SRAM, as it is necessary to wait roughly 3 s between reboots to allow the memory to be fully reset. The remaining time was spent on CRP identification and key generation (see Fig. 8). Although 11 s is relatively long, it does not introduce communication latency, as this phase only runs once and precedes the operational phase. In terms of memory consumption, the dongle must allocate a significant amount of its RAM (160 KB out of 256 KB available in our implementation). However, the data that needs to be stored during operation is relatively small: 36 B on the dongle (SK_D and helper data for $Fuzzy(R)$), and 176 B on the user's device (C, PK, $(C)_{SK_D}$, and $(PK)_{SK_D}$).

The enrolment phase (II), by contrast, introduces minimal overhead. In terms of execution time, only 2 ms are required, which is deemed negligible. Moreover, the user's device is only required to store PK_D (32 B) for dongle verification while the server additionally stores C and PK (48 B in total). The network overhead is also minor, especially when compared to the typical volume of data transferred during web communication [42].

In the operation phase (III), the primary concern is the execution time, as the PUSH protocol potentially can introduce latency that would negate its lightweight nature. The most time-consuming operation here is the cookie signing. Our measurements showed that signing 1 KB cookies takes an average of 419 ms (see Fig. 8), which would lead to noticeable delays if performed on every request. To address this, cookie signatures are updated every 4 minutes, with a validity period of 5 minutes (see Sect. 3.5). However, in this case, a trade-off between security and latency is inevitable. More frequent signature updates increase security but also introduce higher latency, whereas less frequent updates minimise latency at the cost of reduced security.

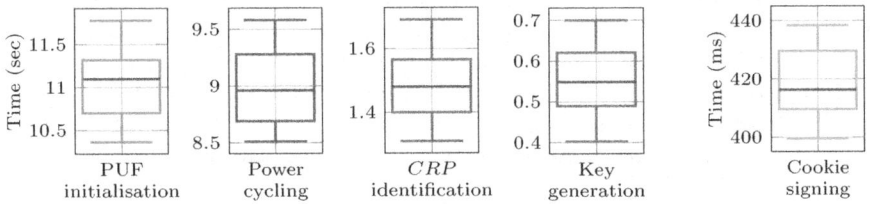

Fig. 8. Time required to complete the PUF initialisation fully, its individual steps (power cycling, CRP identification, key generation), and the signing of 1 KB cookies.

The power overhead introduced by the dongle remains constant across all phases, as the dongle (Arduino) operates in a constant power mode; this consumption is minimal and can be considered negligible. The power overhead from operations on the user's device and the server is similarly low. It was undetectable during measurements and thus considered negligible.

In summary, PUSH introduces very low overhead. Its modest memory requirements make it suitable for resource-constrained devices (e.g., Arduino).

However, using larger CRP sets, longer keys, or alternative cryptographic algorithms may require more powerful hardware. Notably, despite two relatively time-consuming phases, PUSH adds no latency during regular communication.

3.5 Challenges

The following three key areas of concern can be identified in the implementation and deployment of PUSH: latency, scalability, and applicability.

Latency: The evaluation results indicate that the operation phase may introduce latency if cookies and nonce signing are performed on every request. To address this, the following signature update strategy is used: Assume that the signature remains valid and the session is legitimate for a predefined time interval $T_{validity}$. When the signature expires, the server terminates the session. Thus, the signature must be updated before its expiration, i.e., $T_{update} < T_{validity}$. For example, one minute before expiration, the server includes a signature request in a response to a user's request. The updated signature is then sent to the server with a subsequent request. This process runs in the background, without user interaction or disruption to ongoing communication. As mentioned earlier, there is a trade-off between security and latency. If $T_{validity}$, and consequently T_{update}, are set very short, a higher security level can be achieved, but at the cost of increased delays. Conversely, longer $T_{validity}$ and T_{update} reduce latency but also decrease the security level.

Scalability: The scalability of PUSH refers to the number of concurrent sessions that can be associated with a single dongle. Assume that each session (originating from a different server) is linked to a unique and independent (i.e., non-overlapping) CRP. Consequently, the total number of such $CRPs$ is the maximum number of supported sessions. In our prototype, 976 $CRPs$ (16 B) can be derived from SRAM. Increasing CRP's length to 32 B would enhance security but reduce the number of usable $CRPs$ to 448. This limitation can be addressed by using a larger SRAM or adding an extra SRAM module, both of which would increase monetary costs; or by using an alternative PUF (e.g., arbiter PUF [17]), which may require protocol modifications.

Applicability: In this paper, we describe the session binding to a USB dongle, which ensures cross-platform compatibility and facilitates development. However, the dongle is an external device and is inherently resource-constrained due to its compact form factor. Moreover, it could potentially be stolen and used for future attacks, which may not be immediately noticed by the user. To address these limitations, we see the potential for implementing PUSH without relying on a dongle. For example, the session could be bound directly to the SRAM module of the user's device, e.g., a laptop. This approach would eliminate the need for additional hardware and reduce resource constraints while maintaining cross-platform compatibility. Nevertheless, such an implementation would likely require cooperation from device manufacturers, as SRAM is generally not externally accessible.

4 Security Analysis

To analyse the security of PUSH, we define an adversary model that operates within the system model described in Sect. 3.1. Subsequently, we discuss the protocol's resistance to potential attacks carried out by the defined adversary.

4.1 Adversary Model

The adversary $\mathcal{A}$ aims to disrupt the correct operation of PUSH by performing various attacks within their capabilities and limitations [14]. It is assumed that $\mathcal{A}$ can communicate with the PUSH parties; intercept, modify, replay, or drop protocol messages; and compromise the browser (e.g., through malicious browser extensions). However, $\mathcal{A}$ cannot physically access or tamper with the dongle or its SRAM; generate the secret key (SK) without the dongle's PUF response; forge or guess cryptographic primitives (e.g., digital signatures, nonces).

4.2 Resistance of the Protocol to Attacks

We evaluate the resistance of PUSH not only against session hijacking attacks [10,22], but also against other potential attacks that $\mathcal{A}$ may attempt to disrupt the correct operation of the protocol [21,27].

Sniffing Attack: During passive monitoring of traffic between protocol parties, $\mathcal{A}$ may obtain public data (C, PK), $Cookies$, N, and signed values (N_{SK}, $Cookies_{SK}$). Even if this data is transmitted in plain text (which is not the case, as PUSH operates on top of HTTPS) and the session ID is exposed, it would not enable successful future attacks. This is because each authentication requires a fresh server-generated nonce N and its valid signature, both of which $\mathcal{A}$ cannot forge according to the assumed adversary model.

Cross-Site Scripting (XSS) Attack: $\mathcal{A}$ injects a malicious script (typically written in JavaScript) into a trusted website. When the user visits this website, the script is triggered to send cookies that are not marked as HTTP-only to $\mathcal{A}$. However, even in this scenario, PUSH remains secure because successful session hijacking also requires a fresh, signed nonce N, which $\mathcal{A}$ cannot forge (see Sect. 4.1).

Reply Attack: PUSH is resistant to replay attacks, because even if $\mathcal{A}$ intercepts messages over time, they can only obtain PK, C, N, $Cookies$ and their signatures. However, this data is not reusable, as the nonce N is fresh, and the server detects and rejects any attempt to replay the old one.

Man-in-the-Middle (MitM) Attack: Although $\mathcal{A}$ may attempt to inject or modify C, N or signatures, as allowed by the adversary model (see Sect. 4.1), the periodic requirement for fresh digital signatures, their validation, and the use of HTTPS ensure data integrity and protect against potential MitM attacks.

Side-Channel Attack, Device Capturing or Cloning: In our analysis, we focus on an online $\mathcal{A}$, typical in web communication, who cannot physically access the dongle and thus cannot perform side-channel attacks, theft, or cloning. As a result, physical protection of the dongle is beyond the scope of this paper but can be addressed in future work through hardware-level countermeasures [28]. Nevertheless, such attacks remain relevant in broader security contexts. Although PUSH does not inherently protect against them, the absence of permanent storage of secret data in the dongle, combined with the unclonability and the unpredictability of PUFs, prevents the disclosure of confidential information, cloning, or long-term simulation. Moreover, the user would likely detect the dongle's absence before its reverse engineering is successfully completed.

Brute Force or Phishing Attack: Assume that $\mathcal{A}$ obtains a session ID, either by guessing it or by sending a seemingly trustworthy phishing email containing malicious links or malware, and the user falls for the trick. Using this session ID, $\mathcal{A}$ can hijack the session. However, PUSH introduces an additional layer of security by requiring the session cookies and a freshly generated nonce N to be periodically signed using the dongle. $\mathcal{A}$ cannot derive SK from the dongle, cannot clone PUF, and cannot forge signatures. Therefore, even if the session is hijacked, it will be terminated once the valid signature expires.

Impersonation Attack: To impersonate the user, $\mathcal{A}$ must be able to sign cookies and nonces in response to the server's requests. This would require collusion with one of the protocol parties, which is excluded under the system model. Alternatively, $\mathcal{A}$ would need to replicate the dongle's SRAM to reconstruct SK (see Sect. 4.1), which is infeasible due to the inherent properties of PUF.

Denial-of-Service (DoS) Attack: All parties in the PUSH protocol can be potential targets of DoS attacks. A direct attack on the dongle is only possible if PUFMAN is compromised, which is excluded by the system model (see Sect. 3.1). However, flooding PUFMAN with requests can indirectly block access to the dongle. The browser and the server may also be attacked by a large number of requests, consuming resources and disrupting their operation. While PUSH does not inherently protect against DoS attacks, it allows the integration of common countermeasures, e.g., rate limiting, API access controls, etc.

Browser Compromise: Since the browser may be exposed to malicious extensions (see Sect. 3.1), we evaluate the impact of its compromise. In general, compromising the browser is ineffective, as it has no access to secret data, and previously signed cookies cannot be reused due to the requirement for a fresh nonce. However, if the browser is compromised before enrolment, $\mathcal{A}$ could potentially bind the session to their dongle, thereby performing a session fixation attack. Thus, even without revealing secret information, the session could still be compromised.

For all the attacks discussed above in which $\mathcal{A}$ may obtain cookies, such as sniffing, it is accurate to state that the cookies could potentially be used until the dongle's signature expires. However, we believe this poses minimal risk and is unlikely to enable $\mathcal{A}$ to cause significant damage, as the signature validity period can be flexibly configured to limit the time during which the cookies remain usable. This period can be set quite short without introducing noticeable delays (e.g., four minutes in our implementation).

5 Related Work

In this section, we review existing works on countermeasures against session hijacking, which are considered to be most relevant to our study.

Non-PUF-Based Approaches aim to protect web communication and typically involve binding a unique user or session ID to device-specific attributes, e.g., geolocation [1] or hardware characteristics [18]. Moreover, protection is often implemented through the use of expiration limits applied to sessions [35], cryptographic keys [36], or tokens [13,37]. Some methods are also designed to provide continuous authentication [2,33], while others aim to obfuscate session IDs [34]. The disadvantages of these approaches include their often non-lightweight and complex design, which leads to delays, system overloads, and maintenance challenges; as well as reliance on additional hardware and the need to store secret keys, both of which broaden the attack surface and increase security risks.

Considering *PUF-based approaches*, it can be observed that none of them are applied to web communication. Instead, they primarily target the IoT domain, where PUFs are used to establish authentication between devices, typically serving as a source of unique identifiers [3,25], cryptographic keys [24,38], or random numbers [4,6]. Similar to non-PUF-based approaches, PUF-based ones often require additional hardware and storage of secret cryptographic primitives, increasing security risks. Additionally, some solutions rely on time synchronisation, which introduces further challenges in terms of reliability and implementation.

6 Discussion

This section presents the comparative analysis of PUSH and the approaches discussed in Sect. 5. Since existing solutions have been evaluated from different perspectives by their authors, a unified framework is adopted for the analysis. Specifically, each approach is assessed according to nine characteristics and resistance to eleven common attack types. For objectivity, the comparison relies on assumptions and measurements reported by the original authors, aligned with our threat model. The consolidated results are presented in Table 2.

Applicability in Web Communication (⊕): As mentioned in Sect. 5, the non-PUF-based approaches primarily target session hijacking in web communication, whereas PUF-based solutions focus on the IoT domain. This distinction highlights the novelty of PUSH, which is the first protocol to employ PUFs specifically for securing web sessions.

PUF type (⊛) applies exclusively to PUF-based approaches. In most works, the type is unspecified and treated generically. Only one solution relies on a

Table 2. Comparison of PUSH with the existing approaches against session hijacking.

Authors	Advantages					Limitations			Attacks										
	🌐	📡	▨	↕	🔑	📶	❓	⏱	SA	XSS	RA	MM	SC	BF	PA	IA	DoS	DCC	BC
Non-PUF-based Approaches																			
Ahmed et al. [1]	✓	–	✓	✗	✓	✗	✗	✓	○	●	●	●	●	●	●	●	○	●	○
Al-Sadi et al. [2]	✓	–	✗	✗	✓	✗	✗	✓	●	○	●	●	○	●	●	●	○	–	○
Dacosta et al. [13]	✓	–	✓	✗	✓	✗	✗	✗	●	●	●	●	○	●	●	●	○	○	○
Hwang et al. [18]	✓	–	✓	✗	✓	✓	✗	✗	●	●	●	●	○	○	●	●	○	●	○
Monsen et al. [33]	✓	–	✗	✗	✗	✗	✗	✗	●	●	●	○	○	○	●	●	○	○	○
Nikiforakis et al. [34]	✓	–	✓	✗	✗	✓	✗	✗	○	●	○	●	●	○	●	○	●	–	●
Ogundele et al. [35]	✓	–	✗	✗	✗	✓	✗	✗	●	●	●	●	○	○	●	●	○	–	–
Pothumarti et al. [36]	✓	–	✓	✗	✓	✓	✗	✗	●	●	●	●	○	●	●	●	●	●	–
Prapty et al. [37]	✓	–	✗	✗	✗	✓	✗	✗	●	●	●	●	○	●	●	●	○	●	○
PUF-based Approaches																			
Aljrees et al. [3]	✓	n	✗	✓	✓	✗	✗	✗	●	–	●	●	○	○	●	●	●	●	–
Alshaeri et al. [4]	✓	s	✗	✗	✓	✓	✗	✗	–	●	●	●	○	○	●	●	●	○	–
Badshah et al. [6]	✓	n	✗	✓	✓	✗	✗	✗	●	–	●	●	○	○	●	●	○	●	–
Lo et al. [24]	✓	n	✗	✓	✓	✗	✗	✗	●	●	●	●	○	○	●	●	○	●	–
Lounis et al. [25]	✓	n	✗	✓	✗	✓	✗	✗	–	●	●	●	○	○	●	●	○	●	–
Siddiqui et al. [38]	✓	n	✓	✗	✓	✓	✗	✗	○	●	●	●	○	○	●	●	●	●	○
PUSH	✓	w	✓	✓	✓	✗	✗	✗	●	–	●	●	○	○	●	●	⊙	●	◐

🌐: applicability in web communication; 📡: lightweightness; ▨: obfuscation of data; ↕: prior mutual authentication; 🔑: independent cryptographic primitives; 📶: need for additional hardware; ❓: security level highly depends on implementation; ⏱: time synchronisation requirement. **Attacks: SA:** Sniffing; **XSS:** Cross-Site-Scripting; **RA:** Reply; **MM:** Man-in-the-Middle; **SC:** Side-Channel; **BF:** Brute Force; **PA:** Phishing; **IA:** Impersonation; **DoS:** Denial-of-Service; **DCC:** Device Capturing & Cloning; **BC:** Browser Compromise. ✓/✗: yes/no; ●/◐/○: secure/partially secure/not secure; ⊙: can be integrated; –: not applicable. PUF type (not specified, strong, weak).

strong PUF with many $CRPs$ [4], while PUSH supports even weak PUFs as SRAM-based, which can provide only a limited number of $CRPs$.

Lightweightness (⚖): All PUF-based solutions are lightweight in terms of resources, whilst this applies to only about half of the non-PUF-based approaches.

Obfuscation (✺): Most approaches, with a few exceptions [2,6,9,35], apply techniques to conceal sensitive data, e.g., $CRPs$, to ensure confidentiality and prevent reuse. In PUSH, vulnerable data (e.g., cookies) is encrypted both at rest (using DPAPI) and in transit (via HTTPS). Furthermore, in PUSH, the secret key SK is neither stored nor transmitted, because it is generated on demand.

Prior Mutual Authentication (↔) is incorporated in nearly half of the reviewed approaches (e.g., [18,36]), reducing the risk of potential attacks and establishing a secure foundation for session setup. In PUSH, mutual authentication is achieved using manufacturer-issued keys: the secret key SK_D is embedded in the dongle, while the corresponding public key PK_D is provided to the user.

Independent Cryptographic Primitives (🔑) are featured in eight of the reviewed approaches (e.g., [2,13]). Using entirely different primitives enhances resistance to cryptanalysis and side-channel attacks. PUSH leverages this principle in several ways: a secret key SK is derived from a unique SRAM PUF; each distinct CRP enables a unique SK; and a fresh nonce N is included in signature requests.

Need for Additional Hardware or Protocol Parties (▉) such as a Trusted Platform Module (TPM) [33], is a common limitation among the existing approaches. PUSH employs a dongle for binding; however, this could be replaced by the user device's SRAM (see Sect. 3.5). Although this alternative would require manufacturer support, it would eliminate the need for external hardware.

Security Level Highly Depends on Selected Mechanisms (❓): Most of the approaches reviewed emphasise the need for careful selection of methods used (e.g., hashing) to ensure security. Our analysis (see Sect. 4) has shown that PUSH provides strong protection by design, with minimal dependence on specific techniques, though security recommendations, e.g., regarding key lengths, should still be followed [7,8].

Time Synchronisation (⏲) is required for some approaches [1–3,6]. Although this is a reasonably robust and common way to mitigate some attacks, reliance on synchronisation increases implementation and deployment complexity. In contrast, PUSH does not rely on time synchronisation, but uses a random nonce N to ensure request freshness.

Resistance to Attacks: To evaluate the resistance of each approach to the attacks, we relied on the authors' claims, which typically covered only mitigated ones. If an attack was not mentioned, we attempted to assess the resistance of the presented approach based on available details. When this was infeasible, the approach was marked as not secure (○). The detailed security analysis of PUSH can be found in Sect. 4. While some attacks, e.g., DoS, are not addressed, and protection against impersonation and browser compromise is only partial,

PUSH demonstrates resistance to a broader range of attacks compared to other approaches under the defined adversary model (see Sect. 4.1).

Among the reviewed approaches, Device Bound Session Credentials (DBSC) is most similar to PUSH and merits a more detailed comparison [33]. Both aim to enable continuous session verification, yet differ in implementation and compatibility. DBSC relies on a TPM, which is slow and not universally supported across devices. For instance, while a TPM is mandatory on Windows 11, users of other operating systems (OS) may lack TPM support and thus cannot use DBSC. In contrast, PUSH uses a USB-connected dongle that is OS-independent, as USB is universally supported. Alternatively, PUSH could leverage internal SRAM (see Sect. 3.5), removing the need for external hardware altogether. Another difference lies in the introduced latency. DBSC requires an additional server port to avoid delays, while PUSH does not introduce any latency issues.

In summary, PUSH is a secure and efficient protocol for binding web sessions to physical devices using an SRAM PUF. It is significantly distinct from existing approaches and represents the first use of PUF for this purpose. PUSH ensures continuous verification of session legitimacy, providing strong protection against session hijacking and other attacks. Notably, PUSH avoids persistent storage of cryptographic keys, thereby also enhancing resistance to physical and memory-based attacks. Designed for lightweight operation, PUSH is well-suited to resource-constrained environments and integrates seamlessly into web communication without introducing latency. Moreover, it is cross-platform and works on any operating system that supports USB. Although the prototype is implemented with an external dongle, PUSH can be adapted to use the device's internal SRAM, eliminating the need for additional hardware.

7 Conclusion and Future Work

In this paper, we propose a novel SRAM PUF-based hardware-binding protocol, PUSH, which associates a web session with the user's device (dongle) and enables continuous verification of session legitimacy to mitigate session hijacking and related attacks. The results of a comprehensive evaluation of PUSH, including performance and security analysis, and comparison with existing approaches, have shown that PUSH is a secure, lightweight, and flexible protocol. It addresses the limitations of existing solutions and demonstrates great potential to enhance the security of web communication.

The following aspects are not covered in this paper but represent interesting directions for future research: evaluating the impact of different implementation choices on the security of PUSH; exploring the possibility of using alternative types of PUFs; and implementation of PUSH without a dongle, relying solely on the internal SRAM module of the user's device.

Acknowledgments. This work was funded by the Bavarian State Ministry of Science and Arts (BayStMWK), under the project "Secure Encapsulation" of the Bavarian Research Association "FORDaySec" ("Security in Everyday Use of Digital Technologies") and by the Interreg VI-A Programme Germany/Bavaria–Austria

2021–2027 – Programm INTERREG VI-A Bayern–Österreich 2021–2027, as part of Project BA0100016: "CySeReS-KMU: Cyber Security and Resilience in Supply Chains with focus on SMEs", which is co-funded by the European Union.

References

1. Ahmed, A.A., Ahmed, W.A.: An Effective multifactor authentication mechanism based on combiners of hash function over internet things. Sensors **19**(17) (2019). https://doi.org/10.3390/s19173663
2. Al-Sadi, M., Di Pietro, R., Lombardi, F., Signorini, M.: LENTO: Unpredictable Latency-based continuous authEntication for Network inTensive IoT envirOnments. Future Gener. Comput. Syst. **139**, 151–166 (2023). https://doi.org/10.1016/j.future.2022.09.023
3. Aljrees, T., Kumar, A., Singh, K.U., Singh, T.: Enhancing IoT security through a green and sustainable federated learning platform: leveraging efficient encryption and the quondam signature algorithm. Sensors **23**(19) (2023). https://doi.org/10.3390/s23198090
4. Alshaeri, A., Younis, M.: Distributed hardware-assisted authentication and key agreement protocol for internet of things. In: 2024 IEEE 21st Consumer Communications & Networking Conference (CCNC), pp. 152–158 (2024). https://doi.org/10.1109/CCNC51664.2024.10454706
5. Arduino: Nano 33 BLE Documentation (2025). https://docs.arduino.cc/hardware/nano-33-ble/
6. Badshah, A., et al.: USAF-IoD: ultralightweight and secure authenticated key agreement framework for internet of drones environment. IEEE Trans. Veh. Technol. **73**(8), 10963–10977 (2024). https://doi.org/10.1109/TVT.2024.3375758
7. Barker, E.B., Kelsey, J.M., McKay, K.A., Roginsky, A.L., Turan, M.S.: Recommendation for Random Bit Generator (RBG) Constructions. Tech. Rep. NIST SP 800-90C (Fourth Public Draft), National Institute of Standards and Technology (NIST), Gaithersburg, MD (2024). https://doi.org/10.6028/NIST.SP.800-90C.4pd
8. Barker, E.B., Roginsky, A.L.: Transitioning the use of cryptographic algorithms and key lengths. Tech. Rep. NIST SP 800-131A Rev. 3, National Institute of Standards and Technology (NIST), Gaithersburg, MD (2024). https://doi.org/10.6028/NIST.SP.800-131Ar3.ipd
9. Bharti Kumar, A., Chaudhary, M.: Prevention of session hijacking and ipspoofing with sensor nodes and cryptographic approach. Int. J. Comput. Appl. **76**(9), 22–28 (2013). https://doi.org/10.5120/13275-0821
10. Bugliesi, M., Calzavara, S., Focardi, R., Khan, W.: CookiExt: Patching the browser against session hijacking attacks. J. Comput. Secur. **23**(4), 509–537 (2015). https://doi.org/10.3233/jcs-150529
11. Cherupally, S.K., Yin, S., Kadetotad, D., Bae, C., Kim, S.J., Seo, J.s.: A smart hardware security engine combining entropy sources of ECG, HRV, and SRAM PUF for Authentication and Secret Key Generation. IEEE J. Solid-State Circ. **55**(10), 2680–2690 (2020). https://doi.org/10.1109/JSSC.2020.3010705
12. Clark, L.T., Medapuram, S.B., Kadiyala, D.K.: SRAM circuits for true random number generation using intrinsic bit instability. IEEE Trans. Very Large Scale Integr. (VLSI) Syst. **26**(10), 2027–2037 (2018). https://doi.org/10.1109/TVLSI.2018.2840049

13. Dacosta, I., Chakradeo, S., Ahamad, M., Traynor, P.: One-time cookies: Preventing session hijacking attacks with stateless authentication tokens. ACM Trans. Internet Technol. **12**(1) (2012). https://doi.org/10.1145/2220352.2220353
14. Dolev, D., Yao, A.: On the security of public key protocols. IEEE Trans. Inf. Theory **29**(2), 198–208 (1983). https://doi.org/10.1109/TIT.1983.1056650
15. D'silva, K., Vanajakshi, J., Manjunath, K.N., Prabhu, S.: An effective method for preventing SQL injection attack and session hijacking. In: 2017 2nd IEEE International Conference on Recent Trends in Electronics, Information & Communication Technology (RTEICT), pp. 697–701 (2017). https://doi.org/10.1109/RTEICT.2017.8256687
16. Guajardo, J., Kumar, S.S., Schrijen, G.-J., Tuyls, P.: FPGA intrinsic PUFs and their use for IP protection. In: Paillier, P., Verbauwhede, I. (eds.) CHES 2007. LNCS, vol. 4727, pp. 63–80. Springer, Heidelberg (2007). https://doi.org/10.1007/978-3-540-74735-2_5
17. Hemavathy, S., Bhaaskaran, V.S.K.: Arbiter PUF-a review of design, composition, and security aspects. IEEE Access **11**, 33979–34004 (2023). https://doi.org/10.1109/ACCESS.2023.3264016
18. Hwang, W.S., Shon, J.G., Park, J.S.: Web session hijacking defense technique using user information. HCIS **12**, 16 (2022)
19. Kapko, M.: Slack resets passwords en masse after invite link vulnerability. Cybersecurity Dive (2022). https://www.cybersecuritydive.com/news/slack-password-vulnerability/629026/. Accessed 04 Jan 2025
20. Katzenbeisser, S., Schaller, A.: Physical unclonable functions: sicherheitseigenschaften und anwendungen. Datenschutz und Datensicherheit - DuD **36**(12), 881–885 (2012). https://doi.org/10.1007/s11623-012-0295-z
21. Kumar, A., Saha, R., Conti, M., Kumar, G., Buchanan, W.J., Kim, T.H.: A comprehensive survey of authentication methods in Internet-of-Things and its conjunctions. J. Netw. Comput. Appl. **204**, 103414 (2022). https://doi.org/10.1016/j.jnca.2022.103414
22. Kumar Baitha, A., Vinod, S.: Session hijacking and prevention technique. Int. J. Eng. Technol. **7**(2.6), 193–198 (Mar 2018). https://doi.org/10.14419/ijet.v7i2.6.10566
23. Linus Tech Tips: My Channel Was Deleted Last Night (2023). https://www.youtube.com/watch?v=yGXaAWbzl5A. Accessed 4 Jan 2025
24. Lo, N.W., Yohan, A.: BLE-Based Authentication Protocol for Micropayment Using Wearable Device. Wirel. Pers. Commun. **112**(4), 2351–2372 (2020). https://doi.org/10.1007/s11277-020-07153-0
25. Lounis, K., Zulkernine, M.: T2T-MAP: A PUF-Based Thing-to-Thing Mutual Authentication Protocol for IoT. IEEE Access **9**, 137384–137405 (2021). https://doi.org/10.1109/ACCESS.2021.3117444
26. Maes, R.: Physically unclonable functions: properties. In: Physically Unclonable Functions. LNCS, pp. 49–80. Springer, Heidelberg (2013). https://doi.org/10.1007/978-3-642-41395-7_3
27. Mall, P., Amin, R., Das, A.K., Leung, M.T., Choo, K.K.R.: PUF-based authentication and key agreement protocols for IoT, WSNs, and smart grids: a comprehensive survey. IEEE Internet Things J. **9**(11), 8205–8228 (2022). https://doi.org/10.1109/JIOT.2022.3142084
28. Mangard, S., Oswald, E., Popp, T.: Power Analysis Attacks. Lecture Notes in Computer Science, Springer, Boston, MA (2007). https://doi.org/10.1007/978-0-387-38162-6

29. Mexis, N.: A Comprehensive Comparison of Fuzzy Extractor Schemes Employing Different Error Correction Codes. M.Sc. Thesis, University of Passau, Passau, Germany (Oct 2023). https://doi.org/10.15475/ccfesedecc.2023
30. Microchip Technology Inc.: 23LC512 - 512 Kbit SPI Serial SRAM (2025). https://www.microchip.com/en-us/product/23lc512#Documentation
31. Microsoft: CNG DPAPI (Data Protection API). Microsoft Learn. https://learn.microsoft.com/de-de/windows/win32/seccng/cng-dpapi#:~:text=DPAPI%20ist%20Teil%20von%20CryptoAPI,zu%20verschl%C3%BCsseln%20und%20zu%20entschl%C3%BCsseln
32. Microsoft: Pipes (Interprocess Communications) (2021). https://learn.microsoft.com/en-us/windows/win32/ipc/pipes
33. Monsen, K., Birgisson, A.: Fighting Cookie Theft Using Device-Bound Keys. https://blog.chromium.org/2024/04/fighting-cookie-theft-using-device.html (Apr 2024)
34. Nikiforakis, N., Meert, W., Younan, Y., Johns, M., Joosen, W.: SessionShield: lightweight protection against session hijacking. In: Erlingsson, Ú., Wieringa, R., Zannone, N. (eds.) ESSoS 2011. LNCS, vol. 6542, pp. 87–100. Springer, Heidelberg (2011). https://doi.org/10.1007/978-3-642-19125-1_7
35. Ogundele, I.O., Akinade, A.O., Alakiri, H.O.: Detection and prevention of session hijacking in web application management. IJARCCE **9**, 1–10 (Jun2020). https://doi.org/10.17148/IJARCCE.2020.9601
36. Pothumarti, R., Jain, K., Krishnan, P.: A lightweight authentication scheme for 5G mobile communications: a dynamic key approach. J. Ambient. Intell. Humaniz. Comput. 1–19 (2021). https://doi.org/10.1007/s12652-020-02857-4
37. Prapty, R.T., Azmin Md, S., Hossain, S., Narman, H.S.: Preventing session hijacking using encrypted one-time-cookies. In: 2020 Wireless Telecommunications Symposium (WTS). pp. 1–6 (2020). https://doi.org/10.1109/WTS48268.2020.9198717
38. Siddiqui, Z., Gao, J., Khurram Khan, M.: An improved lightweight PUF–PKI digital certificate authentication scheme for the internet of things. IEEE Internet Things J. **9**(20), 19744–19756 (2022). https://doi.org/10.1109/JIOT.2022.3168726
39. Statista: Beyond Passwords: Biometrics, Multifactor, and Passwordless Authentication. Study (Jul 2023). https://www.statista.com/study/116099/beyond-passwords-biometrics-multifactor-and-passwordless-authentication/
40. Statista: Worldwide digital population (Oct 2024). https://www.statista.com/statistics/617136/digital-population-worldwide/
41. SurfShark: Number of user accounts exposed worldwide from 1st quarter 2020 to 3rd quarter 2024 (in millions). Chart (Oct 2024). https://www.statista.com/statistics/1307426/number-of-data-breaches-worldwide/
42. The Chromium Projects: SPDY: An Experimental Protocol for a Faster Web (2009). https://www.chromium.org/spdy/spdy-whitepaper/
43. Wang, R., Selimis, G., Maes, R., Goossens, S.: Long-term continuous assessment of SRAM PUF and source of random numbers. In: Proceedings of the 23rd Conference on Design, Automation and Test in Europe, pp. 7–12. DATE '20, EDA Consortium, San Jose, CA, USA (2020). https://doi.org/10.23919/DATE48585.2020.9116353
44. Weatherley, R.: Crypto Library for Arduino. Rweather Arduino Libraries. https://rweather.github.io/arduinolibs/crypto.html
45. Zhang, Y., Ge, Y.: Evaluation of microcontroller-based SRAM PUF and the authentication scheme. In: Proceedings of the 4th International Conference on Computer, Internet of Things and Control Engineering, pp. 79–86. CITCE '24, Association for Computing Machinery, New York, NY, USA (2025). https://doi.org/10.1145/3705677.3705691

Hardening HSM Clusters: Resolving Key Sync Vulnerabilities for Robust CU Isolation

Sarat Chandra Prasad Gingupalli[✉]

Marvell Technology, Hyderabad, India
sgingupalli@marvell.com

Abstract. This paper exposes critical vulnerabilities in key syncing within Hardware Security Module (HSM) clusters, revealing design flaws that bypass user authorization and make cluster objects accessible to anyone within the cluster. In an ideal HSM cluster, objects should be shared across partitions for availability, yet their usage must remain restricted to their creating user for security. However, when using the Partition Crypto Officer (PCO) for syncing, objects become cluster-shared, but encrypting them with a masking key—unique per partition yet accessible to all users of the partition—compromises the user-owned property. We demonstrate how this lack of user isolation can be exploited to extract sensitive information from clusters. The issue is further exacerbated by data encryption/decryption APIs that fail to enforce segregation between key-wrapping and data-encryption algorithms, exposing plaintext keys at the HSM boundary. To counter these threats, we propose two robust solutions: (1) a nonce-based approach, where the Hierarchical Deterministic (HD) wallet [3] is path-restricted per user, and users derive transport keys for masking objects using a combination of a nonce and the masking key; and (2) a public-key-based model, where each Crypto User (CU) in the HSM is assigned an independent key pair upon creation and uses this user-specific key pair to encrypt their respective objects in the cluster. Through detailed demonstrations, we illustrate how these approaches establish CU isolation in widely deployed cloud HSM clusters, effectively mitigating the identified vulnerabilities.

Keywords: HSM clusters · key synchronization · user isolation · nonce-based key derivation · path-restricted HD wallets

1 Introduction

Hardware Security Modules (HSMs) are the backbone of cryptographic key protection, yet flawed designs can turn them into liabilities [9]. This paper uncovers devastating weaknesses in HSMs' key management—exploiting the use of a masking key (partition master key) that encrypts all cluster objects, combining it with API misuse and key attribute misconfigurations, we were able to sabotage cluster keys, bypass M-of-N authentication, and show how the security of all keys in an HSM cluster reduced to cracking user logins.

HSM clusters use APIs like `extractMaskedObject` and `insertMaskedObject` to sync keys between partitions. Since cluster sync is an automated process, the entity that operates it usually has access to all the keys—some vendors do this sync through PCO (Partition Crypto Officer) and some do it through AU (Appliance User)—yet these mechanisms falter under unique shared-key designs.

To counter this, we introduce two solutions, novel compared to generic key isolation approaches: a nonce-based approach, where the HD wallet [3] is path-restricted per user, and users derive transport keys for masking objects using a combination of a nonce and the masking key, and a public-key-based model where each user in the HSM is assigned an independent key pair upon creation [6], blocking unauthorized access and eliminating shared-key risks. We explore the problem, dissect attacks, present our fixes, analyze their strength, and conclude with a path forward—offering a blueprint to secure HSM key management for cloud HSM clusters specifically.

2 Background

HSMs safeguard keys using hardware-enforced isolation. Each HSM comprises several partitions, and each partition operates independently from the others. In HSM terminology, there is one master partition (MP) and multiple user partitions (UPs). The MP is managed by the Master Crypto Officer (MCO), who oversees the creation and deletion of user partitions. Within each UP, the Partition Crypto Officer (PCO) manages operations, creating and overseeing Crypto Users (CUs), who in turn create and manage keys. Given that keys are highly critical security components, user partitions operate in clusters to ensure High Availability (HA). A cluster consists of several identical partitions holding the same set of keys, enabling HA and load balancing of cryptographic operations. To maintain consistency across cluster partitions, keys are synced regularly using APIs such as `extractMaskedObject` and `insertMaskedObject`. This synchronization, an automated process, is typically handled by either the PCO or an Appliance User (AU)—entities unique across partitions with elevated privileges to access CU objects. All cluster objects are encrypted with a masking key, generated within the HSM during partition initialization. Ideally, this masking key should never leave the HSM unless there is a need to create an identical partition for clustering. Since only identical partitions participate in a cluster, the masking key is transferred from an existing partition to a newly uninitialized one via a trusted pathway—often a secure cloning protocol using a handshake session key. Once the new partition acquires this masking key, it can encrypt and decrypt masked objects, joining the cluster seamlessly.

Some terminology used throughout this paper:

- **MCO**: Master Crypto Officer, responsible for managing the creation and deletion of User Partitions.

- **PCO**: Handles key synchronization in clusters and user management within the partition.
- **CU**: Crypto User, tasked with key management and cryptographic operations.
- **Masking Key**: A unique master key per partition (some HSM vendors call it the Scalable Master Key, or SMK, designed to scale HSM partitions), used to wrap and unwrap cluster objects.
- **Wrap/Unwrap Algorithm**: Most clusters employ NIST SP 800-38F algorithms, predominantly AES-KWP, for wrapping and unwrapping operations [8].
- **extractMaskedObject**: Wraps keys and attributes using the Masking Key for secure extraction.
- **insertMaskedObject**: Unwraps keys and attributes using the Masking Key, storing them in the database (DB) with the original key handle. If the PCO inserts it, the original CU will be the owner of this key; else, the CU who inserts it becomes the owner.
- **extractMaskedObjectWithUserInfo**: Extracts the masked object with CU identity embedded, as the name implies.
- **insertMaskedObjectWithUserInfo**: Validates and enforces that the CU in the masked object becomes the owner, regardless of the inserting entity.
- **M-of-N Authentication**: A threshold-based security control where at least M of N authorized users must approve to perform sensitive operations.
- **USE_KEY and MANAGE_KEY**: These are custom-defined attributes used by HSM vendors and cloud providers. USE_KEY includes cryptographic operations (encrypt/decrypt, sign/verify) while MANAGE_KEY includes key life-cycle management (wrap/unwrap, key share, delete, etc.).

Relevance to Existing HSM Architectures: The reliance on a single masking key per partition is not an abstract flaw but a pervasive design choice in widely deployed HSM cluster architectures, including those from major vendors. These implementations exemplify the vulnerabilities we target, as their synchronization mechanisms prioritize cluster consistency over CU isolation, exposing keys to unauthorized access within the partition.

- **Thales Luna HSMs**: Thales Luna HSMs employ a single masking key—termed the Scalable Master Key (SMK)—per partition to encrypt all cluster objects for synchronization across their High Availability (HA) group. This key, generated at partition initialization, is shared across all HSMs and accessible to all CUs and PCOs within that partition for wrap/unwrap operations, undermining CU-specific isolation. This design, detailed in public documentation [12], enables seamless HA but exposes keys to any authorized user, aligning with the vulnerabilities we exploit in subsequent attacks.
- **Marvell LiquidSecurity**: This HSM family uses a cluster key functioning as a single masking key, generated at partition initialization and synced across cluster partitions via a cloning protocol. This key, unique to the cluster, is accessible to all authorized users within the partition and, if deployed in cloud, within the tenant boundary without per-CU restrictions via extract/insert.

This synchronization ensures consistency but allows any CU to potentially unwrap synced keys, mirroring the shared-key flaw we target.
- **Cloud HSM Deployments**: Cloud HSMs sync objects across HA pairs or regions using shared masking keys accessible to all privileged roles (CUs/PCOs). As documented [12], this setup lacks user-level isolation and remains vulnerable to shared-key and re-registration flaws discussed in our work.

In subsequent sections, we demonstrate attacks on major cloud HSMs, exploiting the lack of CU isolation. Examples include one CU accessing another's keys, PCOs viewing CU keys, key duplication to bypass M-of-N, and recovery of deleted CU keys via re-registration. These attacks compromise high-stakes use cases like exchange wallets and firmware signing, collapsing cluster integrity.

We also highlight how APIs like `aesWrapUnwrap`, commonly used for data operations, allow key extraction due to lack of separation between data and key operations. Passing a wrapped key as data with the correct handle can expose plaintext at the boundary. Additionally, misuse of PKCS#11 attributes like `USE_KEY` and `MANAGE_KEY` amplifies the risk under weak user isolation [10].

2.1 Related Work

Prior solutions, such as [13,14], achieve multi-tenancy via isolated execution environments but do not address key transport or storage isolation at the cluster level. Unlike these runtime-focused approaches, our work enforces cryptographic isolation across HSM clusters. Existing cloud HSM clusters use a common masking key per partition to protect all keys, with no per-user wrapping or binding. Most HSMs encrypt backend storage with a single database-level key, offering no user-level segregation at rest. Existing M-of-N schemes rely on metadata and tokens without cryptographic enforcement, enabling bypasses via API misuse [14]. To our knowledge, no prior work proposes cryptographically enforcing user-specific key isolation across both transport and storage layers within HSM clusters. Our work addresses this systemic gap.

3 Problem Statement

Current HSM cluster key management fails to enforce user isolation, exposing keys through a fundamentally flawed reliance on a partition-unique masking key that is accessible to every user within the partition for extract/insert operations. This key, used to encrypt all cluster objects, undermines the user-owned property of keys despite objects being cluster-shared, allowing any CU or PCO within the partition to decrypt sensitive keys. The synchronization process, driven by APIs like `extractMaskedObject` and `insertMaskedObject`, exacerbates this vulnerability—automated cluster sync, operated by privileged entities (PCO or AU), compromises key authorization due to this shared-key design. Further compounding the issue, APIs such as `aesWrapUnwrap` and exportPrivateKey—misused due to a lack of segregation between key wrapping and data encryption/decryption operations [10]-enable plaintext key exposure at HSM boundaries. HSMs manage key functionality through USE_KEY and MANAGE_KEY attributes. Since these are vendor-defined attributes, there is no mandate to disable USE_KEY when MANAGE_KEY is set. If M-of-N isn't strictly applied on all key operations, any CU or PCO can exploit this loophole to bypass M-of-N controls. Since the shared masking-key design lacks CU isolation, without CU authorization on extracted objects in HSM clusters, a CU or PCO can duplicate keys via extractMaskedObject and insertMaskedObject, evading usage audits by creating copies to trick other CUs into using duplicate keys. If USE_KEY remains enabled with MANAGE_KEY set and M-of-N isn't enforced on USE_KEY operations, a single CU can wrap an M-of-N key and re-import it as new with sole ownership; worse, APIs like aesWrapUnwrap allow plaintext exposure, fully compromising M-of-N security. In widely deployed cloud HSMs, M-of-N bypassing is possible, as demonstrated in our attacks section. This systemic collapse—demonstrated across cloud HSMs—demands CU-specific isolation to prevent cross-user and PCO access, secure key transport mechanisms to eliminate boundary leaks, and robust multi-party enforcement to uphold M-of-N integrity, all unaddressed by existing shared-key architectures. Our proposed solutions address these critical gaps with novel approaches like nonce-based path-restricted key derivation and associating users with a key pair.

4 Attacks on Cluster HSMs with a Unique Masking Key

This section outlines vulnerabilities in HSM cluster key management, exposing keys via a shared masking key and misused APIs. We detail critical exploits using cloud HSM sync APIs: extractMaskedObject, insertMaskedObject, extractMaskedObjectWithUserInfo, insertMaskedObjectWithUserInfo, which wrap/unwrap keys with attributes (and user info) using the masking key.

4.1 Key Exposure via Shared Masking Key in HSM Cluster Sync

Description. Keys are synced across partitions using a shared masking key. The extractMaskedObject API wraps the key with the masking key, and insertMaskedObject unwraps it, allowing any CU to import it. A CU can then use wrapKey with a controlled key (e.g., kh 4) and by passing this wrapped key buffer as data buffer to aesWrapUnwrap to extract the plaintext key, bypassing authorization.

Attack Flow

1. CU1 in Partition 1 creates K1 using genSymKey.
2. PCO wraps K1 with the masking key via extractMaskedObject, syncing the masked object.
3. CU2 in Partition 2 inserts it with insertMaskedObject, unwrapping with the masking key to get a new handle.

4. CU2 uses `wrapKey` with kh 4, then `aesWrapUnwrap` to extract K1 in plaintext.

Impact. Total key compromise occurs due to no CU authorization—any CU can insert masked objects and extract keys using a shared masking key, bypassing authorization. CU2 can use K1 in the HSM or, if "Plaintext Key Extraction" is feasible, obtain it in plaintext at the boundary.

4.2 Plaintext Key Extraction via Exposed Cloud-Based Key Management Systems Wrap/Unwrap APIs

Description. The `aesWrapUnwrap` API, meant for wrapping/unwrapping, processes key material and outputs plaintext keys into a user buffer due to poor segregation of algorithms used in encryption/decryption APIs and wrap/unwrap APIs.

Attack Flow

1. CU1 creates K1 and K2.
2. CU1 wraps K1 with K2 using `wrapKey`.
3. CU1 unwraps with K2 via `aesWrapUnwrap`, outputting K1 in plaintext at the HSM console.

Impact. In widely deployed cloud HSMs, any key can be extracted in plaintext by a CU with API access, breaking key confidentiality. HSMs should wrap keys into handles, not dump raw keys—this poor design choice and wrong labeling exposes all key material via a misused data API that needs removal.

4.3 User Re-registration Key Theft

Description. The HSM's `extractMaskedObjectWithUserInfo` embeds usernames into masked objects wrapped with the masking key. A malicious CU collects these, and after a user deletion (tracked via `listUsers`), re-registers the username to insert them with `insertMaskedObjectWithUserInfo`, recovering zeroized keys.

Attack Flow

1. A malicious CU collects masked objects from `extractMaskedObjectWithUserInfo`.
2. After a user is deleted (via `listUsers`), the CU re-registers the username.
3. The CU inserts collected objects with `insertMaskedObjectWithUserInfo` to recover the original keys.

Impact. In widely deployed cloud HSMs, keys remain recoverable post-deletion if masked objects persist, allowing a new CU with the same username to access old keys. HSMs must invalidate such objects—failing this, deletion becomes a vulnerability, exposing keys to anyone tracking user changes.

4.4 M-of-N Provisioning Bypass via Attribute Misconfiguration

Description. HSM supports $MofN$ via attributes: USE_KEY and MANAGE_KEY. USE_KEY alone doesn't restrict wrap/unwrap, allowing a single CU to bypass $MofN$ authorization with the masking key, while MANAGE_KEY can't stop extract/insert duplication.

Attack Flow

1. A CU generates an $MofN$ key with M = 2 with USE_KEY, but wrap/unwrap succeeds solo as it's unrestricted.
2. With MANAGE_KEY M = 2, a CU extracts the key via extractMaskedObject, duplicates it with insertMaskedObject, and tricks another CU into obtaining $MofN$ approval for a wrapKey operation, enabling the key to be wrapped, exported, and later imported with sole ownership or retrieved as plaintext data using exposed aesWrapUnwrap APIs.

Impact. In widely deployed cloud HSMs, USE_KEY's flaw lets a CU wrap an $MofN$ key with $M \geq 2$ solo, bypassing $MofN$ authorization intent. MANAGE_KEY restricts wrap/unwrap but not extract/insert, enabling duplication and exploitation, compromising key confidentiality despite trust assumptions.

5 Proposed Solutions

To address vulnerabilities in HSM cluster key management, we propose two approaches—nonce-based using BIP32-style wallets and public-key using elliptic curve (EC) pairs—to enforce CU isolation and eliminate reliance on a shared masking key. These mechanisms derive user-specific transport keys, ensuring CUs remain isolated from each other and the PCO. Each method is detailed in the following subsections, followed by evaluation and security analysis against known exploits.

5.1 Nonce-Based HD Wallet Approach

Description. In this approach, we use a master seed m to create a BIP32-based hierarchical deterministic (HD) wallet and assign a unique derivation path to each user. A specific BIP32 path of the form m/x/y is allocated at the time of user creation, where x denotes the role ($x = 0$ for PCO, $x = 1$ for CU) and y is a forward-only user index (e.g., PCO has m/0/0, PCO1 gets m/0/1, CU has m/1/0, CU1 gets m/1/1). These derivation paths yield user-specific child keys (nonces) used to generate transport keys.

To enforce isolation, the HSM ensures that CU derivations (m/1/y) are only accessible to their respective owners, preventing the PCO from accessing them. In PCO access mode (Fig. 1a), PCO has access to both m/0 and m/1 paths. In the restricted mode (Fig. 1b), PCO access is limited to only m/0.

We pair these role-based nonces with the masking key (mk) to derive a unique transport key for each user, eliminating the risk of shared masking keys across

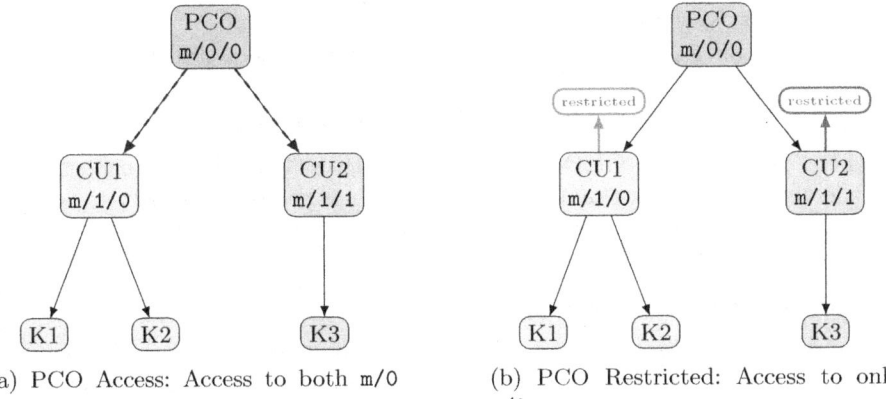

(a) PCO Access: Access to both m/0 and m/1.

(b) PCO Restricted: Access to only m/0.

Fig. 1. HD wallet tree: (a) Full access by PCO; (b) CU paths restricted from PCO.

users. This method maintains CU isolation and enforces strict partition-level separation. The HD wallet structure mirrors a role-based hierarchy: PCO manages CUs, and CUs manage keys. Leaf nodes (keys) are transported using derived transport keys formed from their parent's nonce and mk. For example, CU keys use PBKDF2(mk || cu_nonce), and CU objects use PBKDF2(mk || pco_nonce). This ensures seamless synchronization while preserving object ownership and security boundaries.

Mechanism

1. **Master Seed and HD Wallet Setup**:
   During partition initialization, a cryptographically secure master seed m (e.g., 256-bit) and masking key mk are generated and locked within the HSM. During partition cloning, the PCO securely transfers both m and mk to the new partition via a secure channel. The HSM enforces strict role-based derivation: m/0/y derivations are PCO-only, while m/1/y derivations are CU-only.

2. **Nonce Derivation (via CKDpriv)**:
   For each user, a BIP32-compliant nonce is derived using the CKDpriv (Child Key Derivation) function:

   $$\texttt{CKDpriv}(k_{\text{par}}, c_{\text{par}}, i) \rightarrow (k_{\text{child}}, c_{\text{child}})$$

   where:
   - k_{par}: Parent private key,
   - c_{par}: Parent chain code,
   - i: Index for derivation.

   The child key is computed as:

   $$I = \texttt{HMAC-SHA512}(c_{\text{par}}, k_{\text{par}} \parallel 0x00 \parallel i), \quad k_{\text{child}} = I_L + k_{\text{par}} \bmod n, \quad c_{\text{child}} = I_R$$

   For instance, for CU1 with path m/1/1:

   $$(k_{\text{CU1}}, c_{\text{CU1}}) = \texttt{CKDpriv}(k_{\text{m/1}}, c_{\text{m/1}}, 1)$$

3. **Transport Key Derivation**:
   Once the nonce is derived, the transport key for object transfer is computed as:

   $$K\_CU1 = \text{PBKDF2}(\text{mk} \parallel \text{nonce\_CU1})$$

   where `nonce_CU1` is CKD-derived from path `m/1/1`. This transport key is then used in `extractMaskedObject` and `insertMaskedObject` to securely wrap and unwrap CU1's keys.

5.2 Public-Key EC Pair Approach

Description. In this approach, each user is assigned a unique elliptic curve (EC) key pair at the time of creation, generated securely inside the HSM. The HSM creates an EC key pair (e.g., NIST P-256 in FIPS mode, secp256k1 or Curve25519 in non-FIPS mode) for the PCO at partition initialization and for each CU upon user creation, attaching the private key securely to the HSM and exposing only the public key. While users may register asymmetric key pairs of other types (e.g., RSA, or post-quantum schemes like Kyber, as standardized by NIST), this section assumes EC key pairs for consistency with ECIES transport encryption and standard cluster synchronization.

The cloning protocol used to establish identical partitions remains unchanged. Specifically, the protocol, executed by the PCO, transfers the masking key (mk) from the original partition to the new one. After cloning, PCO and CU objects are synchronized using `extractMaskedObject` and `insertMaskedObject` calls. During this synchronization: - The PCO object is encrypted using `mk`. - Each CU object is encrypted using the public key of the PCO (`PCO_pub`) via ECIES. - Each key object (e.g., `K1`) is encrypted using the public key of its creator CU (e.g., `CU1_pub`) via ECIES.

Thus, objects are protected by the public key of their creator, ensuring that only the creator's private key (e.g., `CU1_priv`) can decrypt them, preserving confidentiality and CU isolation. In non-isolation mode (Fig. 2a), the PCO has access to all CU private keys and can decrypt all objects during synchronization. In isolation mode (Fig. 2b), CU private keys are not part of the cloning protocol and are never transferred—only `mk` is transferred—so the PCO lacks decryption capability for CU-encrypted objects post-cloning. This model eliminates the shared-key vulnerability present in traditional cluster sync and supports both automated and M-of-N manual approval mechanisms for secure CU isolation and controlled key sharing.

Mechanism.

1. **EC Key Pair Setup**:
   During partition initialization, the HSM generates a secure EC key pair (`PCO_priv`, `PCO_pub`) for the PCO, along with a masking key (`mk`), attaching them to the PCO object. Each CU (e.g., CU1) at user creation gets its own EC key pair (`CU1_priv`, `CU1_pub`), generated independently of any seed or derivation logic.

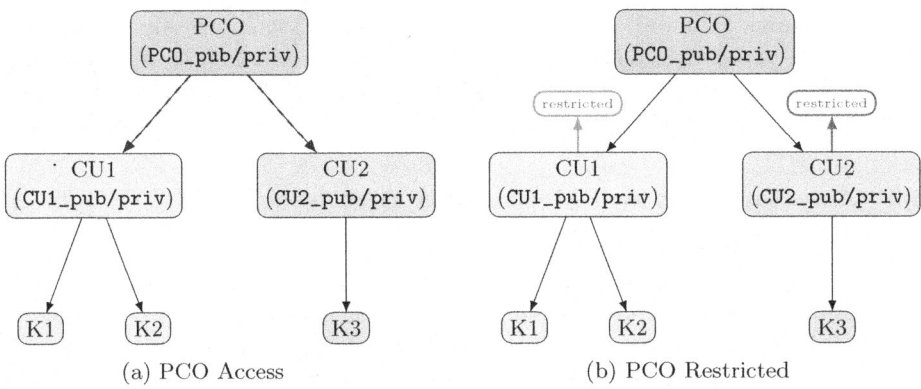

Fig. 2. EC key pair tree: (a) PCO has access to all CU private keys (non-isolation); (b) PCO has restricted access to CU private keys (isolation).

2. **Object Creation and Key Pair Association**:
   When a CU object (e.g., CU1) is created, its key pair is attached to its identity inside the HSM. Key objects (e.g., K1, K2) do not have associated key pairs—they are instead encrypted using the public key of their creator CU.
3. **Transport Key Encryption**:
   To transfer an object (e.g., a key) securely across partitions, the HSM uses ECIES encryption based on the object's creator.
   Consider K1, a key created by CU1 on a sender partition.
   – *Sender-side (Non-isolation mode)*:
   The PCO has access to CU1_pub and encrypts the key object K1 using ECIES:
   $$\mathtt{masked\_k1} = \mathtt{ECIES\_Enc}(K1, \mathtt{CU1\_pub})$$
   This encrypted blob is exported from the sender via extractMaskedObject.
   – *Receiver-side (Non-isolation mode)*:
   Since CU1 is the creator (and parent) of K1, it is typically synchronized before K1. In non-isolation mode, the PCO has access to all CU private keys, including CU1_priv, allowing it to decrypt the object using:
   $$K1 = \mathtt{ECIES\_Dec}(\mathtt{masked\_k1}, \mathtt{CU1\_priv})$$

   In **isolation mode**, however, CU private keys like CU1_priv are not available to the PCO. As a result, while the PCO can synchronize the encrypted object masked_k1, it cannot decrypt it. Instead, the HSM on the receiving partition makes masked_k1 available only to the local instance of CU1, which holds CU1_priv and can perform:
   $$K1 = \mathtt{ECIES\_Dec}(\mathtt{masked\_k1}, \mathtt{CU1\_priv})$$

This ensures that only the original creator (CU1) can decrypt its own key material, preserving confidentiality and CU isolation. In $M$of$N$ cases (e.g., $M = 2$), Shamir-split secret sharing or token authentication further isolates access, detailed below.

5.3 Assessing Proposed Mechanisms Effectiveness in HSM Cluster Scenarios

This section evaluates both nonce-based and public-key approaches against current HSM cluster scenarios, focusing on CU isolation from other CUs and the PCO across cluster and non-cluster setups. Each approach replaces the shared masking key with user-specific encryption keys: the nonce-based mechanism derives symmetric transport keys from HD wallet paths [3], while the public-key mechanism uses elliptic curve (EC) key pairs with ECIES-based encryption [6]. We assess both single-owner cases ($M = 1$), where the CU is the sole owner of the key, and shared multi-user cases ($M = 2$, M-of-N), where a key is shared among N users and requires M approvals to access or use.

CU Isolation from Other CUs

This mechanism enforces strict isolation between CUs within the same partition or cluster by preventing unauthorized access to a CU's key K1. The nonce-based approach uses unique nonce derivation and role-restricted paths, while the public-key approach uses unique EC key pairs. PCO has access to CU nonces or keys, facilitating cluster operations without compromising CU-to-CU isolation—since PCO isolation is not the objective.

1. *Cluster (PCO Extract/Insert) - $M = 1$ (Simple Case):*

In this cluster scenario, the goal is to sync a CU's key using PCO with M = 1 while ensuring CU isolation. CU1 creates K1. The nonce-based approach uses nonce-derived keys, while the public-key approach uses EC key pairs.
Nonce-Based: CU1 is assumed to be created under path m/1/0. PCO derives cu1_nonce = CKDpriv(k_1, c_1, 0)[0] and computes K_CU1 = PBKDF2(mk || cu1_nonce). It then encrypts K1 to masked_k1 = Enc(K_CU1, K1), embeds attributes (owner = "CU1"), and syncs via extractMaskedObject. Receiver HSMs decrypt with K_CU1 and store K1. CU2 can't access K1. PCO supports sync without breaking isolation.
PubKey-Based: PCO encrypts K1 with CU1's public key: masked_k1 = ECIES_Enc(K1, CU1_pub) and syncs it. Since CU1 is typically synced before K1, and CU1's private key is available in non-isolation mode, the PCO on the receiving partition decrypts with K1 = ECIES_Dec(masked_k1, CU1_priv). CU2 can't access K1. PCO supports sync without breaking CU-to-CU isolation.

2. *Cluster (PCO Extract/Insert) - $M = 2$ (M-of-N Case):*

In this cluster scenario, the goal is to sync a CU's key using PCO with M = 2, ensuring single-CU isolation while allowing multi-CU access. CU1 creates K1, with attributes: owner = "CU1", assumed to be under path m/1/0. The nonce-based approach uses Shamir shares with nonce-derived keys [11], while the public-key approach uses EC key pairs. *Nonce-Based:* PCO generates a random 256-bit symmetric key S, splits it into 2-of-3 Shamir shares: S_share1, S_share2, S_share3. It then encrypts K1 as encrypted_k1 = Enc(S, K1). Each share is encrypted with a nonce-derived key:

- cu1_nonce = CKDpriv(k_1, c_1, 0)[0],   K_CU1 = PBKDF2(mk || cu1_nonce),   enc_share1 = Enc(K_CU1, S_share1)
- Similarly for CU2 and CU3.

PCO syncs the object as masked_k1 = encrypted_k1 || enc_share1 || enc_share2 || enc_share3 via extractMaskedObject. Upon receiving, PCO decrypts two valid shares using CU1 and CU2's keys, reconstructs S, decrypts K1, and stores it. CU2 alone cannot access K1 without another share. PCO enables multi-CU access without breaking isolation.

PubKey-Based: PCO generates a random secret S, encrypts K1 as masked_k1 = Enc(S, K1). It splits S into 2-of-3 Shamir shares: S_share1, S_share2, S_share3, and encrypts each using the respective CU's public key:

- enc_share1 = ECIES_Enc(S_share1, CU1_pub), etc.

PCO syncs the full object masked_k1 || enc_share1 || enc_share2 || enc_share3. In non-isolation mode, PCO uses CU1 and CU2's private keys to decrypt two shares, reconstructs S, decrypts K1, and stores it. CU2 alone cannot decrypt without additional share. PCO ensures secure multi-CU access.

3. *Non-Cluster (CU Extract/Insert) - M = 1/M = 2 Cases:*

In this non-cluster scenario, the goal is to extract/insert a CU's key locally, ensuring isolation from other CUs without involving the PCO. CU1 creates K1, with attributes: owner = "CU1", and is assumed to be under path m/1/0. The nonce-based approach uses HD-derived transport keys, while the public-key approach uses EC key pairs. M = 2 additionally enforces token-based multi-user approval.

Nonce-Based: CU1 derives cu1_nonce = CKDpriv(k_1, c_1, 0)[0], computes K_CU1 = PBKDF2(mk || cu1_nonce), and encrypts K1 as masked_k1 = Enc(K_CU1, K1). Extraction is gated by M = 1 or M = 2 token auth, and insertion uses insertMaskedObject. CU2 cannot access K1; CU1 fully manages it.

PubKey-Based: CU1 encrypts K1 with its public key using ECIES: masked_k1 = ECIES_Enc(K1, CU1_pub). Extraction uses M = 1 or M = 2 token auth, and insertion is done using CU1's private key. CU2 cannot decrypt K1; CU1 retains exclusive control.

CU Isolation from Other CUs and PCOs. This mechanism extends CU isolation by preventing both other CUs and the PCO from accessing a CU's key K1, ensuring only the CU that created it can manage it. It enforces strict isolation within the same partition or cluster. The nonce-based approach uses HD-derived transport keys, with the PCO denied access to nonce derivation paths. The public-key approach uses unique EC key pairs, where the private key remains inaccessible to the PCO. HSM policy enforces this segregation, allowing encrypted object sync without revealing CU secrets.

1. *Cluster (PCO Extract/Insert) $M = 1$ (Simple Case):*
   In this scenario, the goal is to sync a CU's key with $M = 1$, ensuring it remains inaccessible to other CUs and the PCO. CU1 creates K1, with attributes `owner = "CU1"`, under path m/1/0. The nonce-based approach encrypts K1 using a nonce-derived key; the public-key approach uses CU1's EC public key. PCO performs blind sync without decryption.
   Nonce-Based: CU1 derives `cu1_nonce = CKDpriv(k_1, c_1, 0)[0]`, computes `K_CU1 = PBKDF2(mk || cu1_nonce)`, and encrypts K1 as `masked_k1 = Enc(K_CU1, K1)`. PCO syncs `masked_k1` using `extractMaskedObject` and `insertMaskedObject`, without nonce access. Receiver HSM decrypts with K_CU1 upon CU1 authentication. CU2 and PCO cannot access K1.
   PubKey-Based: CU1 encrypts K1 using ECIES: `masked_k1 = ECIES_Enc(K1, CU1_pub)`. PCO syncs this blindly without CU1's private key. Receiver decrypts using CU1's private key. CU2 and PCO cannot access K1.

2. *Cluster (PCO Extract/Insert) $M = 2$ (M-of-N Case):*
   Similar to $M = 1$, except CU1 wraps K1 locally after $M = 2$ token auth. PCO performs blind sync without key access.
   Nonce-Based: After $M = 2$ auth, CU1 derives `cu1_nonce = CKDpriv(k_1, c_1, 0)[0]`, computes `K_CU1 = PBKDF2(mk || cu1_nonce)`, and wraps K1 as `masked_k1 = Enc(K_CU1, K1)`. PCO syncs it without nonce access.
   PubKey-Based: After $M = 2$ auth, CU1 encrypts K1 as `masked_k1 = ECIES_Enc(K1, CU1_pub)`. PCO syncs it blindly; only CU1 can decrypt. CU2 and PCO remain isolated.

3. *Non-Cluster (CU Extract/Insert) $M = 1/M = 2$ Cases:*
   In this non-cluster setup, CU1 extracts/inserts its key K1 locally with $M = 1$ or $M = 2$ authorization. Attributes: `owner = "CU1"`, path m/1/0. PCO is not involved.
   Nonce-Based: CU1 derives `cu1_nonce = CKDpriv(k_1, c_1, 0)[0]`, computes `K_CU1 = PBKDF2(mk || cu1_nonce)`, encrypts K1 as `masked_k1 = Enc(K_CU1, K1)`. Extraction/insertion is done locally with token auth if $M = 2$. CU2 cannot access K1.
   PubKey-Based: CU1 encrypts K1 as `masked_k1 = ECIES_Enc(K1, CU1_pub)`. It extracts and inserts locally, using its private key. CU2 has no access.

5.4 Security Analysis

This section analyzes how nonce-based and public-key approaches mitigate key vulnerabilities in cluster HSM exploits, focusing on key exposure, user re-registration, and M-of-N bypass (e.g., plaintext extraction depends on specific API behavior).

Key Exposure via Shared Masking Key in HSM Cluster Sync. The legacy shared masking key allows any CU to decrypt synced keys, exposing them cluster-wide. Both proposed approaches eliminate this, restricting decryption solely to the CU that created the object.

Nonce-Based: Objects are locked to CU-specific nonces (e.g., `cu1_nonce = CKDpriv(k_1, c_1, 0)[0]`), so `K_CU1 = PBKDF2(mk || cu1_nonce)`. CU2's m/1/1 or PCO's m/0/x path cannot derive `K_CU1`, and `insertMaskedObject` fails without it.

PubKey-Based: CU1 encrypts K1 using `CU1_pub`. Only `CU1_priv` can decrypt; `insertMaskedObject` fails for CU2 or PCO, ensuring isolation.

User Re-registration Key Theft. Legacy systems allow new CUs to reuse old masked objects via the same masking key. These approaches prevent that with per-CU identifiers.

Nonce-Based: Each CU uses a unique `m/1/x` path. Nonces derived from different paths (e.g., `m/1/1`) yield different transport keys. Old masked objects tied to `m/1/0` are invalid for the new CU.

PubKey-Based: A new EC key pair is generated per CU. Once a CU is deleted, its EC key is destroyed, rendering its old masked objects undecryptable.

M-of-N Provisioning Bypass via Attribute Misconfiguration. Attribute-based control allows misuse (e.g., a single CU bypassing M-of-N policies). These approaches bind keys to CUs at the cryptographic level.

Nonce-Based: Each share is encrypted with a CU-specific key (e.g., `K_CU1 = PBKDF2(mk || CKDpriv(k_1, c_1, 0)[0])`). `insertMaskedObject` fails without required shares. Shamir splits enforce M-of-N [11].

PubKey-Based: Each share is encrypted with the corresponding `CU_pub`. `insertMaskedObject` fails without the required `CU_priv` keys. M-of-N is enforced via ECIES-encrypted Shamir shares [11].

6 Performance Evaluation

We evaluate our nonce-based and public-key-based approaches for object synchronization in HSM clusters against the traditional shared masking key (mk) method, which is critical for High Availability (HA). Extract, insert, and sync times highlight trade-offs—traditional mk prioritizes speed, while our solutions enhance security with minimal performance overhead.

Setup: We simulated a 4-partition HSM cluster on a 2 GHz HSM (2M cycles/sec) with 256-bit operations and 4-core parallelism. The mk approach uses AES-KWP; the nonce-based approach uses HMAC-SHA256(mk || `cu_nonce`) + AES-KWP; and the public-key-based approach uses ECIES hybrid encryption (ECDH using `secp256k1` or `Curve25519`, with AES-GCM). Clusters sync one object at a time.

6.1 Single Key Evaluation

Analysis: The mk approach is the fastest at 0.10 μs extract/insert (200 cycles), totaling 0.22 μs including 0.02 μs simulated coordination, but it suffers from key exposure due to the shared masking key. The nonce-based approach takes 0.42 μs for extract and insert (HMAC-SHA256 0.32 μs + AES-KWP 0.10 μs on both ends), totaling 0.86 μs— 3× slower than mk, adding 0.64 μs for CU isolation. ECIESsecp256k1 takes 100.70 μs extract (201,400 cycles) and 115.00 μs insert (230,000 cycles), totaling 215.72 μs. ECIESCurve25519 is faster, with 28.90 μs extract (57,800 cycles) and 33.00 μs insert (66,000 cycles), totaling 61.92 μs. Compared to mk, ECIES introduces a 280×980× slowdown for robust isolation.

Approach	Extract Time (μs)	Insert Time (μs)	Sync Time (μs)
Traditional (mk)	0.10	0.10	0.22
Nonce-Based	0.42	0.42	0.86
ECIESsecp256k1	100.70	115.00	215.72
ECIESCurve25519	28.90	33.00	61.92

6.2 Key and Attributes Evaluation

Analysis: The mk method achieves 6.40 μs for extract and insert (12,800 cycles), totaling 12.82 μs. Nonce-based performs similarly: 6.72 μs for extract and insert (HMAC-SHA256 0.32 μs + AES-KWP 6.4 μs), totaling 13.46 μs— only 0.64 μs (5%) higher than mk. For ECIES, symmetric wrapping adds attribute-handling overhead: - secp256k1 totals 107.10 μs extract and 121.40 μs insert, for 228.90 μs total. - Curve25519 totals 35.30 μs extract and 39.40 μs insert, for 74.90 μs total.

Compared to mk, ECIESCurve25519 is 5.84x slower, and ECIESsecp256k1 is 17.85x slower. These results show that while ECIES ensures stronger CU isolation, nonce-based remains the most efficient secure option in key+attribute sync scenarios.

Approach	Extract Time (μs)	Insert Time (μs)	Sync Time (μs)
Traditional (mk)	6.40	6.40	12.82
Nonce-Based	6.72	6.72	13.46
ECIESsecp256k1	107.10	121.40	228.90
ECIESCurve25519	35.30	39.40	74.90

7 Comparison Between Nonce-Based and Public-Key-Based Approaches

In this section, we compare our proposed nonce-based and public-key-based approaches for managing HSM cluster keys. We analyze their integration ease, trade-offs, and limitations, and evaluate their effectiveness in addressing key management vulnerabilities.

- The nonce-based approach initializes with a master seed and mk, deriving unique per-CU nonces (e.g., cu1_nonce = CKDpriv(k_1, c_1, 0)[0]) where (k_1, c_1) comes from the seed. Symmetric masking uses PBKDF2(mk || cu1_nonce) [3]. Secure transfer of just the master seed and mk suffices for deterministic regeneration across the cluster. The public-key approach assigns EC key pairs (e.g., secp256k1 or Curve25519) per CU [6], eliminating seed management. It uses ECIES to encrypt keys and only requires cloning mk for auxiliary symmetric operations.
- Ownership proof differs sharply. Nonce-based masked objects (e.g., masked_k1 = Enc(PBKDF2(mk || cu1_nonce), K1)) lack external verifiability—there's no digital signature, and verification requires internal CU metadata. Public-key objects can be signed using a CU's private key (e.g., CU1_priv) and verified externally via CU1_pub, enabling independent cryptographic ownership validation.
- Sharing mechanics distinguish the two. In the nonce-based model, CU-to-CU transfer of keys (e.g., CU1 to CU2) requires mediation—either HSM or PCO rewraps K1 under CU2's derived key. In the public-key model, CU1 directly encrypts K1 with CU2_pub, enabling peer-to-peer transfer without intermediaries.
- Both approaches support M-of-N policies. In the nonce-based approach, cluster $M = 2$ sync uses a random secret split into 2-of-3 Shamir shares [11], encrypted under CU nonce-derived keys; decryption requires any two shares. The public-key approach performs similar splitting, but each share is encrypted using the respective CU's public key (e.g., Enc(CU2_pub, share2)), enforcing M-of-N access asymmetrically. For non-cluster $M = 2$, both rely on token-based approval: nonce-based uses CU-authenticated wrapping; public-key-based requires CU's private key for unwrap.
- Rotation differs: rotating mk or the master seed in the nonce-based system disrupts derivation and requires cluster downtime. In contrast, the public-key approach supports independent CU and PCO key rotation with no downtime, allowing continuous availability.

8 Conclusion

This paper uncovers critical flaws in HSM cluster key management, where a partition-unique masking key—shared across all users and used by the PCO to encrypt all cluster objects—breaks user isolation, enabling attacks that allow unauthorized access to CU keys during cluster sync and M-of-N bypass via attribute misconfigurations [1,2,5]. Our local replication of major cloud HSM architectures (detailed in the appendix) confirms the feasibility of these exploits across existing implementations. We propose two robust solutions: a nonce-based approach leveraging HD wallet-derived, path-restricted transport keys [3], and a public-key-based model employing unique, independent EC key pairs per user [6]. Both approaches enforce user-specific key encryption across clusters-restoring *CU isolation from other CUs*, and, where applicable, *CU isolation from CUs and PCOs*, securing key transport, and reinforcing M-of-N integrity. These solutions directly address systemic weaknesses in current shared masking key designs and offer a practical blueprint for hardening HSM clusters.

A Full Attack Demonstrations

Below are demonstrations of critical attacks on cluster HSMs using a shared Masking Key, replicated to mirror cloud setups.

A.1 Attack 1: Key Exposure via Shared Masking Key

In HSM clusters, a shared Masking Key (kh 1) syncs keys across partitions, accessible to all users via PCO-managed replication-intended for seamless sharing but fatally flawed. The extractMaskedObject API wraps keys with kh 1, and insertMaskedObject unwraps them-any CU can import these objects, then use wrapKey and aesWrapUnwrap (AES-KWP) with a controlled key (e.g., kh 4) to extract plaintext, bypassing authorization. This eliminates CU isolation-a single kh 1 becomes a backdoor, risking total key compromise cluster-wide.

Attack: CU2 generates K1 (kh 7604, 81bb 9df0 3a4d 22f7 0846 6f32 a49f 37fc) with genSymKey -s 16 -l aes -t 31. CU2 extracts it via extractMaskedObject -o 7604 -out 7604_masked_object. CU1 inserts with insertMaskedObject -f 7604_masked_object (kh 3110), wraps with wrapKey -k 3110 -w 4 -m 4 -out 3110_wrap_4, and unwraps last 24 bytes using aesWrapUnwrap -w 4 -f last_24.bin -m 0 -mech 1 -out 3110_key_buf, yielding K1 plaintext-masked objects float free for any CU.

```
1   # CU2: genSymKey -s 16 -l aes -t 31
2   Key kh: 7604 (81bb 9df0 3a4d 22f7 0846 6f32 a49f 37fc)
3   # CU2: extractMaskedObject -o 7604 -out 7604
        _masked_object
4   Object written to "7604_masked_object"
5   # CU1: insertMaskedObject -f 7604_masked_object
6   New kh: 3110
7   # CU1: wrapKey -k 3110 -w 4 -m 4 -out 3110_wrap_4
8   Key Wrapped to "3110_wrap_4"
9   # CU1: aesWrapUnwrap -w 4 -f last_24.bin -m 0 -mech 1 -
        out 3110_key_buf
10  Result: 81bb 9df0 3a4d 22f7 0846 6f32 a49f 37fc
```

A.2 Attack 2: Plaintext Key Extraction via Exposed APIs

The `aesWrapUnwrap` API, meant for AWS KMS wrapping (AES-KWP), outputs plaintext keys to user buffers, misusing key-wrapping as data decryption. This violates PKCS#11-keys should export wrapped, not raw-yet any CU with access can extract synced or wrapped keys in plaintext, breaching HSM confidentiality and exposing all key material cluster-wide-a flaw needing urgent API removal.

Attack: CU2 creates K1 (kh 7604, 81bb...37fc) and K2 (kh 2404) with `genSymKey -s 16 -l aes -t 31`. CU2 wraps K1 with K2 via `wrapKey -k 7604 -w 2404 -m 4 -out key.file`, unwraps last 24 bytes with `aesWrapUnwrap -w 2404 -f last_24.bin -m 0 -mech 1 -out actual_key.file`, exposing K1 plaintext at the console-a catastrophic security lapse.

```
1  # CU2: genSymKey -s 16 -l aes -t 31 (K1)
2  Key kh: 7604 (81bb 9df0 3a4d 22f7 0846 6f32 a49f 37fc)
3  # CU2: genSymKey -s 16 -l aes -t 31 (K2)
4  Key kh: 2404
5  # CU2: wrapKey -k 7604 -w 2404 -m 4 -out key.file
6  Key Wrapped to "key.file"
7  # CU2: aesWrapUnwrap -w 2404 -f last_24.bin -m 0 -mech 1
       -out actual_key.file
8  Result: 81bb 9df0 3a4d 22f7 0846 6f32 a49f 37fc
```

A.3 Attack 3: User Re-registration Key Theft

Lack of CU isolation lets masked objects persist with usernames via `extractMaskedObjectWithUserInfo` (kh 1). Attackers collect these, track deletions with `listUsers`, re-register usernames, and insert objects with `insertMaskedObjectWithUserInfo` to recover zeroized keys-exploiting no invalidation post-deletion. This keeps keys alive indefinitely, risking exposure across user lifetimes.

Attack: "crypto_user200" extracts kh 3218 with `extractMaskedObjectWithUserInfo -o 3218 -out 3218_info`. CO deletes it via `deleteUser -u CU -n crypto_user200`. Attacker re-registers with `createUser -u CU -s crypto_user200 -p user12345`, inserts 3218_info using `insertMaskedObjectWithUserInfo -f 3218_info`, recovering kh 8578-keys persist post-deletion for re-use. Even though some HSM vendors provide masking key rotation, it doesn't fix this vulnerability as masking key rotation causes cluster downtime, and it is practically infeasible to rotate the masking key after each user deletion.

```
1  # _crypto_user200: extractMaskedObjectWithUserInfo -o
       3218 -out 3218_info
2  Object written to "3218_info"
3  # _cc: deleteUser -u CU -n crypto_user200
4  User deleted
5  # _cc: createUser -u CU -s crypto_user200 -p user12345
6  New user registered
```

```
7  # _crypto_user200: insertMaskedObjectWithUserInfo -f
      3218_info
8  New kh: 8578
```

A.4 Attack 4: M-of-N Bypass via Attribute Misconfiguration

HSM's M-of-N splits duties with MANAGE_KEY (encrypt/sign) and USE_KEY (wrap/unwrap). MANAGE_KEY $M = 2$ doesn't block wrap/unwrap, letting one CU bypass M-of-N with kh 1. USE_KEY $M = 2$ restricts wrap/unwrap but not extract/insert, enabling duplication exploitable solo if misconfigured-subverting secure multi-CU provisioning for firmware signing or UTXOs.

Attack: CU11 sets a key with USE_KEY $M = 2$ (kh 8302) via genSymKey -s 16 -l aes -t 31 -use_key_mvalue 2 -users crypto_user12,crypto_user13. CU11 extracts with extractMaskedObjectWithUserInfo -o 8302 -out 8302_extract, inserts as kh 4512 with insertMaskedObjectWithUserInfo -f 8302_extract, wraps via wrapKey -k 4512 -w 4 -m 4 -out 4512_wrap, unwraps solo with aesWrapUnwrap -w 4 -f last_24.bin -m 1 -mech 1 -out key.file, exposing plaintext (e65b...c8a0)-$M = 2$ fails.

```
1   # CU11: genSymKey -s 16 -l aes -t 31 -use_key_mvalue 2 -
       users crypto_user12,crypto_user13
2   Key kh: 8302
3   # CU11: extractMaskedObjectWithUserInfo -o 8302 -out
       8302_extract
4   Object written to "8302_extract"
5   # CU11: insertMaskedObjectWithUserInfo -f 8302_extract
6   New kh: 4512
7   # CU11: wrapKey -k 4512 -w 4 -m 4 -out 4512_wrap
8   Key Wrapped to "4512_wrap"
9   # CU11: aesWrapUnwrap -w 4 -f last_24.bin -m 1 -mech 1 -
       out key.file
10  Result: e65b 29c0 3396 0c0f 0095 3aa3 53f3 d307...
```

A.5 Special Mention: aesWrapUnwrap Collapse

aesWrapUnwrap reduces HSM security to a password guess-a CU exports owned keys in plaintext (Attack 2) or others' via masked objects (Attack 1). Attackers with stolen objects need one password to unwrap all keys cluster-wide. Shared KEK (kh 4) worsens it-unwraps without auth, bypassing controls. This flaw-plaintext from a wrapping API-collapses HSM integrity into a fragile shell.

References

1. Amazon Web Services: AWS CloudHSM user guide. AWS documentation, latest version as of 2025; Marvell Technology, Inc.: LiquidSecurity HSM Datasheet. Marvell, latest version as of 2025 (2025)
2. Microsoft corporation: Azure dedicated HSM overview. Microsoft Learn, latest version as of 2025 (2025)
3. Wuille, P.: Hierarchical deterministic wallets. Bitcoin Improvement Proposal 32, (2012). https://github.com/bitcoin/bips/blob/master/bip-0032.mediawiki
4. Checkoway, S., et al.: On the practical exploitability of dual EC in TLS implementations. In: Proceedings of the 23rd USENIX Security Symposium (2014)
5. Chen, X., et al.: Attacking the TrustZone: a practical approach to exploit ARM TrustZone. In: Proceedings of the 26th USENIX Security Symposium (2017)
6. IEEE STD 1363a-2004: Standard Specifications for Public Key Cryptography - Amendment 1: Additional Techniques. Institute of Electrical and Electronics Engineers (2004)
7. National institute of standards and technology: Security requirements for cryptographic modules. In: FIPS PUB, pp. 140–143 (2019)
8. Dworkin, M.: Recommendation for Block Cipher Modes of Operation: Methods for Key Wrapping, SP 800–38F. National Institute of Standards and Technology, Special Publication (2012)
9. Barker, E., et al.: Recommendation for Key Management, Part 1: General. National Institute of Standards and Technology, Special Publication, pp. 800–857 (2016)
10. RSA security Inc.: PKCS #11 cryptographic token interface base specification version 2.40. OASIS Standard (2015)
11. Shamir, A.: How to share a secret. Commun. ACM **22**(11), 612–613 (1979)
12. Thales group: Luna network HSM product guide. Thales customer support portal, latest version as of 2025 (2025)
13. Yun, H. J., Kim, I., Kim, S., Son, S., Han, D.: Scalable and secure virtualization of HSM with ScaleTrust. IEEE/ACM Trans. Netw. **31**(4), 1595–1610 (2023). https://doi.org/10.1109/TNET.2022.3220427
14. Utimaco: U.Trust General Purpose HSM Se-Series Datasheet. Utimaco Technical Documentation (2024). https://go.utimaco.com/l/848133/2024-04-17/3ld3sv/848133/1713340754fcnmfM7d/u.trust_GP_HSM_Se_Series_Datasheet_EN.pdf

AcouListener: An Inaudible Acoustic Side-Channel Attack on AR/VR Systems

Fengliang He[1], Hong-Ning Dai[1(✉)], Hanyang Guo[2], Xiapu Luo[3], and Jiadi Yu[4]

[1] Hong Kong Baptist University, Kowloon Tong, Kowloon, Hong Kong
hndai@ieee.org
[2] Sun Yat-sen University, Zhuhai, Guangdong, China
[3] The Hong Kong Polytechnic University, Hung Hom, Kowloon, Hong Kong
[4] Shanghai Jiao Tong University, Minhang District, Shanghai, China

Abstract. Although augmented reality (AR) and virtual reality (VR) systems have garnered extensive attention from both industry and academia, their built-in sensors continuously collect sensitive user data, making them potential targets for malicious attacks. To assess the threat of inaudible acoustic channels in AR/VR, we propose AcouListener, a novel side-channel attack that uses inaudible acoustic signals emitted and received by off-the-shelf VR headsets or mobile phones. Variations in the acoustic channel caused by hand movements allow attackers to reconstruct user input (e.g., passwords). AcouListener is implemented as a camouflaged mobile app that runs on AR/VR or mobile platforms. We evaluate it across three common VR attack scenarios: (1) inferring victims' unlocking patterns, (2) handwriting patterns and (3) typing words and passwords on virtual keyboards. AcouListener achieves an average F1-score of 84%, 95% and 80%, respectively. Furthermore, we present countermeasures against this inaudible acoustic attack.

Keywords: Side-channel Attacks · Augmented Reality · Virtual Reality

1 Introduction

Recent advances in augmented reality (AR) and virtual reality (VR) technologies provide users with immersive interactions and experiences in seamless physical-virtual worlds. These technologies are proliferating across diverse industrial sectors, such as gaming, education, smart manufacturing, and healthcare [13,15,28,31]. The commercially available off-the-shelf (COTS) VR headsets (such as the Meta Quest Series, HTC Vive and Bytedance Pico) typically feature Head-Mounted Displays (HMDs) for immersive visuals and controllers for interactive tracking, facilitated by various sensors such as speakers and microphones.

However, while these multi-channel sensors provide users with an immersive experience, they also increase the potential side-channel attack surface for privacy and security on AR/VR systems [31]. For example, an attacker can use cameras (video channels) to monitor a VR user's hand movement, allowing them to infer input on the virtual keyboard (such as login passwords, browsing URLs, etc.) [12,

(a) Adversary's mobile phone emitting (b) Adversary's HMD emitting (c) Malware of victim's HMD emitting (d) Malicious website emitting

Fig. 1. Four types of side-channel acoustic attacks in AR/VR scenarios.

37]. Similarly, other side channels, such as VR device motion sensors [22,30,36], connected Wi-Fi [4], or external IR [26] or mmWave [24], can also compromise user privacy via the tracked controller. These attacks pose serious security risks, including sensitive information leakage, spoofed accounts, stolen identities, and social network leakage. Therefore, it is crucial to comprehensively understand the side-channel threats to AR/VR systems so as to design effective countermeasures to promptly remedy the vulnerabilities.

In this paper, we investigate emerging threats in AR/VR systems by conducting a concealed active side-channel attack through inaudible acoustic signals. We refer to this attack system as AcouListener, which can be easily launched using built-in microphones and speakers in COTS VR headsets or mobile phones, requiring minimal hardware and software support. In this attack, a speaker emits inaudible acoustic signals that are imperceptible to human ears. When a victim moves their hands in an AR/VR scenario, the resulting variations in the acoustic channel can be captured by a nearby concealed mobile phone or AR/VR device. Notably, different hand movements produce distinct acoustic responses, each with unique characteristics. By processing the received signals, the adversary can recover gestures for privacy intrusion. Figure 1 depicts four typical attack scenarios of AcouListener (more details given in § 3). For example, when a VR user holds controllers to input information (such as handwriting or virtual keyboard typing), local or remote attackers emitting inaudible sounds can capture variants in the acoustic channel caused by hand movements, thus inferring sensitive information (such as the device's unlock password). However, it is *non-trivial* to implement AcouListener, which requires overcoming the following challenges.

Challenge 1: Attack Concealment. Existing methods often rely on external devices (e.g., cameras [12], radar [24], Leap Motion [26]) that are visible and easily detected. Designing a stealthy attack channel using only built-in COTS hardware requires careful design, particularly for broad applicability.

Challenge 2: Capturing Motion Patterns. In-air gestures in AR/VR are unconstrained and motion-induced acoustic disturbances are weak and easily masked by environmental noise, making passive and low-frequency active sensing unreliable. Accurately capturing these subtle channel variations remains technically challenging.

Challenge 3: Lightweight and Deployable Design. While high performance devices (e.g., high-power audio systems) may offer better signal quality, they are typically less accessible or portable. Building a low-power, efficient sensing and inference pipeline that runs on COTS devices without dedicated modifications is essential for practical deployment.

To address these challenges, we design AcouListener with three key components (detailed in § 4): (1) *Acoustic Transceiver.* We emit high-frequency acoustic signals (above 18 kHz), which are inaudible to humans, ensuring attack concealment. (2) *Channel Estimator.* We employ the channel impulse response (CIR) method to capture fine-grained motion patterns. Compared to Doppler and Frequency Modulated Continuous Wave (FMCW) techniques, the CIR has demonstrated state-of-the-art performance in gesture recognition [20]. (3) *Hand-Movement Recognizer.* We use well-trained deep convolutional neural networks (CNNs) that require minimal computational and storage resources, enabling lightweight and portable deployment. We develop the whole system as a camouflaged mobile application (app), which can be deployed to mobile phones or VR devices with a compact size (around 70 MB). To further verify the effectiveness of this easily overlooked attack, we conduct extensive experiments in three attack scenarios (detailed in § 5). Results show that AcouListener achieves an average F1-score of 84% for unlocking pattern recognition, 95% for handwriting, and 80% for word typing. In addition, we propose countermeasures to mitigate such an attack (discussed in § 7). Moreover, we also provide countermeasures to mitigate such an attack (detailed in § 7). In summary, we highlight the following contributions of this paper.

- **Novel Side-Channel Attack Vector.** We demonstrate that adversaries can actively launch a side-channel attack in AR/VR using built-in microphones and speakers to infer user behaviors. This covert attack is largely imperceptible to victims, as it operates primarily through an inaudible acoustic channel.
- **Customized Attack Design.** We develop an attack system as a camouflaged mobile application that can be seamlessly deployed on various AR/VR devices or nearby mobile phones. By leveraging a lightweight CNN model trained on CIR graphs that capture human gesture patterns, the app can accurately recognize a wide range of victim gestures from the received acoustic signals.
- **Comprehensive Evaluations.** We conduct extensive experiments across three representative attack scenarios commonly found in AR/VR applications. Experimental results confirm the effectiveness of this concealed acoustic side-channel attack, for example, achieving a 96% F1-score in handwritten numbers recognition. In addition, we propose countermeasures to mitigate this attack.

2 Background, Motivation, and Related Work

Acoustic Side-Channel Leakage. Modern AR/VR devices and mobile phones are typically equipped with speakers and microphones to enable immersive human-computer interaction. However, improper permission configurations can introduce a hidden risk of *acoustic side-channel leakage* [11]. Notably, COTS speakers can emit high-frequency acoustic signals (e.g., above 20 kHz) that are inaudible to most adults (typically below 17 kHz [18]), yet highly sensitive to ambient disturbances caused by human movement. When such signals interact with moving objects like hands or fingers, the resulting variations can be captured by microphones and analyzed, enabling accurate gesture recognition using deep CNNs [20,35]. Since the CIR characterizes signal fading, scattering, and delay in the channel [6], the differential CIR (dCIR), defined as $dCIR(t_1) = CIR(t_1) - CIR(t_0)$ (between t_0 and t_1), can be used to model motion-induced channel variations for gesture recognition tasks [20].

Motivation. Most COTS AR/VR devices and mobile phones have microphones and speakers, enabling gesture inference from acoustic channels. These facts naturally raise the question: *Can inaudible acoustic signals be leveraged for a concealed side-channel attack?* To explore this, we investigate (1) how to accurately infer common gestures and (2) which scenarios are vulnerable. To the best of our knowledge, this is the first study to report an *active attack* on the inaudible acoustic side-channel of AR/VR systems to infer private inputs (e.g., unlocking patterns, handwriting, and typing). This attack is distinct from prior mobile-based approaches, as it targets immersive AR/VR settings where users wear HMDs and draw in the air with controllers-scenarios not replicable on standard mobile devices. Compared to earlier acoustic gesture recognition on phones [34,38], AcouListener expands the motion range from 10 cm to 3060 cm, enabling large-scale motion tracking with power-limited devices. We hope this study raises awareness of such hidden risks in the AR/VR community to prevent potential privacy breaches.

Related Work. We survey related work on side-channel attacks targeting AR/VR devices through various approaches.

(1) *Acoustic-Based Activity Recognition.* Content inference via acoustics has been studied [7]. Passive methods such as Keylistener [21], Acoustictype [25], and WordRecorder [8] rely on microphones to capture typing or writing sounds, making it inapplicable to in-air AR/VR typing. Active approaches emit sound to track fingers or short-range hand gestures [34,35,38]. However, they mainly focus on mobile interactions and neglect large-scale hand movements in AR/VR. In contrast, AcouListener reveals that acoustic channels are also capable of capturing large-scale gestures and exposing sensitive information.

(2) *Side-Channel Attacks in AR/VR.* External cameras [12,27] and virtual avatar tracking [32,37] have been used for privacy inference. Motion, optical, and eye-tracking sensors can also leak private data, such as keystrokes and voice content [30,36]. Other side channels, including performance counters [39] and power traces [19], can reveal user activities. Active-signal-based systems reconstruct hand motions via Leap Motion [26], WiFi [1,4], or mmWave [24]. In contrast, AcouListener systematically explores novel inaudible acoustic side-channel risks in AR/VR. Although weak and easily masked by noise, passively captured mechanical button sounds have been used for in-air keystroke inference [23].

In contrast, AcouListener distinguishes itself as an *active* and *inaudible* attack, offering greater robustness to low-frequency noise.

3 Threat Model

Acoustic System. We utilize inaudible sound emitted from AR/VR devices or mobile phones to capture the victim's hand trajectory and infer their inputs. The victim's hand movement may affect the received acoustic signals. The fluctuations of received acoustic signals at the microphones can represent the victim's unique gesture features [17]. Considering signal attenuation, our attack operates within an effective range (detailed in § 6). Moreover, we also assume that the input process is one-time without any input errors or modifications.

Threats. According to different signal sources received by the adversary, we consider two types of side-channel attacks: local attacks and remote attacks. Regarding local attacks, the adversary may sit near the victim (e.g., a public coffee shop) and "hear" the victim's gesture by his/her mobile phone or HMD. In contrast to local attacks, the remote attack can be launched by an infectious malware installed on the victim's HMD or mobile phone, as assumed in many previous studies (e.g., [29,40,41]). Figure 1 summarizes four types of side-channel acoustic attacks in AR/VR scenarios.

Attack 1. As shown in Fig. 1a, the adversary deliberately places his mobile phone on the victim's desk. This phone emits and receives inaudible acoustic signals, enabling the adversary to track the victim's hand movements, such as when she unlocks her HMD.

Attack 2. As shown in Fig. 1b, the adversary sits near the victim in a public setting (e.g., a coffee shop) and uses their own HMD to emit and capture inaudible signals. This allows the adversary to monitor the victim's hand movements, such as typing on a virtual keyboard.

Attack 3. As shown in Fig. 1c, malware installed on the victim's HMD carries out the attack. The malware uses inaudible acoustic signals to monitor fine-grained hand movements, such as writing or drawing in the air.

Attack 4. As shown in Fig. 1d, the attack can also be launched by a malicious WebVR website that can access sensors on the HMD for interaction purposes [36]. In this case, the malicious website infects the victim's HMD, emitting and collecting inaudible acoustic sounds to track the victim's hand movements, such as entering a URL.

Attack Scenarios. Adversaries can launch the above four types of attacks (either locally or remotely) in the following three scenarios.

Scenario 1 (Inferring Unlocking Patterns). Many COTS HMDs utilize unlocking patterns for device access [31], e.g., Meta Quest 2 (MQ-2). In AR/VR, users draw the unlocking pattern in the air using a controller, in contrast to touchscreen input on mobile devices [31]. In this proposed side-channel attack, adversaries capture acoustic fluctuations caused by the victim's hand movements via microphones and infer the unlocking pattern by analyzing the resulting dCIR patterns using deep CNNs.

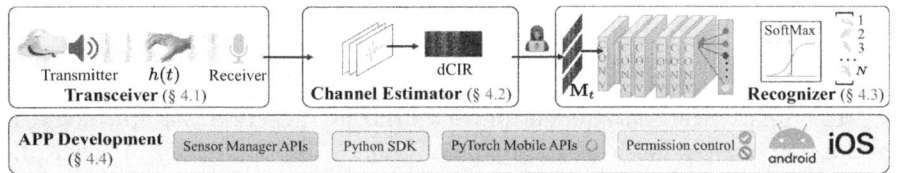

Fig. 2. System overview of AcouListener.

Scenario 2 (Inferring Handwritten Inputs). In AR/VR collaborative applications, such as virtual meetings (e.g., Meta Horizon Workrooms), victims may use an MQ-2 controller to write or draw on a virtual screen. During this process, the resulting acoustic signal variations produce unique dCIR patterns, which can be captured and analyzed (either locally or remotely) by adversaries to infer the written content.

Scenario 3 (Inferring Hand Typing on Keyboards). Typing is another common hand movement. Current VR HMDs provide various input methods [12,36]. For instance, the MQ-2 supports both beam-style and drum-style virtual keyboards. This opens up several attack opportunities: (1) monitoring web activity by capturing inputted URLs, which can be used for profiling or targeted attacks; (2) inferring passwords, including credentials for meetings or games; and (3) recovering typed content such as meeting notes or other sensitive information entered during VR sessions.

4 System Framework

This section details the design of AcouListener, as illustrated in Fig. 2.

4.1 Acoustic Transceiver

Our acoustic transceiver consists of two main functions: transmitting the target signal frames and receiving them for subsequent acoustic feature extraction.

Generation. Figure 3 illustrates five steps for generating the acoustic signal used to detect channel information affected by moving objects (e.g., hand movements via VR controllers). We utilize a 26-bit GSM training sequence, which is widely used in single carrier communication due to its high efficiency in channel estimation and synchronization [20]. Furthermore, a 24-bit zero padding is added to prevent inter-frame interference. Subsequently, the frame is upsampled using replication interpolation, with each element repeated 12 times, resulting in a total of 600 symbols within the signal frame. A low-pass filter with a cut-off frequency of 2 kHz is then applied to eliminate discontinuities, ensuring a smooth signal. Each signal frame takes 12.5 ms to play at a 48 kHz sample rate, allowing for the transmission of 80 frames within 1 s. From these received sequences, 80 dCIR feature graphs can be extracted to characterize the acoustic channel variations associated with object movements. This intensity is sufficient to distinguish between different hand input movements.

Up-Conversion. Speakers integrated into VR devices or mobile phones typically operate at a sampling rate of 48 kHz [18]. According to the Nyquist sampling theorem, the maximum playable frequency can theoretically reach 24 kHz. To enhance the concealment of sound during detection, we up-convert the signal frame to an inaudible band by modulating with $\sqrt{2}\cos(2\pi f_c t)$, where f_c is set to 20 kHz. This process shifts the signal's center frequency to f_c, ensuring it remains within an inaudible frequency range that is imperceptible to adults [18]. Next, we apply an 18-22 kHz band-pass filter (at a 48 kHz sample rate) to the signal to eliminate interference and noise. Finally, we save the sequence S as a Wave file in 16-bit PCM format, preserving high-quality audio data while ensuring compatibility and versatility for playback and processing across various audio applications and devices.

4.2 Channel Estimator

After receiving the reflected signal sequences containing key features of the VR user's hand movements, we segment them into frames and extract channel variations using dCIR graphs.

Demodulation. The signal R is transmitted at a high frequency, with a center frequency of 20 kHz. We down-convert it by modulating with the carrier $\sqrt{2}\cos(2\pi f_c t)$. A low-pass filter with a cutoff frequency of 2 kHz processes the signal. Environmental noises (e.g., voices, music, footsteps, and air-conditioning sounds), typically fall within the low-frequency band [35]. These noises are naturally eliminated through down-conversion and the low-pass filter, enhancing the robustness of our recognition system. To identify the start index and segment the signal into frames containing the 600 training symbols for channel estimation, we calculate the Pearson Correlation Coefficients between the received 1200-bit signal and a 600-bit transmitted signal frame S. The peak of this correlation indicates the start index. The signal is then segmented into target frames, starting from this initial point and cut every 600 data points.

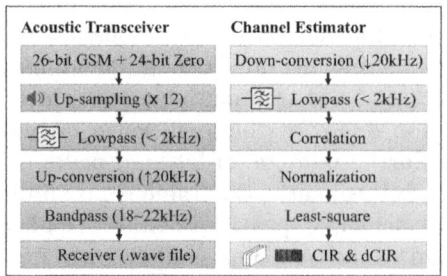

Fig. 3. Audio signals generation, transmission and estimation.

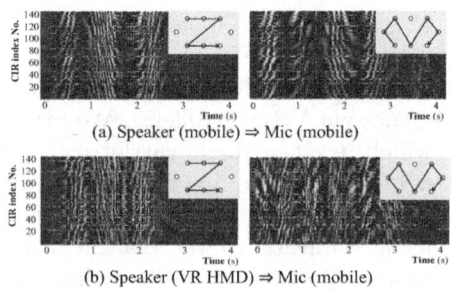

Fig. 4. dCIR patterns under different transceiver settings.

Normalization. The signal received by the microphone is influenced by factors such as the distance between the user's hand and the receiver, obstructions of the sound source, and the level of environmental noise. To address this issue, the keystroke data is normalized by dividing each data point by the maximum value in the dataset. This process compresses the data to a range between 0 and 1, ensuring uniformity and comparability across the dataset.

CIR Estimation. We employ the least squares (LS) channel estimation method, which offers lower computational complexity, to estimate the CIR of the collected signals reflected by the target object (i.e., the hand). The core idea of LS estimation is to derive the CIR, denoted as H, by solving the equation $R = S * H$, where $*$ represents convolution, and S and R are the transmitted and received signals, respectively. To obtain an accurate H, it is essential to have a sufficiently large S, although this may increase computational costs. Specifically, we define the length of the training sequence as $T = P + L$, where L represents the memory length needed to account for multipath effects and P is the reference length used for channel information calculation. Therefore, the training sequence is represented as $S = \{s_1, s_2, \ldots, s_{L+P}\}$, while the calculated CIR sequence is $H = \{h_1, h_2, \ldots, h_L\}$. The received signal sequence is denoted by $R = \{r_1, r_2, \ldots, r_{L+P}\}$. Based on LS channel estimation, the CIR can be obtained using the following equation:

$$\underbrace{\begin{pmatrix} s_1 & s_2 & \cdots & s_L \\ s_2 & s_3 & \cdots & s_{L+1} \\ \vdots & \vdots & \ddots & \vdots \\ s_P & s_{P+1} & \cdots & s_{P+L-1} \end{pmatrix}}_{\text{Training Matrix } \mathbf{M}_t} \cdot \underbrace{\begin{pmatrix} h_1 \\ h_2 \\ \vdots \\ h_L \end{pmatrix}}_{\text{CIR } H} = \underbrace{\begin{pmatrix} r_{L+1} \\ r_{L+2} \\ \vdots \\ r_{L+P} \end{pmatrix}}_{\text{Received Sequence } R}. \tag{1}$$

We then obtain the estimated CIR denoted by $\hat{H}$ as follows,

$$\hat{H} = (\mathbf{M}_t^T \mathbf{M}_t)^{-1} \mathbf{M}_t^T R. \tag{2}$$

In our system, we set $L = 140$ and $P = 172$ to achieve adequate accuracy while maintaining low computational complexity. Each signal frame produces 140 channel taps, reflecting the channel status over a duration of 12.5 ms, resulting in 80 updates per second. The value of dCIR is calculated by subtracting the CIR value of the previous frame from that of the current frame: $\text{dCIR}(t_1) = \text{CIR}(t_1) - \text{CIR}(t_0)$. This value represents the extent of change in the CIR, characterizing channel fluctuations caused by object motion (i.e., hand movements).

Transceiver Setting. Attacks can be launched using various combinations of acoustic transceivers: (1) a VR device as the speaker and a mobile device as the receiver (microphone); (2) a VR device as both the speaker and receiver; (3) a mobile device as the speaker and a VR device as the receiver; and (4) a mobile device as both the speaker and receiver. We conduct preliminary experiments using the first and fourth combinations of experimental settings. The results are presented in Fig. 4. It is evident that different gesture trajectories exhibit unique patterns on the dCIR graph in each scenario. Each gesture corresponds to a distinct trajectory pattern in terms of shape and distribution, which provides a crucial foundation for gesture recognition. By analyzing these patterns, we can extract key features to differentiate between various gestures. Furthermore, the results indicate that different transceiver combinations do not affect the unique dCIR patterns generated by hand movements. Therefore, for simplicity, we primarily consider the fourth combination as the basic setting for our system.

4.3 Hand-Movement Recognizer

The dCIR sequences of the acoustic channel are obtained from the sound signals reflected by the hands of the VR user. To identify and analyze hand movements, we employ a CNN, training it with a series of dCIR sequences (images).

CNN-Based Recognizer. Due to their exceptional performance, deep CNNs have been widely employed in various computer vision tasks [5,9]. After processing the CIR signals, we obtain dCIR sequences, which can effectively be considered as images. We then train a deep CNNs model on these dCIR images to accurately recognize different types of hand movements.

Data Augmentation. One of the challenges in using CNNs in our system is the limited availability of dCIR data for training. To tackle this challenge, we employ data augmentation. Specifically, we apply various image transformation operations, including random rotations, translations, scaling, cropping, and flipping. By applying these random transformations to the obtained dCIR images, we expand the training dataset, increasing both the diversity and quantity of samples. This strategy enables the model to learn from a more varied dataset during training, thereby enhancing its generalization capability and robustness. The system can effectively handle various factors such as gesture speed, distance, and high-frequency noise by using this enriched data to train the final model.

4.4 Camouflaged App Development

To implement the aforementioned processes on mobile devices (e.g., AR/VR HMDs), we develop a camouflaged app that encapsulates the above functional modules, thus enabling its deployment on mobile or AR/VR devices (e.g., Meta Quest Series). Since speakers require no permissions, this app only requests access to the `MICROPHONE` for the collection of inaudible sound data while this permission can be easily obtained by masquerading as a benign application (e.g., video conferencing software) or injection attacks [14]. The recognizer model is developed by using `PyTorch` and saved as a script model by `torch.jit.trace` so that it can perform without relying on the original Python interpreter. We adopt `pytorch_android` API to load the trained model on the Android platform for dCIR images recognition. While our primary focus is on Android development, a similar approach can be applied to iOS or other platforms.

(a) Unlocking   (b) Hand writing   (c) Hand typing

Fig. 5. Experimental Setup.

5 Experiment

We conducted extensive experiments to validate the feasibility of the proposed side-channel attack across different scenarios.

5.1 Experimental Setup

Hardware Devices. In our experiments, we selected the Honor X10 and iPhone 12 Pro as mobile platforms, with the MQ-2 serving as the default VR device, currently one of the most popular VR hardware options available [36]. Generally, AcouListener can be adapted for use with other AR/VR devices by developing similar mobile applications.

Experiment Design. In the attack scenarios, a volunteer sits in a chair at a desk, wears the MQ-2 HMD, and holds controllers in both hands while performing designated hand movements. Simultaneously, a mobile phone (i.e., Honor X10) emits and receives corresponding inaudible audio signals and captures the volunteers' hand movements, as illustrated in Fig. 5. The speed, amplitude, and distance of the volunteers' inputs are tailored to their usage habits (on average, participants complete scenarios 1 and 2 within 3-5 s, and scenario 3 within 6-10 s). The experiments were conducted in a public office room (11 m × 15 m), where there was audible noise interference from the environment (approximately 55 dB), but no moving objects.

Data Collection. We collect a total of 9,400 samples across three attack scenarios. We recruited 10 volunteers in the experiments[1]. They vary in age (20-30 years), height (158-185 cm), and gender (70% males and 30% females). Among them, two participants are familiar with VR devices, while the others had no prior exposure. Before the experiments, we provided the volunteers with essential training to ensure they were comfortable with basic operations. Consistent with prior studies [2,10,33], we employed a training-test split, allocating 80% for training and validation, and 20% for testing. Theoretically, a well-trained model with sufficient data can generalize effectively and perform consistently on new users, just as it does on the test set.

Training CNN Models. We developed a mobile CNN model based on MobileNet V2 for gesture classification tasks (refer to Appendix A for more details). This lightweight and portable model delivers excellent performance on

---

[1] Ethical approval has been obtained (SCI-COMP-2024-25_002).

mobile devices while maintaining efficiency. After being resized to a specified dimension of 224 × 224 pixels with 3 color channels, a dCIR image is then normalized using a mean of [0.485, 0.456, 0.406] and a standard deviation of [0.229, 0.224, 0.225]. To enhance the model's robustness and generalization ability, we apply data augmentation techniques on dCIR images. The model is initialized with a learning rate of 0.001, a batch size of 32, and is trained for 100 epochs using stochastic gradient descent (SGD) as the optimization algorithm.

The trained model with a size of approximately 70 MB, has been deployed on a mobile device as described in § 4.4. Experimental measurements on the Honor X10 smartphone indicate that the model takes approximately 80 ms to predict a dCIR image, thereby meeting practical application requirements.

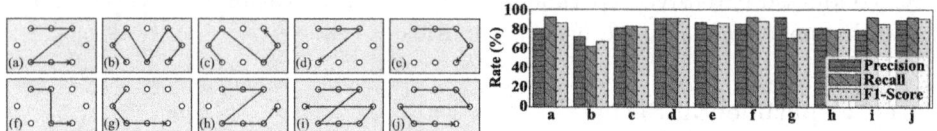

Fig. 6. Top-10 unlocking patterns. **Fig. 7.** 10 unlock patterns results.

5.2 Attack Scenario 1: Unlocking Pattern Inference

Unlocking Action on VR Device. The MQ-2 supports pattern-based unlocking, allowing users to select and connect points on a virtual screen using the controller, as shown in Fig. 6. Each pattern typically includes four to eight points, which can be seen as a direct extension of similar features on mobile phones [31]. During startup or standby, once the controller is paired and activated, a virtual unlocking interface appears. The user moves a cursor using the controller, presses a button to select a point, and continues connecting at least four points. If the drawn pattern matches the preset configuration, the device is successfully unlocked.

Attack Scenario. In this scenario, we assume that the victim, wearing a VR HMD, is seated at a desk attempting to unlock the VR device. Simultaneously, a mobile phone, casually placed on the table, runs a camouflaged (spy) application that continuously sends and receives inaudible sounds. This application utilizes the trained mobile CNN model to recognize the victim's hand gestures. Our objective is to accurately infer the victim's unlock patterns by analyzing the signal changes in the surrounding sound channel.

Experimental Description. As shown in Fig. 6, we invited volunteers to enter 10 different unlocking patterns, which were primarily designed based on the most common unlocking patterns found in the Android system [3]. Each pattern was repeated 50 times, resulting in a total of 1,400 data samples collected.

Attack Results. The result is shown in Fig. 7. The average precision, recall, and F1-score all exceed 84%, indicating an acceptable inference performance for the adversary from the perspective of side-channel attacks. It can be found that pattern j has the highest F1-score (91%). The reason is that the lines in the pattern j are complex enough and require connecting all eight points,

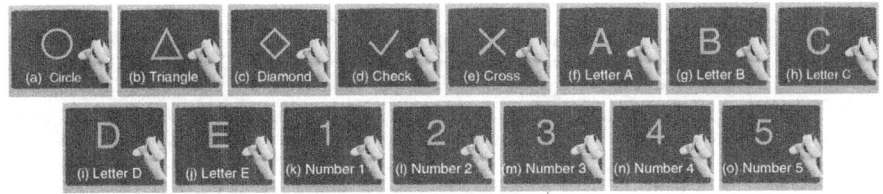

Fig. 8. Handwritten patterns.

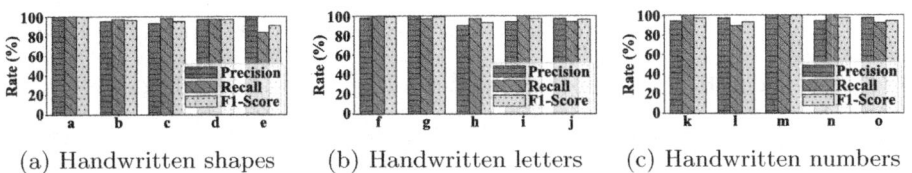

(a) Handwritten shapes (b) Handwritten letters (c) Handwritten numbers

Fig. 9. Recognition of 15 handwritten drawings.

making it significantly different from other patterns observed in the trajectory. While pattern i (F1-score: 85%) also involves eight points, the intertwining of its trajectory increases the similarity between different segments.

5.3 Attack Scenario 2: Hand-Written Content Inference

Handwriting in Virtual Meetings. In VR video conferencing applications, users engage in immersive communication and collaboration. For example, in Horizon Workrooms, a user can write or draw on a virtual whiteboard. In this scenario, the user first designates an area on the physical desk as the virtual whiteboard, then holds and moves the controller like a pen to write on it.

Attack Scenario. We consider a situation where a victim sits at a desk and participates in video conferences on the Horizon Workrooms platform using the MQ-2 device. During the meeting, the victim writes and draws on the virtual whiteboard. A mobile phone running a camouflaged application secretly analyzes the victim's hand movements by emitting and collecting inaudible sounds. By analyzing the acoustic signals, attackers can track the victim's hand movements and recognize the content being written on the virtual whiteboard.

Experimental Description. Each participant sits at their desk, entering the Horizon Workroom virtual conference room through the MQ-2 HMD. Using the hand controllers as pens, they write a series of shapes, letters, and numbers on the table. Figure 8 illustrates the main shapes, letters, and numbers evaluated in our experiments. These drawing actions are rendered in the virtual space as inscriptions on the virtual whiteboard. Meanwhile, the mobile device placed next to the table sends and records inaudible sounds to capture variations in the acoustic signals. In total, 2,550 data samples were collected.

Attack Results. As shown in Fig. 9, the experiment yields an average precision, recall, and F1-score of 95%. Handwritten numbers exhibit the highest score (over 96%) due to their distinct shapes, which distinguish them from each other.

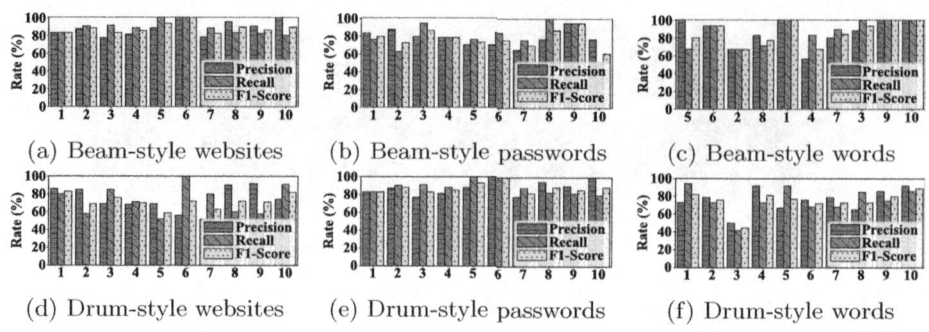

Fig. 10. Recognition of beam-style and drum-style typing.

Furthermore, each type of handwritten pattern achieved an F1-score greater than 90%, demonstrating better recognition performance compared to the recognition of unlock patterns. This may be attributed to the relatively fixed trajectory of handwriting actions, making the patterns easier to capture than unlock patterns.

5.4 Attack Scenario 3: Hand Typing Inference

Besides unlocking patterns and handwriting, typing on virtual keyboards is another common interaction method in VR. We focus on two representative VR typing techniques. *Beam-style Keyboard.* In this method, the user holds a controller that emits a visible virtual beam (e.g., a laser pointer) to select keys on the virtual keyboard by pointing and clicking. *Drum-style Keyboard.* In this method, the controller becomes a drumstick in the virtual environment, used to strike virtual keys in mid-air, resembling the action of drumming but without any physical contact. We consider three types of hand-typing attacks:

(1) Monitoring Web-Surfing Habits. Peeping into MQ-2's keyboard input can reveal the website URLs entered by the user in the browser, thereby allowing for wiretapping their web-surfing habits. When users utilize MQ-2's browser, they must use their hand controller to input various web addresses and search terms on the virtual keyboard. During this process, an adversary can employ inaudible sound to capture the user's hand movements and infer the URLs being entered. Once the adversary successfully obtains this website information, they can deduce the user's browsing preferences, interests, and potentially sensitive data. The misuse of this information could lead to targeted advertising, personal data analysis, or other malicious purposes.

(2) Inferring Passwords. When using the MQ-2, users often need to enter various passwords via the virtual keyboard, such as login credentials or unlocking codes in virtual meetings or games. This input process can present security risks. Attackers can use inaudible sound to capture the user's hand movements and infer the entered password through analysis of these movements. By emitting inaudible sound around the user, attackers can leverage the device's microphone or other sensing techniques to obtain continuous input recognition (CIR) features during the user's hand movements. By analyzing these features, attackers can deduce which keys the user has pressed, thereby guessing the composition and order of the password. This method poses a significant threat to the confidentiality of the user's sensitive information, such as passwords, personal identification numbers (PINs), and other confidential data. If an attacker successfully infers the user's password, they may exploit this information for unauthorized access, theft of sensitive personal information, or identity fraud.

(3) Inferring Words. Similar to typing URLs and passwords, users may also type on a virtual keyboard using beam-style or drum-style inputs. During this process, confidential information may be exposed to attackers who can use inaudible sound to capture changes in dCIR during the user's hand movements and analyze these changes to infer the content being entered. This attack poses a potential threat to the user's input and privacy. Once attackers infer the user's input, they can monitor the user's activities, obtain sensitive information, or engage in other forms of abuse. For instance, if a user is participating in a video conference using the VR device and types important information such as meeting notes on a virtual keyboard, the attacker could infer the user's input and monitor their behavior during the meeting.

Experimental Description. In this experiment, volunteers sit at their desks and type content using the MQ-2 HMD. Table 2 in Appendix B lists the typing contents, which are divided into three scenarios as mentioned above. (1) For the password inference scenario, we selected the top 10 most commonly used passwords[2]. (2) For the keyword inference scenario, we selected the first word from the names of the 10 most popular VR apps[3]. Users typically only need to enter the first word when downloading or searching for an app, making this word a strong indicator of the app they intend to run. (3) For the web-surfing habits inference scenario, we selected the top 10 most popular websites[4] as test subjects. The layout of the virtual keyboard is set to the default QWERTY configuration. A total of 5,450 data samples were collected.

Attack Results. The results are shown in Fig. 10. Across the three types of attacks, the average F1-score for beam-style typing is 84%, while that for drum-style typing is 79%, resulting in an overall average F1-score of 80%.

(1) In website URL inference, beam-style typing (average F1 88%) demonstrates superior performance compared to drum-style typing (average F1 80%). This is primarily due to the longer lengths of website URLs. When using single-hand beam typing, the method better captures continuous trajectories, allowing for more significant differentiation. Further, the keyboard layout plays a crucial role. For instance, when typing facebook.com (average F1 93%) and amazon.com (average F1 89%), a volunteer must move back and forth across the keyboard, resulting in salient hand movements and distinct trajectory differences.

---

[2] https://techcult.com/most-common-passwords/.
[3] https://shardeum.org/blog/best-metaverse-platform/.
[4] https://www.expireddomains.net/alexa-top-websites/.

(2) In password inference, drum-style typing with an average F1-score of 83%, outperforms beam-style typing with an average F1-score of 78%. This difference may be attributed to the short length and proximity of these simple passwords on the keyboard. Shorter input lengths lead to more similar trajectories in single-handed beam-style typing, while the use of both hands in drum-style typing separates the input into two parts, thereby amplifying the differences between them. This input method enhances the ability to distinguish between different typing contents more effectively.

(3) In word inference, beam-style typing (average F1-score: 87%) demonstrates a higher degree of distinguishability compared to drum-style typing (average F1-score: 81%). One possible reason is that the letters forming these words (such as VR app names) are often distributed across different positions on the keyboard, allowing one-handed beam-style typing to produce significantly more distinguishable trajectories. In summary, the overall accuracy of content recognition is influenced not only by the length of the content but also by its specific distribution on the keyboard.

6 Real-World Impact Factors

We summarize the following factors in real-world deployments based on extensive experimental observations and results (detailed in § 5.1).

Environmental Noise. Environmental noises, such as voices, music, footsteps, and air-conditioning sounds, typically fall within the low-frequency band [35]. AcouListener is robust against low-frequency noise because it utilizes only the high-frequency band during transmission and filters out signals below 18 kHz during demodulation (detailed in § 4.2).

Attack Range. The feasibility is experimentally validated within a recognition distance of approximately 1.2 m. Beyond this range, the strength of acoustic signals diminishes rapidly, making them unrecognizable. This limitation is primarily due to the power constraints of portable mobile and AR/VR devices. We propose a future solution for this problem in § 7.2.

Bystanders. We have observed that the movement of bystanders can affect the received acoustic signals, as recognition depends on variations in the acoustic channel caused by moving objects. However, this effect is confined to a limited range (approximately 1.2 m) due to the devices' power limitations. Therefore, we primarily focus on scenarios where their impact is negligible (beyond the attack range), which is typical in home or private settings when using AR/VR.

Inconsistent Position and Posture. AcouListener imposes no strict constraints on the relative position or posture of the victim. While distance affects CIR strength, this effect can be mitigated through normalization (§ 4.2). Variations in angle, posture, hand movement speed, and motion range may deform CIR patterns though data augmentation (§ 4.3) enables the model to handle such distortions.

7 Discussion

7.1 Potential Countermeasures

To defend against various side-channel attacks, we recommend implementing the following countermeasures from both hardware and software perspectives.

Automatic Elimination of Inaudible Sound at 18 kHz. Most AR/VR devices possess advanced audio processing capabilities that operate effectively within the range of human hearing. AR/VR devices need to filter out inaudible sounds with frequencies exceeding 18 kHz.

Secure Your Applications. AR/VR users should ensure that their devices have the latest security updates installed and only download new applications from official app stores (e.g., Meta Store) or other trusted sources.

Restrict Application Permissions. AR/VR users should carefully evaluate permission requests from each application, especially for microphones and sensors, authorizing them only when required [16].

7.2 Limitations

This study still has room for improvement, which we will enhance in future work.

Limited Attack Range. Constrained by AR/VR hardware and the restricted sound propagation, AcouListener has a limited attack range. Future work may use high-power emitters, sensitive microphone arrays and collaborative devices to form distributed sensing systems that expand spatial coverage.

Limited Inference Content. The current framework can only classify straightforward gestures (e.g., unlocking patterns, handwriting letters, and typing words). Future work includes developing more accurate tracking algorithms, incorporating microphone arrays, and exploring multimodal sensor fusion and deep learning techniques to support more diverse hand gestures.

8 Conclusion

In this paper, we investigate a novel inaudible acoustic side-channel attack within emerging AR/VR scenarios. We primarily leverage the unique characteristics of received acoustic signals generated by a victim's hand movements, which reflect inaudible signals emitted by a camouflaged VR device or mobile phone. After processing the received signals into dCIR sequences, we employ a portable deep CNN to effectively extract key features from the collected dCIR images. Moreover, we have developed a user-friendly mobile application that seamlessly integrates the entire system for practical use. Extensive experiments conducted with ten volunteers in three different scenarios have demonstrated that our attack system can accurately infer victims' unlocking patterns, handwriting styles, and typed words across two types of virtual keyboards. Furthermore, we also propose several effective countermeasures to mitigate this new and potentially dangerous acoustic side-channel attack, thereby improving user security in AR/VR.

Acknowledgments. This work is partially supported by HKBU (with no. RC-SFCRG/23-24/R2/SCI/06) and NSFC (with no. 62172277).

Appendix A CNN Model

We have developed an Android-based application (app) to infer hand gestures[5]. Table 1 lists the detailed settings of our adopted MobileNet V2 model.

Table 1. The adopted CNN model structure.

Input	Operator	t	c	n	s
$224^2 \times 3$	conv2d	–	32	1	2
$112^2 \times 32$	bottleneck	1	16	1	1
$112^2 \times 16$	bottleneck	6	24	2	2
$56^2 \times 24$	bottleneck	6	32	3	2
$28^2 \times 32$	bottleneck	6	64	4	2
$14^2 \times 64$	bottleneck	6	96	3	1
$14^2 \times 96$	bottleneck	6	160	3	2
$7^2 \times 160$	bottleneck	6	320	1	1
$7^2 \times 320$	conv2d 1 × 1	–	1280	1	1
$7^2 \times 1280$	avgPool 7 × 7	–	–	1	–
$1 \times 1 \times 1280$	conv2d 1 × 1	–	k	–	–

- t denotes the expansion factor, which is the factor by which the number of channels is expanded in the bottleneck layer.
- c denotes the number of output channels from each layer.
- n denotes the number of repetitions, meaning how many times the operation is repeated.
- s denotes the stride of the convolution or pooling operation.
- k denotes the number of classes ($k = 10$ in Attack Scenario 1 (§ 5.2) and Attack Scenario 3 (§ 5.4); $k = 15$ in Attack Scenario 2 (§ 5.3)).

Appendix B Typing Content

Table 2 lists major typing contents inferred by adversaries in § 5.4.

---

[5] https://github.com/adhakdh/AcouListener.

Table 2. Typing contents.

ID	(1) Websites	(2) Passwords	(3) Words
1	google.com	123456	gym
2	youtube.com	123456789	first
3	baidu.com	qwerty	virtual
4	bilibili.com	password	netflix
5	facebook.com	1234567	bigscreen
6	qq.com	12345678	deovr
7	twitter.com	12345	skybox
8	zhihu.com	iloveyou	fitxr
9	wikipedia.org	111111	vr
10	amazon.com	123123	win

References

1. Ali, K., Liu, A.X., Wang, W., Shahzad, M.: Keystroke Recognition Using WiFi Signals. In: Proceedings of the 21st Annual International Conference on Mobile Computing and Networking, pp. 90–102 (2015)
2. Alla, I., Olou, H.B., Loscrì, V., Levorato, M.: From sound to sight: audio-visual fusion and deep learning for drone detection. In: Proceedings of the 17th ACM Conference on Security and Privacy in Wireless and Mobile Networks (WiSec), pp. 123–133. ACM (2024)
3. Andriotis, P., Oikonomou, G.C., Mylonas, A., Tryfonas, T.: A study on usability and security features of the android pattern lock screen. Inf. Comput. Secur. **24**(1), 53–72 (2016)
4. Arafat, A.A., Guo, Z., Awad, A.: VR-Spy: a side-channel attack on virtual keylogging in VR headsets. In: IEEE Virtual Reality and 3D User Interfaces, VR 2021, Lisbon, Portugal, March 27 – April 1, 2021, pp. 564–572. IEEE (2021)
5. Bae, S.H., Choi, I.K., Kim, N.S.: Acoustic scene classification using parallel combination of LSTM and CNN. In: Proceedings of the Workshop on Detection and Classification of Acoustic Scenes and Events (DCASE), pp. 11–15 (2016)
6. Bai, Y., Lu, L., Cheng, J., Liu, J., Chen, Y., Yu, J.: Acoustic-based sensing and applications: a survey. Comput. Networks **181**, 107447 (2020)
7. Deshotels, L.: Inaudible sound as a covert channel in mobile devices. In: 8th USENIX Workshop on Offensive Technologies (WOOT 14) (2014)
8. Du, H., Li, P., Zhou, H., Gong, W., Luo, G., Yang, P.: Wordrecorder: accurate acoustic-based handwriting recognition using deep learning. In: IEEE Conference on Computer Communications (INFOCOM), pp. 1448–1456 (2018)
9. Espi, M., Fujimoto, M., Kinoshita, K., Nakatani, T.: Exploiting spectro-temporal locality in deep learning based acoustic event detection. EURASIP J. Audio Speech Music Process. **2015**(1), 1–12 (2015). https://doi.org/10.1186/s13636-015-0069-2
10. Fu, C., Du, X., Zeng, Q., Zhao, Z., Zuo, F., Di, J.: Seeing is believing: extracting semantic information from video for verifying IoT events. In: Proceedings of the 17th ACM Conference on Security and Privacy in Wireless and Mobile Networks (WiSec), pp. 101–112. ACM (2024)
11. Genkin, D., Nissan, N., Schuster, R., Tromer, E.: Lend me your ear: Passive remote physical side channels on pcs. In: 31st USENIX Security Symposium, USENIX, pp. 4437–4454. USENIX Association (2022)

12. Gopal, S.R.K., Shukla, D., Wheelock, J.D., Saxena, N.: Hidden reality: caution, your hand gesture inputs in the immersive virtual world are visible to all! In: 32nd USENIX Security Symposium, pp. 859–876. USENIX Association (2023)
13. Guo, H., Dai, H.N., Luo, X., Zheng, Z., Xu, G., He, F.: An empirical study on oculus virtual reality applications: Security and privacy perspectives. In: Proceedings of the IEEE/ACM 46th International Conference on Software Engineering, pp. 1–13 (2024)
14. Huang, W., Tang, W., Chen, H., Jiang, H., Zhang, Y.: Unauthorized microphone access restraint based on user behavior perception in mobile devices. IEEE Trans. Mob. Comput. **23**(1), 955–970 (2024)
15. Kaminska, D., et al.: Virtual reality and its applications in education: survey. Information **10**(10), 318 (2019)
16. Kim, Y., Goutam, S., Rahmati, A., Kaufman, A.E.: Erebus: access control for augmented reality systems. In: 32nd USENIX Security Symposium, USENIX Security 2023, pp. 929–946. USENIX Association (2023)
17. Li, D., Liu, J., Lee, S.I., Xiong, J.: Fm-track: pushing the limits of contactless multi-target tracking using acoustic signals. In: Nakazawa, J., Huang, P. (eds.) SenSys 2020: The 18th ACM Conference on Embedded Networked Sensor Systems, Virtual Event, Japan, November 16–19, 2020, pp. 150–163. ACM (2020)
18. Li, D., Liu, J., Lee, S.I., Xiong, J.: Room-scale hand gesture recognition using smart speakers. In: Proceedings of the 20th ACM Conference on Embedded Networked Sensor Systems (SenSys), pp. 462–475. ACM (2022)
19. Li, J., Meng, Y., Zhan, Y., Zhang, L., Zhu, H.: Dangers behind charging VR devices: hidden side channel attacks via charging cables. IEEE Trans. Inf. Forensics Secur. **19**, 8892–8907 (2024)
20. Ling, K., Dai, H., Liu, Y., Liu, A.X., Wang, W., Gu, Q.: Ultragesture: fine-grained gesture sensing and recognition. IEEE Trans. Mob. Comput. **21**(7), 2620–2636 (2022)
21. Lu, L., et al.: Keylistener: inferring keystrokes on QWERTY keyboard of touch screen through acoustic signals. In: 2019 IEEE Conference on Computer Communications, INFOCOM 2019, Paris, France, April 29 – May 2, 2019, pp. 775–783. IEEE (2019)
22. Luo, S., Hu, X., Yan, Z.: Hololgger: keystroke inference on mixed reality head mounted displays. In: IEEE Conference on Virtual Reality and 3D User Interfaces, VR 2022, Christchurch, New Zealand, March 12–16, 2022, pp. 445–454. IEEE (2022)
23. Luo, S., Nguyen, A., Farooq, H., Sun, K., Yan, Z.: Eavesdropping on controller acoustic emanation for keystroke inference attack in virtual reality. In: The Network and Distributed System Security Symposium (NDSS), vol. 2 (2024)
24. Mei, L., et al.: mmSpyVR: exploiting mmwave radar for penetrating obstacles to uncover privacy vulnerability of virtual reality. Proc. ACM Interact. Mob. Wearable Ubiquitous Technol. **8**(4), 172:1–172:29 (2024)
25. Meteriz-Yidiran, Ü., Yildiran, N.F., Mohaisen, D.: Acoustictype: smartwatch-enabled cross-device text entry method using keyboard acoustics. In: CHI Conference on Human Factors in Computing Systems Extended Abstracts, pp. 352:1–352:7. ACM (2022)
26. Meteriz-Yildiran, Ü., Yildiran, N.F., Awad, A., Mohaisen, D.: A keylogging inference attack on air-tapping keyboards in virtual environments. In: IEEE Conference on Virtual Reality and 3D User Interfaces, VR 2022, Christchurch, New Zealand, March 12–16, 2022, pp. 765–774. IEEE (2022)

27. Nguyen, A., Zhang, X., Yan, Z.: Penetration vision through virtual reality headsets: identifying 360-degree videos from head movements. In: 33rd USENIX Security Symposium. USENIX Association (2024)
28. Pensieri, C., Pennacchini, M.: Overview: virtual reality in medicine. J. Virtual Worlds Res. **7**(1) (2014)
29. Qamar, A., Karim, A., Chang, V.: Mobile malware attacks: review, taxonomy & future directions. Future Gener. Comput. Syst. **97**, 887–909 (2019)
30. Slocum, C., Zhang, Y., Abu-Ghazaleh, N.B., Chen, J.: Going through the motions: AR/VR keylogging from user head motions. In: 32nd USENIX Security Symposium. pp. 159–174. USENIX Association (2023)
31. Stephenson, S., Pal, B., Fan, S., Fernandes, E., Zhao, Y., Chatterjee, R.: Sok: authentication in augmented and virtual reality. In: 43rd IEEE Symposium on Security and Privacy, SP 2022, San Francisco, CA, USA, May 22–26, 2022, pp. 267–284. IEEE (2022)
32. Wang, H., Zhan, Z., Shan, H., Dai, S., Panoff, M., Wang, S.: Gazeploit: remote keystroke inference attack by gaze estimation from avatar views in VR/MR devices. In: Proceedings of the 2024 on ACM SIGSAC Conference on Computer and Communications Security, CCS 2024, Salt Lake City, UT, USA, October 14–18, 2024, pp. 1731–1745. ACM (2024)
33. Wang, R., Huang, L., Madden, K., Wang, C.: Enhancing QR code system security by verifying the scanner's gripping hand biometric. In: Kim, Y., Kim, J., Koushanfar, F., Rasmussen, K. (eds.) Proceedings of the 17th ACM Conference on Security and Privacy in Wireless and Mobile Networks, WiSec 2024, Seoul, Republic of Korea, May 27–29, 2024, pp. 42–53. ACM (2024)
34. Wang, W., Liu, A.X., Sun, K.: Device-free gesture tracking using acoustic signals. In: Proceedings of the 22nd Annual International Conference on Mobile Computing and Networking (MobiCom), pp. 82–94. ACM (2016)
35. Wang, Y., Shen, J., Zheng, Y.: Push the limit of acoustic gesture recognition 566–575 (2020)
36. Wu, Y., et al.: Privacy leakage via unrestricted motion-position sensors in the age of virtual reality: a study of snooping typed input on virtual keyboards. In: 44th IEEE Symposium on Security and Privacy, SP 2023, San Francisco, CA, USA, May 21–25, 2023, pp. 3382–3398. IEEE (2023)
37. Yang, Z., Sarwar, Z., Hwang, I., Bhaskar, R., Zhao, B.Y., Zheng, H.: Can virtual reality protect users from keystroke inference attacks? In: 33rd USENIX Security Symposium. USENIX Association (2024)
38. Yun, S., Chen, Y., Zheng, H., Qiu, L., Mao, W.: Strata: fine-grained acoustic-based device-free tracking. In: Proceedings of the 15th Annual International Conference on Mobile Systems, Applications, and Services (MobiSys), pp. 15–28. ACM (2017)
39. Zhang, Y., Slocum, C., Chen, J., Abu-Ghazaleh, N.B.: It's all in your head(set): side-channel attacks on AR/VR systems. In: Calandrino, J.A., Troncoso, C. (eds.) 32nd USENIX Security Symposium, USENIX Security 2023, Anaheim, CA, USA, August 9–11, 2023, pp. 3979–3996. USENIX Association (2023)
40. Zhou, W., Zhou, Y., Jiang, X., Ning, P.: Detecting repackaged smartphone applications in third-party android marketplaces. In: Second ACM Conference on Data and Application Security and Privacy, CODASPY 2012, San Antonio, TX, USA, February 7–9, 2012, pp. 317–326. ACM (2012)
41. Zhou, Y., Wang, Z., Zhou, W., Jiang, X.: Hey, you, get off of my market: detecting malicious apps in official and alternative android markets. In: 19th Annual Network and Distributed System Security Symposium, NDSS 2012, San Diego, California, USA, February 5–8, 2012. The Internet Society (2012)

Verifying DRAM Addressing in Software

Martin Heckel[1,2](✉), Florian Adamsky[1], Jonas Juffinger[2], Fabian Rauscher[2], and Daniel Gruss[2]

[1] Hof University of Applied Sciences, Hof, Germany
martin.heckel.2@hof-university.de
[2] Graz University of Technology, Graz, Austria

Abstract. In this paper, we introduce a novel approach to reliably verifying DRAM addressing functions and function components from software. We perform the first systematic analysis of 5 DRAM function reverse-engineering tools on 2 different DDR3, 4 DDR4, and 4 DDR5 system configurations, revealing a significant variance in the success rate of these tools, from 0% to 92.9%. We discover the previously unknown rank selection side channel and reverse engineer its function on two DDR4 and two DDR5 systems. These results enable novel DDR5 row-conflict side-channel attacks, which we demonstrate in two scenarios: First, we evaluate the DDR5 row-conflict side channel in a covert channel with 1.39Mbit/s. Second, we evaluate the channel in a website fingerprinting attack with an F_1 score of 84% on DDR4 and 74% on DDR5.

1 Introduction

Software-level security often assumes that hardware is functioning correctly and without side effects. However, physical effects can undermine system security with side-channel and fault attacks. One attack target is DRAM, the main memory in modern computers. There are side channels [27,41], fault attacks [5,14], and slowdown attacks [24] on DRAM, undermining a system's confidentiality, integrity, and availability. DRAM addressing functions can be used in performance optimization, such as application-aware memory channel partitioning [25] or variable page sizes [38] for more efficient row-buffer usage. However, DRAM side-channel and fault attacks also often use these functions: Pessl et al. [27] presented the first DRAM side-channel attacks exploiting reverse-engineered addressing functions. Seaborn [33,34] used DRAM addressing functions for the first practical *Rowhammer* exploit. Rambleed [17] exploits bit flips in attacker memory, depending on inaccessible victim data bits and addressing functions.

DRAM addressing functions are defined by the CPU's memory controller, i.e., specific to the CPU model and the memory configuration. Consequently, it is necessary to reverse-engineer the functions **anew** for every system. Prior works utilize DRAM access timings [4,8,27,40]. Helm et al. [9] reverse-engineered the DRAM functions using performance counters. Most works did not verify the functions systematically but only tested whether an attack succeeded. However, Rowhammer bit flips can also occur with incorrect or even without addressing functions, e.g., One-Location Rowhammer [5]. Only Pessl et al. [27] and Jattke et al. [12] verified addressing functions using high-bandwidth oscilloscopes.

In this paper, we present a novel methodology to verify the correctness of DRAM addressing functions purely in software. Our approach is based on the fact that the theoretical success rate of DRAM side channel tests changes with each function component. Consequently, we can verify the correctness of even single output bit of the DRAM addressing functions purely from software. Thus, we can identify incorrect function components and combine the outputs of multiple reverse-engineering tools to a complete and correct a set of functions. We evaluate our approach on 10 systems and show that the maximum deviation from theoretical values for correct functions is 0.76% on DDR3, 0.52% on DDR4, and 0.49% on DDR5, indicating the high precision of our approach.

Based on our novel verification methodology, we present the first systematic analysis of DRAM addressing function reverse-engineering approaches. We observe success rates of 92.9% on DDR3, 85.6% on DDR4, and 87.3% on DDR5 for the full DRAM addressing functions with the best respective reverse-engineering tool [4,8,12,27,40]. We show that 3 tools yield good results (i.e., ≈90% correct) on our DDR3 systems (Intel), 4 tools yield good results (i.e., ≈80% correct) on our DDR4 systems (Intel), and only 1 tool yields moderate results (i.e., ≈60% correct) on DDR4 (AMD) and good results (i.e., ≈85% correct) on DDR5 (Intel). No tool yields good results on DDR5 (AMD).

Using our approach, we found an additional layer in DRAM addressing: There is a measurable timing difference between addresses of the same rank and those of different ranks. We strongly suspect this is due to the rank select commands sent between accesses to different ranks. We are the first to reverse-engineer *rank addressing functions* and show that using such functions increases the success rate by 18.36% to 36.11% on different systems.

We built the first row-conflict covert channel on DDR5 with a true capacity of up to 2.23 Mbit/s on DDR3, 0.66 Mbit/s on DDR4, and 1.39 Mbit/s on DDR5. Additionally, we evaluate our approach in a row-conflict side-channel website-fingerprinting attack, identifying a single website out of 100 with an F_1 score of 84% on DDR4 and 74% on DDR5.

In summary, in this paper, we make the following contributions:

1. We present a new approach for DRAM address function verification in software[1] based on computing deviations from the theoretical behavior.
2. We systematically evaluate 5 reverse-engineering tools on 2 DDR3, 4 DDR4, and 4 DDR5 systems and show that none produce good results on all systems.
3. We discover a novel rank selection timing channel and reverse-engineer the corresponding rank function on two DDR4 and two DDR5 systems.
4. We present the first row-conflict covert channel on DDR5[2]. with 1.39Mbit/s.
5. We demonstrate a novel row-conflict-based side-channel attack on DDR5, allowing to distinguish 100 websites with an F_1 score of 74%.

---

[1] https://github.com/iisys-sns/DramaVerify.
[2] https://github.com/iisys-sns/DramaNg.

Outline. Section 2 provides background. Section 3 describes our setup. Section 4 presents our new function verification approach. Section 5 presents our DRAM rank addressing insights. Section 6 presents our covert channel on DDR5, and Sect. 7 our website-fingerprinting attack. Section 8 concludes.

2 Background and Related Work

This section discusses DRAM and DRAM addressing, covert channels, website fingerprinting, and related work.

DRAM. DRAM cells consist of capacitors and transistors organized in rows and columns, forming DRAM banks grouped into ranks on a DIMM [27]. DIMMs are connected to the CPU's memory controller via channels. Activating cells (reading the data into a row buffer) is destructive, so content must be written back before activating another row. Since capacitors lose charge over time, DRAM needs periodic recharging, e.g., every 64 ms.

DRAM Addressing Functions. Addressing functions map consecutive memory into different banks, ranks, and channels to minimize bank conflicts. The memory controller translates physical addresses via addressing functions into DRAM components, i.e., channels, DIMMs, ranks, banks, rows, and columns.

Linear Addressing functions are used on systems where the number of all DRAM components is a power of two. They are represented as a hexadecimal bitmask, indicating which bits need to be XORed. For example, the addressing function $0x88000$ corresponds to 10001000000000000000_2, indicating that the 19th and the 15th bit of the physical address needs to be XORed. Each function distinguishes two states, meaning there are $log_2(n_{banks})$ addressing functions on a system with n_{banks} DRAM banks. Reverse-engineering non-linear addressing functions (which use operations other than XOR) remains an open problem.

Covert Channels. Various microarchitectural elements have been used in covert communication channels [18], e.g., via CPU load [26], CPU caches [7, 21–23, 28, 31, 42, 45, 46], and the memory bus [43, 44]. Covert channels have become a best practice to evaluate the capacity of side channels. Semal et al. [35] present a DRAMA covert channel on DDR3 and DDR4 systems with up to 729 bit/s. Wang et al. [41] show that this channel also affects Intel SGX. Van der Veen et al. [39] amplify the DRAMA channel by making all memory uncacheable. In a simulation, Kushwaha et al. [16] showed certain *secure* cache designs can also amplify the DRAMA channel from a simulated range of 2.73 Mbit/s to 4.61 Mbit/s to 4.53 Mbit/s to 6.82 Mbit/s. The fastest DRAM covert channel to date [27] achieves a capacity of up to 2Mbit/s on DDR4.

Website-Fingerprinting Side Channels. A common scenario for side-channel evaluation with low spatial resolution is website fingerprinting. Fingerprinting attacks exploited Android data usage [37], browser memory usage [10], the power side channel [29], cache occupancy [36], interrupt timing [3, 30, 47], SSD contention [13], and timing side channels in the operating system [19], often achieving high F1 scores in open- and closed-world scenarios on the top 100 websites.

Related Work. Several Rowhammer exploits do not use DRAM bank addressing functions [5,14,32]. However, newer and sophisticated Rowhammer exploits [4,6,11,15,32] use DRAM addressing functions to increase the number of bit flips with more targeted hammering.

Pessl et al. [27] reverse-engineered DRAM bank addressing functions from software and used physical memory-bus probing for verification. Barenghi et al. [2] and Marazzi et al. [20] also use the timing-based approach to reverse-engineer DRAM addressing functions. Prior work often determines the correctness through success rates of resulting attacks, e.g., the overall success rate of the full set of addressing functions. In contrast, we demonstrate that the *theoretical influence of correct functions can be leveraged as ground truth to verify the correctness of single reverse-engineered functions*. While we also discover the rank selection side channel that was previously unknown, we focus our verification on the known row-conflict side channel with addressing functions from prior work (which did not include rank selection functions).

DRAMDIG [40] is a knowledge-assisted tool to determine DRAM address mappings and then run a double-sided rowhammer test for verification. Zhang et al. [48] extended DRAMDIG to a Rowhammer testing tool using reverse-engineered addressing functions. Frigo et al. [4] trigger bit flips in TRR-enabled DIMMs using a many-sided pattern with many aggressor rows, relying on reverse-engineering DRAM addressing functions. Helm et al. [9] use performance-counter-based reverse-engineering, focusing on Intel Haswell, Broadwell, and Skylake. Since we also cover AMD, we cannot use their approach in our measurements.

Fewer works focused on AMD. AMD published functions on older CPUs [1] but not for newer ones, where Heckel et al. [8] and Jattke et al. [12] recently reverse-engineered DRAM addressing functions. They also reverse-engineered DRAM addressing functions on DDR5 utilizing the row-conflict side-channel we utilize for the attacks presented in this paper. Jattke et al. [12] verify the function correctness with an oscilloscope, like Pessl et al. [27].

3 Experimental Setup

Our experimental setup consists of 2 systems with DDR3, 4 with DDR4, and 4 with DDR5 DRAM. Each system has a unique ID that follows the format: S⟨DDR Version⟩⟨Counter⟩. All systems run a current version of Arch Linux (6.8.7-arch1-1). Since rank addressing functions are a significant part of the experimental evaluation, we use DIMMs with one or two ranks. If we have multiple similar systems, we use a DIMM with one rank in one system and a DIMM with two ranks in the other (see Table 1 for details). We use /proc/self/pagemap to get physical to virtual addresses mappings.

Table 1. Systems used for experimental evaluation. The number of banks (n_{bnk}) is the number of all banks in the system, e.g., there are $\frac{n_{\text{banks}}}{n_{\text{rnk}}}$ banks per rank.

	System	CPU	Memory	n_{bnk}	n_{rnk}		System	CPU	Memory	n_{bnk}	n_{rnk}		System	CPU	Memory	n_{bnk}	n_{rnk}
DDR3	S301	i5-3320M	4 GiB	8	1	DDR4	S401	i9-10900K	8 GiB	16	1	DDR5	S501	i7-13700	16 GiB	64	1
	S302	i7-4800MQ	4 GiB	16	2		S402	i9-10900K	8 GiB	32	2		S502	i7-13700	16 GiB	64	1
							S403	5950X	8 GiB	16	1		S503	7700X	16 GiB	64	1
							S404	5950X	8 GiB	32	2		S504	7700X	16 GiB	64	1

4 Verification of DRAM Addressing Functions

This section shows how we verify DRAM bank addressing functions based on DRAMA [27]. Rather than exploiting the varying timings between row hits and conflicts to create a covert channel, we utilize this side channel to confirm the accuracy of the bank addressing functions. Although we use the same side channel from DRAMA, we utilize it *differently*, as discussed in Sect. 4.1 We verify our approach using DRAM bank addressing functions reverse-engineered by five existing tools [4,8,12,27,40]. Our criterion for selecting the tools was that they were published in the last ten years and do not require features available only on one architecture. We omitted Helm et al. [9] since their approach uses performance counters exclusive to Intel CPUs from Haswell to Skylake.

4.1 Verification Steps

This section describes the steps to verify reverse-engineered DRAM bank addressing functions. First, we measure the threshold between a row hit and a conflict before allocating 1 GiB of memory. We resolve the physical addresses with elevated privileges, group the allocated memory based on the given addressing functions, and run the DRAMA side channel. We compute a success rate for the addressing function from the number of row hits and conflicts.

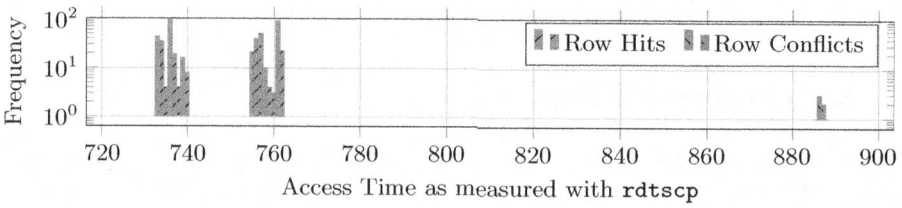

Fig. 1. Histogram of access times when accessing randomly selected pairs of addresses in a flush and reload loop. The gap around 825 TSC cycles hints at the threshold between row hits and misses on *S404*.

Measure the Threshold between Row Hit and Row Conflict. We allocate one 2 MiB Transparent Huge Page (THP) (512 single 4 KiB pages) and measure the access time using the rdtsc instruction of the first (offset 0) and second (offset 4 KiB) page within the THP. We repeat this for all other pages within the THP, e.g., comparing the first and the third, and so on. Between measurements, we clear the CPU cache with clflush.

A histogram from the measured access times is shown in Fig. 1. While we expect the histogram to have two peaks, one for fast row hits and one for slow row conflicts, there are three, two with row hit timings. This can be explained by the fact that *S404* has two ranks. We also performed this experiment on *S401*, which has only one rank and only one row-hit peak. Accesses to addresses on the same rank (*rank hits*) do not require the memory controller to issue a rank select command between them. Access to addresses on different ranks (*rank conflicts*) required the memory controller to issue rank select commands. For this reason, those accesses are slightly slower. There are two ranks on *S404*, and the addresses are equally distributed over both ranks, so there are two peaks of similar size. The histogram is analyzed to identify the threshold t_T between the *row hit* peak and the *row conflict* peak (around 825 for the histogram shown in the plot).

Grouping Addresses. We allocate 1 GiB and get the physical addresses from /proc/self/pagemap. With 2^{30} single addresses in 1 GiB, only a fraction (1% by default) is used. We apply all reverse-engineered DRAM addressing functions under test to the physical addresses. The bits are XORed, and the resulting bit is considered a bit of the bank number. When n addressing functions are applied to a physical address, there is an n-bit bank number. Finally, the virtual address is added to the group to match the bank number computed before.

Verification. After address grouping, the row-conflict side channel [27] is used for group verification. Only correct addressing functions lead to correct groups, so it is sufficient to verify that the groups are correct to derive that the addressing functions are correct. There are 2^n groups for n functions. Several address pairs (a_1, a_2) (we use 5000 by default, since this number yielded good results in a brief comparison) are randomly selected for each group. Additionally, an address (b_1) from another randomly selected group is selected.

Then, we measure the timing of alternatingly accessing (a_1, a_2), expecting a row conflict $(t_c > t_T)$, and (a_1, b_1), expecting a row hit $(t_h < t_T)$. Each of these timing measurements is performed a few hundred times, and the median of the measurements is used as the resulting value. If both timings are correct, $t_c > t_T$ and $t_h < t_T$, the address pair is considered to be grouped correctly.

Evaluation. We compute the share of correctly grouped pairs from all address pairs, resulting in a correctness measure for reverse-engineered DRAM bank addressing functions. In Sect. 4.2, we experimentally evaluate our approach.

4.2 Experimental Evaluation

We evaluate our approach with the following reverse engineering tools: DARE [12], DRAMA [27], DRAMDIG [40], TRRESPASS RE Tool [4], and

AMDRE [8]. After **identifying the addressing functions with these tools**, we ran our verification method on these functions 10 times. We report the average percentage of cases where the assumed banks are correct. We show a graphical representation of all bits identified to belong to at least one DRAM bank addressing function. Therefore, it is possible to see how stable the functions were over multiple measurements. Additionally, to function correctness, we evaluate the stability of the tools as follows: **Stable** tools yield the same result upon every execution. **Mostly Stable** tools yield the same result in $\geq$70% of runs and only 1 or 2 bits difference in the other cases, or no result in at most 3 runs. **Unstable** tools yield the same result in $\geq$70% of runs, but other runs vary. **Completely Unstable** tools have varying results for all runs. **Failed** tools crashed or returned nothing.

Table 2. Experimentation results of multiple PoCs [4,8,12,27,40] on our DDR3 systems. 10 measurements were performed. AFn Mask shows a graphical representation of all bits belonging to at least one DRAM bank addressing function. The average percentage %$_{avg}$ is lower than %$_{max}$ when some runs failed and some succeeded.

	PoC	AFn Mask	%$_{avg}$	σ	%$_{min}$	%$_{max}$		PoC	AFn Mask	%$_{avg}$	σ	%$_{min}$	%$_{max}$
S301	AMDRE		83.5%	27.4	1.4%	92.9%	S302	AMDRE		90.1%	0.1	90.0%	90.3%
	DRAMDIG		92.7%	0.1	92.5%	92.8%		DRAMDIG		89.8%	0.8	87.3%	90.2%
	DRAMA		43.9%	34.1	8.3%	92.7%		DRAMA		42.3%	35.4	0.0%	90.1%
	DARE		0.0%	0.0	0.0%	0.0%		DARE		0.0%	0.0	0.0%	0.0%
	TRRESPASS		0.0%	0.0	0.0%	0.0%		TRRESPASS		0.0%	0.0	0.0%	0.0%

DDR3. Table 2 summarizes our results on two DDR3 systems. DRAMDIG consistently identified *stable* addressing functions with success rates around 92%. AMDRE produced *mostly stable* results but with high variance (1.4 % to 92.9 %). In contrast, DRAMA was *completely unstable*, ranging from 0% to 92.7%. DARE and TRRESPASS *failed* on both systems.

DDR4. As shown in Table 3, on *S401* and *S402*, AMDRE, DRAMDIG, and TRRESPASS returned *stable* functions, DARE reported *mostly stable* functions and DRAMA reported *completely unstable* functions. DRAMA has a success rate of 0 % to 44.9 %. The maximum success rate for AMDRE, DRAMDIG and DARE is around 77 % to 85 % and around 42 % to 85 % for TRRESPASS. The minimum success rate is approximately 85% for AMDRE and DRAMDIG, it is 79.6 % for TRRESPASS and 0 % to 42 % for DARE.

On *S403* and *S404*, DRAMDIG and TRRESPASS *failed*. The masks of DARE are *stable* and *mostly stable*. AMDRE returns *completely unstable* and *stable* results. The success rates are generally lower than for the other two systems.

DDR5. Table 3 shows the results for our four DDR5 systems. No tool has stable results across all machines. DRAMDIG *failed* on all machines and AMDRE and TRRESPASS on *S503* and *S504*. AMDRE is only *stable* on one machine,

Table 3. Experimentation results [4,8,12,27,40] on our DDR4 systems (left) and DDR5 systems (right), analogue to Table 3.

	PoC	AFn Mask	%$_{avg}$	σ	%$_{min}$	%$_{max}$		PoC	AFn Mask	%$_{avg}$	σ	%$_{min}$	%$_{max}$
S401	AMDRE		85.4%	0.1	85.2%	85.5%	*S501*	AMDRE		42.9%	42.9	0.0%	86.0%
	DRAMDIG		84.8%	0.2	84.4%	85.1%		DRAMDIG		0.0%	0.0	0.0%	0.0%
	DRAMA		15.3%	15.6	0.0%	44.9%		DRAMA		5.1%	1.8	1.6%	6.3%
	DARE		76.8%	25.6	0.0%	85.5%		DARE		6.3%	0.0	6.3%	6.4%
	TRRESPASS		84.1%	2.1	79.6%	85.6%		TRRESPASS		5.4%	1.2	2.9%	6.1%
S402	AMDRE		77.2%	0.2	76.9%	77.4%	*S502*	AMDRE		87.0%	0.2	86.7%	87.3%
	DRAMDIG		42.3%	0.1	42.0%	42.5%		DRAMDIG		0.0%	0.0	0.0%	0.0%
	DRAMA		6.7%	6.5	0.0%	21.3%		DRAMA		4.0%	2.2	0.0%	5.5%
	DARE		29.6%	19.4	0.0%	42.4%		DARE		4.6%	1.7	0.0%	5.4%
	TRRESPASS		42.2%	0.1	42.0%	42.4%		TRRESPASS		5.4%	0.1	5.2%	5.5%
S403	AMDRE		23.2%	13.0	0.0%	38.8%	*S503*	AMDRE		0.0%	0.0	0.0%	0.0%
	DRAMDIG		0.0%	0.0	0.0%	0.0%		DRAMDIG		0.0%	0.0	0.0%	0.0%
	DRAMA		13.9%	9.7	0.0%	23.1%		DRAMA		22.7%	0.6	21.8%	23.7%
	DARE		14.4%	6.0	0.0%	21.6%		DARE		1.2%	1.2	0.0%	2.6%
	TRRESPASS		0.0%	0.0	0.0%	0.0%		TRRESPASS		0.0%	0.0	0.0%	0.0%
S404	AMDRE		62.3%	0.5	61.8%	63.4%	*S504*	AMDRE		0.0%	0.0	0.0%	0.0%
	DRAMDIG		0.0%	0.0	0.0%	0.0%		DRAMDIG		0.0%	0.0	0.0%	0.0%
	DRAMA		16.0%	5.8	7.3%	21.8%		DRAMA		20.6%	6.9	0.0%	23.6%
	DARE		18.5%	1.6	16.1%	20.5%		DARE		18.9%	9.5	0.0%	23.7%
	TRRESPASS		0.0%	0.0	0.0%	0.0%		TRRESPASS		0.0%	0.0	0.0%	0.0%

TRRESPASS is *unstable* on the two machines where it works. DRAMA was *unstable* or *completely unstable* across all machines. The success rates are generally lower than for DDR4, with AMDRE reaching the highest success rates of approximately 87% on two systems. DARE has *stable* and *mostly stable* results with maximum success rates of 2.6 % to 23.7 %.

4.3 Verification of Single Addressing Functions

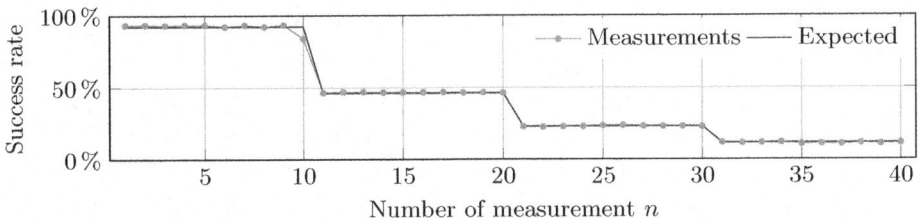

Fig. 2. Success rate reported depending on the number of addressing functions submitted. The measurement was done on *S401* with 4 addressing functions. For each number of addressing functions, 10 measurements were performed.

We verify the entire set of addressing functions in Sect. 4.2. However, with that, we cannot make any statement about single functions. This section extends the approach from Sect. 4.2 to verify single addressing functions within a set.

192   M. Heckel et al.

If a system has n_{fn} correct DRAM bank addressing functions, the number of banks is $n_{\text{banks}} = 2^{n_{\text{fn}}}$. If we remove one of these functions, the number of banks addressable halves: $2^{n_{\text{fn}}-1} = \frac{2^{n_{\text{fn}}}}{2} = \frac{n_{\text{banks}}}{2}$. No addresses can be added to half of the banks because they can not be addressed with the reduced number of functions. This results in 50% of the DRAM banks no longer being accessible via addressing functions and reduces the success rate by 50%, as shown in Fig. 2.

In the range $0 < n \leq 10$ we use all DRAM addressing functions 0x2040, 0x24000, 0x48000, and 0x90000. The average success rate is 92.08%. For $10 < n \leq 20$, we remove 0x90000 and the average success rate halves to 46.61%. In the $20 < n \leq 30$ range, we remove 0x48000 resulting in an average success rate of 23.09%. Finally, for $30 < n \leq 40$, the function 0x2040 is used, and the average success rate is 11.35%, with an expected success rate of 11.51%.

We conclude that all the DRAM addressing functions used above are correct. However, this approach has the disadvantage that the differences between using or not using a function get lower the more functions were removed before. For example, the expected difference for removing the first function is 46.04%, which decreases to 11.51% for removing the third function. However, as DRAM bank addressing functions are not ordered, we remove every function from the initial set of all functions individually, comparing the new success rate to the initial one. If a correct function is removed, the success rate is expected to halve.

We evaluate our verification on DDR3, DDR4, and DDR5, each with the set of addressing functions reverse-engineered in Sect. 4.2 that yields the highest percentage on the respective system. Then, we manually modify some of the DRAM addressing functions. Afterward, we repeat the experiment with the modified function to verify that our approach can detect the modified, now wrong, addressing functions. The results of this evaluation are shown in Table 4.

Table 4. Evaluation of single addressing functions grouped by system. The value of $\%_{\text{exp}}$ is always 50% of the measured initial success rate for the entire function set. Manual manipulation to obtain wrong functions (see the ✓ under *Mod*).

	Function	Mod.	$\%_{\text{meas}}$	$\%_{\text{exp}}$	$\%_{\text{diff}}$	Cor.		Function	Mod.	$\%_{\text{meas}}$	$\%_{\text{exp}}$	$\%_{\text{diff}}$	Cor.
S302	0x22000	✗	47.6%	46.1%	1.5%	✓	S302	0x23000	✓	23.1%	10.7%	12.4%	✗
	0x44000	✗	47.6%	46.1%	1.5%	✓		0x44000	✗	10.9%	10.7%	0.2%	✓
	0x88000	✗	47.8%	46.1%	1.7%	✓		0x89000	✓	22.6%	10.7%	11.9%	✗
	0x110000	✗	47.7%	46.1%	1.6%	✓		0x110000	✗	10.9%	10.7%	0.2%	✓
S401	0x2040	✗	46.1%	46.6%	0.5%	✓	S401	0x2040	✗	10.4%	10.4%	0.0%	✓
	0x24000	✗	46.4%	46.6%	0.2%	✓		0x25000	✓	20.8%	10.4%	10.4%	✗
	0x48000	✗	46.4%	46.6%	0.2%	✓		0x48000	✗	10.5%	10.4%	0.1%	✓
	0x90000	✗	46.3%	46.6%	0.3%	✓		0x110000	✓	22.6%	10.4%	12.2%	✗
S501	0x6300	✗	43.6%	43.3%	0.3%	✓	S501	0x6100	✓	9.43%	3.11%	6.32%	✗
	0x10000	✗	43.6%	43.3%	0.3%	✓		0x10000	✗	3.07%	3.11%	0.04%	✓
	0x20000	✗	43.8%	43.3%	0.5%	✓		0x24000	✓	9.19%	3.11%	6.08%	✗
	0x42300	✗	43.4%	43.3%	0.1%	✓		0x42300	✗	3.08%	3.11%	0.03%	✓
	0x81100	✗	43.5%	43.3%	0.2%	✓		0x82100	✓	9.36%	3.11%	6.25%	✗
	0x108000	✗	43.3%	43.3%	0.0%	✓		0x108000	✗	3.08%	3.11%	0.03%	✓

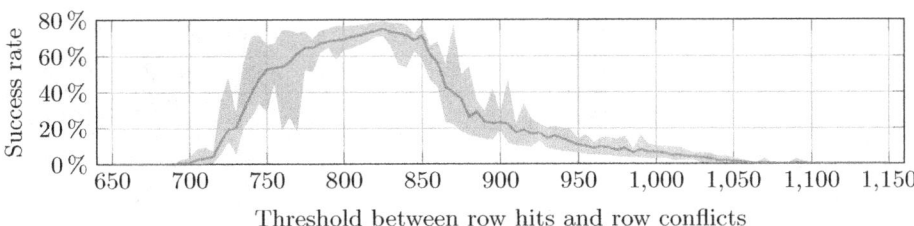

Fig. 3. Success rate of our verification approach depending on the threshold. The graph shows average, minimum, and maximum values over 10 measurements.

For *S301*, *S401*, and *S501*, the submitted addressing functions were identified to be correct, with a maximum difference of 0.76% between the expected and the measured values when no modifications were performed. Without any modified functions, all systems' base success rate ($2 \times \%_{\text{exp}}$) is approximately 90%. With two modified functions, the success rate drops to 21.34% on *S301*. Both incorrect functions were identified, with differences of 11.43% and 11.80%. The correct function was identified with a difference of 0.71%. On *S401*, two modified addressing functions resulted in an overall success rate of 20.88%. The incorrect functions were identified, with differences of 10.39% and 12.18%. Both correct functions were identified, with differences of 0.01% and 0.08%. The three modified addressing functions on *S501* resulted in a drop in the overall success rate of 6.22%. The incorrect functions have differences of 6.32%, 6.08%, and 6.25%. In contrast, the three correct functions have differences of 0.04%, 0.03%, and 0.03%. Our approach identifies correct and incorrect DRAM bank addressing functions in all cases within this experiment.

5 Rank Timing Analysis

To analyze the lower-than-expected success rate (see Sect. 4.2), we perform multiple measurements and finally show that a second layer of addressing functions is used to determine the rank of a physical address.

5.1 Rank Addressing Functions

We use the same timing notation introduced in Sect. 4.1 and find four timing cases, **C1**, with $t_c > t_T$ and $t_h < t_T$, **E1**, with $t_c < t_T$ and $t_h < t_T$, **E2**, with $t_c < t_T$ and $t_h > t_T$, and **E3**, with $t_c > t_T$ and $t_h > t_T$. When the addresses are correctly grouped, and both addresses from the same group are not in the same row, t_c cannot be smaller than t_h since a row hit (t_h) is faster than a row conflict (t_c). Depending on the addresses chosen, the case labeled E2 might occur even when correct addressing functions are used. The probability of this happening is discussed below. By default, 1% of the available addresses is grouped, which is 10 MiB of 1 GiB. If all selected addresses are contiguous, 10 MiB of

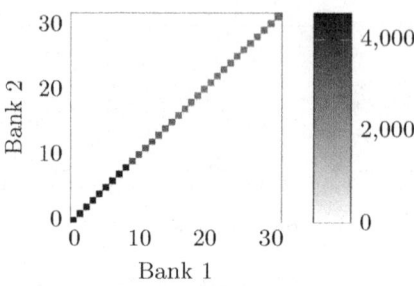
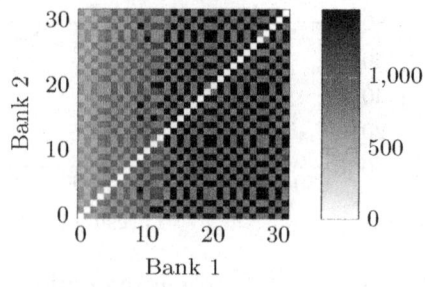

(a) Number of too fast row conflicts.   (b) Number of too slow row hits.

Fig. 4. Heat maps of both errors: too fast row conflicts and too slow row hits. The x-axis shows the group of the first address, the y-axis the second selected address. Measurements on *S404* (with threshold 495), averaged over 10 measurements.

memory are distributed over n_{banks} banks. In the case of 32 DRAM banks, this results in $\frac{10\,MiB}{32} = 320\,KiB$ per DRAM bank. With the assumption that the addresses completely populate contiguous rows with a row size of 8 KiB, the selected addresses populate $\frac{320\,KiB}{8\,KiB} = 40$ rows. So, the probability of one randomly selected address being in one chosen row is $\frac{1}{40} = 2.5\%$. Following this, the probability of two randomly selected addresses being in the same DRAM bank is 2.5%. Therefore, case E2 is doubtful when correct DRAM bank addressing functions are used, since two randomly selected addresses from the same DRAM bank would have to be in the same row, which happens at a probability of 2.5% in the worst case. Under the assumption that the tested DRAM bank addressing functions are correct, the cases E1, C1, and E3 are statistically relevant.

In contrast to the approach described in Sect. 4.1, the threshold is manually specified and not measured for this experiment. The threshold impacts the success rate, as shown in Fig. 3. The statistically relevant cases E1, C1, and E3 depend on the selected threshold as shown below:

E1: Since both timings (t_c and t_h) are lower than the threshold, row conflicts are misclassified as row hits. The threshold is selected too high (for $t_T \geq 875$ in the graph shown in Fig. 3).
C1: Since row conflicts (t_c) are slower and row hits (t_h) are faster than the threshold, both cases are classified correctly. The threshold is set correctly (for $875 \geq t_T \geq 795$ in the graph shown in Fig. 3).
E3: Since both timings (t_c and t_h) are higher than the threshold, hits are misclassified as conflicts. The threshold is too low (for $t_T \leq 795$ in Fig. 3).

Note that the three cases overlap and merge, so the submitted threshold values describe a range and not a specific value. In these measurements, two types of single errors can occur: **(e1)** a row hit is too slow and misclassified as conflict; and **(e2)** a row conflict is too fast and misclassified as hit.

Figure 4 shows heat maps for both errors. Row conflicts are expected when comparing addresses from the same DRAM bank, so there are n_{banks} different cases (one for each DRAM bank), as shown in Fig. 4a. Row hits are expected between addresses from one DRAM bank and addresses from any other DRAM bank, as shown in Fig. 4b. The heat map shows no values on the diagonal since addresses from the same bank are not expected to be row hits.

As shown in Fig. 4b, there is a pattern in the error number depending on the addresses of which DRAM banks are compared to each other. When comparing an address from bank 0 to another address, the number of errors is lower for the following banks: (2, 5, 7, 9, 11, 12, 14, 16, 18, 21, 23, 25, 27, 28, 30). Similarly, comparing an address from bank 1 with another address has fewer errors for the following banks: (3, 4, 6, 8, 10, 13, 15, 17, 19, 20, 22, 24, 26, 29, 31). So, there are two groups of DRAM banks for which the error rate is lower when addresses are selected from banks within the same group. At the same time, the error rate is higher when selecting two addresses from banks in different groups.

This grouping can be described by a *grouping function* taking bank number (0–31) as input and returning an output of one bit equivalent to the number of the groups. The function can be represented by a bitmask that selects bits of the input and applies a bitwise XOR to them. When bank numbers are represented in binary, the addressing function 0xd (0b01101) can be applied similarly to the DRAM bank addressing functions to get a resulting bit determining the group.

The error rate is lower when two addresses from different banks within the same bank group are selected, so we restrict the measurements only to those cases. We compare the success rates with or without applying the additional DRAM addressing function. The result of this experiment is shown in Fig. 5.

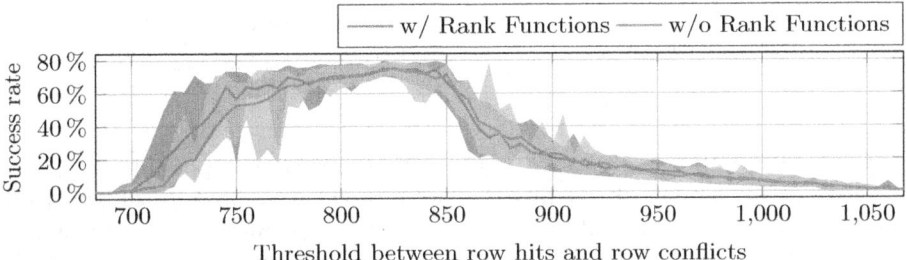

Fig. 5. Average, minimum and maximum success rate (10 measurements) of our verification approach with and without using rank addressing functions. The graph without rank addressing functions is the same one shown in Fig. 3.

When additional rank addressing functions are used, the success rate is higher in the $700 \leq t_T \leq 780$ range. For $t_T \leq 700$, the success rate is nearly 0 for both graphs. When $t_T \geq 780$, the success rates for both graphs are similar.

The range $700 \leq t_T \leq 780$ has a similar upper border as $t_T \leq 795$, as discussed in case *E3*, in which both timings (t_c and t_h) are higher than the threshold. So, the number of row hits misclassified as row conflict is lower when rank addressing functions are used.

Some row hits are faster than others, as shown in Fig. 4b. However, in contrast to the patterns in the heatmaps that occurred in the range $920 \leq t_T \leq 980$ as well, the differences in the success rate graph are only relevant in the range of row hits being misclassified as row conflicts.

The memory controller issues *Rank Select* commands every time the rank changes, so it is assumed that accessing two addresses from the same rank that are on different banks (e.g., row hit) is faster than accessing two addresses from different ranks (e.g., row hit). This effect occurs only on systems with multiple ranks (we tested systems with 1 and 2), as further evaluated in Sect. 5.2. Therefore, we conclude that the effect is related to the DRAM rank.

5.2 Experimental Evaluation

We perform the steps described in Sect. 5.1 for experimental evaluation. If a DRAM rank addressing function is derived, it is submitted to the verification tool. The maximum distance between the success rates with and without using the rank addressing function is measured. The results are shown in Table 5.

Table 5. Success rate at the threshold (t_T) with a maximum difference with and without DRAM rank addressing functions (RF) yielding the best results in Sect. 4.2 (10 measurement average). No rank functions found on other systems.

System	RF	t_T	% w RF	% w/o RF	Δ_{RF}
S402	2	540	66.16 %	38.77 %	27.40 %
S404	13	730	38.54 %	20.18 %	18.36 %
S501	6,8,10	255	77.32 %	42.86 %	34.46 %
S502	6,8,10	230	55.63 %	19.52 %	36.11 %

On both DDR3 systems (*S301* and *S302*), it was not possible to see any patterns in the number of row hits that were too slow, similar to the one shown in Fig. 4b. Therefore, we could not apply a rank addressing function and skipped the evaluation of the rank addressing function.

For the DDR4 systems, patterns occurred only on systems with two ranks (*S402* and *S404*), there were no recognizable patterns for the systems with one rank (*S401* and *S403*). Therefore, we evaluate rank addressing functions only on *S402* and *S404*. On *S402*, we identify the rank addressing function 2. We observe a maximum difference of 27.40%. On *S404*, the rank addressing function is 13. The same data as in Sect. 5.1 was used for the evaluation. The maximum distance of 18.36% was reached at a threshold of 730.

As the DRAM addressing functions on *S503* and *S504* reached very low success rates in our experiments (see Sect. 4.2), these systems were excluded from the evaluation of rank addressing functions. In contrast to the DDR4 systems discussed before, *S501* and *S502* had correct DRAM addressing functions. Recognizing a pattern in the number of row hits that were too slow was also possible.

From this pattern, we derived the rank addressing functions 6,8,10 for both systems. On *S501*, the maximum difference between using and not using the rank addressing functions is 34.46%. For *S502* it is 36.11%.

The row-conflict side-channel can be used to detect rank functions equivalent to bank functions, which is the case when only a single bit is set in the rank function mask (e.g., 2, 8). However, most rank function masks (e.g., 13, 6, 10) have multiple bits set, e.g., combine more than one bank addressing function. Thereby, the row-conflict side-channel itself is not sufficient to detect them.

6 Row-Conflict Covert Channel on DDR5

This section presents the first row-conflict covert channel on DDR5, including cross-VM, with transmission speeds up to 2.23 Mbit/s. The sender and receiver have *no shared memory* and encode data into same-bank row conflicts, similar to previous covert channel designs: A low timing (absence of a row conflict) corresponds to a '1' and a high timing (row conflict) corresponds to a '0'.

We use a time-sliced protocol, synchronized via rdtsc and a 75%-majority vote to decide whether the accesses within a time slice were mainly row conflicts or not, i.e., a '0'-bit or not. For cross-VM, the Time Stamp Counter (TSC) can have different values but run at the same speed in each VM. Hence, we synchronize by transmitting a predefined sequence at a predefined rate. The receiver reads the sequence and can adjust its offset to the timestamp counter. After 8 bits were received, the receiver increases the offset by $\frac{1}{20}$ of the specified transmission window.

Suppose the receiver encounters a byte that is either 10101010, i.e., 0xaa, or 01010101, i.e., 0x55 (one bit shifted); the current offset is stored for the first valid sequence. Likewise, the offset of the first following sequence that is neither 0xaa nor 0x55 is stored for the following invalid sequence. Afterward, the average of both offset values is used as offset during the rest of the transmission.

Next, it is required to synchronize the border of bytes. This is done by transmitting two bytes of 0x00. Because the sequence 10101010 ends with a 0, the receiver should receive $1 + 8 \times 2 = 17$ zeroes in a row. After receiving 17 zeroes in a row, the receiver starts to receive a new byte. Finally, the byte 0xaa is sent again to verify that the synchronization was successful.

Experimental Evaluation. We transmit 6000 randomly generated bytes. The raw capacity, i.e., the number of bits sent divided by the transmission time, and the error rate, i.e., bit-edit distance divided by the number of bits, is in Fig. 6.[3] We tested 25 gradually decreasing window sizes per system. The true capacity varies slightly with the error rate.

We perform experiments on multiple test systems and calculate the true capacity. Table 6 shows the raw capacity, the error rate, and the true capacity we reach. The covert channel did not work on the systems with AMD CPUs

---

[3] Shannon's noisy-channel coding theorem yields the true capacity T as $T = r \cdot (1 + ((1-p) \cdot \log_2(1-p) + p \cdot \log_2(p)))$.

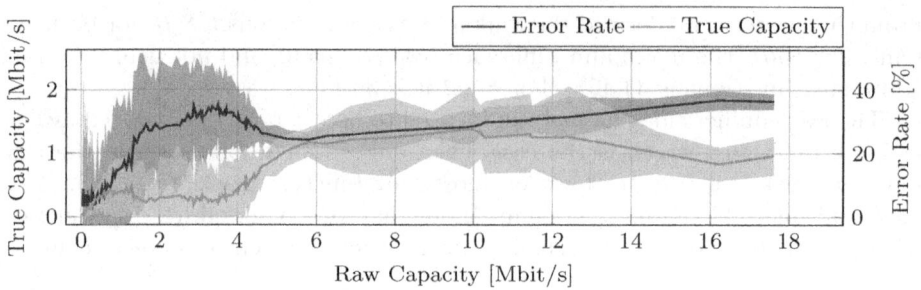

Fig. 6. Raw and true capacity of our covert channel on *S502* with 99% confidence intervals.

Table 6. True capacity of the covert channel on multiple systems where it worked.

System	Error Rate	Raw Capacity	True Capacity	System	Error Rate	Raw Capacity	True Capacity
S301	39.22%	0.27 Mbit/s	0.01 Mbit/s	*S402*	24.01%	3.21 Mbit/s	0.66 Mbit/s
S302	21.74%	9.14 Mbit/s	2.23 Mbit/s	*S501*	25.88%	7.39 Mbit/s	1.29 Mbit/s
S401	43.66%	3.72 Mbit/s	0.16 Mbit/s	*S502*	28.30%	9.89 Mbit/s	1.39 Mbit/s

(*S403, S404, S503, S504*). The reason might be that Jattke et al. [12] found that AMD requires offsets for specific physical addresses, which was not considered.

On the Intel systems with DDR3, the true capacity differs significantly. This can be explained by the error rate on *S301*, which is significantly higher than on *S302*, even though the raw capacity is significantly lower. The error rate on *S301* was even higher at higher capacities. Therefore, the true capacity of 0.01Mbit/s was reached at a raw capacity of 0.27Mibit/s. In contrast, the true capacity on *S302* is 2.23Mbit/s at a raw capacity of 9.14Mbit/s.

On *S401*, the error rate of 43.66% is significantly higher than 24.01% on *S402*. Even though a raw capacity of 3.72Mbit/s and 3.21Mbit/s is close, the big difference in the error rates leads to a significantly different true capacity. Therefore, the true capacity is 0.16Mbit/s on *S401* and 0.66Mbit/s on *S402*.

In contrast to the previous experiments, the true capacity of both DDR5 systems is similar. On *S501*, the true capacity is 1.29Mbit/s at a raw capacity of 7.39Mbit/s with an error rate of 25.88%. On *S502*, the true capacity is 1.39Mbit/s at a raw capacity of 9.89Mbit/s with an error rate of 28.30%.

7 Website Fingerprinting Attack

We utilize the DRAMA side channel to mount a website fingerprinting attack. We measure memory access patterns while accessing websites using Firefox. We hypothesize that the browser's memory access patterns depend on the website rendered at that moment. For evaluation, we train a machine learning (ML) model to classify the websites based on measured memory accesses. We verify our fingerprinting approach by classifying 100 websites with an F_1 score of 84% on DDR4 and 74% on DDR5.

Fingerprinting Procedure. First, we spawn a process that measures the access times to addresses on different system memory banks. At the same time, we access a website with Firefox and wait 8 s for the website to be rendered. We then stop Firefox and the measuring process, aggregate the data to reduce data size, and prepare them for ML model training or evaluation. Afterward, we use the aggregated data to train our ML model. Finally, we reaccessed the websites, measured and aggregated memory access data, and used our ML model to predict which website we had accessed.

Access Time Measurements. We take DRAM addressing functions, allocate two 2 MiB hugepages on the system. Then, we resolve the mapping of the virtual addresses to physical addresses using /proc/self/pagemap. Pagemap is **unnecessary** for an actual attack because Heckel et al. [8] showed that we can dynamically group addresses based on access times. However, for the purpose of demonstration, we used it to reduce the initialization time and increase the stability for the experimental evaluation. We then start n threads for measuring. Each thread measures the memory access times of a specific DRAM bank. If the measured access time was bigger than the threshold between row hit and row conflict, the access time and timestamp are stored in a buffer. We measure the loading of each website for approximately 8 S. The number of threads n is set to $n_{\text{proc}} - 2$, where n_{proc} is the number of logical CPU cores in the system. Hence, there are still two CPU cores left for Firefox and system.

Aggregation of Data. Next, we take the files created in the previous step. We specify a window size and aggregate the number of row conflicts in that window. We then store the data in a three-dimensional array. We use a window size of 100 μs. The first dimension contains the number of row conflicts within the specified window. The second dimension contains the banks, e.g., one first-dimension list for each bank measured. The third dimension contains multiple measurements; in our case, 100 accesses the same website.

Description of the ML Model. Our ML model consists of 9 convolutional layers in groups of three with max pooling and dropout layers in between. The output of the convolutional layers is then flattened, and the final prediction is made after three dense layers. The input of a single website to the model is a 3 dimensional spectrogram with the dimensions time, frequency, and DRAM bank.

Experimental Evaluation. For experimental evaluation, we access 100 websites 100 times each. Afterward, we use 80% of the measurements to train our ML model and 20% to test our model. On a test system with DDR5 ($S502$), we reach an overall F_1 score of 74% and plot the predictions of our model in Fig. 7b. On a test system with DDR4 ($S401$), we reach an overall F_1 score of 84% and plot the predictions of our model in Fig. 7a. $S502$ has 24 logical cores (22 threads for measurement) and $S401$ has 20 logical cores (18 threads for measurement). Because each thread measures a single DRAM bank, we can measure 16 of 16 banks on $S401$, so we measure accesses of Firefox to all DRAM banks. On $S502$, we can only measure 22 of 64 banks, so 34.38% of the DRAM accesses performed by Firefox (assuming equal distribution of accesses over all banks). We hypothesize that this is the reason for the lower accuracy on *S502*.

8 Conclusion

In this paper, we introduced a novel approach to reliably verifying DRAM addressing functions and function components from software. A first systematic analysis of 5 DRAM function reverse-engineering tools on 10 different system configurations showed significant variance in the success rate of these tools, from 0% to 92.9%. We discovered the previously unknown rank selection side channel and reverse engineer its function on two DDR4 and two DDR5 systems. These results enable novel DDR5 row-conflict side-channel attacks, which we demonstrated in two scenarios: a covert channel with 1.39Mbit/s, and a website fingerprinting attack with an F_1 score of 84% on DDR4 and 74% on DDR5. We conclude that as reverse-engineering of DRAM address functions remains relevant, our new verification methodology provides a cheap and reliable alternative to verification using expensive physical measurements.

Acknowledgments. This work was funded by the Deutsche Forschungsgemeinschaft under grant number 503876675 and the Austrian Science Fund under grant number 10.55776/I6054, as well as the European Union under grant number ROF-SG20-3066-3-2-2.

A Confusion Matrix Website Fingerprinting

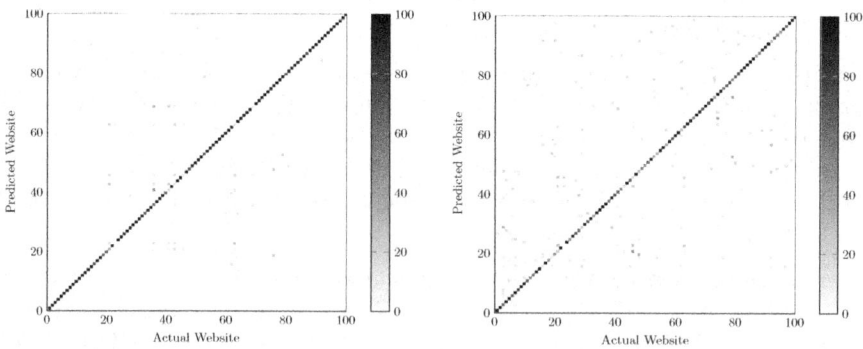

(a) Website confusion matrix on DDR4 (*S401*), with F_1 score 86.7 %.

(b) Website confusion matrix on DDR5 on *S502*, with F_1 score 74.0 %.

Fig. 7. Confusion matrices. The actual website is shown on the x axis, the website predicted by the model is shown on the y axis.

References

1. AMD. BIOS and Kernel Developer's Guide (BKDG) for AMD Family 16h Models 00h-0Fh Processors (2015)
2. Barenghi, A., Breveglieri, L., Izzo, N., Pelosi, G.: Software-only reverse engineering of physical DRAM mappings for Rowhammer attacks. In: International Verification and Security Workshop (IVSW) (2018)
3. Cook, J., Drean, J., Behrens, J., Yan, M.: There's always a bigger fish: a clarifying analysis of a machine-learning-assisted side-channel attack. In: ISCA (2022)
4. Frigo, P., et al.: TRRespass: exploiting the many sides of target row refresh. In: S&P (2020)
5. Gruss, D., et al.: Another flip in the wall of Rowhammer defenses. In: S&P (2018)
6. Gruss, D., Maurice, C., Mangard, S.: Rowhammer.js: a remote software-induced fault attack in JavaScript. In: DIMVA (2016)
7. Han, Y., Kim, J.: A novel covert channel attack using memory encryption engine cache. In: DAC (2019)
8. Heckel, M., Adamsky, F.: Reverse-Engineering Bank Addressing Functions on AMD CPUs. In: DRAMSec Workshop (2023)
9. Helm, C., Akiyama, S., Taura, K.: Reliable reverse engineering of intel DRAM addressing using performance counters. In: Modeling, Analysis, and Simulation of Computer and Telecommunication Systems (MASCOTS). IEEE (2020)
10. Jana, S., Shmatikov, V.: Memento: learning secrets from process footprints. In: S&P (2012)
11. Patrick Jattke, van der Veen, V., Frigo, P., Gunter, S., Razavi, K.: BLACKSMITH: Rowhammering in the frequency domain. In: S&P (2021)
12. Jattke, P., Wipfli, M., Solt, F., Marazzi, M., Bölcskei, M., Razavi, K.: ZenHammer: Rowhammer attacks on AMD zen-based platforms. In: USENIX Security (2024)
13. Juffinger, J., Rauscher, F., La Manna, G., Gruss, D.: Secret spilling drive: leaking user behavior through SSD contention. In: NDSS (2025)
14. Kim, Y., et al.: Flipping bits in memory without accessing them: an experimental study of DRAM disturbance errors. In: ISCA (2014)
15. Kogler, A., et al.: Half-double: hammering from the next row over. In: USENIX Security (2022)
16. Kushwaha, A., Jain, A., Patel, M., Panda, B.: Golmaal: thanks to the secure Time-Cache for a faster DRAM covert channel. In: DRAMSec (2022)
17. Kwong, A., Genkin, D., Gruss, D., Yarom, Y.: RAMBleed: reading bits in memory without accessing them. In: S&P (2020)
18. Lampson, B.W.: A note on the confinement problem. Commun. ACM (1973)
19. Maar, L., Juffinger, J., Steinbauer, T., Gruss, D., Mangard, S.: KernelSnitch: side-channel attacks on kernel data structures. In: NDSS (2025)
20. Marazzi, M., Razavi, K.: RISC-H: Rowhammer attacks on RISC-V. In: DRAMSec Workshop (2024)
21. Maurice, C., Le Scouarnec, N., Neumann, C., Heen, O., Francillon, A.: Reverse engineering intel complex addressing using performance counters. In: RAID (2015)
22. Maurice, C., Neumann, C., Heen, O., Francillon, A.: C5: cross-cores cache covert channel. In: DIMVA (2015)
23. Maurice, C., et al.: Hello from the other side: SSH over robust cache covert channels in the cloud. In: NDSS (2017)
24. Moscibroda, T., Mutlu, O.: Memory performance attacks: denial of memory service in multi-core systems. Technical report (2007)

25. Muralidhara, S.P., Subramanian, L., Mutlu, O., Kandemir, M., Moscibroda, T.: Reducing memory interference in multi-core systems via application-aware memory channel partitioning. In: MICRO (2011). https://doi.org/10.1145/2155620.2155664
26. Okamura, K., Oyama, Y.: Load-based covert channels between xen virtual machines. In: Symposium on Applied Computing (SAC) (2010)
27. Pessl, P., Gruss, D., Maurice, C., Schwarz, M., Mangard, S.: DRAMA: exploiting DRAM addressing for cross-CPU attacks. In: USENIX Security (2016)
28. Purnal, A., Verbauwhede, I.: Advanced profiling for probabilistic prime+probe attacks and covert channels in ScatterCache. arXiv:1908.03383 (2019)
29. Qin, Y., Yue, C.: Website fingerprinting by power estimation based side-channel attacks on android 7. In: TrustCom/BigDataSE (2018)
30. Rauscher, F., Kogler, A., Juffinger, J., Gruss, D.: IdleLeak: exploiting idle state side effects for information leakage. In: NDSS (2024)
31. Saileshwar, G., Fletcher, C.W., Qureshi, M.: Streamline: a fast, flushless cache covert-channel attack by enabling asynchronous collusion. In: ASPLOS (2021)
32. Seaborn, M.: Exploiting the DRAM Rowhammer bug to gain kernel privileges (2015)
33. Seaborn, M.: How physical addresses map to rows and banks in DRAM (2015)
34. Seaborn, M., Dullien, T.: Exploiting the DRAM Rowhammer bug to gain kernel privileges. In: Black Hat USA (2015)
35. Semal, B., Markantonakis, K., Akram, R.N., Kalbantner, J.: Leaky controller: cross-VM memory controller covert channel on multi-core systems. In: ICT Systems Security and Privacy Protection (SEC) (2020)
36. Shusterman, A., et al.: Robust website fingerprinting through the cache occupancy channel. In: USENIX Security (2019)
37. Spreitzer, R., Griesmayr, S., Korak, T., Mangard, S.: Exploiting data-usage statistics for website fingerprinting attacks on Android. In: ACM Conference on Security & Privacy in Wireless and Mobile Networks (2016)
38. Sudan, K., Chatterjee, N., Nellans, D., Awasthi, M., Balasubramonian, R., Davis, A.: Micro-pages: increasing DRAM efficiency with locality-aware data placement. In: ASPLOS (2010). https://doi.org/10.1145/1735970.1736045
39. van der Veen, V., Gras, B.: DramaQueen: revisiting side channels in DRAM. In: DRAMSec (2023)
40. Wang, M., Zhang, Z., Cheng, Y., Nepal, S.: DRAMDig: a knowledge-assisted tool to UncoverDRAM address mapping. In: Design Automation Conference (DAC) (2020)
41. Wang, W., et al.: Leaky cauldron on the dark land: understanding memory side-channel hazards in SGX. In: CCS (2017)
42. Wang, Z., Lee, R.B.: Covert and side channels due to processor architecture. In: ACSAC (2006)
43. Wu, Z., Xu, Z., Wang, H.: Whispers in the hyper-space: high-bandwidth and reliable covert channel attacks inside the cloud. ACM Trans. Netw. (2014)
44. Wu, Z., Xu, Z., Wang, H.: Whispers in the hyper-space: high-speed covert channel attacks in the cloud. In: USENIX Security (2012)
45. Xu, Y., Bailey, M., Jahanian, F., Joshi, K., Hiltunen, M., Schlichting, R.: An exploration of L2 cache covert channels in virtualized environments. In: CCSW (2011)
46. Yarom, Y., Falkner, K.: Flush+reload: a high resolution, low noise, L3 cache side-channel attack. In: USENIX Security (2014)

47. Zhang, R., Kim, T., Weber, D., Schwarz, M.: (M)WAIT for it: bridging the gap between microarchitectural and architectural side channels. In: USENIX Security (2023)
48. Zhang, Z., et al.: BitMine: an end-to-end tool for detecting Rowhammer vulnerability. TIFS **16**, 5167–5181 (2021)

Epistemology of Rowhammer Attacks: Threats to Rowhammer Research Validity

Martin Heckel[1,2(✉)], Hannes Weissteiner[2], Florian Adamsky[1], and Daniel Gruss[2]

[1] Hof University of Applied Sciences, Hof, Germany
[2] Graz University of Technology, Graz, Austria
martin.heckel.2@hof-university.de

Abstract. The Rowhammer effect is a disturbance error in DRAM that attackers can trigger from software. The first publication on Rowhammer in 2014 evaluated 129 Dual In-line Memory Modules (DIMMs) on an FPGA and showed that 110 DIMMs are affected, indicating that Rowhammer is a widespread issue. However, until now, no case outside of academia is known in which Rowhammer was used for attacks, indicating a stark discrepancy between the attention Rowhammer receives and its real-world relevance.

This paper systematically analyzes 32 offensive Rowhammer papers, including 48 experiments. However, we avoid finger-pointing but identify six threats to the validity and relevance of Rowhammer research results and give multiple examples. The threats include small sample sizes, overestimated attacker capabilities, unrealistic attack scenarios, non-comparability of the results, age and wear of hardware, and suboptimal attack performance metrics. Additionally, we provide recommendations with detailed justification to the scientific community to mitigate those threats: (1) pre-experimental testing of DIMM integrity, (2) increasing and broadening the DIMM sample size, (3) expanding reproduction studies of published work, (4) defining attacks in real-world conditions and distinguishing them from theoretical ones, (5) publishing DIMM manufacturing data, (6) documenting DIMM wear and, (7) leveraging multiple metrics for bit flip evaluations.

1 Introduction

The main memory, Dynamic Random-Access Memory (DRAM), remains crucial in all computer devices. The demand for higher storage capacity yields a high density of DRAM memory cells. However, the industry has reached a point where scaling becomes a problem. Scaling the capacitors and transistors beyond 40 nm is challenging [32] and can result in disturbance errors.

These disturbance errors were initially assumed to have little to no security implications [50]. Later, Kim et al. [28] showed that an attacker can trigger bit flips in DRAM rows by reading from nearby rows rapidly, which is known as *Rowhammer*. In recent years, researchers developed sophisticated exploits

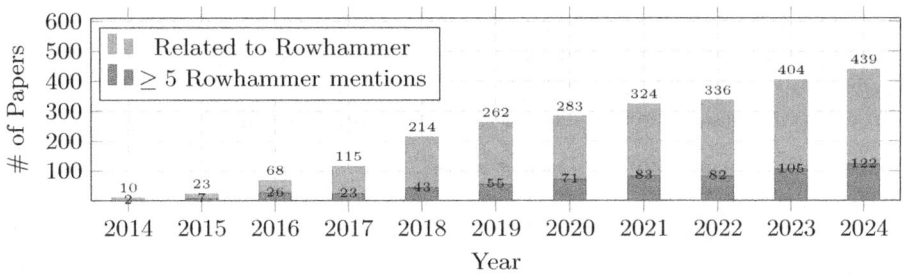

Fig. 1. Number of published research papers related to Rowhammer per year, and number of papers that mention rowhammer multiple times. We analyzed 2509 papers identified by a Google Scholar search and counted the number of occurrences of the word "Rowhammer". If a paper has ≥ 5 occurrences of that word, we count it as a Rowhammer paper. This metric might include some paper that focuses on another topic, but still provides an estimation of the number of publications related to Rowhammer.

based on Rowhammer. These exploits achieve, for instance, privilege escalation on desktop computers [1,8,9,12,13,17–19,25,26,31,36,47,49,51,54,57], mobile devices [9,30,34,58,62], and even on cloud systems [4,48,55,60], all without a software vulnerability. Over the years, the number of scientific papers related to Rowhammer[1] increased, as shown in Fig. 1.

With so many scientific publications, system administrators ask: *Should we integrate Rowhammer into our threat analysis?* However, to the best of our knowledge, Rowhammer has not been used in real-world attacks, such as malware or ransomware. It might be unrealistic to see malware or ransomware based on Rowhammer, but *we don't know if Rowhammer would be an attack vector usable for such attacks.* National or state actors could use Rowhammer as part of their attack chain. Overall, the lack of real-world attacks contradicts the number of Rowhammer publications from academia. There is a stark discrepancy between the attention Rowhammer's research has in the academic community and the relevance of Rowhammer in real-world attacks.

In this paper, we show multiple threats to Rowhammer research validity and discuss their influence on the overall validity of Rowhammer research. We analyze 32 publications that perform 48 experiments regarding these threats and show how relevant these threats are regarding these publications. We focus on offensive Rowhammer research since these publications typically perform experiments on how good attacks work on specific systems, resulting in the difference between academic and real-world estimation of exploitability. Finally, we show how researchers can prevent those threats in future research.

We point out cases where specific threats undermined the validity of previous work's experimental evaluation. *Identifying these threats would not have been possible without the tremendous effort put into these prior works.* We crucially

---

[1] The results for the keyword "hammer" were almost identical.

build upon them for identification and do not want to point fingers at previous work. Instead, we want to provide recommendations to improve the validity of Rowhammer's research in general for future work.

We identify the following threats to Rowhammer research validity:

***T*1 Small Sample Sizes.** Most of the publications related to Rowhammer use a small sample size for their experimental evaluation, sometimes only a sample size of 1. Small sample sizes are insufficient to show that an attack works in general, and it raises the question of the prevalence of Rowhammer. An attack might only work under specific conditions or not work and yield results because the Dual In-line Memory Module (DIMM) is not functioning correctly, e.g., Target Row Refresh (TRR) is not working properly.

***T*2 Overestimated Attacker Capabilities.** The assumption of unrealistic capabilities of attackers leads to an overestimation of the impact of an attack. Many attacks require specific preconditions, e.g., elevated privileges to get the physical addresses mapped to virtual addresses or access to 1 GB hugepages, etc. Some preconditions render an attack ineffective for practical exploitation, e.g., requiring elevated privileges to perform a privilege escalation attack.

***T*3 Unrealistic Attack Scenarios.** In some publications, the authors use special hardware like FPGAs to have fine control over the DRAM commands or overclock DIMMs in the BIOS. These are unrealistic attack scenarios, and it is unclear if such attacks would work in a real-world scenario.

***T*4 Results are Not Comparable with Other Publications.** The susceptibility of systems to Rowhammer depends strongly on the system itself and environmental parameters. For example, Orosa et al. [44] showed that the number of bit flips triggered depends on the temperature. Due to the lack of specifying and monitoring environmental parameters and the fact that each research group uses different systems for experimental evaluation, the results of multiple experimental evaluations are not comparable.

***T*5 Age and Wear of Hardware not Specified.** There are indicators that Rowhammer bit flips may "burn in", similar to the malicious aging of circuits [27]. Thus, when a specific bit flip is triggered many times in DRAM, the number of activations to trigger the bit flip can decrease. TRR, a proprietary Rowhammer mitigation, might have to be adjusted over time to mitigate new patterns or improve performance. Therefore, the age of a DIMM is relevant information for estimating specific properties of a DIMM.

***T*6 The Number of Bit Flips is a Bad Comparison Metric.** Typically, the number of bit flips is used as a comparison metric. However, it strongly depends on the system used for experimental evaluation. Therefore, it is impossible to compare the effectiveness of different existing approaches without repeating them in the same setup. Additionally, this metric does not provide any information regarding exploitability.

Contributions. Our work makes the following contributions:

1. We perform a meta-analysis and evaluate potential threats to Rowhammer research validity using 32 publications that performed 48 experiments.
2. We identify six threats to the validity of Rowhammer research and provide a detailed justification.
3. We identify 8 recommendations to our community that help mitigate threats to validity in Rowhammer research.

Outline. Sect. 2 provides background. Section 3 overviews threats to Rowhammer research validity. Section 5 analyzes sample sizes of prior work, Sect. 6 analyzes attack scenarios, Sect. 7 analyzes empirical results and comparability, and Sect. 8 discusses the influence of aging and wear. Section 9 analyzes comparison metrics from prior works. Section 10 concludes.

2 Background and Related Work

This section provides background on DRAM, Rowhammer, and related work.

DRAM. In DRAM, data is stored in cells consisting of capacitors and transistors, organized in an array of rows and columns. A *wordline* connects all transistors in a row, i.e., all cells in a row are accessed at once. The charge from the cells is amplified and forwarded to the *row buffer* (either SRAM or a feedback loop of the *bitlines*). Reading a cell drains the capacitor's charge, i.e., the row buffer has to be written back to the DRAM array before another row can be loaded. The memory controller must periodically refresh capacitors that lose charge over time. DDR3 [20] and DDR4 [21] use a refresh interval of 64 ms for each cell, and DDR5 [22] uses 32 ms, i.e., refresh commands must be issued for each row within this interval. Refreshes are typically performed in batches [11].

DRAM banks are located on multiple DRAM chips, and are organized in *ranks*, with one or more ranks on a DIMM. DIMMs are connected to the CPU with buses called *channels*.

DRAM Addressing. The kernel maps virtual to physical addresses using page tables. Physical addresses are mapped to different devices and their spatial components by the memory controller. For DRAM, the memory controller determines, e.g., channel, DIMM, rank, bank, row, and column, using *DRAM addressing functions*. These functions can be linear, essentially an XOR combination of physical address bits, or non-linear. Addressing functions were published for some models [2,16] but not recent ones.

Reverse-engineering linear DRAM addressing functions has been demonstrated using, e.g., timing [9,14,19,45,59] and performance counters [15]. However, non-linear DRAM addressing functions remain a challenge.

Rowhammer. When two rows in the same DRAM bank are accessed alternatingly, they are loaded into the row buffer and written back every time they are accessed, incurring numerous accesses the DRAM array. A high number of accesses to the DRAM array can lead to disturbance errors, typically in spatially nearby cells [28], called *Rowhammer*. If DRAM cells leak enough charge, their value is inverted at the sense amplifier. These bit flips have to happen before the next refresh, as cell charge is restored at refresh, i.e., fully charged or discharged. The accessed rows are called *aggressor rows*, and the rows likely to have bit flips afterward are called *victim rows*. Initially, different patterns like Single-Sided [28], Double-Sided [13], or One-Location [12] were used. Newer approaches [9,18,19] fuzz these patterns to bypass TRR.

In 2014, Kim et al. [28] published the first scientific analysis of Rowhammer. They showed that 110 of the 129 DIMMs in their FPGA-based setup are affected by Rowhammer. They also demonstrated bit flips on one Intel Sandy Bridge, Ivy Bridge, Haswell, and one AMD Piledriver system using one 2 GB DDR3 DIMM.

In 2015, Seaborn and Dullien [52] presented two Rowhammer exploits: A NaCl sandbox escape and a local privilege escalation based on flipping bits in page-table entries (PTEs). One year later, Razavi et al. [48] showed that Rowhammer can be exploited in a cross-VM scenario.

In 2014, vendors started to deploy mitigations against Rowhammer [6]. One of the first approaches was to double the refresh rate, as suggested by Kim et al. [28]. However, they already reported that lowering the refresh interval from 64 ms to 8.2 ms may degrade performance by 11 %35 %.

Another approach is to use Error Correction Code (ECC) DRAM to correct bit flips. However, Cojocar et al. [7] showed that even ECC does not prevent Rowhammer when high numbers of bit flips occur. Later, vendors introduced Target Row Refresh (TRR), a mechanism that tracks DRAM accesses and refreshes potential victim rows between regular refreshes. TRR implementations are proprietary and adjusted for new DIMMs when new attacks are published. Still, multiple publications bypassed TRR [9,12,18,19]. However, there are multiple other approaches for mitigations: Some are based on counting activations [3,43], and some on the location of rows in DRAM [5], some on cryptographic checksums [24].

Related Work. Mutlu and Kim [39] were the first to provide a retrospective of Rowhammer attacks and defenses. They surveyed the existing research papers at that time and discussed them in detail. Additionally, they focused on their previously proposed hardware mitigation PARA [28]. They also discussed Rowhammer attacks on other memory technologies, such as NAND flash.

Loughlin et al. [35] created a taxonomy for existing mitigations and proposed a memory controller extension against future attacks. They also described the limitations of countermeasures and argued that there is a disconnect between existing hardware and proposed software mitigations from the community. On the meta-level, they suggested DRAM vendors should publish precise information about their defenses to help build more effective mitigations.

Naseredini [40] surveyed of Rowhammer attacks and defenses, categorizing research into attack techniques and mitigation strategies. He analyzed them year by year and created an overview of different approaches over the years.

Recently, Zhang et al. [63] systematized Rowhammer attacks and defenses on commodity systems. They establish a unified framework to analyze Rowhammer attacks, grouping them by origins, methodologies, and objectives. They also classify various defense mechanisms including ECC and TRR.

These works provide an excellent overview of Rowhammer but do not systemically analyze problems in the research methodology that threaten validity.

3 Threats to Rowhammer Research Validity

In this section, we describe six threats to Rowhammer research validity. We identify potential problems and propose mitigations to establish a rigorous scientific process for future Rowhammer research, based on a representative set of Rowhammer publications. The results of these high-quality, peer-reviewed publications led to the insights and recommendations presented in this paper.

3.1 *T*1 Sample Sizes is Too Small

With small sample sizes, deriving general claims in empirical settings is impossible. Testing a Rowhammer attack on a single DIMM shows an attack is theoretically possible. However, a DIMM is a complex piece of electronics. Multiple potential causes exist for bit flips [38]:

- **Bad memory cells** can introduce random bit-flips.
- **Temperature** outside the operating range can impact reliability.
- **Cosmic rays** can hit DIMMs, yielding completely random bit flips.
- **Voltage fluctuations** by the power supply can introduce faults.
- **Manufacturing variations** can make a DIMM more vulnerable.
- **Electrical properties** of the motherboard (e. g., path length differences, impedance issues, or faulty contacts) can affect reliability.

Some attacks may only work due to undocumented preconditions or faulty hardware. These attacks are not reproducible, reducing trust in their validity. To reduce the influence of these factors, a higher sample size is required, ideally using different test systems. Additionally, higher sample sizes allow for the estimation of the prevalence of Rowhammer, i. e., the fraction of affected DIMMs.

A reasonable estimation of the prevalence of Rowhammer is essential: If the estimate is too low, Rowhammer research may become underrepresented despite of it's high impact. If the estimate is too high, too much effort might be put into solving a problem that only has little real-world implications.

3.2 *T*2 Dependence on Elevated Attacker Privileges

In 2015, Seaborn and Dullien [52] demonstrated two exploits based on Rowhammer: A NaCl sandbox escape and a local privilege escalation based on PTEs.

Consequently, obtaining virtual-to-physical address mappings was made privileged [29]. In newer attacks, other concepts like uncached memory [30], Transparent Hugepages (THPs) [26,48], or 1 GB Hugepages [18,19] were used. Many exploitation techniques from prior work rely on very particular prerequisites and *have been mitigated as a reaction to the publication of these techniques* by changing default configurations or requiring elevated privileges for vulnerable interfaces. Therefore, most systems with default configurations do not meet these prerequisites anymore. Elevated attacker privileges make the attack more difficult to reproduce and may decrease trust in the empirical results. As a result, Rowhammer research may become a niche area where findings are only relevant to other Rowhammer studies and lack broader implications.

3.3 $\mathcal{T}$3 Uncertain Practical Applicability

Another threat to the validity of Rowhammer research is the uncertain practical applicability of results on off-the-shelf hardware. Some experimental evaluations of Rowhammer attacks are performed on specialized hardware, e.g., FPGAs, with the advantage of fine-grained control over DRAM commands.

Additionally, some Rowhammer attacks work on commodity hardware, yet require extreme parameters for DRAM operation, e.g., extreme overclocking. Thus, these attacks require physical access and control over firmware settings.

Rowhammer simulators like Hammertime [53] and Hammulator [56] enable faster development of Rowhammer attacks and defenses by providing faster and more deterministic bit flips. However, while this enables better comparability of different Rowhammer attacks, it has the disadvantage of not being a real system. Emulators provide good metrics for comparisons, but replacing experimental evaluation with simulators might increase the difference between academic results and the real-world exploitability of Rowhammer. Such research is essential for understanding the Rowhammer effect. However, such foundational research cannot be directly applied to real-world attacks. Follow-up work is needed.

3.4 $\mathcal{T}$4 Comparability across Publications

The position and number of bit flips during a Rowhammer attack depend on environmental parameters such as temperature [44]. Additionally, they rely on the systems and DIMMs that are evaluated. Thus, directly comparing different approaches is impossible, as most publications use different setups.

In some publications, the experimental setups are not described sufficiently. For example, CPU models, DIMM model numbers, Kernel versions, etc. are often missing. The memory controller is directly integrated into the CPU. Thus, different CPU models may have different memory access behaviors. Other kernel versions may influence the attack. For example, the change in the permission of /proc/pid/pagemap [29] made the attacks more difficult, as users cannot obtain physical memory addresses. Thus, due to undocumented hard- and software, experiments are often not reproducible anymore.

The physical environment is often not documented, e.g., the temperature of the DIMMs depends on whether the test system is in an office environment or a climate-controlled server room. Therefore, the environmental effects that affect experimental results are unknown, making it hard to compare them.

Another problem is that different DIMMs, even if they are the same model, are affected differently by Rowhammer [33]. While one DIMM might yield a high number of bit flips, another DIMM of the same model might not be susceptible to Rowhammer at all. This diversity makes results hard to reproduce and hinders comparing novel and existing attacks.

3.5 $\mathcal{T}$5 Unspecified Age and Wear of Hardware

Typically, the DIMMs used in experimental setups are not documented. Scientific papers aim for general applicability rather than singling out specific manufacturers, but documentation of the used hardware is essential for reproducibility. Additionally, aging generally affects circuits and their reliability, and Karimi et al. [27] showed that this can be sped up maliciously. Thus, the DIMMs' manufacturing date and wear are crucial to contextualizing the experimental evaluation.

In DRAM, bit flips induced by Rowhammer can *"burn in"* [27], i.e., they can become more likely when triggered many times. Consequently, the susceptibility of DIMMs used for Rowhammer research has increased over the years. Typically, the usage in prior Rowhammer experiments is not documented for the DIMMs used in the experimental evaluation. Therefore, it is hard to compare the effectiveness of attacks between experiments on different DIMMs.

The algorithms used for Rowhammer attack detection in TRR are not specified, most likely differ between manufacturers and even DIMM models. Therefore, effectiveness of TRR depends on the specific model or even manufacturing date of a DIMM. Vendors may adjust TRR to mitigate published attacks in newer DIMM generations. However, when the DIMM model is unknown, it is impossible to estimate which specific attacks are mitigated by TRR.

Age and usage of a DIMM may affect the Rowhammer susceptibility and, thus, they may influence the results of empirical evaluations. However, both parameters are usually not documented, increasing the difficulty of reproducing results. In addition, it decreases the comparability of publications. Both effects might reduce the trust in experimental results.

3.6 $\mathcal{T}$6 Suboptimal Metrics for Comparison

In the current research, the susceptibility of a system to Rowhammer is often expressed in the number of bit flips found in a given time or memory area. However, these metrics are not standardized. For example, Kang et al. [26] used bit flips per hour. Other work [41] used minimal activations until the first bit flips occurred, which is also known as *hammer count*. In contrast, Jattke et al. [18] used multiple measurements, including a total bit flips found in a given time

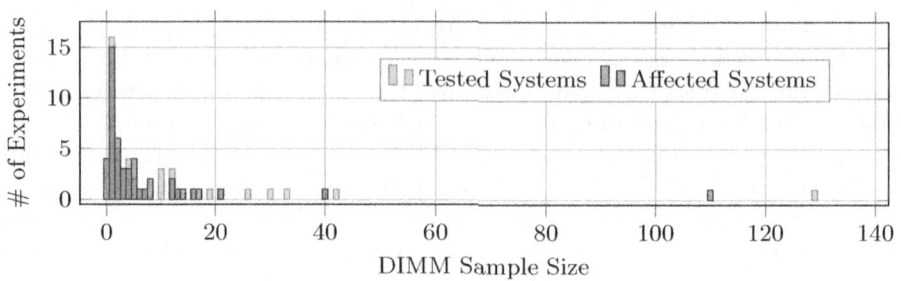

Fig. 2. Number of experiments for specific sample sizes and number of affected items.

and total number of bit flips over a sweep[2] of 256 MiB. Ridder et al. [49] used the percentage of times they observed bit flips at a vulnerable location. Thus, the metrics presented in different publications can not be used to compare the performance of attacks across publications. Therefore, to compare a novel attack to existing work, researchers must reproduce the prior attack on their hardware with their measurements. Due to the limited reproducibility of Rowhammer attacks, this is an unrealistic demand. Thus, the number of unique exploitable bit flips can be a better metric to estimate the performance of novel attacks.

Different exploitation strategies depend on *exploitable* bit flips, e. g., bit flips that occur at specific offsets and in particular directions. Typically, only one exploitable bit flip is required for a successful exploit chain. Thus, the attack runtime until the first exploitable bit flip may express a good estimation of the real-world applicability of a specific attack. Additionally, new insights on exploitation techniques may lead to novel exploit chains, allowing better estimations of the importance of Rowhammer outside the academic world. While the raw number of bit flips, either scaled by time or a number of accesses, can still be used to compare different attack strategies on a consistent test setup, it does not provide a universally comparable metric across different machines.

4 Methodology

We started with a Google Scholar search for the word "Rowhammer" and found 2509 publications. Google Scholar also includes publications that mention the word only once. Thus, we checked if a paper has ≥ 5 occurrences of that word; we ended up with 463 publications (including presentation, bachelor theses, etc.). Then, we manually filtered for peer-reviewed papers that perform Rowhammer attacks and ended up with 55 papers. Then, we filtered for papers in highly ranked conferences (CORE ranking A or A*) and ended up with 22 papers. After that, we had multiple meetings with researchers from different groups that have published Rowhammer attack papers in the past to discuss the papers and

---

[2] When Blacksmith [18] found an effective pattern, it *sweeps* over the same contiguous memory region and reports the number of bit flips.

ask if relevant papers were missing. In the end, we selected 32 publications with 48 experimental evaluations. Some of the selected studies include experimental evaluations for different approaches to different types of systems. The list of papers we used in our analysis is in Appendix 10.

5 Analysis of Sample Sizes

We survey the sample sizes of 32 publications with 48 experimental evaluations. The results are shown in Fig. 2.

The average sample size (e.g., tested DIMMs, mobile phones, single-board computers, etc. depending on the experiment) is 10.60, and the median sample size is 3.5, while most experiments used a sample size of 1. Of 48 experiments we analyzed, 16 used a sample size of 1, which limits the ability to draw general conclusions. We cannot exclude the possibility that these experiments depend on broken or faulty DIMMs and do not work on other systems. For these experiments, there is no information regarding the prevalence.

There are 19 experiments with a sample size between 2 and 10, and 6 with a sample size between 11 and 20. Three experiments have a sample size between 21 and 30, 2 between 31 and 40, and 1 between 41 and 50. After that, there is a gap until 129 DIMMs are analyzed by Kim et al. [28]. On average, 7.33 items are affected with a median of 2.0. Most experiments report 1 affected item.

The number of affected items (DIMM, Mobile Device, etc. depending on the experimental setup) was 0 in 4 experiments, so a specific attack or approach did not work. We group experiments based on the type of system verified, so it is possible that an attack worked on one system type but not the other: The experimental evaluation of HalfDouble [30] shows that it works on ARM-based devices but not on any x86-based devices. Most experiments identified 1 affected item. The small affected sample size does not allow for general conclusions, as the results may depend on broken or not correctly working DIMMs.

There are 20 experiments with a number of affected items between 2 and 10. 6 experiments show that 11 to 20 items are affected, 1 experiment reports 21, and 1 experiment reports 40 affected items. The experiment from Kim et al. [28] reports 110 affected DIMMs, the highest number of affected items. As discussed in Sect. 3.1, there are multiple reasons that bit flips can occur that are not caused by Rowhammer. While some effects, like cosmic rays, are uncontrollable and very rare, other issues, like bad memory cells, can affect multiple measurements. Therefore, our first recommendation, $\mathcal{R}1$, is to test DIMMs for any faults that may affect the accuracy of the experimental results.

> $\mathcal{R}1$: DIMMs used in empirical research must be tested for other problems, e.g., using Memtest86 (except for integrated Rowhammer tests), to ensure that no other (non-Rowhammer) problems are present.

Our second recommendation $\mathcal{R}2$ is to increase the sample size to ≥ 30 DIMMs. This number is more of a rule-of-thumb from the central limit theorem than a strict cut-off for every experiment. Still, it is frequently referenced as a minimum viable sample size to achieve at least some diversity and statistical reliability. Additionally, we recommend including multiple manufacturers, different capacities, and various speeds to demonstrate a broader coverage.

> **R2**: Increase the sample size to $\geq$ 30 DIMMs total, spread across 3 major vendors, each with at least 2 different capacities.

Our third recommendation **R3** is to encourage the scientific community to do more reproduction studies, like Gerlach et al. [10].

> **R3**: Do more reproduction studies of published work to gain more insights regarding the prevalence. More venues should accept reproduction studies.

6 Dependence on Elevated Attacker Privileges

This section reviews 32 publications and analyzes the experimental setup of 48 experiments. Figure 3 illustrates the results. The majority (68.57 %) of experimental setups use x86 systems. We hypothesize that this is the case because many tools already exist for x86, so they can be reused and adjusted. In 6 setups (12.5 %), mobile devices, such as smartphones and Chromebooks, were analyzed. Seven experimental setups (14.6 %) use an FPGA to send commands directly to the tested DIMMs. A RISC-V-based lab system was used in 1 experimental setup. For two setups, test systems were not described in detail, making it hard to reproduce them and impossible to estimate their practical impact.

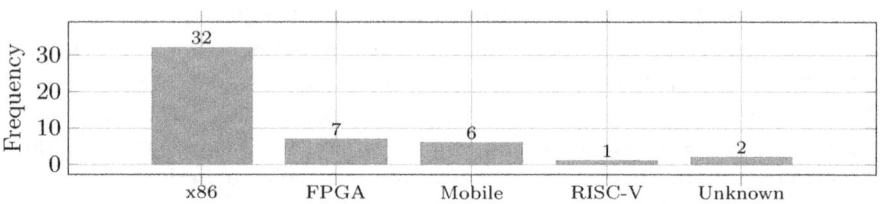

Fig. 3. Frequencies of the different experimental setups for Rowhammer experiments.

FPGA Experiments do not Reflect Realistic Attack Scenarios. FPGA-based setups send commands directly to the DIMMs. While allowing for greater control over the behavior of the DIMMs, this approach does not reflect a realistic attack scenario, where an attacker can only indirectly instruct the memory controller to access specific regions. Also, these setups may use specific parameters, e.g., timings, that are unavailable or uncommon on commodity systems. Also, it may not even be possible to configure a commodity system to use the parameters, e.g., timings, used by the FPGA-based setups. While the results of these experiments show essential insights into the DIMMs' low-level behavior, they do not represent a realistic attack scenario. Therefore, the relevance of these experiments for real-world attacks is limited.

Attacks Require Access to Pagemap File. In Linux, /proc/⟨pid⟩/pagemap maps virtual to physical addresses. Access to this file is limited to privileged users since 2015 [29]. We found that 5 experimental setups require access to the pagemap file. Therefore, this requires either a severely outdated kernel or privileged access. In the first case, many other exploits, e.g., DirtyCOW [46], can be used to escalate privileges. In the second case, the attacker already has elevated privileges, so no further escalation is necessary.

Attacks Require Elevated Privileges. We found that 6 experimental evaluations require 1 GB Hugepages. Once these Hugepages are requested from the kernel and mounted somewhere, they can be mapped without elevated privileges. However, requesting and mounting Hugepages require elevated privileges. Therefore, these attacks are only realistic when the attacker has elevated privileges, or the system has requested and mounted 1 GB Hugepages which are not used by another process (otherwise, the process of the attacker would not be able to map it). In the first case, no privilege escalation is necessary since the attacker already has root privileges. The latter case is exploitable but requires a specific, non-default system configuration.

Attacks Require Special OS Settings. Razavi et al. [48] showed that exploiting Kernel Same-page Merging (KSM) combined with Rowhammer to trigger bit flips on another KVM guest on the same host is possible. However, this requires KSM to be enabled, which is not the case by default for most Linux distributions, except for special ones like Proxmox VE. The attack also requires the attacker's process to be started in the attacker's VM before the process of the victim is started—similarly, Bosman et al. [4] exploited memory deduplication on Windows with a Rowhammer attack. Memory deduplication is a feature from Hyper-V and is not enabled by default on Windows Server. In our survey, we found that only 11 experimental evaluations assume a realistic attack scenario exploitable on a commodity system with default configuration. Since the prevalence of affected systems is not known as described in Sect. 5, no statistically significant estimations on the number of systems affected by Rowhammer can be made. Most publications introduce attacks assuming unrealistically high capabilities of the attacker or uncommon system configurations. Other publications require a custom memory controller based on an FPGA. Therefore, attacks should be classified based on the required preconditions. For example, attacks that require specific, non-standard configurations, should provide a reasonable explanation of why this configuration is realistic. Attacks that assume an unrealistically capable adversary should be clearly labeled as such. We recommend in $\mathcal{R}4$ distinguishing between attacks that are possible in theory and attacks exploitable in a realistic experimental setup.

R4: Attacks should only be classified as such when assessed under realistic attack scenarios, and there should be a more apparent distinction between actual attacks and potential (theoretical) attacks.

7 Comparability across Publications

Orosa et al. [44] showed that the number and position of bit flips depend on environmental parameters, e. g., temperature. Thus, comparing results from the same experimental setup is difficult when environmental parameters are unknown. Out of 48 experimental setups inspected, only 2 [36,44] verified the impact of the temperature. In 2 other experiments, the authors reported a constant temperature [37,61]. Two experiments measured the impact of the refresh interval t_{REFI}, but did not specify the temperature. 44 (91.6 %) did not specify the temperature and 46 experiments (95.83 %) did not specify t_{REFI}. The refresh interval t_{REFI} is defined to be 64 ms on DDR3 and DDR4 and 32 ms on DDR5. However, some mitigations set t_{REFI} to 32 ms on DDR3. In total, 42 experimental evaluation setups did not document any environmental parameters. Typically, no experimental evaluation of prior work is performed when a new attack is published. Due to the variability between experimental setups, new attacks' performance can not be compared to prior work.

Environmental parameters known to have effects on the susceptibility of systems to Rowhammer should be controlled, monitored, and documented in future work, In the case of temperature, we recommend keeping the room at a fixed, measured temperature or measuring the temperatures with the integrated sensors of the lab systems. t_{REFI} should be measured and documented for each system. Additionally, we should encourage reproducing prior experiments on different test setups to gain some "ground truth", which allows for better confidence when comparing different approaches.

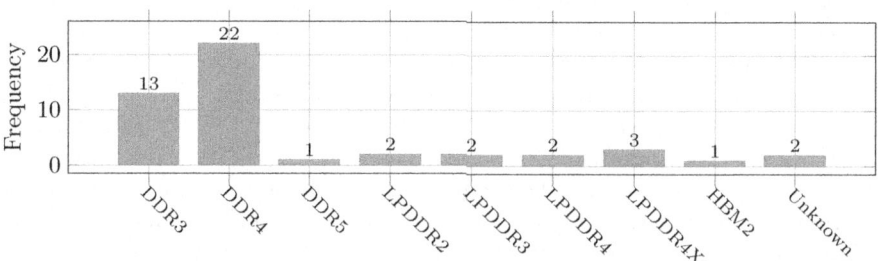

Fig. 4. Frequencies of different DRAM types in the analyzed experimental evaluations.

8 Unspecified Age and Wear of Hardware

DIMMs used for security research could be highly susceptible to Rowhammer because bit flips could "burn in" [27,28]. However, most publications do not include the manufacturing date or wear of the DIMMs. This can lead to a self-increasing effect as DIMMs are used in more experiments over time [27,28]. Since DDR4, most DIMMs support TRR, a Rowhammer mitigation based on detecting Rowhammer patterns. However, TRR is an umbrella term for many different (proprietary) vendor implementations. We assume that more recent TRR versions protect against more recent Rowhammer attacks. However, only 7 of the experimental evaluations we analyzed specify the manufacturing dates. It is impossible to estimate whether the hypothesis that older DIMMs are more strongly affected by older attacks is true. We recommend in $\mathcal{R}5$ that authors should publish the manufacturing date of DIMMs.

$\mathcal{R}5$: Authors should publish the manufacturing data of the DIMMs used in experimental evaluation.

In contrast to the manufacturing data, most papers specify the DRAM generation used in the experimental evaluation. Figure 4 gives an overview of different DRAM generations and the number of experimental evaluations that used them. We show that 13 experimental setups utilize DDR3 DIMMs and 22 utilize DDR4 DIMMs. In contrast, only 1 experimental evaluation was done on DDR5, even though it was released in 2020. The number of experiments performed on LPDDR is much lower: There are 2 experiments on LPDDR2, LPDDR3, and LPDDR4 each. For LPDDR4X, there are 3 experiments. Only 1 experiment analyzed Rowhammer on HBM2. Two publications did not mention which DRAM generation they used for experimental evaluation.

The generation of DRAM can be used to derive information regarding the age of the tested DIMM. Taking the year of the publication and the DRAM standard into account, and assuming that the DIMM was not manufactured after the standard for the next generation was available, we calculate the potential age of DIMMs used for experimental evaluation. The results are shown in Fig. 5

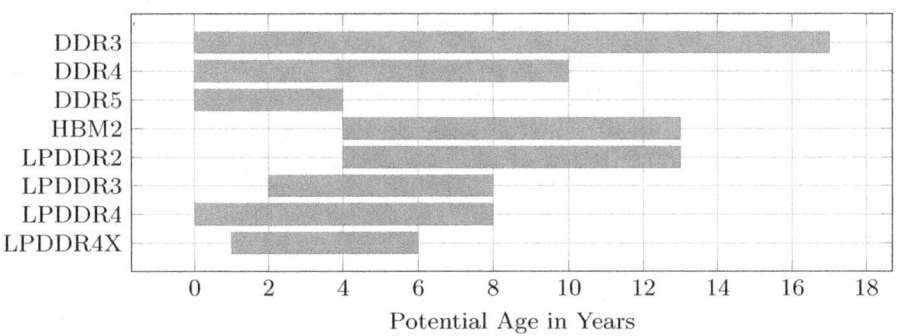

Fig. 5. Estimated potential age of DIMMs at the time of experimental evaluation.

When using this approach, the potential minimum age of a DDR3 DIMM, while used in an experiment, is 0 years for a publication from 2014 [28] when assuming the DIMM was manufactured in 2014 since the DDR4 standard was released in 2014. The maximum age of DDR3 DIMMs used in any studies is 17 years in the case of a publication from 2024 [26] when assuming the DIMM was manufactured in 2007, immediately after the standard was launched. Different DRAM generations and standards have varying age ranges, affecting the reliability and features of DIMMs. Therefore, $\mathcal{R}6$ states that authors should document the actual manufacturing dates of the used DIMMs. Additionally, they should provide an estimation of the wear of the DIMMs, e. g., how long and often they were used for Rowhammer evaluation. This would allow estimations on the reliability on the DIMMs, based on their age and wear.

> $\mathcal{R}6$: Authors should submit information about the DIMMs' wear in experimental evaluation.

9 Suboptimal Metrics for Comparison

Kim et al. [28] were the first to use the number of bit flips as an absolute metric. This metric depends on the execution strategy, e. g., if the same memory area is scanned multiple times. Also, some works count only unique bit flips, while others count all. In that context, *uniqueness* may be based on the same memory cell, access patterns, and data stored in cells before performing the Rowhammer attack. Additionally, the number of bit flips strongly depends on the experiment's runtime or the size of the scanned memory area. This approach is used in multiple papers in our survey [9,26,28,34,36,58,62].

Some papers use the relative number of bit flips as an alternative. This approach aims to make the absolute number of bit flips comparable. By normalizing the number of bits flips against a reference value, e. g., the size of the scanned memory area or the scan time, this metric estimates how affected a single setup, or DIMM, actually is. However, these relative metrics are still influenced by the same factors as the absolute number of bit flips. This approach is used in multiple publications [10,12,19,25,28,30,37,42,49,55,58,60]. In contrast to counting all bit flips, other publications count only exploitable bit flips. Exploitable bit flips is a better metric for estimating the impact of potential exploitation. However, this strongly depends on the definition of *exploitable*: Attacks based on bit flips in the Page Frame Number (PFN) part of a PTE [7,18,19,30]. It was also shown that cryptographic algorithms can be attacked by flipping bits in the keys [7,18,19,48]. Bit flips can target opcodes in binaries and libraries [7,12,18,19]. There are also attacks based on bit flips in URLs [48]. Thus, in ℛ7, authors should include multiple metrics for bit flips.

> **ℛ7**: Authors should use multiple metrics for bit flips to allow for better comparisons to other works.

10 Conclusion

We systematically analyzed 32 publications with 48 experimental evaluations and identified six major threats to Rowhammer's research validity. We have shown that in 33 % of the experiments, the sample size is only 1; therefore, many other factors could be the reason for bit flips. From the overall 32 x86 consumer hardware, only 22 described an approach to get physical addressing information. Half of these 22 experiments on x86 required unrealistically high capabilities of an attacker (e. g., root privileges), making them an isolated problem in academia. We found that the experimental results are often incomparable because environmental parameters are not controlled or documented, and inconsistent units for bit flips have been used. Additionally, 25 analyzed publications do not document the age and wear of used hardware. We developed the following 7 recommendations with detailed justification to improve future Rowhammer research: pre-experimental testing of the DIMMs, increasing sample size, value reproduction studies, defining attacks in real-world conditions and distinguishing them from theoretical ones, publishing more information about the used DIMMs, including wear, and using multiple units for bit flips evaluation.

Acknowledgments. This work was funded by the Deutsche Forschungsgemeinschaft under grant number 503876675 and the Austrian Science Fund under grant number 10.55776/I6054, as well as the European Union under grant number ROF-SG20-3066-3-2-2.

Appendix

Table 1 overviews the analyzed Rowhammer studies.

Table 1. Overview of the analyzed Rowhammer studies.

Author	Pattern	Memory Type	Environment	Test Setup	Focus	Sample size	Flips observed on	Year
Kim et al. [28]	One-Location	DDR3	Unspecified	FPGA	Bit Flips	129 DIMMs	110 DIMMs	2014
Qiao and Seaborn [47]	?	?	Unspecified	Unspecified	Exploitation	?	?	2016
Bosman et al. [4]	Double-Sided	DDR3	Unspecified	1 Lab System	Exploitation	1 DIMM	1 DIMM	2016
Veen et al. [58]	Double-Sided	LPDDR2	Unspecified	1 Smartphone	Exploitation, Bit Flips	1 Smartphone	1 Smartphone	2016
Veen et al. [58]	Double-Sided	LPDDR3	Unspecified	26 Smartphones	Exploitation, Bit Flips	26 Smartphones	17 Smartphones	2016
Veen et al. [58]	Double-Sided	LPDDR4	Unspecified	1 Smartphone	Exploitation, Bit Flips	1 Smartphones	0 Smartphones	2016
Razavi et al. [48]	Double-Sided	DDR3	Unspecified	1 Lab System	Exploitation	1 DIMM	1 DIMM	2016
Xiao et al. [60]	Single-Sided, Double-Sided	DDR3	Unspecified	5 Lab Systems	Exploitation, Bit Flips	5 DIMMs	4 DIMMs (only done on 4)	2016
Xiao et al. [60]	Single-Sided, Double-Sided	DDR4	Unspecified	1 Lab System	Exploitation, Bit Flips	1 DIMM	0 DIMMs (not done on DDR4)	2016
Gruss et al. [13]	Double-Sided	DDR3	Unspecified	2 Lab Systems	Bit Flips	6 DIMMs	5 DIMMs	2016
Gruss et al. [13]	Double-Sided	DDR4	tREFI	2 Lab Systems	Bit Flips	4 DIMMs	2 DIMMs	2016
Jang et al. [17]	Double-Sided	DDR4	Unspecified	1 Lab System	Exploitation, Bit Flips	1 DIMM	1 DIMM	2017
Aga et al. [1]	Single-Sided, Double-Sided	DDR3	Unspecified	1 Lab System	Bit Flips	4 DIMMs	3 DIMMs	2018
Gruss et al. [12]	One-Location	DDR3	Unspecified	2 Lab Systems	Exploitation, Bit Flips	4 DIMMs	4 DIMMs	2018
Gruss et al. [12]	One-Location	DDR4	Unspecified	1 Lab System	Exploitation, Bit Flips	2 DIMMs	2 DIMMs	2018
Tatar et al. [54]	Single-, Double-Sided, Amplified	DDR3	Unspecified	2 Lab Systems	Exploitation	33 Memory Setups?	14 Memory Setups?	2018
Lipp et al. [34]	Double-Sided	DDR4	Unspecified	3 Lab Systems	Exploitation, Bit Flips	1 DIMM	1 DIMM	2018
Lipp et al. [34]	One-Location	LPDDR2	Unspecified	1 Smartphone	Exploitation, Bit Flips	1 Smartphone	1 Smartphone	2018
Tatar et al. [55]	Double-Sided	DDR3	Unspecified	2 Lab Systems	Bit Flips	4 DIMMs	4 DIMMs	2018
Zhang et al. [62]	Double-Sided	LPDDR3	Unspecified	1 Single Board Computer	Bit Flips	1 Single Board	1 Single Board	2018
Cojocar et al. [7]	Double-Sided	?	Unspecified	?	Exploitation	?	?	2019
Ji et al. [23]	Single-Sided, Double-Sided	DDR3	Unspecified	1 Lab System	Bit Flips	16 DIMMs	12 DIMMs	2019
Kwong et al. [31]	Many-Sided	DDR4	Unspecified	1 Lab System	Bit Flips	2 DIMMs	2 DIMMs	2020
Frigo et al. [9]	Many-Sided	LPDDR4X	Unspecified	13 Mobile Devices	Bit Flips	42 DIMMs	13 DIMMs	2020
Frigo et al. [9]	Many-Sided	DDR4	Unspecified	3 Lab Systems	Bit Flips	13 Mobile Devices	5 Mobile Devices	2020
Ridder et al. [49]	Fuzzed (Blacksmith)	DDR4	Unspecified	10 Lab Systems	Bit Flips	5 DIMMs	3 - 5 DIMMs (not clarified)	2021
Jattke et al. [18]	Fuzzed (Blacksmith)	LPDDR4X	Unspecified	JEDEC developer board	Bit flips	40 DIMMs	40 DIMMs	2022
Jattke et al. [18]	Half-Double	DDR4	Unspecified	FPGA	Bit Flips	19 Chips	16 Chips	2022
Kogler et al. [30]	Half-Double	LPDDR4X	Unspecified	7 Mobile Devices	Bit Flips	3 DIMMs	2 DIMMs	2022
Kogler et al. [30]	Half-Double	DDR4	Unspecified	1 Notebook	Bit Flips	7 Mobile Devices	5 Mobile Devices	2022
Kogler et al. [30]	Half-Double	LPDDR4	Unspecified	2 MiniPCs	Bit Flips	1 Notebook	0 Notebooks	2022
Tobah et al. [57]	Double-Sided	DDR3	Unspecified	1 Lab System	Exploitation, Bit Flips	2 MiniPCs	0 MiniPCs	2022
Tobah et al. [57]	Many-Sided	DDR4	Unspecified	3 Lab Systems	Exploitation, Bit Flips	3 DIMMs	3 DIMMs	2022
Orosa et al. [44]	Double-Sided	DDR4	Temperature	FPGA	Bit Flips	12 DIMMs	12 DIMMs	2022
Yağlıkçı et al. [61]	Double-Sided	DDR3	50C	FPGA	Exploitation	30 DIMMs (272 Chips)	64 DIMMs	2022
Fahr Jr et al. [8]	Fuzzed (Blacksmith)	DDR4	Unspecified	1 Lab System	Bit Flips	2 DIMMs	¿= 1 DIMM	2023
Gerlach et al. [10]	Double-Sided	DDR4	Unspecified	4 Lab Systems	Bit Flips	10 DIMMs	8 DIMMs	2023
Olgun et al. [42]	Double-Sided	HBM2	Unspecified	FPGA	Bit Flips	1 Chip	1 Chip	2023
Luo et al. [36]	Single-Sided	DDR4	Temperature	FPGA	Bit Flips	21 DIMMs	21 DIMMs	2023
Luo et al. [36]	Single-Sided	DDR4	Unspecified	1 Lab System	Bit Flips	1 DIMM	1 DIMM	2023
Juffinger et al. [25]	Fuzzed (Blacksmith)	DDR4	Unspecified	Lab Systems	Bit Flips	12 DIMMs	6 DIMMs	2024
Juffinger et al. [25]	Single-Sided	DDR4	Unspecified	Lab Systems	Bit Flips	12 DIMMs	2 DIMMs	2024
Marazzi and Razavi [37]	Double-Sided	DDR4	23C	1 Lab System (RISC-V)	Bit Flips	1 DIMM	1 DIMM	2024
Kang et al. [26]	Many-Sided	DDR3	Unspecified	1 Lab System	Bit Flips	1 DIMM	? DIMMs	2024
Kang et al. [26]	Many-Sided	DDR4	Unspecified	1 Lab System	Bit Flips	2 DIMMs	2 DIMMs (not clarified)	2024
Jattke et al. [19]	Fuzzed (Zenhammer)	DDR4	Unspecified	3 Lab Systems	Bit Flips	10 DIMMs	8 DIMMs	2024
Jattke et al. [19]	Fuzzed (Zenhammer)	DDR5	Unspecified	1 Lab System	Bit Flips	10 DIMMs	1 DIMM	2024

References

1. Aga, M.T., Aweke, Z.B., Austin, T.: When good protections go bad: exploiting anti-DoS measures to accelerate Rowhammer attacks. In: HOST (2017)
2. AMD: BIOS and Kernel Developer's Guide (BKDG) for AMD Family 16h Models 00h-0Fh Processors (2015)
3. Aweke, Z.B., et al.: ANVIL: Software-based protection against next-generation Rowhammer attacks. In: ACM SIGPLAN Notices, vol. 51, pp. 743–755 (2016)
4. Bosman, E., Razavi, K., Bos, H., Giuffrida, C.: Dedup est machina: memory deduplication as an advanced exploitation vector. In: S&P (2016)
5. Brasser, F., Davi, L., Gens, D., Liebchen, C., Sadeghi, A.R.: CAn't touch this: software-only mitigation against Rowhammer attacks targeting kernel memory. In: USENIX Security (2017)
6. Chromium Issue Tracker: Security: NaCl sandbox escape via DRAM "rowhammer" memory corruption (2014)
7. Cojocar, L., Razavi, K., Giuffrida, C., Bos, H.: Exploiting correcting codes: on the effectiveness of ECC memory against Rowhammer attacks. In: S&P (2019)
8. Fahr Jr, M., et al.: When Frodo Flips: End-to-End key recovery on FrodoKEM via Rowhammer. In: CCS (2022)
9. Frigo, P., et al.: TRRespass: exploiting the many sides of target row refresh. In: S&P (2020)
10. Gerlach, L., Thomas, F., Pietsch, R., Schwarz, M.: A Rowhammer reproduction study using the Blacksmith Fuzzer. In: European Symposium on Research in Computer Security (2023)
11. Google: Measuring the DRAM refresh rate by timing memory accesses (2015)
12. Gruss, D., et al.: Another Flip in the wall of Rowhammer defenses. In: S&P (2018)
13. Gruss, D., Maurice, C., Mangard, S.: Rowhammer.js: a remote software-induced fault attack in JavaScript. In: DIMVA (2016)
14. Heckel, M., Adamsky, F.: Reverse-engineering bank addressing functions on AMD CPUs. In: Workshop on DRAM Security (DRAMSec) (2023)
15. Helm, C., Akiyama, S., Taura, K.: Reliable reverse engineering of intel DRAM addressing using performance counters. In: Modeling, Analysis, and Simulation of Computer and Telecommunication Systems (MASCOTS). IEEE (2020)
16. Intel: Intel Xeon Processor E5 v4 product family: datasheet volume 2: registers (2016)
17. Jang, Y., Lee, J., Lee, S., Kim, T.: SGX-bomb: locking down the processor via Rowhammer attack. In: SysTEX (2017)
18. Jattke, P., van der Veen, V., Frigo, P., Gunter, S., Razavi, K.: BLACKSMITH: Rowhammering in the frequency domain. In: S&P (2021)
19. Jattke, P., Wipfli, M., Solt, F., Marazzi, M., Bölcskei, M., Razavi, K.: ZenHammer: Rowhammer attacks on AMD Zenbased Platforms. In: USENIX Security (2024)
20. JEDEC Solid State Technology. DDR3 SDRAM Standard (2012)
21. JEDEC Solid State Technology. DDR4 SDRAM Standard (2021)
22. JEDEC Solid State Technology. DDR5 SDRAM Standard (2024)
23. Ji, S., Ko, Y., Oh, S., Kim, J.: Pinpoint Rowhammer: suppressing unwanted Bit Flips on Rowhammer attacks. In: AsiaCCS (2019)
24. Juffinger, J., Lamster, L., Kogler, A., Eichlseder, M., Lipp, M., Gruss, D.: CSI: Rowhammer - cryptographic security and integrity against Rowhammer. In: S&P (2023)

25. Juffinger, J., Raghav Neela, S., Heckel, M., Schwarz, L., Adamsky, F., Gruss, D.: Presshammer: Rowhammer and Rowpress without physical address information. In: DIMVA (2024)
26. Kang, I., et al.: SledgeHammer: amplifying Rowhammer via bank-level parallelism. In: USENIX Security (2024)
27. Karimi, N., Kanuparthi, A.K., Wang, X., Sinanoglu, O., Karri, R.: MAGIC: malicious aging in circuits/- cores. In: ACM TACO (2015)
28. Kim, Y., et al.: Flipping Bits in memory without accessing them: an experimental study of DRAM disturbance errors. In: ISCA (2014)
29. Shutemov, K.A.: Pagemap: do not leak physical addresses to non- privileged userspace (2015)
30. Kogler, A., et al.: Half- double: hammering from the next row over. In: USENIX Security (2022)
31. Kwong, A., Genkin, D., Gruss, D., Yarom, Y.: RAMBleed: reading bits in memory without accessing them. In: S&P (2020)
32. Lee, B.C., Ipek, E., Mutlu, O., Burger, D.: Architecting phase change memory as a scalable DRAM alternative. In: International Symposium on Computer Architecture (ISCA) (2009)
33. Li, D., et al.: FPHammer: a device identification framework based on DRAM fingerprinting. In: TrustCom (2023)
34. Lipp, M., et al.: Nethammer: inducing Rowhammer faults through network requests. In: SILM Workshop (2020)
35. Loughlin, K., Saroiu, S., Wolman, A., Kasikci, B.: Stop! Hammer time: rethinking our approach to Rowhammer mitigations. In: Workshop on Hot Topics in Operating Systems (2021)
36. Luo, H., et al.: RowPress: amplifying read disturbance in modern DRAM chips. In: ISCA (2023)
37. Marazzi, M., Razavi, K.: RISC-H: Rowhammer attacks on RISC-V. In: Workshop on DRAM Security (DRAMSec) (2024)
38. Memtest86: Troubleshooting Memory Errors (2021)
39. Mutlu, O., Kim, J.S.: RowHammer: a retrospective. In: IEEE TCAD (2020)
40. Naseredini, A.: Exploring the horizon: a comprehensive survey of Rowhammer. arXiv preprint arXiv: 2310.06950 (2023)
41. Olgun, A., et al.: Variable read disturbance: an experimental analysis of temporal variation in DRAM read disturbance. In: HPCA (2025)
42. Olgun, A., et al.: An experimental analysis of RowHammer in HBM2 DRAM chips. In: DSN (2023)
43. Olgun, A., et al.: ABACuS: all-bank activation counters for scalable and low overhead RowHammer mitigation. In: USENIX Security (2024)
44. Orosa, L., et al.: Spyhammer: using Rowhammer to remotely spy on temperature. arXiv preprint arXiv:2210.04084 (2022)
45. Pessl, P., Gruss, D., Maurice, C., Schwarz, M., Mangard, S.: DRAMA: exploiting DRAM addressing for cross-CPU attacks. In: USENIX Security (2016)
46. Oester, P.: CVE-2016-5195 (2016)
47. Qiao, R., Seaborn, M.: A new approach for Rowhammer attacks. In: HOST (2016)
48. Razavi, K., Gras, B., Bosman, E., Preneel, B., Giuffrida, C., Bos, H.: Flip Feng Shui: hammering a needle in the software stack. In: USENIX Security (2016)
49. de Ridder, F., Frigo, P., Vannacci, E., Bos, H., Giuffrida, C., Razavi, K.: SMASH: synchronized many-sided Rowhammer attacks from JavaScript. In: USENIX Security (2021)

50. Jerome, H., Saltzer, M., Kaashoek, F.: Principles of Computer System Design: An Introduction (2009)
51. Seaborn, M.: Exploiting the DRAM Rowhammer bug to gain kernel privileges (2015)
52. Seaborn, M., Dullien, T.: Exploiting the DRAM Rowhammer bug to gain kernel privileges. In: Black Hat USA (2015)
53. Tatar, A.: Hammertime: a software suite for testing, profiling and simulating the Rowhammer DRAM defect (2018)
54. Tatar, A., Giuffrida, C., Bos, H., Razavi, K.: Defeating software mitigations against Rowhammer: a surgical precision hammer. In: RAID (2018)
55. Tatar, A., Krishnan, R., Athanasopoulos, E., Giuffrida, C., Bos, H., Razavi, K.: Throwhammer: Rowhammer attacks over the network and defenses. In: USENIX ATC (2018)
56. Thomas, F., Gerlach, L., Schwarz, M.: Hammulator: simulate now - exploit later. In: DRAMSec (2023)
57. Tobah, Y., Kwong, A., Kang, I., Genkin, D., Shin, K.G.: SpecHammer: combining Spectre and Rowhammer for new speculative attacks. In: S&P (2022)
58. van der Veen, V., et al.: Drammer: deterministic Rowhammer attacks on mobile platforms. In: CCS (2016)
59. Wang, M., Zhang, Z., Cheng, Y., Nepal, S.: Dramdig: a knowledge-assisted tool to UncoverDRAM address mapping. In: Design Automation Conference (DAC) (2020)
60. Xiao, Y., Zhang, X., Zhang, Y., Teodorescu, R.: One Bit Flips, one cloud flops: cross-VM row hammer attacks and privilege escalation. In: USENIX Security (2016)
61. Giray Yağlık, A., et al.: Understanding RowHammer under reduced wordline voltage: an experimental study using real DRAM devices. In: DSN (2022)
62. Zhang, Z., Zhan, Z., Balasubramanian, D., Koutsoukos, X., Karsai, G.: Triggering Rowhammer hardware faults on ARM: a revisit. In: ASHES Workshop (2018)
63. Zhang, Z., et al.: SoK: Rowhammer on commodity operating systems. In: Asia CCS (2024). https://doi.org/10.1145/3634737.3656998

Personalized Password Guessing via Modeling Multiple Leaked Credentials of the Same User

Fugeng Huang[1], Jiahong Yang[1], Haibo Cheng[1](✉), Wenting Li[2], and Ping Wang[1](✉)

[1] Peking University, Beijing 100871, China
huangfugeng@stu.pku.edu.cn, {jiahongyang,hbcheng,pwang}@pku.edu.cn
[2] Beijing Institute of Graphic Communication, Beijing 102600, China
wentingli@pku.edu.cn

Abstract. As password breaches increase, users frequently face multiple password leaks. Because of memory limitations, users often reuse or slightly modify their passwords across different accounts. This behavior makes targeted password-guessing attacks, which leverage leaked passwords, a serious security threat. While previous studies have primarily focused on single-leak scenarios, where the attacker possesses only one leaked password, multi-leak scenarios remain insufficiently explored.

In this work, we propose Pass2Pass-T, a model designed to capture similarities across multiple passwords from the same user. Pass2Pass-T leverages Transformers to predict a target password from multiple leaked passwords of the same user. Additionally, we are the first to empirically evaluate the multi-leak attacks on real-world password datasets.

In multi-leak scenarios, Pass2Pass-T enhances the Transformer with input compression and segmented positional encoding, tailored to the distinct characteristics of password sequences unlike natural language texts.

It also utilizes transfer learning to effectively model patterns across multiple passwords. With five leaked passwords, our model compromises 4.87% of user accounts on the first guess, achieving a 7.27× improvement over state-of-the-art strategies that process each leaked password individually. In single-leak scenarios, Pass2Pass-T matches existing models at 1,000 guesses and achieves a 4.46% improvement at 10^7 guesses.

Keywords: Password Reuse · Password Guessing · Multi-Password Model · Credential Tweaking

1 Introduction

Text passwords remain one of the most widely used methods of user authentication, despite the availability of various alternative methods [6,11,13]. The rapid expansion of the Internet has led users to manage an ever-increasing number of accounts; indeed, a 17-country survey by NordPass reveals that the average Internet user manages 255 passwords [15]. Driven by memory constraints, users often generate passwords based on predictable semantic patterns [10]. Moreover, the sheer volume of accounts often leads them to reuse passwords across numerous services [4,7,14,16,18]. Consequently, because of these user password behaviors, passwords become highly susceptible to guessing attacks [12,17,21].

The pervasive issue of password breaches further amplifies the risk, as these breaches frequently expose users to multiple leaked passwords, thereby providing attackers with richer data for more sophisticated guessing techniques. Empirical evidence consistently highlights this widespread problem: a 2018 study [3] found 14,979 breach events across 5,000 email accounts—an average (and median) of three leaks per account. Further demonstrating the scale, the aggregated RaidForums Massive Database Collection (RMDC) compiled by Cheng et al. [2] reveals that 6.9 million users have at least five passwords leaked. Consistent with these findings, our analysis indicates that approximately 25% of users had password exposures across at least five distinct domains (as shown in Fig. 1), based on querying 1,000 randomly sampled email addresses from RMDC using the *Have I Been Pwned* API [9].

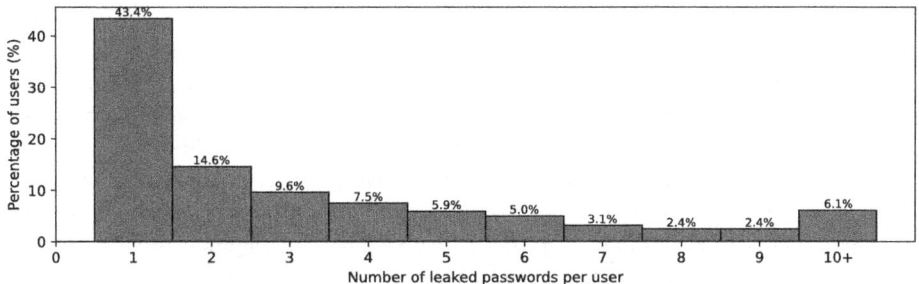

Fig. 1. Distribution of per-user password exposures across distinct domains

Several guessing algorithms have been proposed to characterize password security when attackers have access to leaked passwords. These include approaches by Das et al. [4], Pal et al. [16] (Pass2Path), Wang et al. [20] (Pass2Edit), and Xiu and Wang [21] (PointerGuess). However, these studies primarily focus on *single-leak* scenarios, also leak as credential tweaking, where an attacker has access to only one leaked password per user. In contrast, *multi-leak* scenarios, where users may leak *varying numbers* of passwords, remain largely unexplored. Even so, a few preliminary approaches have been proposed to tackle this setting. Pal et al. [16] propose a straightforward round-robin strategy, which applies a single-leak model (e.g., Pass2Path) to each available leaked password in turn and interleaves the resulting guess lists. However, neither their study nor subsequent work has evaluated the practical performance of the round-robin strategy. Xiu and Wang [21] proposed MSPointerGuess, a multi-leak password model designed to combine clues from multiple leaked passwords. MSPointerGuess encodes leaked passwords from each website using separate encoders that share only architecture but not parameters, and then employs a learnable soft gate to dynamically determine the information drawn from each source.

Despite these advancements, MSPointerGuess [21] faces significant limitations. In multi-leak settings, the number of leaked passwords for each user and their source websites vary widely. Consequently, requiring a distinct encoder for each leaked password severely hinders the model's scalability. Even with shared encoder architecture, this design implies a rigid model structure that must be specifically tailored or trained for each distinct number of leaked passwords a user possesses. This makes it poorly adaptable to the wide variability in leak counts observed in real-world scenarios, thereby limiting its practical applicability and effectiveness.

Our Contributions

In this paper, we focus on multi-leak scenarios and aim to build a probability model that accurately captures the similarity among multiple passwords from the same user for password guessing.

We propose Pass2Pass-T, a Transformer-based [19] password probability model, for predicting a target password from one or multiple leaked passwords of the same user. Fundamentally, it operates by concatenating leaked passwords into a single sequence which is then fed into the Transformer for guess generation. Recognizing that these concatenated password sequences differ from natural language in three key aspects: their semi-structured nature, high repetitiveness, and lack of typical syntax, we introduce several adaptations. First, we refine the positional encoding by introducing a segment-wise scheme tailored to password sequences. For data augmentation, we also apply epoch-level random shuffling of leaked passwords. Second, departing from common tokenization techniques, we propose a repetition-aware compression scheme to represent the relationships among leaked passwords more clearly and concisely. Finally, we leverage transfer learning by pre-training on extensive single-leak data and fine-tuning on comparatively smaller multi-leak data.

We evaluate existing models under single-leak and multi-leak scenarios.

In the *single-leak scenario*, where the attacker holds exactly one leaked password per user, our method achieves a 4.46% attack-success advantage over the best models at the 10^7-guess mark.

In the *multi-leak scenario*, where the attacker has access to multiple leaked passwords per user, our method surpasses previous state-of-the-art methods: it compromises 4.87% of user accounts on the first guess—a 7.27× improvement over the best prior multi-leak attack—and breaks 16.36% of accounts within the first five guesses, a 58.9% relative gain. We provide the first systematic empirical evaluation of round-robin guessing, comparing it directly with our multi-leak model.

To summarize, we mainly have the following contributions.

- We focus on multi-leak scenarios, propose Pass2Pass-T, to predict a target password based on several leaked passwords from the same user. Our model

mainly leverage Transformer and enhances it with input compression and segmented positional encoding, tailored to the distinct characteristics of password sequences unlike natural language texts.
- We evaluate Pass2Pass-T and show it outperforms existing attacks in both multi-leak scenarios and single-leak scenarios.
- Our multi-similarity model adapts to an arbitrary number of leak passwords, whereas MSPointerGuess requires training and testing on a fixed number of leak passwords.

2 Related Work

2.1 Password Reuse Behaviors

Due to cognitive limitations, users frequently reuse or only slightly modify passwords across different online services. Florencio and Herley [5] first documented the widespread prevalence of password reuse and weak passwords in a large-scale user study in 2007; later, Das *et al.* [4] corroborated these findings using website data at NDSS'14. Subsequent studies, such as Pearman *et al.* [18], found that passwords containing special characters or numbers are more likely to be reused. These findings highlight the persistent and multifaceted nature of password reuse.

2.2 Personalized Password Guessing via Leaked Passwords

Attackers can exploit users' habit of reusing or slightly modifying existing passwords across different websites. In 2019, Pal *et al.* [16] proposed *Pass2Path*, a sequence-to-sequence model that converts old passwords into sequences of character-level edits, cracking nearly 48% of accounts within 1,000 guesses. However, it cannot capture the mutual influence among edit operations and the transformation effects they produce, nor can it leverage popular password dictionaries. At USENIX Security 2023, Wang *et al.* [20] introduced *Pass2Edit*, which breaks password transformation into multi-step classification, improving success rates by 43% over *Pass2Path* in the first 100 guesses for normal users, and by another 24% when adding a global dictionary. Yet both *Pass2Edit* and *Pass2Path* only perform single-character edits and remove dissimilar pairs during training, limiting their ability to model long-range transformations. In 2024, Xiu and Wang [21] proposed *PointerGuess*, which builds on Bahdanau et al.'s attention mechanism [1] and Long Short-Term Memory (LSTM) networks [8], and uses a pointer network to jointly model copying old characters and generating new ones, supporting both personalized and population-level reuse behaviors without external dictionaries, and further extended it to multi-leak settings as *MSPointerGuess*.

3 Multi-leak Password-Guessing Attack

In this section, we introduce the data processing methods and analyze the password reuse behavior and characteristics of passwords across multiple accounts. Based on this analysis, we propose our model, Pass2Pass-T.

3.1 Dataset Collection and Pre-Processing

We use the RMDC email aggregation dataset as multi-leak data. Originally, it was a password vault dataset covering aggregated data from 28 sites, with each user having a different number of leaks.

Terminology. This paper directly employs the RMDC dataset that is released in work [2]. To familiarise readers with its properties, we briefly summarise the main cleaning steps below.

Data Source and Preprocessing. The raw RMDC archive (182 sites, about 427GB) was collected from public hacker forums. We keep only 28 plain-text dump files and apply three sequential filters: (i) remove passwords containing non-printable ASCII characters; (ii) retain entries whose user-name length is ≥ 3 and password length is 4–25; (iii) require the e-mail field to contain the "@" symbol.

Aggregation Strategy. After cleaning, they aggregate accounts by e-mail address rather than user name. This prevents extremely common user names (e.g. "abc") from merging passwords belonging to different individuals into the same vault, which would otherwise contaminate cross-user data. Although e-mail aggregation can occasionally split a single user's credentials across multiple vaults, its impact on subsequent evaluation is smaller than that of user-name aggregation.

Full details can be found in the paper [2]. The dataset and preprocessing scripts are available at https://zenodo.org/records/15646753.[1]

3.2 Password Reuse Behaviors

Beyond the single-password–reuse behavior noted in prior work [16,20], there are also significant or potential relationships between multiple passwords of a user. We show examples of these relationships in Table 1. For some passwords, users simply reuse strings from different previous passwords. For example, in Example 1, "xslfly" and "512" come from "xslfly118" and "1990512" respectively. In addition to direct password reuse, there is also latent information between multiple passwords. For instance, in Example 7, "B4cp7eii" and "Bcpeiim" exhibit a corresponding relationship.

Additionally, passwords from the same user are often highly repetitive and syntax-free. As shown in Examples 3 and 4, strings like "1995622" and "282026" appear repeatedly within the passwords. In Examples 2 and 8, even though passwords like "B4cp7eii" and "Bcpeiim", as well as "mar1na" and "mari", are similar, they exhibit flexibility in their expression.

---
[1] the dataset requires an ethics-compliance application

Table 1. Typical examples of similarity among multiple passwords

Reuse Type	No.	Leak password				Target
Password segment concatenation	1	1990512	xslfly118	1990512	1990512	xslfly512
	2	mar1na	bill1950	chick1968	mari03	mar1na03
	3	1995622	1995622	1995622	dengbinjun	jun1995622
	4	denglei1112	282026	282026	282026	deng282026
Considering users' reuse habits	5	6sasha6	sasha66	sasha00022	sasha6665	00022sasha
	6	131192	Julio92	julio	julio100	julio100
	7	mamzelja	Mamzelja	7f074b	7F074b4	7f074b4
	8	B4cp7eii	Bcpeiim1910	eleon1910	1910Bcpeiim	B4cp7eiim

Note: All displayed passwords have been anonymized and rewritten to protect user privacy.

3.3 Multi-password Model

We made some simple adaptations to password data based on Transformer [19] and constructed the Pass2Pass-T model, which is a multi-leakage password model. The choice of Transformer is due to its prominence in natural language processing, where password generation can be seen as a character-level language modeling task, and Transformer is the mainstream model for this task. For the multi-leak scenario, we concatenate all leaked passwords of the same account with <sep> into a single sequence, compress it with a dedicated strategy, and employ a *decoder-only Transformer* [19] for autoregressive modeling to fully exploit its long-context capacity and high training throughput. We adapted to the data characteristics of multiple password sequences.

Input Data Handling Strategies. We considered three processing methods, of which the first two have already been tried in password processing, while the third is a new strategy we propose.

1) *BPE subword segmentation*: BPE subword segmentation is a mainstream approach in NLP. However, passwords are morphologically diverse, and the same semantic fragment may appear in many spellings (e.g., p@ssword, Pa55word, p4w0rd), yielding non-unique tokenization paths and unstable Monte-Carlo estimates at high guess ranks.
2) *Keyboard-mapping*: Following Pass2Edit / Pass2Path, each character is mapped to its US-keyboard coordinate to shorten edit sequences. This chiefly benefits edit-distance models (e.g., transforming abcdefg to ABCDEFG needs only one <CAP> insertion). Our experiments show negligible impact on character-level generators.
3) *Repetition-aware compression*: When the current password is identical to any *previous* one in the same account, we replace the entire string with a pointer symbol < s_j>, where j denotes the position of its *first* occurrence in the sequence. For example, if the 3rd password repeats the 1st, we encode it as < s_1>. This compression shortens the input and improves performance, so

Pass2Pass-T adopts it. Under credential-stuffing defenses, repetition-aware compression markedly boosts top-5 success rates (see Table 5).

Segment-Wise Positional Encoding. The vanilla sinusoidal positional encoding presumes a globally monotonically increasing index, which multi-leak inputs obviously violate. We therefore reset the positional index at every password boundary and append a one-hot segment tag to avoid spurious inductive bias. Concretely, within each password we keep the original Transformer sin–cos encoding, while across passwords we add a one-hot vector to distinguish segments, as illustrated in Fig. 2. During training, we randomly shuffle the order of password blocks at the epoch level to weaken the model's dependence on a pseudo-timeline.

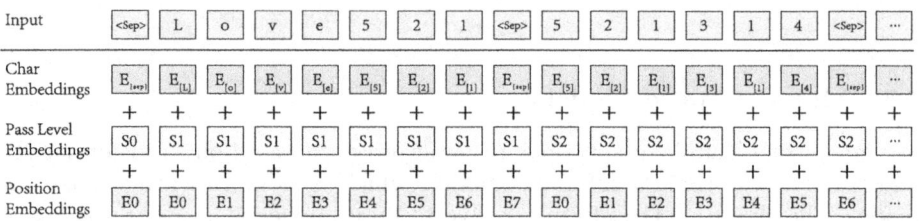

Fig. 2. Segment Level embedding

Pre-training. A large corpus of single-password samples enhances brute-force capacity; we pre-train on it and fine-tune on multi-password data, enabling the model to learn cross-password similarities.

In sum, by combining repetition-aware compression, segment-wise positional encoding, and pre-training, Pass2Pass-T captures multi-password reuse patterns more accurately.

3.4 Monte-Carlo PPSM

We propose to pre-sample password-similarity trajectories offline so that a newly entered password could be scored with a *single* forward pass. While attractive for small candidate sets on compute-rich devices, the overall cost would still scale as $O(n^2)$ with the number n of stored passwords, and quantifying this trade-off is left for future experiments.

4 Empirical Evaluation

We evaluate our model in two single-leak attack scenarios and six multi-leak attack scenarios (when the number of given passwords is one, our model automatically degenerates to the single-leak model, so we include that scenario as well). Next, we assess the performance of our similarity model under high guess counts to reflect the threat of offline attacks, which prior work has not revealed. Finally, we perform ablation studies to demonstrate the contribution of each component to the model's performance.

4.1 Experimental Setting

For the multi-similar experiment settings, We chose RMDC because we regard MSPointerGuess's multi-leak setting as unrealistic: their attacker knows at most two historical passwords per user, both taken from only two identical datasets. Therefore, their setting diverges sharply from real-world conditions—where the number of leak passwords per user varies and originates from diverse sites—and cannot faithfully reflect the true threat landscape.

We follow the experimental setup of Pass2Path [16]. We evaluate the attacker's capabilities when they know different numbers of passwords, under two conditions: one where direct reuse of leak passwords is removed (referred to as "no repeat" hereafter) and one where it is not . Additionally, we set different numbers of leak passwords for the attacker to reflect the impact of leak passwords on the success rate of account compromise.

For the multi-leak experiments we use the RMDC dataset and adopt the Pass2Path [16] evaluation protocol. We vary the number of leak passwords available to the attacker and compare their success against two site configurations: with and without credential-stuffing protection.

Specifically, we use the other passwords to predict the final password. To control input length, we truncate each record to the first six passwords. The last password in the truncated list is used as the attack target, and the preceding entries serve as leak inputs.

In this chapter, we use *Leak Num* to denote the number of passwords the attacker possesses.

- ≥ 1 **scenario**—keep the original RMDC distribution and treat the last password of each account as the prediction target.
- ≥ 2 **scenario**—select accounts with *3–6* passwords, using the first $n-1$ to predict the n-th.
- $= 5$ **scenario**—select accounts with *6–10* leaked passwords and retain the first six (i.e., five leak plus one to predict).

The "≥ 1" bucket preserves the dataset's natural distribution, whereas the "≥ 2" and "$= 5$" buckets simulate moderate and severe leakage conditions, respectively, enabling us to evaluate attack accuracy under different leakage levels.

We used the RMDC open-source 7 million data, with 90% as the training set, and the remaining 10% was filtered using the method mentioned earlier to extract 10,000 samples from each of the 6 scenarios for testing.

Hyperparameter Settings. For our model, we configured the model dimensions to 512, employed 8 attention heads and 8 layers, set a dropout rate of 0.1, limited the maximum sequence length to 128 tokens, used a training set ratio of 0.95, trained for 15 epochs, and applied gradient accumulation with 2 steps. We used a batch size of 128. This arrangement was chosen because the loss had essentially converged by the 15th epoch.

Regarding the training strategy, we adopted a learning rate of 1e-4, a warmup of 1000, and a cosine annealing learning rate.

For the Pass2Edit[2] and Pass2Path models, we follow the original data pipeline and train on the similar password pairs.[3] In terms of pair count, our new dataset is comparable to 4iQ. Since we observed that validation loss continues to decrease beyond three epochs, for a fair comparison we also train Pass2Edit for 15 epochs and save the checkpoint with the lowest validation loss.

For our model, we pre-trained for 1.5 days on two RTX 3090 GPUs (using 10% of the merged single-password dataset) and then fine-tuned for 0.6 days on a single RTX 3090.

4.2 Ethical Considerations

This dataset has been widely disseminated through BitTorrent (BT). In our study, it is used solely to advance password protection technologies rather than to inflict further harm.

We treat each password as confidential during processing; no real user passwords appear in this paper, and all displayed passwords are edited variants of the originals. Access to the data is restricted to the participants of this study, and authentication via certificates is required.

4.3 Estimation for Crack Rate

The optimal strategy for password guessing is: *to strictly attempt all candidate passwords in descending order of model probability.* However, sampling probabilities that strictly decrease monotonically from the model is impractical, so estimation methods are needed. We use Beam Search and Monte Carlo methods for evaluation.

Beam Search explicitly enumerates and attacks the $k = 1\,000$ highest-probability passwords generated by the model. It has been adopted in prior work such as Pass2Path, Pass2Edit, and PointerGuess [16,20,21]. Its exhaustive nature, however, makes evaluation at very large guess budgets computationally prohibitive.

Monte Carlo is a statistical estimator that samples passwords from the model and applies inverse-probability weighting, yielding an unbiased estimate of the crack rate even at extremely high guess counts.

4.4 Experimental Results in Multi-leak Attack Scenarios

We first employed Beam Search to evaluate performance with a low number of guesses. We observed that, under such conditions, our model exhibits a significant improvement in accuracy within the first 100 attempts—particularly on

---

[2] Pass2Edit [20] was not open-sourced, we reimplemented the method described in the paper. We evaluated our implementation under the original authors' experimental Scenario 1; the results are shown in Table 2. Our reproduction yields results approximately 1% higher than those reported in the original work, with the discrepancy within an acceptable margin, indicating that the reproduction is essentially accurate.

[3] In the previous paper, approximately 116 million password pairs from the 4iQ dataset were used for training. Applying the Pass2Edit filtering algorithm to 10% of that data produced 112 million pairs.

Table 2. Crack Rate in Multi-Leak Scenarios

Leak num	Guess num	FLA [12]	Pass2Edit [20]	Pass2Path [16]	PointerGuess	Transformer	Pass2Pass-T
≥ 1	1	2.59%	43.51%	43.51%	46.26%	47.03%	**47.23%**
	5	2.98%	55.65%	55.23%	56.32%	57.41%	**57.61%**
	10	3.68%	56.95%	56.29%	57.47%	58.68%	**58.91%**
	100	5.94%	60.29%	58.22%	60.72%	61.88%	**62.00%**
	1000	8.44%	63.26%	59.61%	62.88%	64.37%	**64.67%**
	10^7	40.49%	\	\	76.27%	79.25%	**79.40%**
≥ 2	1	2.76%	49.11%	48.34%	54.38%	55.34%	**55.95%**
	5	3.20%	67.18%	67.84%	68.25%	69.65%	**69.81%**
	10	3.79%	68.65%	69.08%	69.62%	71.09%	**71.27%**
	100	6.12%	72.07%	71.14%	72.72%	73.96%	**74.02%**
	1000	8.76%	74.94%	72.40%	74.81%	76.02%	**76.18%**
	10^7	41.30%	\	\	83.65%	85.95%	**86.43%**
= 5	1	3.25%	45.03%	45.13%	57.02%	58.50%	**59.70%**
	5	4.11%	74.60%	76.98%	76.02%	78.58%	**78.89%**
	10	4.76%	77.00%	78.90%	78.21%	80.63%	**80.84%**
	100	7.12%	80.81%	81.09%	81.87%	83.17%	**83.29%**
	1000	9.65%	83.58%	82.09%	83.48%	84.35%	**84.43%**
	10^7	37.42%	\	\	88.68%	89.80%	**89.96%**
≥ 1 (no repeat)	1	2.17%	0.73%	0.61%	1.00%	1.08%	**1.27%**
	5	2.95%	11.08%	7.87%	10.82%	12.38%	**12.74%**
	10	3.16%	13.12%	9.88%	12.99%	15.01%	**15.34%**
	100	4.90%	18.61%	13.95%	19.07%	21.08%	**21.40%**
	1000	7.34%	23.83%	16.51%	23.45%	26.19%	**26.71%**
	10^7	36.94%	\	\	49.89%	**56.99%**	56.84%
≥ 2 (no repeat)	1	2.67%	0.18%	0.23%	0.69%	1.12%	**1.98%**
	5	3.18%	10.92%	7.27%	9.76%	12.75%	**13.48%**
	10	3.67%	14.19%	10.96%	13.49%	17.00%	**17.49%**
	100	5.89%	21.82%	16.71%	22.07%	24.93%	**25.39%**
	1000	8.47%	27.90%	20.52%	27.16%	30.54%	**31.21%**
	10^7	38.84%	\	\	53.03%	59.87%	**60.48%**
= 5 (no repeat)	1	2.93%	0.18%	0.24%	0.67%	2.02%	**4.87%**
	5	3.92%	9.64%	4.95%	8.39%	13.58%	**16.36%**
	10	4.28%	15.84%	12.38%	13.57%	21.02%	**21.99%**
	100	7.21%	25.95%	21.54%	26.02%	31.54%	**32.01%**
	1000	9.93%	33.49%	26.52%	32.59%	36.49%	**36.93%**
	10^7	39.44%	\	\	53.35%	58.70%	**59.33%**

Note: Bolded entries indicate the best-performing model when attacking based on leaked passwords.

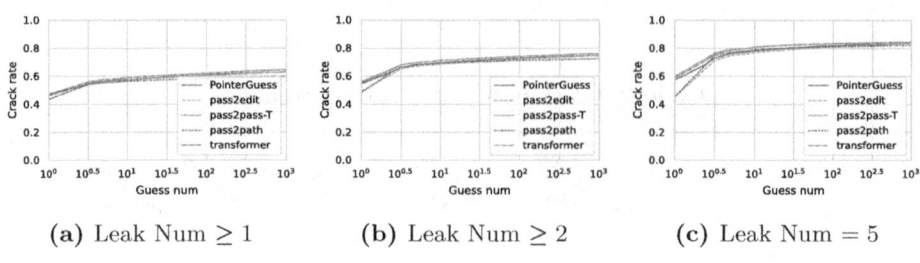

Fig. 3. Attack Success Rate within the Top 1,000 Guesses on the Repeat Multi-Leak Attack Scenarios

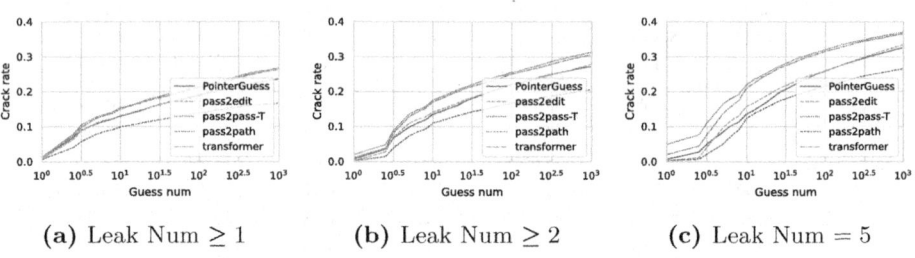

Fig. 4. Attack Success Rate within the Top 1,000 Guesses on the No-Repeat Multi-Leak Attack Scenarios

the very first guess. The results are shown in Figs. 4, 3, and Table 2. On the very first guess, our method cracked 4.87% of accounts, revealing that round-robin attacks severely underestimate an attacker's early-stage cracking power.

In the repeat scenario, when attackers possess more than five Leak passwords, our method—compared to the best previous approach—increases the first-guess success rate from 57.02% to 59.70%. In the no-repeat scenario, the success rate improves from 0.67% to 4.87%, representing a 7.27-fold increase.

We observe that although PointerGuess is the most recent model, its actual attack performance in multi-leak scenarios is worse than that of the round-robin-based Pass2Edit. We speculate that this performance gap stems from the architectural design of PointerGuess, which first generates multiple separate password distributions and only combines them at the final stage. As a result, interactions between different Leak passwords occur too late in the process, making it difficult for the model to capture cross-password dependencies effectively.

In addition, we find it achieves better first-guess accuracy than its round-robin variant but loses this advantage by the 10th guess, indicating limited generalization (see Appendix B for details).

Our analysis reveal that, compared to our multi-leak model, the single-leak model tends to directly reuse passwords on the first attempt (unlike Pass2Edit, where we did not force the first guess to be a reuse; otherwise, the first-guess success rate would be zero) due to the lack of additional user information. In contrast, our multi-leak model enables the attacker can infer the user's password habits, whether they tend to reuse passwords or make slight modifications.

4.5 Result Analyze

Table 3. Comparison examples of single-leak and multi-leak attacks: top 5 and top 31–40

Leak pw	gurgled123 sparkie123		houxiaochao xiaochao521		B4cp7eii Bcpeiim1910 191991 eleon1910 1910Bcpeiim	
Target	salle123		houxiaochao521		173232	
Rank	Pass2Edit	Ours	Pass2Edit	Ours	Pass2Edit	Ours
1	gurgled123	sparkie123	houxiaochao	xiaochao521	B4cp7eii	**B4cp7eiim**
2	sparkie123	gurgled123	xiaochao521	houxiaochao	Bcpeiim1910	B4cp7eii
3	gurgled	gurgled	123456	xiaochao	191991	b4cp7eii
4	sparkie	sparkie	xiaochao52	xiaochao52	eleon1910	eleon1910
5	gurgled1	sparkie12	houxiaochao1	**houxiaochao521**	1910bcpeiim	Eleon1910
...						
31	gurgled23	gurgled13	163.com	houxiao521	1910acpei	Eleon191
32	sparkie2	123gurgled	houchao	xiaochao521.	Acp7eii	19191991
33	gurgled12345	neopets123	a123456	houxiaochao0	19911991	Bcpeiim191
34	sparkie14	love123	1314521	xiaochao521521	eleon10	123456
35	Gurgled	spark123	1314520	5201314	a1cp7eii	1991Eleon
36	sparkie12345	dragon123	woaini	Xiaochao521	BCPEIIM1910	B4cp7eiim1910
37	sparkie01	sparkie12345	houda	7758521	111111	191910
38	gurgled14	princess123	xiaochao521.	woaini	B4cp7eii	4cp7eiim
39	Sparkie	sparkie101	houxiaochao2	houxiaocha	Bcpeiim191	eleon1991
40	gurgled2	gurgled22	chao521	hdchao521	191991a	1991bcpeiim

For our example, we selected the Pass2Edit + round-robin scheme—shown to achieve the best empirical attack performance among earlier methods—rather than the more recent MSPointerGuess.

In the no-repeat scenario, with 100 guesses and five leak passwords, our multi-leak model still delivers an improvement of nearly 5.99% in success rate, which is 23.02% higher compared to Pass2Edit. As presented in Table 3, for select data samples with such improvements, we examined both the first five attack attempts and the list of attacks from the 31st to the 40th guesses.

We found that our multi-leak model can capture the intrinsic relationships among samples to launch more precise attacks. For instance, when "gurgled123" and "sparkie123" are leak passwords, the single-leak plus round-robin method typically generates numerous variants of "gurgled" and "sparkie"—as observed in the 31st to 40th guesses—whereas our multi-leak model identifies common patterns across the passwords, attempting to break the password pair using

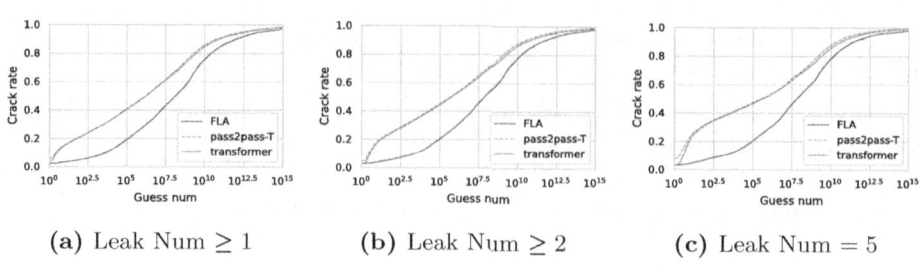

Fig. 5. Comparative experiments with the state-of-the-art no-leak attack FLA under the no-repeat scenario

strategies such as combining an English word with "123". In the second example, a simpler cross-password reuse is observed by concatenating "521" from the leak passwords "houxiaochao" and "xiaochao521", which allowed our multi-leak model to break the password in just 5 guesses.

In the third example, where a greater number of leak passwords are available, the model deduced the target password on the very first guess. It inferred that the relation between "Bcpeiim" and "B4cp7eiim" involves the insertion of two digits within "Bcpeiim", and, taking into account previous accounts suggesting that users might avoid directly reusing passwords, it opted for a combination strategy.

4.6 Advantage of Multi-Leak Attacks Under High Guess Numbers

We refer to attacks that do not rely on leaked passwords as *no-leak attacks*. In previous research, only Pass2Path compared *single-leak attacks* and *no-leak attacks*. Since it did not consider non-similar passwords, their experimental results showed that after 100,000 guesses, the single-leak attack had no advantage over the no-leak attack.

In contrast, our model, during training, learns from less similar password pairs. Using the Monte Carlo method for evaluation, we found, contrary to previous conclusions, that under almost all guess numbers, the performance of no-leak attacks is worse than that of multi-leak attacks.

We find that the primary advantage comes from samples that exhibit partial similarity combined with enumerative patterns. In such cases, the model can leverage partial similarity information to achieve orders-of-magnitude improvements in attack success rates. See Table 4.

Since Pass2Edit and Pass2Path are edit-based—where a single password corresponds to multiple generation paths and accurate probability computation is infeasible—we did not include them in the high-guess-count evaluation (Fig. 5).

Table 4. Attack Results of Different Methods on Two Target Passwords

Target pw	zq534126514			fadednegro33		
Method	FLA [12]	Pass2Pass-T	Pass2Pass-T	FLA [12]	Pass2Pass-T	Pass2Pass-T
Leak pw	\	\	wangqi890519	\	\	domything33
Rank	8.48e+11	4.78e+11	9.60e+9	3.84e+14	4.51e+13	2.10e+12

Table 5. Ablation experiment results (percentage)

Guess num	Pass2Pass-T (Transformer +zip_pw +new_pos_finetune)	Transformer +zip_pw	Transformer	Transformer sspm	Pass2Edit [20]
Ablation Variants	org	A	B	C	D
		Leak Num = 5 and no repeat			
1	**4.87%**	4.22%	2.02%	0.22%	0.18%
5	**16.36%**	15.25%	13.58%	6.80%	9.64%
10	**21.99%**	20.64%	21.02%	17.37%	15.84%
100	**32.01%**	31.50%	31.54%	29.90%	25.95%
1000	**36.93%**	36.72%	36.49%	35.53%	33.49%

4.7 Ablation Study

In order to validate the impact of the methods proposed in this paper, we designed a series of ablation experiments. Specifically, based on the complete model, we individually removed the following key factors, as shown in Table 5:

A) Removal of the new positional encoding and pretraining strategy;
B) Disabling the compression strategy;
C) Replacing the multi-leak method with standard round-robin;
D) Replacing the Transformer module with the Pass2Edit model.

4.8 Single-Leak Scenario Evaluation

In addition to the multi-leak scenario, we have also evaluated the model's performance under the single-leak scenario.

We conduct two *single-leak* experiments. Setting A trains on *Tianya* → *Dodonew* and is evaluated on *Tianya* → *Taobao*. Setting B setup uses 90% of the 7 million data from the RMDC dataset for training, and the remaining portion is filtered to test the cases where *Leak Num* = 1 (Table 6).

Table 6. Comparison of Results (%) on Two Datasets

Leak Num	Guess num	Pass2Edit [20]	PointerGuess [21]	Pass2Pass-T
Setting A: Tianya→Dodonew (train); Tianya→Taobao (test)				
$=1$	1	27.28%	**27.73%**	26.94%
	5	31.10%	31.10%	**31.24%**
	10	32.15%	31.99%	**32.26%**
	100	34.09%	34.20%	**34.33%**
	1000	36.40%	36.27%	**36.58%**
	10^7	–	50.14%	**52.38%**
Setting B: RMDC 7M (train); RMDC 100K (test)				
$=1$	1	40.42%	40.21%	**40.64%**
	5	46.88%	47.05%	**48.05%**
	10	48.19%	47.92%	**49.23%**
	100	51.13%	51.45%	**52.41%**
	1000	53.94%	53.55%	**55.42%**

Using the same training and testing setup as Scenario 1 in Pass2Edit—Tianya → Dodonew for training and Tianya → Taobao for testing—we conduct a fair comparison between the prior method and ours. We observe no significant performance difference, indicating that the previous approach is already sufficient to capture single-password modification patterns within 1,000 guesses.

5 Conclusion

We focus on multi-leak scenarios and propose Pass2Pass-T to predict a target password from several leaked passwords of the same user. Pass2Pass-T leverages the Transformer, enhanced with input compression and segmented positional encoding tailored to passwords. This design enables Pass2Pass-T to outperform existing methods in both single-leak and multi-leak scenarios. Additionally, we introduce a password strength estimator based on Monte Carlo methods, helping users select appropriate passwords in multi-leak situations.

Acknowledgment. This research is supported by National Natural Science Foundation of China (No. 62202012 and No. 62072010), BIGC Project Ea202515 and Publishing Think Tank Platform Development Project KYCPT202514. We also thank the anonymous reviewers for their valuable comments and suggestions.

Appendix

A MSPointerGuess Implement

In the original PointerGuess formulation [21], several implementation details are left unspecified, which undermines reproducibility. To address this, we now present a complete account of our multi-source PointerGuess implementation.

We noticed an inconsistency in the PointerGuess paper between the calculation of Pg in Eq. 5 and its depiction in Fig. 3. Therefore, we follow the method in Eq. 5 when computing Pg.

Second, although MSPointerGuess defines a multi-source fusion mechanism for the copy distribution P_{copy}, it omits any description of how the generation distribution P_{vocab} is obtained. To fill this gap, we compute individual context vectors $C_t^{(i)}$ for each leaked password, weight each vector by its learned soft-gate score, and sum them to form a global context C_t. We then concatenate C_t with the decoder state s_t and project the result to produce P_{vocab}.

Third, we observe that Eq. (5) applies two successive linear mappings without intervening non-linearities; since such mappings can be algebraically merged into a single affine transformation, we implement this step using a single fully connected layer.

Finally, We observe that in the original MSPointerGuess design, the number of projection matrices W_c equals the number of leak passwords, giving a one-to-one correspondence between each W_c and its context vector C_t (see Eq. 9 in the MSPointerGuess paper). In our setting, however, every sample contains a variable number of leak passwords and the websites are shuffled, so no position conveys extra information. Hence, we train a single global W_c to project all C_t vectors and reuse the same encoder to encode each password multiple times.

B Comparison Between Simple Round-Robin and MSPointerGuess Approaches

We compare three strategies whose results are summarized in Table 7:

1. **Original MSPointerGuess**: feed the *entire* set of leak passwords for a user at once; the model computes probabilities for all candidates in a shared context and guesses in descending order of these scores.
2. **Round-robin**: run MSPointerGuess *separately* on each leak-password sequence, take the current top-scoring candidate from every sequence in turn, and remove duplicates.
3. **Global sort**: also compute probabilities separately for each sequence, but pool *all* candidates and sort them globally by probability before guessing.

In the leak-num = 5 setting, MSPointerGuess (MSPG) outperforms round-robin in one-guess (top-1) accuracy. However, its performance degrades significantly under the leak-num = 5 (no-repeat) condition.

Table 7. Crack rates of three guessing strategies on the RMDC dataset (percentage)

Leak num	Guess num	Round-robin (dedup)	Global sort	MS-PointerGuess
≥ 1	1	43.38%	43.11%	**46.26%**
	5	55.12%	**56.48%**	56.32%
	10	56.34%	**57.70%**	57.47%
	1000	62.76%	62.85%	**62.88%**
$= 5$	1	44.68%	44.76%	**57.02%**
	5	71.95%	**76.83%**	76.02%
	10	74.21%	**78.97%**	78.21%
	1000	82.82%	83.37%	**83.48%**
≥ 1 (no repeat)	1	0.85%	0.87%	**1.00%**
	5	10.91%	**10.93%**	10.82%
	10	12.83%	**13.11%**	12.99%
	1000	23.29%	23.31%	**23.45%**
$= 5$ (no repeat)	1	0.07%	0.21%	**0.67%**
	5	7.57%	5.61%	**8.39%**
	10	12.21%	13.54%	**13.57%**
	1000	31.57%	32.32%	**32.59%**

To further investigate this phenomenon, we compare the distribution of target password repetition rates between the two methods for their first-guess advantage samples (i.e., samples where MSPG ranks the correct password higher than round-robin) under the leak-num = 5 setting. The results are shown in Fig. 6:

(a) The target password repetition rates of MSPG's first-guess advantage samples;

(b) The target password repetition rates of the leak-num = 5 test set;

(c) The target password repetition rates of the leak-num = 5 (no-repeat) test set.

It can be observed that MSPG's advantage mainly comes from cases where the target password appears multiple times in the leak set. When the target passwords are non-repeating, as in (c), its top-1 success rate drops significantly. This indicates that MSPG lacks generalization ability under multi-password conditions with non-repetitive targets.

This limited effectiveness likely results from its origins as a lightweight (0.5 M-parameter) extension of the PointerGuess model, which was originally designed for single-leak scenarios and thus struggles to capture correlations across multiple leaked passwords.

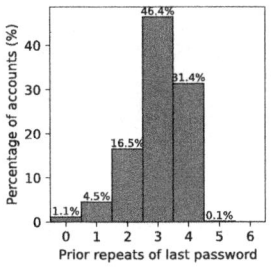
(a) MSPointerGuess's first guess advantage samples

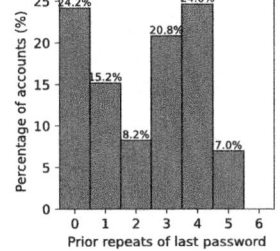
(b) the leak-num = 5 test set

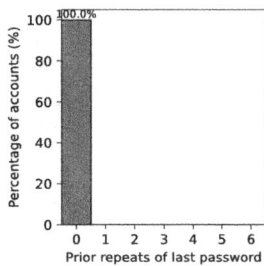
(c) the leak-num = 5 (no-repeat) test set

Fig. 6. Target password repetition rate distributions under the leak-num = 5 setting

C Impact of the Estimation Method

MC is slightly more optimistic because it avoids beam-search pruning, as theory predicts (Table 8).

Table 8. Crack rate comparison between Transformer and Pass2Pass-T under different estimation methods (percentage form)

Guess num	Monte Carlo ↑		Beam Search ↑	
	Transformer	Pass2Pass-T	Transformer	Pass2Pass-T
10	21.09%	23.10%	21.02%	21.99%
100	31.58%	32.39%	31.54%	32.01%
1000	36.88%	37.52%	36.49%	36.93%

References

1. Bahdanau, D., Cho, K., Bengio, Y.: Neural machine translation by jointly learning to align and translate. In: Proceedings of the International Conference on Learning Representations (ICLR) (2015)
2. Cheng, H., Huang, F., Yang, J., Li, W., Wang, P.: Practically secure honey password vaults: new design and new evaluation against online guessing. In: Proceedings of the 34th USENIX Security Symposium (USENIX Security) (2025)
3. Cor, K., Sood, G.: Pwned: How often are Americans' online accounts breached? arXiv preprint arXiv:1808.01883 (2018)
4. Das, A., Bonneau, J., Caesar, M., Borisov, N., Wang, X.F.: The tangled web of password reuse. In: Proceedings of the 21st USENIX Security Symposium (NDSS '14), San Diego, CA, USA (2014)

5. Florencio, D., Herley, C.: A large-scale study of web password habits. In: Proceedings of the 16th International Conference on World Wide Web, WWW '07, pp. 657–666, New York, NY, USA. Association for Computing Machinery (2007)
6. Ghorbani Lyastani, S., Schilling, M., Neumayr, M., Backes, M., Bugiel, S.: Is fido2 the kingslayer of user authentication? A comparative usability study of fido2 passwordless authentication. In: 2020 IEEE Symposium on Security and Privacy (SP), pp. 268–285 (2020)
7. Hanamsagar, A., Woo, S.S., Kanich, C., Mirkovic, J.: Leveraging semantic transformation to investigate password habits and their causes. In: Proceedings of the 2018 CHI Conference on Human Factors in Computing Systems, CHI '18, pp. 1–12, New York, NY, USA. Association for Computing Machinery (2018)
8. Hochreiter, S., Schmidhuber, J.: Long short-term memory. Neural Comput. **9**(8), 1735–1780 (1997)
9. Hunt, T.: Have I been pwned (2025). https://haveibeenpwned.com
10. Ma, J., Yang, W., Luo, M., Li, N.: A study of probabilistic password models. In: IEEE S&P 2014, pp. 538–552 (2014)
11. Mainka, C., Mladenov, V., Schwenk, J., Wich, T.: Sok: single sign-on security — an evaluation of OpenID connect. In: 2017 IEEE European Symposium on Security and Privacy (EuroS&P), pp. 251–266 (2017)
12. Melicher, W., et al.: Fast, lean, and accurate: modeling password guessability using neural networks. In: USENIX Security 2016, pp. 175–191 (2016)
13. Negi, P., Sharma, P., Jain, V., Bahmani, B.: K-means++ vs. behavioral biometrics: one loop to rule them all (2018)
14. Nicholas, M.: 68 million reasons why your small business needs a password manager. Dashlane Blog (2017). https://blog.dashlane.com/68-million-reasons-why-your-small-business-needs-a-password-manager/
15. NordPass: How many passwords does the average person have? Average user holds 168 personal and 87 work passwords (2024)
16. Pal, B., Daniel, T., Chatterjee, R., Ristenpart, T.: Beyond credential stuffing: password similarity models using neural networks. In: 2019 IEEE Symposium on Security and Privacy (SP), pp. 417–434 (2019)
17. Pasquini, D., Ateniese, G., Troncoso, C.: Universal neural-cracking-machines: self-configurable password models from auxiliary data. In: IEEE S&P 2024, pp. 1365–1384, Los Alamitos, CA, USA, May 2024. IEEE Computer Society (2024)
18. Pearman, S., et al.: Let's go in for a closer look: observing passwords in their natural habitat. In: Proceedings of the 2017 ACM SIGSAC Conference on Computer and Communications Security, CCS '17, pp. 295–310, New York, NY, USA. Association for Computing Machinery (2017)
19. Vaswani, A., et al.: Attention is all you need. In: NIPS 2017, vol. 30 (2017)
20. Wang, D., Zou, Y., Xiao, Y.-A., Ma, S., Chen, X.: Pass2Edit: a multi-step generative model for guessing edited passwords. In: 32nd USENIX Security Symposium (USENIX Security 23), pp. 983–1000, Anaheim, CA, August 2023. USENIX Association (2023)
21. Xiu, K., Wang, D.: PointerGuess: targeted password guessing model using pointer mechanism. In: 33rd USENIX Security Symposium (USENIX Security 24), pp. 5555–5572, Philadelphia, PA, August 2024. USENIX Association (2024)

WelkIR: Flow-Sensitive Pre-trained Embeddings from Compiler IR for Vulnerability Detection

Hao Huang[1], Xiuwei Shang[1], Junqi Zhang[1,2(✉)], Shaoyin Cheng[1,2], Weiming Zhang[1,2(✉)], and Nenghai Yu[1,2]

[1] University of Science and Technology of China, Hefei, China
{huanghao2023,shangxw}@mail.ustc.edu.cn
[2] Anhui Province Key Laboratory of Digital Security, Hefei, China
{jqzh,sycheng,zhangwm,ynh}@ustc.edu.cn

Abstract. While most vulnerability detection methods rely on source code features, such as Abstract Syntax Tree (AST), some have adopted compiler intermediate representations (IRs) for their efficient code representations. However, IR-based methods struggle with modeling long-range dependencies, exhibit limitations in semantic extraction, and suffer from inadequate model evaluation. To address these challenges, we propose WelkIR, a two-tier IR-based Transformer model for vulnerability detection, which is fine-tuned from a flow-sensitive pre-trained model on task-specific data. During pre-training, we introduce three novel pre-training tasks to capture the program semantics: Control Flow Prediction (CFP), Data Def-Use Prediction (DDP), and Data Reachability Prediction (DRP). The pre-trained model is then fine-tuned on task-specific data to refine its understanding of vulnerable code patterns, resulting in a specialized vulnerability detection model. We evaluate WelkIR through comprehensive experiments. On the Juliet benchmark, WelkIR achieves a 7.01%–23.26% improvement in macro F1-score compared to state-of-the-art baselines. We additionally construct ARVul, which, to the best of our knowledge, is the first large-scale LLVM IR-based vulnerability dataset, comprising 3,732 vulnerable functions from 217 real-world projects. On ARVul, WelkIR outperforms baselines by 9.01%–32.74% in F1-score. Ablation studies confirm that the proposed pre-training tasks contribute to WelkIR's performance in vulnerability detection.

Keywords: Vulnerability Detection · Flow-Sensitive Pre-training · Intermediate Representations

1 Introduction

Software vulnerabilities represent a significant security threat to modern information systems, with over 40,000 Common Vulnerabilities and Exposures (CVEs) disclosed in the latest annual reporting cycle [1]. Exploitation of these vulnerabilities by attackers can lead to severe consequences, including data breaches, service disruptions, and unauthorized privilege escalation. Consequently, vulnerability detection is crucial for the protection of software ecosystems.

Driven by rapid advances in artificial intelligence, numerous studies have employed deep learning methods for vulnerability detection, achieving encouraging results. While the predominant research focuses on the source code of high-level programming languages [6,9,14,31,36,43,46,47], several studies instead leveraged IR to explore more effective detection methods [20,30].

The Low-Level Virtual Machine (LLVM) [18] leverages a language-agnostic intermediate representation (IR) to decouple program semantics from language-specific syntax. As an encoded structure in Static Single Assignment (SSA) form, LLVM IR enables precise modeling of memory dependencies and provides formally verifiable control-flow information. Compared with high-level source code, IR-based code eliminates ambiguous constructs such as syntactic sugar and implicit type conversions, while preserving richer program semantics.

IR-based vulnerability detection approaches [20,30] typically employ graph-based code abstractions, such as ASTs and Program Dependency Graphs (PDGs), to model program syntax and semantics. These methods parse instructions into graph nodes, extract explicit attributes (e.g., operators, constants, library calls), and construct node embeddings. The resulting graph representation is subsequently fed into neural networks, such as Bidirectional Recurrent Neural Network (BRNN) [37] and Structure2Vec (S2V) [11], to learn vulnerability patterns.

Despite these advances, current IR-based vulnerability detection methods face four limitations that directly impact their practical effectiveness. First, these methods rely on manual extraction of instruction features, which disrupts syntactic structures, causes semantic loss, and introduces out-of-vocabulary (OOV) issues, resulting in decreased detection accuracy for complex vulnerability patterns [17]. Second, existing data-flow modeling techniques predominantly focus on define–use relationships while ignoring data-reachability properties, leading to incomplete flow representations that lack the contextual information essential for accurate vulnerability detection [39]. Third, current models struggle to handle long-range dependencies, which severely limits their ability to detect vulnerabilities [24]. Finally, the evaluation datasets for the IR-based methods lack sufficient diversity, as exemplified by VulChecker [30], which uses the synthetic Juliet dataset and real-world cases containing only 35 vulnerabilities in 19 open-source projects.

To address these challenges, the following methods are employed: (1) We apply subword tokenization to IR instructions, which effectively mitigates OOV issues and preserves syntactic patterns. (2) We propose an IR program representation based on Control Flow Graphs (CFGs), Def-Use Flow Graphs (DFGs), and Reaching Definition Graphs (RDGs), in which distinct flow types are assigned to instruction-level dependencies. This representation is then fed into a flow-sensitive pre-training model, which is trained through four tasks: Masked

Language Modeling (MLM), Control Flow Prediction (CFP), Data Def-Use Prediction (DDP), and Data Reachability Prediction (DRP), to capture flow information in the program. (3) We employ a two-tier Transformer model [40], in which the first tier embeds each instruction and the second-tier Graph Transformer uses attention-driven message propagation to learn representations of the entire IR program, effectively addressing long-range dependency challenges. (4) We construct ARVul, a vulnerability dataset based on LLVM IR to evaluate the models. The dataset is compiled from 217 real-world software projects and comprises 3,732 vulnerable functions, which can be processed through the LLVM toolchain for optimization and static analysis.

In summary, we make the following contributions:

- **Flow-Sensitive Vulnerability Detection Model**. We propose WelkIR, a flow-sensitive vulnerability detection model for IR, which introduces a novel multi-task pre-training strategy to assist in capturing comprehensive program semantics.
- **Large-Scale Benchmark Dataset**. To the best of our knowledge, ARVul is the first large-scale vulnerability dataset based on LLVM IR from real-world software projects. The dataset and source code are publicly released to advance research and practical applications in vulnerability detection and program analysis [44].
- **Extensive Experimental Evaluations**. We conduct comprehensive experiments on both the Juliet and ARVul datasets. The results show that WelkIR outperforms all baseline models and each of the proposed pre-training tasks effectively improves the model's capability in vulnerability detection.

2 Related Work

2.1 Vulnerability Detection Models

Modern approaches employ deep neural networks to learn vector representations of source code and make vulnerability predictions through a classifier. Early research [36] focused on the features of code sequences, but sequence-based methods often fail to capture the structural information inherent in programs. To address this limitation, subsequent studies integrated data flow and control flow into convolutional neural networks (CNNs) [19,48,49], recurrent neural networks (RNNs) [21,22,51], and graph neural networks (GNNs) [5,7,8,39,42,45,50]. Despite these advances, these methods still struggle to model long-range dependencies and may lose positional information of code statements. Recent approaches, such as PDBERT [26] and TRACED [13], employ Transformer models enhanced with control and data dependency prediction objectives during pre-training to address these challenges. However, their effectiveness is limited by inherent ambiguities in high-level language constructs. Moreover, most approaches lack inter-procedural analysis, further constraining their applicability.

Research on IR-based vulnerability detection remains limited, with VulChecker [30] being a representative approach. The method first constructs a PDG, where nodes represent IR instructions and edges represent control flow and data flow dependencies between them. The PDG is then encoded as an adjacency matrix, which is fed into S2V to generate embeddings of the entire program. However, the effectiveness of VulChecker is constrained by its reliance on manually extracted instruction features and limited ability to model complex data flow patterns.

2.2 IR-Based Code Embedding Models

IR-based code embedding models [2,4,10,23,32,33,41] have been widely applied to tasks such as code retrieval, algorithm classification, heterogeneous device mapping, and optimization of thread coarsening factors. Representative works include IR2VEC [41] and FAIR [32]. IR2VEC converts instructions into triplets of opcodes, data types, and parameters, employing the TransE model [3] to generate initial embeddings. These embeddings are subsequently augmented with structural information from CFGs and RDGs to produce program representation vectors. However, this approach to instruction feature extraction fails to capture critical semantic information within instructions, such as pointer offset computation and type conversion constraints, which are essential for vulnerability pattern recognition. FAIR addresses these challenges through a two-tier Transformer architecture. The first tier encodes basic blocks (BBs) and variables to learn the semantics of IR tokens, while the second tier integrates these representations with control dependencies among BBs and data flow dependencies among variables to construct the overall IR embeddings. While this hierarchical approach allows FAIR to process extended program contexts effectively, it struggles to capture flow information within the instructions and ignores the impact of constants on data flow. Additionally, the 256-token limit per basic block further restricts its ability to preserve semantic details. Therefore, it may not be well-suited for tasks that require fine-grained modeling and precise semantic capture, such as vulnerability detection.

3 Methodology

This section delineates the overall workflow of the WelkIR framework and elaborates on its three core components: input representation, pre-training model architecture, and multi-task pre-training tasks.

3.1 Framework Design

Figure 1 illustrates the WelkIR framework, which consists of four stages for vulnerability detection. First, the Control Flow Graphs (CFGs), Def-Use Flow Graphs (DFGs), and Reaching Definition Graphs (RDGs) are generated from the IR code. These property graphs, along with the instruction sequences, are tokenized and encoded into feature matrices that capture syntactic structures and contextual dependencies. The resulting representations are then fed into the pre-training model, which is trained through four tasks: Masked Language Modeling (MLM), Control Flow Prediction (CFP), Data Def-Use Prediction (DDP), and Data Reachability Prediction (DRP). In the final stage, the pre-trained model is fine-tuned on the vulnerability dataset.

3.2 Input Representation

We propose an IR program representation based on CFG, DFG, and RDG for the WelkIR model. As shown in Fig. 2, nodes represent instructions, while edges denote the relationships between these instructions. The function comprises a signature and a body. The body contains one or more basic blocks (BBs), each beginning with a label and consisting of a sequence of instructions without branches. The instruction typically consists of a destination register (e.g., sum), an opcode (e.g., add), a set of operands (e.g., a), and type identifiers (e.g., i32).

Before constructing the property graph, we apply LLVM optimizations to enhance semantic representation. Specifically, the following optimizations are applied: (1) function inlining that replaces call sites with callee implementations, (2) dead code elimination to remove unreachable instructions and redundant computations, (3) jump instruction optimization to transform indirect control transfers into direct branch instructions, and (4) control flow simplification to merge redundant BBs and simplify conditional branches.

CFG Construction. Figure 2.b shows the CFG of an example IR function. The CFG represents the execution order of instructions within a program, reflecting

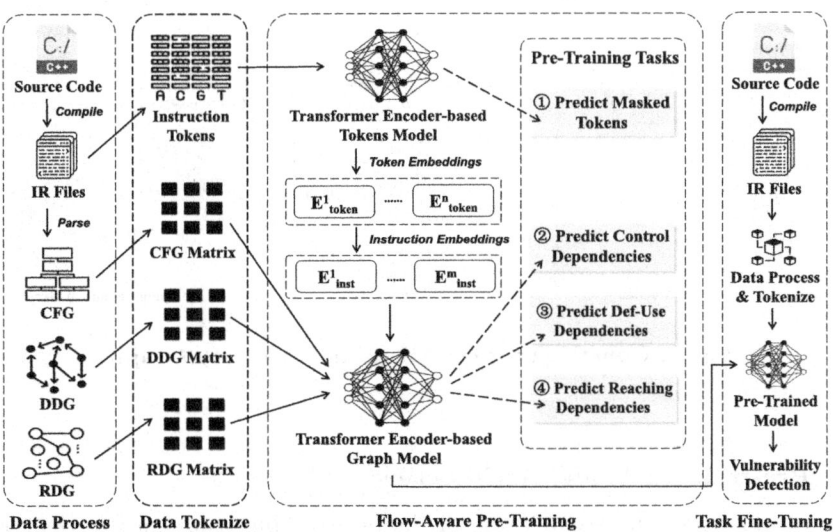

Fig. 1. The Overview of WelkIR

its control flow and potential execution paths. We begin by partitioning the IR module into BBs, where the first instruction serves as the entry, and the last instruction serves as the exit. Each instruction is then mapped to a corresponding node in the CFG. We connect adjacent instructions within the same BB, labeling these edges as `Intra_block`. For cross-block jumps, we connect the exit instruction of the source block to the entry instruction of the target block, labeling edges by jump types (e.g., `BrTrue`). For termination instructions (e.g., `ret`), no outgoing edges are added as no subsequent paths exist.

DFG Construction. Figure 2.c shows the DFG of an example IR function. The Def-Use relationship models data flow dependencies between program points, where a variable is defined at a statement and subsequently used in computational or control-dependent operations. Similarly to the construction of the CFG, each IR instruction maps to a node in the DFG. We first identify the variables defined by each instruction and then locate all subsequent instructions that use them. Edges are established between the definition instructions and their subsequent use instructions, with the data type of the defined variable (e.g., `integers`) serving as the edge type.

RDG Construction. Figure 2.d shows the RDG of an example IR function. The Reaching Definition relationship determines whether a variable's definition can reach a specific program point along a control flow path. Following the approach proposed in IR2Vec [41], we construct the Reaching Definition relationships between instructions. To enhance semantic representation, we use the opcode of each defining instruction (e.g., `load`) as the edge type in the RDG.

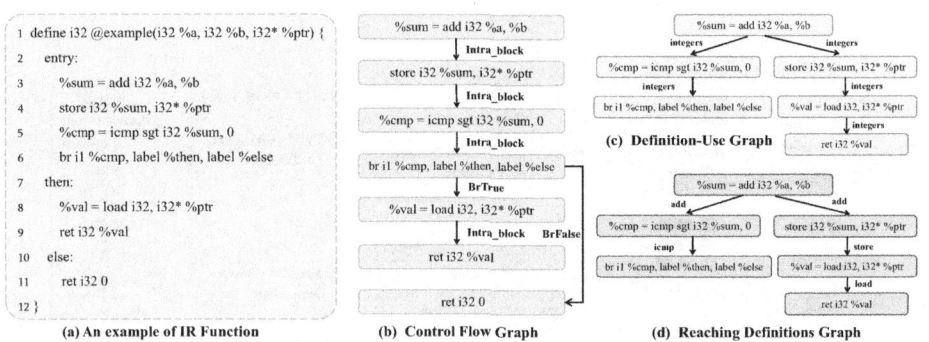

Fig. 2. Constructing the IR-based Property Graphs

3.3 Pre-training Model Architecture

Figure 3 illustrates the architecture of the pre-training model, a two-tier Transformer Encoder [40]. The first tier encodes instruction tokens to derive instruction representations, while the second tier constructs the embedding of the entire

IR code by integrating these representations with structural information from CFG, DFG, and RDG.

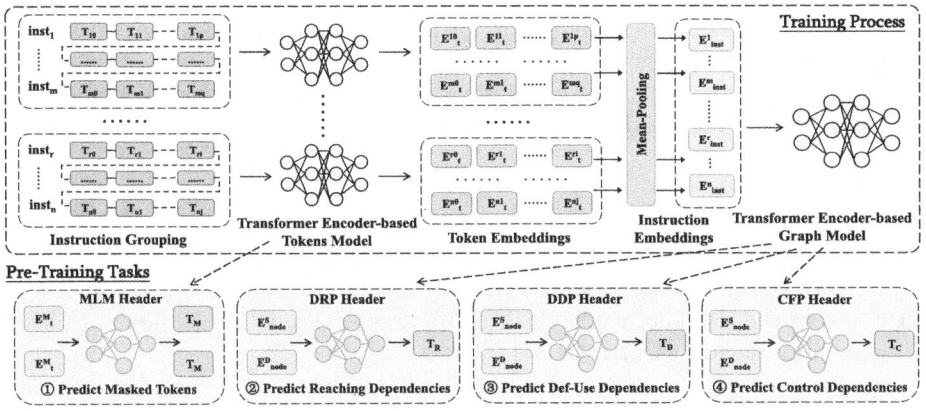

Fig. 3. The Architecture of the Pre-training Model.

Transformer Encoder-Based Tokens Model. To address the token length limitation of a single Transformer model, we employ a structure comprising multiple Transformer Encoders in the first tier. In this tier, the input consists of tokens extracted from IR instructions, and the output includes token embeddings and instruction vector representations.

Given an IR function f, we denote the set of extracted instructions as $\{\text{inst}_1, \ldots, \text{inst}_n\}$. Each instruction inst_i is represented as a sequence of tokens $\{T_{i0}, \ldots, T_{ik}\}$, where k is the number of tokens in inst_i. These tokens are partitioned into coherent groups $\{G_1, \ldots, G_m\}$, where each group consists of multiple complete instructions, and the total number of tokens in each group satisfies $|G_j| \leq L$, with L being the maximum number of tokens allowed in each group. Each group G_j is processed by a corresponding Transformer Encoder, from which the final hidden states are extracted to obtain token-level embeddings $\{E_t^0, \ldots, E_t^n\}$. To obtain instruction representations, we perform mean-pooling aggregation over the token embeddings $\{E_t^{i0}, \ldots, E_t^{ik}\}$ for each instruction inst_i, resulting in the instruction vector representation E_{inst}^i.

Transformer Encoder-Based Graph Model. To effectively integrate flow information, we use a Graph Transformer as the second-tier encoder. This tier takes as input the instruction representations produced by the first tier, along with three matrices representing inter-instruction relationships. These matrices G_c^C, G_c^D, and $G_c^R \in \mathbb{R}^{m_c \times m_c}$, are derived from the CFG, DFG, and RDG, respectively. Here, m_c denotes the length of the instruction sequence, and each element $G[i][j]$ in the matrices indicates a specific type of directed relationship between a pair of IR instructions. The Graph Transformer learns syntactic patterns and program behaviors from these matrices, producing instruction embeddings enriched with flow information and an embedding representation of the entire IR code.

In the implementation, we follow the methodology proposed by FAIR [32], which integrates graph structural priors into the attention mechanism. Specifically, relationship matrices are used as graph bias terms during attention computation, injecting flow information between instructions into the attention matrix at each layer. For other components, such as the feed-forward network and layer normalization, WelkIR adopts the standard Transformer Encoder architecture.

3.4 Pre-training Tasks

As shown in Fig. 3, WelkIR employs four pre-training tasks: MLM, CFP, DDP, and DRP. MLM helps the model capture the semantic information and syntactic structure of the IR code, while CFP, DDP, and DRP enable the model to learn the flow information within the code.

Masked Language Modeling (MLM). MLM is a widely used pre-training strategy in Transformer models, such as BERT [12], RoBERTa [25], and GraphCode-BERT [16]. To generate instruction tokens, we apply Byte-pair Encoding (BPE), a subword tokenization algorithm proposed by [15], to decompose IR code into subword units. Following standard practice [12], we randomly sample 15% of the tokens from the input sequence. Of these, 80% are replaced with the [MASK] token, 10% with random tokens, and the remaining 10% are unchanged.

In the pre-training phase, the first-tier encoder produces hidden representation E_t^{Mi} of each [MASK] token. These representations are then fed through a Multi-Layer Perceptron (MLP), followed by a SoftMax classifier to predict the original tokens from the vocabulary. The MLM training objective aims to minimize the following loss function:

$$P(T_i \mid E_t^{Mi}) = \text{Softmax}_{T_i \in V}(\text{MLP}(E_t^{Mi})) \tag{1}$$

$$\mathcal{L}_{MLM} = \frac{1}{|M^t|} \sum_{i \in M^t} -\log P(T_i \mid E_t^{Mi}) \tag{2}$$

where $P(T_i \mid E_t^{Mi})$ is the probability of predicting token T_i from the hidden representation E_t^{Mi}, V is the token vocabulary, M^t is the set of masked token indices, and $|M^t|$ is the total number of masked tokens.

Relation Type Prediction. To capture flow information from CFG, DFG, and RDG, we introduce a masked prediction task based on the relation matrix. As an example, in the CFP task, we mask 10% of the entries in the relation matrix with [MASK] tokens. WelkIR then generates flow-aware vector representations for each instruction from the second-tier encoder, treating each instruction as a node in the CFG. For each masked relation $G_c^C[i][j]$, we define instruction i as the source node and instruction j as the destination node. The edge representation E_{edge}^i is constructed by concatenating the node embeddings $[E_{node}^s : E_{node}^d]$, where

E_{node}^s and E_{node}^d denote the embeddings of the source and destination node, respectively. This edge representation is processed by an MLP, followed by a SoftMax classifier, to predict the control flow type from a predefined vocabulary V_c. The objective of CFP is to minimize the following loss function:

$$P_c(T_i \mid E_{edge}^i) = \text{Softmax}_{T_i \in V_c}(\text{MLP}_c(E_{edge}^i)) \tag{3}$$

$$\mathcal{L}_{CFP} = \frac{1}{|M_c^t|} \sum_{i \in M_c^t} -\log P_c(T_i \mid E_{edge}^i) \tag{4}$$

where V_c is the vocabulary of the control flow types, and M_c^t represents the set of masked elements in the relation matrix G_c^C.

DDP and DRP share the same structure with separate MLPs and vocabularies. The objective of DDP is to minimize the following:

$$P_d(T_i \mid E_{edge}^i) = \text{Softmax}_{T_i \in V_d}(\text{MLP}_d(E_{edge}^i)) \tag{5}$$

$$\mathcal{L}_{DDP} = \frac{1}{|M_d^t|} \sum_{i \in M_d^t} -\log P_d(T_i \mid E_{edge}^i) \tag{6}$$

where V_d is the vocabulary of the Def-Use type, and M_d^t is the set of masked elements in G_c^D. Similarly, the DRP objective is to minimize:

$$P_r(T_i \mid E_{edge}^i) = \text{Softmax}_{T_i \in V_r}(\text{MLP}_r(E_{edge}^i)) \tag{7}$$

$$\mathcal{L}_{DRP} = \frac{1}{|M_r^t|} \sum_{i \in M_r^t} -\log P_r(T_i \mid E_{edge}^i) \tag{8}$$

where V_r is the vocabulary of the Reaching Definition relationships, M_r^t is the set of masked elements in G_c^R.

4 Experimental Design

To evaluate the utility of WelkIR for vulnerability detection, we seek to answer the following questions:

RQ1: How effective is WelkIR compared to state-of-the-art baselines in vulnerability detection?

To evaluate the model's vulnerability detection capabilities, we compare WelkIR with five state-of-the-art baselines: TRACED [13], PDBERT [26], EPVD [49], IR2VEC [41], and FAIR [32]. TRACED, PDBERT, and EPVD detect vulnerabilities based on source code, while IR2VEC and FAIR focus on IR.

RQ2: How does function length affect WelkIR's vulnerability detection performance in real-world projects?

In the Juliet dataset, we employ LLVM's function inlining optimization to obtain complete contextual information for function-level vulnerability detection. In contrast, real-world applications exhibit more complex structures and diverse scenarios. Variations in function lengths within the source code may lead to significant differences in the availability of contextual information, which could impact model performance. This study aims to evaluate how the performance of WelkIR is affected by functions of varying lengths in real-world applications.

RQ3: How do different pre-training tasks in WelkIR affect the performance?

One of the key contributions of our approach is integrating four pre-training tasks into the WelkIR model. To investigate the impact of different pre-training tasks on vulnerability detection effectiveness, we compare WelkIR with four variants: (1) WelkIR w/o MLM, which excludes the MLM pre-training task; (2) WelkIR w/o CFP, which excludes the CFP pre-training task; (3) WelkIR w/o DDP, which excludes the DDP pre-training task; and (4) WelkIR w/o DRP, which excludes the DRP pre-training task.

RQ4: How does the separability of feature vectors across vulnerability categories in WelkIR compare to baseline methods in the Juliet dataset?

We compare the topological structures of feature spaces generated by WelkIR and baseline methods using t-distributed Stochastic Neighbor Embedding (t-SNE) [28]. As a nonlinear dimensionality reduction technique, t-SNE projects high-dimensional feature vectors into a low-dimensional space by matching probability densities. This visualization reveals inter-class separation and intra-class clustering, reflecting the separability of vulnerability categories.

RQ5: How does WelkIR perform on line-level vulnerability localization in real-world projects?

For vulnerability localization, we define vulnerable statements as the lines of code within vulnerable functions that require modification. Our approach leverages the Transformer's attention mechanism to localize these statements. Specifically, we utilize the [CLS] token embedding from the second-tier Transformer Encoder as a global semantic representation. When the model identifies a vulnerability function, we compute the vulnerability coefficients for individual code lines based on the attention weights between the [CLS] token and each statement. The coefficient for each line is derived by averaging attention weights across all heads, with higher coefficients prioritizing lines as potential vulnerability locations.

5 Experimental Setup

5.1 Data Collection

Our experimental datasets consist of two components: (1) Juliet, a widely used security benchmark, and (2) ARVul, a real-world vulnerability dataset derived from the Arvo project [29].

Juliet Dataset. The Juliet dataset is a widely recognized benchmark for evaluating vulnerability detection methods. The functions within this dataset are labeled at the function level, where those containing `bad` in their names are marked as vulnerable, while those with `good` are designated as non-vulnerable. Additionally, each vulnerable function is annotated with the corresponding Common Weakness Enumeration (CWE) identifier, extracted directly from the source filenames, to denote its vulnerability type.

However, the original Juliet dataset contains identifiers with vulnerability indicators (e.g., `CWE122_Heap_Based_Buffer_Overflow_bad`), which directly reveal weakness types (e.g., CWE-122) and severity labels (e.g., bad). Such naming conventions may inadvertently enable models to overfit lexical patterns rather than learning authentic vulnerability features derived from code semantics.

To address this issue, we normalize the dataset by replacing developer-defined identifiers with generic labels (e.g., *func1*, *var1*). This procedure ensures that the models focus on learning semantic features for vulnerability detection, rather than relying on labeled identifiers. Table 1 summarizes the post-processed Juliet corpus, including its CWE distribution.

Table 1. The statistics of Juliet dataset

Vulnerability Category	#Vul	#Non-Vul	#Total
CWE121	3,078	3,078	6,156
CWE122	3,608	3,608	7,216
CWE190	2,538	2,538	5,076
CWE191	1,929	1,929	3,858

ARVul Dataset. Although the Juliet dataset provides a security benchmark through artificially constructed vulnerability cases, its complexity and diversity still differ significantly from vulnerabilities in real-world software. Therefore, we construct the ARVul dataset using the Arvo project infrastructure. The Arvo project reproduces 5,001 memory vulnerabilities from 273 OSS-Fuzz projects [38], providing patches and Docker environments to facilitate vulnerability replication.

As shown in Fig. 4, we use Bear [35] to capture the compilation commands for each file in Arvo projects. For source files with code modifications, we recompile them with adjusted Clang flags (e.g., `-S`, `-emit-llvm`) to generate the corresponding LLVM IR files. Our labeling strategy designates functions modified by security patches as vulnerable and unmodified functions as non-vulnerable.

In total, we produce a dataset comprising 3,732 vulnerable functions and 145.2K non-vulnerable functions from 217 projects. For evaluation, we combine all 3,732 vulnerable functions with 12,000 randomly sampled non-vulnerable ones to form the benchmark dataset and reserve the remaining non-vulnerable functions for pre-training.

5.2   Pre-training Model Configurations

The first-tier encoder uses 32 Transformer models, each processing up to 512 tokens with a hidden dimension of 768 and 12 attention heads. The second-tier

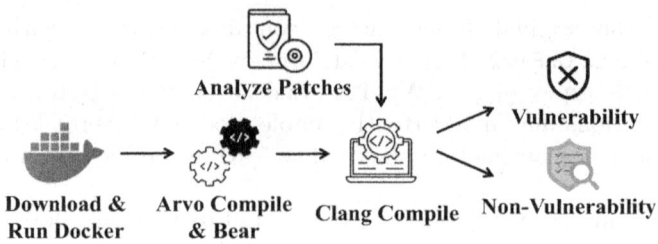

Fig. 4. ARVul Dataset Collection Process.

encoder employs a single Transformer with the same configuration as the Transformers in the first tier. The maximum sequence length for the pre-training model is 500 instructions. For functions that exceed this length, we apply a sliding window of size 256 to segment them and meet the model's input requirements.

The instructions are tokenized using the BPE tokenizer provided by FAIR [32], which has a vocabulary size of 30,000. The vocabulary sizes for the edge types in the CFG, DFG, and RDG are 22, 24, and 69, respectively.

We train the model for 10 epochs on 8 NVIDIA RTX 3090 GPUs, using AdamW [27] for optimization. The objective is to minimize the combined loss from four pre-training tasks:

$$\mathcal{L} = L_{\text{MLM}} + L_{\text{CFP}} + L_{\text{DDP}} + L_{\text{DRP}} \qquad (9)$$

5.3 Vulnerability Detection Configuration

For the Juliet dataset, which consists mostly of short examples, we apply tail truncation to functions that exceed 500 IR instructions. In contrast, for the more complex and diverse ARVul dataset, we employ a sliding window approach with a size of 256 to segment functions exceeding 500 instructions. To focus on security-critical code, we exclusively preserve the code snippets within vulnerable functions that require fixes, while discarding the rest.

To ensure fair comparisons with the baseline models, we standardize vulnerability detection at the function level. For functions split into multiple snippets, we adopt a conservative prediction strategy: a function is classified as non-vulnerable only if all snippets are predicted as such; otherwise, it is predicted as vulnerable.

We split the dataset into 80% for training, 10% for validation, and 10% for testing. The performance of WelkIR and the baseline models is evaluated using four widely recognized metrics: accuracy, precision, recall, and F1-score [34].

6 Results and Analysis

6.1 Answering RQ1: Comparison with Baselines

We perform two distinct vulnerability detection tasks using the Juliet and ARVul datasets. The Juliet dataset contains function-level samples, each labeled as either non-vulnerable or associated with one of four CWE types: CWE-121 (Stack-Based Buffer Overflow), CWE-122 (Heap-Based Buffer Overflow), CWE-190 (Integer Overflow), and CWE-191 (Integer Underflow). This setup defines a multi-class classification problem, requiring the model to not only detect the presence of vulnerabilities but also accurately identify their types.

In contrast, the ARVul dataset employs a binary labeling scheme, where each function is classified as either vulnerable or non-vulnerable, without distinguishing between specific vulnerability categories. Consequently, the vulnerability detection task on ARVul is treated as a binary classification problem.

Comparison on Juliet Dataset. As shown in Table 2, WelkIR outperforms baseline models in multi-class vulnerability detection. Specifically, it achieves relative improvements over the baselines with accuracy gains from 5.16% to 18.07%, macro precision improvements from 9.04% to 18.74%, macro recall increases from 3.87% to 19.81%, and macro F1-score improvements from 7.01% to 23.26%.

Comparison on ARVul Dataset. As demonstrated in Table 2, which presents both code snippet and function-level detection results for WelkIR, we focus on function-level comparisons to maintain methodological consistency with the baseline models. The experimental results show that, although WelkIR's precision is slightly lower than TRACED, it still outperforms the baseline models in overall metrics, with F1-Score showing an improvement range of 9.01%–32.74%.

Table 2. Evaluation Results on the Juliet and ARVul Dataset

Model	Juliet				ARVul			
	A (%)	P (%)	R (%)	F1 (%)	A (%)	P (%)	R (%)	F1 (%)
TRACED	89.05	82.29	90.89	85.58	81.38	71.89	35.56	47.58
PDBERT	91.48	86.25	90.65	87.98	82.21	69.72	46.79	56.00
EPVD	88.77	81.30	89.69	84.80	81.32	66.66	42.78	52.11
IR2VEC	78.57	76.55	74.95	71.74	75.73	47.89	24.33	32.27
FAIR	81.14	81.71	79.11	79.35	79.61	61.17	42.97	50.48
WelkIR$_{func}$	**96.64**	**95.29**	**94.76**	**95.00**	**84.74**	71.25	59.79	65.01
WelkIR$_{snippet}$	-	-	-	-	81.82	**75.29**	**60.46**	**67.07**

Analysis of Sample Cases. Figure 5(a) shows a vulnerability where `func2` reads external input into `data` without bounds checking and passes it to `func1` for indexing `buffer`. If `data` exceeds 9, a heap-based buffer overflow occurs. The patched version in Fig. 5(b) fixes the issue by having `func2` assign `data` a constant value of 7, ensuring all buffer accesses remain within valid bounds.

As outlined in the Related Work section, the source code-based baselines EPVD, TRACED, and PDBERT lack inter-procedural analysis capabilities, leading to failures in distinguishing vulnerable and non-vulnerable scenarios in our case. In contrast, IR-based approaches leverage the LLVM's function inlining optimization during IR generation. This process replaces function calls (e.g., func2 invoking func1) with the callee's inlined code, thereby consolidating cross-function contexts within a unified IR function for analysis.

Unfortunately, both IR2VEC and FAIR misclassify non-vulnerable scenarios as vulnerabilities in our case. This misclassification occurs because IR2VEC converts instructions into triplets of opcodes, data types, and parameters, which makes it difficult to capture the complex semantic relationships (e.g., at line 4 in Fig. 5(b)). On the other hand, FAIR struggles to capture precise program semantics (e.g., at line 12 in Fig. 5(b)), due to the lack of fine-grained data-flow modeling. In contrast, our approach can correctly detect this case due to its ability to capture comprehensive and fine-grained program semantics.

```
1   static int var3;
2   static void func1() {
3       int data = var3;
4       int * buffer = (int *)malloc(10 *
            sizeof(int));
5       ...
6       if (data >= 0)
7           buffer[data] = 1;
8       ...
9   }
10  void func2(){
11      ...
12      data = atoi(inputBuffer);
13      var3 = data;
14      func1();
15  }
```
(a) Case Study of Vulnerability in CWE-122

```
1   static int var3;
2   static void func1() {
3       int data = var3;
4       int * buffer = (int *)malloc(10 *
            sizeof(int));
5       ...
6       if (data >= 0)
7           buffer[data] = 1;
8       ...
9   }
10  void func2(){
11      ...
12      data = 7;
13      var3 = data;
14      func1();
15  }
```
(b) Case Study of Non-Vulnerability in CWE-122

Fig. 5. Case Study in CWE-122.

6.2 Answering RQ2: Effect of Function Length

As shown in Table 3, sample functions with fewer than 50 lines, although the most numerous, exhibit the lowest precision, recall, and F1-score. In comparison, functions containing 100–150 lines of source code achieve the highest recall 82.86%, while functions with 150–200 lines show the best precision 82.76%. In particular, functions exceeding 200 lines attain the optimal F1-score of 81.48%. Our analysis suggests that longer functions typically provide richer contextual information, enabling WelkIR to capture vulnerability patterns more effectively and thus improve detection performance.

Table 3. Impact of Function Length on Performance

Range	#Vul	#Non-Vul	Precision	Recall	F1-score
(0, 50]	173	948	65.62%	48.55%	55.81%
(50, 100]	79	169	67.74%	53.16%	59.57%
(100, 150]	35	33	72.50%	**82.86%**	77.33%
(150, 200]	32	20	**82.76%**	75.00%	78.69%
(200, +∞)	54	30	81.48%	81.48%	**81.48%**

6.3 Answering RQ3: Model Ablation

We conduct an ablation study to assess the impact of each pre-training task on WelkIR's vulnerability detection performance. Model variants are created by excluding individual pre-training tasks, fine-tuning them on the detection task, and comparing the results. As shown in Tables 4, excluding any pre-training task results in varying degrees of performance degradation. These results confirm that each of the proposed pre-training tasks effectively enhances the model's capability in vulnerability detection.

Table 4. Ablation Study Results

Model	Juliet				ARVul			
	A (%)	P (%)	R (%)	F1 (%)	A (%)	P (%)	R (%)	F1 (%)
WelkIR	**96.64**	**95.29**	**94.76**	**95.00**	**84.74**	71.25	**59.79**	**65.01**
- w/o MLM	95.79	94.00	92.43	92.92	84.17	72.30	53.89	61.75
- w/o CFP	94.91	92.34	91.81	92.01	83.74	70.11	52.81	60.24
- w/o DDP	94.23	90.61	90.06	90.25	84.42	**72.54**	55.23	62.71
- w/o DRP	95.40	93.32	93.07	93.16	83.03	68.66	52.28	59.36

6.4 Answering RQ4: Class Separability

Figure 6 presents the t-SNE plots of WelkIR and the baseline models, derived from the feature vectors of the Juliet test set. It is observed that the baseline models exhibit both more significant inter-class overlap and greater intra-class dispersion than WelkIR. This suggests that WelkIR achieves superior class separability compared to the baselines.

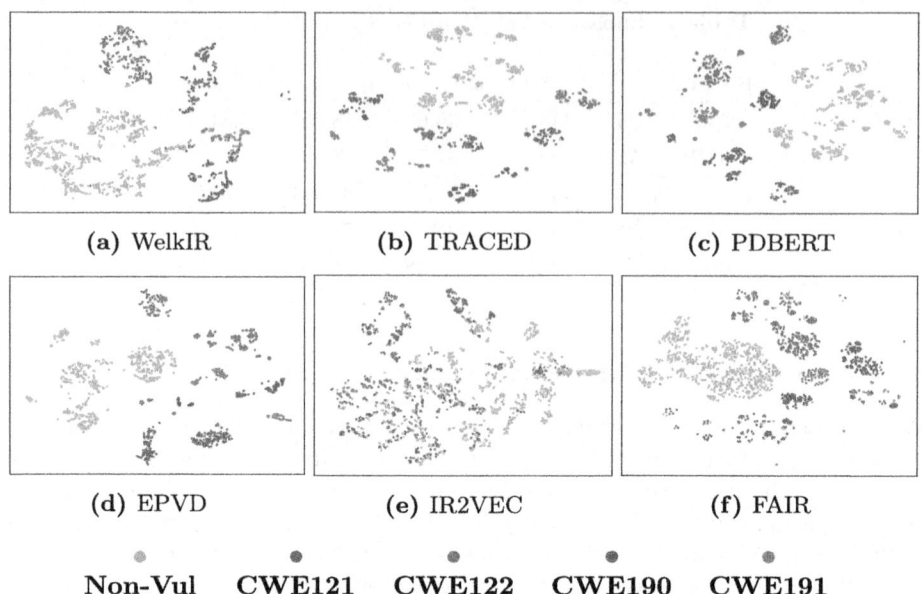

Fig. 6. t-SNE Plots of Model Representations

6.5 Answering RQ5: Localization Precision Evaluation

To evaluate the precision of line-level vulnerability localization, we perform the following experiment. For each correctly predicted vulnerability, we extract the line numbers of the top-n IR instructions with the highest vulnerability coefficient to form the set L. Let M represent the known vulnerable code lines. If L overlaps with M, the prediction is considered valid; otherwise, it is invalid. Localization precision is defined as the ratio of valid predictions to the total number of correctly predicted vulnerabilities. When selecting the top-n IR instructions based on vulnerability coefficients, the experimental results show that the localization precisions are 35.92%, 44.70%, 52.71%, and 57.36% for top-5, top-10, top-15, and top-20, respectively. These indicate that we can leverage the attention mechanism of the Transformer architecture in WelkIR to effectively locate vulnerable lines.

7 Limitations

This study has several limitations. First, the ARVul dataset contains incomplete vulnerability code snippets in the Arvo project, primarily due to issues such as missing patch information, unavailable compilation resources, and incomplete interception of compilation commands by the Bear tool. Second, the ARVul dataset is constructed by compiling individual source files, which limits the exploitation of LLVM's global optimization capabilities. Third, WelkIR requires the source code to be compiled into IR, making it unusable when compilation fails. Finally, our dataset is based on compiling C/C++ source code into LLVM IR using the Clang compiler. It remains unclear whether WelkIR performs differently on IR generated by other compiler front-ends.

8 Conclusion and Future Work

In this paper, we present WelkIR, a vulnerability detection model based on a flow-sensitive pre-trained architecture. By integrating multiple pre-training tasks, including MLM, CFP, DDP, and DRP, WelkIR effectively learns vulnerability patterns from both code semantics and program structures. Experimental results demonstrate that WelkIR outperforms state-of-the-art baseline models in vulnerability detection.

For future work, we plan to explore the integration of WelkIR with components of the LLVM toolchain, such as LibFuzzer, to enhance vulnerability detection by combining static and dynamic analysis techniques. Additionally, we will investigate the model's ability to detect adversarial or obfuscated code designed to bypass detection. This integration represents a promising direction for future research, potentially leading to more robust and comprehensive vulnerability detection systems.

Acknowledgments. This work was supported in part by the Natural Science Foundation of China (Grant No. U20B2047, 62072421, 62002334, 62102386, and 62121002), by the Postdoctoral Fellowship Program of CPSF (Grant No. GZC20252180), and by the Anhui Provincial Natural Science Foundation (Grant No. 2508085QF213).

References

1. Cve details. https://www.cvedetails.com/. Accessed 24 June 2025
2. Ben-Nun, T., Jakobovits, A.S., Hoefler, T.: Neural code comprehension: a learnable representation of code semantics. Adv. Neural Inf. Process. Syst. **31** (2018)
3. Bordes, A., Usunier, N., Garcia-Duran, A., Weston, J., Yakhnenko, O.: Translating embeddings for modeling multi-relational data. Adv. Neural Inf. Process. Syst. **26** (2013)
4. Brauckmann, A., Goens, A., Ertel, S., Castrillon, J.: Compiler-based graph representations for deep learning models of code. In: Proceedings of the 29th International Conference on Compiler Construction, pp. 201–211 (2020)
5. Cao, S., Sun, X., Bo, L., Wei, Y., Li, B.: BGNN4VD: constructing bidirectional graph neural-network for vulnerability detection. Inf. Softw. Technol. **136**, 106576 (2021)
6. Cao, S., Sun, X., Bo, L., Wu, R., Li, B., Tao, C.: MVD: memory-related vulnerability detection based on flow-sensitive graph neural networks. In: Proceedings of the 44th International Conference on Software Engineering, pp. 1456–1468 (2022)
7. Cheng, X., Wang, H., Hua, J., Xu, G., Sui, Y.: Deepwukong: statically detecting software vulnerabilities using deep graph neural network. ACM TOSEM **30**(3), 1–33 (2021)

8. Cheng, X., et al.: Static detection of control-flow-related vulnerabilities using graph embedding. In: 2019 24th International Conference on Engineering of Complex Computer Systems (ICECCS), pp. 41–50. IEEE (2019)
9. Cheng, X., Zhang, G., Wang, H., Sui, Y.: Path-sensitive code embedding via contrastive learning for software vulnerability detection. In: Proceedings of the 31st ACM SIGSOFT International Symposium on Software Testing and Analysis, pp. 519–531 (2022)
10. Cummins, C., Fisches, Z.V., Ben-Nun, T., Hoefler, T., O'Boyle, M.F., Leather, H.: ProGraML: a graph-based program representation for data flow analysis and compiler optimizations. In: International Conference on Machine Learning, pp. 2244–2253. PMLR (2021)
11. Dai, H., Dai, B., Song, L.: Discriminative embeddings of latent variable models for structured data. In: International Conference on Machine Learning, pp. 2702–2711. PMLR (2016)
12. Devlin, J., Chang, M.W., Lee, K., Toutanova, K.: Bert: pre-training of deep bidirectional transformers for language understanding. In: Proceedings of the 2019 Conference of the North American Chapter of the Association for Computational Linguistics: Human Language Technologies, Volume 1 (Long and Short Papers), pp. 4171–4186 (2019)
13. Ding, Y., Steenhoek, B., Pei, K., Kaiser, G., Le, W., Ray, B.: Traced: execution-aware pre-training for source code. In: Proceedings of the 46th IEEE/ACM International Conference on Software Engineering, pp. 1–12 (2024)
14. Fu, M., Tantithamthavorn, C.: LineVul: a transformer-based line-level vulnerability prediction. In: Proceedings of the 19th International Conference on Mining Software Repositories, pp. 608–620 (2022)
15. Gage, P.: A new algorithm for data compression. C Users J. **12**(2), 23–38 (1994)
16. Guo, D., et al.: Graphcodebert: Pre-training code representations with data flow. arXiv preprint arXiv:2009.08366 (2020)
17. Hanif, H., Maffeis, S.: Vulberta: Simplified source code pre-training for vulnerability detection. In: 2022 International Joint Conference on Neural Networks (IJCNN), pp. 1–8. IEEE (2022)
18. Lattner, C., Adve, V.: LLVM: a compilation framework for lifelong program analysis & transformation. In: International Symposium on Code Generation and Optimization, 2004. CGO 2004, pp. 75–86. IEEE (2004)
19. Li, X., Wang, L., Xin, Y., Yang, Y., Chen, Y.: Automated vulnerability detection in source code using minimum intermediate representation learning. Appl. Sci. **10**(5), 1692 (2020)
20. Li, Z., Zou, D., Xu, S., Chen, Z., Zhu, Y., Jin, H.: VulDeeLocator: a deep learning-based fine-grained vulnerability detector. IEEE Trans. Dependable Secure Comput. **19**(4), 2821–2837 (2021)
21. Li, Z., Zou, D., Xu, S., Jin, H., Zhu, Y., Chen, Z.: SySeVR: a framework for using deep learning to detect software vulnerabilities. IEEE Trans. Dependable Secure Comput. **19**(4), 2244–2258 (2021)
22. Li, Z., et al.: VulDeePecker: a deep learning-based system for vulnerability detection. arXiv preprint arXiv:1801.01681 (2018)
23. Li, Z., et al.: Unleashing the power of compiler intermediate representation to enhance neural program embeddings. In: Proceedings of the 44th International Conference on Software Engineering, pp. 2253–2265 (2022)
24. Liu, J., Kawaguchi, K., Hooi, B., Wang, Y., Xiao, X.: EIGNN: efficient infinite-depth graph neural networks. Adv. Neural. Inf. Process. Syst. **34**, 18762–18773 (2021)

25. Liu, Y., et al.: Roberta: a robustly optimized BERT pretraining approach. arXiv preprint arXiv:1907.11692 (2019)
26. Liu, Z., Tang, Z., Zhang, J., Xia, X., Yang, X.: Pre-training by predicting program dependencies for vulnerability analysis tasks. In: Proceedings of the IEEE/ACM 46th International Conference on Software Engineering, pp. 1–13 (2024)
27. Loshchilov, I., Hutter, F.: Decoupled weight decay regularization. arXiv preprint arXiv:1711.05101 (2017)
28. Van der Maaten, L., Hinton, G.: Visualizing data using t-sne. J. Mach. Learn. Res. **9**(11) (2008)
29. Mei, X., et al.: ARVO: atlas of reproducible vulnerabilities for open source software. arXiv preprint arXiv:2408.02153 (2024)
30. Mirsky, Y., et al.: {VulChecker}: graph-based vulnerability localization in source code. In: 32nd USENIX Security Symposium (USENIX Security 23), pp. 6557–6574 (2023)
31. Nguyen, V.A., Nguyen, D.Q., Nguyen, V., Le, T., Tran, Q.H., Phung, D.: ReGVD: revisiting graph neural networks for vulnerability detection. In: Proceedings of the ACM/IEEE 44th International Conference on Software Engineering: Companion Proceedings, pp. 178–182 (2022)
32. Niu, C., Li, C., Ng, V., Lo, D., Luo, B.: Fair: flow type-aware pre-training of compiler intermediate representations. In: Proceedings of the 46th IEEE/ACM International Conference on Software Engineering, pp. 1–12 (2024)
33. Peng, D., Zheng, S., Li, Y., Ke, G., He, D., Liu, T.Y.: How could neural networks understand programs? In: International Conference on Machine Learning, pp. 8476–8486. PMLR (2021)
34. Powers, D.M.: Evaluation: from precision, recall and f-measure to roc, informedness, markedness and correlation. arXiv preprint arXiv:2010.16061 (2020)
35. Rizsotto: Bear. https://github.com/rizsotto/Bear. Accessed 30 Jan 2023
36. Russell, R., et al.: Automated vulnerability detection in source code using deep representation learning. In: 2018 17th IEEE International Conference on Machine Learning and Applications (ICMLA), pp. 757–762. IEEE (2018)
37. Schuster, M., Paliwal, K.K.: Bidirectional recurrent neural networks. IEEE Trans. Sig. Process. **45**(11), 2673–2681 (1997)
38. Serebryany, K.: {OSS-Fuzz}-Google's continuous fuzzing service for open source software (2017)
39. Steenhoek, B., Gao, H., Le, W.: Dataflow analysis-inspired deep learning for efficient vulnerability detection. In: Proceedings of the 46th IEEE/ACM International Conference on Software Engineering, pp. 1–13 (2024)
40. Vaswani, A., et al.: Attention is all you need. Adv. Neural Inf. Process. Syst. **30** (2017)
41. VenkataKeerthy, S., Aggarwal, R., Jain, S., Desarkar, M.S., Upadrasta, R., Srikant, Y.: IR2Vec: LLVM IR based scalable program embeddings. ACM TACO **17**(4), 1–27 (2020)
42. Wang, H., et al.: Combining graph-based learning with automated data collection for code vulnerability detection. IEEE Trans. Inf. Forensics Secur. **16**, 1943–1958 (2020)
43. Wang, W., Nguyen, T.N., Wang, S., Li, Y., Zhang, J., Yadavally, A.: DeepVD: toward class-separation features for neural network vulnerability detection. In: 2023 IEEE/ACM 45th International Conference on Software Engineering (ICSE), pp. 2249–2261. IEEE (2023)
44. WelkIR: Online package (2025). https://github.com/HH-USTC/WelkIR

45. Wu, Y., Lu, J., Zhang, Y., Jin, S.: Vulnerability detection in C/C++ source code with graph representation learning. In: 2021 IEEE 11th Annual Computing and Communication Workshop and Conference (CCWC), pp. 1519–1524. IEEE (2021)
46. Wu, Y., Zou, D., Dou, S., Yang, W., Xu, D., Jin, H.: VulCNN: an image-inspired scalable vulnerability detection system. In: Proceedings of the 44th International Conference on Software Engineering, pp. 2365–2376 (2022)
47. Yuan, B., et al.: Enhancing deep learning-based vulnerability detection by building behavior graph model. In: 2023 IEEE/ACM 45th International Conference on Software Engineering (ICSE), pp. 2262–2274. IEEE (2023)
48. Zagane, M., Abdi, M.K., Alenezi, M.: Deep learning for software vulnerabilities detection using code metrics. IEEE Access **8**, 74562–74570 (2020)
49. Zhang, J., Liu, Z., Hu, X., Xia, X., Li, S.: Vulnerability detection by learning from syntax-based execution paths of code. IEEE Trans. Softw. Eng. **49**(8), 4196–4212 (2023)
50. Zhou, Y., Liu, S., Siow, J., Du, X., Liu, Y.: Devign: effective vulnerability identification by learning comprehensive program semantics via graph neural networks. Adv. Neural Inf. Process. Syst. **32** (2019)
51. Zou, D., Wang, S., Xu, S., Li, Z., Jin, H.: μ VulDeePecker: a deep learning-based system for multiclass vulnerability detection. IEEE Trans. Dependable Secure Comput. **18**(5), 2224–2236 (2019)

Edge Coverage Feedback of Embedded Systems Fuzzing Based on Debugging Interfaces

Weihua Jiao[1]( ), Qingbao Li[1], Xilong Li[1], Zhifeng Chen[1], Weiping Yao[1], Guimin Zhang[1,2], and Fei Cao[1]

[1] Information Engineering University, Zhengzhou 450000, China
jiao_weihua@163.com
[2] Laboratory for Advanced Computing and Intelligence Engineering, Zhengzhou 450000, China

Abstract. Fuzzing is one of the most widely used dynamic testing techniques for identifying bugs and vulnerabilities. However, the lack of accurate and generalized hardware-based coverage feedback methods hinders the application of Coverage-based Gray-box Fuzzing (CGF) on embedded systems. To cope with this problem, we propose an edge-coverage feedback method based on debugging interfaces for the first time and implement the prototype tool HIFuzz. HIFuzz first utilizes hardware breakpoints and debug probes to obtain information about a single node on the execution path. Other nodes on the path are then traced based on the dominance relations between nodes in the Control-Flow Graph (CFG). Finally, HIFuzz analyzes the edges contained in the execution path to obtain edge coverage feedback. In addition, we customize the breakpoint setting strategy and seed scheduling strategy for HIFuzz to improve the probability of hitting breakpoints and discovering new paths. Experiments show that HIFuzz can efficiently trace execution paths based on breakpoints and dominance relations. In tests using the MSP430, ESP32, and STM32, an average of 2.3 to 4.1 new edges can be tracked per breakpoint hit, saving 56.5% to 75.6% of the probing task. Compared with the state-of-the-art fuzzer GDBFuzz and black-box fuzzing, HIFuzz achieves the highest coverage in 8 of the 9 scenarios. In addition, our approach achieves high performance without impacting execution efficiency.

Keywords: Fuzzing · Embedded System · Edge Coverage · Debugging Interface

1 Introduction

In the era of rapid development of information technology, embedded devices such as the Internet of Things (IoT) have been widely used in various industries and human life. However, due to the limitations of hardware resources and the performance of MCUs, it is often necessary to balance between efficiency and security. In addition, firmware security is not adequately considered due to code quantity, response time, memory allocation patterns, etc. That leads to a higher likelihood of security vulnerabilities and a higher risk of attacks on embedded devices. To mitigate the problem, extensive security testing of embedded devices is necessary.

Coverage-based Gray-box Fuzzing (CGF) is one of the most widely used testing techniques for identifying security vulnerabilities. CGF is constantly moving towards increasing the coverage, thus improving the adequacy of the tests as well as the likelihood of triggering bugs [4]. High code coverage and more unique crashes indicate high performance of CGF. In addition, high coverage is often necessary to trigger an error.

However, applying CGF on embedded systems faces several challenges. First, the diversity of MCUs, peripherals, and firmware type makes simulation-based fuzzing unable to reproduce hardware behavior accurately. Second, we usually do not have access to the source code of embedded systems, but only the binary, which makes source code instrumentation no longer applicable. Even in the case of static binary instrumentation, the hardware needs to provide sufficient storage space. Finally, fuzzers need to receive feedback through the hardware interface and dynamically adjust their test strategies. Therefore, deploying fuzzers for embedded hardware often requires customizing the coverage collection scheme for different devices.

1.1 Related Work

To cope with the above challenges, researchers have tried to improve the performance of embedded device fuzzing through various methods, including full simulation testing, hardware-in-the-loop testing, and hardware interface-based testing.

Full emulation testing runs the firmware in a virtual environment and does not require access to any physical peripherals. The methodology enables scalable testing of embedded devices, provided that the target system and all peripherals are successfully simulated. In 2020, Abraham et al. decoupled hardware from firmware using the hardware abstraction layer (HAL) as a basis for re-hosting and analyzing firmware [5]. However, not all embedded devices provide HAL. In 2021, μEmu [16], which is based on S2E, utilizes concolic execution techniques to build a peripheral model for blob firmware. This method not only reaches deep paths and finds appropriate peripheral readings, but also mitigates the path explosion problem. In 2022, Fuzzware [13] implements fine-grained access modeling for blob firmware based on symbolic execution. It allows the fuzzing engine to change only meaningful hardware-generated values, thus drastically reducing the input load. However, Fuzzware does not support DMA, and a significant overhead often accompanies symbolic execution. In summary, existing full simulation-based approaches do not accurately model the behavior of hardware devices, resulting in inaccurate test results.

Hardware-in-the-loop testing was first proposed by Avatar [15]. Its main idea is to run the firmware only in an emulator and forward access packets to the physical peripheral through the emulator when the firmware interacts with the peripheral. This approach avoids emulating various peripherals. In 2018, the dynamic testing framework Charm [14] runs the driver on a virtual machine, where a monitoring program obtains the driver's I/O access requests and sends them to physical I/O devices over USB channels. In the same year, Inception [6], based on KLEE's Inception Symbolic Virtual Machine, used multiple strategies to handle different levels of memory abstraction, interactions with peripherals, and interrupts. However, this approach also requires source code for firmware and is not in line with our research scenario.

Hardware-based testing dynamically tests the firmware code running on the MCU directly through the physical interface of the embedded device. While this method is the most convenient way, existing research requires expensive tracking devices and special interfaces when obtaining coverage feedback, or the coverage metric does not accurately reflect code behavior. For example, in 2021, Snipuzz [8] used a dynamic testing approach based on syntactic reasoning, which somewhat solved the problem of low validity of test-case mutations. However, Snipuzz is still only a black-box test and does not obtain feedback on the execution state (only the response) of the MCU. In 2022, Maximilian Beckmann et al. [2] and μAFL [12] trace the execution state of embedded devices based on the Single Wire Output (SWO) interface and the Embedded Trace Macrocell (ETM) interface, respectively, and sample the way to obtain instruction-level coverage information. However, the bandwidth of SWO limits the accuracy of sampling and the ETM interface is only available for a few ARM devices. In addition, they both require expensive specialized tracking equipment. In 2023, GDBFuzz [7] utilized debugging interfaces to perform fuzzing on embedded systems. However, the basic block coverage GDBFuzz uses does not accurately describe the execution path and code behavior. In addition, its completely random selection of breakpoints affects test performance.

1.2 Our Approach and Contribution

To mitigate the limitations of existing research, we propose an edge coverage feedback method and implement the prototype tool HIFuzz. HIFuzz is the first general-purpose embedded system fuzzer that uses hardware interfaces to feedback edge coverage.

HIFuzz first gathers information about a single node on the current execution path using hardware breakpoints. Then, tracing which edges are located on the execution path based on the dominance relations and the adjacency relations between nodes in the Control-Flow Graph (CFG). In addition, we customize the breakpoint setting strategy for HIFuzz to improve the hit probability of breakpoints. Since breakpoint-based path tracing does not determine the complete execution path, traditional seed scheduling strategies (e.g., those employed by AFL) are no longer applicable. Therefore, we customize an new seed schedule strategy for HIFuzz. Finally, we evaluate the performance of HIFuzz on development boards with multiple architectures. The experimental results show that HIFuzz can effectively realize edge coverage feedback for embedded device fuzzing. Based on the dominance relations between nodes, on average, HIFuzz can track 2.3 to

4.1 edges per breakpoint hit, saving 56.5% 75.6% of cost. Compared with state-of-the-art fuzzer GDBFuzz and black-box fuzzing, HIFuzz achieves the highest coverage in 8 out of 9 scenarios. In summary, our main contributions include:

- We propose a general edge coverage feedback method for embedded system fuzzing based on hardware interfaces.
- We develop a breakpoint setting strategy that automatically and rationally selects hardware breakpoint addresses.
- We design a new seed scheduling strategy that determines the saving of new seeds and seed selection for the next round.
- We implemented the prototype tool HIFuzz and evaluated it experimentally.

2 Background

2.1 CGF

Gray-box fuzzing lies between white-box and black-box fuzzing. It can obtain satisfactory test results by relying only on limited knowledge of the target program and appropriate testing strategies rather than needing a detailed and comprehensive analysis of the program's internal structure.

Accurately tracking coverage is critical for CGF. Typically, three types of coverage metrics are basic block coverage, edge coverage, and path coverage. Keeping track of all paths (especially the order of edges) at runtime is usually not feasible due to, for example, the large number of paths [9]. In addition, edge coverage can provide more information than basic block coverage. In general, we can compute the basic block coverage from edge coverage, but we cannot infer the edge coverage from the basic block coverage.

As shown in Fig. 1, the example function EX processes two inputs in $Run1$ and three inputs in $Run2$. The basic blocks covered by the two runs are the same, while the edge $C3 \rightarrow C2$ exists only in $Run1$, and the edge $C3 \rightarrow D$ exists in $Run2$. Compared to the other two coverage metrics, the edge coverage balances the feasibility and accuracy and has been adopted by most gray-box fuzzers.

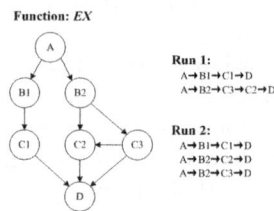

Fig. 1. CFG and example of execution path for function EX.

2.2 Hardware-Supported Trace Channel

Embedded devices need to monitor the operational state of the embedded software during development and debugging, which can often be accomplished using hardware-level execution trace interfaces. These interfaces capture processor instruction streams, memory access patterns, and peripheral interactions through dedicated pins.

Joint Test Action Group (JTAG) is a general-purpose debugging interface based on IEEE 1149.1. It accesses internal chip registers, performs breakpoint debugging, accesses memory data, and detects physical defects in hardware connections through the Test Access Port (TAP) controller. JTAG has broad compatibility, and about 90% of commercially available chips integrate a JTAG interface [10].

Serial Wire Debug (SWD) is a 2-wire debugging protocol developed by ARM. It realizes the basic debugging function equivalent to JTAG through SWCLK and SWDIO. In addition, SWD has an extended channel, Serial Wire Output (SWO), which supports asynchronous transmission of instruction execution time, logs, and other data to facilitate remote device diagnosis.

Embedded Trace Macrocell (ETM) is an instruction-level trace technology. It non-intrusively records processor execution information through hardware logic. ETM can capture fine-grained information, including branch prediction results, data load/store addresses, etc. However, ETM must rely on the hardware buffering and compression capabilities of expensive specialized debuggers such as J-Trace. In addition, ETM is not supported by devices other than particular series of ARM processors.

2.3 Firmware Reverse and CFG

Firmware reverse analysis is a cross-cutting technique for parsing the internal logic of embedded system firmware utilizing disassembly, dynamic debugging, and semantic recovery. Its core lies in: 1. crossing the differences between hardware architecture and software packaging. 2. transforming the functional logic of firmware from non-open-source machine code into comprehensible explicit expression. Then, on top of further analysis of the logical structure, data flow, control flow, etc., it reveals potential vulnerabilities, backdoors, or undisclosed functions.

CFG, as a basic abstraction model, is an important means of characterizing a program's execution logic. CFG demonstrates the jump and return relationships between basic blocks through nodes and edges. In firmware reverse, CFG not only helps to understand a program's normal execution path but also reveals where abnormal behavior or potential vulnerabilities lie.

2.4 Hardware Breakpoints and Debugging

Hardware breakpoints are hardware-supported mechanisms that rely on the processor's built-in debug registers. Debug registers are used to store the addresses of instructions to be monitored. When the program executes an instruction at that address, the processor automatically generates an interrupt signal and pauses program execution. Compared to software breakpoints, hardware breakpoints can monitor and control program execution without affecting program logic and are more suitable for debugging long-running tasks.

Debugging supported by hardware breakpoints is a common means of observing the execution state of a target device. It is typically used to interrupt the execution of the target device at a specified location, check memory values, and single-step the execution. When the target device execution reaches a breakpoint, the processor suspends program execution, hands control to the tester through the debugger, and allows checking the devices' execution status.

3 Design and Implementation

3.1 Overview

In order to obtain accurate coverage information in a more generalized way when fuzzing embedded devices, we propose an edge coverage feedback method based on debugging interfaces. As shown in Fig. 2, our approach consists of three main parts: (1) Setting hardware breakpoints for embedded devices based on the breakpoint setting strategy and obtaining breakpoint hit information. (2) Trace the edge coverage based on the breakpoint hit information and the dominance relationship between nodes in the CFG. (3) Based on the coverage feedback to further guide the selection of breakpoints and seed scheduling. Based on the above approach, we implement the prototype tool HIFuzz.

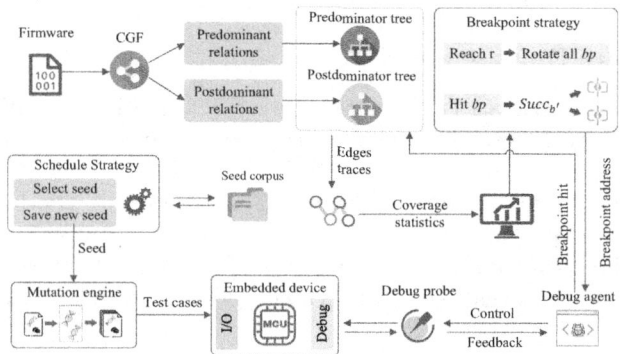

Fig. 2. HIFuzz design overview.

3.2 Low-Level Device Control

HIFuzz uses debugging interfaces such as JTAG and SWD interfaces to provide low-level control of the target device, enabling functions such as setting breakpoints, controlling the running state, and reading data. In addition, HIFuzz needs to send test-cases to the device's I/O interface (e.g., serial port). Through the cooperation of the test-case generation module and the embedded device control module, HIFuzz realizes the control and status monitoring of the embedded device's processing of input data.

Debug adapters have direct access to device memory and processor registers including memory-mapped system configuration registers [12]. When the target device is unresponsive during testing, HIFuzz can automatically force a reset via low-level commands without human involvement.

Due to the diversity of device architectures and debugging interfaces, the debugging framework adopts the form of GDB Server and GDB Client. GDB Server realizes cross-layer debugging services by coordinating the debug probe and remote stub. The debug probe is responsible for converting debug instructions from the host side to physical signals recognized by the target device and performing underlying hardware operations. Common debug probes include MSP430-FET, J-Link, ST-Link, etc. The remote stub acts as a protocol translation intermediary, translating high-level debugging commands into instructions executable by the debug probe and maintaining debugging session state. In this way, the GDB Client makes it possible to debug various devices via the serial protocol.

3.3 Dominance Relations of Basic Blocks and Edge Coverage

There may be dominance relationships between nodes in the CFG, which helps in tracking execution paths containing multiple nodes based on a single node. The edges between neighboring nodes on the execution path are the elements that form the edge cover. As shown in Fig. 1, if the program executes node $C1$ while processing an input, the execution path must contain entry node A and node $B1$, and reach exit node D. Thus, we can infer richer information about the path when we know only one node.

In order to obtain edge coverage information with lower overhead during fuzzing, we utilize the aforementioned domination relationship between nodes in calculating edge coverage. In addition, we introduce the concepts of Predomination and Postdomination derived from Agrawal [1] to describe this relationship [7].

Predomination. The entry node of CFG C is s and node $u \in C$, $v \in C$. If every path from s to u contains v, then we call v predominates u, denoted $v \xrightarrow{pre} u$.

Postdomination. The exit node of CFG C is s' and node $v \in C$, $w \in C$. If every path from v to s' contains w, then we call w postdominates v, denoted $w \xrightarrow{post} v$.

In CFG, the predominating node of the entry node s is only itself, and the predominating nodes of other nodes contain at least itself as well as s. Among the predominating nodes of u, the node v' closest to u other than itself is called the direct predominating node of u, denoted as $iPredom(u) = v'$. Every node except s has a unique direct predominating node and does not constitute a cycle. Thus, the predominance relation constitutes a predominance tree. Similarly, every node except the exit node s' has a unique postdominating node. A postdominance tree is formed based on the postdominance relation.

During fuzzing, if we know that the execution path contains node b based on the breakpoint hit information, we can analyze other nodes that are necessarily on the execution path based on dominance relations. For example, if the parent node of b in the predominance tree is the predecessor node of b in the CFG, we can determine that the execution path contains the edge $a \to b$. Then, iteratively determines if a predecessor node of a is also located on the execution path. This way, we can determine the set E_{pre} of edges on the current path and located before node b. Similarly, the set E_{post} of edges on the execution path after b can be known based on the postdominance relation. Thus, when hitting a hardware breakpoint, we can determine the edges $E_{cover} = E_{pre} \cup E_{post}$ covered by this execution.

For Fig. 1, if the hardware breakpoint set at node $C1$ is hit, it can be inferred that the execution path contains at least three edges $A \to B1$, $B1 \to C1$, and $C1 \to D$. If the breakpoint at node $C3$ is hit, it can be determined that $A \to B2$ and $B2 \to C3$ are located in the execution path.

3.4 Breakpoint Setting Strategy

Since each basic block corresponds to a node in the CFG, HIFuzz uses the addresses of all basic blocks as the selection range of breakpoint addresses. That effectively minimizes the number of alternative addresses and avoids setting multiple breakpoints in the same basic block. The number of breakpoint registers in the MCU determines the maximum number of breakpoints max_{BP}.

When HIFuzz sets breakpoints for the first time, the address is chosen randomly among all basic blocks. If a breakpoint is hit during testing, HIFuzz clears and resets all existing breakpoints. Why not only reset the hit breakpoint? Intuitively, if one of the $max_{BP} - 1$ breakpoints (other than the one hit) is located on a node that can be tracked based on dominance relationships, execution will necessarily be interrupted at that breakpoint while the device continues. Since the node at which the breakpoint is located has already been traced, the hit is meaningless, adds time overhead, and wastes hardware resources.

In addition, our analysis suggests that resetting all breakpoints increases the probability of hitting a breakpoint, which helps to obtain more accurate coverage and discover more complete execution paths. Since the complete execution path cannot be restored based on the trace of breakpoints, there may be an unknown segment of the path $Path_{head}$ and $Path_{tail}$ at the beginning and end of the execution path, respectively. Assuming that the test hits a breakpoint p on node b_{hit}, and another breakpoint p' is located on the execution path $Path_{tail}$ after b_{hit}, we call p' a preparatory breakpoint. Since this type of breakpoint is inevitably hit when the device continues execution, it can continue tracing and refining the current execution path with a small overhead.

Suppose the total number of nodes in the CFG is N. The n_{pre} and n_{post} denote the number of nodes covered before and after performing the trace. After the trace, the number of nodes on $Path_{tail}$ is m. At this point, whether the other $max_{BP} - 1$ breakpoints should be reset can be seen as a variant of the Monty Hall problem paradox. Therefore, we can calculate the probability that a breakpoint is a preparatory breakpoint in each of the two cases of keeping and resetting these breakpoints. The results are as follows:

$$P_{keep} = \frac{m}{N - n_{pre}}$$
$$P_{reset} = \frac{m + (n_{post} - n_{pre})}{N - n_{pre}} \qquad (1)$$

According to Eq. 1, resetting breakpoints can increase the probability of hitting breakpoints during testing, which is conducive to improving the accuracy of coverage information. How to choose the breakpoint location (node in CFG) when resetting? We categorize the selection of the breakpoint location into two cases: 1. selecting the successor node of the traced execution path. 2. Select randomly among the uncovered nodes.

When tracing an execution path, if node b' has multiple branches (outgoing edges) in the CFG that can reach the exit, it is impossible to determine which branch the execution path passes through based on dominance relations.

If it is possible to determine which branch the path passes through when execution continues, an execution path closer to completeness can be obtained. Therefore, we set a breakpoint on the successor node to b'. When the debugger controls the device to continue execution, the breakpoint on the branch is hit. At this point, we already know where the execution path is going, so we continue to trace it to get a more complete execution path.

Since the relationship between the number of available hardware breakpoints max_{BP} and the number of successor nodes $Succ_{b'}$ to node b' is uncertain. If $max_{BP} \leq Succ_{b'}$, set all breakpoints on the successor nodes of b'. If $max_{BP} > Succ_{b'}$, first set breakpoints on all successor nodes, and then randomly select $max_{BP} - Succ_{b'}$ nodes among those that have not been covered.

If no nodes similar to b' are found during tracing, all breakpoints are chosen randomly from the nodes that have not been covered. In addition, all breakpoints need to be reset if no breakpoint is hit after a certain number (threshold r) of executions. In this case, all breakpoints are similarly chosen randomly from the nodes that have not been covered.

3.5 Seed Schedule Strategy

An important feature of gray-box fuzzing is saving interesting test-cases to the corpus as new seeds. Since breakpoint-based tracing cannot determine the complete execution path, so the current execution path may still be a new path even if all edges traced have been covered. Therefore, it is inappropriate to base the decision to save the current test-case on whether a new path is found (as AFL does). In addition, if the device can trigger a breakpoint when processing an input, it indicates that the current input executes at least part of the code. Therefore, it somewhat conforms to the formatting requirements. Mutating the current input has a higher potential to generate valid test cases. Therefore, to avoid missing test-cases that cover new paths and enrich the corpus's diversity, HIFuzz adds the current test-case to the corpus each time a breakpoint is hit.

When selecting a seed for the next round from the corpus, HIFuzz prioritizes entries that have been selected a low number of times. Essentially, selecting low-frequency seeds means selecting low-frequency paths. This choice has two reasons: 1. Since low-frequency paths are not adequately tested, they are more likely to have potential bugs or vulnerabilities. 2. Exploiting low-frequency paths has a higher probability of discovering new paths. CGF was abstracted as a Markov chain model by Marcel Böhme et al. Based on this model, they show that using seeds that execute low-frequency paths improves the probability of transitioning to unknown paths, thus contributing to improved test coverage [3]. Although the seeds and execution paths in HIFuzz's corpus are not a one-to-one correspondence, the number of times a seed has been selected can also reflect the execution frequency of the paths. Therefore, HIFuzz uses the entry with the least number of selections as the seed for the next rounds.

4 Implementation and Evaluation

HIFuzz is based on GDBFuzz and implemented by adding about 500 lines of Python code. We implemented an edge-tracking module to track edges bound to locate in the execution path based on a known node. Combined with breakpoint hit information, the tracking module can obtain edge coverage feedback for the current execution path. In addition, we design a new breakpoint strategy file to improve the utilization of hardware breakpoint resources by refining the breakpoint address selection method. Finally, we customize the strategy to save interesting seeds and select seeds based on the characteristics of HIFuzz.

We will experimentally evaluate the performance of HIFuzz and the effectiveness of our method. Moreover, answer the following questions during the evaluation:

- Is HIFuzz able to efficiently track edges on the execution path?
- Is HIFuzz able to achieve higher coverage than existing work?
- Does our breakpoint setting strategy increase the probability of hitting a breakpoint?
- Does our seed saving and selection strategy help improve the performance of HIFuzz?
- How does the number of breakpoints affect HIFuzz performance?
- Does our approach affect test efficiency?

4.1 Setup

We evaluated HIFuzz using a variety of common development boards. Table 1 lists the architecture of each board, the debug probes used, and the number of hardware breakpoints supported. We deployed three different applications, JSON, Buggy, and Sensor, on each board. JOSN and Buggy were selected from the experimental setup of GDBFuzz. GDBFuzz uses four applications, of which only JOSN and Buggy are available for all three MCUs in Table 1. Sensor is the application we developed to process the sensor data. These three development boards and three applications constitute nine test scenarios. We refer to the three boards as MSP430, ESP32, and STM32. Besides, we use "board_application" to denote specific scenarios, such as MSP430_JSON.

Table 1. Detailed information about the development board, including the architecture, debug probes used, and the number of available hardware breakpoints.

Development Boards	Arch.	Debug Probe	#HW Br.
MSP-EXP430F5529LP	MSP430	eZ-FET lite	8
ESP-WROOM-32	Xtensa	J-Link Plus	2
Apollo STM32F429	ARM	STLink v2	6

For each application, each board uses an initial corpus containing only the same input file. Each set of experiments contains multiple independent tests to reduce the impact of fuzzing's randomness on the results. The total test duration is over 600 h. HIFuzz runs on a device with an Intel Core i7-10700K CPU, 128 GB RAM, and an operating system of Ubuntu 20.04.

4.2 Effectiveness of Tracking

To analyze the benefits of tracing for coverage feedback, we recorded information about each breakpoint hit during testing. Using ESP32 as an example, the recorded results are shown in Fig. 3. The horizontal axis indicates the number of new edges tracked per hit. For JSON, the statistics show 77.3% of the hits track new edges, and the number of new edges tracked is concentrated between 1 and 10. For Sensor, 91.7% of the hits can discover at least one new edge by tracking, and the number of edges is concentrated between 1 and 5. Buggy can discover more than 2 new edges for each hit.

In addition, we count the ratio of the number of edges traced to the number of breakpoint hits. The results show that, on average, 2.3 to 4.1 new edges can be traced per breakpoint hit. That means the number of breakpoint hits can be reduced by 56.5% to 75.6% with the same coverage. The above results indicate that the edges on the execution path that are around the hit nodes can be effectively restored through the dominance relation. As for the case where a breakpoint is hit but no new edge is found, it may be because the node's direct dominator node is not its neighboring node or all of the tracked edges have already been covered.

Since dominance relations include both predominance and postdominance, do traces based on them both contribute to path recovery? To explore the question, the number of edges obtained using forward tracking and backward tracking, respectively, was recorded each time a breakpoint was hit.

As shown in Fig. 4, both tracing types can effectively restore edges on the execution path. In contrast, forward tracing restored more edges than backward tracing. Our analysis reveals that this is due to the structure of the CFG. When a node has multiple outgoing edges, the node may not have a postdominance node, or the postdominance node is not a successor of the node. This situation leads to a break in path tracking. Similarly, the number of incoming edges affects forward tracking. CFGs typically have one entry and multiple exits, resulting in more

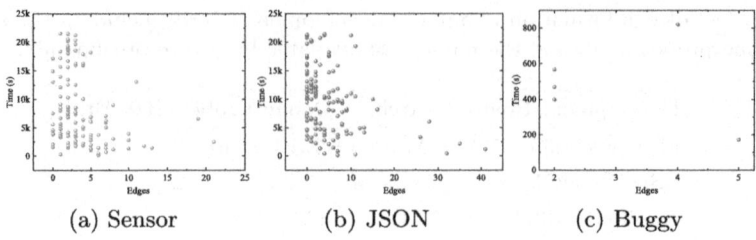

(a) Sensor (b) JSON (c) Buggy

Fig. 3. The time of each hit breakpoint and the number of new edges tracked. The development board is ESP32.

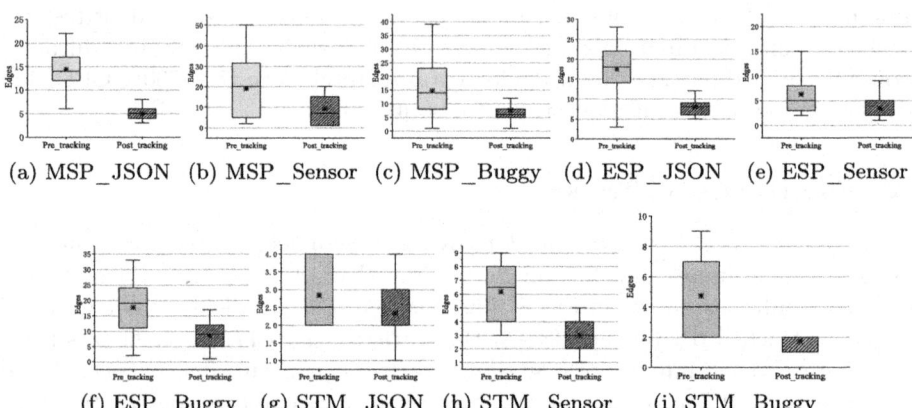

(a) MSP_JSON (b) MSP_Sensor (c) MSP_Buggy (d) ESP_JSON (e) ESP_Sensor

(f) ESP_Buggy (g) STM_JSON (h) STM_Sensor (i) STM_Buggy

Fig. 4. The number of edges that can be tracked by forward tracking and backward tracking in 2 h, respectively (Includes edges that have been previously covered).

nodes having a single incoming edge than nodes having a single outgoing edge. As a result, the predominance tree will generally be deeper than the postdominance tree, which results in more edges being available for forward tracing.

4.3 Coverage

Table 2 records the edge coverage achieved by HIFuzz in all 9 scenarios. However, no other fuzzer is currently able to achieve edge coverage feedback under the same interface conditions, making it impossible to compare with existing work. For this reason, we recorded the basic block coverage of HIFuzz to compare with the current state-of-the-art work GDBFuzz and BlackFuzz. Where BlackFuzz is modified from HIFuzz by not saving new seeds during testing, i.e., by keeping the initial corpus unchanged. We use HIFuzz, GDBFuzz, and BlackFuz on all test scenarios for three separate runs, each lasting 6 h. The basic block coverage they achieved is shown in Fig. 5.

Table 2. Edge coverage achieved by HIFuzz in 9 test scenarios. Each scenario was tested three times independently for 6 h each.

Boards	JSON		Buggy		Sensor	
	Max.	Avg.	Max.	Avg.	Max.	Avg.
MSP430	218	179.3	23	20.3	90	90
ESP32	740	699	19	17.7	469	454
STM32	644	607.7	18	17	495	493

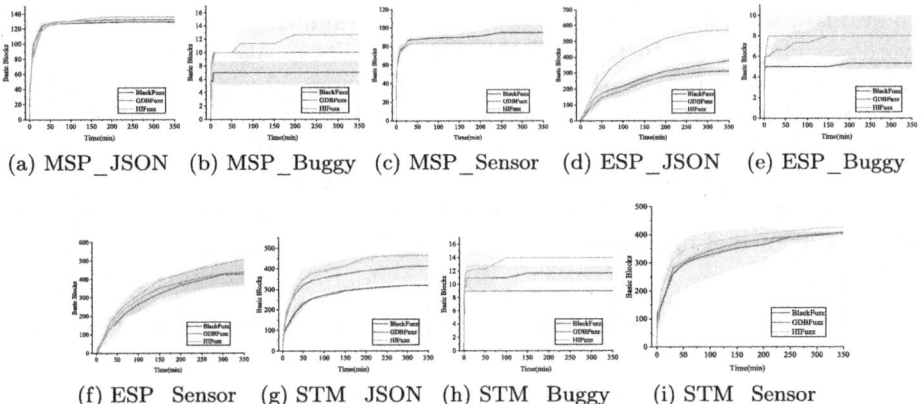

(a) MSP_JSON (b) MSP_Buggy (c) MSP_Sensor (d) ESP_JSON (e) ESP_Buggy

(f) ESP_Sensor (g) STM_JSON (h) STM_Buggy (i) STM_Sensor

Fig. 5. Basic block coverage achieved by HIFuzz, GDBFuzz, and BlackFuzz for the 9 test scenarios, shaded for standard deviation.

HIFuzz and GDBFuzz obtained higher coverage than BlackFuzz in 8 of the 9 scenarios, indicating that the feedback information they obtained can effectively guide the fuzzing engine to make relevant decisions. In addition, HIFuzz achieved higher coverage than GDBFuzz in 7 scenarios. In the ESP32-Buggy scenario, although HIFuzz and GDBFuzz finally achieved the same coverage, HIFuzz reached the highest coverage 140 min earlier. The above results show that HIFuzz has better performance, mainly due to HIFuzz's edge coverage providing more accurate feedback on the test status and a reasonable strategy for setting breakpoints.

However, a counterintuitive phenomenon occurs in the MSP430_Sensor scenario, where BlackFuzz achieves higher coverage than HIFuzz and GDBFuzz. Our analysis reveals that this is mainly due to the characteristics of MSP430 and the processing logic of Sensor. Due to factors such as architecture and dependent libraries, Sensor compiles far fewer basic blocks on MSP430 than ESP32 and STM32. In addition, MSP430 has more hardware breakpoints than the other two boards, which allows the fuzzers to cover those easily covered nodes. Sensor decides whether to perform certain computations by determining whether a particular byte satisfies a condition. Since the judgment conditions are strict, it is challenging for the mutation to generate test-cases fulfilling the requirements. That leads to some code regions being hard to cover. In contrast, BlackFuzz has only one seed in its corpus, which provide more ample mutations and thus is more likely to generate inputs that satisfy conditions.

4.4 Vulnerability Discovery

To evaluate the ability of HIFuzz to detect vulnerabilities, we implanted a stack overflow vulnerability in Buggy and ran it on STM32. We conducted multiple independent tests using HIFuzz and GDBFuzz respectively, and recorded the time it took to detect the overflow vulnerability. As shown in Table 3, both HIFuzz and GDBFuzz can detect the vulnerability in Buggy in all 5 tests. In addition, HIFuzz outperforms GDBFuzz in both average and shortest time spent. That suggests our proposed edge coverage feedback is more helpful in improving the performance of fuzzing compared to basic block coverage used in GDBFuzz.

Table 3. Time taken by HIFuzz and GDBFuzz to discover the stack overflow vulnerability in Buggy, respectively.

	1st	2nd	3rd	4th	5th	Avg.
GDBFuzz	6 min 8 s	1 h 29 min 28 s	17 min 58 s	21 min 13 s	18 min 6 s	30 min 35 s
HIFuzz	11 min 39 s	52 min 54 s	**4 min 50 s**	22 min 40 s	5 min 31 s	**19 min 31 s**

4.5 Breakpoint Setting Strategy

To evaluate the effectiveness of our breakpoint setting strategy, we recorded the number of times HIFuzz set breakpoints, and the number of breakpoint hits in each run. By calculating and comparing their ratios, we can compare the breakpoint hit probability of HIFuzz and GDBFuzz. Breakpoint setting include setting after a hit and resetting after r is reached. As shown in Table 4, HIFuzz has a higher probability of hitting breakpoints than GDBFuzz in most scenarios. That illustrates that our breakpoint setting strategy helps achieve more accurate coverage feedback, which further contributes to improving test performance. However, we can see that in both the ESP32_Sensor and STM32_Sensor scenarios, although HIFuzz has more hits, the percentage is lower. The reason is that HIFuzz records a large number of duplicate crashes, resulting in frequent switching of breakpoints.

Table 4. The number of times breakpoints were set and hit, as well as the ratio of them. The results were taken from three tests of 6 h each.

Application	Board	Fuzzer	Avg. set times	Avg. hit times	Percentage
JSON	MSP430	HIFuzz	407.3	75	**18.4%**
		GDBFuzz	387.7	70.3	18.1%
	ESP32	HIFuzz	1161.3	153.3	**13.2%**
		GDBFuzz	891.6	85.7	9.6%
	STM32	HIFuzz	1088	187	**17.2%**
		GDBFuzz	1121.3	159.3	14.2%
Buggy	MSP430	HIFuzz	589.7	22.7	**3.80%**
		GDBFuzz	629	22	3.50%
	ESP32	HIFuzz	1574	126.7	**8.00%**
		GDBFuzz	1427	102.7	7.20%
	STM32	HIFuzz	240.7	116.7	**48.40%**
		GDBFuzz	272	130.3	47.90%
Sensor	MSP430	HIFuzz	350.3	8.7	**24.60%**
		GDBFuzz	347	8.3	23.90%
	ESP32	HIFuzz	1477.3	7	0.47%
		GDBFuzz	792	6.7	**0.85%**
	STM32	HIFuzz	1813.3	9	0.50%
		GDBFuzz	794.3	7.3	**0.92%**

According to the breakpoint setting strategy, breakpoints can be categorized into two types: 1. Randomly selected uncovered nodes. 2. Successor nodes of the traced path. In order to verify the reasonableness of the second type of breakpoints, we recorded the number of times the two types of breakpoints were hit respectively. In the case of the STM32_JSON scenario, for example, there are 187 hits per run on average, of which 8.5 hits are for the second type of breakpoints. Although the percentage of the second type of breakpoints is only 4.5%, it improves the coverage with almost negligible overhead. Therefore, this type of breakpoint is important for improving test efficiency and performance, which shows the rationality and effectiveness of our breakpoint setting strategy.

As described in Sect. 3.4, if execution reaches r and still does not hit any breakpoints, all breakpoints need to be reset. So how should r be set? How does the difference in r affect the performance of HIFuzz? In order to explore the above questions, we set r to vary from 1 to 50k and record the number of edges that HIFuzz can cover in two hours, respectively. This setup aims to analyze the effect of r on edge coverage with the same MCU but different applications and with the same application but different MCUs (Fig. 6).

As shown in subplots (a) and (b) of Fig. 7, in the ESP32_Sensor scenario, the change of r does not affect the performance of HIFuzz with a significant trend.

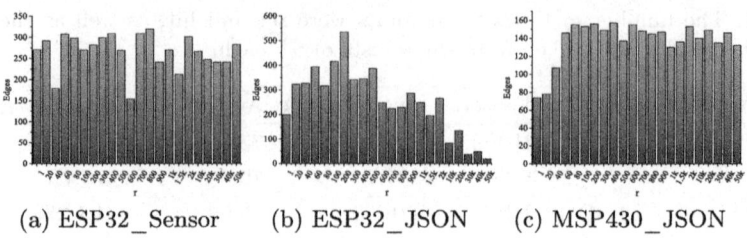

(a) ESP32_Sensor   (b) ESP32_JSON   (c) MSP430_JSON

Fig. 6. The edge coverage that HIFuzz can achieve when r takes different values between 1 and 5W.

For ESP32_JSON, if r is set too large, it will affect the performance of HIFuzz. The highest coverage is achieved when r is set to around 200. However, for MSP430_JSON, the performance is degraded when r is lower than 60. It can be concluded that r impacts the performance of HIFuzz. However, the optimal range of r differs in different scenarios and is affected by both MCU and application.

In order to explore how r affects performance, we recorded the amount of data processed by the development board (i.e., the execution count) and the times of hit breakpoints when r took different values. Then, we performed curve fitting for the relationship between r and the amount of data on scales of 1 100 and 1 50K, respectively. The fitting results are shown in Fig. 7.

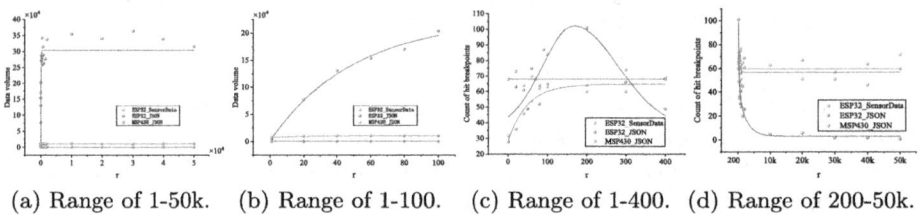

(a) Range of 1-50k.   (b) Range of 1-100.   (c) Range of 1-400.   (d) Range of 200-50k.

Fig. 7. Simple curve fitting between r and data volumes in the ranges 1–100 and 1–50k, respectively. And the fits between the number of hit breakpoints and r in the intervals 1–400 and 200–50k, respectively.

In the ESP32_Sensor scenario, the amount of data processed by the development board in two hours is hardly affected by r. As for MSP430_JSON, it only causes a decrease in data volume when r is 1. The most affected is ESP32_JSON. When r is less than 100, the data volume increases rapidly as r increases. When r exceeds 100, data volume gradually stabilizes at around 300k. In contrast, the volume of data (about 5k) when r is 1 is only 1.6% of normal. This phenomenon is because breakpoints are frequently switched when r is too small. That introduces a huge extra overhead, which reduces the number of test inputs processed by the embedded device. The impact of r is greater in scenarios where processing is faster.

In order to analyze the effect of r on the number of hits, we performed a preliminary curve fitting of their relationship over two intervals, 1–400 and 200–50k. The results are as shown in subplots (c) and (d) of Fig. 7. In the two scenarios running JSON, if r is between 1–200, the number of hits increases as r increases. Subsequently, the hit count of ESP32_JSON decreases rapidly as r continues to increase. When r is 50k, there is only one hit in two hours. In contrast, ESP32_Sensor is hardly affected by r.

Our analysis shows that even though r is very large, if the breakpoint can be hit after fewer executions, the breakpoint will be reset without being affected by r. If the breakpoint is located in a code region that is difficult to reach, HIFuzz can only wait for r executions before resetting the breakpoint. This situation does not affect the amount of data processed by the embedded system, but it does cause a significant reduction in the number of breakpoint hits.

4.6 Seed Scheduling Strategies

As described in Sect. 3.5, HIFuzz does not save new seeds to the corpus only when a new edge is found, but saves the current test-case when a breakpoint is hit. Since a new edge may or may not be found when a breakpoint is hit, the seeds saved to the corpus are categorized into two types: (1) seeds saved when a new edge is covered, and (2) seeds saved when a breakpoint is hit but no new edge is covered.

We recorded the categorization of the seeds selected each time hit to verify whether our strategy of saving seeds is of practical significance for improving test performance. Using Sensor as an example, we ran for two hours on each board (every selected seed was mutated once). The percentage of the second type of seeds in the three test scenarios are 22.4%, 15.4% and 12.5%, respectively. That suggests that the second type of seed plays an important role in exploring the code path as valid test-cases, thus validating the rationale for saving the seed when a breakpoint is hit but no new edges are covered.

4.7 Number of Hardware Breakpoints

The number of available hardware breakpoints varies between MCU families. How does the number of breakpoints affect the performance of fuzzing? In order to explore the problem, we used different numbers of hardware breakpoints in multiple tests and recorded the growth of edge coverage over 2 h. MSP430 and STM32 are divided into 4 cases. Since the ESP32 has only two hardware breakpoints, it is only divided into two cases. Taking JSON as an example, the results are shown in Fig. 8.

The results show that the higher the number of hardware breakpoints, the higher the edge coverage and the growth rate that HIFuzz can achieve. How does the number of breakpoints affect the test performance? To figure this out, we recorded how many breakpoints HIFuzz was able to hit in 2 h when using different numbers of breakpoints. As shown in Fig. 9, the number of hardware breakpoints positively correlates with the number of breakpoints hit. That is

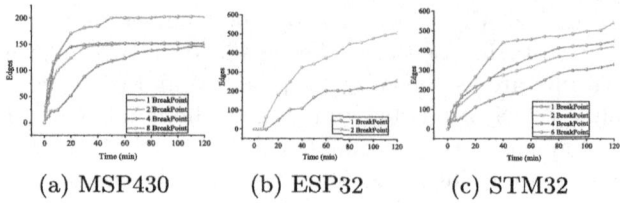

(a) MSP430 (b) ESP32 (c) STM32

Fig. 8. For JSON, the edge coverage achieved by HIFuzz with varying numbers of hardware breakpoints.

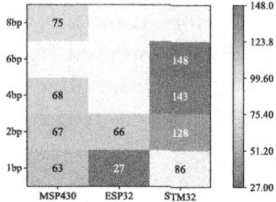

Fig. 9. The number of times HIFuzz hits breakpoints within two hours when using different numbers of hardware breakpoints.

why a larger number of breakpoints can improve edge coverage. However, this also reveals the limitation of using hardware breakpoints to obtain coverage, i.e., it is limited by the number of breakpoints.

5 Discussion

According to Sect. 4.4, r may have a significant impact on test performance. Additionally, the impact of r varies with different MCUs or applications. Due to the diversity of MCUs and applications, it is difficult to predict the suitable r before running. However, we believe that this does not diminish the applicability of HIFuzz. When r takes the value of 200, HIFuzz performs well in all three of our test scenarios. Thus, several short trial runs with different r (around 200) before the formal testing will allow us to find the suitable r for the current scenario.

The performance of HIFuzz is related to the accuracy of CFG. In cases where the actual paths detected by HIFuzz do not match the paths in the CFG, the problem of CFG accuracy can be mitigated by dynamically refining the CFG during the testing process. We will try to address this issue in future research. In addition, how to obtain more accurate CFG through reverse analysis is not within our research scope.

6 Conclusion

Hardware-based fuzzing can conveniently and quickly test the real state of embedded systems. However, existing research lacks a general and accurate coverage feedback method. To cope with this problem, we propose an edge coverage feedback solution based on debugging interfaces and implement a prototype tool HIFuzz. HIFuzz utilizes hardware breakpoints to obtain information about a node on the execution path and then traces the edges based on the nodes' dominance relations. In addition, we customize the breakpoint setting strategy and seed scheduling strategy to improve the performance of HIFuzz. Compared with the basic block coverage, edge coverage can more accurately describe the coverage state. Thus, it can more effectively guide the fuzzing engine in making relevant decisions.

The evaluation results show that HIFuzz can effectively feedback edge coverage. As for basic block coverage, HIFuzz significantly outperforms the current state-of-the-art fuzzer GDBFuzz and black-box fuzzing. In addition, our breakpoint setting strategy can effectively improve the hit probability of breakpoints. The seed saving strategy is also significant for improving performance. However, HIFuzz also has some limitations, i.e., its performance is constrained by the number of hardware breakpoints and the performance of the MCU. In future work, we will try to address the above limitations and then combine HIFuzz with mutation strategies [11] to further improve the fuzzing performance for embedded systems.

Acknowledgments. This research was supported by the National Key Research and Development Program of China under Grant (2021YFB3101804) and the fund of Laboratory for Advanced Computing and Intelligence Engineering (2023-LYJJ-01-032).

References

1. Agrawal, H.: Dominators, super blocks, and program coverage. In: Proceedings of the 21st ACM SIGPLAN-SIGACT Symposium on Principles of Programming Languages, pp. 25–34. POPL 1994, Association for Computing Machinery, New York, NY, USA (1994). https://doi.org/10.1145/174675.175935
2. Beckmann, M., Steffan, J.: Coverage-guided fuzzing of embedded systems leveraging hardware tracing. In: Computer Security. ESORICS 2022 International Workshops: CyberICPS 2022, SECPRE 2022, SPOSE 2022, CPS4CIP 2022, CDT&SECOMANE 2022, EIS 2022, and SecAssure 2022, Copenhagen, Denmark, 26–30 September 2022, Revised Selected Papers, pp. 362–378. Springer-Verlag, Berlin, Heidelberg (2022). https://doi.org/10.1007/978-3-031-25460-4_21
3. Böhme, M., Pham, V.T., Roychoudhury, A.: Coverage-based GreyBox fuzzing as Markov chain. IEEE Trans. Softw. Eng. **45**(5), 489–506 (2019). https://doi.org/10.1109/TSE.2017.2785841
4. Chen, C., Cui, B., Ma, J., Wu, R., Guo, J., Liu, W.: A systematic review of fuzzing techniques. Comput. Secur. **75**, 118–137 (2018). https://doi.org/10.1016/j.cose.2018.02.002
5. Clements, A.A., et al.: HALucinator: firmware re-hosting through abstraction layer emulation. In: USENIX Security Symposium (2020). https://api.semanticscholar.org/CorpusID:209379845

6. Corteggiani, N., Camurati, G., Francillon, A.: Inception: system-wide security testing of real-world embedded systems software. In: Usenix (ed.) USENIX 2018, 27th Usenix Security Symposium, 15-17 August 2018, Baltimore, MD, USA. Baltimore (2018). copyright Usenix. Personal use of this material is permitted. The definitive version of this paper was published in USENIX 2018, 27th Usenix Security Symposium, 15-17 August 2018, Baltimore, MD, USA and is available at :
7. Eisele, M., Ebert, D., Huth, C., Zeller, A.: Fuzzing embedded systems using debug interfaces. In: Proceedings of the 32nd ACM SIGSOFT International Symposium on Software Testing and Analysis (2023). https://api.semanticscholar.org/CorpusID:259844933
8. Feng, X., et al.: Snipuzz: black-box fuzzing of IoT firmware via message snippet inference. In: Proceedings of the 2021 ACM SIGSAC Conference on Computer and Communications Security, pp. 337–350. CCS 2021, Association for Computing Machinery, New York, NY, USA (2021). https://doi.org/10.1145/3460120.3484543
9. Gan, S., et al.: CollAFL: path sensitive fuzzing. In: 2018 IEEE Symposium on Security and Privacy, SP 2018, Proceedings, 21-23 May 2018, San Francisco, California, USA, pp. 679–696. IEEE Computer Society (2018). https://doi.org/10.1109/SP.2018.00040
10. IEEE: IEEE standard for test access port and boundary-scan architecture. IEEE Std 1149.1-2013 (Revision of IEEE Std 1149.1-2001), pp. 1–444 (2013). https://doi.org/10.1109/IEEESTD.2013.6515989
11. Jiao, W., Li, X., Li, Q., Cao, F., Li, X., Yue, S.: Adaptive mutation based on multi-population evolution strategy for GreyBox fuzzing. Inf. Sci. **705**, 121959 (2025). https://doi.org/10.1016/j.ins.2025.121959, https://www.sciencedirect.com/science/article/pii/S002002552500091X
12. Li, W., Shi, J., Li, F., Lin, J., Wang, W., Guan, L.: μAFL: non-intrusive feedback-driven fuzzing for microcontroller firmware. In: 2022 IEEE/ACM 44th International Conference on Software Engineering (ICSE), pp. 1–12 (2022). https://api.semanticscholar.org/CorpusID:246634279
13. Scharnowski, T., et al.: Fuzzware: using precise MMIO modeling for effective firmware fuzzing. In: USENIX Security Symposium (2022). https://api.semanticscholar.org/CorpusID:240302533
14. Seyed Talebi, S.M., Tavakoli, H., Zhang, H., Zhang, Z., Sani, A., Qian, Z.: Charm: facilitating dynamic analysis of device drivers of mobile systems. In: USENIX Security Symposium (2018)
15. Zaddach, J., Bruno, L., Francillon, A., Balzarotti, D.: Avatar: a framework to support dynamic security analysis of embedded systems' firmwares. In: NDSS (2014). https://doi.org/10.14722/ndss.2014.23229
16. Zhou, W., Guan, L., Liu, P., Zhang, Y.: Automatic firmware emulation through invalidity-guided knowledge inference (extended version). In: USENIX Security Symposium (2021). https://api.semanticscholar.org/CorpusID:235469057

Cache Demote for Fast Eviction Set Construction and Page Table Attribute Leakage

Taehun Kim, Hyerean Jang, and Youngjoo Shin(✉)

Korea University, Seoul, Republic of Korea
{taehunk,hr_jang,syoungjoo}@korea.ac.kr

Abstract. ISA extensions are increasingly used to enhance performance for specialized workloads without major architectural redesign. However, these enhancements can unintentionally introduce new microarchitectural attack surfaces. This paper examines security implications of Intel's new cldemote extension, which optimizes data sharing by transferring cache lines from upper to lower-level caches. Our analysis shows the cldemote facilitates efficient eviction set construction in non-inclusive LLCs without helper threads or extensive memory operations. Our method reduces eviction set construction time by 36% with high success rates. Additionally, we find cldemote's execution latency leaks sensitive data such as TLB states, page table permissions, and translation termination levels. Leveraging these leaks, we successfully derandomize the kernel base address in 2.49 ms on Linux. Finally, we discuss potential mitigations, emphasizing the broad security impacts of emerging ISA extensions.

1 Introduction

Modern processors continuously evolve to support a wider range of workloads efficiently. A key driver of this evolution is the introduction of Instruction Set Architecture (ISA) extensions. These extensions enhance processor capabilities without significant architectural redesigns. While ISA extensions offer substantial benefits, they can introduce unintended interactions between software and hardware layers. Such interactions often involve microarchitectural components—such as caches [12,32,47] and execution units [1,4]—which are susceptible to side-channel attacks.

This paper analyzes the security implications of Intel's cldemote extension, introduced by the 4th Gen Intel Xeon Scalable Processors (Sapphire Rapids). Intel designed this instruction to optimize performance in multi-threaded workloads with frequent inter-core data sharing [2,17,20]. The cldemote instruction moves a cache line from an upper-level cache to a lower-level cache, increasing the likelihood of Last-Level Cache (LLC) hits.

Despite its performance benefits, the cldemote instruction has introduced new potential security threats. Prior work [37] showed that the latency of the cldemote instruction depends on the cache level where the targeted data resides, and exploited this characteristic for new cache side-channel attacks. Building upon and extending this observation, our work demonstrates that the `cldemote` instruction can further be leveraged to: (1) efficiently construct eviction sets by directly targeting the cache coherence directory, and (2) precisely leak sensitive attributes from the page table.

Constructing eviction sets in non-inclusive LLCs presents significant challenges. Unlike inclusive LLCs, which allocate accessed cache lines in both private caches and the LLC, non-inclusive LLCs retain cache lines exclusively in private caches. Consequently, an attacker must explicitly move cache lines from private caches into the LLC to successfully create an eviction set. Previous approaches tackled this by inducing cache conflicts through extensive memory operations [26,46] or using additional cores to run helper threads [35,46,49], both of which introduce substantial overhead.

To overcome these limitations, we exploit the `cldemote` instruction, which directly moves cache lines to the LLC, enabling efficient eviction set construction without relying on cache conflicts or helper threads. Utilizing `cldemote` effectively requires detailed knowledge of the LLC and directory structures of Intel's Sapphire Rapids processors. Since Intel does not publicly disclose such architectural details as set associativity or address mapping hash functions, we conducted reverse engineering to uncover these internals. Based on the reversing result, we propose a novel and highly efficient eviction set construction method. Integrating this approach with existing algorithms [42,49], we achieve a 36% reduction in eviction set construction time while maintaining high success rates.

Next, we demonstrate that the execution latency of `cldemote` can leak critical page table attributes. We find that this latency varies based on several factors: (1) the presence of a corresponding entry in the TLB, (2) the permission bits set in the page table entry, and (3) the specific level of the page table at which address translation terminates. We further investigate how `cldemote` interacts with the recently introduced TLB architecture in Sapphire Rapids processors. Leveraging these insights, we demonstrate the ability to reliably derandomize the kernel base address in just 2.49 ms on Linux systems. Lastly, we discuss potential mitigations to address and prevent the presented attack.

Contributions. Our main contributions are as follows:

- We reverse-engineered the LLC and directory structure in Intel Sapphire Rapids processors, uncovering microarchitectural details required for eviction set construction.
- We propose a fast and efficient eviction set construction method for non-inclusive LLCs. This technique reduces the construction time by 36% while maintaining comparable success rates.
- We demonstrate that the execution time of `cldemote` leaks page table attributes, including TLB state, permission bits, and page table level. Based on this timing behavior, we break the KASLR from user space.

Responsible Disclosure. Our attacks discovered during the study were reported to Intel on January 23, 2025 under a responsible disclosure process. At the time of finalizing this paper, we have not yet received any response from Intel.

2 Related Work

Side-Channel Attack with `cldemote` Extension. Recently, Rauscher et al. [37] systematically evaluated various cache attacks utilizing Intel's `cldemote` extension. They introduced attacks such as Demote+Reload and Demote+Demote, primarily emphasizing performance benchmarking and attack efficiency compared to previous approaches (e.g., Flush+Reload and Prime+Probe). However, they did not propose detailed methodologies for constructing eviction sets for non-inclusive LLCs. Our work, on the other hand, introduces a comprehensive and optimized eviction set construction algorithm specifically exploiting `cldemote`. Furthermore, their analysis mainly focuses on timing differences exploited for KASLR breaks without detailed consideration of page table attributes and address translation vulnerabilities. In contrast, our work explicitly explores how `cldemote` can leak precise information regarding page table properties.

Eviction Set Construction. Constructing an eviction set is essential for *evict-* and *prime-*based cache attacks. Early research primarily focused on Intel processors with inclusive LLC architectures. Liu et al. [32] and Irazoqui et al. [22] leveraged huge pages to construct eviction sets without physical address information. Other studies utilized group testing approaches [36, 40, 42], categorizing candidate addresses and filtering irrelevant ones. However, recent transitions to non-inclusive LLC designs have complicated eviction set construction. Yan et al. [46] addressed this by using helper threads and inducing cache conflicts at the directory level. Additionally, several works reverse-engineered hash functions of cache slices [23, 33, 48] and TLB sets [9] to map cache lines directly to target sets. In this paper, we introduce a novel eviction set construction technique tailored for non-inclusive LLCs. Our method significantly simplifies the construction process and achieves a 36% reduction in construction time by leveraging the cache demote operation.

KASLR Breaking Attack. This attack aims to infer the kernel base address by exploiting microarchitectural components such as the TLB or branch target buffer. As directly accessing a kernel address from user space triggers a page fault, previous studies have utilized ISA extensions to manage or suppress these faults. For instance, software-based prefetch instructions [11, 29, 30], Intel TSX [25], and AVX extensions [8] have been employed to bypass KASLR. Other approaches rely on speculative execution mechanisms for fault suppression. Phantom [44] and Inception [41] exploit instructions executed speculatively at early pipeline stages (before instruction decoding). More recently, SysBumps [24] leveraged Spectre-v1 type gadgets within system calls to bypass KASLR on macOS for Apple Silicon. In contrast, Meltdown-type attacks, such as Meltdown [31], Data Bounce [38], EchoLoad [6], and FlushConflict [43], utilize fault handlers or Intel TSX to achieve similar outcomes. Our work exploits Intel's newly introduced `cldemote` ISA extension, which inherently supports fault suppression. Unlike previous studies, we specifically target the TLB for store operations, a capability first introduced in Sapphire Rapids processors.

3 Background

3.1 Cache Organization

Modern processors utilize a multi-level cache hierarchy to mitigate the high latency associated with accessing main memory. This hierarchy generally comprises (1) private caches (L1 and L2) within each core, and (2) a shared Last-Level Cache (LLC) situated in the processor's uncore, which is divided into slices corresponding to individual cores. Data stored closer to the core in this hierarchical structure benefits from significantly reduced access latencies.

An essential characteristic of cache architectures is inclusiveness. Initially, Intel employed an inclusive LLC design, ensuring any cache line residing in a private cache was also present in the LLC. However, with the increase in core count, Intel shifted toward a non-inclusive LLC architecture to better optimize cache capacity and coherence management.

Intel processors achieve data consistency by using a cache directory, which tracks cache lines located within private caches [15]. This directory, already existing prior to the transition to a non-inclusive LLC, is positioned adjacent to the LLC. The directory is structured as a set-associative cache and utilizes an address-mapping hashing function to determine the appropriate set for each cache line allocation. While prior studies [46] confirmed that older Intel architectures, such as Skylake-SP, employed identical mapping functions for both the LLC and directory, this has not yet been validated for newer architectures like Sapphire Rapids.

3.2 Address Translation and TLB

Virtual memory systems abstract physical memory to achieve process isolation and efficient memory management. In this system, each process operates with its own independent virtual address space. When a memory access occurs, the virtual address must be translated into their corresponding physical address. This crucial task is typically managed by the Memory Management Unit (MMU), a key hardware component that mediates the interaction between the CPU and the physical memory system. The MMU translates the virtual address using a process-specific page table stored in main memory. However, the page table walk requires multiple physical memory accesses, making address translation inherently time-consuming.

To address this, MMUs include the Translation Lookaside Buffer (TLB) to accelerate the address translation process. The TLB stores recently used virtual-to-physical address mappings. This enables fast address translation by eliminating repetitive page table walks for subsequent accesses to the same virtual address. When accessing memory, if the target address is already cached in the TLB, (i.e., TLB hit), the time required for address translation is substantially reduced. Conversely, if the address is not found in the TLB (i.e., TLB miss), the MMU must perform a page table walk to complete the translation.

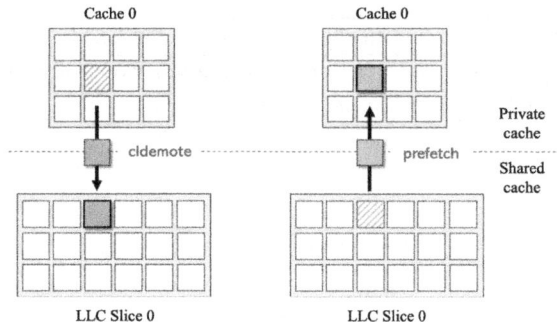

Fig. 1. Comparison of cldemote and prefetch behavior.

3.3 Cache-Based Side-Channel Attack

Caches are designed to reduce memory access latency by leveraging temporal and spatial locality. However, they have become a source of side-channel attacks [7, 12,22,32,35,39,46,47,49] as cache state influences the access latency, which can be exploited to extract sensitive data. To achieve this, an attacker must be able to manipulate the cache state into a known state and monitor the state transition.

For this purpose, three types of attack are typically employed. The *flush*-based attack [12,14,47] uses the clflush instruction to flush a target cache line, and observes the change in the cache state by using timing information. While this method is straightforward, it relies on both clflush and memory sharing between the attacker and the victim. To overcome the dependency on the clflush, the *evict*-based attack [13] evicts the desired cache line using an eviction set *i.e.*, a collection of addresses mapped to the same cache set. However, this attack still relies on memory sharing to infer the victim's behaviors. The third, *prime*-based attack [9,22,28,32,39], does not require both the clflush and memory sharing. The attacker primes the target set with the eviction set and probes the state transitions of the primed cache lines.

The LLC is a common target for cross-core attacks due to its shared nature across processor cores. However, on non-inclusive LLCs, *evict*- and *prime*-based attacks become ineffective, as memory accesses by the victim influence only the private caches, leaving the shared LLC unaffected. Consequently, attackers must instead exploit the directory structure, which preserves inclusivity for private caches [35,46,49].

3.4 Cache Demote Operation

Since the launch of the 4th Gen Intel Xeon Scalable Processors, codenamed Sapphire Rapids, Intel has introduced several architectural advancements to better support data center data center workloads [16]. In particular, Intel has added

Algorithm 1: Reverse engineering procedure for LLC and directory.

Input: Target address *addr*, the maximum number of congruent addresses N
Output: The measured timing information *result*

1 **procedure** *Prime* ($\mathcal{E}$):
2   **for** *each ϵ in $\mathcal{E}$* **do**
3   maccess(ϵ)
4   **end**
5 **end**
6
7 **for** $n \leftarrow 1$ **to** N **do**
8   tmp $\leftarrow 0$
9      $\mathcal{E} \leftarrow$ construct_EVSet(*addr*, n)
10   **for** $i \leftarrow 1$ **to** 100 000 **do**
11   Prime($\mathcal{E}$)
12   start $\leftarrow$ *rdtsc()*
13   maccess(*addr*)
14   end $\leftarrow$ *rdtsc()* - start
15   tmp $\leftarrow$ tmp + end
16   **end**
17   result[n] $\leftarrow$ tmp / 100 000
18 **end**

new ISA extensions to address bottlenecks in multi-threaded, large-scale workloads. Such bottlenecks frequently arise when requested data resides in another core's private cache rather than in the shared LLC, resulting in increased access latency. To reduce this delay, Intel has implemented a new `cldemote` extension, which explicitly moves cache lines from a private cache to the LLC [17,19,20]. By doing so, `cldemote` can enhance the overall efficiency of multi-threaded workloads. This operation contrasts with prefetch instructions (e.g., the `prefetchX` family in x86), which bring data closer to the core, as illustrated in Fig. 1.

4 Fast Eviction Set Construction on Directory

To perform *evict-* and *prime*-based cross-core attacks on non-inclusive LLCs, attackers must target the directory, which maintains inclusivity for private caches [26,46]. Constructing an eviction set $\mathcal{E}$ for a target set $\mathcal{S}$ is crucial to achieve this. Using this eviction set, an attacker can reset the state of $\mathcal{S}$ by filling it with addresses $\epsilon \in \mathcal{E}$, which we refer to as congruent addresses.

Prior work [46] has demonstrated that the directory and LLC have an identical number of sets and use the same address-mapping hash function to determine the corresponding LLC or directory slice. However, such details have previously only been disclosed for Intel's Skylake-X microarchitecture. Assuming that Sapphire Rapids processors have a similar directory structure, we begin by reverse-engineering their LLC architecture. From our analysis, we uncover detailed properties of the directory (see Sect. 4.1). Leveraging these insights, we

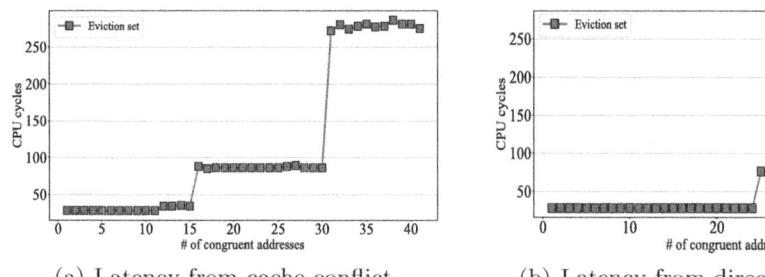

(a) Latency from cache conflict. (b) Latency from directory conflict.

Fig. 2. Execution latency induced by cache and directory conflict.

introduce a novel and efficient eviction set construction method utilizing the cldemote instruction (see Sect. 4.2).

4.1 Reverse Engineering Directory Structure in Sapphire Rapids

Reverse Engineering LLC. Algorithm 1 outlines the reverse-engineering procedure. First, we construct an eviction set $\mathcal{E}$ for an LLC set $\mathcal{S}$ that shares the same set and slice index bits as the target address *addr* (line 9). To construct $\mathcal{E}$ on non-inclusive LLCs, we follow the check_conflict technique proposed by Yan et al. [46]. Next, we prime $\mathcal{S}$ by accessing each address $\epsilon \in \mathcal{E}$ (lines 1–5). Finally, we measure the access latency for *addr* using rdtsc (lines 12–15). We repeat this procedure while varying the number of congruent addresses n in $\mathcal{E}$.

Figure 2(a) shows the reverse-engineering results, revealing three distinct latency peaks when the size of $\mathcal{E}$ reaches 12, 16, and 31. These latency peaks correspond to an L2 hit, an LLC hit, and a physical memory access, respectively, as illustrated in Fig. 3. These findings indicate that L1d is 12-way associative, L2 is 16-way associative, and L2 is inclusive of L1d. They also confirm that the LLC slice is 15-way associative and non-inclusive of the private caches. Additionally, we examine the physical addresses of all congruent addresses to determine the number of sets in each LLC slice. Our analysis shows that bits 16:6 of the physical address remain consistent across these congruent addresses. This consistency indicates that each LLC slice contains 2048 sets.

Comparison to Cache Parameters from CPUID. Cache parameters can be retrieved via the CPUID instruction by querying leaf 0x4 with sub-leaves 0x0, 0x1, 0x2, and 0x3. However, our analysis revealed unusual information regarding the structure of the LLC. While CPUID reports a 30 MiB LLC with 15-way associativity and 32,768 sets—consistent with Intel's specifications [21]—this conflicts with the fact that our processor has 12 physical cores (i.e., 12 LLC slices), making 32,768 sets not evenly divisible by 12. Our reverse engineering results show that each LLC slice is 15-way associative with 2048 sets, for 22.5 MiB of LLC capacity. Due to the inaccurate structural information from CPUID, we decided to base our eviction set construction on these reverse-engineering results, despite the discrepancy with Intel's specifications.

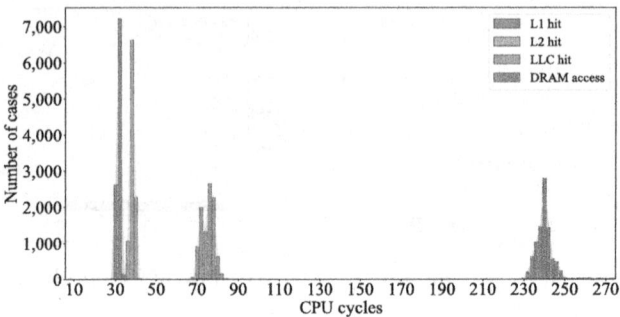

Fig. 3. The access latencies according to the location of data in cache hierarchy.

Reverse Engineering Directory. We hypothesize that the directory follows the same architectural design as the LLC, except for the number of ways. To verify this hypothesis, we conduct the following experiment. We begin our experiment by preparing two threads, referred to as the main and the evictor thread. We then run them on separate physical cores. The main thread first selects a target address $\mathcal{T}$ and accesses it to load a cache line into the L1d cache. Next, the evictor thread creates an eviction set $\mathcal{E}$ for the target directory set, where $\mathcal{T}$ will be placed. We then access each address $\epsilon \in \mathcal{E}$ to allocate cache lines into the directory. Finally, the main thread measures the access latency for $\mathcal{T}$. If a directory conflict occurs, the main thread experiences increased access latency. We repeat this procedure, varying the number of congruent addresses in $\mathcal{E}$.

Figure 2(b) shows the experimental results. The graph reveals two prominent spikes in access latency when the number of congruent addresses reaches 25 and 31. These spikes correspond to L3 cache hits and physical memory accesses, respectively (see Fig. 3). Since a conflict in the directory moves a cache line from the private cache to the shared LLC [46], this timing behavior indicates that the directory slice has 25-way associativity and employs the same address mapping hash function as the LLC. Furthermore, analyzing the physical addresses of all congruent addresses within each directory slice shows that bits 16:6 of the physical address remain identical across these congruent addresses, indicating that each directory slice consists of 2048 sets. Our reverse engineering results are summarized in Table 1.

4.2 Efficient Eviction Set Construction

We present a novel eviction set construction technique for the directory. This technique streamlines the construction process, significantly reducing the building time.

Overcoming the Limitations of Existing Methods. Multiple studies have introduced efficient eviction set construction algorithms to facilitate *evict*- and *prime*-based attacks in various computing environments [32,34,35,40,42,45,49].

Table 1. Architectural details on Sapphire Rapids.

	Intel Xeon Silver 4510T
L1 data	48KiB, 64 sets, 12 ways
L1 inst	32KiB, 64 sets, 8 ways
L2	2MiB, 2048 sets, 16 ways, inclusive to L1
LLC slice	1.875MiB, 2048 sets, 15 ways, non-inclusive to L1/L2
Directory slice	3.125MiB, 2048 sets, 25 ways

Most of them have primarily focused on constructing eviction sets in inclusive LLCs. In contrast, constructing eviction sets on non-inclusive LLCs has not received as much attention as on inclusive LLCs. This is because the non-inclusive property gives rise to intricate challenges.

Specifically, processors with a non-inclusive LLC allocate cache lines to the private cache (i.e., L1 and L2) rather than an LLC slice when performing memory accesses. Consequently, an attacker must move the cache line from the private cache to the LLC slice to construct an eviction set on the directory. To address this challenge, prior works [35,46,49] proposed two methods: (1) inducing cache conflicts and (2) using a helper thread. However, each method has limitations. The cache conflict method demands multiple memory accesses to evict a single cache line from private caches into the LLC. In addition, achieving a low false negative eviction rate requires up to 10 iterative memory accesses on the L2 eviction set [46]. The helper thread method is based on the observation that if two threads running on different physical cores access the same data, it resides in the LLC [35,46]. However, this method requires at least two physical cores, limiting its applicability in single-core attack scenarios.

To address these issues, we propose a novel method for efficient eviction set construction by leveraging the `cldemote`. The `cldemote` instruction is explicitly designed to demote a cache line from a private cache to the LLC. This functionality offers a practical and efficient alternative to prior techniques based on cache conflicts or helper threads. Integrating our method into existing eviction set construction algorithms requires minimal changes. Specifically, it replaces prior methods with a single invocation of the `cldemote` instruction.

Evaluation. To demonstrate the effectiveness of our approach, we compare it with the helper thread under two eviction set construction algorithms: (1) the widely used baseline algorithm by Vila et al. [42] and (2) the Function-as-a-Service oriented algorithm by Zhao et al. [49]. Although we evaluate our approach using two specific eviction set construction algorithms and compare their results with helper threads, our method is not restricted to these two cases. Our approach does not alter the fundamental logic of eviction set construction; rather, it replaces the mechanism for transferring cache lines from private caches to the LLC with a single `cldemote` instruction. This design choice allows our

Table 2. Performance evaluation of eviction set constructions.

		Vila et al. [42]	Zhao et al. [49]
Helper thread	Succ. rate	97%	100%
	Build. time	82.153 ms	19.470 ms
Our work	Succ. rate	97%	98%
	Build. time	54.842 ms	10.792 ms

method to be readily integrated with a wide range of eviction set construction algorithms targeting non-inclusive LLCs.

For a thorough evaluation, we reproduced both algorithms in our experimental setup using a 4 KiB page size. We integrated our proposed method and a helper thread into each algorithm to demote a cache line into the LLC. We then performed each eviction set construction procedure 100 times. We excluded the cache conflict method from our evaluation because it is not commonly used, exhibits a high false negative rate, and incurs a substantial number of memory operations. Table 2 presents their success rates and building times.

The results show that the helper thread achieves success rates exceeding 97%. Similarly, our method experiences comparable or slightly lower success rates. However, this method reduces construction time by 36% through a single cldemote instruction without relying on a helper thread. As a result, our method not only reduces construction time, but also overcomes the limitations of existing methods that require either two physical cores or multiple memory accesses.

While we successfully integrated our method into existing eviction set construction algorithms [42,49], our approach is incompatible with Prime+Scope [35] due to fundamental differences in how Prime+Scope constructs eviction sets. Unlike previous works [32,34,40,45,49], Prime+Scope starts with an empty set and gradually adds congruent addresses to build an eviction set. This process relies on a key observation regarding the cache's replacement policy: memory accesses served by upper-level caches do not affect the replacement policy of the lower-level caches holding the same data.

To construct an eviction set with Prime+Scope, an attacker first selects a target address T and accesses it through a helper thread, placing T in both a private cache and the shared LLC. The attacker then accesses candidate addresses and measures the access latency for T to check if it has been evicted from the cache hierarchy. If T is evicted, the candidate address is considered congruent. Otherwise, the attacker repeats this procedure with other candidates.

However, if the attacker employs cldemote to move the cache line for T into the LLC rather than using a helper thread, the private cache does not contain a copy of that cache line. Consequently, when the attacker accesses T, a private cache miss occurs, causing a fetch from the LLC. This behavior prevents the attacker from utilizing the cache replacement policy, making it impossible to construct an eviction set with cldemote.

5 Page Table Attribute Leakage

In this section, we demonstrate that the timing behavior of cldemote reveals three properties of a given kernel address: (P1) the TLB state, (P2) the permission bits of the corresponding page table entry, and (P3) the level of the page table at which address translation terminates (See Sect. 5.1). We then analyze the interaction between cldemote and the recently redesigned TLB architecture in the Sapphire Rapids (See Sect. 5.2). Finally, we present the KASLR breaking attack by using cldemote (See Sect. 5.3).

Table 3. The execution time of prefetch and cldemote on memory pages with various permission bits and memory types.

Permission bits*		Memory types	prefetch		cldemote	
P U D NX	A		TLB hit	TLB miss	TLB hit	TLB miss
●●●●	●	Write-back	113 ($\sigma = 6.08$)	133 ($\sigma = 7.76$)	160 ($\sigma = 6.42$)	180 ($\sigma = 6.07$)
●○●●	○	Write-back	132 ($\sigma = 5.92$)	132 ($\sigma = 7.46$)	137 ($\sigma = 6.78$)	136 ($\sigma = 5.30$)
●●●●	○	Write-back	132 ($\sigma = 6.94$)	133 ($\sigma = 7.00$)	137 ($\sigma = 6.54$)	136 ($\sigma = 4.78$)
●○●●	●	Write-back	112 ($\sigma = 5.04$)	132 ($\sigma = 7.37$)	114 ($\sigma = 5.38$)	136 ($\sigma = 4.87$)
○●●●	●	Write-back	115 ($\sigma = 5.23$)	133 ($\sigma = 7.00$)	139 ($\sigma = 7.09$)	148 ($\sigma = 6.39$)
○○●●	●	Write-back	115 ($\sigma = 5.76$)	132 ($\sigma = 6.45$)	138 ($\sigma = 6.24$)	149 ($\sigma = 7.88$)
●●● ○	●	Write-back	113 ($\sigma = 5.92$)	132 ($\sigma = 6.32$)	160 ($\sigma = 5.86$)	180 ($\sigma = 6.10$)
●●○●	●	Write-back	112 ($\sigma = 5.68$)	134 ($\sigma = 7.98$)	160 ($\sigma = 6.38$)	180 ($\sigma = 5.14$)
○○●●	○	Write-back	132 ($\sigma = 5.96$)	132 ($\sigma = 7.05$)	148 ($\sigma = 6.99$)	148 ($\sigma = 6.48$)
●●●●	●	Write-protected	113 ($\sigma = 6.04$)	132 ($\sigma = 7.13$)	114 ($\sigma = 5.07$)	137 ($\sigma = 7.03$)
●●●●	●	Uncacheable	113 ($\sigma = 5.79$)	135 ($\sigma = 8.31$)	115 ($\sigma = 6.06$)	138 ($\sigma = 7.92$)

* **P** denotes Present bit, **U** denotes User/Supervisor bit, **D** denotes Dirty bit, **NX** denotes Non eXecutable bit, and **A** denotes Accessed bit.
The symbol (●) indicates that the bit is set to 1, and the symbol (○) indicates that the bit is set to 0.

5.1 Timing Behavior of cldemote According to Page Table Attributes

As cldemote does not trigger faults, it can be executed on kernel addresses without requiring fault handling or suppression. We show that the execution latency of cldemote for a given kernel address leaks sensitive information on its page table attributes, referred to as P1, P2, and P3 below.

P1: Distinguishing TLB State. To evaluate how effectively cldemote distinguishes between TLB hits and misses, we conducted an experiment and compared its results with those obtained from software-based prefetch instructions [11,30]. We allocated a target page $\mathcal{P}$ and cleared its user/supervisor bit to 0. Subsequently, we measured the execution latency of the cldemote instruction one million times.

Our experiment comprised two scenarios representing distinct TLB states: TLB hits and TLB misses. To induce a TLB hit, we executed `cldemote` twice consecutively; the first execution populates the TLB, ensuring a TLB hit on the subsequent execution. For the TLB miss scenario, we flushed the TLB before each measurement by invoking `tlb_flush_page()` in a custom kernel module. We repeated this procedure using the `prefetch` instruction for comparative purposes.

As expected, both instructions showed increased execution latency for TLB misses compared to TLB hits. Specifically, the average latency of `prefetch` was 112 cycles ($\sigma = 5.04$) for TLB hits and 132 cycles ($\sigma = 7.37$) for TLB misses. Similarly, the average latency of `cldemote` was 114 cycles ($\sigma = 5.38$) for TLB hits and 136 cycles ($\sigma = 4.87$) for TLB misses.

P2: Distinguishing Permission Bits in the Page Table. To evaluate the effectiveness of our primitive in distinguishing permission bits in the page table, we repeated the previous experiment on various pages with different permission bits and memory types. Table 3 presents the experimental results with `cldemote` and `prefetch`.

When the `A` bit in the accessed page table entry was set to 0, TLB hits and misses exhibited similar execution times. This behavior stems from two architectural features of Intel processors. First, the processor caches a virtual-to-physical address pair only if the `A` bit is set to 1 in every page table entry involved in address translation [18]. Second, neither `cldemote` nor `prefetch` sets the `A` bit to 1 in the page table entry. In addition, we observed that `cldemote`'s execution time is influenced by both the `P` bit and the `U` bit, whereas `prefetch` is not. When the `P` bit was set to 1 and the `U` bit was set to 0, `cldemote` required 114 cycles for a TLB hit and 136 cycles for a TLB miss. In contrast, when the `P` bit was set to 0 and the `U` bit was set to 1, the execution time increased to 139 cycles for a TLB hit and 148 cycles for a TLB miss. Furthermore, when both the `P` and `U` bits were set to 1, `cldemote` exhibited its longest execution times, reaching 160 cycles for a TLB hit and 180 cycles for a TLB miss.

The experimental results show that page fault handling times vary depending on the type of fault. In particular, a page fault caused by a privilege violation (i.e., protection fault) is resolved faster than one caused by accessing a non-present page. Also, executing the `cldemote` instruction on a page where both the P and U bits are set to 1 results in the longest handling time. This increased latency occurs because the processor must traverse the cache hierarchy to locate the corresponding cache line traverse the cache hierarchy to locate cache line that will be moved into the LLC. Additionally, Intel's documentation states that *"performing cldemote on an uncacheable type of page may cause the instruction to be ignored"* [19]. Nevertheless, our observations show that, even if the execution is ignored on uncacheable memory, the processor still records the resolved virtual-to-physical address pair in the TLB.

P3: Distinguishing Page Table Level. Several prior works [11,30] have demonstrated that the page table level at which address translation terminates can be inferred by exploiting the timing behavior of software-based prefetch

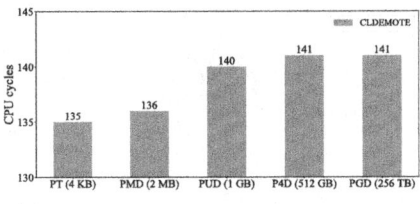 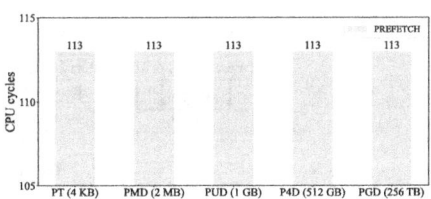

(a) Execution latency with `cldemote` (b) Execution latency with `prefetch`

Fig. 4. Execution latency of `cldemote` and `prefetch` across page table levels.

instructions. In contrast, our work achieves this by leveraging the newly introduced `cldemote` extension. It is noteworthy that, since the 4th Gen Intel Xeon processor, previously proposed techniques [11,30] can no longer leak this information.

To evaluate whether page table levels can be distinguished via the execution latency of `cldemote`, we design and conduct an experiment. In this experiment, we prepare five distinct virtual addresses within an inaccessible address space, where address translation for each address terminates at a different page table level (i.e., PGD, P4D, PUD, PMD, and PT). We configure the page table entries for these addresses with both the present bit and the user/supervisor bit cleared to 0. For each address, we measure the execution time of the `cldemote` one million times. On the Intel processor, the TLB caches the address translation only when the virtual address being accessed has the present bit set to 1 and the reserved bits set to 0 [18]. Therefore, we do not perform a TLB flush as memory accesses to these addresses consistently trigger a page table walk.

Figure 4(a) illustrates the experimental results for five distinct virtual addresses, with the average execution latency of `cldemote` displayed at the top of each bar. These results show that as the number of page table mappings associated with an address increases, the time required for address translation via a page table walk decreases. This behavior aligns with Lipp et al. [30], where they observed similar behavior with software-based prefetch instruction at various page table levels. Although this timing behavior may appear counterintuitive, it can be explained by the design of the Paging-Structure Caches [3]. According to Intel's documentation [18], the paging-structure caches first attempt to retrieve the physical address of the Page Table (PT) by indexing virtual address bits 56:21. They then traverse higher cache levels up to the Page Global Directory (PGD), using virtual address bits 56:48. As a result, when the address translation completes at the PT level, the execution time of `cldemote` is minimized, measured at 113 cycles.

In contrast, when we repeat the experiment using `prefetch` under the same setup, we do not observe the same results as with `cldemote`. Figure 4(b) shows an experimental result obtained with `prefetch`. Unlike `cldemote`, `prefetch` exhibits consistent execution times regardless of the page table level. This result indicates that software-based prefetch instructions do not expose the specific

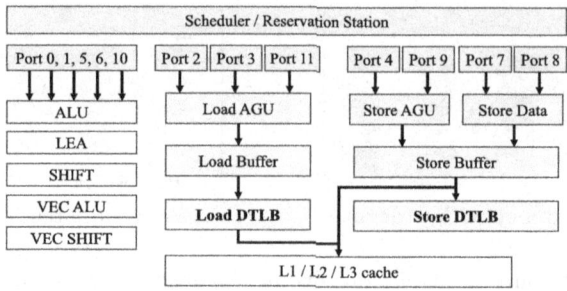

Fig. 5. Overview of Golden Cove microarchitecture.

page table level where address translation is terminated. To explain this different timing behavior between `cldemote` and `prefetch`, we analyze how these instructions interact with the recently redesigned TLB architecture in Sapphire Rapids (see Sect. 5.2).

Security Implications. Our experimental results show that the execution latency of `cldemote` serves as a powerful attack primitive for leaking sensitive information. Specifically, P1 demonstrates that `cldemote` reliably distinguishes between TLB hits and misses, enabling attackers to deduce the presence of specific pages and infer memory access patterns of the kernel or victim processes based on the TLB state. P2 indicates that `cldemote` can expose page table permission bits, such as the Accessed (A) and User/Supervisor (U) bits, through timing variations. Knowledge of the A bit allows attackers to monitor access patterns to specific pages utilized by the kernel or targeted processes. Additionally, information regarding the U bit can facilitate identifying potential target page table entries for rowhammer attacks. P3 shows that `cldemote` can distinguish the page table level at which address translation concludes, providing insight into the hierarchical structure of the page table for specific addresses. Furthermore, the capabilities demonstrated in P1 and P2 can be leveraged to successfully circumvent Kernel Address Space Layout Randomization (KASLR), as detailed in Sect. 5.3.

5.2 An In-Depth Analysis of the TLB in Golden Cove

To analyze the interaction between TLB and memory operations such as `cldemote` and `prefetch`, we examine the microarchitectural properties of the Sapphire Rapids processor, which is based on the Golden Cove architecture. According to Intel's documentation [17], Golden Cove introduces several microarchitectural modifications, including changes to the TLB structure. Specifically, Golden Cove separates data TLBs into two types: one for load operations ($dTLB_{load}$) and another for store operations ($dTLB_{store}$), as illustrated in Fig. 5.

To investigate the properties of these TLBs, we conduct an analysis using performance monitoring events. We prepare two addresses: one is a valid kernel address and the other is an invalid kernel address. We then execute cldemote and prefetch one million times for each address, measuring the change in the $dTLB_{load}$ miss events (DTLB_LOAD_MISSES.WALK_COMPLETED) and $dTLB_{store}$ miss events (DTLB_STORE_MISSES.WALK_COMPLETED). Since cldemote is a store-type memory operation and prefetch is a load-type memory operation, they utilize different data TLBs respectively.

The experimental results are shown in Table 4. Our findings indicate that in Golden Cove, $dTLB_{load}$ caches virtual-to-physical address translations even when the kernel address is invalid (i.e., not present in memory). In contrast, $dTLB_{store}$ updates the TLB only when the address is valid. We also observed that executing cldemote with an invalid address triggers two page table walks. This behavior aligns with observations on AMD's Zen microarchitecture, where issuing a prefetch to an invalid address also results in two page table walks [30].

Executing prefetch on an inaccessible kernel address allocates a TLB entry, regardless of its validity. However, the execution time differs slightly between valid and invalid addresses, even though both trigger TLB hits. We measure 108 cycles for a valid address and 112 cycles for an invalid address. This result suggests that handling a TLB hit on an invalid address requires extra time because there is no physically backed memory.

Table 4. The number of measured TLB miss events when executing the cldemote and prefetch 1 million times.

Instruction	Address type	$dTLB_{load}$ misses	$dTLB_{store}$ misses
cldemote	Valid addr	0	0
	Invalid addr	0	2,000,000
prefetch	Valid addr	0	0
	Invalid addr	0	0

5.3 Breaking KASLR

Threat Model. We assume that an unprivileged attacker who can execute arbitrary code in user space. We also assume that the target system has no implementation flaws or bugs that could leak the kernel base address.

Attack Strategy. In modern operating systems, the kernel is loaded into a predetermined memory region rather than a fully randomized location. This region is divided into fixed-size units, known as slots, where each slot represents a potential base address for loading the kernel text. During the boot process, the kernel is randomly placed into one of these slots. For instance, in Linux, the kernel is loaded with 2 MiB granularity within the address range 0xffffffff80000000 to 0xffffffffc0000000, resulting in 512 possible slots.

Our attack exploits the behavior of $dTLB_{store}$ on Sapphire Rapids. Specifically, the processor allocates a $dTLB_{store}$ entry for a valid address, even if the

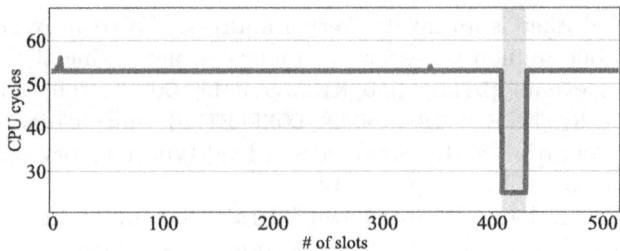

Fig. 6. KASLR breaking attack with `cldemote`.

address is inaccessible from user space. As a result, subsequent memory accesses to the same address result in $dTLB_{store}$ hits, leading to faster execution time. In contrast, accesses to invalid addresses result in $dTLB_{store}$ misses, causing longer execution time. Based on this behavior, we identify the base address of the kernel text by iteratively measuring the execution latency of `cldemote` across all candidate slots within a specified range. Specifically, when the kernel resides in a given slot, the execution latency of `cldemote` in that slot decreases due to $dTLB_{store}$ hits. In contrast, when the kernel is not mapped to a slot, the execution latency increases as a result of $dTLB_{store}$ misses. Figure 6 presents the measured execution latencies for each slot on Linux. The gray-shaded region, spanning slots 409 through 430, consistently exhibits low execution latencies, indicating that the kernel is located within this range. Based on this observation, we infer that the kernel base address is `0xffffffffb3200000`.

Evaluation. We evaluate the performance of our attack on Ubuntu 24.04 (kernel version 6.8.0-38). Specifically, we performed 1,000 attacks to measure both accuracy and execution time. After each set of 100 attacks, we rebooted the system to reset the kernel base address. This process resulted in 10 reboots in total. For each slot, we measured the execution time of 100 consecutive `cldemote` instructions to reduce potential noise. In terms of accuracy, the attack succeeded with a rate of 99.8% on Ubuntu 24.04, reliably locating the kernel base address. We also found the kernel base address in an average of 2.49 ms.

5.4 Countermeasure

We discuss potential mitigations against our page table attribute leakage attack.

Mitigation Against `cldemote`-Based Attacks. Our work demonstrates that the timing behavior of `cldemote` can be exploited to leak page table attributes. To mitigate this attack, one promising approach is to introduce random noise into the execution latency of `cldemote`, thereby disrupting precise timing measurements and preventing an attacker from extracting meaningful information through timing analysis. Another effective countermeasure is to restrict `cldemote` execution to privileged users, preventing unprivileged users from invoking it. This restriction would render `cldemote`-based microarchitectural attacks infeasible.

Mitigation Against KASLR Breaking Attack. Kernel Page-Table Isolation (KPTI) [10] is a widely used mitigation against KASLR breaking attacks. The main strategy of KPTI is to isolate the kernel address space from user space, preventing an unprivileged user from accessing kernel addresses without switching to kernel mode. However, despite this isolation, certain kernel segments (e.g., the trampoline region) remain mapped in user space, allowing attackers to infer the kernel base address [5,27,30,43]. An alternative mitigation [5] instead maps invalid kernel addresses to dummy physical pages. This technique ensures all kernel addresses are physically backed, making used and unused kernel memory indistinguishable.

6 Discussion

In this section, we investigate the applicability of our work to other processors.

Other Intel Processors. While cldemote is not supported on Intel Core processors, it has been available since the Sapphire Rapids (4th Gen) Intel Xeon processor. We have verified that both Emerald Rapids (5th Gen) and Sierra Forest (6th Gen) Intel Xeon processors support cldemote, and that its behavior on these platforms remains consistent with that we observed on Sapphire Rapids. Therefore, our approach is not restricted to Sapphire Rapids, but it can be extended to later generations of Xeon processors.

AMD and ARM Processors. Since cldemote is an ISA extension exclusively supported by Intel processors, other vendors such as AMD and ARM do not implement this instruction on their processors. As a result, our work cannot be feasible for these platforms.

7 Conclusion

In this paper, we conducted a comprehensive security analysis of Intel's new cldemote extension, uncovering previously unnoticed security implications. By reverse-engineering the LLC and directory structures of Sapphire Rapids, we identified undocumented architectural details. Leveraging these insights, we developed a novel eviction set construction technique tailored for non-inclusive LLCs, significantly reducing construction time by 36%. Moreover, we demonstrated that the execution latency of cldemote leaks critical page table attributes, including TLB state, permission bits, and page table levels. Exploiting this vulnerability, we showed that an unprivileged attacker could successfully derandomize KASLR in only 2.49 ms on Linux. Our findings underscore the necessity for rigorous security assessments prior to integrating new ISA extensions, as neglecting thorough evaluations may inadvertently introduce serious security risks.

Acknowledgement. This research was supported by a National Research Foundation of Korea (NRF) grant, funded by the Korean government (MSIT) (RS-2023-NR077166, RS-2023-00227165). This research was supported by the Korea University Grant.

References

1. Aldaya, A.C., Brumley, B.B., ul Hassan, S., García, C.P., Tuveri, N.: Port contention for fun and profit. In: IEEE Symposium on Security and Privacy (SP), pp. 870–887 (2019)
2. Atul, K.: intel labs' contributions to latest intel® Xeon® scalable processor. https://community.intel.com/t5/Blogs/Tech-Innovation/Data-Center/Intel-Labs-Contributions-to-Latest-Intel-Xeon-Scalable-Processor/post/1441731
3. Barr, T.W., Cox, A.L., Rixner, S.: Translation caching: skip, don't walk (the page table). In: International Symposium on Computer Architecture (2010)
4. Bhattacharyya, A., et al.: SMoTherSpectre: exploiting speculative execution through port contention. In: ACM SIGSAC Conference on Computer and Communications Security, pp. 785–800 (2019)
5. Canella, C., Schwarz, M., Haubenwallner, M., Schwarzl, M., Gruss, D.: KASLR: break it, fix it, repeat. In: ACM Asia Conference on Computer and Communications Security, pp. 481–493 (2020)
6. Cassell, B., Szepesi, T., Wong, B., Brecht, T., Ma, J., Liu, X.: Nessie: a decoupled, client-driven key-value store using RDMA. IEEE Trans. Parallel Distrib. Syst. **28**(12), 3537–3552 (2017)
7. Chen, Y., Hajiabadi, A., Pei, L., Carlson, T.E.: PrefetCHX: cross-core cache-agnostic prefetcher-based side-channel attacks. In: IEEE International Symposium on High-Performance Computer Architecture, pp. 395–408 (2024)
8. Choi, H., Kim, S., Shin, S.: AVX timing side-channel attacks against address space layout randomization. In: ACM/IEEE Design Automation Conference, pp. 1–6 (2023)
9. Gras, B., Razavi, K., Bos, H., Giuffrida, C.: Translation leak-aside buffer: defeating cache side-channel protections with TLB attacks. In: USENIX Security Symposium, pp. 955–972 (2018)
10. Gruss, D., Lipp, M., Schwarz, M., Fellner, R., Maurice, C., Mangard, S.: KASLR is dead: long live KASLR. In: International Symposium on Engineering Secure Software and Systems, pp. 161–176 (2017)
11. Gruss, D., Maurice, C., Fogh, A., Lipp, M., Mangard, S.: Prefetch side-channel attacks: Bypassing SMAP and kernel ASLR. In: ACM SIGSAC Conference on Computer and Communications Security, pp. 368–379 (2016)
12. Gruss, D., Maurice, C., Wagner, K., Mangard, S.: Flush+flush: a fast and stealthy cache attack. In: International Conference on Detection of Intrusions and Malware, and Vulnerability Assessment, pp. 279–299 (2016)
13. Gruss, D., Spreitzer, R., Mangard, S.: Cache template attacks: automating attacks on inclusive last-level caches. In: USENIX Security Symposium, pp. 897–912 (2015)
14. Gülmezoğlu, B., Inci, M.S., Irazoqui, G., Eisenbarth, T., Sunar, B.: A faster and more realistic flush+reload attack on AES. In: International Workshop on Constructive Side-Channel Analysis and Secure Design, pp. 111–126 (2015)
15. Gupta, A., Weber, W.D., Mowry, T.: Reducing memory and traffic requirements for scalable directory-based cache coherence schemes. In: Scalable Shared Memory Multiprocessors (1990)
16. Intel: Architecture day 2021. https://download.intel.com/newsroom/2021/client-computing/intel-architecture-day-2021-presentation.pdf
17. Intel: Intel® 64 and IA-32 architectures optimization reference manual. https://www.intel.com/content/www/us/en/content-details/814198/intel-64-and-ia-32-architectures-optimization-reference-manual-volume-1.html

18. Intel: Intel® 64 and IA-32 architectures software developer's manual combined volumes 3A, 3B, 3C, and 3D: system programming guide. https://cdrdv2.intel.com/v1/dl/getContent/671447
19. Intel: Intel® 64 and IA-32 architectures software developer's manual, Volume 2 (2A, 2B, 2C, & 2D): instruction set reference, A-Z. https://www.intel.com/content/www/us/en/developer/articles/technical/intel-sdm.html
20. Intel: Intel® architecture instruction set extensions and future features, programming reference. https://cdrdv2-public.intel.com/819680/architecture-instruction-set-extensions-programming-reference.pdf
21. Intel: Intel® Xeon® Silver 4510T processor. https://www.intel.com/content/www/us/en/products/sku/236638/intel-xeon-silver-4510t-processor-30m-cache-2-00-ghz/specifications.html
22. Irazoqui, G., Eisenbarth, T., Sunar, B.: S$a: A shared cache attack that works across cores and defies VM sandboxing–and its application to AES. In: IEEE Symposium on Security and Privacy, pp. 591–604 (2015)
23. Irazoqui, G., Eisenbarth, T., Sunar, B.: Systematic reverse engineering of cache slice selection in intel processors. In: Euromicro Conference on Digital System Design, pp. 629–636 (2015)
24. Jang, H., Kim, T., Shin, Y.: SYSBUMPS: exploiting speculative execution in system calls for breaking KASLR in MACOS for apple silicon. In: ACM SIGSAC Conference on Computer and Communications Security (2024)
25. Jang, Y., Lee, S., Kim, T.: Breaking kernel address space layout randomization with Intel TSX. In: ACM SIGSAC Conference on Computer and Communications Security, pp. 380–392 (2016)
26. Kim, S., Han, M., Baek, W.: DPRIME+DABORT: a high-precision and timer-free directory-based side-channel attack in non-inclusive cache hierarchies using intel TSX. In: IEEE International Symposium on High-Performance Computer Architecture, pp. 67–81 (2022)
27. Kim, S., Shin, S., Choi, H.: AVX-TSCHA: leaking information through AVX extensions in commercial processors. Comput. Secur. **134**, 103437 (2023)
28. Kim, T., Park, H., Lee, S., Shin, S., Hur, J., Shin, Y.: Devious: device-driven side-channel attacks on the IOMMU. In: IEEE Symposium on Security and Privacy, pp. 2288–2305 (2023)
29. Kim, T., Shin, Y.: ThermalBleed: a practical thermal side-channel attack. IEEE Access **10**, 25718–25731 (2022)
30. Lipp, M., Gruss, D., Schwarz, M.: AMD prefetch attacks through power and time. In: USENIX Security Symposium (2022)
31. Lipp, M., et al..: Meltdown: reading kernel memory from user space. In: USENIX Security Symposium, pp. 973–990 (2018)
32. Liu, F., Yarom, Y., Ge, Q., Heiser, G., Lee, R.B.: Last-level cache side-channel attacks are practical. In: IEEE Symposium on Security and Privacy, pp. 605–622 (2015)
33. Maurice, C., Le Scouarnec, N., Neumann, C., Heen, O., Francillon, A.: Reverse engineering intel last-level cache complex addressing using performance counters. In: International Symposium on Research in Attacks, Intrusions, and Defenses, pp. 48–65 (2015)
34. Oren, Y., Kemerlis, V.P., Sethumadhavan, S., Keromytis, A.D.: The spy in the sandbox: practical cache attacks in Javascript and their implications. In: ACM SIGSAC Conference on Computer and Communications Security, pp. 1406–1418 (2015)

35. Purnal, A., Turan, F., Verbauwhede, I.: Prime+scope: overcoming the observer effect for high-precision cache contention attacks. In: ACM SIGSAC Conference on Computer and Communications Security, pp. 2906–2920 (2021)
36. Qureshi, M.K.: New attacks and defense for encrypted-address cache. In: ACM/IEEE International Symposium on Computer Architecture, pp. 360–371 (2019)
37. Rauscher, F., Fiedler, C., Kogler, A., Gruss, D.: A systematic evaluation of novel and existing cache side channels. In: Network and Distributed System Security Symposium (2025)
38. Schwarz, M., Canella, C., Giner, L., Gruss, D.: Store-to-leak forwarding: leaking data on meltdown-resistant CPUS (updated and extended version). arXiv:1905.05725 (2019)
39. Shusterman, A., Agarwal, A., O'Connell, S., Genkin, D., Oren, Y., Yarom, Y.: Prime+probe 1, Javascript 0: Overcoming browser-based side-channel defenses. In: USENIX Security Symposium, pp. 2863–2880 (2021)
40. Song, W., Liu, P.: Dynamically finding minimal eviction sets can be quicker than you think for side-channel attacks against the LLC. In: International Symposium on Research in Attacks, Intrusions, and Defenses, pp. 427–442 (2019)
41. Trujillo, D., Wikner, J., Razavi, K.: Inception: exposing new attack surfaces with training in transient execution. In: USENIX Security Symposium (2023)
42. Vila, P., Köpf, B., Morales, J.F.: Theory and practice of finding eviction sets. In: IEEE Symposium on Security and Privacy, pp. 39–54 (2019)
43. Weber, D., Ibrahim, A., Nemati, H., Schwarz, M., Rossow, C.: Osiris: automated discovery of microarchitectural side channels. In: USENIX Security Symposium, pp. 1415–1432 (2021)
44. Wikner, J., Trujillo, D., Razavi, K.: Phantom: exploiting decoder-detectable mispredictions. In: IEEE/ACM International Symposium on Microarchitecture (2023)
45. Xue, Z., Han, J., Song, W.: CTPP: a fast and stealth algorithm for searching eviction sets on intel processors. In: International Symposium on Research in Attacks, Intrusions, and Defenses, pp. 151–163 (2023)
46. Yan, M., Sprabery, R., Gopireddy, B., Fletcher, C., Campbell, R., Torrellas, J.: Attack directories, not caches: side channel attacks in a non-inclusive world. In: IEEE Symposium on Security and Privacy, pp. 888–904 (2019)
47. Yarom, Y., Falkner, K.: Flush+reload: a high resolution, low noise, l3 cache side-channel attack. In: USENIX Security Symposium, pp. 719–732 (2014)
48. Yarom, Y., Ge, Q., Liu, F., Lee, R.B., Heiser, G.: Mapping the intel last-level cache. Cryptology ePrint Archive (2015)
49. Zhao, Z.N., Morrison, A., Fletcher, C.W., Torrellas, J.: Last-level cache side-channel attacks are feasible in the modern public cloud. In: ACM International Conference on Architectural Support for Programming Languages and Operating Systems, pp. 582–600 (2024)

WaitWatcher and WaitGuard: Detecting Flush-Based Cache Side-Channels Through Spurious Wakeups

Lukas Lamster[(✉)], Fabian Rauscher, Martin Unterguggenberger, and Stefan Mangard

Institute of Information Security (ISEC), Graz University of Technology, Graz, Austria
{Lukas.Lamster,Fabian.Rauscher,Martin.Unterguggenberger, Stefan.Mangard}@tugraz.at

Abstract. Flush+Reload and Flush+Flush attacks target CPU caches and allow malicious actors to leak confidential data across different CPU cores. Typically, detection mechanisms against such attacks leverage hardware performance counters to observe architectural and microarchitectural events. However, recent research has shown that state-of-the-art security monitors can effectively be bypassed by camouflaged Flush+Reload attacks. Thus, flush-based cache side-channel attacks are still a significant threat to system security.

In this work, we present *WaitGuard*, a novel detection technique with a >99.9% detection rate based on the userspace monitor and wait instructions. Our framework automatically profiles internal CPU interactions of userspace monitor/waits with other unprivileged instructions. We use WaitWatcher to analyze 7 different server and desktop-class x86 CPUs from Intel and AMD. In our analysis, we uncover 5 spurious wakeup triggers and 18 user-mode instructions that completely bypass the wakeup mechanisms. Based on our analysis, we develop *WaitGuard*, a novel detection mechanism that repurposes the recently introduced userspace monitor and wait instructions to detect flush-based cache side-channel attacks on modern x86 hardware. We implement WaitGuard as a drop-in security monitor that reliably detects Flush+Reload and Flush+Flush attacks with a detection rate of >99.9%, even when introducing heavy system noise. Moreover, we find that WaitGuard also detects the previously invisible camouflaged Flush+Reload attacks. Finally, we demonstrate the real-world applicability of WaitGuard by showing its effectiveness in detecting Flush+Reload attacks on the OpenSSL AES T-table implementation.

Keywords: Side Channels · Cache Attacks · Userspace monitor/wait

1 Introduction

Computing systems require the strong isolation of shared system resources. For instance, modern cloud computing systems co-locate mutually distrusted tenants with code execution privileges on the same physical machine. While computer systems offer strong architectural isolation for memory resources, *i.e.*, through process isolation, side-channel attacks still allow a malicious actor to leak secret data. Concretely, side-channel attacks facilitate shared system resources (*e.g.*, the cache) to extract secret information from software running on shared hardware by observing measurable side effects caused by the victim's execution.

Cache side-channel attacks take advantage of the shared cache between attacker and victim on modern CPUs. Flush+Reload [33] and Flush+Flush [13], in particular, flush cache locations that contain shared data or code, *e.g.*, shared libraries. Subsequently, by timing a memory access or a second flush operation after executing the victim code, the attacker can learn whether the victim accessed the flushed location to infer secret information, such as cryptographic key material [13,33]. As modern CPUs utilize caches that are shared or can be manipulated across cores, an attacker is not constrained to attacking victims on the same core, thus significantly increasing the attack surface through potential cross-core data leakage [13,33].

Common detection techniques for flush-based side-channel attacks rely on hardware performance counters [3,18], which measure low-level system events such as cache evictions or TLB misses [3]. While these detection mechanisms were assumed to be sufficient to detect Flush+Reload and Flush+Flush attacks, recent research by Kosasih et al. [18] demonstrated that it is possible to circumvent performance counter-based detection completely. They present a camouflaged Flush+Reload attack that bypasses state-of-the-art detection mechanisms, successfully leaking secret information from a victim.

In this work, we present *WaitGuard*, a novel approach for detecting flush-based side-channel attacks by repurposing the userspace monitor and wait instructions on commodity x86 Intel and AMD machines. *WaitGuard* is capable of detecting Flush+Reload and Flush+Flush attacks with a detection rate of >99.9%. Furthermore, we introduce *WaitWatcher*, a framework for systematically analyzing the behavior of userspace monitor/wait instructions.

With WaitWatcher, we provide a framework that automatically analyzes the recently introduced userspace monitor and wait instructions, originally intended to reduce the CPU energy consumption of busy waits. We perform a comprehensive study, analyzing 7 different server and desktop-class x86 CPUs from Intel and AMD using WaitWatcher. Our study uncovers five different spurious wakeup triggers and 18 instructions that completely bypass the wakeup mechanisms.

With WaitGuard, we present a drop-in security monitor for detecting flush-based cache side-channel attacks by repurposing the unprivileged userspace monitor and wait instructions. While these instructions are intended for detecting writes to monitored addresses, we find that flushing the monitored addresses also causes the wait to abort. Combining this address monitoring with an access latency measurement after each wakeup allows us to detect flush-based attacks with an accuracy of >99.9%, even under heavy system load. Furthermore, WaitGuard is capable of detecting camouflaged Flush+Reload attacks, which can bypass traditional performance counter-based detection mechanisms [18].

We introduce two variants of WaitGuard that allow for flexible use of our detection mechanism. First, we propose a self-contained variant in which a process monitors its own memory using a dedicated monitor thread. This variant can be implemented without involving the host operating system (OS) and allows the process to determine whether it wants to continue execution in the case of a potential attack. Second, we detail a delegated variant, which hands the monitoring task to the operating system. The OS uses a dedicated thread to protect the data of the victim process.

We implement the self-contained variant of WaitGuard and evaluate its effectiveness. Using three different Flush+Reload attacks, we find that WaitGuard can reliably detect side-channel attacks with a detection rate of >99.9%. Furthermore, we find that the rate of false positives is vanishingly low, thus underlining the feasibility of our approach.

Contributions. In this work, we make the following key contributions:

- **WaitWatcher.** We present WaitWatcher, an open-source[1] framework that automatically analyzes the behavior of the recently introduced x86 userspace monitor and wait instructions.
- **Insights on Monitor/Wait Instructions.** We provide a comprehensive study with overall 7 Intel and AMD CPUs with different microarchitectures, showcasing undocumented CPU behavior, such as spurious wakeup triggers and unprivileged instructions that can bypass the wakeup mechanisms.
- **WaitGuard.** We present a novel mechanism that reliably detects cache-based side-channel attacks by repurposing the userspace monitor/wait instructions available on commodity x86 hardware.
- **Proof-of-Concept and Evaluation.** We evaluate WaitGuard, showcasing the detection of flush-based side-channel attacks with a high accuracy of >99.9%, including camouflaged Flush+Reload attacks.

Outline. The remainder of this work is organized as follows. Section 2 provides the background of this work and discusses related work. Section 3 introduces the WaitWatcher framework and presents the analysis results for 7 Intel and AMD machines. In Sect. 4 we introduce WaitGuard, a novel drop-in security monitor that detects flush-based cache side-channel attacks. Section 5 discusses the implementation and evaluation of WaitGuard. Section 6 concludes this work.

2 Background and Related Work

This section provides the required background on cache side-channels, flush-based side-channel attacks, and proposed detection mechanisms. Furthermore, we discuss the recently introduced userspace monitor and wait instructions that provide the foundation of our approach.

---

[1] The WaitWatcher Framework.

2.1 Cache Side-Channels

The cache hierarchy of modern CPUs consists of multiple *levels*, which are categorized depending on their proximity to the CPU cores. The Level 1 (L1) and Level 2 (L2) caches are usually small and deeply integrated in the core to allow for minimal access latencies. While the L1 and L2 are not shared across physical cores, with hyperthreading they can be shared across logical cores which share the same execution engine. The last-level cache (LLC) is furthest away from the cores, provides more storage space, and is typically shared across multiple physical cores. Cache side-channels exploit timing variations that depend on whether data is cached or not, *e.g.*, a load access that results in a cache hit is significantly faster than a cache miss that results in a main memory access (*i.e.*, the DRAM) [33]. Through measuring timing differences, an attacker can determine whether a value was recently accessed (*i.e.*, cached) or not.

2.2 Flush-Based Side-Channel Attacks

Flush-based cache side-channel attacks are based on flushing an address from the cache, waiting for victim activity, and measuring whether the victim accessed the address. This attack relies on the availability of shared memory between the victim and the attacker to flush the victim address. While these attacks are typically performed on shared libraries, they are also possible on arbitrary memory and cross-VM due to page deduplication [27,30]. Depending on how the attacker determines whether the victim address was accessed, we distinguish between Flush+Reload and Flush+Flush attacks [13,33].

Flush+Reload. In 2014, Yuval et al. [33] introduced a cache side-channel attack dubbed Flush+Reload. They use the `clflush` instruction, which evicts victim data from all cache levels, to build a cross-core attack. The basic principle of Flush+Reload is to evict a shared address using `clflush`, wait for or trigger victim execution, and measure the access latency for the evicted address. If the access is fast (cache hit) the victim accessed the memory location. If the access is slow (cache miss) the victim did not accessed the memory location.

In their proof-of-concept attack, they use Flush+Reload to leak the RSA private key of GnuPG [1]. The targeted program executes different code paths depending on the secret key bits. Thus, the execution behavior measured with Flush+Reload allows the attacker to reconstruct the key bits.

Flush+Flush. Gruss et al. [13] refined Flush+Reload by timing the `clflush` instruction instead of a separate memory access and dubbed this attack Flush+Flush. Flush+Flush is based on latency variations of the flush instruction that depend on whether the flushed address is present in the cache. `clflush` has to perform significantly more work when a cache line is present as it has to evict it from all cache levels. Thus, measuring the latency of `clflush` allows the attacker to determine the cache state of the victim address. The attack consists of a loop that executes `clflush` and measures the latency. Gruss et al. [13] also implement covert channels using Flush+Reload and Flush+Flush. Their evaluation showcases that Flush+Flush achieves high transmission rates while staying largely undetected. Furthermore, Flush+Flush does not have a blind spot, unlike Flush+Reload, which can miss victim accesses if they occur between the attackers memory access and the flush which restores the cache state [29].

2.3 Side-Channel Attack Detection

Due to the threat of side-channel attacks, researchers proposed a multitude of possible solutions. One promising approach is to *detect* side-channel attacks using hardware performance counters (HPC) [4–6, 9, 10, 19, 21–23, 28, 32, 35]. HPCs monitor certain architectural and micro-architectural events occurring on a system. Many defenses use the values reported by HPCs to assess the current state of the system. Due to the distinct behavior of side-channel attacks, they either cause detectable anomalies in the performance counter behavior or follow certain signatures [3].

While HPCs were generally thought to allow for the accurate detection of cache side-channel attacks, issues arise with this approach. Recently, Kosasih et al. [18] introduced a camouflaged Flush+Reload attack that bypasses all considered detection classifiers. Furthermore, the set of available performance counters is hardware-specific, varies between CPU vendors, and also varies between CPU generations and families. It is, thus, challenging to provide a *generic* detection mechanisms that does not require tedious adaption for each specific hardware platform. Also, granting userspace programs access to low-level performance counters can facilitate further side-channel attacks, by introducing another potential attack surface [8, 12, 31].

2.4 Userspace Wait Instructions

Recent AMD and Intel processor generations introduced new instructions for reducing the CPU power consumption while waiting for certain events, such as write accesses. Both vendors provide dedicated userspace monitoring and waiting instructions [7, 16] that eliminate the need for busy waits by replacing them with efficient alternatives. For Intel CPUs, the new instructions are dubbed umonitor and umwait, while AMD denotes them as monitorx and waitx. They allow userspace code to set up a monitor for a certain memory granule and subsequently call the corresponding wait instruction to hint the CPU to enter a low-power state. Write accesses to the monitored address wake up the waiting thread. However, other events, such as non-maskable interrupts or a wait time exceeding an operating-system-defined limit may cause spurious wakeups. In the case of Intel CPUs, a flag indicates whether a wakeup was due to the operating system timeout or any other source.

Recently, Zhang et al. [34] demonstrated that not only *architectural* write accesses to the monitored addresses act as wakeup triggers. They find that speculative write accesses also cause the waiting thread to exit its low-power state. Thus, they illustrate that undocumented, implementation-specific sources can also act as a wakeup trigger for the novel wait instructions. In their work, Zhang et al. [34] use these spurious wakeups to improve the leakage achieved with speculative execution attacks and to perform website fingerprinting attacks.

Terminology. In the remainder of this work, we use the term `monitor` and `wait` to refer to the userspace monitoring instructions of both Intel and AMD. In cases where it is important to distinguish between vendor-specific behavior, we use the corresponding instruction names, *i.e.*, `umonitor`/`umwait` for Intel and `monitorx`/`waitx` for AMD.

3 WaitWatcher Framework

Previous research explored specific parts of the new `wait` instructions. Despite this, there is no openly available framework for analyzing how `monitor` and `wait` instructions are influenced by other instructions on different CPUs. Furthermore, there is no comprehensive study on wakeup triggers and the behavior of the `monitor`/`wait` instructions across different CPU architectures. While the corresponding documentations describe modification of the monitored memory location as a wakeup trigger [7,16], we will show that this is not always the case. Additionally, there might exist further undocumented wakeup triggers. As the x86 instruction set architecture consists of thousands of instructions, a manual analysis even on a single platform would require an extensive amount of time. Thus, performing a manual analysis on multiple platforms and microarchitectures is infeasible. Therefore, an automated approach for both Intel and AMD systems is needed. To solve this issue, we develop the WaitWatcher framework. Our WaitWatcher framework implements an automated analysis for finding interactions between `monitor`/`wait` instructions and all other instructions available on the system under test. We base our implementation on the opensource Minefield framework developed by Kogler et al. [17]. Their framework is designed to test instructions for their susceptability to undervolting fault attacks. However, we find that Minefields' instruction gathering and sample generation is a suitable starting point for WaitWatcher.

3.1 Framework Design and Analysis Approach

The analysis performed by our framework can be divided into three distinct steps. We denote these steps as *Instruction Gathering*, *Sample Generation*, and *Interaction Analysis*. After executing these three steps, the framework produces a list of instructions and how they interact with the `monitor`/`wait` instructions.

Instruction Gathering. First, we gather a list of all instructions that are available on the target ISA, in this case x86. We obtain this data by using publicly available sources provided by Abel et al. [2]. The data is provided as an XML file that contains detailed information about the available instructions as well as their source and destination operands. Furthermore, each instruction entry in the list

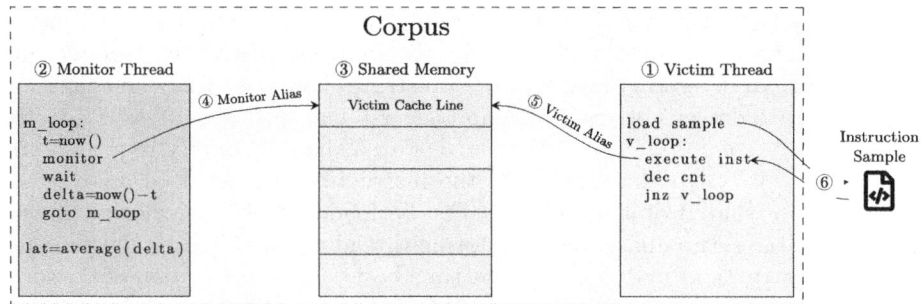

Fig. 1. An overview of the *Instruction Analysis* step of our framework. The monitor thread monitors a victim cache line and measures the time spent waiting in a loop. The victim thread executes the instruction sample on the victim cache line. The average waiting duration determines whether an instruction affects the wakeup behavior.

contains information on the required privilege level and if the instruction is part of an ISA extension. We consider this list as the ground truth for all further steps of the analysis.

Sample Generation. Next, we generate a distinct dynamically loadable file for each of the available instructions. During this step, we filter out instructions that require a higher privilege level than CPL 3 (*i.e.*, userspace mode). This is due to the fact that we are only interested in analyzing the interaction of userspace instructions and wait instructions. Based on the source and destination operands, our framework instruments the instructions with a prologue and epilogue. Both of them are required to set up registers and memory locations such that they are contextually meaningful for the analyzed instruction. This is especially vital for instructions that interpret register values as addresses, as a faulty setup will cause crashes. Due to the operand-dependent instrumentation, we consider operations with different operand types as distinct instructions. Thus, a mov from register to memory and a mov from register to register are compiled into two separate files. Note that this step also compiles instructions that may not be supported by the system under test. Reducing the set of compiled instructions to potentially executable instructions is a possible optimization for speeding up the sample generation step. However, the sample generation is only executed once and, even on our slowest system, takes only minutes of execution time due to the parallel nature of our implementation. During this step, the framework excludes instructions that are not supported by the currently used compiler version. Instructions that are affected by this exclusion belong to currently unimplemented extensions. Furthermore, we exclude instructions that perform control-flow transfers as we only focus on data-oriented instructions.

Interaction Analysis. In the third step, we perform the actual analysis of the interaction between instructions and the monitor/wait instructions. For that, the previously compiled and instrumented samples are dynamically linked by a test program denoted as the *corpus*. The corpus handles the logic to detect an interaction between the currently analyzed instruction sample and the `monitor`/`wait` instructions. Figure 1 illustrates how the corpus and the samples interact to detect potential wakeup triggers. The corpus creates ① a *victim thread* and ② a *monitor thread*. It then sets up a shared memory region ③ and two aliases (④,⑤) to the region. As the instructions we want to analyze are compiled to a shared object, they need to be loaded ⑥ by the victim thread. After the initial setup phase, the monitoring thread repeatedly calls the `monitor` and `wait` instructions and measures the time between the invocation of the `wait` instruction and the subsequent wakeup. When invoking the `monitor` instruction, the monitor thread uses ④ the monitor alias for its target address. Meanwhile, the victim thread executes the currently loaded sample in a tight loop. The samples are instrumented such that they use ⑤ the victim alias as their destination operand. The victim thread halts once a configured number of iterations is reached. Once the victim thread is finished, the monitor thread averages the latency values measured during the monitoring phase.

Our framework uses the average wait duration to distinguish between the samples that interact with `wait` (*i.e.*, cause wakeups) and those that do not cause wakeups. As the latency is significantly lower on wakeups, ambiguities in the form of false positives and false negatives are highly unlikely. Combining the average latency with a check that tests whether the monitored location was actually modified after invoking the sample loop allows us to detect two types of atypical behavior. A high average wakeup latency combined with a memory modification indicates that the analyzed instruction does not act as a wakeup trigger and bypasses the wakeup logic. Contrarily, a low average wakeup latency and an unmodified victim memory imply that the analyzed instruction is a wakeup trigger without actually writing to memory. We denote these instructions as *spurious* triggers. Overall, we classify instructions into four categories based on the averaged wait times and the state of the data after sample invocation. Besides the atypical cases listed above, the other two categories contain the instructions that behave according to their expected wakeup behavior.

At the end of the interaction analysis, our framework generates a report for all instruction samples that were compiled during sample generation. For each sample, we log the exact operation and operands, the averaged wakeup latency, and the category in which the operation was classified. Furthermore, the report contains information on which instructions are unimplemented on the current system and which samples encountered runtime errors. We execute the analysis in two configurations where the monitor and victim thread are either sibling threads or pinned to unrelated cores.

Transient Execution. While the main focus of WaitWatcher lies on regular instruction execution, we also implement the analysis of transiently executed instructions. When using the transient execution mode, the instruction sample is modified such that the analyzed instruction is never executed architecturally. Thus, when measuring positive interaction with the analyzed instruction, we can conclude that transient effects also act as wakeup triggers. Note that the

Table 1. The analysis results of our framework for architectural execution. Depending on the microarchitecture, multiple spurious wakeup triggers are identified. We also find that some instructions are able to modify data without causing a wakeup. Results reported for AMD systems assume sibling threads.

CPU Generation	Analyzed Instructions	Data Mod. 👁	Data Mod. 🚫	No Data Mod. 👁	No Data Mod. 🚫
🖥 Zen 2	2996	385	14	4	2593
🖥 Zen 3	3005	399	0	4	2602
🖧 Zen 4c	12 880	655	6	4	12 215
🖥 Alder Lake	3044	389	12	3	2640
🖥 Arrow Lake	3124	418	12	0	2692
🖧 Sapphire Rapids	15 039	647	18/0†	5	14 369
🖧 Emerald Rapids	15 040	647	18/0†	5	14 370

👁 Wakeup Trigger   🚫 No Wakeup Trigger
🖧 Server CPU   🖥 Desktop CPU   † Arbitrary Thread/Sibling Thread

transient execution version of WaitWatcher may require manual optimizations depending on the analyzed system due to differences in the underlying hardware.

3.2 Analysis Results

We find that our analysis approach and instruction instrumentation work reliably for most of the instructions implemented on our tested systems. A small subset of all instructions triggers runtime errors. This is usually the case for instructions where the operands are contextually bound to a range that is not documented in the ground truth used for instrumenting the instructions. As our framework logs crashing instructions, they can be manually analyzed if required.

We execute our framework on multiple microarchitectures from both Intel and AMD. In our analysis, we target an overall of seven systems containing both server-grade and desktop CPUs. Table 1 lists the quantitative results of our automated analysis. As in the sample generation step, we distinguish between invocations of the same operation using different source and destination types when counting instructions. The main focus of our analysis lies on instructions that either modify data without causing a wakeup or, conversely, do not modify data but act as wakeup triggers. We find that all considered systems except for Arrow Lake CPUs have at least three spurious wakeup triggers. Furthermore, on some of the analyzed systems, we find instructions that can completely bypass the monitoring logic and modify memory without causing wakeups. A detailed description of the results of our analysis is given below.

Spurious Wakeup Triggers. Our framework allows us to reproduce the findings regarding undocumented wakeup triggers provided by previous work [34].

However, we also observe previously unreported additional triggers. Specifically, we find that `clflush` and `clflushopt` also cause wakeups on Intel Sapphire Rapids and Emerald Rapids. Previous research only analyzed Intel desktop CPUs and reported that `clflush` only causes wakeups for AMDs `mwaitx` instructions [34]. Furthermore, we find that on Emerald Rapids and Sapphire Rapids, both `prefetch` and `prefetchwt1` cause wakeups in addition to the previously reported `prefetchw` instruction. Thus, for Emerald Rapids and Sapphire Rapids we find an overall of five spurious wakeup triggers. Our measurements indicate that on Intel server-grade CPUs, spurious triggers reliably cause a wakeup *independently* of the core on which the monitor and victim thread are running. Furthermore, we find that Intel's desktop CPUs do not experience the same spurious wakeup triggers as their larger counterparts. On Alder Lake, we find that `prefetch`, `prefetchw`, and `prefetchwt1` cause spurious wakeups, while on Arrow Lake, no spurious triggers are detected.

On AMD systems, `clflushopt`, `clflush`, `clwb`, and `prefetchw` cause spurious wakeups. For AMD machines, we find no difference between server-grade and desktop CPUs.

Undetected Data Modification. Besides spurious wakeup triggers, we also identify instructions that bypass the monitoring functionality. We find that `movnt*` and `vmovnt*` instructions allow for data modification without triggering the wakeup of the `wait` instructions on all considered Intel machines. We observe this behavior for the regular and `evex` encoded instructions. However, we also find that both `vmovnt*` and `movnt*` instructions *do* trigger wakeups when using the ZMM register or running the victim and monitor threads on the same core, *i.e.*, as sibling threads. On Zen 4c, we find that `vmovnt*` instructions encoded using the `evex` prefix modify data without triggering a wakeup of `mwaitx`.

Non-conformant Behavior. Surprisingly, we find that on all analyzed AMD systems it is necessary to run the monitoring thread and the victim thread as sibling threads. When pinning one of the two threads to a different core, no instruction will reliably trigger a wakeup. This directly contradicts the description of the `mwaitx` instruction given in the Architecture Programmer's Manual, which states that *a store from another processor* shall cause a wakeup of the instruction [7].

Contrarily, on the analyzed Intel machines, we find that the wakeup behavior of *most* instructions does not depend on the cores on which the monitor and victim thread are executed. Only the non-temporal move instructions discussed above experience different behavior when executed on non-sibling threads.

Wakeups on Transient Execution. We find that transiently executed instructions also cause spurious wakeups, thus confirming the results of Zhang et al. [34]. Interestingly, we find that not only write accesses trigger wakeups. Instructions such as `prefetchw`, which do not actually perform a write, may also act as transient spurious wakeup triggers. However, we find that transient invocations of `clflush` do *not* trigger spurious wakeups. Note that while some data-modifying instruction instructions cause wakeups when executed transiently, some fail to do so. We assume that this behavior depends on the latency of the instruction and the size of the speculation window. Instructions that finish within the speculation window cause wakeups while those that do not finish do not trigger wakeups.

4 Detecting Flush-Based Side-Channel Attacks

In this section, we show how the insights gained in our analysis allow us to implement a performance-counter agnostic detection method for flush-based side-channel attacks on Intel CPUs.

First, we discuss the general idea of our new side-channel detection mechanism and introduce WaitGuard. WaitGuard is the first side-channel detection using userspace `wait` instructions to detect Flush+Flush and Flush+Reload attacks. We elaborate on the monitoring approach and show how WaitGuard can detect malicious flush operations on monitored data on Intel CPUs. We then propose two variants of WaitGuard and elaborate on their respective use cases. Theoretically, the presented approach also applies to AMD systems given that the behavior of `mwaitx` would reflect the description given in the architecture programmer's manual.

Attacker Model. For our detection approach, we assume a Flush+Reload or Flush+Flush attacker that aims to extract secret information from a victim process. The attacker can perform `clflush` operations on cache lines that the attacker process shares with the victim process. Without loss of generality, we assume that victim cache lines contain read-only data. We assume that the attacker has full knowledge of the victim process. Furthermore, we assume that the attacker process and the victim process are completely synchronized. Thus, the attacker knows precisely which victim operations are currently being executed. We do not consider attacks that use a contention-based approach to evict victim cache lines. Attacks like Prime+Probe or Evict+Reload [14,26] were relatively straightforward to mount across cores on older machines using fully inclusive L3 caches. However, newer CPU generations, such as the ones supporting userspace wait instructions, utilize L3 caches that are not fully inclusive. Evictions from the shared L3 do not cause evictions from the private L1 and L2 caches of the victim, making the eviction step of both Prime+Probe and Evict+Reload no longer possible across cores. Additionally, accesses that can be served by the L1 or L2 do not result in the cache line being written into the L3. Therefore, the probing step of Prime+Probe on the L3 can not detect memory accesses that can be served from these private caches [29].

4.1 Design of WaitGuard

Our analysis results show that `clflush` acts as a wakeup trigger for both Intel and AMD CPUs. Hence, we propose to use the `monitor/wait` instructions as a detection mechanism for flush-based side-channel attacks. Given that we can monitor a cache line using `monitor` and `wait`, a `clflush` instruction that targets this cache line will cause a wakeup without a write access. As `clflush` constitutes the core operation of Flush+Reload and Flush+Flush attacks, it should thus be possible to detect such attacks by observing the behavior of `wait` when monitoring a currently targeted cache line. Based on this general idea, we develop WaitGuard. WaitGuard is the first detection mechanism for flush-based side-channels that leverages the novel `monitor` and `wait` instructions. While doing so, our approach does not require access to any hardware performance counters besides the time stamp counter (TSC).

Monitoring Logic. WaitGuard implements a *monitoring logic* which aims to detect all flushes to a monitored cache line. The core of our monitoring logic is a tight loop that calls `monitor` followed by a `wait` instruction. We measure the time passed between executing the `wait` instruction and the subsequent wakeup. This wait time is the first indicator on whether the cache line is being targeted by a flush-based attack. The monitoring loop is, in this aspect, equivalent to the loop used in our Interaction Analysis. However, we cannot purely rely on this metric to detect flush-based attacks. There are multiple sources that can wake up a waiting thread. Additionally to a write access to the monitored cache line, interrupts and an OS-defined timeout can cause spurious wakeups [34]. Thus, using a single measurement causes too many false positives as spurious wakeups may be interpreted as write accesses. To avoid this issue, we use an additional metric to improve the results of our detection: after the wakeup, we measure the access latency to the monitored cache line. In the case of Flush+Reload or Flush+Flush attacks, the access latency is high as the data was flushed and must be fetched again from memory. Given that `monitor` performs a 1-byte fetch operation, the monitored cache line is always cached [7,16]. Thus, accessing the cache line after a wakeup due to a timer interrupt or any other trigger will result in a fast access. We combine the access latency measurement with a rolling average over the latest wakeup latencies to improve our detection reliability. This allows us to detect anomalies due to the significant increase of flush operations during Flush+Reload and Flush+Flush attacks.

4.2 WaitGuard Variants

We propose two variants of how WaitGuard can be implemented. When elaborating on the variants, we use the term *victim* process or cache line to refer to the potential target of a side-channel attack. Figure 2 schematically depicts both variants of WaitGuard.

Drop-In Variant. First, we propose a self-contained variant of WaitGuard, which is illustrated in Fig. 2 (a). This variant requires the victim process to be able to create threads. The victim creates a list of cache lines that require monitoring. This list can either be generated manually or by using a profiling approach such as the one proposed by Gruss et al. [14]. For each of these cache lines the victim spawns one thread that monitors the corresponding cache line ①.

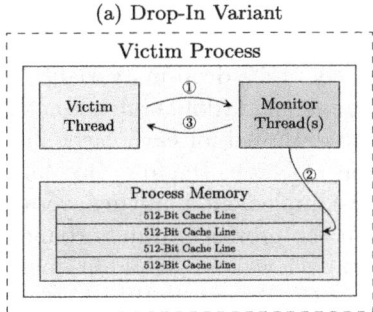 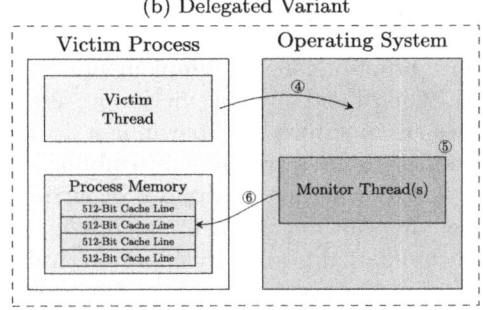

Fig. 2. Two variants of WaitGuard. The drop-in variant can be deployed by any process and does not require OS support. The delegated variant spawns a dedicated monitoring thread which is managed by the OS.

Subsequently, the monitoring thread calls `monitor` followed by a `wait` on the to-be-monitored cache line ②. After waking up from the wait, the monitor thread checks how long it was waiting and the access latency when reading from the monitored cache line. Depending on the measured values, the monitor thread decides whether the cache line was flushed. This approach has the advantage that it can be implemented as a drop-in side-channel detection for userspace processes on off-the-shelf Intel CPUs. Upon detection of `clflush` operations, the monitoring thread informs the victim ③. Thus, the process can decide how to react and whether it is safe to proceed execution. Note, however, that one hardware thread can only monitor one cache line at a time. Thus, monitoring multiple cache lines must either be achieved by monitoring one cache line after the other or by spawning additional monitoring threads.

Delegated Variant. The delegated version of WaitGuard relies on the operating system, as shown in Fig. 2 (b). Like in the drop-in variant, the victim process creates a list of cache lines that require monitoring. This list is passed to the operating system ④ which, in turn, creates one or multiple monitoring threads ⑤ that monitor the given victim cache lines ⑥. Contrary to the drop-in variant, the OS can take measures to isolate the victim from potential attackers (*e.g.*, by providing a non-shared mapping of the shared library under attack). However, the delegated variant requires the operating system to be aware of the side-channel detection approach. While it is possible to modify the Linux kernel, using a kernel module would allow for easier integration in existing systems.

5 WaitGuard Implementation and Evaluation

In this section, we discuss our proof-of-concept implementation and evaluate the detection rate of WaitGuard. We evaluate our implementation on a commodity Intel system and achieve a detection rate of >99.9% for basic Flush+Reload attacks. Furthermore, we show how WaitGuard can be configured to detect stealthy attacks such as the ones proposed by Kosasih et al. [18].

5.1 Implementation

Our proof-of-concept implementation consists of the drop-in variant of WaitGuard and multiple victim processes. In our implementation, multiple cache lines are monitored by spawning a dedicated monitor thread for each cache line. Monitor threads are pinned to sibling threads. Our PoC uses the following logic to classify whether an attack is occurring or not. We implement a moving average over the wait durations to smoothen the values in the presence of disturbances due to interrupts and other spurious wakeups. After each wakeup, we additionally measure the access latency to the monitored data. Combining both values, we decide whether we were woken due to a `clflush` and flag such cases as potential attacks. If the current average wait duration is below a *critical wait duration* and the memory access latency is above a pre-defined threshold, a detection is logged. Both the critical wait duration and the access latency threshold are measured manually and are expected to vary across systems. Note that the requirement for manual measurement is a limitation of our PoC and the calibration can be automated. The PoC logs the timestamp at which the attack was detected. Our implementation is parameterizable with regard to the moving average window size and the critical wait duration.

To show the importance of combining our wait-based approach with memory access timing measurements, we also implement a variant that does *not* use `monitor` and `wait` instructions. Instead, it only measures the cache access latency to determine whether an attack occurred. We refer to this variant as the *measure-only* (MO) variant.

Victim Processes. We implement multiple victims, denoted as $\mathcal{V}_1$ to $\mathcal{V}_3$, to evaluate WaitGuard for Flush+Reload attacks under different attack scenarios. At their core, all victims implement an AES encryption using OpenSSL 3.3.3 [25] and are based on an open-source implementation of a Flush+Reload attack [24]. The cache lines targeted by the attacker hold the T-tables, which are a popular target for side-channel attacks [11,13,15,20]. We compile OpenSSL without hardware acceleration to enforce the usage of software-based T-tables. All victims perform 300 000 encryptions. Depending on the victim, the attacker performs one or multiple measurements for each encryption. We combine the attacker and the victim in the same process to ensure synchronization and a minimal time difference between flushing target cache lines, performing the OpenSSL AES encryption, and measuring whether the relevant T-table entries were accessed.

The attacker in $\mathcal{V}_1$ leaks individual key bytes by attacking one T-table entry at a time. $\mathcal{V}_1$ first performs a fixed number of encryptions where the attacker exclusively targets the first T-table cache line. Next, the attacker targets the second T-table entry. The attacker proceeds like this until all key bytes are leaked. Victim $\mathcal{V}_2$ implements a more efficient attacker that first flushes all targeted cache lines. Then, the victim executes its encryption operation. Subsequently, the attacker measures the access latency for all previously flushed cache lines. For $\mathcal{V}_3$, we implement a stealthy variant of $\mathcal{V}_2$. Each encryption iteration has a

0.2% chance of actually performing the Flush+Reload attack. In all other cases, the victim performs the encryption without being attacked.

5.2 Evaluation Setup

We use the previously described victims to gauge how well WaitGuard can detect the implemented attacks. Each victim invocation executes for a set amount of time and logs the begin and end timestamp of each Flush+Reload attack, thus generating a list of time frames in which an attack occurred. Similarly, WaitGuard logs the time stamps at which it detects an attack. We use the system-wide timestamp counter for these measurements. Once the victim finishes, we compare the detection timestamps with the time frames at which attacks were performed. We consider an attack as detected whenever the victim logs *at least one detection timestamp* during the attack time frame. All victims described above are implemented such that we introduce an artificial delay of several milliseconds after each attack run. We use this delay to create a temporal separation between attack time frames to better catch spurious wakeups and avoid a bias toward overly optimistic detection results.

We use the cpu stressor of stress-ng to evaluate our PoC under varying system loads by generating additional noise. The imposed load increases from 0% to 90% in 10% steps. During our evaluation, we do *not* isolate the cores that are executing the victim and the monitor code.

As mentioned in Sect. 4.1, our PoC uses a windowing approach to reduce noise. We evaluate our implementation for different window sizes to measure their impact on the detection rate. The tested window sizes range from two samples to 256 samples. We perform our evaluation on a commodity Intel Xeon Gold 6530 CPU with 32 cores and 64 threads. Our system is equipped with 512GB DDR5 DRAM and runs the Linux kernel version 6.8.0.

5.3 Detection Rate and False Positive Rate

The left column of Fig. 3 illustrates the detection rates and false positives rates for a 16-sample window PoC. The detection rate is computed as the ratio between the number of actually performed attacks and the number of mounted attacks. For $\mathcal{V}_1$ and $\mathcal{V}_2$ we achieve a >99.9% detection rate. However, we can not detected stealthy attacks like the one implemented in $\mathcal{V}_3$ due to the averaging approach. As the stealthy attack does not flush in every iteration, the computed average waiting time will only drop slightly when seeing a wakeup due to the attack. Thus, a 16-sample window is only suitable for detecting classical Flush+Reload attacks. We find that window sizes that exceed 16 samples do not offer any additional benefits.

Conversely, we find that when using a smaller window size of just two samples we can detect >99.9% of stealthy attacks, as depicted in the right column of Fig. 3. The short sleep duration that is observed when the attack is actually performed is enough to bias the average such that it falls below the detection threshold. Thus, attacks like the one implemented by $\mathcal{V}_3$ can also be detected

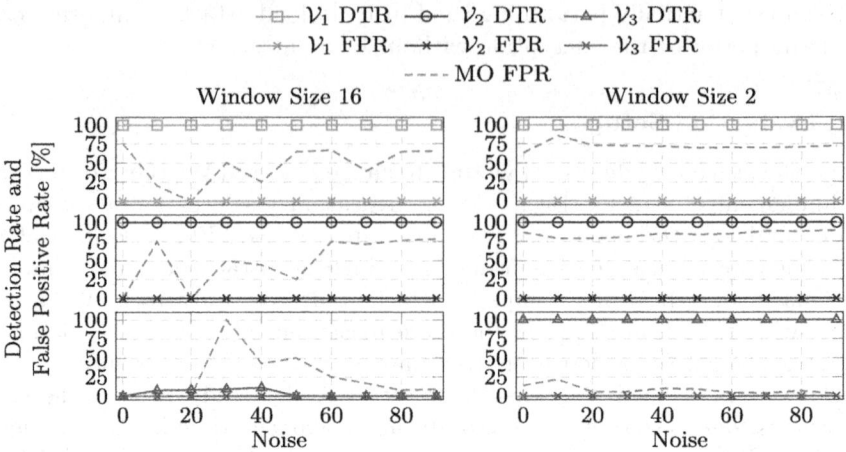

Fig. 3. The detection rate (DTR) and false positive rate (FPR) for WaitGuard using a 16-sample and a 2-sample window. While $\mathcal{V}_1$ and $\mathcal{V}_2$ are detected in both cases, $\mathcal{V}_3$ can only be detected by the 2-sample window configuration. The Measure-Only (MO) false positive rate is infeasibly high.

using WaitGuard. Furthermore, we find that decreasing the window size does not increase the false positive rate. As our PoC only flags an attack if both the wakeup latency and the subsequent memory access latency are low, false positives are rare. For all tested configurations we find that the rate of false positives is vanishingly low. The measured false positive rates are well below the 1% mark, regardless of the imposed system noise. We find that a measure-only variant (MO) is infeasible. While all attacks are flagged as detected, the amount of false positives is overwhelming, as depicted by the dashed lines in Fig. 3. We observe large false positive rates, reaching up to 100%, across all noise levels. We find that the high false-positive rate is due to the monitor claiming to see a large number of attacks during the window between the attack rounds. Even *without* an active attacker, the measure-only variant logs, on average, 15.6 attacks per second. Contrarily, when using `wait` and `monitor`, we see no such behavior.

Scheduled Monitoring. We furthermore investigate whether it is feasible to monitor multiple cache lines using a single thread. For that, we extend the monitor implementation such that each thread holds a list of monitored cache line addresses. All measured and computed values such as the averaged wakeup durations are unique for each monitored cache line. Thus, each monitored cache line is handled independently from all other cache lines. We implement a pseudo-random scheduling and a cache-line focused scheduling. When using the pseudo-random scheduling, the monitor thread picks a cache line at random and installs the monitor for the address at the beginning of each monitoring iteration. After measuring the wakeup time the monitor thread picks the next cache line by

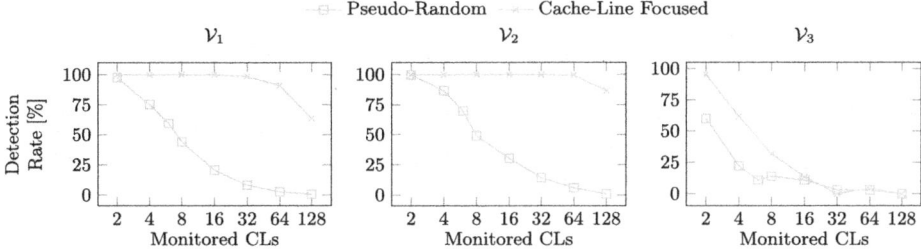

Fig. 4. The detection rates when monitoring multiple cache lines using a single thread. The detection rate drops steadily with the increasing number of monitored cache lines. When focussing on an attacked cache line, the detection rate remains high, even for multiple cache lines.

randomly selecting one from the given list. The cache-line focused scheduling initially operates equivalently. However, as soon as a cache line that is likely under attack is identified, the scheduling algorithm prioritizes this cache line.

Figure 4 illustrates the detection rates for both scheduling approaches. For the pseudo-random scheduling, the detection rate declines with an increasing number of cache lines being monitored by a single thread. The cache-line focused scheduling performs significantly better, especially for $\mathcal{V}_1$ and $\mathcal{V}_2$ victims. Note that all of the given curves were measured using a 2-sample window size as this configuration performed best in the previous experiments.

5.4 Wakeup Distribution

Besides the detection rate, we also determine the empirical distribution of wakeup times within the attack time frames. The distributions are illustrated in Fig. 5. For $\mathcal{V}_1$ and $\mathcal{V}_2$ most of the wakeups occur at the beginning of the attack. Note that $\mathcal{V}_1$ attacks the four victim cache lines sequentially. This is reflected in the distribution of $\mathcal{V}_1$, which shows an increase of wakeups around the points in time at which the attacker flushes the victim cache lines. For $\mathcal{V}_3$ we can observe that the wakeup timings are uniformly distributed. This is due to $\mathcal{V}_3$ distributing its attack phases across the whole attack window.

The distributions suggest that WaitGuard flags attacks early in the attack process or close to the `clflush` invocations. When computing the distributions for noise levels below 50% (not depicted in the figure), we observe even more pronounced peaks in the distribution. This suggests that additional system noise has a negative impact on the latency between the flush operation and the detection by WaitGuard.

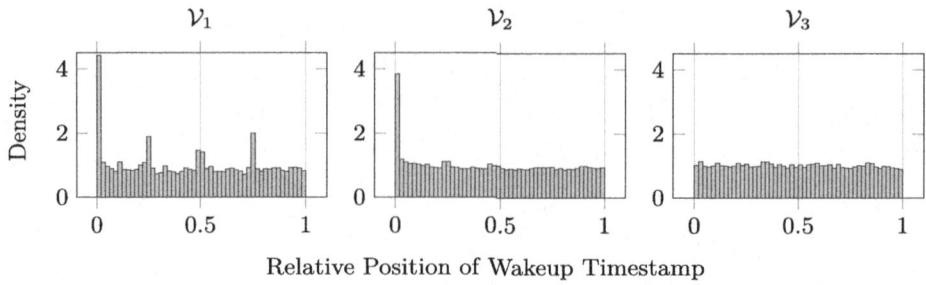

Fig. 5. The empirical distribution of wakeup timings in normalized attack windows for a 2-sample configuration.

6 Conclusion

In this work, we presented *WaitWatcher*, an automated analysis framework that determines how unprivileged instructions interact with the new `umonitor`/`umwait` and `monitorx`/`waitx` instructions. Contrarily to the work of Zhang et al. [34], WaitWatcher analyzes *all* executable userspace instructions with and without transient execution. We performed our analysis on 7 server and desktop-class x86 CPUs, uncovering 5 spurious wakeup triggers as well as 18 instructions that modify memory without causing wakeups. In addition, we found that, on AMD systems, wakeups are only correctly triggered when the monitoring thread and the thread performing the write access are sibling threads.

Based on the spurious wakeup triggers discovered in our analysis, we proposed *WaitGuard*, a novel mechanism that leverages the `umonitor`/`umwait` instructions on Intel x86 hardware to detect Flush+Reload and Flush+Flush attacks. Contrary to many existing detection approaches [3], WaitGuard operates without hardware performance counters and provides a drop-in solution that can be easily included in userspace software. We implemented a proof-of-concept of WaitGuard and evaluated its detection rate for different variants of Flush+Reload, including a stealthy attack. We find that WaitGuard achieves a detection rate of up to >99.9% while reporting close to zero false positives. Furthermore, we find that WaitGuard is resistant to heavy system noise, *i.e.*, the detection accuracy stays constant. Hence, our approach is feasible for detecting flushes on vulnerable cache lines and, thus, Flush+Reload and Flush+Flush attacks. Besides a high detection rate, we find that WaitGuard can detect camouflaged attacks that are not detected by existing side-channel detection approaches [18].

Acknowledgements. We would like to thank the reviewers for their detailed feedback. Furthermore, we would like to thank David Schrammel for his support during the initial phase of this work. This research is supported by the European Research Council (ERC project FSSec 101076409) and the Austrian Research Promotion Agency (FFG) via the AWARE project (FFG grant number 891092). Additional funding was provided by generous gifts from Red Hat and Intel.

References

1. The GNU privacy guard. https://www.gnupg.org/. Accessed 13 Jan 2025
2. Abel, A., Reineke, J.: uops.info: characterizing latency, throughput, and port usage of instructions on intel microarchitectures. In: ASPLOS, pp. 673–686 (2019)
3. Akram, A., Mushtaq, M., Bhatti, M.K., Lapotre, V., Gogniat, G.: Meet the Sherlock Holmes' of side channel leakage: a survey of cache SCA detection techniques. IEEE Access **8**, 70836–70860 (2020)
4. Alam, M., Bhattacharya, S., Mukhopadhyay, D., Bhattacharya, S.: Performance counters to rescue: a machine learning based safeguard against micro-architectural Side-Channel-Attacks. IACR Cryptol. ePrint Arch, p. 564 (2017)
5. Allaf, Z., Adda, M., Gegov, A.E.: A comparison study on flush+reload and prime+probe attacks on AES using machine learning approaches. In: Advances in Computational Intelligence Systems - Contributions Presented at the 17th UK Workshop on Computational Intelligence, 6-8 September 2017, Cardiff, UK. Advances in Intelligent Systems and Computing, vol. 650, pp. 203–213 (2017)
6. Allaf, Z., Adda, M., Gegov, A.E.: ConfMVM: a hardware-assisted model to confine malicious VMs. In: 20th UKSim-AMSS International Conference on Computer Modelling and Simulation, UKSim 2018, Cambridge, United Kingdom, 27-29 March 2018, pp. 49–54 (2018)
7. AMD: AMD architecture programmer's manual. https://www.intel.com/content/www/us/en/developer/articles/technical/intel-sdm.html (2024). 24594 rev. 3.36
8. Bhattacharya, S., Mukhopadhyay, D.: Utilizing performance counters for compromising public key ciphers. ACM Trans. Priv. Secur. **21**, 5:1–5:31 (2018)
9. Briongos, S., Irazoqui, G., Malagón, P., Eisenbarth, T.: CacheShield: detecting cache attacks through self-observation. In: CODASPY, pp. 224–235 (2018)
10. Chiappetta, M., Savas, E., Yilmaz, C.: Real time detection of cache-based side-channel attacks using hardware performance counters. Appl. Soft Comput. **49**, 1162–1174 (2016)
11. Didier, G., Maurice, C.: Calibration done right: noiseless flush+flush attacks. In: DIMVA. LNCS, vol. 12756, pp. 278–298 (2021)
12. Gast, S., Weissteiner, H., Schröder, R.L., Gruss, D.: CounterSEVeillance: performance-counter attacks on AMD SEV-SNP. In: Network and Distributed System Security Symposium 2025: NDSS 2025 (2025)
13. Gruss, D., Maurice, C., Wagner, K., Mangard, S.: Flush+Flush: a fast and stealthy cache attack. In: DIMVA. LNCS, vol. 9721, pp. 279–299 (2016)
14. Gruss, D., Spreitzer, R., Mangard, S.: Cache template attacks: automating attacks on inclusive last-level caches. In: USENIX Security Symposium, pp. 897–912 (2015)
15. Gülmezoglu, B., Inci, M.S., Apecechea, G.I., Eisenbarth, T., Sunar, B.: A faster and more realistic flush+reload attack on AES. In: COSADE. LNCS, vol. 9064, pp. 111–126 (2015)
16. Intel: Intel software developer's manual. https://www.intel.com/content/www/us/en/developer/articles/technical/intel-sdm.html (2024)
17. Kogler, A., Gruss, D., Schwarz, M.: Minefield: a software-only protection for SGX enclaves against DVFS attacks. In: USENIX Security Symposium, pp. 4147–4164 (2022)
18. Kosasih, W., Feng, Y., Chuengsatiansup, C., Yarom, Y., Zhu, Z.: SoK: can we really detect cache side-channel attacks by monitoring performance counters? In: Proceedings of the 19th ACM Asia Conference on Computer and Communications Security, ASIA CCS 2024, Singapore, 1-5 July 2024 (2024)

19. Kulah, Y., Dincer, B., Yilmaz, C., Savas, E.: SpyDetector: an approach for detecting side-channel attacks at runtime. Int. J. Inf. Sec. **18**, 393–422 (2019)
20. Lipp, M., Gruss, D., Spreitzer, R., Maurice, C., Mangard, S.: ARMageddon: cache attacks on mobile devices. In: USENIX Security Symposium, pp. 549–564 (2016)
21. Mushtaq, M., Akram, A., Bhatti, M.K., Chaudhry, M., Lapotre, V., Gogniat, G.: NIGHTs-WATCH: a cache-based side-channel intrusion detector using hardware performance counters. In: HASP, pp. 1:1–1:8 (2018)
22. Mushtaq, M., et al.: Machine learning for security: the case of side-channel attack detection at run-time. In: 25th IEEE International Conference on Electronics, Circuits and Systems, ICECS 2018, Bordeaux, France, 9-12 December 2018, pp. 485–488 (2018)
23. Mushtaq, M., et al.: Whisper: a tool for run-time detection of side-channel attacks. IEEE Access **8**, 83871–83900 (2020)
24. NEPOCHE. https://github.com/nepoche/Flush-Reload (2017). Accessed 13 Jan 2025
25. OpenSSL: OpenSSL 3.3.3. https://github.com/openssl/openssl/tree/openssl-3.3.3 (2025). Accessed 13 Jan 2025
26. Osvik, D.A., Shamir, A., Tromer, E.: Cache attacks and countermeasures: the case of AES. In: CT-RSA. LNCS, vol. 3860, pp. 1–20 (2006)
27. Philippe-Jankovic, D., Zia, T.A.: Breaking VM isolation-an in-depth look into the cross VM flush reload cache timing attack. Int. J. Comput. Sci. Netw. Secur. **17**, 181 (IJCSNS) (2017)
28. Raj, A., Dharanipragada, J.: Keep the Pokerface on! Thwarting cache side channel attacks by memory bus monitoring and cache obfuscation. J. Cloud Comput. **6**, 28 (2017)
29. Rauscher, F., Fiedler, C., Kogler, A., Gruss, D.: A systematic evaluation of novel and existing cache side channels. In: Network and Distributed System Security Symposium 2025: NDSS 2025 (2025)
30. Suzaki, K., Iijima, K., Yagi, T., Artho, C.: Memory deduplication as a threat to the guest OS. In: EUROSEC, p. 1 (2011)
31. Uhsadel, L., Georges, A., Verbauwhede, I.: Exploiting hardware performance counters. In: FDTC, pp. 59–67 (2008)
32. Wang, Z., Peng, S., Guo, X., Jiang, W.: Zero in and TimeFuzz: detection and mitigation of cache side-channel attacks. In: Innovative Security Solutions for Information Technology and Communications - 11th International Conference, SecITC 2018, Bucharest, Romania, November 8-9, 2018, Revised Selected Papers. LNCS, vol. 11359, pp. 410–424 (2018)
33. Yarom, Y., Falkner, K.: FLUSH+RELOAD: a high resolution, low noise, L3 Cache Side-Channel Attack. In: USENIX Security Symposium, pp. 719–732 (2014)
34. Zhang, R., Kim, T., Weber, D., Schwarz, M.: (M)WAIT for it: bridging the gap between microarchitectural and architectural side channels. In: USENIX Security Symposium, pp. 7267–7284 (2023)
35. Zhang, T., Zhang, Y., Lee, R.B.: CloudRadar: a real-time side-channel attack detection system in clouds. In: RAID. LNCS, vol. 9854, pp. 118–140 (2016)

T-Time: A Fine-Grained Timing-Based Controlled-Channel Attack Against Intel TDX

Woomin Lee[1], Taehun Kim[1], Seunghee Shin[2], Junbeom Hur[1], and Youngjoo Shin[1(✉)]

[1] Korea University, Seoul, South Korea
{redcokeb,taehunk,jbhur,syoungjoo}@korea.ac.kr
[2] State University of New York at Binghamton, Binghamton, USA
sshin@binghamton.edu

Abstract. Intel's Trust Domain Extensions (TDX) is a Confidential Virtual Machine (CVM) technology designed to enhance security through Trusted Execution Environments (TEEs). Although TDX effectively mitigates interrupt-based stepping attacks, it remains vulnerable to controlled-channel attacks, which exploit page-level memory access patterns to infer secret-dependent control flows. Current defenses confine sensitive execution within single memory pages to reduce observable access patterns. We challenge this strategy by introducing T-Time, a fine-grained timing-based controlled-channel attack targeting Intel TDX. T-Time precisely measures dwell time—the interval between consecutive page faults—to uncover previously hidden sensitive control flows. We further enhance T-Time's precision through a cache-based amplification technique. We validate T-Time in two practical scenarios: extracting a 4096-bit RSA private key from MbedTLS, and reconstructing a WebP image through timing analysis during decoding. Our findings demonstrate that existing page-level defenses are inadequate against fine-grained timing attacks.

1 Introduction

Intel's Trust Domain Extensions (TDX) is the latest Confidential Virtual Machine (CVM) technology designed to provide robust hardware-enforced isolation through Trusted Execution Environments (TEEs). TDX specifically addresses interrupt-based stepping attacks [8,29,30,36,39], a longstanding and critical security issue prominently associated with its predecessor, Intel SGX. Despite this significant advancement, TDX inherently lacks comprehensive protection against controlled-channel attacks, which remains a fundamental security challenge [1].

Controlled-channel attacks exploit predictable interactions between a victim's control flow and the underlying low-level system, enabling privileged

---

W. Lee and T. Kim—These authors contributed equally to this work.

attackers to infer sensitive information by observing page-level memory access patterns [37]. Due to the persistent nature of this vulnerability, Intel relies heavily on software developers to implement defenses against these attacks [9]. Developers are encouraged to ensure secret-dependent control flows remain within a single memory page, effectively minimizing observable page-level access patterns. This strategy has traditionally been deemed sufficient, as controlled-channel attacks were thought to be inherently limited by page-level granularity.

However, this paper challenges the assumption that restricting secret-dependent execution to a single memory page provides adequate protection. We introduce *T-Time*, a novel fine-grained timing-based controlled-channel attack specifically designed to circumvent the existing page-level defense strategy in Intel TDX. T-Time precisely measures *dwell time*—the time interval between consecutive page faults—to reveal secret-dependent execution flows that were previously undetectable through traditional controlled-channel methods.

To further enhance the precision and effectiveness of T-Time, we propose a novel cache-based amplification technique that significantly increases timing differences between secret-dependent code paths residing within the same page. Our technique flushes target cache lines and measures dwell time, thereby amplifying otherwise subtle timing discrepancies and enabling T-Time to reliably infer sensitive control-flow decisions.

We demonstrate the practical impact and severity of T-Time through two concrete case studies. First, we extract a full 4096-bit RSA private key from the MbedTLS library using only 20 signing operations, highlighting a significant cryptographic vulnerability. Second, we reconstruct a WebP image through detailed timing analysis during its decoding, emphasizing T-Time's capability to infer sensitive data in realistic application scenarios. These examples clearly illustrate that current software-driven defensive practices based on single-page confinement are insufficient against fine-grained timing attacks. Finally, we discuss several mitigation strategies to address the risks posed by T-Time. The source code for our attack is publicly available at https://github.com/koreacsl/T-Time.

Contributions. In this paper, we make the following contributions:

- We present T-Time, a novel fine-grained timing-based controlled-channel attack that circumvents existing page-level defense strategy.
- We propose a technique that precisely measures dwell time via induced page faults and a timing amplification using a cache flush technique.
- We demonstrate T-Time's effectiveness through case studies, recovering an RSA-4096 private key and reconstructing a WebP image.

Responsible Disclosure. We disclosed our findings to Intel's PSIRT team, as well as to the maintainers of MbedTLS, WebP, Google Chrome, and Mozilla Firefox on April 23, 2025. In response, Intel PSIRT informed us that T-Time falls under existing side-channel guidance and requires no further action. The MbedTLS maintainer informed us that T-Time is ineffective against version 3.6.0 and later, since the `mbedtls_mpi_exp_mod()` function was rewritten to use a constant-time implementation. The WebP team responded that T-Time is not specific to libwebp and may impact other media decoders. Furthermore, they noted that, in general, Chrome cannot do much about timing attacks, and remarked that this vulnerability should be addressed at the hypervisor level, rather than by modifying individual libraries.

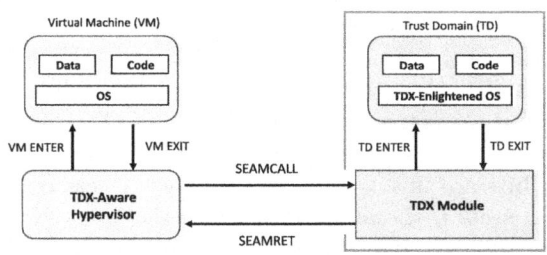

Fig. 1. Architecture of Intel TDX.

2 Background

2.1 Intel Trust Domain Extension

Intel TDX [12] is a hardware-based memory isolation technology that provides TEE for virtual machines (VMs). Intel TDX achieves this by introducing the TDX module, a core component providing hardware-enforced isolation for VMs. A VM protected by TDX is called a Trust Domain (TD). The TDX module [11] is responsible for ensuring secure communication and isolation between the hypervisor and the TD. As shown in Fig. 1, the TDX module acts as an intermediary between the hypervisor and the TD, securely handling communication between them. The hypervisor transfers control to the TD via the TDX module by invoking the SEAMCALL instruction, and control is returned to the hypervisor when the TDX module executes the SEAMRET instruction.

Page Fault Handling. A page fault occurs when a process accesses a virtual address that violates the current page table configuration, such as when the address is not mapped to physical memory. When a page fault occurs within a TD, the exception is intercepted by the TDX module, and control is transferred to the hypervisor via the SEAMRET instruction. The hypervisor, operating outside the TD context, resolves the fault—typically by mapping the required page or updating the page tables. Once the fault is handled, TD execution resumes through the SEAMCALL instruction, which returns control to the TDX module and re-enters the TD.

Memory Encryption. The processor enforces strict access control policies to isolate TD-assigned memory from all other applications, including the host and other TDs. To ensure data confidentiality and integrity, each TD's memory is encrypted using Intel's Multi-key Total Memory Encryption (MKTME) [10] mechanism.

2.2 Controlled-Channel Attack

TEEs are hardware-based isolation technologies designed to protect sensitive workloads [4] or virtual machines (VMs) [12,28] from a potentially compromised OS or hypervisor. However, since the OS or hypervisor still controls low-level resources such as memory management, several new attack surfaces for side-channel attacks have emerged. One notable example is the controlled-channel attack [37], which exploits the attacker's privileged control over memory management to infer the victim's memory access patterns. This attack is performed in four steps. In step 1, the attacker clears the present bits in the page table entries corresponding to memory regions of the TEE-protected application or VM. In step 2, the attacker induces the victim to perform memory accesses. Since the present bits are unset, any such memory access by the victim results in a page fault. In step 3, the attacker handles the trapped fault and logs the page fault sequence triggered by the victim's accesses. In step 4, the attacker analyzes the collected faulting addresses and recovers security-sensitive information. Because the controlled-channel attack relies on page faults to gather access patterns, its spatial resolution is inherently limited to the granularity of a memory page.

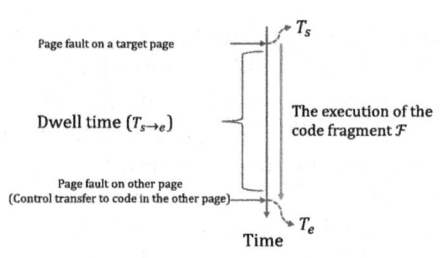

(a) Timing difference in the target page. (b) Content of the target page.

Fig. 2. T-Time attack

3 Building Attack Primitive

The main idea behind T-Time is that different execution flows lead to different execution times. By measuring dwell time—the duration between two consecutive page faults, T-Time uncovers secret-dependent control flows that have been deemed safe.

Figure 2 illustrates the concept of dwell time and provides an example of how it can be utilized in the T-Time attack. As shown in Fig. 2(a), the execution of the code fragment $\mathcal{F}$, whose execution time reveals a secret, is surrounded by two consecutive page faults, occurring at pages P_s and P_e. Dwell time $\mathcal{T}_{s \to e}$ refers to the time interval $(T_e - T_s)$ between the time (T_s) when a fault occurs at page

P_s and the time (T_e) when a fault occurs at page P_e. By measuring this dwell time, we can infer the execution time of $\mathcal{F}$, which in turn leaks the secret.

Figure 2(b) illustrates how dwell time can be leveraged in the T-Time attack. Since different control flows, such as f_1 and f_0, typically execute a different number of instructions, the corresponding dwell times also differ. By precisely measuring these dwell times, an attacker can distinguish between secret-dependent execution paths, even when both reside within the same memory page. Thus, this enables the extraction of sensitive information that would otherwise be assumed secure under page-level confinement. It is noteworthy that traditional controlled-channel attacks cannot infer the secret if both control flows (f_1 and f_0) result in identical page access sequences, highlighting the advantage of T-Time attack.

In Sect. 3.1, we present our attack. In Sect. 3.2, we propose a cache-based amplification technique. In Sect. 3.3, we evaluate the performance of the T-Time attack primitive and the amplification technique.

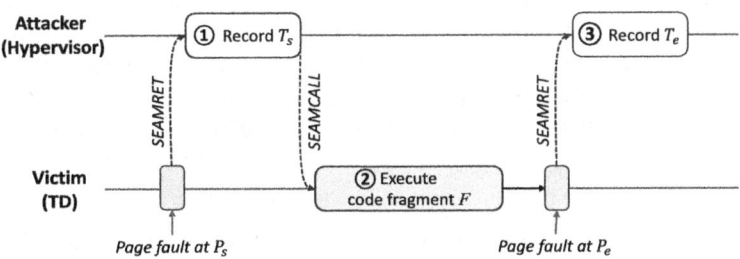

Fig. 3. Measuring dwell time between two successive page faults.

3.1 T-Time Attack

Figure 3 illustrates a T-Time attack. The attacker attempts to infer the execution time of a code path $\mathcal{F}$ (e.g., lines 5–10 in Fig. 2(b)). The attacker chooses two target pages, P_s and P_e, such that a page fault occurs at P_s immediately before the execution of $\mathcal{F}$ (e.g., line 1 in Fig. 2(b)), and another page fault occurs at P_e immediately after the execution of $\mathcal{F}$ (e.g., line 13 in Fig. 2(b)). By measuring the dwell time $T_{s \to e}$, the attacker can infer the execution time of $\mathcal{F}$.

As an initialization step, the attacker clears the present bits of pages P_s and P_e. When a victim begins executing code, the attack proceeds as follows. ① When a page fault occurs at P_s, the attacker's page fault handler is invoked by SEAMRET from the TDX module. The handler then records a timestamp T_s just before re-entering the victim TD via SEAMCALL. ② Upon re-entry, the victim continues to execute code including $\mathcal{F}$. ③ At the second fault at P_e, the attacker's handler records T_e immediately after regaining control and computes the dwell time as $T_{s \to e} = T_e - T_s$.

Precisely measuring dwell time serves as the primitive of the T-Time attack. However, implementing the attack poses two main challenges. The first challenge involves monitoring the victim's execution flow at the page level. Traditional controlled-channel attacks exploit an attacker's high privilege to manipulate the present bit in the page table entry. However, Intel TDX strictly prohibits such manipulation, even for attackers with hypervisor privileges. To address this, we employ a method introduced by Aktas et al. [1], leveraging the TDH.MEM.RANGE.BLOCK API. This API temporarily blocks victim access to targeted memory pages by clearing their present bits. When the victim accesses a blocked page, an extended page table (EPT) violation triggers a VM exit, transferring control to the hypervisor along with the faulting address. The hypervisor can then identify the accessed pages and subsequently unblock them, enabling continuous and non-destructive monitoring of the victim's execution flow.

The second challenge is obtaining highly precise timing information from the TD. To accomplish this, we instrument the KVM hypervisor to capture timestamps immediately before and after interactions with the TD. We record the timestamp counter immediately before invoking SEAMCALL, which transfers control from the hypervisor to the TD. We record it again immediately after SEAMRET, when control returns from the TDX module back to the hypervisor. We record the timestamp counter immediately before invoking SEAMCALL, which transfers control from the hypervisor to the TD. This method ensures accurate measurement of dwell time, facilitating reliable differentiation between distinct execution paths.

3.2 Timing Amplification Using Cache Flush Technique

We introduce a novel cache-based timing amplification technique designed to enhance the distinguishability of subtle timing variations. The key idea is to flush specific cache lines within the target code fragment $\mathcal{F}$ and subsequently measure their dwell time, thus amplifying subtle timing discrepancies. Leveraging this method, the T-Time attack can reliably differentiate secret-dependent control flows that would otherwise appear indistinguishable.

In Intel TDX environments, however, flushing cache lines poses significant challenges. Specifically, memory requests are encrypted and tagged with unique KeyIDs, preventing attackers from directly flushing the target cache lines associated with the victim TD's KeyID. To circumvent this limitation, we adopt the aliased access approach [1]. This method exploits the cache coherence protocol, where memory requests issued with a different KeyID (aliased access) cause existing cache lines associated with the victim's KeyID to be evicted and replaced by data corresponding to the new KeyID. By utilizing aliased access, we achieve an indirect yet effective cache line flush.

Our technique involves the following two steps. ① The attacker flushes a target cache line by performing an aliased access. ② Then, the attacker measures the dwell time of the victim on the target page.

3.3 Performance Evaluation

We performed experiments to evaluate the effectiveness of the T-Time attack. The experiments were conducted on an Intel Xeon Silver 4510T processor with KVM as the hypervisor. The host ran Ubuntu 24.10 (kernel 6.11.0) and Intel TDX 1.5.0.6, while the guest VM operated on Ubuntu 24.04 LTS (kernel 6.8.0-36-generic). To ensure precise timing measurements, we disabled DVFS, C-states, hardware prefetching, and reserved a dedicated physical core for the VM.

```
if (secret)
{
    asm (".rept M"
        "imul %r12, %r13"    // Repeat M times if secret is true.
        ".endr" );
}
else
{
    asm (".rept N"
        "imul %r12, %r13"    // Repeat N times if secret is false.
        ".endr");
}
```

Listing 1: An example of secret-dependent code.

We evaluate the precision of dwell time measurements using T-Time. For this evaluation, we use a code snippet containing conditional branches within a single 4 KB memory page, where execution paths depend on a secret value (see Listing 1). When the secret is true, the code executes the imul r64, r64 instruction M times; otherwise, it executes N times. We measured dwell times over 1,000,000 iterations for the else path, varying N between 20 and 100, while fixing $M = 10$ for the if path. We denote T_n as the average dwell time when the imul instruction executes n times in the secret-dependent path.

We use two metrics for this comparison: the dwell time difference Δ_n and the Fisher score F_n, defined as:

$$\Delta_n = T_n - T_{10}, \ F_n = \frac{(T_n - T_{10})^2}{\sigma_n^2 + \sigma_{10}^2}.$$

Table 1 presents the average dwell times and corresponding Fisher scores between the two execution paths. A Fisher score F_n below 1 indicates that the measured dwell time does not provide sufficient power to distinguish between the execution paths reliably.

To verify the effectiveness of our cache-based timing amplification technique, we compared it against a baseline T-Time attack without amplification. Without amplification, timing differences become noticeable at Δ_{60}, indicating that secret-dependent behavior becomes distinguishable starting at $n = 60$. At this

Table 1. Average dwell time difference (Δ) and Fisher score (F) of the attack.

		20	30	40	50	60	70	80	90	100
T-Time	Delta (Δ_n)	3.20	30.09	30.14	16.64	49.72	82.09	113.45	122.29	161.23
	F-score (F_n)	0.00	0.32	0.31	0.09	0.95	2.19	4.36	4.38	8.14
T-Time (amp)	Delta (Δ_n)	240.36	301.61	276.19	296.60	405.68	416.39	428.92	455.60	497.02
	F-score (F_n)	17.06	19.95	25.87	23.98	55.06	55.03	60.39	63.24	78.06

point, the Fisher score reaches $F_{60} = 0.95$, confirming the reliability of the T-Time attack primitive. When employing our amplification technique, we flush the target cache line (lines 9–11) from the cache hierarchy. With amplification, the dwell time difference at Δ_{20} markedly increases from the baseline 3.20 to 240.36. Correspondingly, the Fisher score improves significantly to $F_{20} = 17.06$, highlighting that the amplification substantially enhances the distinction between execution paths. Thus, cache-based amplification dramatically improves the capability of T-Time, particularly in cases where timing differences would otherwise be too subtle to detect.

4 T-Time Attack on MbedTLS RSA

We demonstrate T-Time attack that recovers complete 4096-bit RSA private keys from multiple traces of the MbedTLS (v3.5.2) signature routine, which is implemented using non-constant time algorithms.

4.1 Signature Process of MbedTLS

MbedTLS [18] implements RSA modular exponentiation through a windowed square-and-multiply method within the function `mbedtls_mpi_exp_mod()`. Since prior work has shown that side-channel attacks against the square-and-multiply algorithm with a window size of 1 can be generalized to arbitrary window sizes [20], our attack similarly targets the setting with a fixed window size of 1 [5,6,19,27].

Listing 2 simplifies `mbedtls_mpi_exp_mod()` function[1]. with setting of window size of 1. The function, which resides on a page P_e, executes modular exponentiation by conditionally branching based on each bit (e_i) of the exponent, resulting in distinct page access sequences. Specifically, when the exponent bit e_i is 0, the function calls `mpi_select()` on page P_s and `mpi_montmul()` on page P_m exactly once, resulting in accesses to two pages in total. Here, `mpi_montmul()` performs a square operation. In contrast, when e_i is 1, each of these functions is called twice, resulting in accesses to four pages. In this case, `mpi_montmul()` executes a square operation and an additional multiply operation.

---

[1] The full source code is available at https://github.com/Mbed-TLS/mbedtls/blob/v3.5.2/library/bignum.c.

```
1  /* mbedtls_mpi_exp_mod(), mpi_select(), and mpi_montmul() are
      located
2     on a page Pe, Ps, Pm respectively. */
3
4  int mbedtls_mpi_exp_mod () {
5      for (int i = 0; i < bit_length; i++) {
6          if (e[i] == 0) {
7              mpi_select();                    /* Page fault at Ps */
8              // Return from mpi_select()      /* Page fault at Pe */
9              mpi_montmul();                   /* Page fault at Pm */
10             // Return from mpi_montmul()     /* Page fault at Pe */
11         } else {
12             mpi_select();                    /* Page fault at Ps */
13             // Return from mpi_select()      /* Page fault at Pe */
14             mpi_montmul();                   /* Page fault at Pm */
15             // Return from mpi_montmul()     /* Page fault at Pe */
16             mpi_select();                    /* Page fault at Ps */
17             // Return from mpi_select()      /* Page fault at Pe */
18             mpi_montmul();                   /* Page fault at Pm */
19             // Return from mpi_montmul()     /* Page fault at Pe */
20         }
21     }
22 }
```

Listing 2: Simplified version of mbedtls_mpi_exp_mod().

Although these functions reside on separate memory pages, traditional controlled-channel attacks have difficulty precisely reconstructing these call sequences. This difficulty arises because different combinations of exponent bits can lead to identical page access patterns. For example, a page fault sequence such as $P_s \to P_m \to P_s \to P_m$ could correspond either to a single exponent bit being 1 ($e_i = 1$) or to two consecutive exponent bits both being 0 ($e_i = 0$, $e_{i+1} = 0$). This ambiguity makes it challenging for traditional attacks to accurately infer secret-dependent execution flows.

4.2 Recovery of RSA Private Keys Using T-Time

The idea underlying our attack is to exploit the fact that mbedtls_mpi_exp_mod() takes secret-dependent control paths that occupy different cache lines. Although the page fault sequences generated by each control path do not show distinct patterns, we can make their dwell times distinguishable by applying our cache-based timing amplification technique presented in Sect. 3.2.

As shown in Table 2, mbedtls_mpi_exp_mod() executes different control paths depending on the exponent bits e_i, with each control path residing at distinct memory addresses. For example, when $e_i = 0$, the control path executes code (lines 7–10 in Listing 2), located at address range 0x25a24 $\sim$ 0x25a6f, whereas when $e_i = 1$, it executes code (lines 12–19 in Listing 2) at 0x25b69 $\sim$ 0x25bc1.

This observation yields two critical insights. First, the page fault sequences triggered by distinct exponent bit occur at different execution code. Second, these execution codes reside on separate cache lines.

Leveraging these characteristics, our cache-based timing amplification technique specifically targets the cache lines associated with the execution path for $e_i = 1$, effectively amplifying its dwell time. As a result, the eight dwell time measurements for $e_i = 1$ (i.e., $T_{s \to e}, T_{e \to m}, T_{m \to e}, \ldots$ listed in Table 2) become significantly larger than those measured when $e_i = 0$. Exploiting this distinct timing difference forms the core principle underlying our attack.

Table 2. The control structure of mbedtls_mpi_exp_mod() (v3.5.2)

Control path	Virtual address	Page fault sequence	Dwell time measurements
$e_i = 0$	0x25a24 $\sim$ 0x25a6f	P_s, P_e, P_m, P_e	$T_{s \to e}, T_{e \to m}, T_{m \to e}, T_{e \to s}$
$e_i = 1$	0x25b69 $\sim$ 0x25bc1	$P_s, P_e, P_m, P_e, P_s, P_e, P_m, P_e$	$T_{s \to e}, T_{e \to m}, T_{m \to e}, T_{e \to s},$ $T_{s \to e}, T_{e \to m}, T_{m \to e}, T_{e \to s}$

Threat Model. We assume a privileged attacker with full access to the operating system, who is capable of inferring guest physical addresses through legacy controlled-channel attacks. The attacker is aware that the victim is running the default MbedTLS library (version 3.5.2) inside a TDX-protected VM. Leveraging this knowledge, the attacker determines in advance target code pages ($P_s, P_m,$ and P_e) whose access patterns make them vulnerable to the T-Time attack. The attacker aims to extract the RSA private key from a victim process executing within the TDX-protected environment on the same host system.

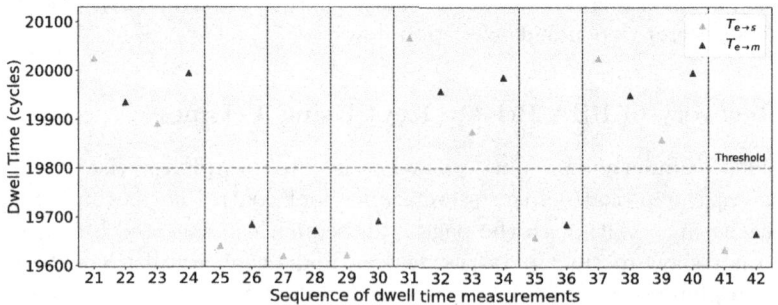

Fig. 4. Trace for exponent bits of RSA private keys.

Attack Process. The attacker aims to extract the victim's RSA private key during RSA signing operations. Specifically, the attacker targets three pages,

P_s, P_m, and P_e, to measure dwell times, applying the cache-based amplification technique to the execution path corresponding to the exponent bit $e_i = 1$, as detailed in Table 2. A sequence of eight consecutive dwell times (i.e., $T_{s \to e}, T_{e \to m}, T_{m \to e}, \ldots, T_{e \to s}$) exhibiting notably high cycle counts indicates that the corresponding exponent bit e_i is 1.

Figure 4 illustrates an example of the dwell time traces obtained from these measurements. For simplicity and clarity, the figure includes only $T_{e \to s}$ and $T_{e \to m}$, which are sufficient for accurately reconstructing the private keys. Sequence numbers 21 through 24 exhibit notably high dwell times, highlighted in red in Fig. 4, indicating that the execution path corresponding to $e_i = 1$ was taken. These high dwell times result from cache misses at the memory addresses associated with this execution path, induced by our amplification technique. Conversely, sequence numbers 25 and 26, highlighted in blue, show significantly lower dwell times due to cache hits, indicating that the execution path for $e_i = 0$ was taken. Based on this distinction, the collected trace allows us to infer the exponent bits as 10001010.

Evaluation. We evaluate our attack on an Intel Xeon Silver 4510T CPU, with the host system running Ubuntu 24.10 and Intel TDX Module version 1.5.0.6, and the guest VM running Ubuntu 24.04 LTS. To mitigate measurement noise, we collect 20 RSA signing traces using the same private key and calculate the average dwell time for each transition. Our attack successfully recovers the complete RSA private key without any bit errors by combining only 20 traces, completing the reconstruction in under 25 s.

5 T-Time Attack on Libwebp

5.1 WebP Image Format and Decoding Process in Libwebp

WebP [7] is a modern image compression format developed by Google, supporting both lossy and lossless compression modes. The lossy mode of WebP uses techniques similar to those used in video encoding, specifically from Google's VP8 video codec [2]. In simple terms, a WebP image is divided into small blocks (16 × 16 pixels), known as macroblocks, which are compressed and later reconstructed during decoding. Each macroblock is further divided into sixteen 4×4 sub-blocks, which serve as the basic units for transformation and coefficient encoding.

Macroblocks encode image information in terms of basic brightness (DC coefficients) and finer details like edges and textures (AC coefficients). WebP uses a method called YUV 4:2:0, where brightness information (luminance or Y) is stored in greater detail than color information (chrominance or U and V), since the human eye is more sensitive to brightness than color details. In this format, all three components (Y, U, V) are encoded using both DC and AC coefficients.

Listing 3 simplifies the decoding process for a single macroblock[2]. During decoding, `ParseResiduals()` in libwebp is responsible for decoding and

---

[2] The full source code is available at https://github.com/webmproject/libwebp/blob/v1.5.0/src/dec/vp8_dec.c.

```
 1  int ParseResiduals() {
 2      if (!is_i4x4_) {
 3          GetCoeffs();                        // Parse Y DC coefficients
 4      }
 5
 6      for (int y=0; y<4; y++) {
 7          for (int x=0; x<4; x++) {
 8              GetCoeffs();                    // Parse Y block coefficients
 9          }
10      }
11
12      for (int ch=0; ch<4; ch=ch+2) {         // U(0), V(2) channels
13          for (int y=0; y<2; y++) {
14              for (int x=0; x<2; x++) {
15                  GetCoeffs();                // Parse U/V block coefficients
16              }
17          }
18      }
19  }
```

Listing 3: Simplified version of `ParseResiduals()`.

reconstructing the macroblock coefficients. As part of the decoding routine, `GetCoeffs()` is repeatedly invoked to extract the transform coefficients from each sub-block. The decoding sequence within this function follows three primary stages. First, if the macroblock is not encoded in a 4 × 4 intra-prediction mode (i.e., `is_i4x4_` is false), `GetCoeffs()` is called once to decode the DC coefficients for the luminance (Y) component. The DC coefficient for the Y component is shared across the macroblock's sixteen 4 × 4 sub-blocks.

In the second stage, the function processes detailed luminance information by iterating over each of the sixteen 4 × 4 sub-blocks within the macroblock. If the macroblock is not encoded in 4 × 4 intra-prediction mode (i.e., `is_i4x4_` is false), `GetCoeffs()` is invoked to recover only the AC coefficients for each sub-block. In contrast, if the macroblock is encoded in 4 × 4 intra-prediction mode (`is_i4x4_` is true), `GetCoeffs()` is called to decode both DC and AC coefficients for each sub-block.

Finally, the function decodes chrominance details (color information) for the U and V channels. Because WebP utilizes YUV 4:2:0 subsampling, chrominance decoding occurs over four 4 × 4 sub-blocks (two for U and two for V). For each chroma block, `GetCoeffs()` is invoked to decode both DC and AC coefficients. In total, `GetCoeffs()` is called 24 times per macroblock: 16 times for Y, and 4 times each for U and V.

5.2 Inferring Image Pixels with T-Time

The fundamental idea behind attacking the WebP decoding process is exploiting differences in execution time within the `GetCoeffs()` function. Specifically,

GetCoeffs() exhibits varying execution times depending on the presence of coefficients in the current block. By measuring these dwell times with a T-Time attack, an attacker can infer the presence or absence of coefficients. High dwell time indicates the presence of more coefficients, which reflects higher visual complexity in the corresponding image block. By repeatedly measuring the dwell times across all 24 invocations of GetCoeffs() per macroblock—16 for luminance and 8 for chrominance—an attacker can recover the coefficient activity pattern across the block. Ultimately, this extracted information enables the reconstruction of structural features of the underlying image, such as edges, contours, and textured regions, without requiring access to actual pixel values.

It is noteworthy that traditional controlled-channel attacks cannot reconstruct the WebP image, as the implementation of libwebp, including the GetCoeffs() function, has no distinguishable patterns at page-level granularity.

Threat Model. The attacker aims to reconstruct a WebP image during its decoding by a victim process (e.g., a web browser) running inside an Intel TDX-protected virtual machine, which is hosted on a system under the attacker's control. The attacker is aware that the victim employs an unmodified, up-to-date libwebp library (e.g., version 1.5.0). By leveraging page tracking techniques, the attacker can determine guest physical addresses of the libwebp library, enabling precise observation of the decoding execution.

Attack Process. The attacker aims to infer the execution time of the GetCoeffs() function by targeting two pages of the libwebp library, P_p and P_g, which contain ParseResiduals() and GetCoeffs(), respectively. By measuring the dwell time $T_{g \to p}$, the time interval between a page fault at P_g (triggered by the invocation of GetCoeffs()) and a subsequent fault at P_p (caused by the return to ParseResiduals()), the attacker can successfully infer its execution time.

When a victim starts image decoding (by browsing an image on a web page), the trace of the dwell times begins. Since one call to ParseResiduals() causes a total of 24 subsequent calls to GetCoeffs() for decoding coefficients, the trace for each macroblock B results in a sequence $C = \{c_i\}_{(0 \leq i < 24)}$, where each c_i represents the execution cycles of a corresponding GetCoeffs() invocation. A higher cycle count of c_i indicates the presence of a coefficient in i-th call of GetCoeffs(), whereas lower counts do not. This provides 24 bits of information about a single macroblock in the image, enough for reconstructing the image's structural content.

For example, Fig. 5 shows the obtained trace for two vertically aligned macroblocks B_1 and B_2. The trace for each macroblock begins with a sharp execution time peak corresponding to the ParseResiduals() function, allowing an attacker to infer macroblock boundaries, followed by a sequence of GetCoeffs() measurements. The number of observed GetCoeffs() executions is different for these two macroblocks, 25 for B_1 and 24 for B_2, due to the different control paths in decoding the DC coefficients. That is, B_1 contains an additional call to GetCoeffs() because it has to decode DC coefficients (i.e., is_4x4 is true in Listing 3).

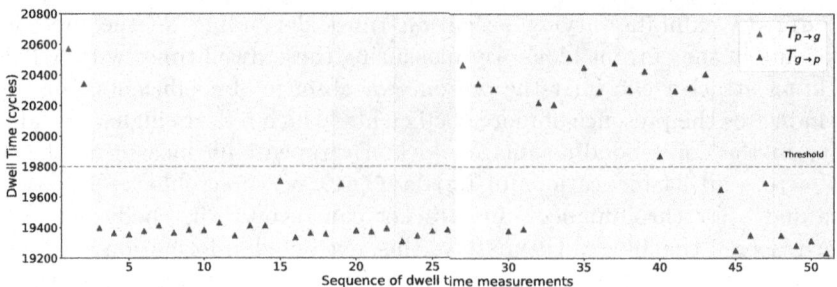

Fig. 5. Attack results.

The first sequence (page fault sequence numbers 1–26) corresponds to the decoding of the first macroblock B_1, which contains both DC and AC coefficients. Specifically, page fault sequence number 1 involves the starting of macroblock decoding. Number 2 involves the decoding of DC coefficients, and numbers 3–18 mark the transition to the AC decoding routine. Numbers 19–22 and 23–26 cover the chroma U and V channels, respectively. The second sequence (page fault sequence numbers 27–51) corresponds to those of B_2, which can be analyzed in the same way except for decoding the DC and AC coefficients. Table 3 shows the obtained information of the coefficients for B_1 and B_2, from which the original image can be inferred.

Table 3. Traces of `GetCoeffFast()` dwell times for AC coefficients (H and L indicate high and low cycles, respectively.)

Macroblock	Y block	U block	V block
B_1	L L L L L L L L L L L L L L L L	L L L L	L L L L
B_2	H H L L H H H H H H H H H H H H	L L L L	L L L L

Evaluation. We conducted our attack on an Intel Xeon Silver 4510T CPU, with the host system running Ubuntu 24.10 and Intel TDX Module version 1.5.0.6, and the guest VM running Ubuntu 24.04 LTS. To evaluate the effectiveness of the proposed T-Time attack, we assembled a test set comprising various images obtained from publicly available sources. The dataset includes complex, high-resolution photographs. For each image, we collected a single trace comprising a page fault sequence and corresponding dwell times, revealing the memory access behavior during the decoding process. These traces were subsequently analyzed using a custom reconstruction tool to produce visual approximations of the original images in PNG format. Figure 6 presents three representative examples of reconstructed images, each derived from a single decoding trace. Figure 6(a) shows an image reconstructed by inferring only the coefficients of the luminance (Y) channel. Figure 6(b) demonstrates improved reconstruction quality achieved by incorporating coefficients from all Y, U, and V channels.

Original   Recovered

(a) Recovered using Y (luma) channel

(b) Recovered using YUV channels

Fig. 6. Trace for two consecutive macroblocks (Grey, blue, and red box indicate decoding phase of Y, U, and V blocks, respectively). (Color figure online)

6 Mitigation

In this section, we propose several mitigation strategies to defend against the T-Time attack.

Constant-Time Algorithms. Since T-Time exploits timing variations, a crucial mitigation involves eliminating timing discrepancies between secret-dependent execution paths. Developers should therefore employ constant-time algorithms [13,14,22] to ensure security-sensitive code executes in a uniform manner, independent of secret values. Achieving constant-time execution involves techniques such as aligning sensitive code within the same cache line and standardizing execution durations across secret-dependent control paths.

Enhancing Intel TDX Security. We propose additional mitigations specifically tailored for Intel TDX environments. First, the TDX module could monitor for abnormal patterns of repeated page faults within the same memory region. By restricting the invocation of the TDH.MEM.RANGE.BLOCK API in these identified regions, the module can effectively reduce the feasibility of frequent page faults used in T-Time. Second, we suggest disabling the timestamp counter while a TD is actively running on a physical core. As T-Time relies heavily on precise timestamp measurements to distinguish secret-dependent execution paths, disabling the timestamp counter upon TD entry and re-enabling it on TD exit can significantly mitigate the attack's effectiveness.

Introducing AEX-Notify on Intel TDX. Constable et al. [3] proposed AEX-Notify, a hardware-software co-designed mitigation technique that defends against interrupt-based side-channel attacks [21,25,31] targeting SGX enclaves. The key idea of AEX-Notify is to make enclaves aware of interrupt events, enabling them to distinguish between normal and adversarial context switches, thereby reducing information leakage through side-channels. Based on this, a similar mechanism, TDExit-Notify [24], has been discussed for Intel TDX. TDExit-Notify allows a TD to detect interrupt events, thereby mitigating attacks like T-Time. Furthermore, with TDExit-Notify support, TLBlur [33]—a compiler-assisted mitigation technique originally developed to protect SGX enclaves from controlled-channel attacks—can be extended to support Intel TDX environments with minimal modification.

7 Related Work

Controlled-Channel Attack. Xu et al. [37] first introduced controlled-channel attacks by exploiting the page-fault side channel in Intel SGX. Subsequent studies [32,34] improved their work by developing stealthier methods to infer enclave memory access patterns without explicitly inducing page faults. Additionally, numerous studies [6,15–17,23,35,36,38] have demonstrated the feasibility of controlled-channel attacks across various TEE platforms, such as AMD SEV and Intel TDX.

In line with our research, Wang et al. [34] introduced the T-SPM attack, a timing-based page-fault side-channel attack against SGX enclaves. Our work differs fundamentally from T-SPM in three critical aspects. First, T-Time explores the applicability of timing-based attacks specifically within the Intel TDX environment rather than SGX. Second, T-SPM can only measure coarse-grained timing differences and thereby struggles to distinguish between execution paths with closely similar runtimes. In contrast, T-Time leverages cache line flushing to amplify subtle timing differences, allowing it to reliably differentiate between such execution paths. Third, our evaluation of T-Time focuses on contemporary implementations of MbedTLS and WebP, where secret-dependent control flows are confined within single memory pages. Despite this defensive strategy effectively mitigating traditional coarse-grained attacks, our findings demonstrate that T-Time can still reliably extract security-sensitive information through fine-grained timing analysis.

Side-Channel Attacks on CVM. Recent research has extensively explored various attacks targeting CVMs. Heckler [26] introduces malicious interrupt injection techniques that manipulate the register states of CVMs. This method enables attackers to alter both data and control flow within applications. Consequently, it effectively bypasses security mechanisms in Intel TDX-protected environments.

Another work, TDXdown [35], addresses vulnerabilities associated with single-stepping mitigations implemented in Intel TDX. It leverages observable instruction execution counts within a TD. This technique successfully performs nonce truncation attacks. It effectively extracts ECDSA private keys from widely-used cryptographic libraries, including wolfSSL and OpenSSL.

Additionally, CounterSEVeillance [6] exploits performance counters to target RSA signature implementations in MbedTLS version 3.5.2 running on AMD SEV platforms. This attack demonstrates the feasibility of extracting a full 4096-bit RSA private key from a single execution trace within eight minutes. However, this attack is ineffective in Intel TDX environments since these platforms disable performance counters by default. In contrast, our proposed attack successfully recovers the same private key within only 30 s. This significantly enhances the practicality and speed of timing-based attacks on Intel TDX.

8 Conclusion

In this paper, we introduced T-Time, a fine-grained timing-based controlled-channel attack on Intel TDX. T-Time measures dwell time within memory pages to bypass existing defenses. To enhance its precision, we also introduced a cache-based amplification technique that magnifies subtle timing variations, enabling the attacker to distinguish sensitive control flows even when confined to a single memory page. In two case studies, we recovered a 4096-bit RSA private key from MbedTLS with only 20 signatures and reconstructed image content from libwebp via fine-grained dwell time analysis. These results underscore the limitations of current page-level defenses against such attacks. Finally, we proposed potential mitigation strategies to harden Intel TDX against such threats.

Acknowledgement. This research was supported by a National Research Foundation of Korea (NRF) grant, funded by the Korean government (MSIT) (RS-2023-NR077166, RS-2025-00563143, RS-2021-NR060143, RS-2023-00227165). This research was supported by the Korea University Grant. This work was supported by NSF CAREER Award CCF-2146475.

References

1. Aktas, E., Cohen, C., Eads, J., Forshaw, J., Wilhelm, F.: Intel trust domain extensions (TDX) security review. Google security review (2023)
2. Bankoski, J., Wilkins, P., Xu, Y.: Technical overview of VP8, an open source video codec for the web. In: 2011 IEEE International Conference on Multimedia and Expo, pp. 1–6. IEEE (2011)
3. Constable, S., et al.: AEX-notify: thwarting precise single-stepping attacks through interrupt awareness for intel SGX enclaves. In: 32nd USENIX Security Symposium (USENIX Security 23), pp. 4051–4068 (2023)
4. Costan, V., Devadas, S.: Intel SGX explained. Cryptology ePrint Archive (2016)
5. Gast, S., et al.: SQUIP: exploiting the scheduler queue contention side channel. In: 2023 IEEE Symposium on Security and Privacy (SP), pp. 2256–2272 (2023)

6. Gast, S., Weissteiner, H., Schröder, R.L., Gruss, D.: CounterSEVeillance: Performance-counter attacks on AMD SEV-SNP. In: Network and Distributed System Security Symposium 2025: NDSS 2025 (2025)
7. Google: An image format for the web (2025). https://developers.google.com/speed/webp
8. Huo, T., et al.: Bluethunder: A 2-level directional predictor based side-channel attack against SGX. IACR Trans. Cryptogr. Hardw. Embed. Syst. 321–347 (2020)
9. Intel: Intel® 64 and IA-32 architectures software developer manuals (2023). https://www.intel.com/content/www/us/en/developer/articles/technical/intel-sdm.html
10. Intel: Intel® architecture memory encryption technologies (2024). Revision 336907-005US
11. Intel: Intel trust domain extensions (intel TDX) modulebase architecture specification (2025). https://www.intel.com/content/www/us/en/products/docs/accelerator-engines/trust-domain-extensions.html. Revision 348549-005US
12. Intel: Intel® trust domain extensions(intel®tdx) (2025). https://www.intel.com/content/www/us/en/products/docs/accelerator-engines/trust-domain-extensions.html
13. Kocher, P.C.: Timing attacks on implementations of Diffie-Hellman, RSA, DSS, and other systems. In: Koblitz, N. (ed.) CRYPTO 1996. LNCS, vol. 1109, pp. 104–113. Springer, Heidelberg (1996). https://doi.org/10.1007/3-540-68697-5_9
14. Langley, A., Hamburg, M., Turner, S.: RFC 7748: elliptic curves for security (2016)
15. Li, M., Wilke, L., Wichelmann, J., Eisenbarth, T., Teodorescu, R., Zhang, Y.: A systematic look at ciphertext side channels ON AMD SEV-SNP. In: 2022 IEEE Symposium on Security and Privacy (SP), pp. 337–351 (2022)
16. Li, M., Zhang, Y., Lin, Z.: Crossline: breaking "security-by-crash" based memory isolation in AMD SEV. In: Proceedings of the 2021 ACM SIGSAC Conference on Computer and Communications Security, pp. 2937–2950 (2021)
17. Li, M., Zhang, Y., Lin, Z., Solihin, Y.: Exploiting unprotected I/O operations in AMD's secure encrypted virtualization. In: 28th USENIX Security Symposium (USENIX Security 2019), pp. 1257–1272 (2019)
18. Linaro: Mbedtls (2025). https://www.trustedfirmware.org/projects/mbed-tls/
19. Lipp, M., et al.: Platypus: software-based power side-channel attacks on x86. In: IEEE SP, pp. 355–371 (2021)
20. Liu, F., Yarom, Y., Ge, Q., Heiser, G., Lee, R.B.: Last-level cache side-channel attacks are practical. In: 2015 IEEE Symposium on Security and Privacy, pp. 605–622 (2015)
21. Moghimi, D., Van Bulck, J., Heninger, N., Piessens, F., Sunar, B.: CopyCat: controlled instruction-level attacks on enclaves. In: 29th USENIX Security Symposium (USENIX Security 2020), pp. 469–486 (2020)
22. Molnar, D., Piotrowski, M., Schultz, D., Wagner, D.: The program counter security model: automatic detection and removal of control-flow side channel attacks. In: Won, D.H., Kim, S. (eds.) ICISC 2005. LNCS, vol. 3935, pp. 156–168. Springer, Heidelberg (2006). https://doi.org/10.1007/11734727_14
23. Morbitzer, M., Huber, M., Horsch, J., Wessel, S.: Severed: subverting AMD's virtual machine encryption. In: Proceedings of the 11th European Workshop on Systems Security, pp. 1–6 (2018)
24. PradyumnaShome: Closing the intel TDX page fault side channel, or, the case for tdexit-notify (2024). https://collective.flashbots.net/t/closing-the-intel-tdx-page-fault-side-channel-or-the-case-for-tdexit-notify/3775

25. Puddu, I., Schneider, M., Haller, M., Čapkun, S.: Frontal attack: leaking control-flow in SGX via the CPU frontend. In: 30th USENIX Security Symposium (USENIX Security 2021), pp. 663–680 (2021)
26. Schlüter, B., Sridhara, S., Kuhne, M., Bertschi, A., Shinde, S.: Heckler: breaking confidential VMs with malicious interrupts. In: 33rd USENIX Security Symposium (USENIX Security 24), pp. 3459–3476 (2024)
27. Schwarz, M., Weiser, S., Gruss, D., Maurice, C., Mangard, S.: Malware guard extension: using SGX to conceal cache attacks. In: Polychronakis, M., Meier, M. (eds.) DIMVA 2017. LNCS, vol. 10327, pp. 3–24. Springer, Cham (2017). https://doi.org/10.1007/978-3-319-60876-1_1
28. Sev-Snp, A.: Strengthening vm isolation with integrity protection and more. White Pap. January **53**(2020), 1450–1465 (2020)
29. Sieck, F., Zhang, Z., Berndt, S., Chuengsatiansup, C., Eisenbarth, T., Yarom, Y.: TeeJam: sub-cache-line leakages strike back. IACR Trans. Cryptogr. Hardw. Embed. Syst. **2024**(1), 457–500 (2024)
30. Van Bulck, J., Piessens, F., Strackx, R.: SGX-step: a practical attack framework for precise enclave execution control. In: SysTEX, pp. 1–6 (2017)
31. Van Bulck, J., Piessens, F., Strackx, R.: Nemesis: studying microarchitectural timing leaks in rudimentary CPU interrupt logic. In: Proceedings of the 2018 ACM SIGSAC Conference on Computer and Communications Security, pp. 178–195 (2018)
32. Van Bulck, J., Weichbrodt, N., Kapitza, R., Piessens, F., Strackx, R.: Telling your secrets without page faults: stealthy page table-based attacks on enclaved execution. In: 26th USENIX Security Symposium (USENIX Security 2017), pp. 1041–1056 (2017)
33. Vanoverloop, D., Sanchez, A., Toffalini, F., Piessens, F., Payer, M., Van Bulck, J.: TLBlur: compiler-assisted automated hardening against controlled channels on off-the-shelf intel SGX platforms. In: USENIX Security (2025)
34. Wang, W., et al.: Leaky cauldron on the dark land: understanding memory side-channel hazards in SGX. In: Proceedings of the 2017 ACM SIGSAC Conference on Computer and Communications Security, pp. 2421–2434 (2017)
35. Wilke, L., Sieck, F., Eisenbarth, T.: TDXdown: single-stepping and instruction counting attacks against intel TDX. In: Proceedings of the 2024 on ACM SIGSAC Conference on Computer and Communications Security, pp. 79–93 (2024)
36. Wilke, L., Wichelmann, J., Rabich, A., Eisenbarth, T.: SEV-step a single-stepping framework for AMD-SEV. IACR Trans. Cryptogr. Hardw. Embed. Syst. 180–206 (2024)
37. Xu, Y., Cui, W., Peinado, M.: Controlled-channel attacks: deterministic side channels for untrusted operating systems. In: 2015 IEEE Symposium on Security and Privacy, pp. 640–656 (2015)
38. Zhang, R., et al.: CacheWarp: software-based fault injection using selective state reset. In: 33rd USENIX Security Symposium (USENIX Security 2024), pp. 1135–1151 (2024)
39. Zhang, Z., Tao, M., O'Connell, S., Chuengsatiansup, C., Genkin, D., Yarom, Y.: BunnyHop: exploiting the instruction prefetcher. In: USENIX Security, pp. 7321–7337 (2023)

Unraveling DoH Traces: Padding-Resilient Website Fingerprinting via HTTP/2 Key Frame Sequences

Baiyang Li[1,2], Yujia Zhu[1,2(✉)], Yuedong Zhang[3], Qingyun Liu[1,2], and Li Guo[1,2]

[1] Institute of Information Engineering, Chinese Academy of Sciences, Beijing, China
zhuyujia@iie.ac.cn
[2] School of Cyber Security, University of Chinese Academy of Sciences, Beijing, China
[3] National Computer Network Emergency Response Technical Team/Coordination of China, Beijing, China

Abstract. DNS-over-HTTPS (DoH) has been widely adopted by major web browsers to enhance the security and privacy of DNS transactions. To mitigate traffic analysis threats such as website fingerprinting (WFP) attacks, many DoH deployments apply EDNS(0) padding at both the client and resolver. As the padding strategy equalizes DNS data sizes, it diminishes the efficacy of previous WFP attacks that exploit TLS-layer length patterns. Moreover, TLS-level features fail to capture the application-layer behavior of HTTP/2, which underlies DoH communication.

In this paper, we propose a novel WFP method for DoH that operates at the application layer. Our approach extracts the sequence of HTTP/2 key frames that encapsulate DNS queries and responses, and then derives time interval features that remain informative even in the presence of padding. Experimental results show that our approach achieves over 87% accuracy in the same-environment settings and maintains robustness across different resolver implementations and operating systems settings. Compared to existing WFP techniques, our method improves accuracy by at least 6% in same-environment tests and 19% in cross-environment scenarios. In addition, we conduct an Internet-scale measurement of 6,617 public DoH resolvers and uncover widespread deficiencies in padding adoption, which exacerbate fingerprint leakage. Based on these findings, we propose practical countermeasures to further strengthen DoH privacy.

Keywords: DNS-over-HTTPS · Website Fingerprinting · HTTP/2 Frames · EDNS(0) Padding

1 Introduction

Encrypted DNS protocols, including DNS-over-TLS, DNS-over-HTTPS, and DNS-over-QUIC, employ TLS encryption to ensure the confidentiality and integrity of DNS transactions, and have been standardized and widely deployed to enhance user privacy and security. Among these protocols, DNS-over-HTTPS (DoH) has achieved particularly broad integration within major web browsers [2,4,7], largely due to its seamless compatibility with the existing HTTP networking stack [3].

However, similar to other encrypted channels such as HTTPS [12,15] and anonymity systems such as Tor [26,27,29,31], DoH remains susceptible to traffic analysis attacks, most notably website fingerprinting (WFP). To mitigate WFP threats, RFC 8467 recommends padding DNS queries to 128-byte boundaries and responses to 468-byte boundaries [24]. Modern browsers (e.g., Chrome since version 83 and Firefox since version 95 [8,20]) and public resolvers such as Google and Cloudflare have implemented EDNS(0) padding. As a result, existing DoH WFP methods that rely on TLS-length patterns [19,25,30] have become substantially less effective. While a prior study achieved moderate success in analyzing DoT traffic with padding [11], similar methods applied in the DoH setting, such as Segram [25], showed limited effectiveness.

Our investigation further reveals that the previous work typically leverages features solely from the transport layer, without reconstructing the application data unit (ADU) exchanged over HTTP/2, which serves as the underlying transport for DoH. As illustrated in Fig. 1, reliance on Internet layer information such as server IP address and Server Name Indication (SNI) is not well-suited for DoH WFP, since the adversary's view is limited to a single destination IP corresponding to the DoH resolver. Transport-layer features derived from TLS are coarse-grained. Because HTTP/2 multiplexes data frames and intermingles flow-control frame with payload-carrying data, transport-level observations alone cannot disambiguate flow-control overhead from actual DNS exchanges, resulting in unstable fingerprints. The lack of application-layer ADU visibility presents a fundamental challenge for reliable DoH website fingerprinting.

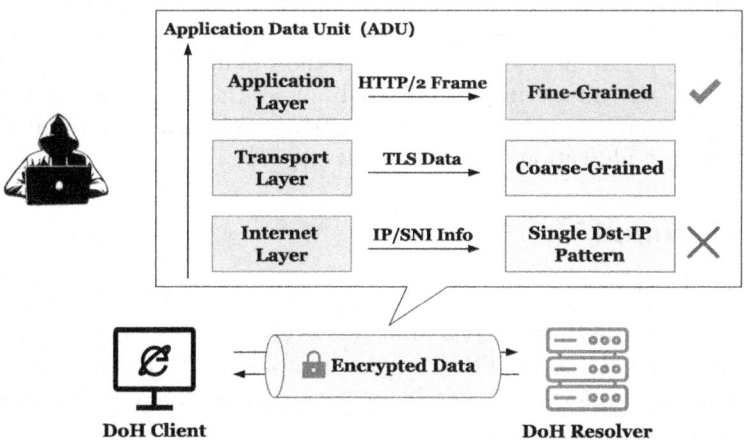

Fig. 1. Comparison of Observable Features Across Network Layers in DoH WFP.

To fill these research gaps in DoH WFP, we present a novel DoH WFP method that leverages sequences of HTTP/2 key frames—the application data units that carry DNS queries and responses. By extracting the time intervals between successive key frames carrying domain queries, our method achieves an accuracy of no less than 87% even in the presence of EDNS(0) padding, reflecting an enhancement of more than 6% compared to current state-of-the-art methods.

In summary, the main contributions of this paper are as follows:

- **A novel HTTP/2 key frame based WFP method for DoH traffic.** We present a two-stage side-channel approach that (a) infers HTTP/2 key frames carrying DNS queries and responses using an HTTP/2 protocol-aware state machine, and (b) eliminates redundant parallel queries through sequence segmentation algorithm using dynamic programming. This produces a compact, application-layer frame sequence that serves as a high-density DoH fingerprint without requiring decryption.
- **Comprehensive evaluation and cross-environment robustness analysis.** Through extensive experiments against six state-of-the-art WFP methods, our method achieves over 87% classification accuracy in controlled environment settings and exhibits the smallest degradation under cross-environment testing. These results highlight the robustness of our approach under real-world deployment variations.
- **Empirical insights and practical defense recommendations.** We conduct an Internet-scale measurement of 6,617 public DoH resolvers and uncover widespread deficiencies in EDNS(0) padding adoption that exacerbate fingerprint leakage. Based on these findings, we propose actionable countermeasures, including correct padding configurations, query scattering, and dummy-traffic injection, which help strengthen the privacy guarantees of DoH without compromising usability.

The remainder of this paper is organized as follows. Section 2 provides an overview of DoH protocol and introduces the threat model for DoH WFP attacks. Section 3 presents our approach for extracting key frame sequences from DoH traffic. Section 4 evaluates the proposed method under both same-environment and cross-environment settings. Section 5 discusses the limitations of our method and offers practical recommendations to mitigate WFP threats. Related work is reviewed in Sect. 6. Section 7 concludes the paper.

2 Background

2.1 DoH Protocol

To improve both performance and privacy, RFC 8484—the prevailing DoH specification– mandates HTTP/2 as the minimum HTTP version and incorporates padding support [16], thereby endowing the protocol with new features.

HTTP/2 Frame. HTTP/2 communication is organized into frames, which serve as the smallest application-layer units. As shown in Fig. 2, DNS messages are first encapsulated in HTTP/2 DATA frames and then encrypted within

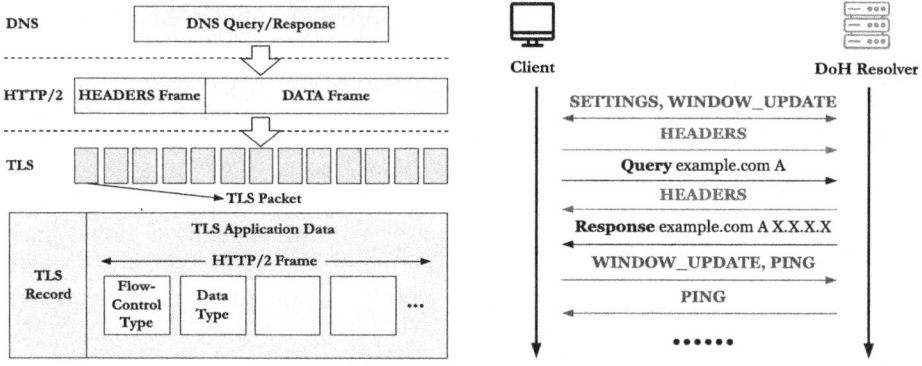

Fig. 2. HTTP/2 Frames in TLS Packets.   **Fig. 3.** DoH Transaction.

TLS packets. HTTP/2 frames can be categorized into flow-control types (e.g., SETTINGS frame, WINDOW_UPDATE frame, etc.) and data types (DATA frame). Only DATA frames consume space in the connection's flow-control window, whereas other frames incur no flow-control cost [32].

Figure 3 illustrates a typical DoH transaction. The client initiates the session with the mandatory connection preface, issues a SETTINGS frame to negotiate parameters and sends one or more WINDOW_UPDATE frames to configure flow-control limits. It then transmits HEADERS frames carrying HTTP metadata followed by DATA frames containing the DNS payload. The server completes its initialization by replying with its own SETTINGS frame; once both endpoints have exchanged SETTINGS, the server returns HEADERS and DATA frames, and bidirectional data transfer proceeds.

Most prior work has focused on transport-layer features, an approach limited in granularity because it overlooks the distinction of mixed data frames and flow-control frames in DoH traffic. Within this coarse-grained view, essential flow-control frames are indistinguishable from DNS payloads, acting as noise that destabilizes the resulting fingerprints. To overcome this, our method moves up the stack to analyze the HTTP/2 frame sequence. We treat each HTTP/2 frame as the fundamental application-layer data unit (ADU) and designate DATA frames that carry DNS queries or responses as **HTTP/2 key frames**, which provide a more precise representation of the DoH exchange, better reflecting the website's resource-loading behavior than transport-layer features.

EDNS(0) Padding. DoH clients and servers commonly implement EDNS(0) padding to mitigate traffic analysis attacks. RFC 8467 recommends a block-length padding scheme, where clients extend DNS queries to the next multiple of 128 bytes, and resolvers pad responses to the next multiple of 468 bytes for optimal obfuscation [24].

To assess real-world adoption, we evaluate DoH padding in three major browsers, Google Chrome, Microsoft Edge, and Mozilla Firefox (all version 120). We confirm that all three browsers follow the RFC's block-length approach for

DoH queries. On the resolver side, we examine padding behavior across public DoH resolvers by sending padded queries and analyzing the corresponding responses. Our measurements reveal four distinct resolver-side strategies:

- **RFC block-length Padding:** Responses are padded to an integer multiple of 468 bytes.
- **Fixed-length Padding:** A constant padding size is applied to every response. (e.g., matching the client's query padding or using a global fixed value.)
- **Random Padding:** The padding length varies unpredictably across responses, even for identical queries.
- **Absent Padding:** The resolver ignores client padding and returns responses at their original lengths.

Notably, fixed-length and absent padding preserve distinctive packet-length fingerprints, while block-length and random padding significantly reduce the effectiveness of packet-length fingerprinting techniques. Among large-scale public resolvers, Google (8.8.8.8) and Cloudflare (1.1.1.1) implement RFC block-length padding, AdGuard (94.140.14.140) employs random padding, ALi (223.5.5.5) has migrated from fixed-length to random padding, and Quad9 (9.9.9.9) does not apply any padding.

2.2 Threat Model

Attacker Model. We adopt a threat model consistent with prior encrypted DNS WFP research [11,19,25,30]. Specifically, we assume a local, passive eavesdropper (e.g., an ISP) positioned on the link between the client and the DoH resolver. This adversary can observe all DoH encrypted traffic but cannot modify, delay, drop, or decrypt any packets. Its goal is to infer, from a predefined set of target sites, which website the user is accessing.

Scope and Realistic Constraints. Our evaluation focuses exclusively on homepage accesses, which represent a common and privacy-sensitive scenario. To reflect practical conditions, we account for differences in resolver-side EDNS(0) padding strategies and variations in operating system and browser networking behaviors. These factors significantly influence the eavesdropper's observational view.

3 Methodology

The core premise of our approach is that a website's unique Document Object Model (DOM) structure dictates a deterministic sequence of DNS queries. When a browser loads a page, it parses the DOM and discovers external resources (e.g., scripts, stylesheets, images), which are often hosted on various third-party domains such as CDNs and analytics services. The specific structure of the

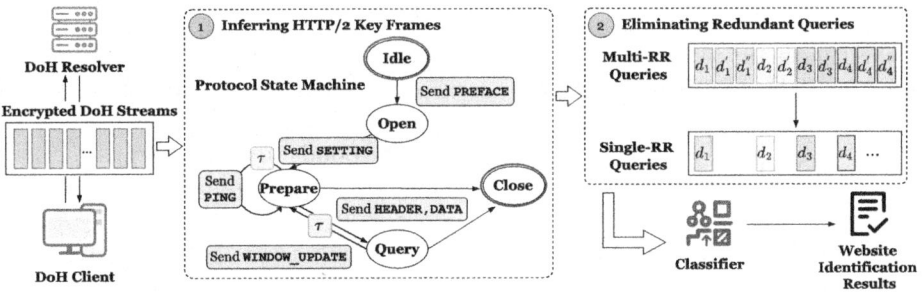

Fig. 4. The process of DoH WFP Attack.

page—including the order of <script> and <link> tags, resource dependencies, and asynchronous loading attributes— governs the precise sequence and timing in which the browser fetch these resources. Since fetching a resource from a new domain necessitates a DNS query, the unique DOM and rendering logic of a website translate directly into a distinct, observable sequence of DNS queries. This sequence is the unique communication pattern that our method leverages for fingerprinting.

Based on this observation, we propose using the time intervals between successive DoH domain queries as a fingerprint for website identification. To account for delays caused by domain blocking, we measure the time interval between the homepage domain's response and the first subsequent domain query. For all other domains, we record the intervals between each pair of consecutive query events.

Two primary challenges arise in generating this sequence. First, DoH traffic intermixes encrypted HTTP/2 key frames with control frames used for flow management; thus, only key frames corresponding to domain queries and responses should be extracted. Second, browsers issue multiple Resource-Record (RR) queries to the same domain in parallel, complicating the interpretation of the query sequence.

To address these challenges, we design a protocol state machine to identify key frames and develop a sequence segmentation algorithm based on dynamic programming to eliminate redundant queries. Figure 4 illustrates the overall process of our proposed DoH WFP attack. The following subsection provides a detailed description of each component.

3.1 Inferring HTTP/2 Key Frames

DoH communication proceeds through three stages: the transport-layer handshake, the TLS handshake for key exchange, and the DoH query and response phase. Our goal is to extract the key frame subsequences in the final phase. We classify traffic as either "outgoing" (client → server) or "incoming" (server → client), and define the first outgoing TLS application data as the beginning of the HTTP/2 transaction. The problem can be formalized as follows.

Given a TLS traffic sequence $S = (p_i)_{i=1}^{N}$, where $p_i = (l_i, d_i)$. Here $l_i \in \mathbb{Z}$ is the length (in bytes) of the i-th TLS data, and $d_i \in \{+1, -1\}$ indicates the direction. The goal is to construct a decision function $F : S \rightarrow \{0, 1\}$, such that

$$F(p_i) = \begin{cases} 1, & \text{if the TLS data } p_i \text{ corresponds to a key frame,} \\ 0, & \text{otherwise (i.e., it is another frame type).} \end{cases} \quad (1)$$

Through protocol analysis and empirical testing across public resolvers, we identify two key observations. First, DoH transactions within a TLS connection exhibit a repetitive query-response pattern, consistent with the state-transition sequence described in Sect. 2.1. Second, key frames carrying DNS queries and responses consistently result in larger TLS data lengths compared to other frame types. The effect of padding on TLS data lengths can be classified into two categories.

- **Uniform Length:** In environments implementing the RFC block-length scheme, key frames display a uniform TLS data size, as queries and responses are padded to a fixed boundary.
- **Dispersed Length:** Conversely, when padding is fixed, random, or absent, the size of each key frame varies according to the actual DNS payload, while control frames maintain a stable, smaller record size across repeated sessions.

Based on these observations, we implement a protocol state machine that leverages the order of HTTP/2 frame sequence and applies length threshold, denoted as τ, to identify key frames within the TLS connection (see Step ① in Fig. 4). To determine τ, we randomly selected 100 domains from the Majestic top 1,000 list and accessed each domain using Chrome configured with Google, Quad9, and ALi DoH resolvers. We recorded the lengths of both outgoing and incoming TLS records and plotted their histograms and kernel density estimates, as shown in Fig. 5.

The resulting distributions reflect the padding strategies employed by Chrome and each resolver. Both the Chrome browser and Google's DoH resolver implement the RFC block-length padding scheme, resulting in a bimodal distribution, where the higher-length peak corresponds to DNS query and response frames. Quad9, which applies no padding, and ALi, which uses random padding, both exhibit a long-tailed distribution for frame lengths, while control frame lengths remain concentrated around smaller values. In all cases, a distinct separation is observed between the lengths of control frames and key frames. Based on this separation, we set $\tau = 100$ bytes: any TLS record with a length l_i exceeding 100 bytes is classified as a candidate HTTP/2 key frame.

3.2 Eliminating Redundant Queries

When using DoH, browsers typically issue two or three RR queries (A, AAAA, and HTTPS) for the same domain in rapid succession. Our preliminary analysis indicates that queries for multiple records of the same domain are clustered

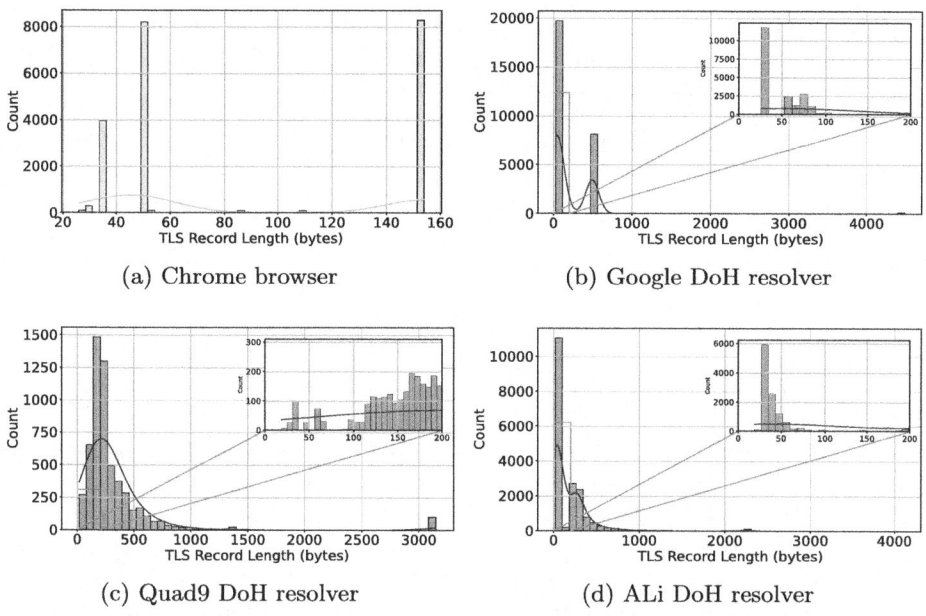

Fig. 5. Distribution of TLS record lengths in DoH packets.

within short inter-arrival times, whereas queries to different domains are separated by longer delays. In our proposed DoH WFP attack, the time interval between queries to different domains serves as a key feature; however, closely spaced same-domain queries can obscure this signal. Due to network variability, intra-domain inter-arrival times fluctuate across sessions, and the number of queries per domain is not fixed. As a result, filtering based solely on a fixed threshold or query order is unreliable.

To address this, we treat each sequence of query arrivals independently and partition it into segments of two or three queries, each representing a single domain. Formally, given a sequence of DoH query intervals

$$\Delta t = (\Delta t_1, \ldots, \Delta t_n) \in \mathbb{R}^n, \qquad n \geq 2,$$

we seek indices $0 = i_0 < i_1 < \cdots < i_k = n$ such that the length of each segment satisfies $i_j - i_{j-1} \in \{2, 3\}$ for all $j = 1, \ldots, k$. Let $S_j = \{\Delta t_{i_{j-1}+1}, \ldots, \Delta t_{i_j}\}$ denote the j-th segment, and define the contribution of each segment as

$$\mathrm{contrib}(S_j) = \Delta t_{i_{j-1}+1}. \tag{2}$$

Among all feasible partitions, we aim to maximize the sum of these contributions, that is,

$$\underset{\substack{k \in \mathbb{N}_{\geq 1},\ 0 = i_0 < \cdots < i_k = n \\ i_j - i_{j-1} \in \{2,3\}}}{\arg\max} \sum_{j=1}^{k} \Delta t_{i_{j-1}+1}. \tag{3}$$

We solve this segmentation problem with dynamic programming. Let OPT[i] denote the maximum sum of first time intervals attainable from the prefix ($\Delta t_1, \ldots, \Delta t_i$). We initialize

$$\text{OPT}[0] = 0, \qquad \text{OPT}[1] = -\infty.$$

Since there is exactly one valid segmentation for $i = 2$ and $i = 3$, we have

$$\text{OPT}[2] = \Delta t_1, \qquad \text{OPT}[3] = \Delta t_1.$$

For every $i \geq 4$ we update OPT[i] according to

$$\text{OPT}[i] = \max\left\{\text{OPT}[i-2] + \Delta t_{i-1},\ \text{OPT}[i-3] + \Delta t_{i-2}\right\}, \tag{4}$$

where the first term corresponds to appending a two-element segment ($\Delta t_{i-1}, \Delta t_i$) and the second term corresponds to appending a three-element segment ($\Delta t_{i-2}, \Delta t_{i-1}, \Delta t_i$). The optimal segmentation is reconstructed using back-pointers stored during the update process. For instance, consider a inter-arrival time sequence (in milliseconds): $[100, 0.01, 30, 0.03, 0.01]$. Our algorithm partitions this sequence into segments of two or three elements to maximize the sum of the first interval in each segment. The optimal partition for this example is $[100, 0.01]$ and $[30, 0.03, 0.01]$. This yields a final feature vector of $[100, 30]$, composed of the first interval from each segment, which serves as as a critical feature for DoH WFP attack.

4 Evaluation

4.1 Datasets

We assembled a comprehensive dataset comprising 1,634 website visits across diverse scenarios to evaluate our method. The candidate sites were collected from two sources: the Citizen Lab list of censorship-tested sites [21] and a random sample of 1,000 domains selected from the top 10,000 domains in the Majestic list [6]. We merged the two sources to form an initial candidate set. Since this set contained unreachable domains and aliases for the same service, we applied the following filtering steps:

- **Discard Inaccessible Sites.** Domains that returned HTTP errors were excluded to ensure that all remaining sites were accessible.
- **Merge Redirects.** For HTTP 30X responses, If both the original and redirected domains appeared in our dataset (e.g., example.com redirecting to www.example.com), we followed the redirect chain and retained only the redirected domain.
- **Merge Duplicate Templates.** Some distinct websites, by using a shared web template, fetch resources from a nearly identical set of domains, making them functionally identical from a traffic analysis standpoint. To address these

Table 1. Overview of the DoH Traffic Datasets.

Dataset	Resolver	OS	Browser	# Websites	# Samples
$\mathcal{D}_1 - \mathcal{D}_5$	Google, Cloudflare, Quad9, ALi, Adguard	Ubuntu 22.04	Chrome v120	1,634	65k
$\mathcal{D}_6$	Google	Windows 11	Chrome v128	1,627	6.4k
$\mathcal{D}_7$	Google	Ubuntu 22.04	Firefox v121 Edge v120	1,634	6.4k

template duplicates, we calculate the Jaccard index, $|D_1 \cap D_2|/|D_1 \cup D_2|$, for the accessed domain sets of any two sites (D_1, D_2). If the index surpasses 0.8, the sites are merged into a single class. This merging process removes websites that are otherwise indistinguishable to DoH fingerprinting due to their nearly identical DNS sequences.
- **Exclude Single-Domain Sites.** Websites that referenced only their own domain were removed, as our analysis depends on intervals between multiple domains.

After filtering, the final dataset comprised 1,634 websites, of which 684 were from the Majestic sample and 950 were from the Citizen Lab list. We automated data collection with *Selenium* for browsing and *TCPDump* for packet capture, conducted across three browsers, two operating systems (OSes) and five DoH resolvers.

Table 1 summarizes the seven collected datasets, denoted $\mathcal{D}_1$ through $\mathcal{D}_7$. Datasets $\mathcal{D}_1$ to $\mathcal{D}_5$ were collected on Ubuntu 22.04 using Chrome under different resolver configurations, with each site visited 40 times. Dataset $\mathcal{D}_6$ was collected on Windows 11 using Chrome with the Google resolver; it excludes a small number of domains that were inaccessible. Dataset $\mathcal{D}_7$ was collected on Ubuntu 22.04 using Firefox and Edge. Datasets $\mathcal{D}_6$ and $\mathcal{D}_7$ are used to assess the robustness of our method across different environments. The datasets are publicly available in our GitHub repository [1].

4.2 Information Leakage Analysis

To gain a deep understanding of the effectiveness of features, we evaluate information leakage [23] to quantify the amount of information that can be inferred by an adversary from the traffic-representation features associated with a website. The information leakage $I(F; C)$ in the closed-world scenario is defined as:

$$I(F; C) = H(C) - H(C \mid F), \tag{5}$$

where C denotes the monitored website, F represents the traffic-representation feature, and $H(\cdot)$ is the entropy.

We selected six state-of-the-art WFP attacks, namely N-Grams [30], Segram [25], AWF [27], DF [31], Tik-Tok [26], and RF-Shen [29], to make a comprehensive comparison with our key frame sequence (**KF-Seq**). Among these, AWF,

Table 2. Information Leakage of Test Features

Attacks	Feature	Information Leakage		
		Google	Quad9	ALi
N-Grams [30], Segram [25]	1-gram	0.443	0.134	0.141
AWF [27], DF [31]	Packet Direction	0.574	0.780	0.542
Tik-Tok [26]	Timing with Direction	1.192	1.232	0.948
RF-Shen [29]	Packets per Second	**1.598**	0.942	1.219
Segram [25]	TLS Data Interval	1.063	0.802	1.114
KF-Seq (our method)	HTTP/2 Key Frame Interval	1.365	**1.862**	**1.538**

DF, Tik-Tok, and RF-Shen were originally devised for the Tor network. For evaluation, we chose the top 100 domains from the selected Majestic list. Using three DoH resolvers (Google, Quad9, and ALi), we collected 40 samples per website. From each trace, we truncated the data to the first 100 TLS application-data packets and limited the total capture duration to 20 s. We then extracted the corresponding feature sets to assess information leakage.

Table 2 reports the average leakage (measured in bits) for each feature. The HTTP/2 key frame interval and the packets-per-second feature exhibit higher leakage compared to the others. Notably, leakage measured from the intervals of HTTP/2 key frame sequences consistently exceeds that derived from TLS data intervals across all three resolvers. The results demonstrate the superior discriminative power of our key frame approach and further corroborate our analysis.

4.3 Same-Environment Evaluation

We first evaluate performance of WFP attacks under identical environmental settings. Our method, KF-Seq, incorporates the intervals of key frames corresponding to DoH queries, as well as the total number of domain queries per website, as representation features. For each DoH trace, we retain the first 30 key frame intervals, truncating any excess and padding with zeros if fewer than 30 intervals are present. We then train a random forest classifier on these feature vectors. For comparison, we reproduce four Tor WFP attacks using the implementations provided by Deng et al. [13]. On datasets $\mathcal{D}_1$ to $\mathcal{D}_5$, deep-learning baselines are trained, validated, and tested with an 8:1:1 split, whereas machine-learning methods are evaluated on training and test partitions. Each deep-learning model adopts its originally reported optimal hyperparameters.

All experiments are conducted on Ubuntu 23.10 server equipped with an Intel Xeon 2.9 GHz CPU, 128 GB of RAM, and an NVIDIA A100 GPU. We implement machine-learning models in Scikit-learn [9] and deep-learning models in PyTorch [10]. Performance is evaluated using accuracy (ACC), precision (P), recall (R), and F1-score (F1), with macro-averaging across all classes.

Table 3. Classification results on Google and Cloudflare Resolvers

Attacks	$\mathcal{D}_1$ (Google)				$\mathcal{D}_2$ (Cloudflare)			
	ACC	P	R	F1	ACC	P	R	F1
N-Grams	39.61	38.12	39.61	36.45	22.83	21.37	22.81	20.66
Segram	57.89	58.05	57.87	54.91	54.72	54.68	54.71	51.68
DF	52.41	51.49	52.40	48.87	50.38	48.56	50.34	46.33
AWF	56.08	57.99	56.09	54.78	57.40	58.66	57.35	55.80
TIK-TOK	69.83	70.28	69.84	67.15	68.27	68.20	68.26	65.08
RF-Shen	76.22	77.73	76.22	74.61	75.97	77.14	75.98	73.94
KF-Seq	**87.68**	**89.04**	**87.68**	**87.49**	**89.80**	**90.74**	**89.78**	**89.47**

Table 4. Classification results on Quad9, ALi, and Adguard Resolvers

Attacks	$\mathcal{D}_3$ (Quad9)				$\mathcal{D}_4$ (ALi)				$\mathcal{D}_5$ (Adguard)			
	ACC	P	R	F1	ACC	P	R	F1	ACC	P	R	F1
N-Grams	88.46	90.38	88.47	87.96	9.43	8.58	9.43	8.05	14.87	13.48	14.89	12.85
Segram	**91.69**	**93.16**	**91.68**	**91.34**	20.86	19.76	20.85	18.32	34.39	32.93	34.41	31.10
DF	39.41	37.09	39.33	35.06	41.33	40.41	41.28	37.69	47.01	45.44	46.98	42.92
AWF	43.78	45.50	43.75	41.91	42.98	44.67	42.93	41.59	51.75	54.91	51.74	50.54
TIK-TOK	59.52	57.95	59.45	55.07	64.28	64.47	64.25	60.84	67.13	68.17	67.08	64.11
RF-Shen	70.21	72.06	70.19	68.17	71.86	73.49	71.84	69.80	81.03	83.14	81.04	80.06
KF-Seq	87.19	88.47	87.13	86.78	**88.15**	**89.20**	**88.13**	**87.80**	**87.06**	**88.33**	**87.04**	**86.64**

The evaluation results are presented in Table 3 and Table 4. In all four padding scenarios, KF-Seq consistently outperforms six state-of-the-art baselines. Compared to RF-Shen, the second-best performing method, KF-Seq improves the accuracy by approximately 10%. Even on dataset $\mathcal{D}_3$, where KF-Seq did not outperform all competing methods, it still achieves 87.19% accuracy and 86.78% F1 score, which is only 4.5% lower than the top-performing method. These results demonstrate that KF-Seq effectively captures differences in DoH traffic across websites.

Packet-length based n-gram methods are effective only when padding is absent. Although Chrome implements RFC padding, the Quad9 resolver does not. Thus, on $\mathcal{D}_3$ (no padding), Segram and N-Grams achieve the highest and second-highest accuracies, respectively. Segram extends N-Grams method by incorporating TLS data interval features, leading to improved performance. However, both approaches experience substantial degradation under padding. In the RFC block-padding scenarios $\mathcal{D}_1$ and $\mathcal{D}_2$, Segram's best accuracy drops to 57.89%. Under random padding conditions ($\mathcal{D}_4$ and $\mathcal{D}_5$), Segram's performance declines to 20.86%, while N-Grams remain around 10% accuracy.

Table 5. Results of Different Testing Methods across resolvers, OS, and browsers

Attacks	Cross-resolver $\mathcal{D}_1 \Rightarrow \mathcal{D}_{2-5}$				Cross-OS $\mathcal{D}_1 \Rightarrow \mathcal{D}_6$				Cross-browser $\mathcal{D}_1 \Rightarrow \mathcal{D}_7$			
	ACC	P	R	F1	ACC	P	R	F1	ACC	P	R	F1
N-Grams	0.33	0.25	0.33	0.14	27.91	27.09	27.96	24.88	2.34	2.03	2.32	1.75
Segram	0.10	0.16	0.10	0.04	30.58	34.71	30.62	29.83	2.69	3.96	2.67	2.73
DF	0.71	0.75	0.70	0.33	34.55	32.40	34.61	30.49	2.74	2.09	2.71	1.96
AWF	0.26	0.39	0.26	0.17	33.63	36.07	33.66	32.22	1.39	1.05	1.38	1.04
TIK-TOK	3.06	3.88	3.07	2.51	<u>48.85</u>	<u>48.64</u>	<u>48.91</u>	<u>44.73</u>	2.75	2.22	2.72	2.05
RF-Shen	<u>20.27</u>	<u>28.69</u>	<u>20.29</u>	<u>19.84</u>	45.34	46.64	45.33	42.08	**17.97**	**24.56**	**17.97**	**17.75**
KF-Seq	**71.20**	**72.09**	**71.18**	**70.39**	**68.15**	**68.62**	**68.17**	**65.53**	8.48	7.42	8.43	6.89

Deep-learning methods for Tor WFP exhibit relatively stable performance across scenarios but achieve lower overall accuracy. DF and AWF, which rely solely on packet-direction sequences, reach at most 57.40% accuracy. By contrast, Tik-Tok and RF-Shen, which incorporate fine-grained timing features, achieve better results. RF-Shen attains the second-best performing accuracy in four datasets. These findings suggest that Tor WFP methods are less effective in the DoH context. We attribute this disparity to fundamental differences in traffic characteristics between Tor and DoH. Tor traffic consists of fixed-length cells that transport complete website request and response payloads, whereas DoH packets involves only domain queries and responses, resulting in a sparser traffic profile. These differences in traffic representation and distribution affect the effectiveness of Tor WFP methods when applied to DoH.

4.4 Cross-Environment Evaluation

The core of our cross-environments evaluation is to assess how well a model trained in one specific environment performs when tested in others, simulating real-world conditions. As established by prior work [30], WFP performance can be sensitive to variations in operating systems, network locations, and DNS resolvers. To systematically evaluate this, We train all methods on the $\mathcal{D}_1$ dataset and testing under three cross-environment conditions: (1) cross-resolver (using the $\mathcal{D}_2$ through $\mathcal{D}_5$ test sets), (2) cross-operating system ($\mathcal{D}_6$), and (3) cross-browser ($\mathcal{D}_7$). Table 5 presents the detailed results.

Cross-Resolver and Cross-OS Evaluation. In both cross-resolver and cross-OS evaluations, KF-Seq consistently achieves the highest classification accuracy and demonstrates the least degradation compared to its baseline on $\mathcal{D}_1$. While inherent latency fluctuations across environments introduce some reduction in KF-Seq's accuracy, particularly for websites with fewer domain queries, its overall robustness remains notable.

In contrast, other evaluated methods experience a more substantial performance decline, especially in the cross-resolve scenario. We attribute this disparity primarily to variations in the composition of HTTP/2 frames within DoH responses emitted by different resolvers, which causes more pronounced shifts in traffic distributions. By comparison, cross-OS variations mainly introduce latency differences while preserving the browser's underlying HTTP/2 framing patterns. KF-Seq's robustness stems from its reliance on the key frame sequence of domain queries, rendering it inherently less sensitive to resolver-specific variations in DoH responses.

Cross-Browser Evaluation. Our results indicate significant performance degradation of all methods when evaluated on unseen browsers. Across the cross-browser test scenarios, RF-Shen achieves the best performance with an accuracy of 17.97%, followed by KF-Seq at 8.48%, while all remaining approaches maintain average accuracies below 3%. This substantial decline can be attributed to browser-specific variations in network request ordering, concurrency strategies, and resource pre-loading mechanisms. Even for identical websites, each browser introduces distinct networking and rendering behaviors into the DoH traffic, leading to feature sets that conflate site-specific and browser-specific patterns. Enhancing the robustness of WFP methods under such heterogeneous environments will likely require training on datasets that incorporate diverse browsers, thereby enabling classifiers to mitigate the influence of browser-specific idiosyncrasies.

5 Discussion

5.1 Limitations

Dependence on Multi-Domain query Sequences. A primary limitation of KF-Seq is its reliance on inter-domain query intervals, rendering the method inapplicable to websites that load resources from only a single domain. To quantify the scope of this applicability boundary, our analysis of the top 100,000 Majestic domains revealed that while 8.71% of sites are single-domain, the vast majority (74.6%) query three or more distinct domains during page load. This finding establishes the set of websites for which our feature engineering approach is viable.

However, a more fundamental challenge affects DoH fingerprinting techniques based on DNS patterns. The prevalence of templated web design means that even among multi-domain websites, some distinct sites share a high degree of domain sequence similarity by loading resources from a common set of third-party services. From a DoH traffic perspective, this similarity makes these websites fundamentally indistinguishable. This points to an inherent limitation of the field: the space of unique websites is larger than the space of unique DoH fingerprints, making it hard for the method based solely on this signal to differentiate all sites.

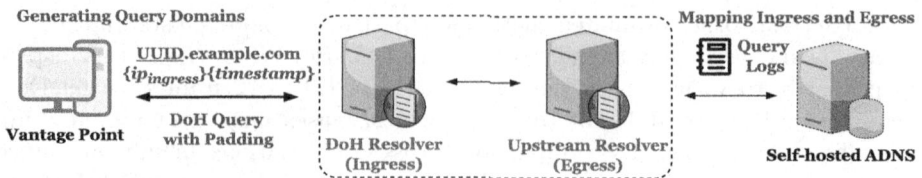

Fig. 6. Active Measurement of DoH Resolver Padding Behavior in the Wild.

Sensitivity to Network and Browser Variability. Although the time intervals in KF-Seq primarily reflect browser rendering delays, they are also influenced by round-trip time (RTT) delays and resolver processing or blocking delays. Distinguishing delays caused by DNS blocking from ordinary network delays in encrypted traffic is challenging, and misclassifications may arise as a result. Moreover, different browsers employ distinct page loading strategies, leading to KF-Seq sequences that embed browser-specific traits. Consequently, KF-Seq does not generalize effectively to unseen browsers. Addressing this limitation requires either training on mixed-browser traffic samples or incorporating a preliminary browser fingerprinting step. For example, using the JA4 method [5] to identify the client browser before applying the WFP model can enhance cross-browser robustness.

5.2 Recommendations

Correct Padding Implementations and Configurations. To assess the real-world adoption of padding mechanisms, we deployed a self-hosted authoritative DNS server (ADNS) and tested 6,617 public DoH resolvers observed in the wild sending encoded queries with padding, as illustrated in Fig. 6. Following the methodology of Li et al. [22], we identified each resolver's vendor and software components. Our measurements show that 5,630 (85%) resolvers returned unpadded responses in all ten query attempts. Notably, NextDNS and AdGuard together account for 69% of these non-padding resolvers; none of the AdGuard forwarders we found applied padding, even when forwarding to padding-capable upstream providers such as Google or Cloudflare. Six resolvers applied padding to only a subset of their responses, suggesting that the unpadded responses originated from upstream resolvers that either lacked padding support or forwarded queries using the traditional DNS protocol.

In the absence of standardized padding, the efficacy of WFP attacks increases substantially. Based on these findings, we recommend the following: For end users, we recommend selecting DoH providers that fully implement block-length padding. For resolver operators and software vendors, we recommend consistently adopting and enabling the RFC-recommended padding scheme, both in direct DoH responses and when forwarding queries, to uphold the privacy guarantees of DoH.

Scattering DNS Queries and Injecting Dummy Queries. When padding effectively obfuscates packet lengths, WFP increasingly relies on the ordering and timing of DNS message sequences. This temporal behavior constitutes the side channel exploited in our study. A practical countermeasure involves distributing queries across independent resolvers and injecting dummy lookups at randomized time intervals. Resolver rotation disrupts the direct association between a browsing session and a single resolver, thereby limiting each resolver's visibility to only a subset of the user's domain sequence. [14,17]. Concurrently, the injection of randomly generated queries, including syntactically valid but semantically irrelevant entries and replays of cached domains, further obscures genuine behavior by disrupting the sequence patterns used by classifiers. The integration of these two methods fragments the traffic into multiple short and incomplete traces punctuated by noise, thereby increasing the complexity of WFP attacks without requiring any alterations to the DoH protocol or upstream resolvers.

6 Related Work

In this section, we review the representative work on website fingerprinting (WFP) against encrypted DNS traffic. Houser et al. [18] represented each TLS packet in DoT flows as a <timestamp, length, direction> triplet and classified the resulting sequences using a random forest model. They showed that both padding and variability in the number of DNS messages per TLS record significantly affect classification accuracy, and that distinguishing broad site categories is generally easier than identifying individual websites. Siby et al. [30] modeled DoH packet-length sequences using n-gram representations and a 100-tree random forest classifier. Their approach achieved high precision and recall when no padding was present, but its performance degraded under padding and failed to generalize across operating systems, network locations, or resolvers. Building upon the work of Siby et al., Shao et al. [28] proposed a lightweight fingerprinting method that analyzes the size and direction of the first 50 outgoing DoH packets, achieving high identification accuracy using a Random Forest classifier. Bushart et al. [11] collected ten traces for 7,699 Tranco-ranked websites using Firefox and the Cloudflare DoT resolver. They used packet-length and timing features with a k-nearest-neighbor classifier, achieving deanonymization of 86.1% of sites and full identification for 65.9%. Hynek et al. [19] evaluated packet-length and inter-arrival-time statistics for Alexa-ranked sites accessed over DoH using HTTP/1.1 and HTTP/2. They observed a noticeable drop in accuracy under HTTP/2, which they attributed to multiplexing and framing behaviors that obscure timing and size features. Mühlhauser et al. [25] assessed four feature sets—including the Segram length-and-timing sequence they proposed—on traffic generated by 118 mobile applications across ten DoT and DoH resolvers. They reported that Segram's accuracy decreased significantly when DNS responses were padded by resolvers.

In summary, most existing DoH fingerprinting methods rely on coarse-grained TLS record-length features, rendering them highly sensitive to padding schemes. In contrast, our approach extracts fine-grained application-layer key frame sequences, aiming to enhance both the effectiveness and robustness of WFP under DoH with standardized padding.

7 Conclusion

This paper presents a novel HTTP/2 key frame-based WFP method for DoH traffic. The proposed method operates in two stages: First, a protocol-aware state machine reconstructs the HTTP/2 frame sequence, and identifies key frames by analyzing distinctive TLS record-length side-channel patterns. Second, a dynamic programming-based segmentation algorithm filters out redundant and parallel RR queries, producing a compact and stable fingerprint representation. The experimental results demonstrate that the method achieves over 87% accuracy under RFC-compliant padding in same-environment settings. It also reaches 71% accuracy across resolvers and 68% across operating systems. Compared with leading WFP methods, the proposed approach exhibits the least performance degradation under cross-environment conditions, indicating high resilience to both padding and deployment variability. The paper also outlines practical countermeasures to mitigate the exposure of DoH traffic to WFP attacks.

Acknowledgements. The authors would like to thank the anonymous reviewers for their valuable comments and helpful suggestions. This work is supported by the Scaling Program of the Institute of Information Engineering, CAS (No. E3Z0041101).

References

1. byron-li/KFSeq-dataset. https://github.com/byron-li/KFSeq-Dataset
2. DNS over HTTPS (aka DoH). https://www.chromium.org/developers/dns-over-https/
3. DNS-over-HTTPS (DoH) FAQs | firefox help. https://support.mozilla.org/en-US/kb/dns-over-https-doh-faqs#w_why-is-firefox-implementing-doh-and-not-dot
4. Firefox DNS-over-HTTPS | Firefox Help. https://support.mozilla.org/en-US/kb/firefox-dns-over-https
5. FoxIO-LLC/ja4. https://github.com/FoxIO-LLC/ja4
6. Majestic million. https://majestic.com/reports/majestic-million
7. Microsoft Edge Privacy Whitepaper - Microsoft Edge Development | Microsoft Docs. https://docs.microsoft.com/en-us/microsoft-edge/privacy-whitepaper/
8. Mozilla, bug 1543811: EDNS padding support for encrypted DNS transports. https://bugzilla.mozilla.org/show_bug.cgi?id=1543811
9. scikit-learn: machine learning in python — scikit-learn 1.6.1 documentation. https://scikit-learn.org/stable/
10. Ansel, J., et al.: PyTorch 2: Faster machine learning through dynamic python bytecode transformation and graph compilation. https://doi.org/10.1145/3620665.3640366. https://docs.pytorch.org/assets/pytorch2-2.pdf. publication Title: 29th ACM International Conference on Architectural Support for Programming Languages and Operating Systems, Volume 2 (ASPLOS '24) original-date: 2016-08-13T05:26:41Z

11. Bushart, J., Rossow, C.: Padding ain't enough: assessing the privacy guarantees of encrypted DNS. In: Ensafi, R., Klein, H. (eds.) 10th USENIX Workshop on Free and Open Communications on the Internet, FOCI 2020, August 11, 2020. USENIX Association (2020). https://www.usenix.org/conference/foci20/presentation/bushart
12. Cheng, Y., et al.: Holmes & watson: a robust and lightweight https website fingerprinting through http version parallelism. In: Proceedings of the ACM on Web Conference 2025, WWW 2025, pp. 1078–1092. Association for Computing Machinery, New York (2025). https://doi.org/10.1145/3696410.3714578
13. Deng, X., Li, Q., Xu, K.: Robust and reliable early-stage website fingerprinting attacks via spatial-temporal distribution analysis. In: Luo, B., Liao, X., Xu, J., Kirda, E., Lie, D. (eds.) Proceedings of the 2024 on ACM SIGSAC Conference on Computer and Communications Security, CCS 2024, Salt Lake City, UT, USA, October 14–18, 2024, pp. 1997–2011. ACM (2024). https://doi.org/10.1145/3658644.3670272
14. Hoang, N.P., Lin, I., Ghavamnia, S., Polychronakis, M.: K-resolver: Towards decentralizing encrypted DNS resolution. In: Proceedings of The NDSS Workshop on Measurements, Attacks, and Defenses for the Web 2020. MADWeb 2020, Internet Societyhttps://doi.org/10.14722/madweb.2020.23009, event-place: San Diego, CA, USA
15. Hoang, N.P., Niaki, A.A., Gill, P., Polychronakis, M.: Domain name encryption is not enough: privacy leakage via IP-based website fingerprinting. Proc. Priv. Enhancing Technol. **2021**(4), 420–440 (2021)
16. Hoffman, P., McManus, P.: DNS queries over HTTPS (DoH).https://doi.org/10.17487/RFC8484. https://www.rfc-editor.org/info/rfc8484
17. Hounsel, A., Schmitt, P., Borgolte, K., Feamster, N.: Encryption without centralization: distributing DNS queries across recursive resolvers. In: ANRW 2021: Applied Networking Research Workshop, Virtual Event, USA, July 24-30, 2021, pp. 62–68. ACM (2021). https://doi.org/10.1145/3472305.3472318
18. Houser, R., Li, Z., Cotton, C., Wang, H.: An investigation on information leakage of DNS over TLS. In: Mohaisen, A., Zhang, Z. (eds.) Proceedings of the 15th International Conference on Emerging Networking Experiments And Technologies, CoNEXT 2019, Orlando, FL, USA, December 09–12, 2019, pp. 123–137. ACM (2019). https://doi.org/10.1145/3359989.3365429
19. Hynek, K., Cejka, T.: Privacy illusion: Beware of unpadded DOH. In: 2020 11th IEEE Annual Information Technology, Electronics and Mobile Communication Conference (IEMCON), pp. 0621–0628 (2020). https://doi.org/10.1109/IEMCON51383.2020.9284864
20. Jerábek, K., Rysavý, O., Burgetova, I.: Measurement and characterization of DNS over HTTPS traffic. CoRR abs/2204.03975 (2022). https://doi.org/10.48550/ARXIV.2204.03975
21. Lab, C., Others: Url testing lists intended for discovering website censorship (2014). https://github.com/citizenlab/test-lists. https://github.com/citizenlab/test-lists
22. Li, B., et al.: From fingerprint to footprint: Characterizing the dependencies in encrypted DNS infrastructures. In: García-Alfaro, J., Kozik, R., Choras, M., Katsikas, S.K. (eds.) Computer Security - ESORICS 2024 - 29th European Symposium on Research in Computer Security, Bydgoszcz, Poland, September 16–20, 2024, Proceedings, Part II. Lecture Notes in Computer Science, vol. 14983, pp. 45–64. Springer (2024). https://doi.org/10.1007/978-3-031-70890-9_3

23. Li, S., Guo, H., Hopper, N.: Measuring information leakage in website fingerprinting attacks and defenses. In: Lie, D., Mannan, M., Backes, M., Wang, X. (eds.) Proceedings of the 2018 ACM SIGSAC Conference on Computer and Communications Security, CCS 2018, Toronto, ON, Canada, October 15–19, 2018. pp. 1977–1992. ACM (2018). https://doi.org/10.1145/3243734.3243832
24. Mayrhofer, A.: Padding policies for extension mechanisms for DNS (EDNS(0)). RFC 8467 (2018). https://doi.org/10.17487/RFC8467
25. Mühlhauser, M., Pridöhl, H., Herrmann, D.: How private is android's private DNS setting? identifying apps by encrypted DNS traffic. In: Reinhardt, D., Müller, T. (eds.) ARES 2021: The 16th International Conference on Availability, Reliability and Security, Vienna, Austria, August 17–20, 2021, pp. 14:1–14:10. ACM (2021). https://doi.org/10.1145/3465481.3465764
26. Rahman, M.S., Sirinam, P., Mathews, N., Gangadhara, K.G., Wright, M.: Tik-tok: the utility of packet timing in website fingerprinting attacks. Proc. Priv. Enhancing Technol. **2020**(3), 5–24 (2020). https://doi.org/10.2478/POPETS-2020-0043
27. Rimmer, V., Preuveneers, D., Juarez, M., van Goethem, T., Joosen, W.: Automated website fingerprinting through deep learning. In: 25th Annual Network and Distributed System Security Symposium, NDSS 2018, San Diego, California, USA, February 18–21, 2018. The Internet Society (2018). https://www.ndss-symposium.org/wp-content/uploads/2018/02/ndss2018_03A-1_Rimmer_paper.pdf
28. Shao, Y., Hernandez, K., Yang, K., Chan-Tin, E., Abuhamad, M.: Lightweight and effective website fingerprinting over encrypted dns. In: 2023 Silicon Valley Cybersecurity Conference (SVCC), pp. 1–8 (2023).https://doi.org/10.1109/SVCC56964.2023.10165086
29. Shen, M., Ji, K., Gao, Z., Li, Q., Zhu, L., Xu, K.: Subverting website fingerprinting defenses with robust traffic representation. In: Calandrino, J.A., Troncoso, C. (eds.) 32nd USENIX Security Symposium, USENIX Security 2023, Anaheim, CA, USA, August 9–11, 2023, pp. 607–624. USENIX Association (2023). https://www.usenix.org/conference/usenixsecurity23/presentation/shen-meng
30. Siby, S., Juarez, M., Díaz, C., Vallina-Rodriguez, N., Troncoso, C.: Encrypted DNS -> privacy? A traffic analysis perspective. In: 27th Annual Network and Distributed System Security Symposium, NDSS 2020, San Diego, California, USA, February 23–26, 2020. The Internet Society (2020). https://www.ndss-symposium.org/ndss-paper/encrypted-dns-privacy-a-traffic-analysis-perspective/
31. Sirinam, P., Imani, M., Juarez, M., Wright, M.: Deep fingerprinting: Undermining website fingerprinting defenses with deep learning. In: Lie, D., Mannan, M., Backes, M., Wang, X. (eds.) Proceedings of the 2018 ACM SIGSAC Conference on Computer and Communications Security, CCS 2018, Toronto, ON, Canada, October 15-19, 2018, pp. 1928–1943. ACM (2018). https://doi.org/10.1145/3243734.3243768
32. Thomson, M., Benfield, C.: HTTP/2. RFC 9113 (2022). https://doi.org/10.17487/RFC9113

NLSaber: Enhancing Netlink Family Fuzzing via Automated Syscall Description Generation

Lin Ma[1], Xingwei Lin[1], Ziming Zhang[2], and Yajin Zhou[1](✉)

[1] Zhejiang University, Hangzhou, China
{linma,xwlin.roy,yajin_zhou}@zju.edu.cn
[2] Hangzhou, China

Abstract. Recently, security researchers have uncovered a significant number of high-severity vulnerabilities in Netlink families, posing serious threats to overall kernel security. Despite these risks, there are no automated methods available to effectively detect bugs in Netlink families. For example, Syzkaller—a state-of-the-art, general-purpose kernel fuzzer—fails to achieve effective fuzzing for Netlink families because it depends on manually written descriptions that are often incomplete or inaccurate. To address this gap, we present NLSaber, the first specialized tool designed for enhancing Netlink family fuzzing. NLSaber uses static taint analysis to construct parse graphs that model the message parsing process, and then automatically generates complete and accurate fuzzing descriptions based on these graphs. In our evaluation on Linux 6.1.70, NLSaber identified 76 target families, encompassing 865 operations. The generated fuzzing descriptions were significantly more complete (supporting 43% more families) and more accurate (93% vs. 33% accuracy) compared to existing descriptions. Using these generated descriptions, our enhanced fuzzer improved code coverage by 9.1% over Syzkaller in families supported by both tools (and by 40.8% when including Syzkaller-unsupported families). Additionally, NLSaber uncovered 19 previously unknown vulnerabilities, all reported and confirmed, with 12 CVEs assigned.

Keywords: System Security · Linux Kernel · Netlink · Fuzzing

1 Introduction

Netlink is a socket-based communication interface that facilitates inter-process communication (IPC) between the kernel and userspace processes. Introduced in Linux 2.2, Netlink offers greater flexibility than the traditional ioctl interface, supporting higher throughput and a richer feature set [37]. Initially, Netlink was designed for exchanging networking-related information. It has since been adopted by other kernel subsystems [24] and integrated into operating systems such as FreeBSD [27].

Z. Zhang—Independent Researcher.

The widespread adoption of Netlink has improved efficiency but also introduced significant security risks. Recently, security researchers have uncovered numerous high-severity vulnerabilities [4,9,15,28,29] in Netlink families, most of which can lead to privilege escalation, threatening the security of the Linux kernel and millions of devices. Thus, automatically detecting Netlink vulnerabilities before they can be exploited in the wild remains a pressing challenge and an open research problem.

Fuzzing is a promising approach for automatically detecting bugs in OS kernels. For example, Syzkaller [35], a state-of-the-art kernel fuzzer developed by Google, has uncovered thousands of Linux kernel bugs since 2017. However, we observed that Syzkaller fails to achieve effective Netlink family fuzzing. A key limitation is that the syscall descriptions it relies on, which enable structure-aware fuzzing, are incomplete or inaccurate (see Sect. 2). Consequently, Syzkaller often fails to perform as expected, leaving many code paths inadequately tested.

The problem is particularly severe for Netlink families because their inputs, known as Netlink messages, are highly complex. These messages use specialized attribute encoding and require a specific parsing process to extract usable payloads. Notably, Netlink messages have an average nesting-depth[1] five times greater than that of `ioctl` arguments used in device drivers according to the existing descriptions. This complexity makes manual description writing both time-consuming and error-prone, while also rendering existing automated description generation approaches for device drivers [6,8,22,33] ineffective.

To address this gap, we propose a dedicated model called the **parse graph** for systematically analyzing the Netlink message parsing process. This graph, constructed using static taint analysis, captures essential parsing details for recovering the complex Netlink messages. By traversing and translating the parse graph, we generate complete and accurate syscall descriptions, thereby enhancing the effectiveness of Netlink family fuzzing. We implemented the prototype system **NLSaber** and evaluated it on Linux 6.1.70. Cross-validation shows that the generated descriptions are more complete (supporting 43% more families) and accurate (93% vs. 33%) than existing descriptions. Additionally, we assessed the system's effectiveness through comprehensive fuzzing experiments. The enhanced fuzzing improved code coverage by more than 9.1% for common families (and by 40.8% when including Syzkaller-unsupported families). NLSaber uncovered 19 previously unknown vulnerabilities, all have been reported and confirmed, with 12 CVEs assigned.

Contributions. In summary, our main contributions are in the following.

- We found that the state-of-the-art fuzzer Syzkaller is ineffective in Netlink family fuzzing due to its incomplete and inaccurate descriptions. Existing device-driver-targeted solutions are difficult to adapt for Netlink due to their inability to analyze the message parsing process.
- We propose a solution that models the Netlink message parsing process using parse graphs constructed with static taint analysis. These graphs capture

---

[1] Syzkaller types are organized in directed-acyclic graph form. We call the depth of the expanded tree from one type as the nesting-depth for this type.

essential parsing details, enabling the generation of complete and accurate syscall descriptions to enhance Netlink family fuzzing.
- We present a prototypical implementation named NLSaber and evaluate its effectiveness on Linux 6.1.70. The evaluation shows that our generated descriptions are more complete and accurate than existing ones. Using these improved descriptions, the enhanced fuzzing improved code coverage by over 9.1% (and by 40.8% when including Syzkaller-unsupported families). Moreover, NLSaber uncovered 19 previously unknown vulnerabilities, with 12 CVEs assigned.

2 Technical Background and Motivation

2.1 Netlink Family and Message Parsing

Netlink facilitates communication between the kernel and userspace processes [25]. Similar to driver interfaces (e.g., char and block device drivers), Netlink provides multiple interfaces, such as NETLINK_ROUTE, the foundation of Linux kernel components for packet routing and device hook frameworks, and NETLINK_NETFILTER, the foundation for packet filtering and iptables. Each Netlink family registers callback functions (called operations) to handle Netlink messages[2]. These messages, sent from userspace via network syscalls like send and sendmsg, consist of a fixed-format metadata header followed by a stream of attributes containing userspace payloads in TLV (Type, Length, Value) format [20]. Figure 1 presents an operation snippet for configuring a virtual network interface, along with its Netlink policies and message structure. The header comprises a 16-byte message header (nlmsghdr) and a family-specific header (ifinfomsg). Each subsequent attribute begins with 4-byte metadata (nlattr), followed by the actual payload. Notably, attributes can be nested, meaning a payload may contain another TLV-formatted attribute stream to carry complex data.

To parse the Netlink message and attributes to get the accessible payload, the rtnl_setlink function takes a parameter nlh (of type struct nlmsghdr *), which points to the message header. Then, nlmsg_data (L2) retrieves the family-specific header, assigning it to the pointer ifm. Next, nlmsg_parse_deprecated (L3) parses nlh into an array of attributes tb. Attribute-type enums, such as IFLA_IFNAME and IFLA_NEW_IFINDEX, are then used as indices to get specific attribute pointers from the array tb (L11,12). Functions like nla_strscpy (L11) and nla_get_s32 (L12) are used to extract the payload from these attributes. For nested attributes, such as tb[IFLA_XDP], the function nla_parse_nested _deprecated (L14) is called to parse the nested payload into another attribute array xdp. Importantly, during parsing, Netlink families may define validation rules through **Netlink policies**. For example, the ifla_policy in Fig. 1 specifies the following constraints: (1) IFLA_IFNAME's payload must be a string shorter

---

[2] Netlink family also transmits messages to userspace via unicast or broadcast. This study focuses on the case where userspace is the sender.

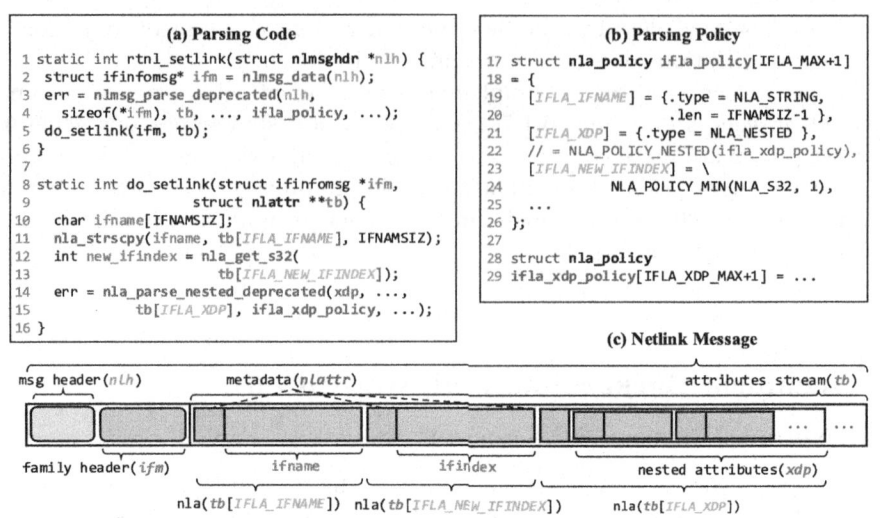

Fig. 1. Simplified code snippet for network link configuration, including Netlink policies and message structure.

than IFNAMSIZ; (2) IFLA_XDP must be a nested attribute; and (3) IFLA_NEW _IFINDEX's payload must be a signed integer with a minimum value of 1. The function nlmsg_parse_deprecated verifies these constraints. If any validation fails, it returns an error and terminates the parsing process. Such validations are flexible yet robust, making them widely used in the Netlink family code for payloads verification.

2.2 Motivation

Recently, security researchers have uncovered numerous high-severity vulnerabilities in Netlink families [9,28,29]. Notably, over half of the kCTF [15] submissions exploit this attack surface to achieve privilege escalation. Despite this, no specialized tool exists for detecting these vulnerabilities. Even Syzkaller, the state-of-the-art advanced general-purpose kernel fuzzer, fails to achieve effective fuzzing of Netlink families due to *incomplete* and *inaccurate* descriptions. In the following, we elaborate on these two issues, which motivate our work to generate *complete* and *accurate* descriptions to enhance Netlink family fuzzing.

Issue I. Current Descriptions are Incomplete. Our analysis on Syzkaller's descriptions reveals the following: (1) Since 2020, Syzkaller has added descriptions for nine new Netlink families, yet eight[3] of them have already existed in the kernel for over two years. (2) Five critical vulnerabilities[4] were reported in kCTF 2023, but their corresponding descriptions were not updated in Syzkaller until over a year later (September 2024). Furthermore, our evaluation shows that

---
[3] netlabels, nl80211, ipset, nfc, batman-adv, smc, nldev, mptcp.
[4] CVE-2023-4147,5197,4569,4015,5345.

over 23 Netlink families still lack descriptions (see Sect. 4.1), with 17 of them present in the kernel for more than five years.

Issue II. Current Descriptions are Inaccurate. Although Syzkaller's descriptions are written by experts, they contain errors. As evidence, we identified and reported 85 errors (see Sect. 4.1) in Netlink-related descriptions. Besides, we also identified many *redundant attributes* (either unused or repeated). Specifically, since there is no available approach to analyze the message parsing process, e.g., the parsing code listed in Fig. 1, the existing descriptions choose to include all specified attributes in the parsing policies into their message structure definitions, regardless of whether their attributes are accessed or not. Consequently, these inaccuracies lead to inefficient generation and mutation, hindering fuzzing performance. For example, in our experiment on the Netlink family in Fig. 1, only 19.3% of the attributes sent by Syzkaller were actually accessed, while over 20.1% were redundant.

Our Solution. We found that both issues stem from the complexity of Netlink messages. Compared to ioctl arguments, Netlink messages exhibit significantly deeper nesting (average depth of 15 vs. 3), as shown in existing descriptions. The complexity makes previous approaches ineffective. For example, we tested SyzGen++ [6], which uses symbolic execution to infer the input structure of the operation shown in Fig. 1. However, the analysis either times out or runs out of memory. To address this, we propose a specialized and systematic solution. It analyzes how these messages are parsed, enabling the generation of complete and accurate descriptions to enhance fuzzing for Netlink families. These automatically generated descriptions solves above issues. First, they remain up to date with new or modified kernel code. Using them, our enhanced fuzzing uncovered 12 vulnerabilities in code unsupported by existing descriptions. Second, the improved accuracy of the descriptions enhances fuzzing efficiency. In our evaluation, our system not only improves code coverage but also detects previously unknown bugs. Notably, it discovered a previously undetected null pointer dereference in the Linux kernel, which had gone unnoticed for over 12 years, despite five years of testing with related descriptions in Syzkaller (see Sect. 4.3).

3 System Design and Implementation

Entrypoint Identification. Similar to prior work [8] that identifies device driver handlers, we use interface-specific models to detect target Netlink families and their corresponding operation functions. For example, the operation `rtnl_setlink` (Fig. 1) is registered via `rtnl_register`[5] (registration details omitted). By analyzing all calls to `rtnl_register`, we can identify other related operations. To our knowledge, this work presents the first systematic summary of models for each Netlink interface. These models allow us to extract all operation functions for Netlink families in the kernel, serving as entrypoints for Netlink message analysis.

---

[5] The latest kernel uses a similar function named `rtnl_register_many`.

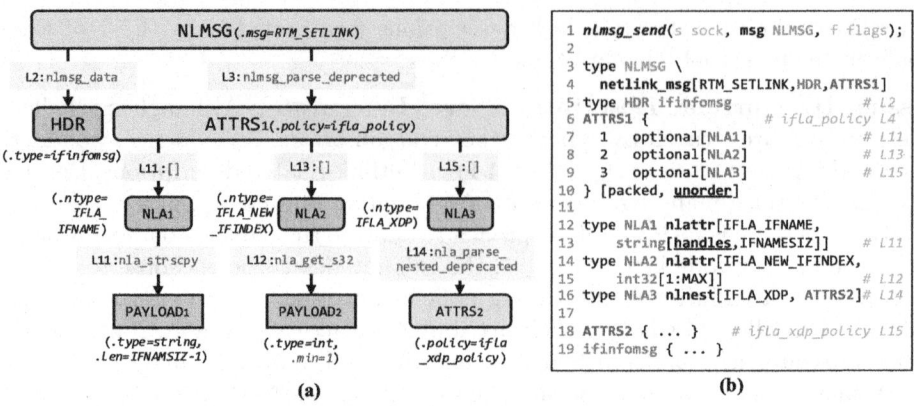

Fig. 2. Example parse graph for Fig. 1 (a) and the demo descriptions (b).

Parse Graph Internal and Construction. To analyze the Netlink message parsing process, we propose a dedicated graph model. This key insight is that the parsing process follows a principled approach, with most parsing actions handled by a limited set of library functions (defined in lib/nlattr.c, highlighted in red in Fig. 1). Hence, we can first model these limited library functions and use them as waypoints to analyze the entire parsing process. Based on this insight, we propose parse graphs to model how Netlink messages are parsed. For example, Fig. 2 (a) presents an example of the code listed in Fig. 1. In this graph, the nodes represent parsing elements in five concluded types: *NLMSG* for the entire message; *HDR* for the family-specific header; *ATTRS* for the stream of attributes; *NLA* for the sole attribute; and *PAYLOAD* for the payload carried in the attribute. Nodes with these types are highlighted with different colors in Fig. 2 (a). The edges represent associated parsing actions, such as the calls to library functions (L2,3,11,12,14) and array expressions of attributes array (L11,13,15). Furthermore, as demonstrated in Fig. 2(a), each node contains additional information. For example, the NLMSG node contains the message type (.msg), which determines the handler function (in this case, rtnl_setlink). The HDR and PAYLOAD nodes contain type information (.type) inferred from related expressions—for example, the ifinfomsg* type inferred from the return value of nlmsg_data. Some types may also have additional constraints, such as length (.len) for string type in PAYLOAD1. The ATTRS node contains the parsing policy (.policy), while the NLA node includes the attribute type (.ntype). In summary, the graph node contains key information and constraints necessary for recovering the message structure and generating accurate descriptions.

To construct the parse graph, we start by identifying all parsing actions and collecting relevant information through an iteration over all basic blocks. Each identified action defines a parsing element (e.g., the call to nlmsg_parse _deprecated (L3) defines ATTRS1), which is marked as a taint source. Using static taint analysis, we trace how this tainted element is used by other actions (e.g., ATTRS1) is used in array expressions (L11,13,15). These tainted elements are then connected to form parse paths, and the collection of all such paths constitutes the complete parse graph (see Table 3 for more details). When the taint is propagated to an indirect call site, apply the MLTA algorithm [26] to determine the possible callee candidates. In addition, our taint analysis also traces all comparisons involving the extracted payloads. This information can be used to refine the payload types. For instance, if the analysis reveals that a payload is involved in an enum-based switch statement, we extract the corresponding enum values and include them in the fuzzing dictionary (represented as *flags* in the Syzlang syntax) when specifying this payload during description generation.

Updating with Netlink Policy. Since our taint analysis does not traverse pre-modeled library functions (e.g., `nlmsg_parse_deprecated`), the resulting graphs lack internal details and are therefore incomplete. To address this, we refine the parse graph using Netlink policies, which reflect the side effects of these library functions and provide more detailed constraints for attribute payloads. Specifically, we first dump all Netlink policies from the kernel and convert them into graphs with a structure compatible with the parse graph. Each policy graph has a parent node of type ATTRS and child nodes of type NLA, containing all defined constraints. If a policy defines nested constraints (e.g., using `NLA_POLICY_NESTED`) for an attribute NLAnested, we first identify the associated nested policy, convert it into another policy graph, and then attach it as a child subgraph of node NLAnested. This process is performed recursively in a depth-first manner, terminating upon encountering a repeated policy to prevent infinite recursion. After preparing all policy graphs, we update each ATTRS node in the parse graph by: (1) Locating the corresponding policy graph based on .policy; (2) Matching child NLA nodes between the parse graph and located policy graph based on .ntype; (3) Merging information and constraints from the grandchild PAYLOAD nodes. This ensures the parse graph incorporates all constraints from Netlink policies. For example, in Fig. 2 (a), the red-marked constraint (.min = 1) in PAYLOAD2 originates from the policy `ifla_policy`. It is worth noting that the update process also helps detect parsing errors. For example, we identify conflicts between the parsing code and the defined parsing policies (refer to Sect. 5.1 for further details).

Resolving Cross-Message Dependency. Once constraints are updated with Netlink policy, the parse graph should contain sufficient information to define valid messages for a *single operation*. To further improve fuzzing performance, we must also account for cross-message dependencies involving *multiple operations*. For example, when a userspace application configures or deletes a network link, the messages must reference an existing link created by prior messages. Unlike the open syscall, which returns a descriptor, such references are not explicitly returned by the kernel in syscall output. That is, cross-message dependency is a type of implicit dependency and the most accurate solution is cross-syscall input propagation analysis via techniques like symbolic execution [23].

However, porting symbolic execution to analyze Netlink messages in the Linux kernel is non-trivial. Instead, inspired by the existing descriptions, we adopt a heuristic approach that leverages our constructed parse graphs to resolve cross-message dependencies. The key insight is that, unlike in device driver targets, where dependency-related payloads are encapsulated in various structures, Netlink families always encapsulate these payloads in the same type of attribute across messages. For instance, the IFLA_IFNAME attribute appears in both link creation and link configuration/deletion messages and contains a payload string for identifying the network device. We refer to such attributes, whose payloads must remain consistent across messages, as Handle Attributes (HAs). To identify HAs based on parse graphs, we investigated the existing descriptions and summarized below heuristic rules: (1) Use Case Rule: a HA-related node should exist in more than one parse graph. (2) Type Rule: a HA-related payload should be of a simple type, such as a string or integer, rather than a more complex structure. (3) Compare Rule: a HA-related payload should be compared with a non-constant value. The first and third rules are straightforward because we know that handle attributes are used in more than one operation, and the payload should be compared to check for existence. The second rule is empirically motivated based on the existing descriptions. To reduce false negatives, based on the found HAs, we do back-propagation from where their payloads are extracted to identify more HAs that serve the same purpose. After identification, we impose constraints to confine HAs' payload values to a limited set, thereby increasing the chance that payload hits the same value across messages during the fuzzing process. Note that potential false positives from our heuristic approach do not negatively impact fuzzing performance for two main reasons. First, we do not apply constraints to payloads that already have defined restrictions (such as value ranges or constant enums). As a result, our method avoids introducing conflicting constraints or reducing the randomness of such payloads. Second, regarding any unnecessary constraints, we observed that Syzkaller's SQUASH trait [19] will randomly convert constrained data structures into random blobs during fuzzing. This mechanism allows the fuzzer to bypass unnecessary constraints and continue exploring the input space effectively.

Description Generation. Finally, we traverse the parse graphs and translate each visited node to the Syzlang type. The node-to-type translation follows the schemas below (all line number references refer to the demo in Fig. 2 (b)):

- *NLMSG* nodes are translated into the Syzlang predefined struct netlink_msg, with message type and references to child nodes (e.g., the L3 NLMSG definition).
- *ATTRS* nodes have two translation methods, depending on how their represented elements are parsed. (1) For ATTRS nodes parsed via loops (e.g., nlmsg_for_each_attr), which allow repeated attributes, we adopt a definition consistent with existing descriptions. Specifically, we use Syzlang union and variable-length array to model the stream as a "permutation with repetition". (2) For ATTRS nodes parsed by library functions (e.g., nlmsg_parse_deprecated) that reject repeated attributes, we introduce a new type

unordered struct, with Syzlang optional type to define the stream as a "permutation without repetition". For example, see the definition of `ATTRS1` at L6. This method can save the fuzzing effort wasted on generating and mutating redundant attributes, thereby improving overall efficiency.
- *NLA* nodes are translated into Syzlang's predefined structs (nlattr and nlnest). For example, the definitions of `NLA1,2,3` at L12,14,16.
- *PAYLOAD* nodes are translated based on their detailed type: For C structs, we use Syzkaller's built-in tool `syz-headerparser` to extract the struct definitions (e.g., the `ifinfomsg` definition at L19). For C scalars (e.g., integers), we use the corresponding Syzlang type (e.g., `int`) and leverage features like min, max, and flags to define constraints (e.g., the NLA2 payload definition at L15). For C strings, we use Syzlang's `string` or `stringnoz` types. Other Syzlang types (e.g., `const`, `void`) are applied as appropriate. Additionally, for identified handle attributes, we use `handles` for string-type handles (e.g., the payload of NLA1 at L13), and `handlei` for integer-type handles. These special types use Syzlang's `proc` type, allocating 16 unique slots per fuzzing process.

After translating all nodes, we wrap the root type with a pseudo-syscall `nlmsg_send` (e.g., L1 in Fig. 2 (b)) to finalize the description for the operation.

Implementation Details. The static analysis component of NLSaber is implemented using CodeQL v2.18.2 [14]. We selected CodeQL due to its efficiency (well-designed multi-process and caching) and complete support for taint analysis. It enables users to define sources and sinks easily to detect desired taint flows. The entire system consists of 7.4K lines of Python code, 5K lines of QL code, and 500 lines of Syzkaller patches (e.g., adding new pseudo-syscalls and types). NLSaber is the first system designed to enhance Netlink family fuzzing by generating descriptions. To promote the development of similar systems and address concerns of reproducibility, the source code is available at https://github.com/TroySysSec/NLSaber.

4 Evaluation

General Setup. We conducted all experiments on a machine equipped with 48 Intel(R) Xeon(R) CPU E5-2678 and 128 GB of RAM, running Ubuntu 20.04 LTS. The target Linux kernel version is 6.1.70 LTS (released in Feb 2024). The Syzkaller and related Syzlang descriptions version is based on commit 8d34fd8d3a26 (released in Feb 2025). Like previous kernel fuzzing research, we use the kernel configuration provided by Syzbot [17], which incorporates the best practices from Google.

Research Questions. This section addresses the following research questions:

- **RQ1:** Are generated descriptions more complete and accurate?
- **RQ2:** Can generated descriptions enhance fuzzing's code coverage?
- **RQ3:** Can generated descriptions help find new vulnerabilities?

4.1 Descriptions Generation (RQ1)

During the target family identification, we consider a family interesting if it contains at least one operation with a PAYLOAD node. These families are then selected as fuzzing targets. Using this criterion, NLSaber identified 76 target families and 865 operations across six Netlink interfaces by scanning the entire 6.1.70 kernel. These targets span over 2,700 files and more than 2,000 KLOC. In addition, the constructed parse graphs contain an average of 285 nodes, and the graph for *route CORE* and the *generic nl80211* family exceeds 3k nodes. Such complexity highlights the need for an automated tool like NLSaber, as manual auditing is insufficient for comprehensive analysis.

To evaluate the correctness of the generated descriptions, we adopted a methodology inspired by previous work [22], cross-validating our results against manually written descriptions. Specifically, we begin by identifying all existing message definitions based on their types (e.g., netlink_msg), and then group them according to the belonging Netlink families. Next, we (reverse-)translate the existing descriptions into parse graphs, enabling the comprehensive comparison with our constructed graphs. We focused on four key aspects: (1) target families (#fam), (2) operation functions (#op), and (3) parse paths (#ppath), which represent how the payload is extracted, (3) handle attributes (#ha), about cross-message dependency. We developed scripts to identify the same contents like nodes, edges, and paths, as well as to highlight differences, between these graphs. Then, we manually verified the true positives and false cases. While the process was primarily manual, it was significantly supported by our static analysis tool, which reports precise code locations for all detected parsing actions (see comments in Fig. 2(b)). Overall, the validation process took approximately a person-month to complete across all target families. The validation results are summarized in Table 1.

Table 1. Descriptions comparison results.

interface	Syzkaller						NLSaber					
	#fam	#op		#ppath		#ha	#fam	#op		#ppath		#ha
		TP	FP	TP	FP			TP	FP	TP	FP	
NETLINK_CRYPTO	1	7	0	2	3	0	1	7	0	2	0	0
NETLINK_GENERIC	22	400	4	2,053	2,808	41	40	583	0	3,428	431	249
NETLINK_NETFILTER	8	65	0	2,390	4,441	51	8	67	0	3,530	12	86
NETLINK_RDMA	1	26	0	73	5	6	3	48	0	134	11	13
NETLINK_ROUTE	20	106	0	2,295	6,010	30	23	136	0	3,812	389	238
NETLINK_XFRM	1	22	2	99	563	1	1	24	0	102	0	1
#total	53	626	6	6,912	13,830	129	76	865	0	11,008	843	587

Overall, the generated descriptions are more comprehensive than the existing ones. They cover 43% more target families (76 vs. 53) and support 38% more operations (865 vs. 626). Among the 23 newly supported families, the oldest was introduced in 2008 (Linux 2.6) and the newest in 2022 (Linux 5.17). Of the 240 previously untested operations, 108 belong to these 23 families, while the remaining 132 are newly added operations in families already supported by Syzkaller. Our analysis shows that 92 of these 132 operations (70%) have been present in the kernel for over three years. During validation, we identified six false positives in the Syzkaller-defined operations. These were caused by missing callback functions in the kernel: two due to deprecated commands and four due to human errors. This underscores the incompleteness and obsolescence of the existing descriptions and demonstrates the value of our automated approach in improving the situation.

In terms of parse path (#ppath) comparison, the generated descriptions contain significantly more true parse paths (11,008 vs. 6,912) and fewer false ones (843 vs. 13,830), indicating that our method can better guide fuzzers in generating and mutating attributes, thereby improving code coverage. This advantage is evident not only in interfaces where NLSaber covers more target families, such as NETLINK_GENERIC, with 67% more paths (3,428 vs. 2,053), but also in NETLINK _NETFILTER (3,530 vs. 2,390). The latter benefits from frequent updates and the addition of new attributes. Two additional observations are noteworthy. First, we identified **85 broken parse paths** in Syzkaller's descriptions, caused by incorrect assumptions about kernel parsing logic, leading to improperly defined structures. These errors have been reported to and confirmed by the Syzkaller team, underscoring the importance of automated approaches in reducing human error. Second, our generated descriptions include 843 false parse paths, all of which arise from challenging corner cases in static analysis. Some attribute types depend on dynamically determined variables, making static resolution infeasible. To preserve soundness, NLSaber includes all possible outcomes, introducing some redundancy. Additionally, certain families use shared callback functions with internal flags to parse different messages, causing our tool to merge multiple parse graphs together and resulting in false positives. Fortunately, such cases are rare, and our approach still achieves a high accuracy of 93%.

NLSaber identifies 587 handle attributes (#ha). To evaluate these, we conduct an inclusion test to determine whether these attributes extracted from Syzlang descriptions are present in the identified set. The test reveals that only five out of 129 cases are missed, indicating that our generated descriptions guide the fuzzer in resolving implicit dependencies at least as effectively as Syzkaller. For the remaining 463 identified handle attributes, they may include false positives, as our method relies on a simple heuristic rather than precise cross-syscall input propagation analysis [23]. Determining whether these attributes correspond to shared resources requires in-depth knowledge of the underlying implementation; thus, we defer more precise verification to future work.

Answer to RQ1: Descriptions generated by NLSaber are more complete (cover 43% more families and 38% more operations) and achieve higher accuracy in parse paths (93% vs. 33%).

4.2 Fuzzing Effectiveness: Coverage (RQ2)

Fuzzing Experiment Setup. In this section, we evaluate the effectiveness of NLSaber by comparing it with other kernel fuzzers. Alongside the original Syzkaller, we include two description-free fuzzers for a comprehensive evaluation. The first is **FuzzNG** [2], a kernel device driver fuzzer based on LibFuzzer [18]. Instead of relying on complex descriptions to define pointer types in driver handlers, FuzzNG instruments kernel I/O functions (e.g., copy_from_user (CFU) to intercept kernel-user space interactions. This enables the LibFuzzer engine to generate structured inputs when the kernel accesses user-provided data. To adapt FuzzNG for fuzzing Netlink families, we modified its agent to: (1) open the appropriate Netlink socket; (2) invoke the send syscall instead of driver-specific read, write, and ioctl; and (3) generate random messages upon CFU happens. The second fuzzer is **WEIZZ** [12], an AFL [16] variant that also operates without predefined descriptions. WEIZZ introduces a "surgical" stage that infers message structures by tagging input bytes. To enable Netlink fuzzing, we developed a harness that: (1) encodes WEIZZ inputs into Netlink messages; (2) sends them to the kernel using send syscall; and (3) collects KCOV coverage and returns it to the fuzzer via shared memory. We used virtme [1] to run the WEIZZ fuzzer in a QEMU KVM environment, consistent with the other fuzzers.

Each Netlink family was tested in a dedicated fuzzing session, with duration based on the number of available operations (#op) : 24 h for fewer than 10 operations, 48 h for fewer than 20, 72 h for fewer than 50, and 120 h otherwise. Netlink families previously exploited in kCTF were always tested for 120 h. In all sessions, the fuzzer was allocated 4 GB of memory and a single CPU core. Following prior work [22], we disabled crash reproduction to focus solely on coverage, and we deleted all seed programs in both Syzkaller and NLSaber to ensure a fair comparison.

Fuzzing Experiment Results. Each fuzzing session ran three times, and the final average coverage (#cov) is summarized in Table 4. Moreover, we calculate Vargha and Delaney's $\hat{A}_{12}$ statistics to estimate the effect size of coverage advantage. The results demonstrate that:

- *Fuzzing with descriptions significantly outperforms the description-free counterparts.* Specifically, Syzkaller and NLSaber achieve higher coverage across all target Netlink families than FuzzNG and WEIZZ (more than doubling the overall coverage). Our analysis of the fuzzing logs shows that the latter two fuzzers often fail early due to attribute checks, which require each attribute in the stream to have a valid type and length. This underscores the benefit of using descriptions to guide Netlink family fuzzing. Additionally, the significant coverage advantage of Syzkaller-based fuzzers is partly attributable to its advanced features, such as support for virtual netdevices, WiFi emulation, and packet injection, which enable exploration of more code paths.
- *WEIZZ outperforms FuzzNG on more targets.* Specifically, it achieved better coverage, with a large effect size ($\hat{A}_{12}(n) \geq 0.71$) in 27 sessions (marked by underlines). Furthermore, it achieved a 9.5% higher overall coverage (90,120

vs. 82.297). This improvement is due to WEIZZ's ability to incrementally infer message structures during fuzzing, enabling the generation of more valid inputs and deeper code path exploration. However, this ability is not sufficient to fully recover the message structures, and the related corpus gets easily rejected when one attribute is mutated erroneously. Worth noting that FuzzNG achieved higher coverage with $\hat{A}_{12}(n) \leq 0.29$ in 15 sessions. Our analysis indicates that this advantage stems from FuzzNG's optimized snapshot-fuzzing engine [2] and its instrumentation of kernel functions such as strncmp and memcmp, which requires kernel modifications not supported by WEIZZ or other fuzzers. These enhancements contribute to FuzzNG's better performance in some targets.

– *NLSaber outperforms Syzkaller and achieves the best coverage for most targets.* Specifically, it achieved better coverage, with a large effect size ($\hat{A}_{12}(d) \geq 0.71$) in 37 sessions (also marked by underlines). Furthermore, it achieved a 9.1% higher overall coverage (163,670 vs. 150,026) than Syzkaller in both supported targets. The improvement increases to 40.8% (211,271 vs. 150,026) if including NLSaber-specific targets. In addition, our tool achieves the highest average coverage in 43/50 sessions (highlighted in bold). Such advantages indicate the effectiveness of the generated descriptions in enhancing the Netlink family fuzzing. Worth noting that, although Syzkaller achieves higher coverage on some targets, there are no cases where it shows a large effect size ($\hat{A}_{12}(d) \leq 0.29$). In five cases, it exhibits a medium effect size, and in two cases, a small effect size, indicating that NLSaber performs comparably. Taking the 802154 session as an example, Syzkaller achieves 3.9% higher coverage. Our analysis reveals that descriptions used by Syzkaller deliberately exclude two operations: NL802154_CMD_DEL_INTERFACE and IEEE802154_DEL_IFACE. These operations can remove fuzzer pre-configured devices, which could disrupt fuzzing. By omitting them, Syzkaller achieves better coverage compared to our approach, which retains these operations. Interestingly, our analysis also shows that the slightly lower coverage in these cases may result from NLSaber detecting more crashes. For instance, in the nbd family, our tool triggered a use-after-free vulnerability that Syzkaller missed.

Answer to RQ2: Descriptions generated by NLSaber improves the fuzzing with more than 9.1% greater code coverage compared to the original Syzkaller.

4.3 Fuzzing Effectiveness: Vulnerability (RQ3)

We used the generated descriptions to guide fuzzing for zero-day vulnerability detection. Specifically, we conducted fuzzing campaigns on interesting kernel versions, like the stable and associated candidate versions. So far, our tool has uncovered in total 19 previously unknown vulnerabilities, all of which were reported and confirmed, with 12 CVEs assigned (Table 2).

Table 2. New vulnerabilities detected by enhanced fuzzing.

	description	lifespan	CVE	effect
1	deadlock in iwpm_hello_cb	6yr 3mo	-	DoS
2	global overflow of ksmbd_nl_policy	2yr 10mo	CVE-2024-26608	DoS
3	global overflow of loggers	8yr 4mo	CVE-2023-6040	Leak
4	heap overflow in xt_find_target	10yr 2mo		Exp
5	global overflow of rmnet_policy	5yr 10mo	CVE-2024-26597	DoS
6	global overflow of wwan_rtnl_policy	3yr 9mo	CVE-2024-50128	DoS
7	heap off-by-one in ieee80211_tx_control_port	2yr 7mo	CVE-2024-56663	Exp
8	information leak in fl_set_geneve_opt	6yr 8mo	CVE-2025-22055	Leak
9	information leak in ip_tun_parse_opts_geneve	5yr 5mo		
10	information leak in nft_tunnel_obj_geneve_init	5yr 2mo		
11	information leak in tunnel_key_copy_geneve_opt	7yr 3mo		
12	information leak in xfrm_address_filter	9yr 4mo	CVE-2023-39194	Leak
13	information leak in xfrm_update_ae_params	1yr 8mo	CVE-2023-3773	Leak
14	null-ptr-deref in xfrm_update_ae_params	12yr 5mo	CVE-2023-3772	DoS
15	stack overflow in nft_set_desc_concat_parse	2yr 4mo	CVE-2022-1972	Exp
16	type confusion in nft_tunnel_obj_geneve_init	5yr 2mo	CVE-2025-22056	Exp
17	type confusion in nft_tunnel_opts_dump			Leak
18	use-after-free in handshake_req_submit	-	-	Exp
19	use-after-free in nfc_genl_llc_get_params	10yr 2mo	CVE-2023-3863	Leak

Among the 19 vulnerabilities, 13 are found in code (either new families or new functions within existing families) not supported by existing descriptions (highlighted in gray in the table). All of them remained in the kernel (and could have been exploited in the wild) for over a year. This again underscores the importance of developing automated tools to keep testing new and updated targets. We also assessed the exploitability and impact of each vulnerability with our best efforts. As shown in the table: (1) *DoS* marks indicate that the corresponding vulnerability leads to Denial of Service in the kernel. For example, the first deadlock bug could be exploited to spray non-killable threads and cause the kernel to hang. (2) *Leak* marks indicate that the corresponding vulnerability could cause kernel information leakage. Take the 11th vulnerability as an example: the root cause of this one is an integer overflow that leads to type confusion. We exploited this to get a heap out-of-bounds read primitive that allows us to read the adjacent kmalloc-512 cache. Then, using heap spraying techniques with `tty_port` as the spray object, we filled the kmalloc-512 cache with controlled data and leaked a function pointer to bypass KASLR. (3) *Exp* marks are the worst, as they enable stronger memory corruption, such as out-of-bounds or arbitrary write primitives. To demonstrate this, we developed a complete exploit for the 16th vulnerability which gains a kernel space arbitrary code execution primitive and achieves the Local Privilege Escalation (LPE). Similar to the aforementioned heap out-of-bounds read one, we also use heap spray techniques on the kmalloc-512 cache to exploit this. Specifically, we choose the nft_object as the victim object and use heap overflow to hijack the code pointer, thereby achieving ROP by pivoting the stack to a controlled heap location. A demonstration of this exploit is also available in our released artifacts.

Answer to RQ3: Descriptions generated by NLSaber help detect new vulnerabilities. As evidence, our enhanced fuzzing uncovered 19 previously unknown vulnerabilities, with 12 CVEs assigned.

5 Discussion

5.1 Finding Parsing Errors via Static Testing

During parse graph construction, e.g., when updating with Netlink policies, we perform static testing to find potential parsing errors. Specifically, we verify the following rules during parsing: *(R1)*. All active Netlink attributes must have corresponding entries in the associated parsing policies. This error typically occurs when new attributes are introduced into the kernel but the corresponding policy is not updated. As a result, there are no constraints on the attribute, allowing attackers to craft malicious payloads for harmful purposes. *(R2)*. Attributes that are validated must also be used; otherwise, the validation is redundant, causing confusing code or even functionality problems. *(R3)*. Library functions must be used correctly. For example, function nlmsg_parse_deprecated requires the user to provide a destination array whose size should be equal to the value of maxtype + 1. In practice, we identified 35 issues: 25 violations of R1, 4 of R2, and 6 of R3. These parsing errors complement fuzzing-based approaches, as they typically do not cause memory corruptions and thus remain undetectable by sanitizers such as KASAN. All findings were reported, confirmed by the kernel community, and fixed successfully.

5.2 Limitations

Inter-Attributes Relation. NLSaber does not account for the relations between attributes within a Netlink message, instead allowing the fuzzer to explore attribute combinations randomly (e.g., using optional type or union type). However, certain attributes are mutually exclusive, while others must appear together. By explicitly modeling these constraints and guiding the fuzzer to generate or mutate inputs accordingly, the fuzzing accuracy can be improved, and fuzzing cycles wasted on wrong relations can be saved. Unfortunately, such relationships are difficult to analyze automatically so they are left as future work.

Other Interfaces. NLSaber targets operation functions that handle userspace messages, as these are observed to be the most vulnerable. However, certain complex Netlink families involve additional interfaces, making operation-level fuzzing insufficient to uncover all bugs. For example, CVE-2022-10155 [9] is a complex vulnerability that is triggered during packet processing by kernel background threads, following a misconfiguration caused by malformed messages in operation functions. Identifying all relevant interfaces and performing comprehensive fuzzing is non-trivial. Therefore, we currently focus on individual operations and leave multi-interface scenarios for future work.

Other Input Structures. NLSaber focuses on Netlink families, so the proposed analysis is primarily designed for the Netlink side. This naturally limits the scope of our tool. Nevertheless, we believe that modeling the parsing process using parse graphs is also effective in other scenarios involving complex input structures, which we leave as future work.

6 Related Work

Structure-Aware Fuzzing. Structure-aware fuzzing uses fuzzers that understand input formats [5,38], allowing them to generate and mutate inputs more effectively, which significantly improves performance [5]. To achieve structure-aware fuzzing, some fuzzers rely on predefined input descriptions. For userspace programs, tools such as AFLSmart [31] and Peach [11] allow users to define complex input formats and protocols using grammar-based representations. For kernel cases, Syzkaller [35] uses syscall descriptions and demonstrates its effectiveness with thousands of reported bugs. Several previous studies [7,21,22,33] aim to automate the generation of these descriptions for Syzkaller. For example, KSG [33] uses dynamic probe analysis targeting device drivers and network protocols. SyzDescribe [22] offers a systematic approach to generating syscall descriptions for Linux kernel drivers. SyzGen++ [6] uses symbolic execution for both Linux device drivers and closed-source macOS IOKit modules. However, none of these approaches is effective in fuzzing Netlink families because they cannot handle complex Netlink messages. For example, we tried using SyzGen++'s type analysis to infer the message structure in Fig. 1, but the symbolic execution failed because it either timed out or ran out of memory.

Some other fuzzers do not rely on pre-existing descriptions. Instead, they infer input structures dynamically using runtime feedback. For instance, WEIZZ [12] infers message fields by analyzing dependencies between input bytes and comparison instructions. Polyglot [3], NestFuzz [10], and AIFORE [32] apply dynamic taint analysis to extract message structure. However, these approaches are difficult to adapt to Netlink families, as they typically rely on frameworks like DFSan [14], which are not supported in the upstream Linux kernel. In our evaluation, we ported the WEIZZ fuzzer since the Linux kernel's KCOV feature supports collecting the comparison coverage it requires. Additionally, we ported FuzzNG [2] as it also operates without relying on syscall descriptions.

Improving Kernel Fuzzing via Other Ways. Rather than focusing on description generation, many existing approaches enhance kernel fuzzing via other solutions. Moonshine [30] derives and refines seed test cases from dynamic execution traces to improve code coverage. SyzVegas [36] applies reinforcement learning to optimize the mutation strategy. Healer [34] proposes a relation learning-based solution to improve the choice table algorithm of Syzkaller. StateFuzz [38] leverages state coverage to guide fuzzing toward deeper program paths. Actor [13] uses action-guided synthesis with specialized templates to help fuzzers discover more bugs. Note that most of these studies require ready-made syscall descriptions, so our work is orthogonal to theirs. That is, the descriptions we generate can serve as a complement to these tools when fuzzing Netlink families.

7 Conclusion

In this paper, we present NLSaber, the first specialized tool that automatically generates complete and accurate descriptions for fuzzing Netlink families. NLSaber employs static taint analysis to construct parse graphs to model the Netlink message parsing process. These graphs capture critical parsing elements, associated actions, and other relevant details, enabling the generation of high-quality descriptions for fuzzing. We evaluated NLSaber on Linux 6.1.70, demonstrating that its generated descriptions are more complete and accurate than existing ones. Using these generated descriptions, our enhanced fuzzing results in over 9.1% improved code coverage. Additionally, it uncovered 19 previously unknown vulnerabilities, with 12 CVEs assigned.

Acknowledgement. This work is partially supported by the National Key R&D Program of China (No. 2022YFE0113200), the National Natural Science Foundation of China (NSFC) under Grant U21A20464. Any opinions, findings, and conclusions or recommendations expressed in this material are those of the authors and do not necessarily reflect the views of funding agencies. We thank all anonymous reviewers for their invaluable comments.

Appendix Tables

Pre-Modeled Parsing Actions. The complete list of pre-modeled parsing actions is provided in Table 3. In each entry, capitalized keywords denote taint elements or essential information values. XXXsrc (XXX could be HDR, NLMSG, ATTRS, NLA, and PAYLOAD) indicates a new taint source introduced by the action, while XXXdst represents a potential taint sink in some expected taint flows. During the taint analysis, we mark all identified XXXsrc as the taint source and track where the taint element flows to. If the flow reaches any of the XXXdst, we wrap a graph node of XXX type and connect it according to the tainted action. Other keywords are about the to-collect information, for example, the POLICY keyword assists the analysis in identifying the corresponding Netlink policy, which provides details such as attribute constraints. NTYPE helps determine the attribute type critical for reconstructing the message structure. MAXTYPE enables further verification, as discussed in Sect. 5.1. Parsing actions 42–48 are special cases that require additional explanation. In these actions, the inner parsing *is not nested;* instead, it occurs at the same "parsing level". In other words, these actions operate directly on the attribute itself, rather than on its payload. When handling these cases, we use sibling nodes rather than child nodes in the parse graph to ensure a correct definition of the message structure.

Table 3. List of pre-modeled parsing actions and to-collect information.

	Parsing Actions
1	HDRsrc=nlmsg_data(NLMSGdst);
2–4	nlmsg_parse{_deprecated}{_strict}(NLMSGdst, ~, ATTRSsrc, MAXTYPE, POLICY, ~);
5	nlsmg_validate_deprecated(NLMSGdst, ~, MAXTYPE, POLICY, ~);
6	NLAsrc = nlmsg_attrdata(NLMSGdst);
7	NLAsrc = nlmsg_find_attr(NLMSGdst, ~, NTYPE);
8	NLAsrc = ATTRSdst[NTYPE];
9–24	PAYLOADsrc = nla_get_{u/s/be/le}{8/16/32/64}(NLAdst);
25	PAYLOADsrc = nla_data(NLAdst);
26–30	PAYLOADsrc = nla_get_{flag/msecs/in_addr/in6_addr/bitfield32}(NLAdst);
31–32	nla_{strscpy/memcpy}(PAYLOADsrc, NLAdst, SIZE);
33	PAYLOADsrc = nla_strdup(NLAdst, ~);
34–35	nla_{strcmp/memcmp}(NLAdst, ~, ~);
36	NLAsrc = nla_data(NLAdst);
37	NLAsrc = nla_find_nested(NLAdst, NTYPE);
38–39	nla_parse_nested{_deprecated}(ATTRSsrc, MAXTYPE, NLAdst, POLICY, ~);
40–41	nla_validate_nested{_deprecated}(NLAdst, MAXTYPE, POLICY, ~);
42	NLAsrc* = nla_next(NLAdst*);
43	NLAsrc* = nla_find(NLAdst*, ~, NTYPE);
44–46	nla_parse{_deprecated}{_strict}(ATTRSsrc*, MAXTYPE, NLAdst*, ~, POLICY, ~);
47–48	nla_validate{_deprecated}(NLAdst*, ~, MAXTYPE, POLICY, ~);

Fuzzing Coverage Experiment Results Due to space limits, we present the fuzzing coverage results for Sect. 4.2 in Table. 4.

Table 4. Fuzzing coverage results.

interface	family	FuzzNG #cov	WEIZZ #cov	$\hat{A}_{12}(n)$	Syzkaller #op	Syzkaller #cov	NLSaber #op	NLSaber #cov	$\hat{A}_{12}(d)$
NETLINK_CRYPTO	-	1,523	1,363	0.0	7	1,819	7	**1,862**	0.89
	802154*	2,257	2,845	1.0	55	**7,989**	57	7,690	0.33
	batadv	1,371	1,403	1.0	19	3,508	19	**3,733**	0.89
	devlink	1,348	1,357	0.56	35	5,970	73	**7,430**	1.0
	ethtool	2,875	1,737	0.0	39	4,121	58	**4,225**	1.0
	fou	1,958	2,148	1.0	4	4,067	4	**4,101**	0.78
	gtp	1,299	1,342	1.0	5	**3,274**	5	3,261	0.44
	hsr	1,230	1,217	0.22	/		2	**2,938**	1.0
	ila	1,647	1,479	0.0	/		5	**3,111**	1.0
	ioam6	1,478	1,373	0.0	/		7	**2,977**	1.0
	ipvs	1,373	1,384	0.67	17	4,337	17	**4,444**	0.78
	l2tp	1,373	2,279	1.0	11	4,141	11	**4,367**	1.0
	macsec	1,281	1,357	1.0	/		11	**3,388**	1.0
	mptcp	1,373	1,404	0.89	12	2,194	12	**2,953**	1.0
	nbd	2,959	2,973	0.67	4	**5,008**	4	4,945	0.33
NETLINK_GENERIC	ncsi	1,322	1,282	0.0	/		7	**3,089**	1.0
	net_dm	1,102	1,499	1.0	2	2,729	5	**3,070**	1.0
	netlabels*	1,468	1,794	1.0	24	3,728	24	**3,734**	0.67
	nfc	1,547	2,999	1.0	19	5,075	20	**5,113**	0.89
	nl80211	4,316	5,108	1.0	114	12,441	122	**14,497**	1.0
	openvswitchs*	1,686	2,287	1.0	/		23	**6,204**	1.0
	seg6	1,261	1,371	1.0	4	2,971	4	**2,978**	0.44
	smbd	1,227	1,424	1.0	/		16	**2,932**	1.0
	smcs*	1,384	1,349	0.11	5	2,955	23	**3,076**	1.0
	taskstats	1,417	1,378	0.11	/		1	**2,980**	1.0
	tcm_user	1,197	1,229	1.0	/		4	**2,828**	1.0
	tcp_metrics	1,337	1,260	0.11	/		3	**2,963**	1.0
	team	1,277	1,326	1.0	4	**3,089**	4	3,084	0.33
	thermal	1,231	1,205	0.11	/		5	**2,785**	1.0
	tipcv2	1,436	1,529	0.78	27	5,540	28	**5,562**	0.67
	vdpa	1,329	1,267	0.22	/		9	**2,490**	1.0
	ACCT	1,301	1,332	0.78	4	**1,994**	4	1,969	0.33
	CONNTRACK*	1,509	1,596	0.78	20	2,613	20	**2,956**	1.0
NETLINK_NETFILTER	IPSET	1,343	1,398	0.78	15	4,927	16	**5,124**	0.67
	NFTABLES	1,399	1,428	0.56	23	3,147	23	**5,418**	1.0
	QUEUE	1,273	1,272	0.56	3	**1,958**	4	1,936	0.33
	IWCM	1,147	1,418	1.0	/		8	**2,431**	1.0
NETLINK_RDMA	LS	1,128	1,217	0.89	/		3	**2,352**	1.0
	NLDEV	1,402	1,397	0.44	26	5,175	37	**5,274**	0.67
	CORE*	7,213	9,744	1.0	54	17,351	75	**19,147**	1.0
	DCB	1,274	1,245	0.33	/		2	**2,056**	1.0
	IPV6SPEC*	1,392	1,419	1.0	8	2,260	8	**2,312**	1.0
	MDB	1,287	1,237	0.11	3	2,296	3	**2,364**	0.89
NETLINK_ROUTE	NEXTHOP*	1,343	1,374	0.78	8	3,662	10	**3,962**	1.0
	NSID	1,330	1,321	0.22	3	**2,796**	3	2,789	0.44
	RULE	1,898	2,020	1.0	7	3,928	9	**3,935**	0.44
	SCHED*	1,804	1,818	0.67	20	5,417	20	**7,831**	1.0
	TUNNEL	1,292	1,241	0.22	/		3	**2,077**	1.0
	VLAN	1,247	1,194	0.0	3	3,010	3	**3,472**	1.0
NETLINK_XFRM	-	1,833	2,481	1.0	22	4,536	24	**5,056**	1.0
#total common	-	61,074	68,241		626	150,026	756	**163,670**	-
#total all	-	82,297	90,120				865	**211,271**	

* means there are multiple families grouped together for better fuzzing;
/ means the family is not supported.

References

1. amluto: an easy way to virtualize the running system. https://github.com/amluto/virtme
2. Bulekov, A., Das, B., Hajnoczi, S., Egele, M.: No grammar, no problem: towards fuzzing the Linux kernel without system-call descriptions. In: Network and Distributed System Security (NDSS) Symposium (2023)
3. Caballero, J., Yin, H., Liang, Z., Song, D.: Polyglot: automatic extraction of protocol message format using dynamic binary analysis. In: Proceedings of the 14th ACM Conference on Computer and communications security, pp. 317–329 (2007)
4. Chao M., Han Yan, T.X.: LinkDoor: a hidden attack surface in the android Netlink kernel modules
5. Chen, C., Cui, B., Ma, J., Wu, R., Guo, J., Liu, W.: A systematic review of fuzzing techniques. Comput. Secur. **75**, 118–137 (2018)
6. Chen, W., et al.: SyzGen++: dependency inference for augmenting kernel driver fuzzing. In: 2024 IEEE Symposium on Security and Privacy (SP), pp. 4661–4677. IEEE (2024)
7. Chen, W., Wang, Y., Zhang, Z., Qian, Z.: SyzGen: automated generation of syscall specification of closed-source macOs drivers. In: Proceedings of the 2021 ACM SIGSAC Conference on Computer and Communications Security, pp. 749–763 (2021)
8. Corina, J., et al.: DIFUZE: interface aware fuzzing for kernel drivers. In: Proceedings of the 2017 ACM SIGSAC Conference on Computer and Communications Security, pp. 2123–2138 (2017)
9. David: How the tables have turned: An analysis of two new Linux vulnerabilities in NF_tables (2022)
10. Deng, P., et al.: NestFuzz: enhancing fuzzing with comprehensive understanding of input processing logic. In: Proceedings of the 2023 ACM SIGSAC Conference on Computer and Communications Security, pp. 1272–1286 (2023)
11. Eddington, M.: Smartfuzzer peach (2021). https://peachtech.gitlab.io/peach-fuzzer-community/
12. Fioraldi, A., D'Elia, D.C., Coppa, E.: WEIZZ: automatic grey-box fuzzing for structured binary formats. In: Proceedings of the 29th ACM SIGSOFT International Symposium on Software Testing and Analysis, pp. 1–13 (2020)
13. Fleischer, M., et al.: {ACTOR}:{Action-Guided} kernel fuzzing. In: 32nd USENIX Security Symposium (USENIX Security 23), pp. 5003–5020 (2023)
14. Github: Codeql: the libraries and queries (2021). https://github.com/github/codeql
15. Google: Public kctf vrp kernelctf responses. https://github.com/google/security-research/tree/master/pocs/linux/kernelctf
16. Google: American fuzzy lop - a security-oriented Fuzzer (2024). https://github.com/google/AFL/tree/master
17. Google: Stable-6.1-Kasan.config (2024). https://github.com/google/syzkaller/blob/master/dashboard/config/linux/stable-6.1-kasan.config
18. Google: Structure-aware fuzzing with libFuzzer (2025). https://github.com/google/fuzzing/blob/master/docs/structure-aware-fuzzing.md
19. Google: Syzkaller Squashany (2025). https://github.com/google/syzkaller/blob/master/prog/mutation.go#L138
20. Group, N.W.: Rfc3549, Linux Netlink as an IP services protocol (2003)

21. Han, H., Cha, S.K.: IMF: inferred model-based Fuzzer. In: Proceedings of the 2017 ACM SIGSAC Conference on Computer and Communications Security, pp. 2345–2358 (2017)
22. Hao, Y., et al.: SyzDescribe: principled, automated, static generation of syscall descriptions for kernel drivers. In: 2023 IEEE Symposium on Security and Privacy (SP), pp. 3262–3278. IEEE Computer Society (2023)
23. Hao, Y., Zhang, H., Li, G., Du, X., Qian, Z., Sani, A.A.: Demystifying the dependency challenge in kernel fuzzing. In: Proceedings of the 44th International Conference on Software Engineering, pp. 659–671 (2022)
24. Lever, C.: Another crack at a handshake upcall mechanism. https://lwn.net/Articles/922553/
25. Linux: Introduction to netlink. https://docs.kernel.org/userspace-api/netlink/intro.html
26. Lu, K., Hu, H.: Where does it go? Refining indirect-call targets with multi-layer type analysis. In: Proceedings of the 2019 ACM SIGSAC Conference on Computer and Communications Security, pp. 1867–1881 (2019)
27. melifaro: netlink: add netlink support. https://reviews.freebsd.org/D36002?id=109872 (2022)
28. Mongodin, A.: Yet another bug into netfilter (2022). https://www.randorisec.fr/yet-another-bug-netfilter
29. Nguyen, A.: Turning \x00 \x00 into 10000$ (2021). https://google.github.io/security-research/pocs/linux/cve-2021-22555/writeup.html
30. Pailoor, S., Aday, A., Jana, S.: Moonshine: optimizing {OS} fuzzer seed selection with trace distillation. In: 27th {USENIX} Security Symposium ({USENIX} Security 18), pp. 729–743 (2018)
31. Pham, V.T., Böhme, M., Santosa, A.E., Căciulescu, A.R., Roychoudhury, A.: Smart Greybox fuzzing. IEEE Trans. Software Eng. **47**(9), 1980–1997 (2019)
32. Shi, J., et al.: {AIFORE}: smart fuzzing based on automatic input format reverse engineering. In: 32nd USENIX Security Symposium (USENIX Security 23), pp. 4967–4984 (2023)
33. Sun, H., Shen, Y., Liu, J., Xu, Y., Jiang, Y.: {KSG}: augmenting kernel fuzzing with system call specification generation. In: 2022 USENIX Annual Technical Conference (USENIX ATC 22), pp. 351–366 (2022)
34. Sun, H., et al.: Healer: relation learning guided kernel fuzzing. In: Proceedings of the ACM SIGOPS 28th Symposium on Operating Systems Principles, pp. 344–358 (2021)
35. Vyukov, D.: Syzkaller: an unsupervised, coverage-guided kernel Fuzzer (2019)
36. Wang, D., Zhang, Z., Zhang, H., Qian, Z., Krishnamurthy, S.V., Abu-Ghazaleh, N.: {SyzVegas}: beating kernel fuzzing odds with reinforcement learning. In: 30th USENIX Security Symposium (USENIX Security 21), pp. 2741–2758 (2021)
37. wikipedia: Netlink. https://en.wikipedia.org/wiki/Netlink (2023). Accessed 21 April 2023
38. Zhao, B., et al.: {StateFuzz}: system {call-based}{state-aware} Linux driver fuzzing. In: 31st USENIX Security Symposium (USENIX Security 22), pp. 3273–3289 (2022)

The Hidden Dangers of Public Serverless Repositories: An Empirical Security Assessment

Eduard Marin[1]([✉]), Jinwoo Kim[2], Alessio Pavoni[1], Mauro Conti[3,4], and Roberto Di Pietro[5]

[1] Telefonica Research, Barcelona, Spain
{eduard.marinfabregas,alessio.pavoni}@telefonica.com
[2] Kwangwoon University, Seoul, Republic of Korea
jinwookim@kw.ac.kr
[3] University of Padua, Padua, Italy
mauro.conti@unipd.it
[4] Örebro University, Örebro, Sweden
[5] King Abdullah University of Science and Technology, Thuwal, Saudi Arabia
roberto.dipietro@kaust.edu.sa

Abstract. Serverless computing has rapidly emerged as a prominent cloud paradigm, enabling developers to focus solely on application logic without the burden of managing servers or underlying infrastructure. Public serverless repositories have become key to accelerating the development of serverless applications. However, their growing popularity makes them attractive targets for adversaries. Despite this, the security posture of these repositories remains largely unexplored, exposing developers and organizations to potential risks. In this paper, we present the first comprehensive analysis of the security landscape of serverless components hosted in public repositories. We analyse 2,758 serverless components from five widely used public repositories popular among developers and enterprises, and 125,936 Infrastructure as Code (IaC) templates across three widely used IaC frameworks. Our analysis reveals systemic vulnerabilities including outdated software packages, misuse of sensitive parameters, exploitable deployment configurations, susceptibility to typo-squatting attacks and opportunities to embed malicious behaviour within compressed serverless components. Finally, we provide practical recommendations to mitigate these threats.

1 Introduction

Serverless computing has become a highly compelling cloud paradigm that abstracts infrastructure management tasks (e.g., load balancing and scaling) from tenants, allowing them to focus entirely on application development [41,48,52,53]. In serverless architectures, applications are implemented as a set of small, interdependent *functions*, each designed to perform a specific task. These serverless functions can communicate with one another and integrate with cloud services like event triggers, message queues or object storage to support a wide range of applications. Serverless computing offers automatic scaling in response to workload demands and follows a pure pay-per-use pricing model, where tenants are billed only for the resources consumed during execution. Due to these advantages, major cloud providers, such as AWS [5], Microsoft [8], Google [18], IBM [20] and Alibaba [2], have incorporated serverless computing into their service offerings.

As serverless adoption has grown, numerous *public serverless repositories* have emerged, enabling developers to share serverless components. These repositories host a wide range of serverless components, many of which have been downloaded thousands to millions of times. However, their increasing popularity has also made them attractive targets for adversaries [31,36]. A key problem is the lack of transparency surrounding the security practices in these repositories. Most repositories provide little to no information about the security checks performed, the approval policies enforced or how security responsibilities are divided among contributing developers, the users who download serverless components and the repository administrators who publish them. For instance, Red Hat Quay claims *"to continuously scan containers for vulnerabilities"* [22], while AWS states *"all applications published by AWS are reviewed to ensure license compliance and code quality"* [33]. Although these claims suggest some level of scrutiny, they are highly generic and offer little detail about the scope, rigour or consistency of the security checks applied. Crucially, we argue that such claims may create a false sense of security, leading users to believe that the serverless components they download have been thoroughly vetted and are safe to integrate without further verification, thus increasing the risk of supply chain attacks [49].

To the best of our knowledge, we present the first comprehensive study of the security state surrounding public serverless repositories. We focus on two fundamental yet previously under-explored research questions: (i) Do public serverless repositories introduce application-level security risks? (**RQ1**); and, (ii) Does the dynamic configuration and deployment model of serverless computing give rise to novel attack vectors? (**RQ2**). To address RQ1, we analyse the prevalence of outdated third-party libraries with known vulnerabilities in serverless components and investigate the potential for embedding malicious behaviour in components distributed as compressed archives. To address RQ2, we conduct a detailed analysis of Infrastructure as Code (IaC) templates to identify possible misconfigurations. Additionally, we discover three sensitive parameters in Docker run commands that can be exploited for malicious purposes and evaluate these repositories' susceptibility to typo-squatting attacks.

To this end, we collect and analyse 2,758 serverless components from five widely-used public repositories: (i) Docker Hub [14]; (ii) GitHub [17]; (iii) AWS Serverless Application Repository (SAR) [7]; (iv) Serverless Framework [25]; and, (v) Red Hat Quay [22]. Our selection includes one repository dedicated to *serverless plugins* and four hosting *serverless functions*, spanning both well-maintained platforms (e.g., AWS SAR and Red Hat Quay) and highly popular but less regulated ecosystems such as Docker Hub and GitHub. Additionally, we analyse 125,936 IaC templates from three widely used frameworks: Terraform [26], AWS CloudFormation [4] and AWS Serverless Application Model (SAM) [6].

Contributions. We summarize our key contributions as follows:

- We conduct a large-scale security analysis of 2,758 serverless components from major public repositories, including AWS SAR, Docker Hub, GitHub, Red Hat Quay and Serverless Framework, along with 125,936 IaC templates across Terraform, AWS CloudFormation and AWS SAM.
- We reveal two new attack vectors: the insertion of malicious behaviour into compressed serverless components and the presence of misconfigurations within IaC templates. Additionally, we discover three previously undocumented sensitive parameters in Docker run commands.
- We provide a set of actionable recommendations aimed at improving the security posture of public serverless repositories and guiding best practices for repository administrators, developers and users.

Responsible Disclosure. We notified the maintainers of the affected repositories, providing detailed descriptions of the issues and recommendations for mitigation.

2 Background and Motivation

2.1 Serverless Deployment Models

Serverless functions can be deployed using various methods, including: (i) packaging the function as a Docker container image [10,12,16], (ii) uploading a prepackaged ZIP folder containing the functions' code and dependencies [11,13,30], (iii) writing code directly in the cloud provider's console editor [3], (iv) using YAML templates or configuration files that specify the deployment details, resources and permissions of the serverless functions to be deployed and (v) using Infrastructure as Code (IaC) frameworks, such as AWS CloudFormation, to automate the deployment and management of serverless functions. Regardless of the method, developers remain responsible for providing the application code. In recent years, it has become increasingly common to accelerate development by integrating components from public repositories. However, this introduces significant security risks, as discussed in the next section.

2.2 Attack Vectors in Public Serverless Repositories

We identify five primary attack vectors (V_1–V_5) that pose significant security risks to public serverless repositories. It is important to note that some attack vectors are relevant only to specific deployment methods (see Table 1).

V_1 **Vulnerable third-party libraries.** Serverless components typically rely on third-party libraries, many of which contain known vulnerabilities that introduce

Table 1. The applicability of attack vectors by deployment model(● Applicable, ○ Not applicable)

Attack Vectors	Container Image	Pre-packaged Zip	Console Editor	YAML Conf. Files	IaC Frameworks
(V1) Vulnerable third-party libraries	●	●	●	●	●
(V2) Malicious serverless components	●	●	○	○	○
(V3) Sensitive parameters in Docker run commands	●	○	○	○	○
(V4) Misconfigurations in IaC templates	○	○	○	●	●
(V5) Typo-squatting attacks	●	●	●	●	●

security risks [39]. Even when patches are available, outdated libraries often remain in use for extended periods, offering adversaries ample opportunities to exploit those weaknesses [49]. The rapid development cycles inherent to serverless applications make them particularly vulnerable to these risks.

(V2) Malicious serverless components. Many repositories allow anyone to upload serverless components after a simple registration process, enabling adversaries to easily distribute malicious components [43,46]. Most serverless platforms also accept pre-packaged compressed archives bundling code and dependencies, which can facilitate more advanced attacks. These formats can further obfuscate malicious behaviour, making detection by traditional security tools significantly more difficult.

(V3) Sensitive parameters in Docker run commands. Some repositories (e.g., Docker Hub) allow contributors to provide execution instructions specifying how their components should be run. Adversaries can exploit this feature and include malicious `Docker run commands` that contain risky parameters (e.g., `-privileged` or `-pid=host`). Users who download these components are likely to follow the provided (malicious) `Docker run commands`, potentially compromising container isolation and jeopardizing the security of the underlying host.

(V4) Misconfigurations in IaC templates. IaC tools (e.g., AWS CloudFormation) are widely used to specify and deploy serverless functions in production environments. They enable developers to declaratively define the serverless functions and their associated resources, configurations, permissions and policies in a structured and repeatable manner through templates. It is common practice for developers to contribute their IaC templates and reuse those shared by others. However, to date, no systematic study has investigated whether these templates contain misconfigurations or assessed the practical security consequences of such misconfigurations.

(V5) Typo-squatting attacks. Various naming conventions such as Docker's Fully Qualified Image Identification (FQID) [50] and AWS's Amazon Resource Names (ARNs) [21] are used to uniquely identify serverless components within repositories. Because developers often enter these names manually (e.g., via terminal or editor), typographical errors are common. Adversaries can exploit this by registering malicious components with names that closely resemble those of popular or trusted ones. This typo-squatting technique leverages human error to surreptitiously distribute malicious serverless components, increasing the likelihood of accidental installation and execution by unsuspecting users.

2.3 Threat Model

We consider adversaries capable of uploading vulnerable (Ⓥ1) or malicious components (Ⓥ2) to these repositories, posing significant risks to unsuspecting users who use them. In doing so, adversaries can also supply execution instructions that include `Docker run commands` with sensitive parameters (e.g., `-privileged`) (Ⓥ3), exploiting the tendency of many users to follow the provided instructions [51]. Similarly, adversaries can upload IaC templates with dangerous configurations to public repositories, causing any developer who uses them to unknowingly misconfigure their serverless applications and inadvertently expose critical information (Ⓥ4). Finally, when uploading components to these repositories, adversaries can select component names that closely resemble popular entries in the repository (Ⓥ5), aiming to exploit typographical errors made by developers when retrieving serverless components [50].

3 Security Analysis Framework for Public Serverless Repositories

In this section, we describe the process we used to discover and retrieve serverless components from public repositories, and we evaluate their susceptibility to the five attack vectors considered in this paper.

① **Data collection.** To automate the extraction of serverless component data from the selected repositories, we developed custom web scrapers using frameworks such as BeautifulSoup [9] and Selenium [24]. Using these scrapers, we collected key metadata, including: (i) the *component name*, (ii) the associated *pull command* or *GitHub URL* and (iii) the recommended *execution instructions* (when available). In some cases, this process required performing authenticated queries and adhering to repository-imposed request limits. For repositories hosting both serverless and non-serverless components, we applied a two-step filtering mechanism to eliminate non-relevant images and keep only the serverless components. We first configured our crawlers to perform queries using the keyword 'serverless' and then examined the metadata associated with each component to detect the presence of a 'serverless.yml' file. This methodology was inspired by the approach used by Eskandani et al. [45].

② **Vulnerability analysis.** Next, we performed a security analysis of the libraries included in the retrieved serverless components using Trivy [28] and Grype [19], two widely used and open-source vulnerability scanners. Both tools extract metadata, package information and libraries from container images or source code, and cross-reference them against multiple vulnerability databases [32]. The identified vulnerabilities are classified into five severity levels according to their CVSS 3.1 scores: (i) *Critical* (9.0–10.0), (ii) *High* (7.0–8.9), (iii) *Medium* (4.0–6.9), (iv) *Low* (0.1–3.9) and (v) *Unknown* (excluded from the analysis). Each serverless component was scanned separately with both tools. Using multiple scanners helps account for tool variability, as each may rely on different vulnerability databases and detection heuristics, potentially identifying distinct sets of vulnerabilities.

③ **Hiding malicious behaviour in compressed serverless components.** To investigate whether compression can be exploited to conceal malicious behaviour in serverless components, we utilised VirusTotal [29], a widely used platform that aggregates results from numerous antivirus engines. We hypothesized that adversaries could leverage common compression formats to evade detection [11,13,30]. To test this, we created serverless components compressed with popular compression formats, including both benign samples and variants embedded with malware. Subsequently, we submitted these samples to VirusTotal and analysed the detection rates reported by its integrated antivirus engines.

④ **Identification of sensitive parameters in Docker run commands.** We analysed the execution instructions provided by component owners to identify `Docker run commands` containing sensitive parameters that could be exploited in security attacks. First, we examined serverless components hosted on Docker Hub for sensitive parameters previously documented in the literature [51]. Next, we extended our analysis and discovered three previously undocumented sensitive parameters that can pose significant security risks. These newly identified parameters could enable adversaries to escalate privileges, bypass security controls or gain unauthorized access, thus increasing the potential impact of compromised serverless components distributed via public repositories.

⑤ **Finding misconfigurations in IaC templates.** We examined a large corpus of IaC templates to assess whether they contained insecure configurations that adversaries could exploit to compromise serverless applications. Using Trivy, we scanned these templates [27] for misconfigurations across widely used frameworks, including Terraform, AWS CloudFormation and AWS SAM, and then classified the identified issues into four severity levels. For parameters frequently associated with security risks, we conducted an in-depth analysis to evaluate their potential impact and trace their underlying root causes. Additionally, we manually reviewed the IaC templates to discover previously undocumented misconfigurations that may not be detected through Trivy's automated analysis.

⑥ **Detection of potential typo-squatting attacks.** To identify potential typo-squatting attacks, we measured the similarity between component names using the Damerau-Levenshtein (DL) distance metric [50], which quantifies the minimum number of operations (insertions, deletions, substitutions, or transpositions) needed to transform one string into another. For each repository, we extracted both the username and image name associated with every serverless component and performed exhaustive pairwise comparisons to detect suspiciously similar naming patterns indicative of potential typo-squatting attacks. We focused on name pairs with low DL distances, as these indicate identical or highly similar names.

Table 2. Vulnerability statistics per repository using data collected from Trivy (blue) and Grype (red), respectively.

Repository	# of Compo.	# of Vulnerabilities				
		Mean	Median	Max	Min	Std Dev
Serverless Framework [25]	355	8/35	0/11	257/611	0/0	24/70
AWS SAR [7]	242	4/21	0/0	127/3437	0/0	13/223
GitHub [17]	712	98/119	6/23	18559/9658	0/0	838/581
Docker Hub [14]	1374	1243/1522	432/519	6897/5781	0/0	1477/1628
Red Hat Quay [22]	75	620/676	135/230	5390/5584	0/0	1057/1157

4 Application-Level Security Risks

In this section, we assess the extent to which the collected serverless components are exposed to application-level security risks (RQ1). We begin by analysing the presence of known vulnerabilities in third-party libraries included in these components (Ⓥ1). We then investigate the potential for concealing malicious behaviour when these components are distributed in compressed formats (Ⓥ2).

4.1 Vulnerability Analysis in Third-Party Libraries

Statistical analysis of vulnerabilities across repositories. To characterize the vulnerability landscape of each repository, we begin by reporting key statistical metrics—including the mean, median, minimum, maximum and standard deviation of vulnerability counts—based on data obtained from both Trivy and Grype (see Table 2). Our findings reveal a consistent discrepancy between both tools, with Grype systematically reporting higher vulnerability counts. This difference is rooted in their distinct design philosophies. Grype prioritizes sensitivity and broad detection coverage at the cost of a higher false positive rate [37,38], while Trivy adopts a more conservative approach focused on minimizing false positives that may occasionally lead to missed vulnerabilities [35]. Among the repositories we analysed, Docker Hub and Red Hat Quay exhibit the highest mean and median vulnerability counts, as well as the largest variability among components. GitHub falls in an intermediate position, with several components exhibiting significant vulnerabilities, though generally fewer than those in Docker Hub and Red Hat Quay. Conversely, we found that the Serverless Framework and AWS SAR consistently report lower vulnerability counts.

Distribution of Vulnerabilities Across Serverless Components. To further understand the distribution of vulnerabilities within repositories, we analyse the Cumulative Distribution Function (CDF) of vulnerability counts per serverless component based on the data obtained from Trivy (see Fig. 1). Our results show that approximately 80% of Docker Hub components and 60% of Red Hat

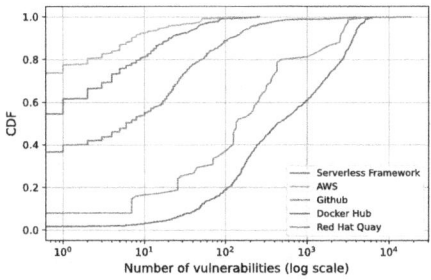
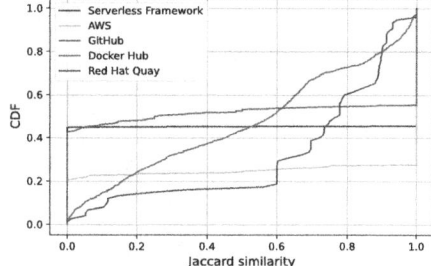

Fig. 1. CDF of vulnerability counts per serverless component.

Fig. 2. Trivy vs. Grype vulnerability similarity.

Quay components have more than 100 vulnerabilities. GitHub presents a slightly better security posture: around 50% of its components contain ten or fewer vulnerabilities, while 10% have more than 100 vulnerabilities. By contrast, serverless components from the AWS SAR and Serverless Framework are significantly less affected. Many components have no known vulnerabilities and most affected ones contain fewer than 10, with few exceeding 100.

Comparison of Grype and Trivy Detection Results. Although Trivy and Grype use similar techniques for vulnerability detection, their results often differ significantly (see Table 2). To quantify this divergence, we computed the Jaccard similarity between the sets of vulnerabilities identified by each tool (see Fig. 2). A score of 1 indicates complete agreement while a score of 0 indicates no overlap. For components from AWS SAR, GitHub and the Serverless Framework, many showed a Jaccard similarity of 1, suggesting identical results. Manual inspection revealed that these components frequently had no detected vulnerabilities. In contrast, components from Docker Hub and Red Hat Quay showed greater discrepancies, with fewer instances of high similarity. These findings underscore the importance of using multiple scanners to obtain a comprehensive assessment of security risks. Importantly, there is no universally accepted 'ground truth' for vulnerability detection. Some organizations prioritize precision by considering only the intersection of scanner outputs to reduce false positives, while others prioritize recall by using the union of results to maximize coverage, even at the expense of increased false positives.

Distribution of Vulnerability Severity Across Repositories. While previous analyses focused primarily on vulnerability counts, we also examined vulnerability severity, a key factor in assessing real-world security risks (see Fig. 3). Although Docker Hub and Red Hat Quay report the highest total vulnerabilities, the proportion of critical and high-severity vulnerabilities in their components is relatively low, only 5% critical and 29% high in Docker Hub, and 3% critical and 23% high in Red Hat Quay. In contrast, AWS SAR and Serverless Framework, which have the lowest average vulnerability counts per component, show the highest proportions of severe vulnerabilities: 68% in AWS SAR and 57% in Serverless Framework are classified as critical or high. For details on the top 10

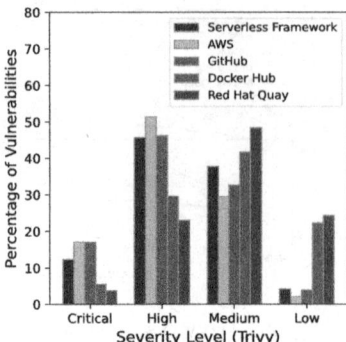 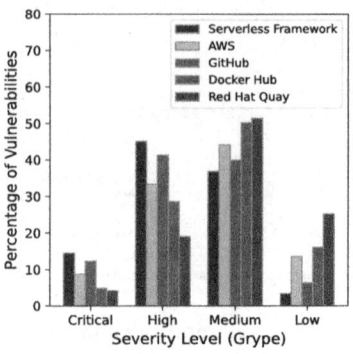

Fig. 3. Vulnerability severity using data from Trivy (left) and Grype (right).

most commonly used packages across five platforms and their associated vulnerabilities and severities, we refer the reader to Appendix A.

4.2 Hiding Malicious Behaviour in Compressed Serverless Components

To evaluate the potential for concealing malicious behaviour within compressed serverless components, we randomly selected 1,794 components from public repositories, including 356 from AWS SAR, 657 from GitHub, 352 from the Serverless Framework, 354 from Docker Hub and 75 from Red Hat Quay. Each component was compressed in its original form using eight widely adopted formats: *7z*, *tar*, *tar.bz2*, *tar.gz*, *tar.lzma*, *tar.xz*, *tar.zst* and *zip*. We first verified that none were flagged as malicious by VirusTotal. Then, using six malicious files sourced from reputable open-source malware repositories[1], including (i) the eicar.txt antivirus test file, (ii) a Python remote access trojan, (iii) a Java infector, (iv) a PHP backdoor, (v) a Python backdoor and (vi) a Python trojan, we generated malicious samples by injecting one file at a time into each component and recompressing them with each compression format.

We examined how the choice of compression format affects the detection of malicious behaviour. Figure 4 presents the CDF of antivirus engines that flagged malicious components for each format. Although all injected files were detected by at least one engine, components compressed with *7z* and *tar.zst* were flagged by significantly fewer engines, indicating lower detection reliability. This is concerning because, due to trade-offs between false positives and false negatives, a component is typically considered malicious only if flagged by a minimum number of engines. In prior work, this threshold was set at five engines [51]. In our analysis, we observed several instances where malicious components compressed with certain formats fell below this threshold, suggesting that embedding malicious behaviour within compressed serverless components could be an effective

---

[1] For example, https://github.com/vxunderground/MalwareSourceCode and https://github.com/nijithneo/DAT.

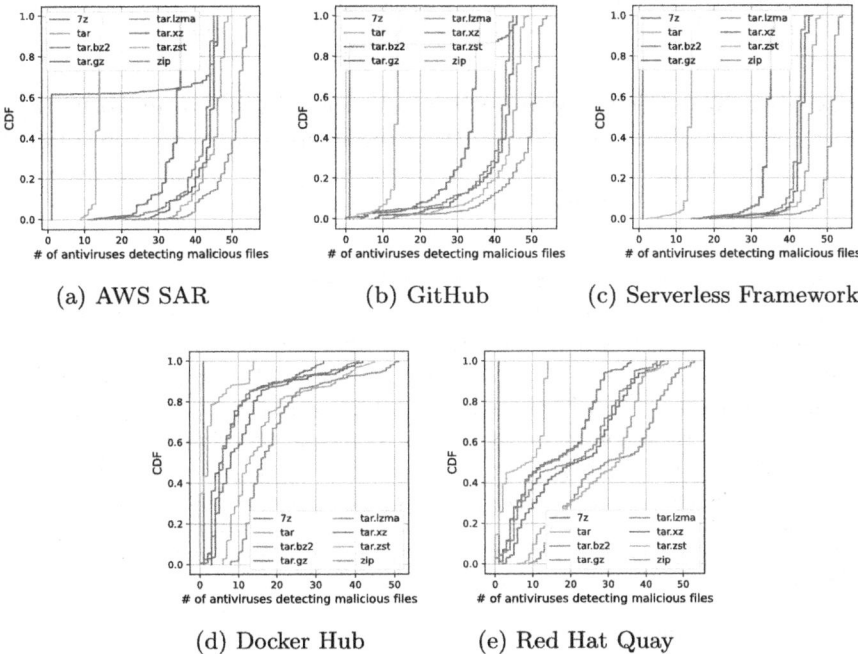

Fig. 4. Relationship between serverless components compressed with various compression algorithms and the number of engines that successfully detect them.

evasion technique. Additionally, we confirmed that such malicious components can be successfully uploaded to public serverless repositories (see Sect. 6).

5 Configuration and Deployment Security Risks

In this section, we examine the security risks in configuring and deploying serverless components (RQ2), focusing on three attack vectors: (i) sensitive parameters in Docker run commands (Ⓥ3); (ii) misconfigurations in IaC templates (Ⓥ4); and, (iii) potential typo-squatting attacks (Ⓥ5).

5.1 Sensitive Parameter Misuse in Docker Run Commands

We analysed the Docker run commands in the execution instructions for serverless components hosted on Docker Hub (Ⓥ3). We first targeted parameters previously identified as sensitive by Liu et al. [51], including -v, -privileged and -pid which can compromise container isolation and host security. For instance, -v <src>:<dest> mounts host directories into a container, potentially leaking sensitive files; -privileged grants unrestricted access to host resources; and -pid=host enables container processes to monitor and interact with all host processes, facilitating reconnaissance or privilege escalation. Our analysis found

137 uses of -v, two instances of -privileged and no occurrences of -pid.

Uncovering New Risky Parameters in Docker Run Commands. Beyond assessing the prevalence of known sensitive parameters in Docker run commands for serverless components hosted in public repositories, our analysis uncovered three previously undocumented parameters that pose significant security risks.

(1) Hard-Coded Credentials. We discovered a case where AWS access keys were hard-coded directly into a Docker run command. Executing such commands may inadvertently expose sensitive credentials, allowing adversaries to take control of the associated cloud environment. This can lead to a range of attacks, including unauthorized access to S3 buckets or launching cryptojacking campaigns [34]. To mitigate this, we recommend avoiding credential injection via command-line arguments and instead using secure methods like Docker secrets (e.g., -secret aws_key and -secret aws_secret) to manage sensitive information.

```
docker run -d --name go-serverless-aws-container
-v $PWD:/usr/src/go/src
-e AWS_KEY=JFHGUFJAKEXAMPLEJDFJHEKF
-e AWS_SECRET=AJDFUEXAMPLESDLKF
-e AWS_REGION=us-east
iamfrisbee/go-serverless-aws
```

(2) Sensitive Information Passed via Environment Variables. We found 47 instances where the -e parameter was used to pass sensitive information, such as credentials, tokens or keys, to containers. Adversaries with access to the Docker daemon (e.g., external adversaries who exploited a misconfiguration) can retrieve these values using commands like `docker inspect`. This exposure could lead to unauthorized access to cloud services, data exfiltration or financial abuse. As with hard-coded credentials, this risk can be mitigated by using Docker secrets.

```
docker run -v $(pwd):/opt/app
-e AWS_DEFAULT_REGION
-e AWS_ACCESS_KEY_ID
-e AWS_SECRET_ACCESS_KEY
andrewoh531/docker-serverless serverless deploy
```

(3) Mounting the Docker Daemon Socket Within Containers. We identified a case where the Docker daemon socket (/var/run/docker.sock) was mounted directly into a container. This configuration effectively grants the container full control over the Docker daemon, allowing an adversary who compromises the container to escalate privileges and gain control over the host system. The security implications are comparable to those of the -privileged flag and are widely regarded as a critical misconfiguration.

```
docker run -p 8080:8080 -v
/var/run/docker.sock:/var/run/docker.sock
furikuri/serverless-to-go
```

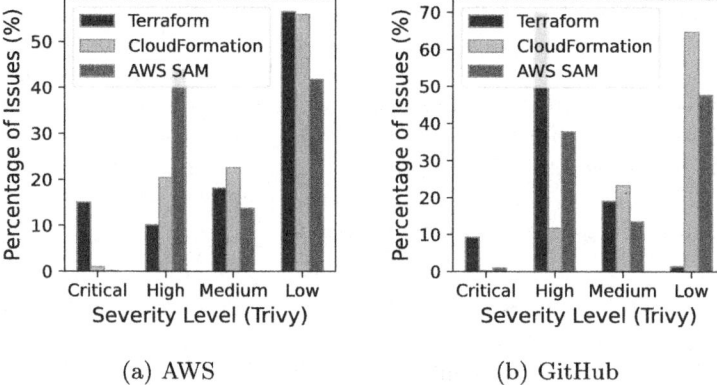

Fig. 5. Misconfigurations severity reported by Trivy for: (a) AWS Serverless Repository; and, (b) GitHub.

Table 3. Breakdown of IaC templates analyzed in our serverless repository dataset.

Repository	Terraform (.tf)	CloudFormation (.yaml, .json)	AWS SAM (.yaml)	Total
AWS	30	5,023	225	5,278
GitHub	1,764	117,860	1,034	120,658
Total	1,794	122,883	1,259	125,936

5.2 Security Analysis of IaC Templates

Given their critical role in automating the deployment of serverless applications, we conducted an in-depth analysis of IaC templates across three widely adopted frameworks: (i) Terraform; (ii) AWS CloudFormation; and, (iii) AWS Serverless Application Model (SAM) (V4). Our dataset includes IaC templates from AWS SAR and GitHub, as container-based platforms such as Docker Hub, Red Hat Quay and Serverless Framework do not include IaC templates. Table 3 provides a breakdown of the analysed IaC templates. To distinguish between frameworks, we classified templates by their extensions: .tf for Terraform and .json or .yaml for AWS CloudFormation. AWS SAM templates, which also use the .yaml format, were identified by detecting the presence of the *Transform: AWS::Serverless-2016-10-31* directive.

We scanned the retrieved IaC templates using Trivy to identify potential misconfigurations. Figure 5 shows the distribution of misconfiguration issues across four severity levels. Our analysis shows that Terraform IaC templates exhibit a significantly higher proportion of critical misconfigurations than AWS CloudFormation and AWS SAM templates. This disparity is likely due to Terraform's broader configurability across multi-cloud environments. Nevertheless, across all frameworks, the proportion of critical and high-severity issues remains substantial, underscoring the systemic risk posed by IaC misconfigurations. We also examined the five most common misconfigurations found in the templates. The most frequent issue, accounting for approximately 19% of the identified misconfigurations, involved the omission of a source ARN in Lambda permissions [15], potentially allowing unrestricted invocation of Lambda functions. Another common issue, accounting for roughly 13% of cases, was the use of default AWS-managed keys instead of customer-managed encryption keys for S3 buckets [23], which weakens control over data protection. A complete overview of the identified misconfigurations is given in Appendix B.

Cross-Origin Resource Sharing. It is well known that using a wildcard ("*") in Cross-Origin Resource Sharing (CORS) policies introduces security risks [42]. Our analysis revealed such misconfigurations in IaC templates configuring CORS for both AWS CloudFormation and AWS SAM. Through manual inspection, we identified seven instances of this issue in AWS SAR and one in GitHub, which were *not* detected by Trivy. The `CorsOrigin` attribute is used to configure CORS policies, which control cross-domain resource sharing (e.g., allowing front-end applications to access resources from AWS S3 buckets) [40]. However, we found that several templates included the configuration `Default: '*'`, which allows unrestricted access from any domain to the serverless application's API Gateway. This wildcard disables CORS protections, posing a significant risk. If adversaries compromise a serverless function, they can exploit the permissive CORS policy to exfiltrate sensitive data to untrusted or attacker-controlled domains [44]. While browsers block credentialed requests (e.g., those involving cookies or authorization headers) [1], our manual inspection of these IaC templates revealed that they provision public APIs without authentication, thereby making even unauthenticated cross-origin requests a security risk.

5.3 Typo-Squatting Attacks

As the final step in our analysis, we assessed the susceptibility of public serverless repositories to typo-squatting attacks (V5), covering components from the Serverless Framework, GitHub, Red Hat Quay and Docker Hub. AWS SAR was excluded since its components are used exclusively within AWS, where the chance of typos by developers is much lower.

Figure 6 shows the CDF of DL similarities for usernames and image names. Our findings revealed two pairs of *user names* with a DL distance equal to 1: one identified on GitHub and one on Docker Hub. Additionally, we identified several *image name* pairs with a DL distance of 1, including two instances in the Serverless Framework, six in GitHub, 191 in Docker Hub and one in Red Hat

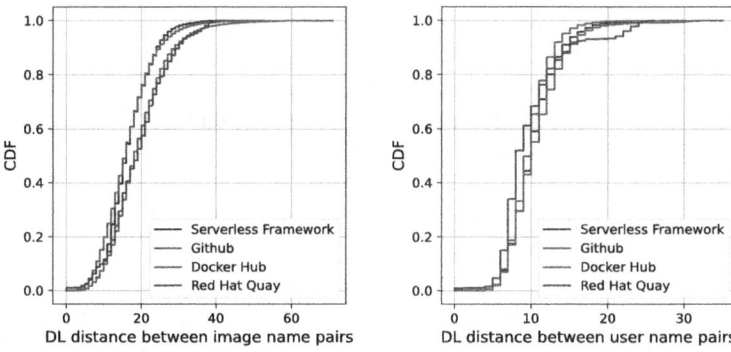

Fig. 6. Lexical analysis based on Damerau-Levenshtein distance, applied to image names (left) and user names (right).

Quay. These results indicate that while typo-squatting risks are present across all repositories, they are particularly pronounced in Docker Hub. Although the intent behind similar usernames or image names within the same repository is unclear, their presence suggests this vector could be exploited by adversaries.

6 Key Findings and Discussion

Our analysis reveals that public serverless repositories often lack rigorous security oversight. Repository administrators typically perform minimal (if any) security checks on the components they host. This is particularly concerning in serverless computing, where applications are rapidly built from many small, interconnected serverless functions. While this enables fine-grained security controls when properly implemented, it also requires each function to be independently configured and secured, increasing the risk of errors and misconfigurations.

Application-Level Security Risks. Although vulnerabilities in third-party libraries are a well-known threat, our findings show that such issues remain widespread even in repositories presumed to maintain strict security controls like AWS SAR. Beyond these, we uncovered new risks tied to how serverless applications are deployed. Specifically, the ability to upload pre-packaged ZIP archives bundling code and dependencies creates a blind spot for traditional scanners, which often fail to properly inspect compressed artifacts. To demonstrate this, we uploaded a malicious ZIP archive with known malware to AWS SAR via a controlled test repository. The upload completed without triggering any alerts, exposing a significant gap in current threat detection. While we deleted the component immediately to comply with ethical research standards, this experiment highlights the need for more advanced security techniques to detect malicious content within compressed serverless packages.

Configuration and Deployment Security Risks. Our study also reveals significant risks arising from serverless application configuration and deployment practices. A common issue is the widespread use of default, overly permissive, or publicly recommended settings. Specifically, both Docker run commands and IaC templates frequently embed risky parameters, making them untrustworthy by default. Although these configuration-related threats are somewhat fewer than third-party library vulnerabilities, they are much harder to detect, as shown by our discovery of three new sensitive Docker parameters and a novel IaC misconfiguration that evaded detection by advanced scanners like Trivy. Furthermore, serverless repositories are vulnerable to typo-squatting attacks, where adversaries register components with names closely resembling popular ones. Critically, serverless automation amplifies the impact of even rare typos, since IaC templates and CI/CD pipelines may automatically fetch and deploy typo-squatted components without manual review, enabling silent integration into production.

Security Model. We advocate for a security model in which public serverless repository administrators are the primary responsible for securing the components they host. To ensure transparency and accountability, they should disclose their security practices, including scanning methods, tools and the frequency of their security assessments. Administrators must implement automated, periodic vulnerability scans using a diverse set of complementary tools, alongside mandatory pre-publication compliance checks. Given the rapidly evolving serverless ecosystem, with frequent emergence of new vulnerabilities in libraries, frameworks and cloud services, continuous monitoring and automated re-evaluation of hosted components are crucial for sustained security. Additionally, repository maintainers should apply automated static analysis to configuration files and enforce blacklists of sensitive parameters (such as those identified in this and prior work) to prevent their inclusion. To mitigate typo-squatting attacks, mechanisms like similarity-based name collision alerts and stricter naming policies should be adopted. Until these security measures become standard, users and developers should assume that any serverless component from a public repository may be compromised and perform thorough independent security evaluations before use.

Possible Limitations of This Work. False positives are a well-known limitation of vulnerability scanners such as Trivy and Grype. These tools may classify a repository as vulnerable if it includes a package with known CVEs in its metadata files. However, if the package is not actually used in the source code, the reported vulnerability may constitute a false positive. To assess the extent of this issue, we randomly selected 30 open-source serverless components (approximately the square root of the total: 242 from AWS and 712 from GitHub). Trivy and Grype collectively reported 1,417 CVEs across these samples. We then manually verified whether the flagged packages were actually referenced in the source code. If a package appeared only in metadata files (e.g., .lock, .gradle, .toml, .yml, .yaml, .json, .xml, .md) but not in source code files (e.g., .py, .js, .ts, .java, .go, .rb, .sh, .c, .cpp), we classified the associated CVE as a false positive. Our analysis found that 1,275 out of 1,417 CVEs were associated with packages present in the source code, resulting in an estimated false positive rate of approximately 10%. These findings suggest that while false positives are present, the rate is within acceptable bounds and does not undermine the overall reliability of our vulnerability analysis.

7 Related Work

Shu et al. [54] were the first to examine the security state of Docker Hub images. Wist et al. [55] conducted a similar study on 2,500 Docker Hub images. Liu et al. [51] provided a comprehensive assessment of the Docker Hub ecosystem, focusing on the detection of malicious images and the identification of exploitable parameters in Docker run commands. Other researchers have focused on analysing specific types of Docker Hub images. For instance, Zerouali et al. [56,57] analysed vulnerabilities and outdated packages in Debian-based and programming language-specific images [58] and Haque et al. [47] evaluated the exploitability of vulnerabilities in base images.

Research Gap. Prior work has mainly addressed security issues in microservices distributed via Docker Hub. In contrast, our study focuses on serverless computing, which is rapidly becoming the dominant cloud application deployment model. We evaluated the vulnerability of serverless components to five distinct attack vectors, including two newly identified in this study, using components from five prominent public repositories. By analysing multiple repositories and diverse attack vectors, we provide a representative overview of current security practices in public serverless repositories.

8 Conclusion

This paper presents the first large-scale empirical analysis of security risks in public serverless repositories. Our study reveals systemic weaknesses across these repositories including (i) widespread use of vulnerable third-party dependencies; (ii) misconfigurations in IaC templates; (iii) sensitive parameters in Docker run commands; (iv) the ability to conceal malicious payloads in compressed serverless components; and (v) exposure to typo-squatting attacks. Based on these findings, we offer actionable recommendations for repository maintainers, developers and users to enhance the security of public serverless repositories.

Acknowledgments. We thank the anonymous reviewers for their insightful feedback and help in improving this paper. This research received funding from the Smart Networks and Services Joint Undertaking (SNS JU) under the European Union's Horizon Europe programme: ELASTIC (GA#101139067); Horizon Europe: FLUIDOS (GA#101070473) and LAZARUS (GA#101070303); and the UNICO I+D Cloud program funded by the Ministry of Economic Affairs and Digital Transformation and the European Union-NextGenerationEU within the framework of the Plan de Recuperación, Transformación y Resiliencia (PRTR) with the CLOUDLESS project. This work was partially supported by project SERICS (PE00000014) under the NRRP MUR program funded by the EU - NGEU. Additionally, this work was partly supported by the National Research Foundation of Korea (NRF) grant funded by the Korea government (MSIT) (No. RS-2024-00457937, Design and implementation of security layers for secure WebAssembly-based serverless environments). The content of this article does not reflect the official opinion of the EU. Responsibility for the information and views expressed lies entirely with the authors.

A Vulnerability Composition

Table 4. Top 10 most commonly used packages across five platforms, along with the number and severity of associated vulnerabilities (C: *Critical*, H: *High*, M: *Medium*, L: *Low*).

AWS Serverless Repository						GitHub						Serverless Framework						Docker Hub						Red Hat Quay					
Package	Rate	C	H	M	L	Package	Rate	C	H	M	L	Package	Rate	C	H	M	L	Package	Rate	C	H	M	L	Package	Rate	C	H	M	L
xml2js	4.96%	0	0	1	0	semver	27.53%	0	0	2	0	xml2js	19.44%	0	0	1	0	tar	74.09%	0	7	6	2	ncurses-base	82.67%	0	1	5	21
follow-redirects	4.55%	0	1	2	0	qs	23.74%	0	4	1	0	lodash	19.15%	1	4	2	1	semver	63.97%	0	0	2	0	ncurses-libs	74.67%	0	0	5	22
axios	4.13%	0	2	2	0	follow-redirects	21.63%	0	1	2	0	semver	18.03%	0	0	1	0	curl	61.72%	25	34	47	16	libgcc	68.00%	0	0	12	14
lodash	3.72%	1	3	1	0	xml2js	21.21%	0	0	1	0	minimatch	17.46%	0	3	0	0	minimist	57.50%	0	3	0	0	pcre2	62.67%	0	0	2	1
minimist	3.72%	1	0	1	0	minimist	21.07%	1	0	1	0	qs	13.80%	0	1	0	0	ncurses-base	57.35%	2	6	13	6	curl	56.00%	13	10	46	24
urllib3	3.72%	0	3	5	0	minimatch	20.22%	0	3	0	0	minimist	13.52%	1	0	1	0	got	57.21%	0	0	1	0	ca-certificates	54.67%	0	2	0	1
minimatch	2.89%	0	1	0	0	lodash	19.52%	1	4	2	1	aws-sdk	11.83%	0	1	0	0	qs	57.21%	0	4	1	0	libxml2	52.00%	2	1	31	7
aws-sdk	2.89%	0	1	0	0	tough-cookie	19.10%	0	1	1	0	axios	9.01%	0	2	2	0	openssl	56.77%	4	29	84	34	tar	52.00%	0	7	3	5
qs	2.48%	0	1	0	0	axios	18.96%	0	2	2	0	follow-redirects	9.01%	0	1	2	0	minimist	54.29%	1	0	1	0	glib2	48.00%	0	2	48	20
semver	2.48%	0	0	1	0	node-fetch	15.73%	0	1	1	1	async	8.45%	0	1	0	0	xml2js	53.28%	0	0	1	0	gnupg2	48.00%	0	1	4	6

To gain deeper insight into the vulnerability landscape, we analysed the top 10 most commonly used packages in each repository (see Table 4). Notably, the *lodash* and *minimist* packages, each affected by one critical vulnerability (CVE-2019-10744 and CVE-2021-44906, respectively) appear in three and four of the analysed repositories, respectively. A cross-repository comparison reveals that versions of these packages hosted in the AWS SAW consistently exhibit fewer vulnerabilities, suggesting that AWS may actively patch or curate its hosted packages. In contrast, Docker Hub and Red Hat Quay show significantly higher vulnerability counts for the same packages, likely due to frequent image reuse and less stringent update practices. Among all analysed packages, *curl* stands out for both its widespread use—particularly in Docker Hub and Red Hat Quay—and its high number of critical and high-severity vulnerabilities.

B Common Misconfigurations in IaC Templates

Figure 7 presents the five most frequently observed misconfigurations across the three analyzed IaC frameworks: Terraform, AWS CloudFormation, and AWS Serverless Application Model (SAM). The obtained results highlight recurring security issues that affect the security posture of serverless deployments.

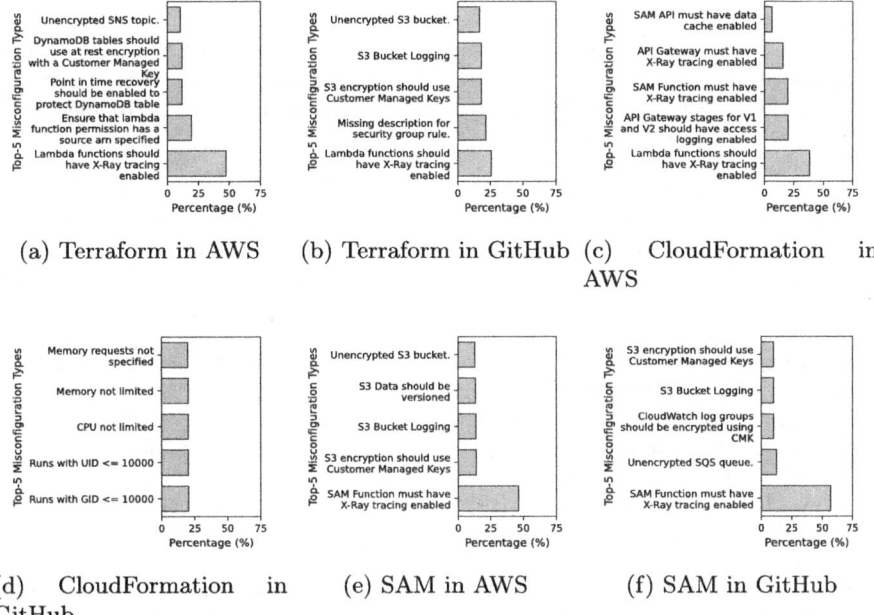

Fig. 7. Top-5 most common misconfigurations in IaC templates from AWS SAR and GitHub.

References

1. Access-Control-Allow-Origin header - HTTP - MDN Web Docs. https://developer.mozilla.org/en-US/docs/Web/HTTP/Reference/Headers/Access-Control-Allow-Origin#directives
2. Alibaba cloud function compute. https://www.alibabacloud.com/en/product/function-compute?_p_lc=1
3. AWS CLI command reference. https://awscli.amazonaws.com/v2/documentation/api/latest/reference/lambda/create-function.html
4. AWS CloudFormation. https://aws.amazon.com/cloudformation/
5. AWS Lambda. https://aws.amazon.com/lambda/
6. AWS SAM. https://aws.amazon.com/serverless/sam/?nc1=h_ls
7. AWS serverless application repository. https://aws.amazon.com/serverless/serverlessrepo/
8. Azure Microsoft. https://azure.microsoft.com/en-us/solutions/serverless
9. Beautifulsoup. https://pypi.org/project/beautifulsoup4/
10. Create your first containerized functions on Azure Container Apps. https://learn.microsoft.com/en-us/azure/azure-functions/functions-deploy-container-apps
11. Deploy a Cloud Function. https://cloud.google.com/functions/docs/deploy
12. Deploy lambda functions with container images. https://docs.aws.amazon.com/prescriptive-guidance/latest/patterns/deploy-lambda-functions-with-container-images.html
13. Deploying lambda functions as .zip file archives. https://docs.aws.amazon.com/lambda/latest/dg/configuration-function-zip.html

14. Docker Hub. https://hub.docker.com/
15. Ensure that lambda function permission has a source ARN specified. https://aquasecurity.github.io/tfsec/v1.0.0-rc.8/checks/aws/lambda/restrict-source-arn/
16. GCP Cloud Run: serverless deployment. https://medium.com/@109manojsaini/serverless-deployment-cloud-run-3332c3817ef9
17. Github. https://github.com/
18. Google cloud serverless. https://cloud.google.com/solutions/serverless?hl=en
19. Grype documentation. https://docs.anchore.com/current/docs/
20. IBM Cloud Functions. https://www.ibm.com/cloud/functions
21. Identify AWS resources with amazon resource names (ARNs). https://docs.aws.amazon.com/IAM/latest/UserGuide/reference-arns.html
22. Red Hat Quay. https://quay.io/
23. S3 encryption should use Customer Managed Keys. https://aquasecurity.github.io/tfsec/v1.6.2/checks/aws/s3/encryption-customer-key/
24. Selenium. https://www.selenium.dev/
25. Serverless framework plugins. https://www.serverless.com/plugins/
26. Terraform. https://developer.hashicorp.com/terraform
27. Trivy - IaC. https://trivy.dev/v0.19.2/misconfiguration/iac/
28. Trivy documentation. https://aquasecurity.github.io/trivy/v0.44/docs/
29. Virustotal. https://www.virustotal.com/
30. Zip deployment for azure functions. https://learn.microsoft.com/en-us/azure/azure-functions/deployment-zip-push
31. Cryptojacking invades cloud. How Modern Containerization Trend is Exploited by Attackers. https://threatpost.com/malicious-docker-containers-earn-crypto-miners-90000/132816/ (2018)
32. Compare Trivy and Grype. https://gitlab.com/gitlab-org/gitlab/-/issues/327174 (2021)
33. AWS Serverless application repository – FAQs and terms. https://aws.amazon.com/serverless/serverlessrepo/faqs/ (2023)
34. EleKtra-Leak Cryptojacking attacks exploit AWS IAM credentials exposed on GitHub (2023). https://thehackernews.com/2023/10/elektra-leak-cryptojacking-attacks.html
35. Multiple false positive and false negative CVEs (2023). https://github.com/aquasecurity/trivy/issues/3010
36. Operation Red Kangaroo: industry's first dynamic analysis of 4M public docker container images (2023). https://www.algosec.com/blog/operation-red-kangaroo-industrys-first-dynamic-analysis-of-4m-public-docker-container-images
37. Stemming the tide of false positive vulnerabilities (2023). https://www.chainguard.dev/unchained/stemming-the-tide-of-false-positive-vulnerabilities
38. Why Chainguard uses Grype as its first line of defense for CVEs (2023). https://www.chainguard.dev/unchained/why-chainguard-uses-grype-as-its-first-line-of-defense-for-cves
39. Hacking serverless runtimes profiling lambda, azure, and more (2024). https://www.blackhat.com/docs/us-17/wednesday/us-17-Krug-Hacking-Severless-Runtimes.pdf
40. Using cross-origin resource sharing (CORS) (2024). https://docs.aws.amazon.com/AmazonS3/latest/userguide/cors.html
41. Castro, P., Ishakian, V., Muthusamy, V., Slominski, A.: The rise of serverless computing. Commun. ACM **62**(12), 44–54 (2019)
42. Chen, J., et al.: We still don't have secure cross-domain requests: an empirical study of CORS. In: USENIX Security, pp. 1079–1093 (2018)

43. Dahlmanns, M., Sander, C., Decker, R., Wehrle, K.: Secrets revealed in container images: an internet-wide study on occurrence and impact. In: ASIACCS, pp. 797–811 (2023)
44. Datta, P., Polinsky, I., Inam, M.A., Bates, A., Enck, W.: ALASTOR: Reconstructing the provenance of serverless intrusions. In: USENIX Security, pp. 2443–2460 (2022)
45. Eskandani, N., Salvaneschi, G.: The wonderless dataset for serverless computing. In: MSR, pp. 565–569 (2021)
46. Franco, J., Acar, A., Aris, A., Uluagac, S.: Forensic analysis of cryptojacking in host-based docker containers using honeypots. In: ICC, pp. 4860–4865 (2023)
47. Haque, M.U., Babar, M.A.: Well begun is half done: an empirical study of exploitability and impact of base-image vulnerabilities (2021). https://arxiv.org/abs/2112.12597
48. Jonas, E., et al.: Cloud programming simplified: a berkeley view on serverless computing (2019). http://arxiv.org/abs/1902.03383
49. Ladisa, P., Plate, H., Martinez, M., Barais, O.: SoK: Taxonomy of attacks on open-source software supply chains. In: S&P, pp. 1509–1526 (2023)
50. Liu, G., Gao, X., Wang, H., Sun, K.: Exploring the unchartered space of container registry typosquatting. In: USENIX Security, pp. 35–51 (2022)
51. Liu, P., et al.: Understanding the security risks of docker hub. In: ESORICS, pp. 257–276 (2020)
52. Marin, E., Perino, D., Di Pietro, R.: Serverless computing: a security perspective. J. Cloud Comput. **11**(1) (2022)
53. Schleier-Smith, J., et al.: What serverless computing is and should become: the next phase of cloud computing. Commun. ACM, pp. 76–84 (2021)
54. Shu, R., Gu, X., Enck, W.: A study of security vulnerabilities on docker hub. In: CODASPY, pp. 269–280 (2017)
55. Wist, K., Helsem, M., Gligoroski, D.: Vulnerability analysis of 2500 docker hub images (2020). https://arxiv.org/abs/2006.02932
56. Zerouali, A., Mens, T., Decan, A., Gonzalez-Barahona, J., Robles, G.: A multidimensional analysis of technical lag in Debian-based Docker images. Empir. Softw. Eng. **26**(2), 1–45 (2021). https://doi.org/10.1007/s10664-020-09908-6
57. Zerouali, A., Mens, T., Robles, G., Gonzalez-Barahona, J.M.: On the relation between outdated docker containers, severity vulnerabilities, and bugs. In: SANER, pp. 491–501 (2019)
58. Zerouali, A., Mens, T., Roover, C.D.: On the usage of JavaScript, Python and Ruby packages in Docker Hub images. Sci. Comput. Program. **207**, 102653 (2021)

CAPMAN: Detecting and Mitigating Linux Capability Abuses at Runtime to Secure Privileged Containers

Alireza Moghaddas Borhan[1], Hugo Kermabon-Bobinnec[1], Lingyu Wang[1,3(✉)], Yosr Jarraya[2], and Suryadipta Majumdar[1]

[1] CIISE, Concordia University, Montreal, QC, Canada
{alireza.moghaddasborhan, hugo.kermabonbobinnec, suryadipta.majumdar}@concordia.ca
[2] Ericsson Security Research, Ericsson Canada, Montreal, QC, Canada
yosr.jarraya@ericsson.com
[3] School of Engineering, University of British Columbia, Kelowna, BC, Canada
lingyu.wang@ubc.ca

Abstract. Linux capabilities represent an important security feature for enabling fine-grained management of privileges. However, limitations in selectively enabling capabilities for processes and lagging adoption from application developers often lead the operators to run containers with unnecessary privileges. Although this can potentially be addressed by modifying the application, minimizing the set of enabled capabilities, assigning capabilities to executable files, or using user space utilities like Ptrace, those solutions typically require manual efforts, only provide partial protection, or incur significant overhead. In this paper, we present CAPMAN, a solution that secures privileged containers by detecting and mitigating potential capability abuses at runtime. Our main idea is threefold. First, CAPMAN examines all capability requests made by system calls to ensure full protection. Second, CAPMAN performs the detection directly inside the Linux kernel to ensure its efficiency. Third, CAPMAN mitigates capability abuses in a transparent manner without requiring any change made to the application or container. Our evaluation of CAPMAN using real-world CVEs and capability abuses shows that it can mitigate all the tested capability abuses (most of which are missed by a state-of-the-art solution) with negligible performance overhead.

1 Introduction

As an important security feature of Linux, capabilities have been around for over two decades [35]. By assigning different privileged operations with different capabilities, this feature allows more fine-grained control of privileges for processes than with the traditional superuser approach. However, the adoption and development of capabilities have been lagging in practice, especially in container environments [25]. For instance, Docker by default enables 14 capabilities for all the processes, and during the whole lifetime of a container [8]. By abusing capabilities enabled in such privileged containers, attackers can cause more serious damages such as escaping the containers to attack

---

A. Moghaddas Borhan and H. Kermabon-Bobinnec—Equal contribution.

the underlying infrastructure [25,35,55,71], which is a common concern of Kubernetes operators [55]. Such security threats, combined with the increasing popularity of cloud-native applications hosted in container environments, make managing capabilities for privileged containers an important area to focus on [13,41,63].

Existing solutions have mostly focused on minimizing the capability sets of binary files, through static analysis (e.g., Decap [25] and LiCA [64]), analyzing system calls (e.g., ConfigWiz [32], TCLP [38] and SysCap [75]), and dynamic analysis (e.g., the RootAsRole framework [3,4,70]). The required capabilities can then be enforced at runtime using Docker's --cap-add and --cap-drop options, or Linux Security Modules (LSMs) such as SELinux or AppArmor. Such solutions can reduce the general attack surface of containers before their execution, but this only provides partial protection since attackers with access to the containers (legitimate or not) can still abuse the remaining capabilities at runtime (as shown in our experiments in Sect. 4). Tools such as SystemTap's *container_check* [46] and BCC's *Capable* [29] can trace capability checks but cannot block suspicious checks. Finally, existing works on limiting system calls for containers (e.g., [7,17,33,39]) can indirectly influence capabilities but do not provide direct solutions for managing capabilities.

To address this research gap, we present CAPMAN, an in-kernel runtime solution for securing privileged containers. CAPMAN analyzes the capability usage of a container offline, and then detects and mitigates capability abuses at runtime. CAPMAN has several unique advantages as follows. First, compared to existing solutions for reducing the attack surface of containers before their execution, CAPMAN provides a complementary solution by extending the protection to runtime. Second, CAPMAN performs its detection entirely inside the kernel, which ensures its efficiency by eliminating the inherent delay for interacting with the user space. Third, CAPMAN mitigates capability abuses by dynamically dropping capabilities in a transparent manner to avoid the need for costly modifications to the container. In summary, our contributions are as follows.

− We propose CAPMAN as the first in-kernel runtime solution for detecting and mitigating capability abuses. Applying CAPMAN to a container environment can prevent attackers from exploiting privileged containers for more severe damages.
− We tackle several key challenges in realizing CAPMAN as follows: i) to ensure CAPMAN can cover every capability request, we develop a kprobe-based kernel module to intercept those requests via a kernel function; ii) to avoid the user space delay, we design CAPMAN to perform its detection completely inside the kernel using lightweight whitelisting and machine learning methods; iii) to safely override the rule that only the container itself can drop capabilities, we develop CAPMAN to perform its mitigation using standard kernel functions and procedures.
− Our evaluation of CAPMAN using real-world capability abuses and CVEs demonstrates its effectiveness and efficiency, e.g., it can mitigate all the 10 tested capability abuses (of which eight are missed by an existing solution) with negligible overhead ($< 0.73\%$) and resource consumption ($< 0.5\%$ CPU and < 40 KB memory).

2 Preliminaries

This section gives background on capabilities, the motivating example, and threat model.

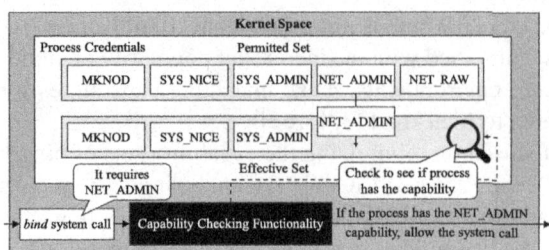

Fig. 1. Examples of Linux capabilities, capability sets, and capability checking functionality.

Table 1. Examples of popular (over-)privileged containers.

	Falco [11]	Sysdig [65]	Calico [67]	Docker (DinD) [9]	Netshoot [30]	Dillinger [45]	rclone-mount [57]	Redroid [58]	Wireguard [72]	Phoenix [33]
NET_ADMIN	✓	✓	✓	✓	✓		✓	✓	✓	✓
NET_RAW	✓	✓	✓	✓	✓					
SYS_ADMIN	✓	✓	✓	✓			✓	✓	✓	✓
Privileged	✓	✓	✓	✓				✓	✓	✓

Capabilities and Capability Abuses. Linux capabilities were introduced to provide more fine-grained separation of privileges than the root vs. non-root design [35]. As illustrated in Fig. 1, the *permitted set* includes capabilities that the process can bring to its *effective set*, and the latter is checked by the kernel to ascertain privileges, e.g., the bind system call requires the NET_ADMIN capability. When a capability is removed from the effective set or the permitted set, it cannot be regained by that process. Although designed to improve security, capabilities are sometimes overloaded with privileges, e.g., SYS_ADMIN (nearly as powerful as the root), NET_RAW, and SYS_MODULE [35]. As such, attackers gaining control of a process with such capabilities can abuse them to lead to more severe security issues such as a container escape [25,35,55,71].

In practice, many *privileged containers* may have such risky capabilities enabled for legitimate reasons, such as security analysis [11,33], logging [65], networking [67], etc., as illustrated in Table 1. Moreover, regular containers may also become privileged due to i) the lack of temporal control, i.e., capabilities will be enabled for the lifetime of a container even if they are only needed at the beginning; ii) the lack of support from application developers (it is known that most applications are written without considering capabilities [10,25,47], and few publishers provide information regarding the required capabilities); iii) the fact that file capabilities are usually not set for common executable files in popular Linux distributions [25]. Running such (over-)privileged containers is a common practice that can lead to serious security concerns.

Motivating Example. Figure 2 illustrates an example of capability abuses in default container environments (left), naive solutions (upper-right), and our ideas (lower-right).

Capability Abuse. A privileged Nginx container requires the NET_RAW capability, which is enabled (but not needed) for the entire lifetime of the container in a default containerized environment. Attackers accessing the container can abuse this capability to escape the container (e.g., via CVE-2020-14386 [48]) and attack the underlying infrastructure.

Existing Solutions. The upper-right corner of the figure shows three categories of potential solutions and their limitations. First, developers can design the application to add a capability from the permitted set to the effective set only when needed, and remove it afterwards. This can significantly reduce the chance of capability abuses. However, as shown in [25], very few applications are capability-aware (e.g., only seven out of 201

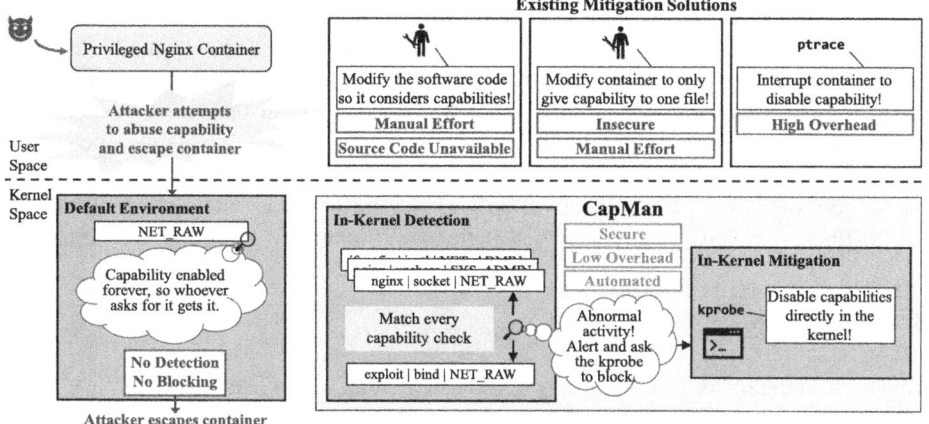

Fig. 2. Motivating example.

setuid programs in Ubuntu even use file capabilities), whereas operators typically lack the means due to the unavailability of source codes or their complexity.

Second, the required capabilities can be assigned to executable files of the main application (e.g., using the setcap command [35]) such that the container can be run with fewer capabilities enabled. However, in reality attackers can still abuse capabilities by attacking the main application (which is usually the case in real-world attacks).

Third, a potential solution is to perform runtime detection by interrupting and matching each system call and its arguments against the existing mapping between system calls and capabilities [25] using a user space tool, e.g., Ptrace. Once an anomaly is detected, we can drop the capability before returning control back to the process, causing the system call to fail. However, such a user space solution can cause prohibitive delay, as shown in our experiments in Sect. 4 (as an extreme case, one of the containers we experimented on completely failed when attaching Ptrace to its processes).

<u>Our Ideas.</u> In contrast to those naive solutions, CAPMAN is designed to run entirely inside the kernel to avoid the delay caused by user space solutions, as illustrated in the lower-right corner of the figure. Specifically, we leverage kprobes, a common tool used to insert breakpoints into a running Linux kernel. Working at the kernel level, kprobes allows CAPMAN to access many kernel functions with very low overhead for efficient detection and mitigation. Moreover, CAPMAN matches every capability check invoked by system calls against the normal usage, which provides full protection without the need to modify the application or container.

Threat Model. Our in-scope threats include attacks involving capability abuses in (over-)privileged containers (e.g., CVE-2022-0492 [49] allows container escape using the SYS_ADMIN capability, and many other capabilities can be abused to elevate privileges [52]). These capabilities may be enabled either because they are legitimately required by the container (as shown in Table 1), or due to misconfigurations [41,55]. We assume an attacker who has already gained access to a container with some privileged capabilities enabled. This could be a legitimate user who has access to the container for normal usage; or an external actor who has gained unauthorized access (e.g., through remote code execution, web-based vulnerabilities, weak credentials, etc.). Zero-days that involve abusing capabilities are also in the scope (as our detection does not rely on signatures of known attacks). Conversely, any attack that does not involve abusing capabilities, or that tampers with the integrity of CAPMAN or the underlying infrastructure, the image and container, or the processed data, is out of the scope of this work. Similarly to most existing whitelisting and detection approaches, we assume the normal capability usage can be effectively captured during the offline phase. This is more feasible for containers since these are commonly used to host microservices and cloud-native applications, which usually have a well-defined and relatively simple functionality.

3 CapMan

This section details the methodology and implementation of CAPMAN.

3.1 Overview of CapMan

As shown in Fig. 3, CAPMAN works in two phases. First, during the offline phase, the target container is executed in a safe environment for CAPMAN to capture the normal capability check events as a whitelist or through machine learning (ML). Second, during the runtime phase, the container is run in the production environment for CAPMAN to detect potential capability abuses through either whitelist matching or ML classification, and CAPMAN either alerts the user about detected abuses, or drops the capability to mitigate such abuses[1]. To achieve these, CAPMAN consists of i) a kernel module based on a kprobe for data collection, detection, and mitigation, and ii) a user space module developed in Python for data processing (only used during the offline phase).

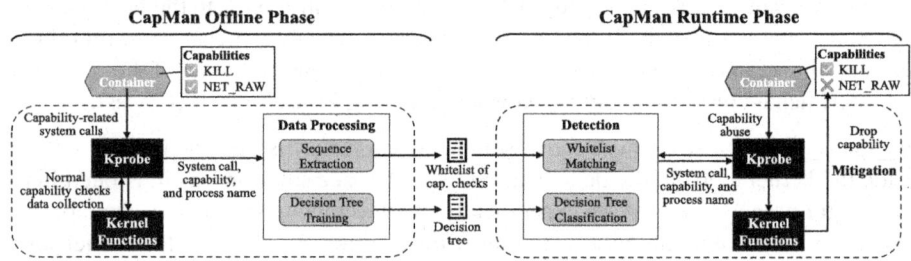

Fig. 3. Methodology Overview.

3.2 Offline Phase

During the offline phase (the left side of Fig. 3), CAPMAN captures and analyzes the normal capability usage of a target container to obtain a whitelist or ML model. The following i) details the data collection using the kernel module; ii) details the data processing using the user space module; iii) details the time-phase separation technique (inspired by SPEAKER [39]); iv) provides an example of how the offline phase works.

---

[1] A future direction is to integrate CAPMAN with container orchestration tools like Kubernetes and Open Policy Agent (OPA) to enforce such policies without re-compiling a kernel module.

Data Collection Using the Kernel Module. To ensure CAPMAN can intercept and collect information about every capability check to provide full protection, we leverage the finding of existing works [21,31,59,70] that the kernel relies on the `cap_capable` kernel function to determine whether a process requesting a capability has that capability inside its effective set. Specifically, CAPMAN installs a `kprobe` as its kernel module to interrupt the `cap_capable` function at the beginning of its execution in order to collect information about capability checks. To ensure `kprobe` only affects the target container, we configure it to only proceed if the namespace ID of the process is the same as the namespace ID of the container (namespaces are used to isolate a container from the rest of the host). We also set a flag in the `kprobe` so it does not block any capability checks and only passively collects information about the passing capability checks.

Various information is collected about each capability check from different sources inside the kernel. First, the capability being checked is obtained from the `dx` register. Second, the system call is obtained by first identifying the reserved process registers using the `task_pt_regs` function, and then obtaining the `orig_ax` register. The namespace ID is deep inside several layers of C structs in the process object in the kernel, namely, `current->nsproxy->pid_ns_for_children->ns.inum`. The PID and process name are obtained from `current->pid` and `current->comm`, respectively. To transmit that information to the user space for processing, we leverage `dmesg` logging [36], a Linux utility for retrieving and displaying information from the kernel ring buffer (we do not consider a `sysfs` file due to its limited size of 4 KB [44]).

Data Processing Using the User-Space Module. The collected data is then processed in the user space to build a whitelist and train an ML model for performing detection in the next stage. Specifically, for the whitelisting method, the goal is to build a whitelist in the form of a set of unique sequences of capability checks, using a sliding window over all the capability check events. For the ML method, since most ML models are known to be too complex and computationally expensive for the kernel space [1,14], we follow the state-of-the-art work [74] to train a decision tree model that can fit into the kernel space, using the *scikit-learn* Python library. For both methods, each capability check is identified by three attributes, i.e., the capability being requested, the system call, and the name of the process. Note that both methods need to be repeated once container behaviors change (e.g., due to software update or new environments), while a future direction is to apply incremental learning techniques to simplify the model update [54].

Time-Phase Separation. Inspired by SPEAKER [39], we study the capability usage of containers, and our results indicate that many capabilities are only used at the startup of a container and then never needed again. Therefore, CAPMAN also employs a time-phase separation technique during its offline phase. Specifically, similarly as in [39], we first find a threshold after which all containers' capability usage stabilizes, and our results show 20 seconds is an acceptable threshold (see Sect. 4). We then collect capability checks before/after this threshold for the booting/running phases, respectively.[2]

Example 1. Figure 4 shows an example of what happens during the offline phase. First, CAPMAN installs its kernel module (`kprobe`). Second, a container is run in a safe

---

[2] More than two fine-grained phases can also be considered [66,76].

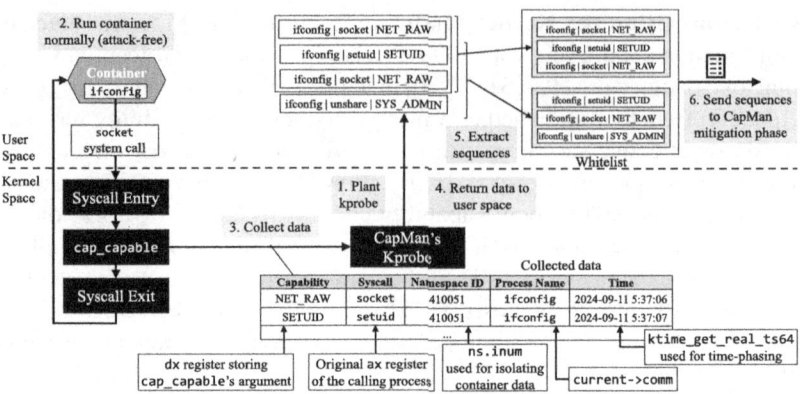

Fig. 4. Example of the offline phase of CAPMAN.

environment, where the `ifconfig` process from this container invokes the `socket` system call, which requires the `CAP_NET_RAW` capability. Therefore, the kernel calls its `cap_capable` function, which is intercepted by our `kprobe`. Third, the `kprobe` collects various information as shown in the table (bottom of the figure). The text boxes below the table show how those attributes are retrieved from the relevant registers, kernel variables, and kernel functions. Fourth, the collected information is sent to the user space for processing. Fifth, considering the whitelisting method, the data is processed to identify a unique list of sequences each of which includes three capability checks.

3.3 Runtime Phase

During the runtime phase (the right side of Fig. 3), CAPMAN detects and mitigates capability abuses as they happen in the target container.[3] The detection is performed on the observed capability checks based on either the whitelist or the ML model obtained during the offline phase. As soon as a potential capability abuse is detected, CAPMAN can either alert the user or mitigate it by removing the requested capability from the effective set of the process. The following discusses the challenges, details the detection and mitigation solutions, and gives an example of how the runtime phase works.

Challenges to Detection. A key challenge when detecting capability abuses at runtime is to keep the delay at an acceptable level. Specifically, CAPMAN can no longer mitigate a capability abuse once the corresponding system call has already taken effect. Therefore, CAPMAN needs to put system calls on hold while it determines whether they are making anomalous capabilities requests. As a result, any time spent on the detection becomes additional delay experienced by the system calls (and the user process). This explains why a naive solution of performing detection in user space would cause unacceptable delay to the system call (user process) or even disrupt the normal operation of the kernel itself. First, as `kprobes` are simply code pieces inserted in the middle of the kernel code [42], making the kernel module of CAPMAN (i.e., `kprobe`) wait for the user space detection results may cause the entire kernel (and hence the host system) to

---

[3] CAPMAN can be selectively disabled/enabled with different policies for individual containers.

be blocked from its normal function (while some parts of the kernel can run system calls in parallel, many other parts do not [2]). Second, the delay introduced by this design consists of the detection time and the time required for exchanging messages between the kernel and user spaces. Such a delay is typically much higher than the average delay between two consecutive system calls (e.g., around 0.003 ms [33]).

Detection. To address the aforementioned challenges, we need to keep the detection lightweight enough such that it may be executed entirely inside the kernel space. For this purpose, we have adopted two lightweight methods, i.e., whitelist matching and decision tree classification (as mentioned earlier, more complex ML models do not fit into the kernel space [1, 14]). These two approaches are complementary and aim at different use cases, i.e., the whitelist matching can achieve higher accuracy if the training data is complete, whereas the decision tree is able to generalize better for previously unseen data. Despite their relative simplicity, those methods can provide reasonable detection accuracy, as demonstrated in our experiments in Sect. 4.

Specifically, to detect capability checks deviating from the normal behavior, the whitelist of unique sequences (of fixed length N) constructed during the offline phase for each process is fed into the kernel module. At runtime, the kernel module of CAPMAN separately keeps track of the N-most recent capability checks requested by each process, and compares these N capability checks (as a sequence) to the whitelist to determine whether there is an anomaly. Here, N is a parameter reflecting the inherent tradeoff between detection accuracy and time (i.e., larger N may give high accuracy but require more time), which will be evaluated through experiments in Sect. 4.

For classification-based detection, the decision tree trained during the offline phase is deployed inside the kernel module. This is achieved by translating the corresponding model conditions (i.e., branches) into C code [74]. To overcome the floating-point limitation of the kernel [43], we only employ integer values for branch conditions. At runtime, the kernel module of CAPMAN saves each capability check in a ring buffer, and assembles a sample data point in the form (*process_name*, *syscall_1*, *capability_1*, ..., *syscall_N*, *capability_N*), with N being the length of the sequence. Finally, the data point is passed through the decision tree for classification.

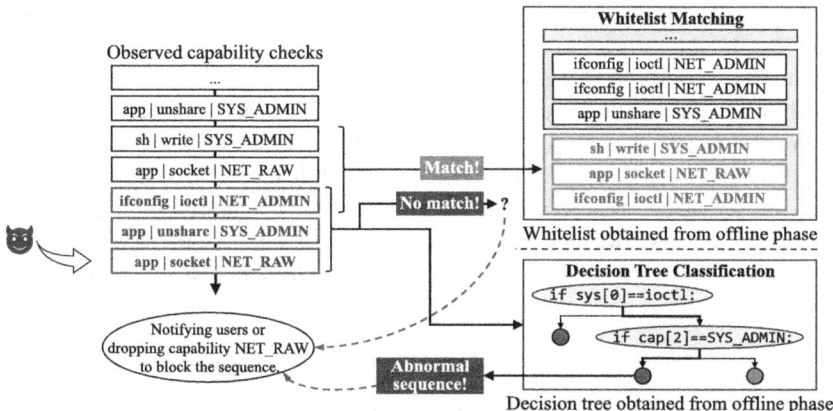

Fig. 5. Example of CAPMAN detection.

Example 2. In Fig. 5, suppose an attacker with access to an Nginx container attempts to escape it by abusing available capabilities. The left side of the figure shows the observed capability checks including those triggered by the attacker (in red color). The upper-right shows how the kernel module of CAPMAN matches each observed sequence of three capability checks against the whitelist. The lower-right shows an excerpt of the in-kernel decision tree (where the nodes show branches written as C code inside CAPMAN's kernel module). For whitelist matching, CAPMAN finds a match in the whitelist for the three latest capability checks when ⟨ifconfig|ioctl|NET_ADMIN⟩ is observed. This is expected since there is nothing abnormal about this capability check by itself, although it is indeed part of the attack, since ifconfig generally requires NET_ADMIN (e.g., as seen in the top two rows). Nonetheless, as the attack progresses, CAPMAN successfully detects the sequence shown completely in red color to be an anomaly that should be mitigated.

Challenges to Mitigation. Once a potential capability abuse is detected, CAPMAN can mitigate it by dropping the requested capability for the process. However, a key challenge here is that the default Linux rules governing the capability sets indicate that a Linux process is not allowed to alter the capabilities of other processes [35], and hence CAPMAN cannot directly drop the capability for a process. Moreover, although overriding such default rules governing the capability sets is possible, this must be done with extra caution in order not to disrupt the normal kernel functionality, and, similarly to the case of detection, this must also be done in an efficient manner to avoid blocking the normal activities of the container and the wider system.

Mitigation. To address those challenges, we study the Linux kernel source code to understand how to change the capabilities of another process (i.e., the target container's) in a safe and efficient manner. Specifically, our study shows that every process is represented as a C struct in the Linux kernel called task_struct, which contains the PID, process name, namespace ID, and the security context of the process stored in another C struct called cred. This cred object contains the cap_permitted and cap_effective data objects, which correspond to the permitted and effective sets of capabilities, respectively. Therefore, CAPMAN can mitigate detected capability abuses by altering those kernel data objects that store the capability sets of each container process. Specifically, since the effective set is what the kernel will check to determine whether the process should be granted access, the kernel module of CAPMAN removes the capability from the effective set of the process, by modifying cap_effective. It also drops the capability from the permitted set by modifying cap_permitted to prevent the process (attacker) from adding the capability back. To ensure those modifications are performed in a safe manner, we choose not to directly modify those data objects in an arbitrary way, but instead follow the existing procedure for updating the cred struct used in the kernel code, and leverage standard kernel functions.

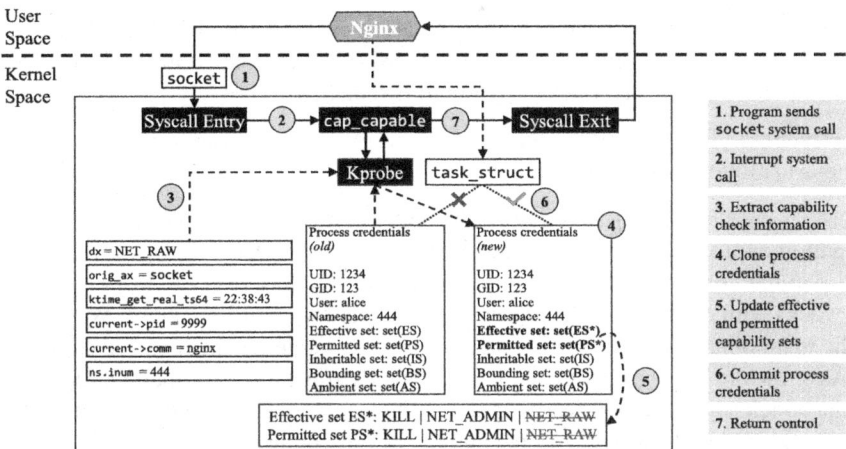

Fig. 6. Example of CAPMAN mitigation.

Example 3. Following Example 2, Fig. 6 shows how CAPMAN mitigates the detected capability abuse. Specifically, the attacker's process makes a socket system call that requests for the NET_RAW capability. This is detected as an anomaly by the kernel module of CAPMAN, which runs at the beginning of the cap_capable function's runtime. The kernel module thus i) clones the cred object of this process using prepare_creds, ii) modifies the cloned cred struct using cap_drop to drop the capabilities from the effective set (and permitted set), iii) commits the new creds struct using commit_creds, and iv) returns the control back to the kernel to continue with the cap_capable function. Consequently, cap_capable finds that the process does not have the required capability, and hence the capability abuse is prevented.

4 Evaluation

This section evaluates CAPMAN by answering the following research questions:
RQ1: How effective is it in mitigating capability abuses compared to existing works?
RQ2: How accurate is its detection compared to existing works using only system calls?
RQ3: How much time/CPU/memory overhead does it incur compared to current works?
RQ4: How much does time-phase separation help it reduce the attack surface?

Evaluation Environment. For our experiments, we use a VirtualBox virtual machine (10 vCPUs and 16 GB RAM) running Ubuntu 18.04 on Linux Kernel v5.4. We create Docker containers with 10 of the most popular images on Docker Hub (totaling over 55 million downloads in one week) to evaluate CAPMAN's effectiveness[4]. We also create images with 10 other popular applications that involve intensive capability checks to evaluate CAPMAN's overhead. To evaluate CAPMAN against real-world capability

---

[4] The signficant amount of manual efforts required to invoke each application's normal behaviors to ensure coverage explains why we would not be able to perform a larger-scale study.

abuses, we implement two exploits of vulnerabilities (CVE-2020-14386 [48] and CVE-2022-0492 [49]), and eight other capability abuses (Table 3a) from the Linux manual and other sources [35,52]. Each experiment is repeated 100 times.

Effectiveness. To answer RQ1, we compare the effectiveness of CAPMAN to two state-of-the-art solutions, Decap [25] and Confine [17].

CAPMAN *vs. Decap [25].* To show the benefits of CAPMAN's runtime detection and mitigation approach over the static analysis approach of Decap [25], we run 10 of the most popular container images from Docker Hub (totaling over 55 million downloads in a week) with default configurations during CAPMAN's offline phase. We run Decap on the main binary file extracted from each image to identify the required capabilities.

As shown in Table 2, CAPMAN is significantly more effective than Decap in reducing the attack surface. Specifically, Decap allows 18.5 more capabilities than CAPMAN on average per application (with no impact on the applications). For instance, for the RabbitMQ image, Decap allows 24 capabilities, whereas CAPMAN allows only one capability. This shows the inherent difficulty for a static approach like Decap to identify the capabilities actually used at runtime (which is a trivial task for a runtime approach like CAPMAN). A few capabilities (e.g., SYS_ADMIN) are allowed by CAPMAN (also by Decap) based on observed capability checks, even though these are not needed (e.g., SYS_ADMIN can be checked when a *fork* or *execve* system call is made by the process [3,70]).

Table 2. Comparing the capabilities allowed by CAPMAN with the capabilities allowed by Decap [25] for 10 of the most popular container images on Docker Hub.

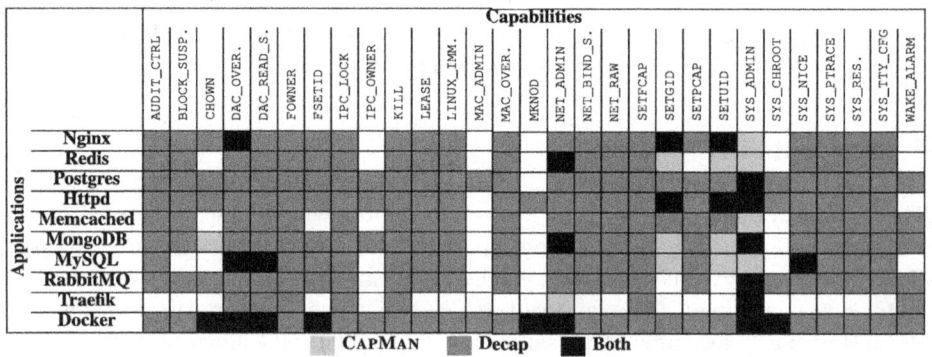

CAPMAN *vs. Confine [17].* To show the benefit of considering capabilities (in addition to system calls), we compare CAPMAN with Confine [17], a widely used system call-based runtime solution. We first apply Confine to a custom Ubuntu container requiring capabilities as mentioned in Table 3a. As Confine turns out to be over-restrictive, disrupting the container's normal operations, we manually unblock the necessary system calls from the generated Seccomp filter to make the containers functional. We then evaluate Confine and CAPMAN (sequence length of three) against capability abuses.

Table 3a presents the results of CAPMAN, Confine, and Docker's default capability check [8]. CAPMAN can detect and mitigate all the capability abuses, whereas Confine only mitigates two out of the 10 abuses (by blocking the system calls shown under the table), and Docker by default cannot mitigate any abuse. One of the capability abuses (installing a kernel module) poses a unique challenge to the mitigation by CAPMAN, i.e., the `cap_capable` function appears too late in the kernel's source code to mitigate this particular abuse, and consequently is replaced with the `capable` function.

Table 3. Comparing the effectiveness and accuracy of CAPMAN

Description	Required Cap.	CAP-MAN	Confine[17]	Docker[8]
Change proc. priorities	SYS_NICE	✓	✓	✗
Clear system logs	SYS_ADMIN	✓	✓	✗
Memory corruption (CVE-2020-14386 [48])	NET_RAW	✓	✗	✗
Bypass ns isolation (CVE-2022-0492 [49])	SYS_ADMIN	✓	✗	✗
Escape cont. via cgroup release agent [52]	SYS_ADMIN	✓	✗	✗
Change iptables rules	NET_ADMIN	✓	✗	✗
Remount read-only filesystem as writable	SYS_ADMIN	✓	✗	✗
Bypass net. restrictions through raw sockets	NET_RAW	✓	✗	✗
Sniff packets and monitor network traffic	NET_RAW	✓	✗	✗
Install kernel modules	SYS_MODULE	✓	✗	✗

(a) Effectiveness of CAPMAN, Confine [17], and Docker [8].

			Sequence Length (N)			
			1	2	3	4
Syscalls (e.g., [5,15,27,33])		TPR (%)	55.14	70.94	79.14	83.41
		FPR (%) / FP	0 / 0	0.007 / 810k	0.017 / 1,968k	0.06 / 6,946k
CAPMAN Whitelist Matching		TPR (%)	72.07	71.99	71.42	70.91
		FPR (%) / FP	0 / 0	0 / 0	0 / 0	1.59 / 3,372k
CAPMAN Decision Tree	Depth 1	TPR (%)	69.94	70.75	70.22	69.96
		FPR (%) / FP	0 / 0	0 / 0	0 / 0	0 / 0
	Depth 3	TPR (%)	87.88	87.85	88.51	87.47
		FPR (%) / FP	0 / 0	0 / 0	0 / 0	0 / 0
	Depth 5	TPR (%)	88.04	99.89	99.90	99.85
		FPR (%) / FP	0 / 0	0 / 0	0 / 0	0 / 0

(b) Detection accuracy of CAPMAN and approaches using only system calls.

Accuracy. To answer RQ2, we evaluate CAPMAN's detection accuracy in comparison to existing approaches using only system calls [5,15,27,33]. We first build a tool to collect sequences of system calls in a per-process manner from a Ubuntu container, while running over 50 common Linux commands using a script, as well as capability abuses. We then re-implement the system call matching approach following existing works, and measure the true positive rate (TPR), the false positive rate (FPR), and the absolute number of false positives (FP). For CAPMAN, we repeat those steps using the capability check data and CAPMAN's whitelist matching and decision tree classification methods (with sequence lengths up to four, since we observe that about 90% of the processes have four or less capability checks). Overall, we collect a dataset of $\approx 39,000$ labeled samples of normal and abuse system calls as well as corresponding capability checks.

As Table 3b shows, the system call-based method (first row) has an increasing true positive rate in the sequence length, ranging from about 55% ($N = 1$) to 83% ($N = 4$). In contrast, CAPMAN with whitelist matching (second row) generally has a more stable true positive rate (between 70% and 72%) across various sequence lengths. The false positive rate of CAPMAN is slightly lower than the system call-based method for $N \leq 3$, and is larger for $N = 4$. However, the absolute number of false positives is more revealing, since for the system call-based method it increases from zero for $N = 1$ to more than 800k for $N = 2$, and almost two and seven million for $N = 3$ and

$N = 4$, respectively. In contrast, the absolute number of false positives stays at zero for CAPMAN for $N \leq 3$, and only becomes prohibitive for $N = 4$. This significant difference shows that, although both methods perform similar sequence matching, examining capability checks in addition to system calls allows CAPMAN to dramatically reduce the false positives (from millions to zero). The worse result of CAPMAN under $N = 4$ is mainly due to the fact that most (around 70%) of the processes are observed to have only three capability checks, and hence in practice N should be limited to three for CAPMAN.

The last three rows of Table 3b report the results for CAPMAN with decision trees of different depths (one, three, and five). We can see that a decision tree of depth three or more can yield higher true positive rates than both the system call-based method and CAPMAN's whitelist matching, and a tree of depth five paired with a sequence length of two or more can achieve almost perfect results ranging between 99.85% and 99.90%. In all cases, the false positive rate (and absolute number) remains zero. Clearly, despite its simplicity, the decision tree model can help CAPMAN achieve accurate detection. Moreover, more complex ML models (which do not fit in kernel [1,14]) can transfer their knowledge to tree-based models [74], paving the way to further improve accuracy.

Overhead. To answer RQ3, we evaluate CAPMAN's overhead compared to that of a user space solution based on Ptrace [34] and a kernel space solution for observability based on the eBPF toolkit BCC [29]. The experiment is based on 10 short-lived containerized applications under test usage that involve intensive system call and capability check activities. Those applications are run under seven different settings: i) the *baseline* setting without CAPMAN, ii) a *BCC capable* setting where we collect capability checks using an eBPF-based tool [29], iii) an *offline* setting where CAPMAN only records the capability checks, iv) a *whitelist* setting with $N = 1$, where CAPMAN performs whitelist matching with a sequence length of one, v) a *whitelist* setting with $N = 3$ (based on our detection accuracy results), vi) a *decision tree* setting, with a tree depth of five and $N = 3$, and vii) a *Ptrace* setting where Ptrace is used to trace the activity of every spawning process within the container.

Table 4a compares the overhead in terms of application performance under those different settings. The overall results show that CAPMAN has a negligible level of overhead on the performance of applications, with an average overhead increase of 0.40%, 1.33%, and 2.51% among these containers, for the *offline* setting, and the *whitelist* settings with $N = 1$ and $N = 3$, respectively. The *decision tree* setting incurs 0.73% overhead on average, comparatively less than the *whitelist* setting, since the former does not require searching in a whitelist, and thus is more efficient. In contrast, Ptrace introduces up to 786.14% overhead (156.59% on average) and even causes the *OpenJDK* container to fail (marked as F), which confirms the benefit of CAPMAN's in-kernel detection. The overhead of BCC Capable and CAPMAN's *offline* setting is similar, which is expected since both do not involve detection or mitigation.

Table 4. Comparing the response time of CAPMAN with BCC Capable and Ptrace.

	BCC Capable	CAPMAN				Ptrace
		Offline	Whitelist $N=1$	Whitelist $N=3$	Decision Tree	
Alpine	1.41%	1.28%	1.98%	2.48%	1.44%	67.26%
Golang	0.02%	0.05%	1.18%	2.02%	0.23%	62.21%
Node	0.02%	0.08%	0.97%	2.21%	0.65%	102.15%
OpenJDK	1.07%	1.47%	2.08%	2.40%	1.77%	F
Python	0.23%	0.11%	0.26%	0.45%	0.21%	49.58%
Stress-ng	0.11%	0.11%	3.13%	7.15%	0.49%	786.14%
MySQL	0.23%	0.25%	1.45%	1.68%	1.24%	85.04%
GCC	0.14%	0.15%	0.85%	1.94%	0.51%	42.68%
Nginx	0.24%	0.15%	0.71%	3.91%	0.38%	167.41%
Redis	0.27%	0.35%	0.65 %	0.83%	0.37%	46.89%
Average	**0.37%**	**0.40%**	**1.33%**	**2.51%**	**0.73%**	**156.59%**

F: The container failed when attaching Ptrace to its processes.
(a) Overhead in terms of application response time.

		Average Response Time per System Call
	Baseline	5,447 ns
	BCC Capable	5,499 ns
CAPMAN	Offline	5,593 ns
	Whitelist, $N=1$	5,669 ns
	Whitelist, $N=3$	5,605 ns
	Decision Tree	6,121 ns
	Ptrace	207,237 ns

(b) Overhead in terms of system call response time.

Table 4a shows the overhead in term of the average response time for handling each system call under CAPMAN, in comparison to Ptrace, BCC, and the *baseline* setting. The results translate to around 0.95% and 2.68% overhead for BCC Capable and *offline* settings, 4.08% ($N = 1$) and 2.90% ($N = 3$) for the *whitelist* setting, and 12.37% for *decision tree* (note such overhead only applies to individual system calls, whereas the aggregated impact on the application and users remains negligible, as shown in Table 4a). In contrast, using Ptrace introduces about 3,705% overhead for each system call. This further confirms the benefits of CAPMAN's in-kernel detection approach.

We also compare CAPMAN's CPU and memory consumption with those of Ptrace [34], BCC Capable [29], and the *baseline* setting. Table 5a shows the results, where the *Container* column is for the container in the presence of the corresponding solution, and the *Solution* column is for the solution itself. Specifically, among all the solutions, Ptrace incurs the most overhead both for the container (1.09% CPU) and for itself (0.98% CPU and 9.89 MB of memory). CAPMAN introduces negligible CPU overhead to both the container and itself, even under the most complex methods (maximum 0.56% and 0.44% for decision tree, and 0.55% and 0.41% for whitelist matching, respectively). The memory consumption in all cases remains constant at around 1.53 MB, while the memory consumption of CAPMAN is only that of the kernel module; which represents at most 36 KB when loaded with the whitelist matching engine. BCC Capable includes negligible overhead in terms of both CPU and memory consumption, since it only collects capability checks (no detection/mitigation).

Finally, we also measure the impact of the depth of decision trees on the overhead and CPU consumption of CAPMAN. Although a depth greater than 5 does not significantly improve the accuracy in our experiences, we still report results for such cases. Specifically, Table 5b reports the overhead on the application response time, as well as the overall CPU consumption for the stress-ng container (our most intensive capability-checking application) while varying the tree depth between 1 and 100. Even with an extreme tree depth of 100, CAPMAN only adds 0.38% of CPU consumption, and incurs 4.44% overhead on the response time (which is almost two times less than with whitelist matching, as shown in Table 4a).

Table 5. The performance overhead of CAPMAN.

(a) CPU/memory consumption of the container and CAPMAN, Ptrace [34], and *BCC Capable* [29].

	Container		Solution	
	CPU	Memory	CPU	Memory
Baseline	0.46%	1.53 MB	N/A	N/A
BCC Capable	0.46%	1.52 MB	0.61%	4.64 KB
CAPMAN Offline	0.52%	1.52 MB	0.40%	24 KB
CAPMAN Whitelist, $N=1$	0.55%	1.53 MB	0.42%	24 KB
CAPMAN Whitelist, $N=3$	0.55%	1.54 MB	0.41%	36 KB
CAPMAN Decision Tree	0.56%	1.57 MB	0.44%	24 KB
Ptrace	1.09%	1.53 MB	0.98%	9.89 MB

(b) CPU/Application response time overhead under different tree depths.

Tree Depth	Overhead on CPU Usage	Overhead on Response Time
1	+0.08%	+0.17%
3	+0.09%	+0.21%
5	+0.08%	+0.65%
10	+0.08%	+0.84%
30	+0.12%	+2.52%
50	+0.22%	+3.33%
100	+0.38%	+4.44%

The Effect of Time-Phase Separation. To answer RQ4, Fig. 7 shows that 48 out of the top 50 downloaded container images on Docker Hub perform their capability checks in the first 20 seconds (our threshold). Table 6 shows many more capabilities are needed during booting than running, and many high-risk capabilities (e.g., NET_ADMIN) can be disabled after booting. Appendix provides more detailed discussions of those results.

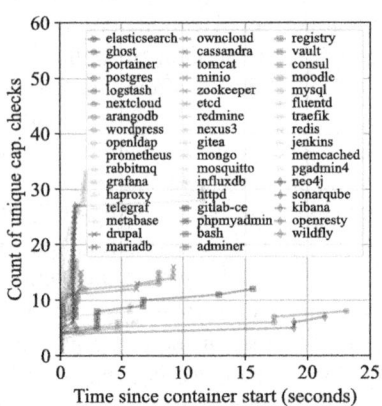

Fig. 7. # of unique capabilities checks over the execution time of containers.

Table 6. Capability checks during booting/running phases of 10 applications.

	Boot.	Run.	Cap. Disabled by CAPMAN in Running Phase	Running Phase Cap.
Nginx	47	1	DAC_OVER., SETGID, SETUID	SYS_ADM.
Redis	21	0	SETUID, NET_ADM., SYS_ADM., SETGID	-
Postgres	25	3	-	SYS_ADM.
Httpd	14	1	SETGID, SETUID	SYS_ADM.
Memcached	9	0	SYS_ADM.	-
MongoDB	39	1	CHOWN, SETGID, SETUID, NET_ADM.	SYS_ADM.
MySQL	49	0	SYS_ADM., SYS_NICE	-
RabbitMQ	35	0	SYS_ADM.	-
Traefik	8	0	NET_ADM., SYS_ADM.	-
Docker	64	4	SYS_CHROOT, CHOWN, MKNOD, [...], NET_ADM., SYS_MOD.	SYS_ADM., DAC_OVER., DAC_READ_S.

5 Discussions and Limitations

Coverage of Normal Behavior. Like most existing solutions involving a learning step [39,69], CAPMAN shares the challenge of ensuring sufficient coverage of normal behavior during its offline phase. Although not a unique challenge to CAPMAN, we make the following best efforts to address it: i) we build our evaluation containers according to best practices of microservices [62], i.e., with a single task in mind, and minimum dependencies (base image and external packages); ii) we apply existing solutions to generate realistic workloads, e.g., Siege [16] and DirBuster [53] for webservers, HammerDB for databases, and compilation benchmarks [20,26] for GCC/Golang. In real-world scenarios, CAPMAN could be applied alongside the program's integration and unit testing framework [37]. It can also be combined with either static analysis tools that take into account the program's configuration and parameters [19], or program fuzzers [40,51] to maximize the coverage. Finally, profiles of capability checks may be constructed for popular applications and shared with the community via crowd-sourcing.

Zero-day Capability Abuses. Since the whitelist and decision tree of CAPMAN are both learned from the normal behavior (capability checks) of a container, CAPMAN does not require prior knowledge about a vulnerability or exploit. Therefore, similar to other anomaly detection approaches [23], CAPMAN can potentially detect (and mitigate) zero-day attacks involving capability abuses.

Advanced Detection Models. Although its in-kernel design currently limits CAPMAN to simple models such as whitelist and decision tree, knowledge distillation [74] can help transfer knowledge from more advanced ML models (which do not fit in the kernel space) to such tree-based models to further improve the detection accuracy.

Security Trade-offs. The in-kernel design of CAPMAN ensures its efficiency but also renders it a critical system component. To minimize the risk, we i) implement it without any external dependencies; ii) develop its kernel module with only $\approx$ 800 LoC to reduce potential bug sites; iii) use only existing kernel functions to update the capability sets of a process. A future direction is to integrate CAPMAN as a Linux Security Module (LSM) hook [60,73], or leverage eBPF to make it more secure and usable.

Removing Capabilities vs. Denying the Checks. Instead of removing capabilities from a process's effective set for mitigation, an alternative is to simply deny the capability check by returning -EPERM. We choose the former approach to ensure consistency/transparency for user space programs, since some programs may behave differently depending on whether a capability is in the effective sets, and denying capability checks at the kernel level could confuse such programs and cause unexpected behaviors.

Evasive Attacks and False Negatives. The stateful models of CAPMAN make it less sensitive to evasive attacks, such as mimicry [68], since it is harder for attackers to mimic *sequences* of capability checks. To reinforce against such attacks, system call arguments [50] and function call stacks [12] can be added to CAPMAN's detection features. Another evasive technique is to attack during the container's *booting* phase (more enabled capabilities), which can be prevented by booting containers offline. Finally, the immutable nature of containers means that CAPMAN's offline phase can occur in a controlled, attack-free environment to prevent adversarial ML attacks. These can all help to keep the false negatives of CAPMAN under control. Allocating more resources to CAPMAN can also reduce false negatives through more capable detection models (e.g., deeper decision trees and longer sequences).

Dynamic Workload. CAPMAN currently does not support dynamic changes in the workload, and its models require re-training for changed behaviors of the container (e.g., software update or new environment). Using incremental learning techniques to dynamically update the models over time can address this [54].

Integration with Orchestration Platforms. CAPMAN is not currently integrated with cloud and container orchestration platforms. While different policies can be selectively enforced for different containers, updating them requires re-compiling the kernel module and keeping track of those policies manually. CAPMAN could benefit from a user space interface to keep track and add/remove policies from the kernel module (e.g., using `ioctl`), and integration with tools like Kubernetes and Open Policy Agent (OPA) will allow central and easier management of CAPMAN's policies.

6 Related Work

Closest to our work, Decap [25] and LiCA [64] employ static analysis to find the necessary and sufficient capabilities set of Linux binaries. Those can be applied to containers, but need manual efforts to identify all binaries in the container, and attackers can still abuse the legitimate capabilities. Similarly, ConfigWiz [32], TCLP [38] and SysCap [75] identify a minimal capabilities set by analyzing the system calls and learning a mapping to capabilities. The RootAsRole framework [3,4,70] implements the *capable* tool to identify a binary's "least privilege" capabilities set, and the *sr* tool to enforce them as RBAC policies in Linux. Those tools can effectively reduce the attack surface of applications, although they do not consider sequence of capabilities nor their runtime and time-phase separation aspects as addressed by CAPMAN. Minicon [31], SystemTap's *container_check* tool [46], and BCC's *Capable* tool [29] all employ a similar in-kernel capability hooking technique as our solution but do not consider sequences of capabilities. SELinux [61] and AppArmor [22] can be used to enforce capability restrictions for each process at runtime, although they do not directly provide any analysis and detection features or consider sequences of capability checks like CAPMAN does.

AutoPriv [28] and CapWeave [24] modify a program at compilation time to add directives for allowing capabilities only when needed. Unlike CAPMAN, these require access to the application's source code. PrivAnalyzer [6] measures the efficacy of capabilities and PeX [77] assesses the soundness of permission checks (including capabilities) in the Linux kernel, while neither provides a solution for mitigating capability abuses. As capabilities are closely related to system calls, existing works on system call filtering for containers are also related to our work. SysFilter [7] uses static analysis to identify the set of system calls required by a program, while Confine [17] extends the work to containers. SPEAKER [39], Ghavamnia et al. [18], SysPart [56], and DynBox [76] restrict unnecessary system calls for different phases of a program's life cycle. Phoenix [33] and SFIP [5] go even further by monitoring sequences of system calls and their arguments. All those works cannot prevent capability abuses employing the same system calls as the application, resulting in more false positives, as shown in Sect. 4.

7 Conclusion

We proposed CAPMAN, an in-kernel runtime solution for protecting privileged containers against capability abuses. Specifically, we developed a `kprobe`-based kernel module for CAPMAN to intercept and collect information about capability checks. We also developed lightweight detection methods that could be deployed inside the kernel to ensure efficiency, and safe mitigation methods leveraging standard kernel functions and procedures for altering capabilities. Our implementation and evaluation showed CAPMAN effectiveness in mitigating capability abuses, with negligible delay and overhead.

Acknowledgements. We thank the anonymous reviewers for their valuable comments. This work was partially supported by the Natural Sciences and Engineering Research Council of Canada (NSERC), Ericsson Canada, Prompt Quebec under Alliance Project 598498, and the Canada Foundation for Innovation (CFI) under JELF Project 38599.

References

1. Bachl, M., Fabini, J., Zseby, T.: A flow-based IDS using machine learning in eBPF. arXiv preprint arXiv:2102.09980 (2022)
2. Billimoria, K.N.: Linux Kernel Programming: A Comprehensive Guide to Kernel Internals, Writing Kernel Modules, and Kernel Synchronization. Packt Publishing Ltd. (2021)
3. Billoir, E., Laborde, R., Wazan, A.S., Rütschlé, Y., Benzekri, A.: Implementing the principle of least privilege using linux capabilities: challenges and perspectives. In: Cyber Security in Networking Conference (CSNet), pp. 130–136 (2023)
4. Billoir, E., Laborde, R., Wazan, A.S., Rütschlé, Y., Benzekri, A.: Enhancing secure deployment with ansible: a focus on least privilege and automation for linux. In: International Conference on Availability, Reliability and Security, pp. 1–7 (2024)
5. Canella, C., Dorn, S., Gruss, D., Schwarz, M.: SFIP: coarse-grained syscall-flow-integrity protection in modern systems. arXiv preprint arXiv:2202.13716 (2022)
6. Criswell, J., Zhou, J., Gravani, S., Hu, X.: PrivAnalyzer: measuring the efficacy of linux privilege use. In: Annual IEEE/IFIP International Conference on Dependable Systems and Networks (DSN), pp. 593–604 (2019)
7. DeMarinis, N., Williams-King, K., Jin, D., Fonseca, R., Kemerlis, V.P.: sysfilter: automated system call filtering for commodity software. In: International Symposium on Research in Attacks, Intrusions and Defenses (RAID) (2020)
8. Docker: Docker Engine Security (2024). https://docs.docker.com/engine/security/#linux-kernel-capabilities. Accessed 15 Nov 2024
9. Docker Hub: Docker in Docker (DinD) (2024). https://hub.docker.com/_/docker. Accessed 25 Dec 2024
10. Edge, J.: Inheriting capabilities (2015). https://lwn.net/Articles/632520. Accessed 25 Dec 2024
11. Falco (2018). https://falco.org. Accessed 15 Nov 2024
12. Feng, H.H., Kolesnikov, O.M., Fogla, P., Lee, W., Gong, W.: Anomaly detection using call stack information. In: IEEE Symposium on Security and Privacy (S&P) (2003)
13. Findlay, W., Barrera, D., Somayaji, A.: BPFContain: fixing the soft underbelly of container security. arXiv preprint arXiv:2102.06972 (2021)

14. Fingler, H., et al.: Towards a machine learning-assisted kernel with LAKE. In: ACM International Conference on Architectural Support for Programming Languages and Operating Systems (ASPLOS), pp. 846–861 (2023)
15. Forrest, S., Hofmeyr, S.A., Somayaji, A., Longstaff, T.A.: A sense of self for UNIX processes. In: IEEE Symposium on Security and Privacy (S&P), pp. 120–128. IEEE (1996)
16. Fulmer, J.: siege - An HTTP/HTTPS Stress Tester (2004). https://linux.die.net/man/1/siege. Accessed 05 Apr 2025
17. Ghavamnia, S., Palit, T., Benameur, A., Polychronakis, M.: Confine: automated system call policy generation for container attack surface reduction. In: International Symposium on Research in Attacks, Intrusions and Defenses (RAID) (2020)
18. Ghavamnia, S., Palit, T., Mishra, S., Polychronakis, M.: Temporal system call specialization for attack surface reduction. In: USENIX Security Symposium (2020)
19. Ghavamnia, S., Palit, T., Polychronakis, M.: C2C: fine-grained configuration-driven system call filtering. In: ACM SIGSAC Conference on Computer and Communications Security (CCS) (2022)
20. Golang: Golang Standard Library (2025). https://pkg.go.dev/std. Accessed 05 Apr 2025
21. Gregg, Brendan: Linux BCC Tracing Security Capabilities) (2016). https://www.brendangregg.com/blog/2016-10-01/linux-bcc-security-capabilities.html. Accessed 05 Apr 2025
22. Gruenbacher, A., Arnold, S.: Apparmor technical documentation. SUSE Labs/Novell (2007)
23. Guo, S., et al.: A zero-day container attack detection based on ensemble machine learning. In: IEEE International Conference on Emerging Technologies and Factory Automation (ETFA), pp. 1–8. IEEE (2023)
24. Harris, W.R., Jha, S., Reps, T., Anderson, J., Watson, R.N.: Declarative, temporal, and practical programming with capabilities. In: IEEE Symposium on Security and Privacy (S&P), pp. 18–32 (2013)
25. Hasan, M.M., Ghavamnia, S., Polychronakis, M.: Decap: depriviliging programs by reducing their capabilities. In: International Symposium on Research in Attacks, Intrusions and Defenses (RAID), pp. 395–408 (2022)
26. Henning, J.: SPEC CPU 2017 Documentation. Standard Performance Evaluation Corporation (SPEC) (2024). https://www.spec.org/cpu2017/
27. Hofmeyr, S.A., Forrest, S., Somayaji, A.: Intrusion detection using sequences of system calls. J. Comput. Secur. **6**(3), 151–180 (1998)
28. Hu, X., Zhou, J., Gravani, S., Criswell, J.: Transforming code to drop dead privileges. In: IEEE Cybersecurity Development (SecDev), pp. 45–52 (2018)
29. IOVisor: capable.py - BCC tools (2024). https://github.com/iovisor/bcc/blob/master/tools/capable.py. Accessed 15 Nov 2024
30. Kabar, N.: Netshoot (2024). https://github.com/nicolaka/netshoot. Accessed 25 Dec 2024
31. Kang, H., Kim, J., Shin, S.: MiniCon: automatic enforcement of a minimal capability set for security-enhanced containers. In: IEEE International IOT, Electronics and Mechatronics Conference (IEMTRONICS), pp. 1–5 (2021)
32. Kavousi, M., et al.: ConfigWiz: automating privilege configuration for containerized applications. Pre-print; SSRN 4995115 (2024)
33. Kermabon-Bobinnec, H., Jarraya, Y., Wang, L., Majumdar, S., Pourzandi, M.: Phoenix: surviving unpatched vulnerabilities via accurate and efficient filtering of syscall sequences. In: Network and Distributed Systems Security Symposium (NDSS) (2024)
34. Kerrisk, M.: Ptrace Man Page (2023). https://man7.org/linux/man-pages/man2/ptrace.2.html. Accessed 15 Nov 2024
35. Kerrisk, M.: Capabilities Man Page (2024). https://man7.org/linux/man-pages/man7/capabilities.7.html. Accessed 15 Nov 2024

36. Kerrisk, M.: dmesg: Diagnostic Message Log Man Page (2024). https://man7.org/linux/man-pages/man1/dmesg.1.html. Accessed 23 Dec 2024
37. Khorikov, V.: Unit Testing Principles, Practices, and Patterns. Simon and Schuster (2020)
38. Lee, S., Seo, J., Nam, J., Shin, S.: TCLP: enforcing least privileges to prevent containers from kernel vulnerabilities. In: ACM SIGSAC Conference on Computer and Communications Security (CCS), pp. 2665–2667 (2019)
39. Lei, L., et al.: SPEAKER: split-phase execution of application containers. In: Detection of Intrusions and Malware, and Vulnerability Assessment (DIMVA) (2017)
40. Li, Y., Chen, B., Chandramohan, M., Lin, S.W., Liu, Y., Tiu, A.: Steelix: program-state based binary fuzzing. In: FSE Joint Meeting on Foundations of Software Engineering (2017)
41. Lin, X., Lei, L., Wang, Y., Jing, J., Sun, K., Zhou, Q.: A measurement study on linux container security: attacks and countermeasures. In: Annual Computer Security Applications Conference (ACSAC), pp. 418–429 (2018)
42. Linux Kernel Docs: Linux Kernel Probes (Kprobes) (2023). https://docs.kernel.org/trace/kprobes.html. Accessed 15 Nov 2024
43. Linux Kernel Docs: Linux Kernel Floating-point API (2024). https://docs.kernel.org/next/core-api/floating-point.html. Accessed 25 Dec 2024
44. Linux Kernel Docs: sysfs: Virtual File System for Kernel Objects (2024). https://www.kernel.org/doc/html/latest/filesystems/sysfs.html. Accessed 23 Dec 2024
45. LinuxServer.io: Dilinger (2024). https://docs.linuxserver.io/deprecated_images/docker-dillinger. Accessed 25 Dec 2024
46. Liu, X.: SystemTap Examples - container_check.stp (2024). https://github.com/boat0/SystemTap-examples/blob/master/container_check.stp. Accessed 15 Nov 2024
47. McCune, R.: Linux Capabilities and When to Drop All (2017). https://raesene.github.io/blog/2017/08/27/Linux-capabilities-and-when-to-drop-all. Accessed 25 Dec 2024
48. MITRE: CVE-2020-14386: Linux Kernel Memory Corruption Vulnerability (2020). https://cve.mitre.org/cgi-bin/cvename.cgi?name=CVE-2020-14386. Accessed 25 Dec 2024
49. MITRE: CVE-2022-0492: Linux Kernel Cgroups Vulnerability (2022). https://cve.mitre.org/cgi-bin/cvename.cgi?name=CVE-2022-0492. Accessed 25 Dec 2024
50. Mutz, D., Robertson, W., Vigna, G., Kemmerer, R.: Exploiting execution context for the detection of anomalous system calls. In: International Symposium on Recent Advances in Intrusion Detection (RAID) (2007)
51. Nagy, S., Nguyen-Tuong, A., Hiser, J.D., Davidson, J.W., Hicks, M.: Breaking through binaries: compiler-quality instrumentation for better binary-only fuzzing. In: USENIX Security Symposium (2021)
52. Nechakhin, V.: Cheat sheets: container escaping - excessive capabilities (2024). https://github.com/0xn3va/cheat-sheets/blob/main/Container/Escaping/excessive-capabilities.md. Accessed 25 Dec 2024
53. OWASP: dirbuster (2009). https://www.kali.org/tools/dirbuster. Accessed 05 Apr 2025
54. Pancholi, M., Kellas, A.D., Kemerlis, V.P., Sethumadhavan, S.: Timeloops: automatic system call policy learning for containerized microservices. arXiv preprint arXiv:2204.06131 (2022)
55. Rahman, A., Shamim, S.I., Bose, D.B., Pandita, R.: Security misconfigurations in open source kubernetes manifests: an empirical study. ACM Trans. Softw. Eng. Methodol. **32**(4) (2023)
56. Rajagopalan, V.L., Kleftogiorgos, K., Göktas, E., Xu, J., Portokalidis, G.: Syspart: automated temporal system call filtering for binaries. In: Proceedings of the 2023 ACM SIGSAC Conference on Computer and Communications Security, pp. 1979–1993 (2023)
57. Rclone: rclone-mount (2024). https://hub.docker.com/r/mumiehub/rclone-mount. Accessed 25 Dec 2024
58. Redroid: Redroid (2024). https://hub.docker.com/r/redroid/redroid. Accessed 25 Dec 2024

59. Robertson, A.: capable.bt - BPFTrace (2025). https://github.com/bpftrace/bpftrace. Accessed 05 Apr 2024
60. senyuuri: Linux Capability - A Kernel Walkthrough (2021). https://blog.senyuuri.info/posts/2021-02-06-linux-capability-a-kernel-workthrough. Accessed 05 Apr 2025
61. Smalley, S., Vance, C., Salamon, W.: Implementing selinux as a linux security module. NAI Labs Rep. **1**(43), 139 (2001)
62. Souppaya, M., Morello, J., Scarfone, K.: Application Container Security Guide. Technical report, National Institute of Standards and Technology (2017)
63. Sultan, S., Ahmad, I., Dimitriou, T.: Container security: issues, challenges, and the road ahead. IEEE Access **7**, 52976–52996 (2019)
64. Sun, M., Song, Z., Ren, X., Wu, D., Zhang, K.: LiCA: a fine-grained and path-sensitive linux capability analysis framework. In: International Symposium on Research in Attacks, Intrusions and Defenses (RAID), pp. 364–379 (2022)
65. Sysdig (2023). https://sysdig.com/. Accessed 15 Nov 2024
66. Thévenon, G., Nguetchouang, K., Lazri, K., Tchana, A., Olivier, P.: B-side: binary-level static system call identification. In: Proceedings of the 25th International Middleware Conference, pp. 225–237 (2024)
67. Tigera: Project Calico - Open Source Networking and Security (2024). https://www.tigera.io/project-calico. Accessed 15 Nov 2024
68. Wagner, D., Soto, P.: Mimicry attacks on host-based intrusion detection systems. In: ACM SIGSAC Conference on Computer and Communications Security (CCS) (2002)
69. Wang, X., Shen, Q., Luo, W., Wu, P.: RSDS: getting system call whitelist for container through dynamic and static analysis. In: IEEE International Conference on Cloud Computing (CLOUD), pp. 600–608 (2020)
70. Wazan, A.S., et al.: RootAsRole: a security module to manage the administrative privileges for linux. Comput. Secur. 102983 (2022)
71. Wenhao, J., Zheng, L.: Vulnerability analysis and security research of docker container. In: IEEE International Conference on Information Systems and Computer Aided Education, pp. 354–357 (2020)
72. WireGuard: WireGuard VPN (2024). https://www.wireguard.com/. Accessed 25 Dec 2024
73. Wright, C., Cowan, C., Smalley, S., Morris, J., Kroah-Hartman, G.: Linux security modules: general security support for the linux kernel. In: USENIX Security Symposium (2002)
74. Xie, G., et al.: Empowering in-network classification in programmable switches by binary decision tree and knowledge distillation. IEEE/ACM Trans. Network. **32**(1), 382–395 (2024)
75. Xing, Y., et al.: SysCap: profiling and crosschecking syscall and capability configurations for docker images. In: IEEE Conference on Communications and Network Security (CNS), pp. 236–244 (2022)
76. Zhang, Q., et al.: Building dynamic system call sandbox with partial order analysis. Proc. ACM Program. Lang. **7**, 1253–1280 (2023)
77. Zhang, T., Shen, W., Lee, D., Jung, C., Azab, A.M., Wang, R.: PeX: a permission check analysis framework for linux kernel. In: USENIX Security Symposium, pp. 1205–1220 (2019)

Digital Twin for Adaptive Adversary Emulation in IIoT Control Networks

Javier Parada[1,2], Cristina Alcaraz[1(✉)], Javier Lopez[1], Juan Caubet[2], and Rodrigo Román[1]

[1] Computer Science Department, University of Malaga, Campus de Teatinos s/n, 29071 Malaga, Spain
{javierparada,alcaraz,javierlopez,rroman}@uma.es
[2] Eurecat, Centre Tecnològic de Catalunya, IT & OT Security Unit, C/Bilbao 72, 08005 Barcelona, Spain
{javier.parada,juan.caubet}@eurecat.org

Abstract. The number of threats in industrial ecosystems is increasing, especially in critical sectors, which have become a particularly lucrative target. These ecosystems have evolved into very complex interconnected systems, driven by the need to adapt to new digitalization and automation trends which extend their attack surface. In addition, the criticality of these systems makes them particularly difficult to test.

For these reasons, this paper covers the application of digital twins as the target of Adversary Emulation for the purpose of improving the security of industrial environments. This is done by involving automated and adaptive adversaries by means of reinforcement learning. Starting from an offensive strategy, these adversaries are able to adapt to the context, attacking the most critical parts of industrial systems. Adversarial attacks are driven by control theory and centrality techniques, providing a safe and efficient way to test critical industrial networks. The proposed methodology also includes the effective training and validation of adversaries by creating a probabilistic model from the analysis of digital twins. The paper provides relevant results on the development of adversarial adversaries and test models, and highlights the importance and opportunities of attack automation in virtualized environments.

Keywords: Adversarial Emulation · Digital Twin · Reinforcement Learning · Industrial Internet of Things

1 Introduction

The current cybersecurity landscape continues to grow, especially in the management of potential threats to strategic industrial sectors [1]. This is due to the current need to create hyper-connected environments in which different technologies are incorporated to automate operational processes and intensify digitization of systems. According to Gartner's radar for 2025, there is a specific technological trend [2] that puts Artificial Intelligence (AI) and hybrid and operational computing in the crosshairs of new emerging adversary profiles [3]. All of this, in turn, leads to the need to invest in the protection of industrial environments, which is projected at USD 166.51 billion by 2032, with a Compound Annual Growth Rate (CARG) of 3.67% during the forecast period 2025–2032 [4]. In this respect, recent AI-assisted methods involving advanced prediction and detection have proven to be especially useful for complex and even unclassified attacks [5]. However, defense systems face problems such as the lack of automatic (re)training data, the use of new strategies and technologies by attackers to evade defense systems, and the strong incentives that the latter currently have against specific critical sectors. Some real cases have already witnessed the consequences of possible attacks, such as the advanced ransomware attack against Schneider Electric in January 2025 [6], and the attack on Key Tronic Corporation in May 2024 that caused data leaks and denial of services in the system's primary operations [7].

One way of tackling these situations from a proactive perspective is through Cyber Threat Hunting (CTH). With the support of Cyber Threat Intelligence (CTI), CTH is positioned within the field of active cyber-defense as one of the most relevant areas for dynamic prevention. This area is so important that it already has an investment forecast of USD 7.66 Billon by 2030 with 13.27% CARG for 2025–2030, especially when AI-based analytical prediction approaches are applied to the field of defense [8]. This is the case of Adversary Emulation (AE) as an effective cybersecurity assessment method within CTH to anticipate threat scenarios and provide guarantees of business and operating continuity [9]. This characteristic has also demonstrated in recent studies such as [10], which applies AE in cyber physical systems, and [9] where AE is applied in general-purpose systems to detect potential threats based on offensive techniques, probably designed with advanced and sophisticated attack approaches. However, the active automation of these evaluation methods and their application in very demanding environments also forces us to explore the use of simulation technologies to emulate attacks without corrupting the integrity and functionality of real systems. Among simulation technologies, the Digital Twin (DT) stands out for its ability to deploy "machines (physical and/or virtual) or computer-based models that are simulating, emulating, mirroring or twinning the life of a physical entity" [11] with high fidelity abstraction [1]. This simulation level, under synchronization and automatic bidirectional communication criteria [12], allows the faithful recreation of scenarios, behaviors and states of the physical counterpart being imitated [1], favoring not only the AE analysis but also feedback to CTH.

Indeed, a DT can help (i) infer security vulnerabilities (probably zero-days) [13–16], (ii) derive emerging exploits, and (iii) identify new and advanced *modus operandi* and attack strategies without infringing the operation and integrity criteria of its real physical counterpart [1,17]. If, in addition, we combine this simulation capacity with AE techniques to enrich CTH processes, it is also possible to contribute to the literature with a new prevention mode, as stated in [18]. Unfortunately, there is not enough related work that uses DT for this purpose, and only [18] comes close to what is presented in this study, proving the role of DT for AE and Internet of Things (IoT) scenarios. However, the relevance of

Industrial Internet of Things (IIoT) control elements and their susceptibility to attack is not explored.

For that reason, **the main contribution of this paper** is to delve deeper into this particular issue, dynamically attacking and evaluating the main control elements of IIoT-based scenarios. Thus, with the help of a DT, referred to here as *HunTwin*, it is possible to illustrate the behavior of IIoT-type control networks and establish an assessment based on emulated offenders, that will be able to dynamically derive security breaches in the control system in an adaptive way. To automate this process, these adversaries must be equipped with a Reinforcement Learning (RL) model that allows them to autonomously learn the integral nature of the system and its implicit vulnerabilities, especially of the main elements with greater dominance and control within an IIoT environment. The RL model is designed to be easily interpretable, establishing the risk and the most critical zones according to the weights assigned by the system's experience. To train adversaries, *HunTwin* also compiles a significant number of (i) digital models characterizing different IIoT control scenarios and (ii) tests based on offensive games to validate a set of threat scenarios (targeted, hybrid and to the network itself or at node level). To promote efficient learning within the approach, inspired in part by [19], multiple digital twins are deployed within *HunTwin*. These virtual representations are attacked and analyzed to create a probabilistic model of the system on which to train the RL algorithm at an early stage. This model is a simulation which represents the vulnerability of the systems's different parts to adversaries, allowing SW agents to be trained on this model efficiently and faster. During the AE stage, the DT is also applied for the validation of this approximation, testing the knowledge generated by the simulations in a real IIoT environment. This abstraction allows the system to execute the RL systems in large simulations, generating useful results for later risk assessment, intrusion impact measurements or to develop adapted early threat prevention measures.

The paper is organized as follows: Sect. 2 adds the related work; Sect. 3 introduces the DT-assisted AE architecture IIoT network deployment process, respecting the properties of structural controllability and extracting maximum control dominance. In Sect. 4, the adversarial model is introduced together with the necessary conditions to characterize the DT models. Section 5 shows the experimental results, all of them performed at different levels and scales of depth of study in the DT, prioritizing the AE models under an adaptive approach in the RL. Section 6 provides the paper's conclusions and outlines the future work.

2 Related Work

The increasing sophistication of malicious actors has led the cybersecurity industry to take a proactive role in dealing with threats. One of the most popular approaches has been the AE, where the defensive characteristics of a system are evaluated by skilled adversary attackers. Thanks to these offenders, it is possible to analyze attacks that are more complex than a simple vulnerability pentest in order to infer techniques and avoid future attacks. However, the main challenge this method has traditionally faced is the large consumption of resources involved, both computational and human, especially in terms of time. This is why numerous efforts have been made to automate the process of emulating a real adversary as closely as possible. The use of AE in this context has been demonstrated in recent studies [10,20–23], which focus on the usefulness of AE in a simple way, showing an offensive approach in IoT and generalist environments. Two studies whose approach is more proximate to this present research are analyzed below.

In [9], a model of CTH via AE is proposed, showing a promising proactive approach rather than relying on traditional ones such as penetration testing, firewalls, and Security Information and Event Management (SIEM) systems. This emulation consists of two main phases: an initial phase in which the system is fed with information from CTI, as well as threat reports, information from blogs and forums from which it extracts the Techniques Tactics and Procedures (TTP); and a second phase comprising the execution of the AE, as well as the construction and validation of a hypothesis with generated data, which are fundamental parts of a CTH. In a nutshell, the proposed model is an effective method compared to typical countermeasures based on known threats, but also an efficient hunting resource compared to more traditional and less automated techniques, such as the creation of red teams.

The AE system presented in [18] is based on DT as an offensive target. MITRE Caldera is used for automated AE tests, where one compromised device attacks another target. This paper demonstrates how DTs can be a crucial tool for securing IoT networks. However, a system that takes into account adaptability, and in particular the structural vulnerabilities of large IIoT systems for its propagation, lateral movement techniques, and TTP in general, could further enrich the contribution that has been made.

Table 1. Some Adversary Emulation Researches

Ref	Year	Industry	TTP sources	Infrastructure	DT	CTI	AI agents	Approach	Large Net
[9]	2021	General	CTI, Forums, Blogs	VM	✗	✓	✗	CTH	✗
[18]	2023	IoT	MITRE ATT&ACK	VM	✓	✓	✗	Offensive	✗
[10]	2020	CPS	Internal Model	Mathematical	✗	✗	✓	Offensive	✗
[20]	2022	IoT	RouterSploit	VM	✗	✓	✗	Offensive	✗
[21]	2023	General	MITRE ATT&ACK	Cloud	✗	✓	✗	CTH	✗
[22]	2024	General	Own Model	VM	✗	✓	✗	Anti-detection	✗
[23]	2024	General	MITRE ATT&CK	Cloud	✗	✓	✓	Deception	✗
HunTwin	2025	Industrial	MITRE ATT&CK, MITRE CVE, ExploitDB, VulDB, Metasploit	Containers	✓	✓	✓	CTH	✓

In respect to the recent literature shown in Table 1, *HunTwin* is comparable in terms of external TTP sources. Furthermore, it presents adaptability to the context in which it is developed by having Artificial Intelligence (AI) models that learn from the IIoT network structural controllability characteristics, explained in Sect. 3.2. On the other hand, considering the infrastructure used, containers are lighter and more efficient compared to other heavier virtualization systems such as Virtual Machine (VM), without losing realism in the simulation, since it is a digital model synchronized with a cyber-physical environment. Taking advantage of this computational efficiency, *HunTwin* simulates adversary emulations over large target networks, assuming large networks such as topologies with more than 50 targets. This makes it possible to develop more sophisticated techniques taking advantage of complex network scenarios and industrial characteristics.

3 DT-Assisted Adversarial Emulation Architecture

Figure 1 illustrates the system architecture discussed in this section. *HunTwin* is based on three main Layers (L): IIoT-based physical layer (**L1**), orchestrator layer (**L2**), and DT layer (**L3**). This division allows to isolate all layers in different systems, enhancing independent scalability and security by functionality.

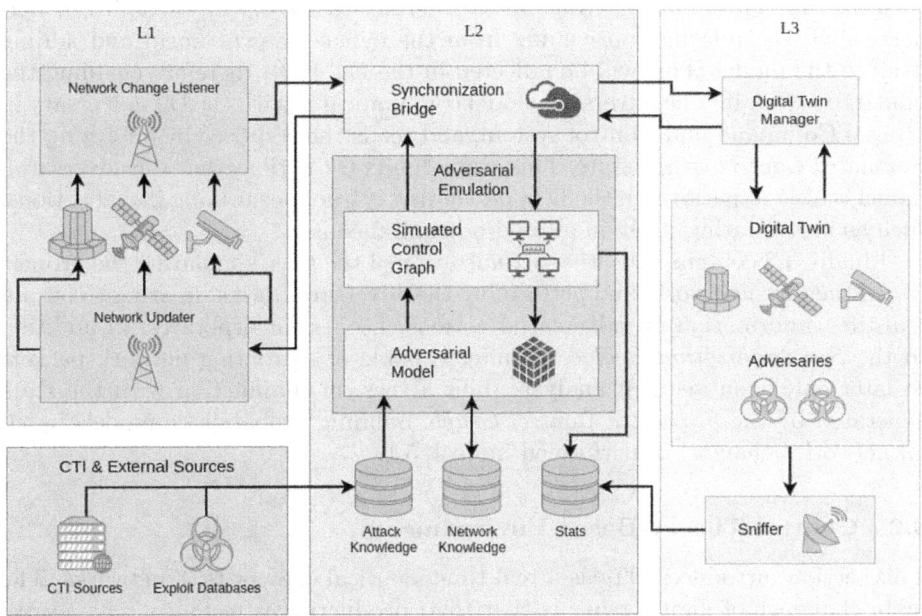

Fig. 1. HunTwin layered architecture: L1, L2 and L3

3.1 Layered HunTwin for Security Assessment

L1 comprises all the physical IIoT elements of the real world, and is in charge of periodically sending synchronization data of current states to L2. This synchronization is performed by two components in a bidirectional flow with L2. The first component is the *Network Change Listener*, which listens for changes in the real physical world and notifies changes through the *Synchronization Bridge* in L2. The second component is the *Network Updater*, which is able to receive updated data from L2 and update the real world infrastructure accordingly.

Additionally, there is a group called *CTI & External Sources* that is not part of L1. It consists of the CTI sources which serve to feed the TTP of the AE models.

In contrast, L2 is responsible for computing received data and synchronizing DTs to their respective counterparts. To do this, L2 relies on a central component called *Synchronization Bridge*, which allows layers to subscribe and emit changes produced in their models. The other element of L2 is the AE module, which has two main responsibilities: the first is to conceptualize the deployment of a graph characterizing the industrial features of real control systems (e.g., controllers, SCADA, etc.). These controllability characteristics define the dominance and control between the different nodes which is a feature of IIoT. This conceptual model is the *Simulated Control Graph*, obtained and synchronized through the *Synchronization Bridge*. The second responsibility is to invoke a set of adversarial software agents (hereinafter illustrated as set A) to attack the threat scenario and verify security gaps. These adversaries have two parts: an RL model acting from L2 as the brain and a real adversary in L3 as the body. The adversary model acts with the *Simulated Control Graph* as an interface to the *Synchronization Bridge*, perturbing the information coming from the cyber-physical world and adding itself to the model. This will be reflected in the DT (L3), therefore enabling the model to attack it. The adversary model communicates with the DT-adversary in L3 as a Command and Control system, and reads the response by analyzing the *Simulated Control Graph* state. This graph limits the actions that the adversarial model is able to perform in the DT, preventing it from performing illegal actions, such as instantiating itself on all nodes simultaneously.

Finally, L3 contemplates the virtualization of the DTs, simulating the properties of the physical world and performing the adversarial tasks. In order to obtain real-time information on adversarial actions, L3 also incorporates, in addition to the *Synchronization Bridge*, a sniffer capable of extracting network packets to later enable subsequent analysis. This allows, in conjunction with the stats generated by the *Simulated Control Graph*, building probabilistic models based on network behavior, as performed in Sect. 5.1.

3.2 Control Theory-Based Environments

This section introduces DTs as a real time identical copy of IIoT networks. The main challenge of digital twins is that their production is technically expensive due to industrial high fidelity. To solve this, an algorithm for the generation of industrial control networks that emulates the structure and organization of such networks is designed. This algorithm also uses images of known systems that have vulnerabilities, which are distributed and replicated throughout the environment according to their functionality, e.g. routers, switches or linux systems.

To characterize this type of scenarios and identify attack targets with higher dominance a network topology that follows a power-law [24] must be first be prepared. Under this assumption, structural controllability rules and power dominance must be reinforced. To do this, it is also necessary to identify among the network elements, hereinafter shown as graph $G(V, E)$, the nodes with the most control that satisfy the rules of control theory [25] and power dominance

[26]. These characteristics are reflected in $OR1$ and $OR2$, two types of groups calculated following the controllability conditions for the entire G network [26]:

- $OR1$: A vertex v_i of degree D observes itself and all its neighbors.
- $OR2$: If a vertex V_i of degree $D \geq 2$ is observed and has adjacent $(D-1)$ observed vertices, the last vertex becomes observed.

Once the environment and control characteristics have been calculated, the next step is to identify the vertices with the highest betweenness centrality, since most of the control passes through them. To do so, the process classifies vertices into different communities using the *Clauset-Newman-Moore* greedy modularity maximization algorithm [27] to find the network's most modularized partitions. This calculation is then used to analyze the different malicious behaviors in small interconnected groups. This is especially interesting in networks that follow a power-law distribution, since they do not contain a large level of interconnection, apart from the zones with the highest centrality. In addition, a criterion involving control characteristics and network centrality $\forall v \in V$ must be defined as a control requirement. To do so, the betweenness centrality of each vertex is calculated. Then, we define the *Scope of Compromise* value for each vertex, which represents a numerical value of how much impact it has to lose a vertex v_i to an attacker, calculated from Eq. 2. This function mixes betweenness centrality, where σ_{mn} is the number of shortest paths from node m to node n, $\sigma_{mn}(v_i)$ those paths that also pass through v_i, and structural controllability-based vertex weighting w_i. These weights depend on whether $v_i \in OR1$, $v_i \in OR2$ or $v_i \notin OR1 \cup OR2$ as shown in Eq. 1.

$$w_i = \begin{cases} p_1 & \text{if } v_i \in OR1 \\ p_2 & \text{if } v_i \in OR2 \quad \forall v_i \in V \quad \text{where} \quad p_1 > p_2 > p_3. \\ p_3 & \text{otherwise} \end{cases} \quad (1)$$

$$com(v_i) = \sum_{m \neq v_i \neq n} \frac{\sigma_{mn}(v_i)}{\sigma_{mn}} \cdot w_i \forall v_i \in V \quad (2)$$

Once the mathematical framework of the topology has been established, including the calculations related to controllability characteristics, the next step is the deployment and digitization of the system. Digital models are generated for each G node, the main information being the copy of the image to be virtually created. In these experiments, images of vulnerable devices are also established to be exploited by agents. Furthermore, some nodes incorporate deception strategies in order to intensify the security testing. Specifically, the position and quantity of these nodes are added randomly, never exceeding a presence of more than 10% of $|V|$ in order to intensify the defense against agents, making topology learning essential to breach the system. The difference between standard and deception nodes is that the deception nodes have no value in quantifying the damage caused to the infrastructure. In other words, these nodes are ignored by the *Scope of Compromise* calculation function in Eq. 3.

$$R(a,t) = \frac{\sum_{i=0}^{|D(a,t)|} com(v_i) \forall v_i \in \{\forall v \in V : (a,v) \in M(t)\}}{\sum_{j=0}^{|V|} com(v_j) \forall v_j \in V} \quad (3)$$

Finally, for the development of an agent's intelligence, the objective function uses the same parameters as the *Scope of Compromise* calculation, but summing the compromise index of all vertices. This assumes that the malicious agent has compromised the system by exceeding a certain threshold calculated by Eq. 3, which aggregates the *Scope of Compromise* of breached vertices by the attacker, establishing a ratio with respect to the total network.

4 DT-Assisted Adversary Model

To formalize the DT and agents-supported emulation, we define each match scenario as an undirected multigraph of type $G = (V, E)$, where V represents the set of vertices illustrating IIoT devices, including those related to control, and E comprises the edges representing the connections between IIoT devices without isolation. Edges are represented as a tuple of two vertices and an index (k), since between two vertices there can be more than one edge representing different physical links $e = (v_i, v_j, k)$. Notice that $\forall\, v \in V$ and $\forall\, e_n \in E$ there is no static allocation of weights because the DT represents illustrations that may vary with the update of its physical counterpart.

4.1 Adversary and Reward Model Formalization

In the agent execution formal system, training and validation matches comprise the following set of variables, conditions and rules:

Time: All the games start at instant $t = 0$ and end at an instant t defined by the starting conditions. An instant t is equivalent to executing an action by $\forall a \in A$.

Players: Agents ($a \in A$) deployed over G are initially randomly assigned to one $v \in V$. This characteristic makes the assignment ($a \rightarrow v$) variables for each match, increasing the number of scenario combinations and avoiding initial disadvantageous situations for a same player. The dominance of vertices by agents is represented by pairs $(a, v) \in M(t)$, where t is a moment and the function M returns a set with all dominance tuples in the instance t.

Teams: Agents ($a \in A$) only belong to a team represented by the set z, which, in turn, belongs to the set of teams represented as Z such that $Z = z_i, ..., z_j$ and $z = a_i, ...a_j$. This property also follows the conditions given by Eq. 4.

$$A = \bigcup_{n=0}^{|Z|} z_n \wedge |A| = \sum_{n=0}^{|Z|} |z_n| \quad (4)$$

Node State: This criterion is based on two possible states. The first state is that an $v \in V$ is dominated by an $a \in A$ (regardless of its z) in an instant t, which means that given $M(t)$ there exists the tuple (a,v). The other state is a neutral state, meaning that the node has not been dominated by any other agent. Node states also follow the restrictions shown in Eq. 5.

$$|\forall v \in V, \forall t \in \mathbb{N}_0 : (a,v) \in M(t)| \in \{1,0\} \tag{5}$$

Movement: An agent's movement is equivalent to *an attempt to join* a $v \in V$ not dominated by an $a \in A$, resulting in adding (a,v) to $M(t+1)$. As the action indicates, this is only an attempt within the game, mainly because the node itself has defensive capabilities against intrusion; even when an $a \in A$ attempts to dominate a $v \in V$, this may result in a failed move.

Cost: Movements do not have a fixed cost. In case of failure in the dominance of a $v \in V$, the cost is given by the loss of the instant t to perform a successful action. Moreover, the difficulty of dominance of a $v \in V$ is not given by v itself, but by the edge $e \in E$ along which the movement takes place. In other words the difficulty is given by attacking $v_i \in V$ through $(v_j, v_i, k) \in E$.

Objective: The objective is given by a function that evaluates whether an $a \in A$, for the end of an instant t has violated the system or not. This function takes into account z_i and the dominance state of all $(a,v) \in M(T)$. Each DT has its own target function since the violation characteristics depend on the physical counterpart it represents.

Reward: It is processed at the end of each match and $\forall a \in A$. There are three types of rewards: *Agent reward*, when $a \in A$ individually wins the match; *Team reward*, when $a \in A$ has not achieved its individual goal but $a \in z \in Z$ and z is the winning team. *Defeat reward*, which involve a defeat of a and the z to which a belongs, in which case a is negatively rewarded.

The execution rules and updates of the system are shown in the Algorithm 1. This algorithm contains two nested loops that iterate A and t, leaving its cyclomatic complexity as shown in Eqs. 6 and 7. On the other hand, the complexity of *update_state* and *has_won* functions are linear to the growth of $|V|$. The complexity of the *next* function grows logarithmically with respect to $|V|$, although its spatial complexity is analyzed in more detail in Sect. 4.2.

$$O(main) = t \cdot |A| \cdot (O(next) + O(update\_state) + O(has\_won)) \tag{6}$$

$$O(main) = t \cdot |A| \cdot (2\,V| + Ln(|V|)) \tag{7}$$

4.2 Adversary Learning Process Modeling

Taking into account the system's flexibility to perform different AI models, this article follows the approach of launching adversarial attackers under RL criteria, and particularly under the *Q-learning* decision policy such as in Eq. 8. In this

Algorithm 1. Simulation loop for the agent execution

Input: 1. A graph $G(V, E)$
Input: 2. A set of Agents A
Input: 3. S_i, where S_i is the strategy of the agent a_i
Input: 4. A function has_won that given an a_i and a game state gs returns whether a_i has won
Input: 6. A function next that receives gs, an a_i, and S_i and returns a (a_i, e_i) to attack
Input: 7. A function update_state that receives gs, an a_i, and (v_i, e_i) and returns the new gs
Input: 8. The initial state of the game game_state
Input: 9. Game run time t

$W \leftarrow \emptyset; \; it \leftarrow 0$
while $LENGTH(W) == 0$ and $it < t$ **do**
    $it \leftarrow it + 1$
    for all $a_i \in A$ **do**
        $(v, e) \leftarrow \text{next}(gs, a_i, S_{A_i})$
        $gs \leftarrow \text{update\_state}(gs, a_i, (v, e))$
        if has_won$(A_i, current\_state)$ **then**
            $W \leftarrow W \cup \{A_i\}$
        end if
    end for
end while
return W

equation, s is the current state of the game, b is the action to perform and Q is a function that returns the learned quality of a b given s.

When applying *Q-learning* policies, a scalability-related challenge is the need to assess the size of the case set to be stored. In a typical approach shown by Eqs. 8 and 9, the possession of each node by $a \in A$ at an instant t is stored as s, and the decision to be made for each $v \in V$ is independently evaluated, leading to an exponential spatial complexity as shown in Eq. 10. This type of strategy is valid in small games such as *tic tac toe* with fewer possible combinations or even in *HunTwin* with small graphs. However, bearing in mind that the match scenarios considered reach up to $|V| = 100$, this complexity is unacceptable, not only because of memory usage but also because of the number of matches that have to be played in order to develop an AI model that has experienced enough casuistry to cover the whole spectrum of possibilities.

$$A(s) = \underset{b}{\operatorname{argmax}} \; Q(s, b) \tag{8}$$

$$s = |\{(a_j, v) \mid v_i \in V, \; a_i \in z_i, \; a_j \in z_i, \; (a_i, v) \in M(t)\}| \tag{9}$$

$$O(f) = 2^{|V|} \tag{10}$$

This is why the approach has been changed for a simpler one, adapted to the type of context to be executed. The foundation of the approach of the designed attack model is inspired by Napoleonic warfare strategies and *Blitzkrieg* [28]. Napoleon's strategy consisted of deep flanking operations in which the enemy's rear was enveloped, with commands advancing along different routes to the point of attack. These characteristics make it ideal for industrial control environments, taking into account the industrial network characteristics detailed in Sect. 3.2. The main focus of this attack is to avoid battles of attrition, emphasizing fast and effective moves; specifically, to surround the enemy's central command area quickly in order to paralyze it and isolate its defenses from the outside.

However, the design of this attack model is more sophisticated than just applying this strategy, in which case we would be ignoring the particular characteristics of industrial network topologies. The idea in this case is to model the agent's knowledge so that the former can learn for itself how to apply it, learning from the network's weakness and evaluating the critical points the strategy talks about.

$$A(s) = \underset{b}{\mathrm{argmax}}\ Q(s,b) \quad s = \{P(a,t), L(a)\} \qquad (11)$$

$$P(a_i, t) = |\{\forall a_j : a_j \in z_k \land a_i \in z_k \land \exists (a_j, v) \in M(t)\}| \qquad (12)$$

$$L(a) = v : (a, v) \in M(0) \qquad (13)$$

$$O(f) = O(P) * O(L) = (|V|-1)^2 * (|z|-1) \qquad (14)$$

In order to perform this Napoleonic-based strategy, as shown in Eq. 11, the policy is decomposed into two functions, P and L, which correspond to Eqs. 12 and 13, respectively. Function L contains the initial position of each $a \in A$, allowing the model to establish optimal attack routes based on each agent's initial position. On the other hand, P consists of enumerating the number of $a \in A$ which belong to the same $z \in Z$. This way, adversaries can learn to distribute themselves over different routes and positions in G. These functions cause agents to not interfere with each other and can change the attack strategy as z decreases. Validation of whether this knowledge modeling translates into this type of strategy is tested in Sect. 5.2. Moreover, thanks to the simplification of the knowledge system, the spatial complexity of the algorithm decreases to quadratic, as shown in Eq. 14.

$$Q(s,a) \leftarrow Q(s,a) + \alpha \left[R(s,a) + \gamma \max_{a'} Q(s',a') - Q(s,a) \right] \qquad (15)$$

The evaluation of victory is based on whether the agent owns a number of $v \in V$ which exceed a certain *Scope of Compromise* threshold. This threshold is given by *Scope of Compromise* calculations, shown at Eq. 3 in Sect. 3.2. This assessment is used to support the reinforcement policy defined in Eq. 15, applying a positive reward to opponents when they win and a negative reward otherwise. This equation allows adversaries to learn based on long-term knowledge, optimizing the decisions that lead to victory. The function updates the quality values of each movement since the last movement performed, propagating backwards. Furthermore, some typical RL parameters like learning and exploration rate are present, and are configured when designing the agent's strategy apart from the DT *Scope of Compromise* calculation.

5 Experimental Cases and Discussion

This section comprises three main experimental studies: (i) Node-level AE (**E1**), (ii) network-level AE (**E2**), and (iii) hybrid (**E3**, combining E1 and E2). E1 consists in creating probabilistic models by attacking DTs to create simulations on which to train the adversaries. On the other hand, E2 consists of training the adversaries in a simulated graph, in which they can learn about the topology and its weaknesses. Finally, E3 consists of running the trained agents on the DT to validate that the generated knowledge is applicable to a real system.

5.1 E1: Node-Level AE Vectors

E1 consists of studying the network's nodes individually, without taking into account the relationships they have at the network level. In this experiment, attack vectors are executed against the nodes in order to perform a probabilistic model that is able to estimate the ability to breach the system by the adversaries.

The first phase of this attack vector consists of performing a scan of all exposed services and vulnerabilities that each node has. The variability of this experiment consists of executing different forms of scanning, such as TCP SYN, UDP Scan, etc., all present in [29], involving characteristics such as the method to use, types of packets to be sent, sizes and intervals of sending, among others. The second phase consists of cross-checking the information obtained by the scan with CTI sources, in which it tries to find vulnerabilities and the corresponding exploits capable of breaching the system. These CTI sources consist mainly of MITRE CVE [30] and VulDB [31]. The third phase consists in executing different exploits from the Exploitdb [32] and Metasploit [33], and TTPs from MITRE ATT&CK [34] in order to control the system. Exploits and TTPs are mixed and concatenated until the agent is able to perform damage to the node and can see the rest of the connections and links to which they propagate. These CTI sources allow to perform real attacks and execute realistic malicious behaviors.

A large number of tests under different conditions and interfaces are performed per image in order to prepare the automatic generation of the control network graph. With these statistics, a ratio is established for each software image approximating the proportion of how many times these elements are breached by adversaries. Thanks to this ratio, fast training of the agents by means of a control graph with a large number of matches can be performed, as shown in Experiment E2, without having to wait for the execution of a real DT.

5.2 E2.1: Net-Level AE Vectors

The next experiments are the simulation of massive matches between different agents to enable them to learn about the network's design. An offensive z_i is configured and must take advantage of these elements to attack the centrality and targets in $OR1$ and $OR2$, further exploiting weaknesses in their design. To improve the efficiency of E2 and to favor the training of agents at an early stage, a simulated control graph is used instead of attacking the DT, as shown in the previous experiment. Moreover, E2 addresses two teams, A and B. Both teams are formed, respectively, of attackers and defenders with the main purpose of competing against each other and finding the fastest way to achieve their goal. Team A is based on an RL model already discussed in Sect. 4. Team B is based on a deterministic algorithm that handles non-dominated nodes propagating through the nodes that are reachable. The idea is that Team B represents a recovery system with a predefined logic and no learning capabilities.

Experiments are conducted on different G, with 10, 20, 50 and 100 nodes, in order to explore the performance of RL. Regarding the games, a total of 10 DTs peer node numbers have been generated, with a total of 100,000 matches for each one. Namely, there is a final total of 1 million matches for each type of scenario, limiting the number of actions to 500 moves per agent. Figure 2 depicts the E2 results.

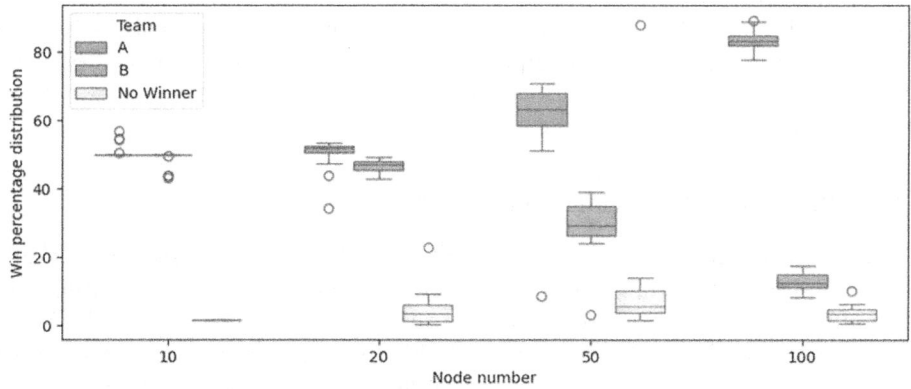

Fig. 2. Distribution of percentage of victories by team

The results obtained on the smallest size graphs, $|V| = 10$ and $|V| = 20$, show a limited performance by the attacking team, unable to overcome a winning ratio higher than that of the defending team. Although there is some dominance of the attacking team, especially in $|V| = 20$, both teams have an approximated winning ratio close to 50%. Based on these results, we conclude the following. On the one hand, victories tend to rely on the initial advantage provided by the assigned starting positions due to the simplicity of the networks. On the other hand, the deviation produced in favor of the attackers in $|V| = 20$ stems from the fact that there is an incipient complexity in the network, which makes the strategic differences between vertices more pronounced.

The results provided by $|V| = 50$ lead to the following conclusions. There is a clear dominance of Team A in the distribution of victories. This is because the network's size is already considerable, with more central and connected zones and more remote isolated zones. The anomaly of games with a clear tendency to the absence of winners is remarkable. This is due to a peculiar network topology with a star-shaped subgraph that has a large number of vertices compared to the general topography. With this interesting topology, there are many possibilities that both teams start the match at one of these points. This in turn, translates into a Nash equilibrium [35] between them to conquer the center, which is the only means of escape from this star but also the only one to be defeated if the opponent passes through it. Moreover, the results obtained by $|V| = 100$ are the most promising. Although the distribution of victories is similar to $|V| = 50$ in tendency, in this case it has greatly increased the number of victories of the attacking team, decreasing victories by the defender team. Complex networks represent an advantage for adversarial attackers, because having more nodes and more connections in the central zones allows them to learn to evade defenses easily without wasting time, and at the same time prioritizing a greater number of critical nodes.

The results of these experiments suggest promising outcomes. In networks with certain complexity and size, the adversaries are able to take advantage of network features by means of some strategies that will be discussed in Sect. 5.3. Although these results do not accurately represent that agents will be able to breach the system, they provide an approximation of how well they will perform in this type of environment. They are also useful to train the AI of agents before running them in a real environment or DT.

5.3 E2.2 Agent Behavior Analysis

Given the predominance of victories of the attacking teams, one additional result that can be extracted from analyzing the previous experiment is the identification of the nodes most relevant to the RL algorithm. This can be done by observing node weights, as shown in Fig. 3 and in the Appendix 6 for all topologies. These topologies are depicted, respectively, with different mathematical representations showing how high the normalized qualities of vertices are through heat graphs. The representation of Fig. 3.a corresponds to the arithmetic mean of the quality per node. The problem with this image is that is difficult to translate into an attacking path to see its short and long-term objectives.

In order to analyze short and long-term thinking, a normalized decay function shown in Eq. 16 is applied to the different representations. This is based on the initial node from which agents start. In consequence, the assigned qualities have a decay, as they are closer from the initial position, thus pondering especially where all paths converge. This is shown in Fig. 3.b, where it can be observed that the relevance falls on the nodes with more centrality, resulting in an initial priority. This criterion is also applied in reverse, setting a negative α parameter in order observe the nodes that are farther from the initial position. This can be seen in the Fig. 3.c, where the objective is clearly to spread to the outer zones without completely renouncing centrality.

$$Q(a, v_i) = \frac{1}{n} \sum_{i=1}^{n} \frac{q_i}{1 + \alpha\, d_G(L(a), v_i)} \tag{16}$$

Analyzing the superimposed results of all the experiments in Fig. 4, there is a positive tendency to value the centrality of both $OR1$ and $OR2$ within the network communities. On the other hand, there is no clear difference between $OR1$ and $OR2$ node qualities, as the attack is performed on both of them. However, when observing the same analysis on the whole network, a negative tendency is seen towards $OR1$ nodes with higher betweenness centrality. This implies that there is a tendency to attack $OR2$ nodes, avoiding $OR1$ nodes with higher centrality, which produces an enveloping effect on them. As a conclusion of these experiments, Rl based agents are able to learn from the characteristics and weaknesses of IIoT networks. Not only have they been able to perform the strategy described in Sect. 4, but have also been able to apply it in the structural controllability context, demonstrating system adaptability.

Finally, following the results obtained and shown in Fig. 4, two individual analyses of performed simulations can be found in Appendix 2. In these figures, the pattern in which the quality of $OR2$ is increasing in centrality while in the case of $OR1$ it is decreasing can be observed more clearly. Taking into account that the topology follows the power-law distribution, the enveloping effect on

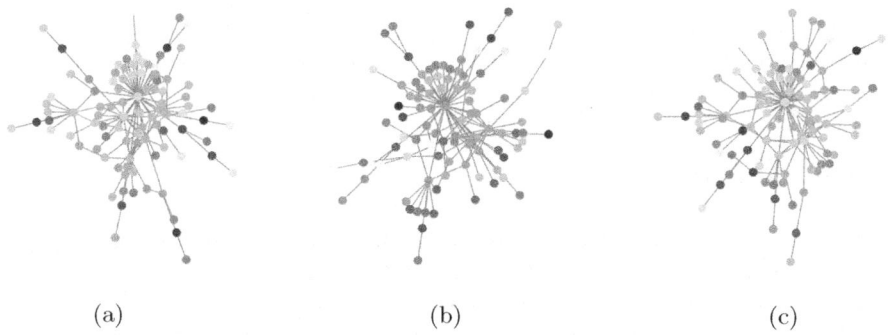

(a) (b) (c)

Fig. 3. Node weights with different representations

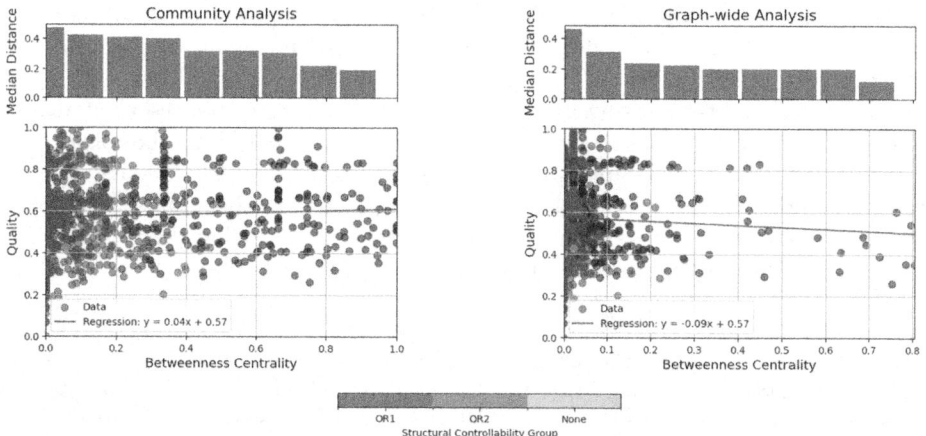

Fig. 4. RL weight analysis by community and graph-wide

$OR1$ and the prioritization of $OR2$ is visible. Moreover, non-overlapping results cause the gradient to be more pronounced, making this conclusion even clearer.

5.4 E3: DT-Assisted Hybrid AE

E3 intends to validate E1 and E2 in a single DT-supported IIoT environment. This experiment is executed on the DT, entailing the assembly of DT with the IIoT structural controllability theory. The most significant results of the previous experiment are taken for this test, namely those performed on industrial networks with $|V| = 100$. For this purpose, E3 launches agents and hybrid-target attacks under one topology used in Sect. 5.2. The results of the experiments designed for $|V| = 100$, with a total of 100 matches, are of 73% for Team A and 27% for Team B. It should be remembered that this was an approximation, so a lower result is justified. However, results are relatively similar to those obtained in E2. Note that a high multi-node DT execution combined with a smaller number of experiments increases the probability of less accurate approximation. Furthermore, the usage of 100 virtualized nodes with all communications and agents running over them implies a large computational burden which may lead to slightly different results. Despite these setbacks, the results are clearly close to the target and the modeled evidence, demonstrating the success of these experiments and of the methodology.

6 Conclusion

This paper has demonstrated the usefulness of DT technology to illustrate IIoT-based scenarios, making it an ideal adversarial target without impacting real infrastructure. In order to conceptualize virtual scenarios, a simulated probabilistic model has been defined, delimiting the offensive rules to be applied within the DT and adapt AE to reality through simulation. The framework allows launching a set of attack strategies and adapting them to the context of the infrastructure using artificial intelligence, evaluating the most critical parts of the system in an autonomous manner. In addition, a methodology for the execution of automated AE actions has also been established. This methodology considers both the suitability of the performed strategy at the network level, as well as an initial performance-oriented approach. The paper describes the development of an innovative AE methodology that uses a DT combined and adapted to control theories to improve the security and prevention of industrial environments. As future improvements, the proposed approach shows limitations in emulating more complex strategies or behaviors as Advanced Persistence Threats that may be the subject of further research.

Acknowledgments. The first author is a fellow of Eurecat's"Vicente López" PhD grant program. Likewise, the work has been partially supported by SecTwin 5.0 (TED2021-129830B-I00) funded by the Ministerio de Ciencia e Innovación, Agencia Estatal de Investigación (10.13039/501100011033), and EU "NextGenerationEU"/Plan de Recuperación, Transformación y Resiliencia; was also partially supported by the AIAS project AIAS (101131292) funded by the European Union under HORIZON-MSCA-2022-SE-01, and the 5G+TACTILE_4 Project (NEXTGENERATION.UE, Spanish UNICO 5G I+D) under Grant TSI-063000-2021-26.

Disclosure of Interests. The authors have no competing interests to declare that are relevant to the content of this article.

APPENDIX 1

Figure 5 shows the results of all the topologies generated in the experiments of Sect. 5.2 with $|V| = 100$, as well as the normalized arithmetic mean of all the RL weights.

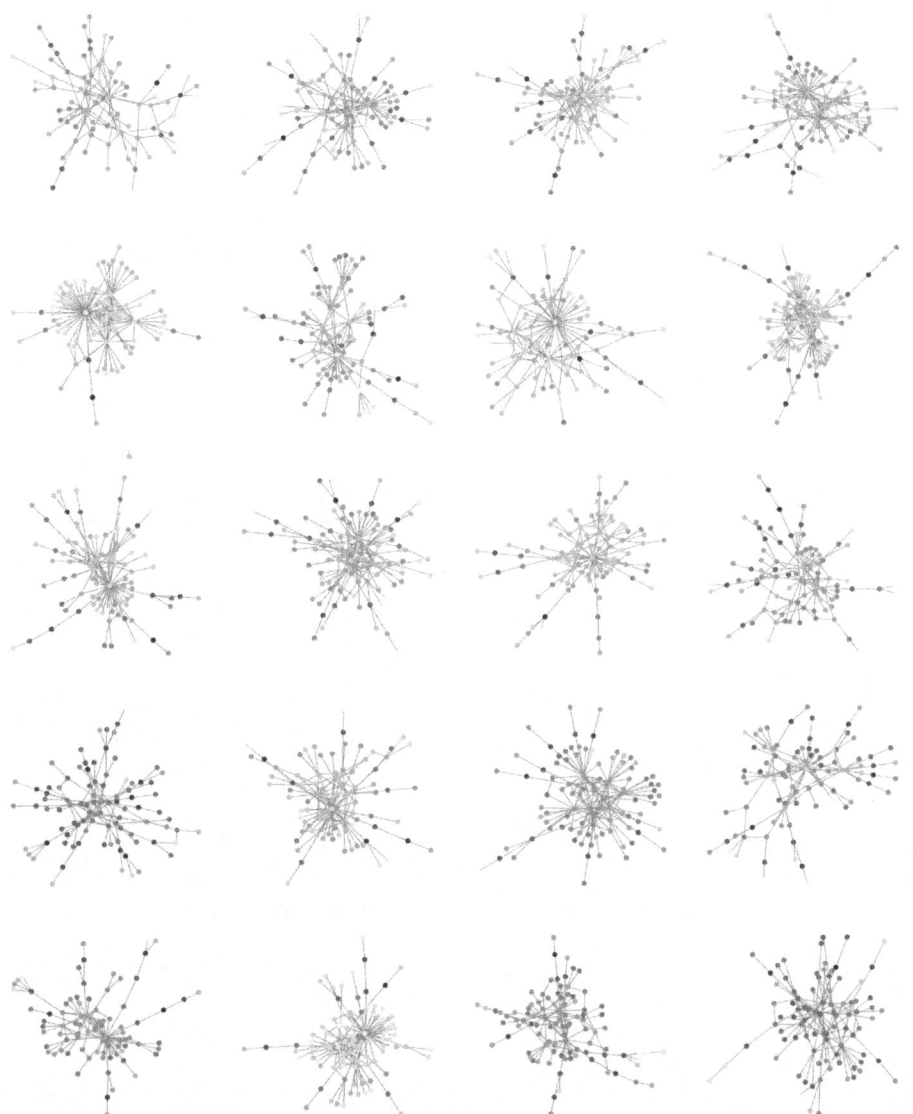

Fig. 5. Topology of the DTs and normalized average RL weights

APPENDIX 2

Figures 6 and 7 show a comparative analysis of centrality, median distance, the structural controllability group to which they belong and a regression with their trend as a function of the quality assigned by the RL algorithm.

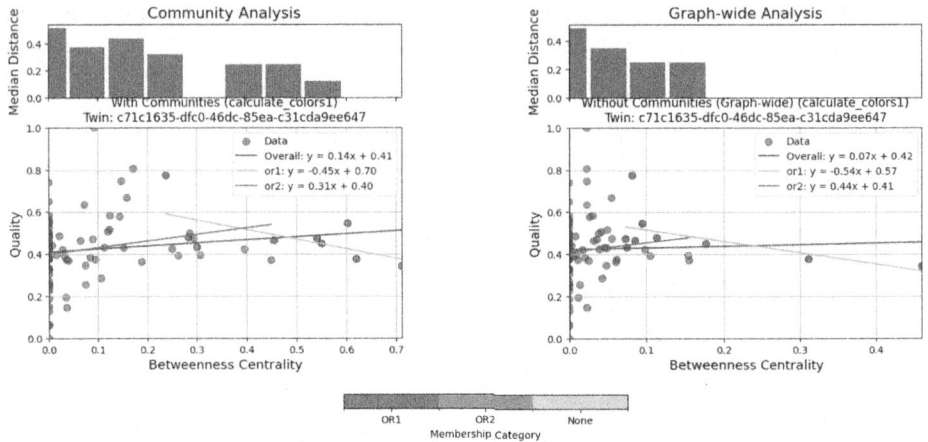

Fig. 6. Centrality analysis over controllability groups 1

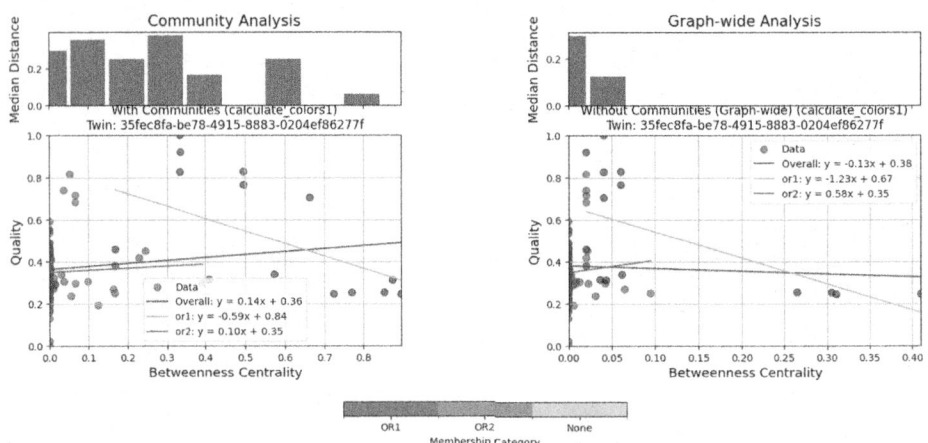

Fig. 7. Centrality analysis over controllability groups 2

References

1. Alcaraz, C., Lopez, J.: Digital twin: a comprehensive survey of security threats. IEEE Commun. Surv. Tutor. **24**(3), 1475–1503 (2022)
2. Gartner. Gartner Top 10 Strategic Technology Trends for 2025, 2025. https://www.gartner.com.au/en/articles/top-technology-trends-2025
3. Möller, D.P.F.: Cyberattacker profiles, cyberattack models and scenarios, and cybersecurity ontology. In: Guide to Cybersecurity in Digital Transformation. Advances in Information Security, LNCS, vol. 103, pp. 181–229. Springer, Cham (2023). https://doi.org/10.1007/978-3-031-26845-8_4
4. Skyquest. Critical Infrastructure Protection Market Size, Share, and Growth Analysis, 2024. https://www.skyquestt.com/report/critical-infrastructure-protection-market
5. Por, L.Y., et al.: A systematic literature review on the methods and challenges in detecting zero-day attacks: insights from the recent crowdstrike incident. IEEE Access (2024)
6. Paganini, P.: Schneider Electric CACTUS Ransomware Attack, 2021. https://securityaffairs.com/158320/data-breach/schneider-electric-cactus-ransomware-attack.html
7. Kaspersky ICS CERT. Q2 2024: A Brief Overview of the Main Incidents in Industrial Cybersecurity, 2024. https://ics-cert.kaspersky.com/publications/reports/2024/11/08/q2-2024-a-brief-overview-of-the-main-incidents-in-industrial-cybersecurity/
8. Research and Markets. Threat Hunting Market by Component, Threat Type, Deployment Mode, Industry Verticals - Global Forecast 2025–2030, 2024. https://www.researchandmarkets.com
9. Ajmal, A.B., Shah, M.A., Maple, C., Asghar, M.N., Islam, S.U.: Offensive security: Towards proactive threat hunting via adversary emulation. IEEE Access **9**, 126023–126033 (2021)
10. Bhattacharya, A., Ramachandran, T., Banik, S., Dowling, C.P., Bopardikar, S.D.: Automated adversary emulation for cyber-physical systems via reinforcement learning. In: 2020 IEEE International Conference on Intelligence and Security Informatics (ISI), pp. 1–6. IEEE, 2020
11. Barricelli, B.R., Casiraghi, E., Fogli, D.: A survey on digital twin: definitions, characteristics, applications, and design implications. IEEE Access **7**, 167653–167671 (2019)
12. Kritzinger, W., Karner, M., Traar, G., Henjes, J., Sihn, W.: Digital twin in manufacturing: a categorical literature review and classification. Ifac-PapersOnline **51**(11), 1016–1022 (2018)
13. Atalay, M., Angin, P.: A digital twins approach to smart grid security testing and standardization. In: 2020 IEEE International Workshop on Metrology for Industry 4.0 & IoT, pp. 435–440. IEEE, 2020
14. Pooyandeh, M., Sohn, I.: A time-stamp attack on digital twin-based lithium-ion battery monitoring for electric vehicles. In: 2024 International Conference on Artificial Intelligence in Information and Communication (ICAIIC), pp. 499–502. IEEE, 2024
15. de Azambuja, A.J.G., Giese, T., Schützer, K., Anderl, R., Schleich, B., Almeida, V.R.: Digital twins in industry 4.0 – opportunities and challenges related to cyber security. Procedia CIRP **121**, 25–30 (2024). 11th CIRP Global Web Conference (CIRPe 2023)

16. Hóu, Z., Li, Q., Foo, E., Dong, J. S., De Souza, P.: A digital twin runtime verification framework for protecting satellites systems from cyber attacks. In: 2022 26th International Conference on Engineering of Complex Computer Systems (ICECCS), pp. 117–122. IEEE, 2022
17. Eckhart, M., Ekelhart, A.: Towards security-aware virtual environments for digital twins. In: Proceedings of the 4th ACM Workshop on Cyber-physical System Security, pp. 61–72, 2018
18. van der Wal, E.W., El-Hajj, M.: Securing networks of iot devices with digital twins and automated adversary emulation. In: 2022 26th International Computer Science and Engineering Conference (ICSEC), pp. 241–246. IEEE, 2022
19. Alcaraz, C., Lopez, J.: Protecting digital twin networks for 6g-enabled industry 5.0 ecosystems. IEEE Netw. Mag. **37**(2), 302–308 (2023)
20. Shahin, S., Soubra, H.: An iot adversary emulation prototype tool. In: 2022 5th International Conference on Information and Computer Technologies (ICICT), pp. 7–12. IEEE, 2022
21. Sheikhi, S., Kostakos, P.: Cyber threat hunting using unsupervised federated learning and adversary emulation. In: 2023 IEEE International Conference on Cyber Security and Resilience (CSR), pp. 315–320. IEEE, 2023
22. Orbinato, V., Feliciano, M. C., Cotroneo, D., Natella, R.: Laccolith: hypervisor-based adversary emulation with anti-detection. IEEE Trans. Dependable Secure Comput. (2024)
23. Kouremetis, M., et al.: Mirage: cyber deception against autonomous cyber attacks in emulation and simulation. Ann. Telecommun. 1–15 (2024)
24. II Power Laws. Generating network topologies that obey power laws
25. Kneis, J., Mölle, D., Richter, S., Rossmanith, P.: Parameterized power domination complexity. Inf. Process. Lett. **98**(4), 145–149 (2006)
26. Alcaraz, C., Miciolino, E.E., Wolthusen, S.: Multi-round attacks on structural controllability properties for non-complete random graphs. In: Desmedt, Y. (eds.) Information Security. LNCS, vol. 7807, pp. 140–151. Springer, Cham (2015). https://doi.org/10.1007/978-3-319-27659-5_10
27. Clauset, A., Newman, M.E., Moore, C.: Finding community structure in very large networks. Phys. Rev. E **70**(6), 066111 (2004)
28. Brands, H.: The New Makers of Modern Strategy: From the Ancient World to the Digital Age. Princeton University Press, Princeton (2023)
29. Lyon, G.: Nmap network scanning - port scanning techniques, 2025. https://nmap.org/book/man-port-scanning-techniques.html
30. The MITRE Corporation. Common vulnerabilities and exposures (cve), 2025. https://www.cve.org/
31. VulDB. Vuldb - the vulnerability database, 2025. https://vuldb.com/
32. Offensive Security. Exploit database (exploit-db), 2025. https://www.exploit-db.com/
33. Rapid7. Metasploit framework - penetration testing software, 2025. https://metasploit.com/
34. MITRE Corporation. Mitre att&ck framework, 2025. https://attack.mitre.org/
35. Kreps, D.M.: Nash equilibrium. In: Game Theory, pp. 167–177. Springer, 1989

Formal Security Analysis of ss2DNS

Ali Sadeghi Jahromi[✉], AbdelRahman Abdou, and Paul C. van Oorschot

Carleton University, Ottawa, Canada
alisadeghijahromi@cmail.carleton.ca, {abdou,paulv}@scs.carleton.ca

Abstract. Motivated by limitations in DNSSEC, ss2DNS has been recently proposed as an alternative scheme that augments recursive resolver and nameserver interactions with stronger real-time security and privacy properties. In this paper, using a symbolic model of ss2DNS in the Tamarin protocol verifier, and the assumption that none of the relevant cryptographic keys are compromised, we formally verify the security and privacy properties of the DNS resolution process with the root zone when using ss2DNS. The validity of these proofs is then extended to the other subordinate zones. We also explore the impact of key and entity compromises on ss2DNS security and privacy properties.

Keywords: DNS Security · Formal Analysis · Tamarin

1 Introduction

Essentially all interactions over the Internet are preceded by a DNS resolution, which translates human-readable domain names into corresponding IP addresses [16,17]. DNS serves as a critical component of the Internet, facilitating the resolution of hundreds of billions of queries everyday.[1] Therefore, the security and privacy of the DNS resolution process impacts all entities and services that depend on its functionality [6]. The DNS resolution process typically involves two stages: the communication between a stub resolver and a recursive resolver (Stage 1), and the interactions between a recursive resolver and authoritative nameservers (ANSes) (Stage 2) [18]. Attackers have exploited the absence of security in Stage 2 to compromise security and privacy [10,12,13].

We recently proposed the ss2DNS protocol, designed to provide real-time security and privacy properties in Stage 2 [18]. Use of ss2DNS in Stage 2 effectively mitigates vulnerabilities within this stage, including cache poisoning [6,12,13], replay attacks using stale responses [1,4,11], eavesdropping [2], and large-scale surveillance [10]. ss2DNS utilizes a delegation mechanism to mitigate the risk of exposure of a zone's long-term key to attacks by avoiding the need to replicate this key throughout the ANSes of the zone. Additionally, it secures

---

In some preliminary versions of this work, the protocol was named DNSSEC+. It was renamed ss2DNS to avoid suggesting it is a direct extension of DNSSEC.

[1] https://vercara.com/resources/2023-dns-traffic-and-trends-analysis.

transmission of DNS messages by employing symmetric authenticated encryption, with encryption keys generated using Diffie-Hellman (DH) key agreement.

The original paper [18], in which ss2DNS was proposed, introduced its design, implemented a prototype, and conducted a performance evaluation. It defines nine properties, including several that hold by design (*e.g.*, properties such as achieving single round-trip DNS resolution are inherently satisfied). As a more robust scheme in terms of security and privacy properties, ss2DNS (if standardized and adopted) could be used to resolve millions (or more) of queries daily. To increase confidence in the security and privacy properties of ss2DNS, a formal analysis is provided herein. To do so, we develop a symbolic model of the protocol using the Tamarin Prover [15] tool. The security and privacy properties of ss2DNS are then formally proven using this model. Finally, the model is used to assess the impact of key and entity compromises, demonstrating the consequences of such compromises on these properties. Our analysis finds that all of the originally defined properties of ss2DNS hold as expected when none of the keys are compromised. Moreover, compromise of any single long-term private key within the protocol does not, in isolation, compromise the validity of the security and privacy properties of responses.

2 Background

In this section, we present an overview of symbolic modeling and property verification of security protocols in Tamarin, followed by background on the components and the theory of operation of ss2DNS. Readers familiar with these may wish to skip over this review section.

2.1 The Tamarin Prover (review)

In symbolic models of security protocols, cryptographic messages are expressed as *terms* (instead of bitstrings), which are used to model data and operations in a protocol. These primitives are used in *rules* that deterministically model protocol behavior, from which properties of interest are defined and verified. Tamarin is a tool used for symbolic modeling and formal verification of security protocols [15]. It offers pre-defined symbolic cryptographic primitives, such as DH key agreement, symmetric encryption, and digital signatures. Tamarin has been employed for modeling and analysis of security protocols such as TLS 1.3 [5], 5G authentication [3], RHINE [9], and other security protocols [19]. Thus, Tamarin is an appropriate tool for a formal security analysis of ss2DNS.

The default attacker model in Tamarin is the Dolev-Yao [8] adversary model, which assumes complete control over the network: the adversary can read, modify, drop, or fabricate and inject network messages. A Tamarin user defines a symbolic model of a protocol in Tamarin syntax and specifies the properties to be proven. Tamarin is capable of automatically generating proofs to establish the validity of the specified properties, without requiring manual interaction. Tamarin also provides an interactive mode with a graphical interface that offers a step-by-step manual proof development process, with visualization of the constraint solver and any discovered attacks.

Protocol Specification. In Tamarin, the allowed protocol interactions and steps are specified using multiset rewriting rules. These rules form a labeled transition system, with a global state composed of *facts* that represent the state information. The transition system begins with an empty multiset of facts, and this multiset evolves as rules are executed. The following example demonstrates a Tamarin rule, named Example_DH. Each rule has a left-hand-side (LHS/premise) and a right-hand-side (RHS/conclusion) that specify the multisets before and after the rule execution. If all the LHS facts exist in the current state, the rule can be executed, resulting in the removal of the LHS facts from the current global state and the addition of the RHS facts to the state.

```
1 rule Example_DH:
2     [Fr(a)] // premise (LHS)
3     --[Secret(a)]→ // action/event facts
4     [!Ltk($A, a), Out(g^a)] // conclusion (RHS)
```

In Tamarin, facts are typically represented as F(t1,...,tn), where F represents the name of the fact, and t1 to tn are the terms that represent variables, messages, functions, and other symbolized elements. On the LHS (line 2), the fact Fr() is a built-in Tamarin fact, used for modeling fresh random values such as keys, and a is a freshly generated term, which will be used as a DH private key in this example. On the RHS, Out() is another built-in fact in Tamarin that models an entity sending out a message to the adversary-controlled network. Here $(g\char`^a)$ models the public component of a DH key in the built-in DH theory of Tamarin. The fact !Ltk() stores identity A with its fresh private key a. The facts within the LHS and RHS are state facts that, upon execution of the rule, are respectively removed and added to the global state. The '!' symbol indicates that a fact is persistent: it will not be removed from the system's state when it is consumed by rules and can be used as often as needed. There is another type of fact, such as Secret() in Example_DH, which is not present in the LHS and RHS and is categorized as an event/action fact. Action facts are not added to or consumed from the system's state. Instead, they serve to label transitions by recording the execution of rules, and they are added to the protocol execution trace. The different possible executions of the rules generate a set of potential execution traces made up from action facts. These traces serve as the basis for defining and verifying properties.

Defining Properties. In Tamarin, the properties are formulated as lemmas, which are guarded first-order logic formulas defined over action facts and timepoints. To verify a security property, its lemma must hold across all possible execution traces with no counterexamples. Tamarin either provides a proof if the property holds in all behaviors or returns a counterexample showing an attack. In some cases, the automatic proof construction process in Tamarin may fail to produce a proof or a counterexample with the allocated time and resources, and the verification process fails to terminate. In this case, the property is neither proved nor disproved. In such cases, the interactive mode of Tamarin can be used to identify the underlying problem and guide the tool by writing special intermediate lemmas and refining the protocol model to help the automatic proof generation process to reach a conclusive termination.

The following example presents a simple secrecy lemma, named `Example_Secrecy`. Here, `K()` (line 4) is a built-in action fact that represents the adversary's knowledge of a specific term, such as a 'key' in this example. The `#i` and `#j` are temporal variables, representing timepoints. This lemma asserts that for all possible protocol behaviors and values of the variable 'key' (line 2), if the 'key' is captured in the execution trace by the action fact `secret()` at timepoint `#i` (line 3), there exists no timepoint `#j` such that (denoted by '.') the adversary knows the 'key' (line 4). If Tamarin identifies a counterexample at which the value 'key' is known to the adversary, it stops the proof process and presents the attack in the output.

```
1 lemma Example_Secrecy:
2    "All key #i .
3     Secret(key) @i
4     ==> not (Ex #j . K(key) @j)"
```

In addition to lemmas used to demonstrate security and privacy properties of a modeled protocol, another type of lemma (executability lemma) is used to ensure that the model can execute to completion properly. These lemmas ensure that the properties are verified in a properly modeled and executable model of the protocol.

2.2 ss2DNS (review)

ss2DNS [18] is a recently proposed protocol aimed at enhancing the security and privacy properties of the DNS resolution process in Stage 2. A security and privacy comparison of ss2DNS with other secure DNS schemes has been conducted in the referenced paper [18]. Additionally, ss2DNS's performance was evaluated in comparison to other secure DNS schemes by measuring resolution time, server-side processing time, CPU utilization, and the impact of network fragmentation on performance.

It provides real-time security and privacy properties while avoiding the replication of long-term private keys (associated with zones) across nameserver instances. This is achieved through a novel delegation mechanism. As demonstrated in Fig. 1, ss2DNS involves the use of three primary components: (1) delegation of authorization within each zone to ANSes, (2) a reverse-tree trust model within the DNS hierarchy, and (3) a secure DNS resolution process between resolvers and ANSes.

Long-Term Keys in ss2DNS: In ss2DNS, a key server integrated with each zone is responsible for managing the zone's long-term keys: the Long-Term Signing Key (`LTSK`) and the Long-Term Agreement Key (`LTAK`). As illustrated in Fig. 1, the root zone keys, denoted $\underline{LTSK}_0$ and $\underline{LTAK}_0$, reside in the root zone's key server (KS_0); the suffix refers to the level of the zone within the DNS hierarchy, with '0' being the root zone, '1' for Top-Level Domain (TLD), and so on. `LTSK` is a signing key, which is used to authorize nameserver instances within a zone, enabling response authenticity. `LTAK` is a DH agreement key used by resolvers to derive query encryption keys, to protect the confidentiality of queries. Underlined keys denote private components of asymmetric key pairs.

Delegation Within Each Zone: The delegation mechanism in ss2DNS involves a zone's key server authorizing ANSes of the zone to securely respond to queries by signing the public part of the Short-Term Signing Key (`STSK`) of ANSes, using the zone's `LTSK`. These STSKs are signature keys with short lifetimes (*e.g.*, hours to days), used for providing response authenticity. ANSes must renew their public part of STSKs (sending them to the zone's key server to be signed) before they expire.

As shown in Fig. 1 (teal dashed boxes, labeled 1), ANSes of a zone send their STSKs to the key server within their zone; the key server signs the STKSs using the zone's LTSK and returns a signature on the public part of STSK ($sig(\text{STSK})$) through a secure Out-Of-Band (OOB) channel to the ANSes of the zone. This approach minimizes the exposure of the private long-term key (LTSK) by eliminating the need for its replication, and also mitigates the risk of compromise of the private STSK, as STSKs automatically expire after a predefined short validity period.

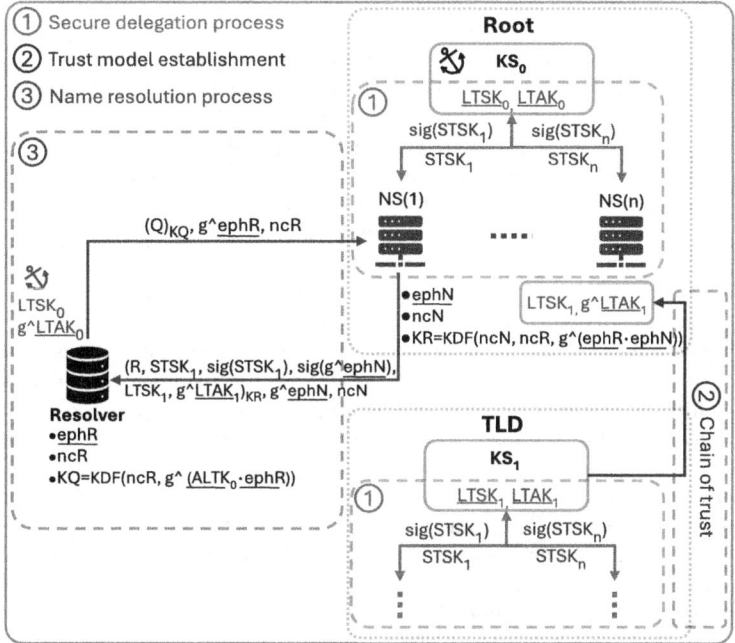

Fig. 1. Workflow of ss2DNS (Underlined keys are private; others are public)

Forming a Trust Model: ss2DNS employs a reverse-tree trust model within the DNS hierarchy, analogous to DNSSEC. To establish this trust model, each zone below the root transmits its long-term public keys (LTSK and LTAK) to its parent zone. For instance, as shown in Fig. 1 (blue dashed box, labeled 2), the TLD zone sends the public components of its $LTSK_1$ and $g\hat{\ }LTAK_1$ keys to the root, forming a chain of trust to the root zone (the trust anchor). Similarly Second-Level Domains (SLDs) send their $LTSK_2$ and $g\hat{\ }LTAK_2$ to their parent TLDs.

The root zone's long-term public keys ($LTSK_0$ and $g\hat{\ }LTAK_0$) are embedded in resolver software as ss2DNS trust anchors. As the resolver traverses the DNS hierarchy, it obtains a child zone's long-term public keys from its parent, enabling secure query encryption and response authentication. This process relies on the chain of trust established through the transmission of public keys from each zone to its parent zone, extending ultimately to the root zone (the trust anchor).

DNS Resolution in ss2DNS: Upon completing the establishment of the chain of trust and the delegation process within the zones, a resolver can use ss2DNS to resolve

DNS records in Stage 2, as illustrated in Fig. 1 (depicted within the dashed purple box labeled 3). The left-hand side purple box demonstrates a DNS resolution instance with nameserver 1 from the root zone. A resolver, with access to the root zone's long-term agreement public key ($g\,\hat{}\,\underline{LTAK_0}$), embedded as a trust anchor, generates a private ephemeral agreement key ($\underline{ephR}$) and a nonce (ncR). It then creates a query (Q) and encrypts it using a symmetric key (KQ), which is derived from the master DH key ($g\,\hat{}\,(\underline{LTAK_0} \cdot \underline{ephR})$) and ncR using a Key Derivation Function (KDF), and sends the encrypted query along with g^ephR and ncR to the root zone's nameserver 1 (demonstrated by the top purple arrow).

Upon receiving the query, Nameserver 1 derives the same KQ, decrypts the query, and prepares a response (R). The symmetric key for response encryption differs from the key for encrypting the query (KQ). The nameserver then generates an ephemeral private agreement key ($\underline{ephN}$) and a nonce (ncN), and subsequently derives a response encryption key (KR) by applying a KDF to ($g\,\hat{}\,(\underline{ephR} \cdot \underline{ephN})$) and ncN with the resolver's nonce (ncR). As illustrated by the purple bottom arrow, the encrypted part of the response includes the response (R) and the nameserver's short-term signature key $STSK_1$ and its signature ($sig(STSK_1)$) obtained in the delegation process. Additionally, a signature of public ephN ($sig(g\,\hat{}\,\underline{ephN})$) generated by $\underline{STSK_1}$ is included by which the resolver can trust g^ephN. The long-term keys of the TLD child zone ($LTSK_1$ and $g\,\hat{}\,\underline{LTAK_1}$) are also included, which will be used by the resolver to securely interact with the child zone in subsequent queries. After encrypting the response, along with the aforementioned signatures and keys, using KR, the nameserver appends g^ephN and ncN, which will be used for response decryption by the resolver.

Upon receiving the response, the resolver uses g^ephN and ncN to generate KR to decrypt the response. It verifies the $sig(STSK_1)$ using $LTSK_0$ (the trust anchor) and thereby authenticates $STSK_1$. Next, it verifies the signature of the ephemeral agreement key ($sig(g\,\hat{}\,\underline{ephN})$) using $STSK_1$, verifying the authenticity of the public agreement key of the nameserver ($g\,\hat{}\,\underline{ephN}$), used for encrypting the response. The resolver also extracts $LTSK_1$ and $g\,\hat{}\,\underline{LTAK_1}$ from the response, which will be used to securely query the TLD child zone. This resolution process continues with the subordinate zones until the resolver queries the authoritative zone for the queried record and obtains the final response, using ss2DNS in Stage 2.

3 Modeling ss2DNS in Tamarin

This section begins by listing the design properties of ss2DNS and specifying the security- and privacy-related subset formally verified by Tamarin. Next, it defines the underlying assumptions and threat model used to develop the symbolic model of ss2DNS and to prove its properties. Finally, it presents an overview of the model used for delegation and DNS resolution processes within ss2DNS.

3.1 Stated Properties of ss2DNS

The original paper [18] defines nine properties to be fulfilled by ss2DNS. Table 1 summarizes these and highlights the subset of these that are security and privacy properties, formally proven in the present paper using Tamarin. ss2DNS encrypts both queries and responses to achieve *message confidentiality*. Additionally, the response encryption keys are freshly generated, with the objective of providing *forward secrecy*. Another security property that ss2DNS provides is *entity authentication* for nameservers, guaranteeing that transmitted responses are both authenticated and *resilient to replay attacks*. The defined entity authentication in ss2DNS is unilateral, as only the nameservers authenticate themselves to the resolvers; the resolvers do not authenticate themselves to the nameservers they query.

For the remaining properties, the original paper [18] demonstrated how the design of ss2DNS satisfies the objectives of *avoiding duplication of long-term secrets* through a secure delegation process, achieving *single round-trip* DNS resolution, and employing an *established trust model*. The property of *minimum amplification* is satisfied by the design of messages that maintain a constant amplification factor compared to DNSSEC [18]. Moreover, the *fail-closed* objective was described as a procedural design choice to mitigate within-protocol downgrade attacks in ss2DNS [18].

Table 1. Properties of ss2DNS: The first four properties are supported by Tamarin proofs herein, while the remaining five were established by design [18].

ss2DNS Property	Target	notes
Message confidentiality	DNS queries/responses	Tamarin proof
Forward secrecy	DNS response keys	Tamarin proof
Entity authentication	Nameservers	Tamarin proof
Mitigate replay	DNS responses	Tamarin proof
Avoid duplicating LTK	DNS zones	by design
Single round-trip	DNS resolution	by design
Established trust model	DNS hierarchy	by design
Minimum amplification	DNS responses	by design
Fail-closed	DNS resolution process	by design

3.2 Assumptions and Threat Model

As outlined in Sect. 2.2, there are three main components in ss2DNS: the delegation of authorization to the nameservers within each zone, a trust model, and the DNS resolution process. The establishment of the trust model, in which the child zones below the root send their long-term public keys to their parent zone, takes place through a secure OOB channel. Thus, it is assumed that this process is securely completed prior to any name resolution. The delegation process involves signing the short-term keys within a zone and sending them to the nameservers through a confidential and authenticated OOB channel established between the zone's key server and its nameservers. The delegation process must also be completed prior to the initiation of any name resolution. The security and privacy properties defined in Table 1 (*i.e.*, the first four properties) are for the DNS resolution process in Stage 2, and the preceding processes of trust model establishment and delegation to nameservers are assumed to be completed via their secure OOB channels [18].

We model the communication between the nameservers and key servers for the delegation process within zones as secure OOB channels whose messages the adversary (in Tamarin) cannot access. Additionally, we assume that there is a trust model established between the zones within the DNS hierarchy through an authenticated OOB channel between the zones. In practice, as seen in DNSSEC, this can be done via a registrar's web interface, where the domain owner adds the Delegation Signer (DS) record to its parent zone. Using these two assumptions, we formally verify the properties of the DNS resolution process in ss2DNS using the Tamarin prover.

In our model, we limit the name resolution to the root zone and do not continue the resolution down the DNS hierarchy. By proving the security and privacy properties for DNS resolution with a root's nameserver, it is assumed that, in ss2DNS, the resolver obtains the child (*i.e.*, TLD) zone's authentic long-term public keys from the root. The long-term public keys of the child zone are assumed to be transmitted authentically to the root during the trust model establishment phase. Thus, in turn, the formal verification of the name resolution for the TLD zone would be similar to the root, but this time with the TLD's long-term keys. In this manner, proving the properties of DNS resolution with the root zone under the defined assumptions ensures that the same properties hold for subsequent resolutions with subordinate zones in the DNS hierarchy, unless the assumptions differ.

The described name resolution process in Sect. 2.2 (Fig. 1) is the *privacy-enforcing* mode of ss2DNS in which the queries are encrypted. ss2DNS also offers a *no-privacy* mode in which the queries are not encrypted but the responses are authenticated and encrypted. Herein, we model and prove the security and privacy properties of ss2DNS in the *privacy-enforcing* mode, for which we can also prove the secrecy of queries. Moreover, in Sect. 5, where we show the implications of key compromises, we demonstrate that the response properties remain verifiable if query secrecy is compromised (*e.g.*, when LTAK is compromised), which is an analogous scenario to the no-privacy mode, wherein the queries are in plaintext.

In addition to the above protocol-related assumptions, in symbolic analysis we exclude computational attacks and primarily focus on the interactions and abstract operation of the protocol. Consequently, symbolic analysis inherently incorporates certain assumptions as part of its abstraction. The first assumption is that the cryptographic primitives within the model are perfect. For example, an adversary can generate a valid signature if and only if it knows the signing private key. Freshly generated random terms, such as nonces and cryptographic keys, are assumed to be unpredictable and unique. Since the information in the symbolic model is abstracted to terms, an entity, including the adversary, either has complete knowledge of a term or no knowledge at all, with no possibility of having partial knowledge of the term.

Common threats in Stage 2 of the DNS resolution include inline adversaries (between a recursive resolver and ANSes). These can be located within distinct Autonomous Systems (ASes), each maintained by different administrative policies. Such entities have access to DNS messages and can read, modify, delete, and inject fabricated messages. Additionally, off-path adversaries can send queries to a recursive resolver and inject false responses, thereby poisoning the cache of the resolver [12,13]. In Sect. 4, we focus on proving the properties of ss2DNS against both in-line and off-path network-based attacks, and we use the default Dolev-Yao [8] attacker in the Tamarin prover. In Sect. 5, in order to analyze the impact of host and key compromises on the properties, we model host-based attacks by adding the private keys of ss2DNS to the adversary's knowledge and analyzing how it affects the verified properties.

3.3 Formal Modeling of ss2DNS in Tamarin

To model the ss2DNS delegation process in Tamarin, we use four Tamarin rules:

D1. The initialization of a key server within the root zone, responsible for generating and securely storing the long-term keys of the zone (*i.e.*, LTSK and LTAK).

D2. The initialization of the zone's ANS instances and their respective short-term signing keys (STSKs), followed by the transmission of these STSKs to the key server via an OOB channel modeled in Tamarin, which assumes that the messages are transferred over a channel not accessible to the adversary.

D3. Receiving the nameserver's STSKs by the initialized key server in Step 1, which then uses the zone's LTSK to sign the STSKs. The signed STSKs are subsequently returned to the nameservers through a secure OOB channel.

D4. Finally, the nameservers receive their signed STSK, enabling their use in the DNS resolution process for responding to queries.

Subsequently, the DNS resolution process between resolvers and the nameserver instances of the zone is modeled using three Tamarin rules.

R1. For a resolver generating and sending an encrypted query to a root zone nameserver: As in Fig. 1, the resolver generates a fresh ephemeral key ephR and ncR, using them with the root zone's public agreement key LTAK (installed as a trust anchor) to derive the query encryption key. Additionally, the resolver generates a fresh query, which is not known to the adversary. The resolver then encrypts the query and transmits it to the network, along with g^ephR and NCR. This message will be received by both the adversary and a root zone nameserver. The resolver also stores the current query state, including the query itself, the ephemeral agreement key ephR, and the nonce NCR. These terms will be used later in Rule 3 for response decryption.

R2. For a nameserver of the root zone that receives an encrypted query and returns an authenticated, encrypted response to the resolver: the nameserver, having access to the private LTAK, decrypts the query using the received g^ephR and ncR terms from the query. The nameserver then generates a fresh ephemeral key ephN and a nonce ncN, which are used alongside the resolver's nonce and ephemeral agreement key to derive the response encryption key. As depicted in the purple box in Fig. 1, the nameserver appends its STSK and the corresponding signature (sig(STSK)) to the response. Additionally, the nameserver signs g^ephN using its STSK and includes the signature sig(g^ephN) in the response before encryption. Finally, the nameserver sends g^ephN, ncN, and the encrypted portion of the response to the network, which will be received by the resolver and adversary.

R3. The resolver that initiated the query in the first rule receives, decrypts, and validates the authenticity of the response. In the Tamarin model, we stored the transmitted query state, including its ephemeral key (ephR), nonce (ncR), and the query itself, in the first rule. The resolver receives the response and obtains the ephemeral agreement key of the nameserver (g^ephN) and the nameserver's nonce (ncN) from the response and uses them along with its ephemeral key and nonce to derive the response decryption key. Upon decrypting the response, the resolver obtains the STSK and sig(STSK) from the response. The resolver then verifies sig(STSK), using the root zone's public LTSK, which is included in its software as a trust anchor. After verifying the authenticity of the STSK, the resolver verifies the signature of the ephemeral key of the nameserver (sig(ephN)) using the public STSK from the response. Once both signatures are verified, the resolver can trust the STSK and ephN used for encryption.

The Tamarin rules D1-D4 are presented in Appendix A.1, and the rules R1-R3 are provided in Appendix A.2.

4 Modeling the Security Properties

In this section, we model the specified security properties of ss2DNS as lemmas using Tamarin's syntax and subsequently verify that these properties hold.

4.1 Secrecy of DNS Messages

Message secrecy in formal verification is generally defined as follows:

$$msg\_secrecy \triangleq \forall \ msg \ i. \ Secret(msg)@i \rightarrow not \ \exists j. \ K(msg)@j$$

This means: the definition of *msg_secrecy* is for all instances of the term *msg*, where *msg* is captured by the *Secret()* action fact at timepoint i, there does not exist a timepoint j at which the adversary knows the *msg*.

Secrecy of Query Data: We formally define the secrecy property of queries generated and sent by a legitimate resolver by the lemma specified in Listing 1.1. This lemma asserts that whenever an encrypted query is sent by a legitimate resolver at timepoint i (captured by the instance of QDataSecret(R, QData) action), and none of the private agreement or signing keys of ss2DNS are compromised (lines 4–8), then there is no timepoint j at which the adversary knows the plaintext of the query message. In the verification of this property in Tamarin, it is assumed that all keys within the protocol remain unknown to the adversary.

```
1 lemma query_secrecy:
2   "All R QData #i .
3     QDataSecret(R, QData) @i & Role('R') @i &
4     not (Ex Z #t1 . RevLTAK(Z) @t1) &
5     not (Ex R #t2 . RevEphR(R) @t2) &
6     not (Ex N #t3 . RevEphN(N) @t3) &
7     not (Ex Z #t4 . RevLTSK(Z) @t4) &
8     not (Ex N #t5 . RevSTSK(N) @t5)
9     ==> not (Ex #j. K(QData) @j)"
```

Listing 1.1. Lemma for query secrecy (verified by Tamarin)

We used the query_secrecy lemma and verified the secrecy of the query data in Tamarin. Additionally, we independently verified the secrecy of the query encryption key using another lemma. In ss2DNS, we assert that the query_secrecy property also implicitly proves the confidentiality of the query session key (*i.e.*, the derived key used for query encryption). If the query encryption key is compromised, this property will be violated, as the adversary can decrypt and access the query data in plaintext.

Secrecy of Response Data: The ss2DNS response encryption key is distinct from the encryption key used for transmitting its corresponding query. In addition to the secrecy of the query data, we also verify the secrecy of the response data received by a legitimate resolver as an answer to a query sent by the same resolver. We define the lemma for response data secrecy, as demonstrated in Listing 1.2, and use Tamarin to prove this lemma. This lemma asserts that for all protocol behaviors, if an encrypted response to a query of a legitimate resolver is received by the resolver at timepoint i (captured by the instance of RDataSecret(RData) action), and none of the private agreement or signing keys are compromised, then there exists no timepoint j at which the adversary knows the plaintext response. In this lemma, similar to query secrecy, we assume that none of the protocol private keys are known to the adversary.

```
1  lemma response_secrecy:
2  "All RData #i .
3     RDataSecret(RData) @i & Role('R') @i &
4     not (Ex Z #t1 . RevLTAK(Z) @t1) &
5     not (Ex R #t2 . RevEphR(R) @t2) &
6     not (Ex N #t3 . RevEphN(N) @t3) &
7     not (Ex Z #t4 . RevLTSK(Z) @t4) &
8     not (Ex N #t5 . RevSTSK(N) @t5)
9     ==> not (Ex #j. K(RData) @j)"
```

Listing 1.2. Lemma for response secrecy (verified by Tamarin)

The proof of the response_secrecy lemma in Tamarin verifies that DNS responses of queries received by a legitimate resolver remain unknown to the adversary. Additionally, we independently verified the secrecy of the response encryption key using a separate lemma. Furthermore, in the context of ss2DNS, the response_secrecy lemma implicitly ensures the secrecy of the response encryption keys; if the response encryption key becomes known to the adversary, this property would not hold, as the adversary would then be able to decrypt and learn the response. Thus, *response encryption key secrecy* is a necessary condition for *response message secrecy* in ss2DNS.

In ss2DNS, if an adversary accesses the plaintext response, query secrecy is also compromised since the query data (*e.g.*, question and ID fields) is included in the response, per the DNS standard [17]. On the other hand, the compromise of the plaintext query does not directly lead to the compromise of the response. This is because the keys used to encrypt queries and responses are distinct, and the response section of data is not included in the query messages. However, given that DNS data is generally public, an adversary with knowledge of the query's question might independently resolve the same query to determine the corresponding response. Thus, while the adversary cannot directly extract the response from ss2DNS queries, access to plaintext queries enables inference of the response through independent resolution. This inherent characteristic of DNS highlights the importance of the confidentiality of both queries and responses, as the lack of secrecy in one may render the secrecy of the other futile.

4.2 Forward Secrecy

In ss2DNS, response session keys are derived from ephemeral keys of both resolvers and nameservers. As a result, these session keys satisfy forward secrecy, meaning that even if the long-term zone and nameserver signing keys (<u>LTSK</u> and <u>STSK</u>) are compromised, the session keys from past DNS resolutions remain unknown to the adversary. As shown in Listing 1.3, the forward secrecy lemma is formally defined and proved in our Tamarin model. For all protocol behaviors, when a resolver receives a response encrypted with a session key at timepoint i (modeled by RKSecret(Rkey) action) and none of the private agreement keys are compromised at any time, and also none of the long-term signing keys are compromised before the response is received (lines 4 and 5), then there is no timepoint j at which the adversary knows the session key.

As stated in lines 4 and 5, the long-term keys LTSK and STSK must not be compromised before the response is received and captured by RKSecret() fact at timepoint i. Therefore, by adding (t1 < i and t2 < i) to the conditions, we are allowing the possibility that the adversary can know LTSK and STSK after the response is received at i. If the signing keys LTSK and STSK are compromised before the response is received, and the adversary has access to a query, the adversary could use these keys to impersonate the zone or nameserver and inject a false response; the encryption key would then be known to the adversary, violating both secrecy and forward secrecy of the response encryption keys. Thus, compromising query secrecy and one of the signing keys undermines the forward secrecy of response keys and secrecy of responses.

```
1  lemma response_sesskey_FwdSecrecy:
2  "All Rkey #i .
3    RKSecret(Rkey) @i & Role('R') @i &
4    not (Ex Z #t1 . RevLTSK(Z) @t1 & t1 < i) &
5    not (Ex N #t2 . RevSTSK(N) @t2 & t2 < i) &
6    not (Ex Z #t3 . RevLTAK(Z) @t3) &
7    not (Ex R #t4 . RevEphR(R) @t4) &
8    not (Ex N #t5 . RevEphN(N) @t5)
9    ==> not (Ex #k. K(RKey) @k)"
```

Listing 1.3. Lemma for response key forward secrecy (verified by Tamarin)

4.3 Unilateral Authentication

Nameserver unilateral authentication is formally defined as a unilateral injective agreement [14,20], as illustrated in the lemma in Listing 1.4. The unilateral authentication lemma is defined as an agreement on a specified set of values, including keys and identities, in the matching runs between resolvers and nameservers [7,14], and then proved using Tamarin. It asserts that for all protocol behaviors, each Commit action by the resolver upon receiving a response with the specified data implies that, if none of the private agreement and signing keys within the protocol are known to the adversary, there exists a unique Running action (lines 10–12) performed by the nameserver with the same data. As there is a unique Running action preceding each Commit action, ss2DNS effectively prevents replay attacks by utilizing a fresh nonce for each response, which is included in the agreed upon data in this lemma.

The proof of the authentication property in Listing 1.4 guarantees that the run between the resolver and nameserver is unique (not replayable) and they have the same view of the data exchanged (one-way injective agreement). However, this lemma does not aim to validate that RES2 is equal to RES, as unilateral authentication implies that only the resolver authenticates the nameserver (*i.e.*, NS in lines 3 and 10 are equal), and the nameserver does not explicitly check the identity of the resolver. This is because in ss2DNS, only resolvers are responsible for authenticating nameservers, whereas the nameservers do not authenticate resolvers.

Summary. In this section, we formally modeled the security and privacy properties of ss2DNS by defining their lemmas. Subsequently, we used Tamarin to automatically

```
1  lemma unilateral_injective_agreement:
2   "All RES NS data #i.
3    Commit(RES, NS, 'Resolver', data) @i &
4    not (Ex Z #t1 . RevLTAK(Z) @t1) &
5    not (Ex R #t2 . RevEphR(R) @t2) &
6    not (Ex N #t3 . RevEphN(N) @t3) &
7    not (Ex Z #t4 . RevLTSK(Z) @t4) &
8    not (Ex N #t5 . RevSTSK(N) @t5)
9    ==> (Ex RES2 #j. Running(NS, RES2, 'NS', data) @j & j < i &
10   not (Ex RES3 NS2 #i2. Commit(RES3, NS2, 'Res', data) @i2
11   & not (i2 = i)))"
```

Listing 1.4. Lemma for unilateral nameserver authentication (verified by Tamarin)

construct proofs for each property in the presence of the Dolev-Yao adversary. The analysis did not yield any counterexamples indicating potential attacks, and the proof for each lemma was generated in Tamarin.

5 Implications of Key and Entity Compromises

In Sect. 4, we defined and proved the properties of ss2DNS under the assumption that if none of the agreement or signing keys within the protocol are compromised, then the defined properties for the protocol are valid and verifiable in Tamarin. In this section, we investigate the implications of key compromises in ss2DNS using Tamarin. To this end, we allow each agreement or signing private key within the protocol to be compromised (become known to the adversary) and then determine whether the properties from Sect. 4 still hold. Subsequently, we extend our analysis for multiple protocol keys being compromised, modeling the compromise of different entities within ss2DNS. As an example, we find that if resolvers are compromised, only the ephemeral private agreement key of the resolvers (ephR) will be compromised.

5.1 Single Key Compromises

Long-term Agreement Key (LTAK): The long-term agreement key of a zone (LTAK) is used by resolvers to derive query encryption keys. We allow this key to become known to the adversary and retry to generate the proofs for the lemmas that were proved in Sect. 4. As summarized in Table 2, if the LTAK is compromised, only the *query secrecy* property can no longer be proved, and Tamarin identifies a corresponding attack. Using the LTAK, with the resolver's nonce and public agreement key, an adversary can derive the query encryption key and thereby decrypt the query. However, since the remaining properties are related to responses and the response encryption keys are different from those for queries, the other properties remain valid.

Long-term Signing Key (LTSK): The long-term signing key (LTSK) of a zone is used by the key server to sign the public signing keys of the nameservers as part of the zone-side delegation process, thereby enabling the nameservers to respond to client queries with verifiable authenticity. We allow this key to become known to the adversary and attempt to recreate the proofs from Sect. 4. The compromise of LTSK alone does not undermine the *query secrecy* property, as it does not impact the confidentiality of queries; thus Tamarin successfully proves it. Similarly, *response secrecy* remains intact and can be proved by Tamarin, since an adversary possessing the LTSK cannot decrypt responses, nor can they generate or inject false responses without access to the corresponding query, which must be included within the response. Furthermore, *response key forward secrecy* remains verifiable in Tamarin, since compromising LTSK does not affect the private agreement keys used for response encryption. An adversary must access the query to impersonate a nameserver and inject a false response.

Finally, when the LTSK is compromised, the resolver can still authenticate the nameserver, preserving the validity of the *entity authentication* property in Tamarin. Since the adversary cannot access the query information and response encryption keys, the adversary cannot compromise the authenticity of the nameserver responses received by legitimate resolvers (as proved by Tamarin).

Short-term Signing Key (STSK): Similar to the long-term signing key (LTSK), as proved by Tamarin, the compromise of private (STSK) does not impact the *query secrecy* property, as this key is not utilized for query encryption. Furthermore, the compromise of a nameserver's STSK alone does not undermine the proof of *response secrecy* in Tamarin. This is because the STSK is not directly used for encrypting responses, and without access to the query data embedded in responses, an adversary cannot generate and inject false responses that are acceptable and known to the adversary.

Regarding the *response forward secrecy* property, possession of the STSK alone does not allow the adversary to compromise the forward secrecy of response keys. Additionally, the adversary cannot impersonate the nameserver, as the query data is still required to generate responses, and this data cannot be accessed by the attacker solely by having access to STSK. Regarding *entity authentication*, it remains verifiable as the adversary does not have access to the query to generate false responses, and also does not have access to response encryption keys to compromise the authenticity of the legitimate nameserver responses directly.

Ephemeral Nameserver Agreement Key (ephN): ephN is the ephemeral private agreement key used on the nameserver-side to derive the response encryption key. Compromise of this key directly undermines the *response secrecy* property in Tamarin, enabling the adversary to derive the response encryption key. Additionally, as the query data is embedded within responses, this compromise would also undermine the *query secrecy* as the adversary obtains query information from its corresponding response.

Regarding the *response key forward secrecy*, the compromise of the ephemeral agreement keys renders the response encryption key accessible to the adversary, thereby violating forward secrecy regardless of the secrecy of the long-term keys. Furthermore, possession of the response encryption key allows the adversary to directly violate the *nameserver authentication* property (*e.g.*, by modifying responses).

Ephemeral Resolver Agreement key (ephR): ephR is the ephemeral private agreement key used for deriving both query and response encryption keys. Thus, if the ephR of resolvers are known to the adversary, then both the *query secrecy* and *response secrecy* would be directly compromised. Additionally, as the response encryption key becomes known to the adversary, the *response key forward secrecy* property does not hold regardless of the secrecy of the long-term keys. Finally, the *nameserver authentication* would also be compromised if ephR is compromised, as an adversary knowing this key can directly modify the nameserver-generated responses.

Table 2. Properties retained under compromise. Columns represent the defined protocol properties, and rows show the keys and entities within ss2DNS. Each table cell indicates whether a property still holds if the corresponding key or entity is compromised. (Keys compromised due to entity compromises in ss2DNS—*Nameserver*: LTAK, STSK, and ephN; *Key server*: LTAK and LTSK; *Resolver*: ephR)

Compromised key/entity	Query Secrecy	Response Secrecy	Response Key Fwd Secrecy	Nameserver Authentication
LTAK	✗	✓	✓	✓
LTSK	✓	✓	✓	✓
STSK	✓	✓	✓	✓
ephN	✗	✗	✗	✗
ephR	✗	✗	✗	✗
Nameserver	✗	✗	✗	✗
Key server	✗	✗	✗	✗
Resolver	✗	✗	✗	✗

5.2 Entity Compromises

We now explain the implication if standalone DNNSEC+ entities, namely the resolver, nameserver, and key server, become compromised or untrusted.

Resolver: In ss2DNS, the only private key that resolvers have access to is the ephemeral private agreement keys (ephR) they generate. Consequently, if resolvers are compromised, the adversary would gain access to ephR. The impact of a resolver compromise on the defined security properties is therefore equivalent to the compromise of ephR itself. Thus, all of the defined query and response properties would be violated by the attacker if resolvers are compromised, as shown in Table 2.

Nameserver: In ss2DNS, nameservers have access to the zone's long-term private agreement key (LTAK), their short-term signing key (STSK), and ephemeral agreement keys (ephN). Consequently, if nameservers are compromised, all these keys become known to the adversary. Possession of the ephemeral agreement key (ephN) alone enables the adversary to compromise all defined security properties (as shown in Table 2), regardless of the secrecy of the other keys. Therefore, the compromise of a nameserver renders all the properties ineffective.

Key Server: In ss2DNS, key servers are responsible for generating and managing the long-term agreement key of a zone (LTAK), which is used for deriving query encryption keys. Furthermore, key servers also manage the long-term signing key of the zone (LTSK), which facilitates the delegation of authorization to the nameservers within a zone. Compromise of the LTAK enables an adversary to decrypt queries, thereby undermining the *query secrecy* property. Access to plaintext queries, combined with the compromised LTSK, allows the adversary to impersonate the zone or associated nameservers and inject false responses. The compromise of these two long-term keys also enables an adversary to impersonate a zone and to inject false responses using arbitrary response encryption keys, violating both *response secrecy* and *response key forward secrecy*. Additionally, the ability to impersonate nameservers and to inject false responses violates the *nameserver authentication* property.

As shown in Table 2's last three rows, compromising any entity in the ss2DNS resolution process defeats all four properties proved in Sect. 4. Aside from securing such entities from attacks that expose private keys, confidentiality and authenticity of communications between all ss2DNS entities are required (otherwise, all four properties could analogously be defeated). This includes the delegation-related message exchanged between each zone's ANSes and key server, and data exchanged (*e.g.,* public keys for long-term key updates; see Sect. 2.2) between parent and child zones.

6 Discussion

Query Compromise. The compromise of a query in ss2DNS alone does not result in the adversary gaining knowledge of its corresponding response. However, since DNS records are not typically secret, an adversary who knows the query can resolve it to obtain its corresponding response. This is not a flaw in ss2DNS, but an inherent property of DNS. While the lack of query confidentiality in DNS allows adversaries to independently resolve the same queries, DNS responses to a single query can vary in specific scenarios. For example, responses may differ when Content Delivery Networks (CDNs) return responses based on the geographic/network location of the query's source IP address, or scenarios where different load-balancing mechanisms are employed.

Additionally, some nameservers are configured to provide different responses based on query metadata and querent profile, including the transport layer protocol, source address, and other metadata parameters. For example, a nameserver might whitelist "`ANY`" queries to specific network locations or addresses. Such configurations may result in different DNS responses for identical queries. Consequently, even when queries are not encrypted, an adversary resolving the same query may not receive a response identical to the one provided to the original querent.

Secrecy in Tamarin. In Tamarin, secrecy is defined as the adversary's lack of knowledge of a specific term, such as a message or a key. In our model, an adversary can gain such knowledge in two main ways: by accessing the plaintext of encrypted messages from a legitimate protocol execution or by impersonating a protocol entity and injecting a forged response, thereby knowing its plaintext. The latter does not constitute a direct secrecy attack but rather an impersonation attack; consequently, the encrypted legitimate protocol interactions are not necessarily compromised. Nevertheless, the adversary's ability to inject an arbitrary message that it is aware of represents a violation of the message secrecy. In this paper, we prove message secrecy in Tamarin's conventional manner and have considered both scenarios as violations of secrecy.

Model Details. Tamarin has a pre-computation phase to determine the sources of protocol and intruder facts to reuse them in later analysis. However, for certain protocols, Tamarin may fail to correctly identify the sources of specific facts, resulting in an incomplete pre-computation phase. To address this issue, users must manually define a special type of lemma, referred to as a "source lemma", which is considered an invariant, to explicitly clarify the origins of values for which Tamarin lacks sufficient information. Alternatively, users can use `auto-sources` to automatically resolve partial deconstructions. In our work, we defined and used a source lemma to enable Tamarin to successfully complete the pre-computation phase. This source lemma and other details defined in the model are included in the publicly available source code of our theory.[2]

---

[2] https://github.com/Ali-Jahromi/FormalAnalysis-ss2DNS.

7 Conclusion

In this paper, using a symbolic model for the secure delegation mechanism and the name resolution process of ss2DNS in the Tamarin prover, we formally verified four security and privacy properties of ss2DNS in its privacy-enforcing mode. The results demonstrate that under the specified assumptions, the name resolution process in ss2DNS satisfies the defined security and privacy properties. We then analyzed the impact of key and entity compromises on these properties. The analysis demonstrated that the compromise of any single signing key within zones does not affect any of the four properties. However, as expected, the compromise of core entities of ss2DNS (*e.g.*, malware on ANSes, key servers, or resolvers) within the protocol can undermine all four security and privacy properties.

Acknowledgments. The last two authors acknowledge support from Natural Sciences and Engineering Research Council of Canada (NSERC) through Discovery Grants.

A Modeling ss2DNS Using Tamarin Rules

A.1 The Secure Delegation Rules

The four rules from Listing 1.5 to 1.8 demonstrate the process of secure delegation by the key server of the root zone to the ANSes of the zone, by signing their short-term signing key (STSK) using the zone's long-term signing key (LTSK) as described in Sect. 3.3.

```
1  rule Key_Server_Init: \\Initializing the key server
2      [ Fr(~LTSK) \\Long-term signing key
3      , Fr(~LTAK) \\Long-term agreement key
4      ]
5      --[OnlyOnce('Key_Server_Init') \\At most one key server
6      , KeyServerInit($K, ~LTSK, pk(~LTSK)) \\Excutability
7      ]->
8      [ !ZKS_Sk($K, ~LTSK) \\Private LTSK
9      , !ZKS_Pk($K, pk(~LTSK)) \\Public LTSK
10     , !ZKA_Sk($K, ~LTAK) \\Private LTAK
11     , !ZKA_Pk($K, 'g' ^ ~LTAK) \\Public LTAK
12     , Out(<pk(~LTSK), 'g' ^ ~LTAK>) \\Publish public keys
13     ]
```

Listing 1.5. Key server initialization.

```
1  rule NS_Sign_Request:
2      [ Fr(~STSK) \\Short-term signing key
3      , Fr(~nid) \\nameserver ID
4      ]
5      --[ NS_Sign_Req($N, ~nid, ~STSK) \\Excutability ]->
6      [ NS_Wait_Sig(< $N, ~nid, ~STSK, pk(~STSK)>)
7      , NS_Sends_to_Sign(<$N, ~nid, pk(~STSK)>)   \\Secure OOB channel
8      ]
```

Listing 1.6. Nameserver requests the signing of its STSK.

A.2 DNS Resolution

Listings 1.9 to 1.11 demonstrate the three steps of the DNS resolution process between a resolver and a nameserver of the root zone in the privacy-enforcing mode, as described in Sect. 3.3.

```
1  rule Key_Server_Signs_NS:
2      [ !ZKS_Sk($K, LTSK) \\Private LTSK
3      , NS_Sends_to_Sign(< $N, nid, stpk >)\\Sign request from OOB
4      ]
5      --[ KS_Signs($N, nid, stpk, sign(<$N, nid, stpk>, ltkKS))
       ]->
6      [ Signed_NS_key(sign(<$N, nid, stpk>, ltkKS), <$N, nid, stpk
       > )]
```

Listing 1.7. Key Server signs the STSK of the nameserver.

```
1  rule NS_Receives_Signed:
2      [ NS_Wait_Sig(< $N, nid, stsk, stpk >) \\Waiting for delegation
3      , Signed_NS_key(sig_stpk, <$N, nid, stpk>) \\Signature from OOB
4      , !ZKS_Pk($K, pkLTSK) \\Public LTSK
5      ]
6      --[
7        Eq(verify(sig_stpk, <$N, nid, stpk> , pkLTSK), true)
8      , NS_Rcv_Signed(sig_stpk, <$N, nid, stpk>)
9      ]->
10     [ !NS_sstk_Signed_PK(sig_stpk, <$N, nid, stpk>)
11     , !NS_sstk_Signed_SK(sig_stpk, <$N, nid, stpk>, stsk)
12     , Out(< stpk, sig_stpk >) \\Public public STSK and signature
13     ]
```

Listing 1.8. Nameserver receives its signed STSK.

```
rule Res_1:
    let
        queryKey = kdf(< ~NCR, ZKAP ^ ~ephR >)
        query_data = < ~query, 'Query' >
    in
    [ !ZKA_Pk($K, ZKAP) \\Public LTAK
    , Fr(~ephR) \\Fresh ephemeral agreement key
    , Fr(~query) \\Fresh query
    , Fr(~NCR) \\Fresh nonce
    ]
    --[
        ResolverSentQuery($R, ~query, ~ephR) \\Executability
    , Role('R') \\Resolver role
    , QKeySecret($R, ~ephR, queryKey) \\Query key secrecy
    , QDataSecret($R, query_data) \\Query data secrecy
    ]->
    [ Out( <~NCR, 'g' ^ ~ephR, senc(query_data, queryKey)>
    )
    , Res_State_1($R, ~ephR, ~query, ~NCR)
    , !EskR($R, ~ephR)
    ]
```

Listing 1.9. Resolver Sends Query

```
rule NS_1:
    let
        queryKey = kdf(<NCR, epkR ^ ZKA>)
        RespKey = kdf(< ~NCN, NCR, epkR ^ ~ephN >)
        query_data = < query, 'Query' >
        ephSig = sign('g' ^ ~ephN, STSK)
        response_data = < 'Response', ~response, query, $N, nid
        , stpk, ephSig, stk_sig >
    in
    [ !ZKA_Sk($K, ZKA) \\Private LTAK
    , In(<NCR, epkR, senc(query_data, queryKey)>) \\Receiving query
    , Fr(~ephN) \\Fresh ephemearl agreement key
    , Fr(~NCN) \\Fresh nonce
    , Fr(~response)
    , !NS_sstk_Signed_SK(stk_sig, <$N, nid, stpk>, STSK)]
    --[
        Role('N') \\Nameserver role
    , NS_Sends_Resp($R, $N, query, 'Response', nid, STSK, stk_sig)
    , Running($N, $R, 'NS', < query, RespKey >)
    ]->
    [ !EskN($N, ~ephN)
    , Out(< ~NCN, 'g' ^ ~ephN, senc( response_data, respKey)>)
    ]
```

Listing 1.10. Nameserver Responds a Query

```
1  rule Res_2:
2     let
3        ResponseKey = kdf(<Nnc, Rnc, epkN ^ ephR>)
4        response_data = <'Response', response, query, $N, nid,
       stpk, sig_epkN, stk_sig>
5     in
6     [
7        In(<Nnc, epkN, senc(response_data, ResponseKey)>)
       \\Response
8        , Res_State_1($R, ephR, query, Rnc) \\Query information
9        , !ZKS_Pk($K, ltkPK) \\LTSK public key
10    ]
11    --[
12       Eq(verify(sig_epkN, epkN, stpk), true) \\Verify sig
13       , Eq(verify(stk_sig, <$N, nid, stpk>, ltkPK), true)\\Verify
       sig
14       , Role('R') \\Resolver role
15       , SecretR(response_data)
16       , ResolverReceivesResponse( response, query)
17       , RKeySecret(ResponseKey)
18       , Commit($R, $N, 'Res', <query, ResponseKey>)
19    ]-> []
```

Listing 1.11. Resolver Receives Response

References

1. Ariyapperuma, S., Mitchell, C.J.: Security vulnerabilities in DNS and DNSSEC. In: IEEE Conference on Availability, Reliability and Security (IEEE ARES) (2007)
2. Atkins, D., Austein, R.: Threat analysis of the Domain Name System (DNS). Request for Comments (RFC3833). IETF RFC Editor (2004)
3. Basin, D., Dreier, J., Hirschi, L., Radomirovic, S., Sasse, R., Stettler, V.: A formal analysis of 5G authentication. In: ACM SIGSAC Conference on Computer and Communications Security (2018)
4. Bernstein, D.J.: DNSCurve: Usable security for DNS (2009). Available: https://dnscurve.org
5. Cremers, C., Horvat, M., Scott, S., van der Merwe, T.: Automated analysis and verification of TLS 1.3: 0-RTT, resumption and delayed authentication. In: IEEE Symposium on Security and Privacy (S&P) (2016)
6. Dai, T., Jeitner, P., Shulman, H., Waidner, M.: From IP to transport and beyond: cross-layer attacks against applications. In: ACM SIGCOMM Conference (2021)
7. Diffie, W., van Oorschot, P.C., Wiener, M.J.: Authentication and authenticated key exchanges. In: Designs, Codes and Cryptography, vol. 2, no. 2, pp. 107–125 (1992)
8. Dolev, D., Yao, A.: On the security of public key protocols. In: IEEE Trans. Info. Theory **29**(2), 198-208 (1983)
9. Duan, H., Fischer, R., Lou, J., Liu, S., Basin, D., Perrig, A.: RHINE: robust and high-performance internet naming with E2E authenticity. USENIX NSDI (2023)
10. Grothoff, C., Wachs, M., Ermert, M.: NSA's MORECOWBELL: Knell for DNS (2017). Technical report
11. Hao, S., Zhang, Y., Wang, H., Stavrou, A.: End-users get maneuvered: empirical analysis of redirection hijacking in content delivery networks. In: USENIX Security (2018)

12. Herzberg, A., Shulman, H.: Fragmentation considered poisonous, or: One-domain-to-rule-them-all.org. In: IEEE Conference on Communications and Network Security (CNS) (2013)
13. Kaminsky, D.: Black ops 2008: its the end of the cache as we know it. In: Black Hat USA (2008)
14. Lowe, G.: A hierarchy of authentication specifications. In: Proceedings of the 10th Computer Security Foundations Workshop. IEEE (1997)
15. Meier, S., Schmidt, B., Cremers, C., Basin, D.: The TAMARIN prover for the symbolic analysis of security protocols. In: Computer Aided Verification (CAV) (2013)
16. Mockapetris, P.: Domain names - concepts and facilities. In: Request for Comments (RFC1034). IETF RFC Editor (1987)
17. Mockapetris, P.: Domain names - Implementation and specification. In: Internet Requests for Comments (RFC1035). IETF RFC Editor (1987)
18. Sadeghi Jahromi, A., Abdou, A., van Oorschot, P.C.: ss2DNS: a secure DNS scheme in stage 2 (2025). Under submission; technical report available at: https://arxiv.org/abs/2408.00968
19. Schmidt, B., Meier, S., Cremers, C., Basin, D.: Automated analysis of Diffie-Hellman protocols and advanced security properties. In: Computer Security Foundations Symposium (CSF). IEEE (2012)
20. Wilson, J., Asplund, M., Johansson, N.: Extending the authentication hierarchy with one-way agreement. In: Computer Security Foundations Symposium (CSF). IEEE (2023)

High-Efficiency Fuzzing Technique Using Hooked I/O System Calls for Targeted Input Analysis

Wenju Sun[1,2,3], Xi Xiao[1,2,3(✉)], Qiben Yan[4], Guangwu Hu[5], Qing Li[2], and Chuan Chen[6]

[1] Shenzhen International Graduate School, Tsinghua University, Shenzhen, China
swj22@mails.tsinghua.edu.cn, xiaox@sz.tsinghua.edu.cn
[2] Peng Cheng Laboratory, Shenzhen, China
liq@pcl.ac.cn
[3] Key Laboratory of Computing Power Network and Information Security, Ministry of Education, Qilu University of Technology (Shandong Academy of Sciences), Shandong, China
[4] Computer Science and Engineering, Michigan State University, Michigan, USA
qyan@msu.edu
[5] School of Computer Science, Shenzhen Institute of Information Technology, Shenzhen, China
hugw@sziit.edu.cn
[6] Key Laboratory of Computing Power Network and Information Security, Ministry of Education, Shandong Computer Science Center (National Supercomputer Center in Jinan), Qilu University of Technology (Shandong Academy of Sciences), Jinan, China

Abstract. Fuzzing is a widely used software testing technique that inputs random data to uncover bugs. Coverage-guided fuzzing (CGF) is one of the most successful approaches, which uses code coverage feedback to guide testing. It randomly mutates bytes of the entire input file to find interesting inputs, which often results in a large search space. Existing fuzzers need to analyze the entire input file for mutation, leading to inefficiencies. To overcome this limitation, we propose Hook-Based Fuzz (HBFUZZ), a heuristic fuzzing method that focuses only on the data that the program actually reads. By tracking data flow through hooking mechanisms, HBFUZZ narrows the search space and significantly improves fuzzing efficiency. We evaluate HBFUZZ on 16 real-world programs and the MAGMA benchmark, which includes various common software vulnerabilities. Experimental results demonstrate that HBFUZZ achieves 2.17%–23.52% higher code coverage compared to other fuzzers and uncovers the highest number of unique vulnerabilities. Additionally, it outperforms competitors in bug discovery speed, emerging as the fastest in uncovering 23 of the evaluated vulnerabilities.

Keywords: Fuzzing · Software Security · Mutation

1 Introduction

Fuzzing is a widely-used technique to find bugs in software by inputting random or modified data into a program and observing its behavior. This method has been particularly useful in detecting vulnerabilities in real-world programs, as shown by projects like OSS-FUZZ [1], which uses fuzz testing to uncover vulnerabilities in open-source software.

Among the different fuzzing techniques, coverage-guided fuzzing (CGF) has become one of the most successful and effective methods [2–12]. CGF works by collecting code coverage information from an instrumented program and using this feedback to guide the fuzzing process.

In CGF, a seed queue is maintained, which holds initial inputs. In each cycle, a seed is selected, mutated, and fed into the target program. The program's behavior is monitored, and its code coverage is checked. If the mutated input triggers new code coverage, it is added to the seed queue, as increasing coverage improves the chance of finding bugs—by 0.92% for every 1% increase in coverage [13]. If no new coverage is found, the input is discarded.

Existing research has mainly focused on improving the efficiency of mutation through seed scheduling optimization [4,14,15], power scheduling [4,6,16,17], and byte inference [7,8,18]. These studies generally treat the entire input file as the target for mutation, analysis, and search. They assume that all parts of the input file should be processed by the program, and therefore, the entire file is analyzed. However, in reality, some bytes are never read or processed by the program because the program reads the input file in segments, depending on its current state and what has already been processed. This is particularly true for programs that exhibit segmented reading behavior. Therefore, by focusing on the segments of the input file that are actually read and processed by such programs, we can optimize the fuzzing process, increasing the chances that mutated bytes will be read, and improving overall efficiency.

In this paper, we propose a lightweight framework called HBFuzz (short for Hook-Based Fuzz), optimized for scenarios where a program reads data partially from a file. For instance, when a program processes a 2MB file, it does not load the entire file into memory but instead reads it in segments as needed. Consider an example where the reading order is (0, 31), (1,024, 1,095), (4,096, 8,191). The probability of mutating a valid byte (defined as a byte that is actually read by the program) for the entire file is $\frac{32+72+4096}{2\times 1024\times 1024} = 0.0095\%$. In contrast, if mutations are based on the program's actual reading pattern, the probability of targeting a valid byte is 100%. This demonstrates that taking the program's I/O behavior into account during mutation operations can significantly improve fuzzing efficiency.

HBFuzz utilizes hooking [19] technology to intercept system calls and standard library functions related to file I/O. This allows to track the specific sections of the file that are accessed by the program during runtime. HBFuzz then optimizes the mutation process by focusing on the portions of the input file that are actually read by the program during execution.

Specifically, we first intercept system calls related to file I/O, capturing detailed information about which sections of the file are accessed at runtime. These reading data are organized into intervals, where each interval includes the file offset (indicating the start of the read) and the length of the data being read. These reading intervals are then organized into a linked list, which HBFuzz uses to determine the parts of the file that are relevant for mutation. We apply two types of mutation strategies to these intervals: coarse-grained and fine-grained. The coarse-grained mutation randomly targets a wide range of intervals, making broad changes to the input. On the other hand, the fine-grained mutation focuses on identifying and modifying specific, critical bytes within the intervals. This is done using a binary search technique to find critical bytes that are most likely to trigger new execution paths, thus improving the likelihood of uncovering new code.

To validate our ideas, we implement a prototype of HBFuzz based on AFL++ and evaluate it on 16 real-world programs (latest version). We selected several well-known fuzzing techniques, including AFL [2], MOPT [17], REDQUEEN [20], FAIRFUZZ [18], HAVOCMAB [21], SEAMFUZZ [22] and AFL++ [3], for comparison.

To further test the ability of our method to discover vulnerabilities, we also evaluate HBFuzz on the MAGMA [23] benchmark, which provides a set of real-world programs with known vulnerabilities for assessing vulnerability discovery. We summarize the main contributions of this paper as follows:

- We identify a key oversight in existing fuzzing techniques, namely, they fail to account for the program's segmented reading behavior, where the input file is read in portions rather than being loaded entirely into memory. This oversight leads to inefficiencies in the fuzzing process.
- We propose the HBFuzz framework, which leverages hooking technology to capture runtime I/O information, allowing us to focus mutation efforts on the specific parts of the input file that the program actually reads.
- We implement HBFuzz based on AFL++ and release it as an open-source tool on GitHub (https://github.com/Ekkosun/HBFuzz). We evaluate HBFuzz on 16 real-world programs and the MAGMA [23] benchmark, demonstrating its effectiveness in improving fuzzing efficiency and vulnerability discovery.

2 Related Work

In recent years, CGF has gained significant attention as a key fuzzing technique, with applications spanning diverse domains. For example, specialized fuzzing tools have been developed for JavaScript engines [24–27], embedded systems [28, 29], and network protocols [30–34]. Unlike prior work, our research focuses on applying fuzzing techniques to command-line applications, addressing the unique challenges posed by this domain.

The primary objective of the mutation strategy in a coverage-guided fuzzing test is to mutate the seeds at specific locations using the selected mutation approach. We conclude that the mutation strategy encompasses a two-fold problem: **"where to mutate"** and **"how to mutate"**.

The current mutation method encompasses multiple types of algorithms, including "bitflip", "arithmetic", "interest", "dictionary", "havoc", and "splice". Among them, "bitflip", "arithmetic", "interest", and "dictionary" are considered part of the deterministic mutation stage in AFL-like fuzzing technique, such as AFL [2] and AFLFast [4]. This stage involves applying fixed mutation strategies to all positions of the seeds. Discussing the deterministic stage's fixed mutation strategy is unnecessary.

Therefore, we exclude the deterministic mutation stage from consideration and instead focus on other mutation methods, such as "havoc", which randomly selects mutation positions and strategies for the seed file. However, using a random selection process that treats all bytes equally results in an overly extensive mutation range. For programs that dynamically read data based on their runtime state, a significant portion of the mutated data may remain unread or unused by the program, the mutation of which would impair the fuzzing efficiency. Furthermore, most AFL-like fuzzing techniques [2–6] adopt similar mutation strategies, often neglecting the influence of the program's runtime state on data processing.

2.1 Where to Mutate

The CGF technique, such as AFL [2], employs a common strategy for identifying mutation locations. This strategy includes performing mutations in the deterministic phase to cover the entire seed file and utilizing random location selection in the large search space. However, despite AFL-like algorithms utilizing effect maps to exclude ineffective locations where mutations do not significantly improve coverage, this approach of locating mutation locations remains inefficient. Therefore, identifying the bytes that need to be mutated becomes more and more crucial.

Taint Analysis. Some researchers use taint analysis techniques to determine the locations of input that are read and utilized by target programs [35–39]. They focus on analyzing and mutating these specific locations to address path constraints effectively. REDQUEEN [20] leverages input-to-state correspondence to address path constraints. PROFUZZER [40] systematically iterates over all possible values and collects the associated execution profiles for each byte. Subsequently, PROFUZZER groups the fields and determines their respective types based on these profiles. GREYONE [41] focuses on exploring the program code space by examining whether changes in specific bytes can influence certain variables within the program. Once such influence is established, GREYONE applies mutations to these variables to achieve the goal of path solving. Moreover, ANGORA [42] uses scalable byte-level taint tracking, context-sensitive branch count, and input length exploration techniques to address path constraints.

Byte Inference. In addition to taint analysis techniques, some researchers analyze runtime states of programs to examine mutations or safeguard specific bytes.

TRUZZ [43], which is grounded on the observation that program error handler code tends to be shorter than functional code. This conciseness enables TRUZZ to deduce bytes that correlate significantly with the availability checksum. The purpose of such analysis is to allow for a more extensive exploration of the program code space.

Some researchers treat the mutation of fuzzing tests as an optimization problem, employing standard optimization algorithms to determine which bytes require mutation and how to perform the mutation. NEUZZ [44] utilizes deep learning techniques to establish the correlation between code coverage and program inputs. Neural networks are utilized to comprehend program branching behavior. At last, gradient descent algorithms aid in determining the optimal mutation position and magnitude during mutation.

2.2 How to Mutate

The strategies for mutating the seed vary depending on the method used. Many AFL-like fuzzing techniques [2–4] use the traditional AFL method. NEUZZ [44] applies gradient descent algorithms to mutate the seed, while TRUZZ [43] determines byte mutation based on their fitness. In this paper, we introduce a new mutation method to improve the efficiency. It is important to note that various mutation methods are tailored to their respective core frameworks and, thus, are not discussed in details here. For instance, HAVOCMAB [21] applies the havoc mutation method exclusively to mutate bytes, while SEAMFUZZ [22] clusters seeds and continuously performs fuzzing to learn effective mutation strategies tailored to each seed group. But HAVOCMAB and SEAMFUZZ still need to analyze the entire input file.

3 Methodology

To enhance fuzzing efficiency, coverage-guided fuzzers require additional techniques, which motivates our investigation into partial reading behavior to ensure that the program processes the mutated bytes. In this section, we study the program's partial reading behavior and introduce our approach's basic framework.

3.1 Motivation

Example Program. We perform a fuzzing experiment on a simple program that only reads two parts of 32 bytes. Then, the target program compares them; the program will crash if they are the same.

We use a 2KB random file as input seed, fuzzing this program 20 times. The average and variance of time to crash of different fuzzers are listed in Table 1. From the experimental results, the fuzzer HBFuzz, optimizing the fuzzing based on reading information, could find the vulnerabilities in the program faster and more stable.

Table 1. Time to crash of the sample program. AFL is the implementation of AFL++, REDQUEEN is the implementation of AFL++ with cmplog mode.

Fuzzers	1	2	3	4	5	6	7	8	9	10	11	12	13	14	15	16	17	18	19	20	Average	Variance
AFL	6	6	6	2	0	2	5	3	2	7	3	11	3	4	10	1	2	13	18	5	5.45	20.37
REDQUEEN	1	0	1	14	0	8	0	25	2	2	1	3	3	2	1	2	10	0	2	6	4.15	37.82
HBFuzz	4	4	2	1	3	4	4	2	3	2	4	1	4	0	4	3	0	2	4	4	**2.75**	**1.99**

Source Code Analysis. To validate our assumption of the program's file reading behavior, we use a program, *"readelf"*, a tool used for analyzing and displaying ELF files, as an example. We study a tiny part of the source code of *"readelf"*, explicitly focusing on the functions that involve read and write operations. Figure 1 illustrates the relationship between input data, program execution, and control flow in *"readelf"*. In the input section, curly brackets and arrows highlight the data read from the input file, with numbers indicating the corresponding code responsible for the reads. In the control flow graph, solid arrows represent the current execution path, while dashed arrows indicate alternative branches. This mapping clearly demonstrates how the program's reading behavior correlates with its current state, validating our theoretical hypothesis.

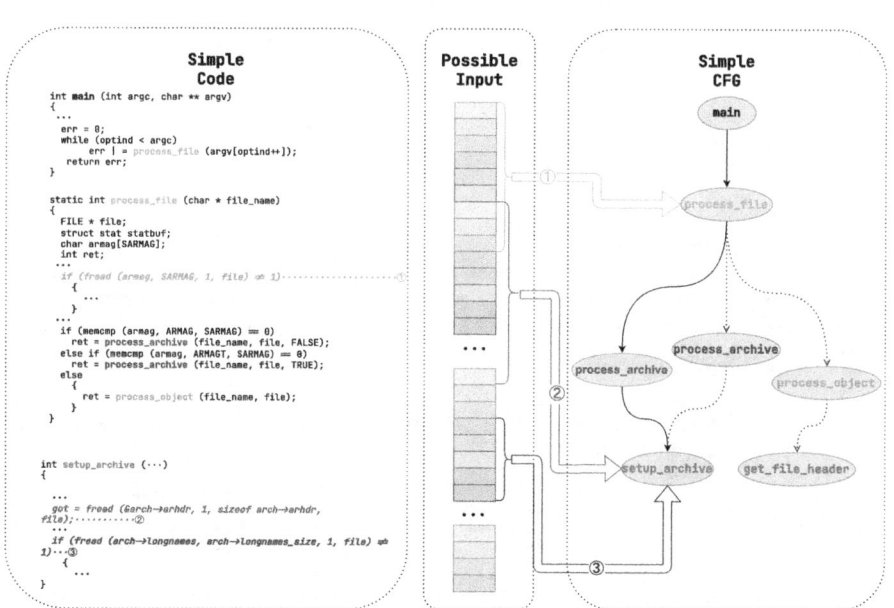

Fig. 1. A motivating example: *"readelf"*

Experimental Evaluation. We leverage hook technology to analyze the file reading behavior of the program. During the experiment, the *"readelf -a"* command-line option is used, and system calls are hooked to capture the data read by *"readelf"* at runtime. Table 2 shows the ranges of intervals accessed by the program during execution (only the first 10 items are displayed). The exported program I/O data confirms the practical accuracy of our assumption. This segmented reading behavior highlights a critical inefficiency in mutation algorithms that treat the entire seed file as the search space.

Table 2. Read information of *"readelf"*

	Read Order									
	1	2	3	4	5	6	7	8	9	10
start	0	0	16	14920	14920	14649	800	1208	64	11792
end	7	15	63	14963	16839	14917	1207	1417	679	12255

For example, if a mutation algorithm such as "havoc" modifies the bytes between (679,800), but the program does not read these bytes at runtime (as indicated in Table 2), these mutations become ineffective and diminish the algorithm's overall efficiency. By accounting for this segmented reading behavior and restricting the mutation range to the portions of the input actually accessed by the program, we can significantly improve the effectiveness of coverage-guided fuzzing.

3.2 Framework Overview

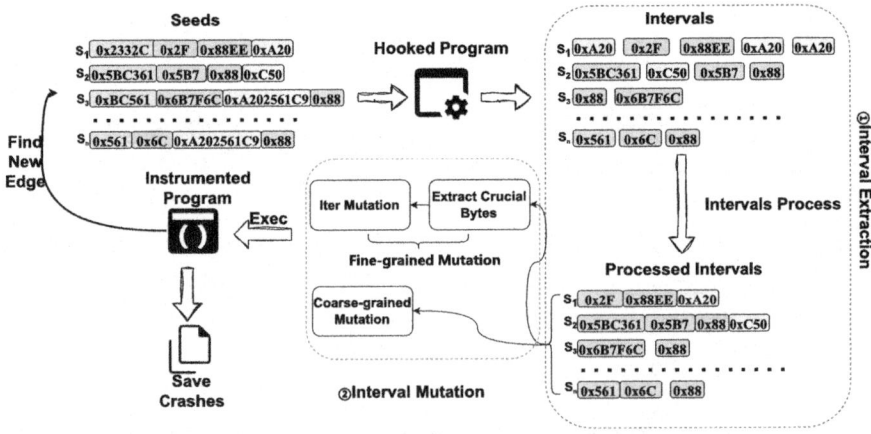

Fig. 2. System design of HBFUZZ

We have developed HBFuzz, a lightweight framework that leverages hook technology to collect runtime I/O information and guide mutation operations. The architecture of HBFuzz is illustrated in Fig. 2. We define our framework as lightweight because it uses the hook mechanism to achieve functionality similar to taint analysis, efficiently identifying the portions of the input file that are read by the program. The framework is composed of two main components: **interval extraction** and **interval mutation**.

In HBFuzz, we use hooks [19] (e.g., on functions like read and fread) to collect I/O information, identifying which parts of the input file are accessed by the program, as illustrated in step ① of Fig. 2. When the input file is provided to the hooked program, HBFuzz analyzes the read portions of the file and organizes them into intervals, which are then subjected to **interval processing**.

Interval processing is essential because, during program execution, specific parts of the input file are often read repeatedly. To eliminate redundancy, we implement an interval deduplication method.

As shown in step ② of Fig. 2, once the read intervals are collected, mutations are performed on them to generate new, interesting inputs. We design mutation methods tailored specifically for intervals, incorporating both **coarse-grained** and **fine-grained** mutation algorithms. The coarse-grained mutation algorithm, akin to the "havoc" operation, introduces significant disruptions to intervals to explore new program edges. In contrast, the fine-grained mutation algorithm, resembling byte-level mutation, targets specific critical bytes within intervals to refine the mutation process. By focusing on these crucial bytes, which are often scattered, we improve the program's code coverage. To locate and mutate these bytes efficiently, we employ a dichotomy method.

In summary, HBFuzz integrates reading information collection, interval processing, and targeted mutation into traditional fuzzing techniques. This framework aligns seamlessly with widely used coverage-guided fuzzing methodologies, enhancing their efficiency and effectiveness.

3.3 Interval Extraction

In this section, we introduce the techniques that we use to collect the reading information of the target program and the subsequent processing of the extracted information, which is called **Interval Extraction**.

Hooking. Hooking [19] is a technique that allows developers to intercept and modify the behavior of a program by inserting custom code at specific points in its execution. This can be done at various levels of a system, including system calls, library functions, or application APIs, to modify the program's flow, gather runtime information, or manipulate data in real time.

In Linux, one of the most common ways to implement hooking is through the LD_PRELOAD environment variable. This variable allows developers to specify a shared library that is loaded before others when a program starts. By using LD_PRELOAD, developers can override existing functions in dynamically linked programs. This allows them to insert custom code that intercepts system calls, such as read or fread, to modify their behavior or capture runtime information, like the data being accessed or the memory addresses involved.

Another approach to implementing hooks in Linux involves modifying the program's dynamic linker, specifically the ELF (Executable and Linkable Format) files. By altering the dynamic linker settings, developers can ensure that a program links to a custom library at runtime, which includes the hook code. This method allows more granular control over which functions or system calls are intercepted and how the program behaves during execution.

HBFuzz leverages hook technology to intercept and monitor system I/O operations, focusing on file access. By inserting hooks into critical I/O functions, such as read, fread, and other file-related APIs, HBFuzz tracks when and which portions of the file are accessed by the program. This enables the collection of precise runtime data, including the offset and size of each read operation. Based on this information, HBFuzz creates a set of reading intervals that represent the sections of the file the program interacts with. These intervals are then used to optimize the mutation process, ensuring that only the relevant portions of the file are mutated, thereby improving fuzzing efficiency.

Interval Processing. Once the parts of the input file accessed by the program during execution are identified, it is necessary to de-duplicate and merge these intervals to minimize redundancy and enable streamline processing.

As described above, deduplication removes repeated intervals caused by the program reading the same sections of the input file multiple times. Additionally, intersecting intervals are merged to form continuous ranges. For example, given the intervals (0,8), (0,8), (4,5), and (9,12), the resulting merged intervals are (0,8) and (9,12). Similarly, if the intervals are (0,8) and (5,12), they are merged into a single interval (0,12). This process ensures a compact and efficient representation of the accessed intervals, reducing unnecessary overhead for subsequent operations.

3.4 Interval Mutation

Based on the processed interval information, we designed two types of mutation algorithms focusing on interval mutation: **coarse-grained** interval mutation and **fine-grained** interval mutation. **Coarse-grained** mutation focuses on disrupting intervals to generate a wide variety of diverse seeds, while **fine-grained** mutation targets critical bytes within intervals, aiming to enhance code coverage through precise traversal-based mutations.

Coarse-Grained Mutation. The coarse-grained interval mutation involves two primary methods. The first method applies our custom havoc mutation algorithm to mutate individual intervals while keeping other intervals unchanged. This approach preserves the overall structure of the input file while focusing mutations on specific intervals. The second method assigns a mutation probability to each interval and iterates through all intervals, mutating those that meet the assigned probability threshold. This method is particularly effective in exploring relationships between intervals, such as cases where one interval determines how others are interpreted. Unlike traditional "havoc" mutation, this approach specifically targets interval-level mutations.

Algorithm 1 outlines the complete coarse-grained mutation process. The "havoc_interval" function is used to apply havoc-like mutations to intervals, while the "execute" function runs the program with the mutated input. In the first stage, we iterate through the set of intervals, completely disrupting the data within each interval while leaving the others unchanged, as shown in lines 3–7 of Algorithm 1. This large-scale disruption aims to explore a broader range of execution paths and generate a diverse set of seeds.

In the second stage, we traverse each interval and apply mutations based on a predefined probability, as detailed in lines 8–16 of Algorithm 1. This method explores potential dependencies or relationships between intervals by selectively mutating intervals with varying probabilities. For example, one interval might influence how others are processed or interpreted by the program. By targeting such interactions, this approach enhances the diversity of the generated seeds and the complexity of explored paths.

Overall, the coarse-grained mutation algorithm is designed to generate a broad variety of diverse input seeds, maximizing code coverage and improving the effectiveness of the fuzzing process. This strategy balances large-scale disruptions and targeted interval mutations to explore a wide range of potential program behaviors.

Algorithm 1 Mutation Method

1: **Input:** I/O intervals M, current seed s, collected crucial bytes D
2: **Variables:** Interval start b, end e, set of (b, e) intervals, max mutations n
3: **for** $i \leftarrow 1$ to length(M) **do**
4:    $(b, e) \leftarrow M[i]$;
5:    $s' \leftarrow$ havoc_interval(s,b,e);
6:    execute(s');
7: **end for**
8: **for** $cur \leftarrow 1$ to n **do**
9:    **for** $i \leftarrow 1$ to length(M) **do**
10:      **if** random_int(0, 100) $\leq p$ **then**
11:         $(b, e) \leftarrow M[i]$;
12:         $s' \leftarrow$ havoc_interval(s,b,e);
13:      **end if**
14:    **end for**
15:    execute(s');
16: **end for**
17: **while** not_empty(D) **do**
18:    $(b, e) \leftarrow$ pop(D);
19:    $s' \leftarrow s$
20:    **for** $i \leftarrow b$ to e **do**
21:      **for** $k \leftarrow 0$ to 255 **do**
22:         $s'[b, e][i] = k$
23:         execute(s')
24:      **end for**
25:    **end for**
26: **end while**

Algorithm 2 Crucial Bytes Analysis

1: **Input:** Seed s, bitmap B_s, interval for analysis I
2: **Variables:** Interval start b, end e, set of intervals W
3: **Output:** Crucial bytes D
4: $W \leftarrow I$
5: **while** not_empty(W) **do**
6:    $(b, e) \leftarrow$ pop(W);
7:    $s' \leftarrow$ flip_all_bits(s,b,e);
8:    **if** not has_new_bit($B_s,B_{s'}$) **then**
9:      continue;
10:    **end if**
11:    $s'' \leftarrow$ flip_all_bits($s,b,(b-e)/2+b$);
12:    $s''' \leftarrow$ flip_all_bits($s,(b-e)/2+b+1,e$);
13:    $B_{s''} \leftarrow$ execute(s'');
14:    $B_{s'''} \leftarrow$ execute(s''');
15:    **if** has_new_bit($B_s,B_{s''}$) or has_new_bit($B_s,B_{s'''}$) **then**
16:      $W \leftarrow W \cup (b, (b-e)/2+b)$;
17:      $W \leftarrow W \cup ((b-e)/2+b+1, e)$;
18:    **else**
19:      $D \leftarrow D \cup (b, e)$;
20:    **end if**
21: **end while**

Fine-Grained Mutation. Fine-grained mutation focuses on addressing specific conditional constraints on bytes to explore new edges and improve code coverage, which, in turn, enhances the detection of program vulnerabilities. While the hook mechanism effectively filters dynamically read intervals during program execution, the space for mutation remains vast. This is because crucial bytes, which significantly affect program behavior, are often sparsely distributed within the input file. Identifying these crucial bytes within intervals is therefore essential.

To find crucial bytes, we employ a dichotomy-based approach. As detailed in Algorithm 2, the "has_new_bit" function checks whether a given input triggers a new edge, while the "flip_all_bits" function inverts all bits within an interval. The process begins by flipping all bits in the interval and observing whether any new edges are triggered (lines 6–10 in Algorithm 2). If no new edges are detected, the interval is deemed non-essential and discarded. If new edges are found, the interval is bisected, and the dichotomy process is repeated until the interval is no longer subdividable (lines 11–20 in Algorithm 2). The crucial bytes identified through this process are stored in an array, and targeted mutations are then applied.

After extracting the crucial bytes, we apply a mutation algorithm (lines 17–26 in Algorithm 1), which modifies each byte by adding a fixed offset and explores the code paths associated with it. This allows us to uncover program behaviors controlled by these bytes and identify additional potential paths.

For example, consider an interval with content 0x7D3AFA82C5E9B1D0. Initially, we invert all its bits, producing 0x82C5F57D3A16E2F. Feeding this inverted result into the program helps determine if the interval is crucial. If no new edges are triggered, the interval is discarded. If new edges are detected we apply dichotomy to locate the critical bytes. The interval is split into two halves: **0x82C5F57DC5E9B1D0** and **0x7D3AFA823A16E2F**, and each half is tested independently. This process continues recursively until the interval length is not further subdividable. For instance, we may eventually identify two crucial intervals: (5,6) and (1,2). These intervals are then mutated individually to explore new code paths, thereby enhancing code coverage.

Through this precise and iterative process, fine-grained mutation efficiently targets the bytes that most influence program behavior, maximizing the effectiveness of fuzzing by focusing on areas with the highest impact.

4 Evaluation

To validate our solution, we implement HBFuzz based on the AFL++ framework, an advanced fuzzing technique that incorporates various state-of-the-art fuzzing algorithms built on AFL. We extend AFL++ by adding functionality to capture I/O information during program execution. Additionally, we develop both coarse-grained and fine-grained mutation algorithms to manipulate this I/O data. In this section, we compare HBFuzz, which leverages runtime information, with other widely-used fuzzing techniques. We conduct experiments on

Table 3. Fuzzed programs

Targets	Input formats	Test option
objdump	ELF	-S @@
nm	ELF,PE,core	-C @@
readelf	ELF,PE,core	-a @@
objcopy	ELF	-S @@
size	ELF,COFF,PE	@@
strip	ELF	@@
addr2line	ELF	-f -C -p -e @@ 0xdeadbeef
pdftotext	PDF	@@ /dev/null
pdftops	PDF	@@ /dev/null
pdffonts	PDF	@@
pdfinfo	PDF	@@
pdfimage	PDF	@@ /dev/null
tcpdump	pcap	-e -vv -nr @@
7za	7z	l @@
psicc	icc	-i @@
dwarfdump	COFF	@@

Table 4. Programs of MAGMA.

Project	Target Programs	Input Format
libpng 1.6.38	libpng_read_fuzzer	PNG
libtiff 4.1.0	read_rgba_fuzzer	TIFF
	tiffcp	
libxml2 2.9.10	libxml2_xml_read_memory_fuzzer	XML
	xmlint	
poppler 0.88.0	pdf_fuzzer	PDF
	pdfimages	
openssl 3.0.0	asn1	Binary blobs
	asn1parse	
	bignum	
	server	
	client	
	x509	
sqlite3 3.32.0	sqlite3_fuzz	SQL queries
libsndfile	sndfile_fuzzer	WAV
lua	lua	LUA
php 8.8.0	exif	IMG
	unserialize	TEXT
	parser	PHP
	json	JSON

multiple programs, collecting data on edge coverage and vulnerability discovery. This analysis seeks to answer the following questions:

- **RQ1**: To what extent does our method improve code coverage?
- **RQ2**: How does our method perform in terms of the speed and stability of code coverage?
- **RQ3**: How effective is our method in discovering vulnerabilities? How many vulnerabilities can it identify?

4.1 Experiment Setup

We use AFL++ and its associated tools, such as *"afl-clang-fast"*, *"afl-clang-fast++"* for program instrumentation, and *"afl-showmap"* for edge counting, to analyze our target programs. We select 16 of the latest open-source software programs for analysis, as documented in Table 3. Some of these programs are sourced from UNIFUZZ [45], while others are widely-used applications selected for their relevance and popularity in real-world scenarios. To ensure consistency, we conduct evaluations over 24-hour periods, and repeat the experiments 5 times.

We also attempted to test these programs with NEUZZ [44] but NEUZZ limits input seed sizes to under 10,000 bytes [46], while our initial seed pool contained larger seeds.

4.2 RQ1: Code Coverage

Code coverage is an indirect measure for evaluating the effectiveness of fuzz testing methods. The probability of discovering vulnerabilities increases with each increment in code coverage. We compare HBFuzz with the well-known fuzzers AFL [2], MOPT [17], AFL++ [3], FAIRFUZZ [18], HAVOCMAB [21], SEAMFUZZ [22] and REDQUEEN [20].

To evaluate code coverage generated by eight fuzzing techniques (HBFuzz, AFL, MOPT, AFL++, REDQUEEN, FAIRFUZZ, HAVOCMAB, and SEAMFUZZ), we conduct 5 trials of 24-hour runs on the selected programs (shown in Table 3). This approach helps mitigate the influence of randomness. We utilize the *"afl-showmap"* tool to calculate the achieved code coverage during these runs.

Table 5. The average number of edge coverage of the fuzzers in 5 trials.

Programs	**HBFuzz**	AFL	REDQUEEN	MOPT	AFL++	FAIRFUZZ	HAVOCMAB	SEAMFUZZ
readelf	6,327	5,387(0.004)[a]	5,456(0.004)	5,332(0.048)	5,547(0.016)	3,949(0.004)	**6,484**(0.345)	6,159(0.345)
objdump	**6,722**	6,594(0.016)	6,587(0.048)	6,391(0.004)	6,560(0.004)	4,335(0.004)	5,419(0.004)	6,310(0.004)
pdftotext	**9,173**	8,650(0.004)	8,913(0.048)	8,381(0.004)	8,732(0.004)	8,432(0.004)	8,722(0.004)	9,069(0.345)
pdffonts	**6,388**	5,449(0.004)	5,186(0.004)	5,280(0.004)	5,366(0.004)	5,961(0.004)	6,085(0.004)	6,188(0.004)
pdfinfo	5,112	4,574(0.008)	4,683(0.004)	4,763(0.004)	4,763(0.048)	4,974(0.345)	4,643(0.004)	**5,202**(0.075)
pdfimage	**8,795**	8,293(0.006)	8,349(0.006)	8,281(0.006)	8,335(0.006)	7,915(0.006)	8,149(0.006)	8,616(0.018)
pdftops	**11,588**	11,151(0.028)	10,995(0.075)	11,089(0.004)	10,981(0.004)	10,819(0.004)	10,866(0.004)	11,377(0.028)
objcopy	**4,403**	3,227(0.004)	3,157(0.004)	3,165(0.004)	3,234(0.004)	3,175(0.004)	3,361(0.004)	3,659(0.048)
nm	3,900	2,703(0.075)	3,042(0.155)	2,751(0.004)	3,085(0.075)	1,817(0.004)	**4,044**(0.111)	3,659(0.048)
size	**2,416**	2,127(0.004)	2,104(0.004)	2,141(0.004)	2,205(0.008)	1,914(0.004)	2,402(0.421)	2,386(0.5)
addr2line	**4,653**	4,190(0.004)	3,909(0.004)	4,238(0.004)	4,201(0.075)	2,989(0.004)	4,357(0.004)	4,409(0.048)
strip	**4,690**	4,337(0.016)	4,340(0.004)	4,348(0.028)	4,230(0.004)	3,637(0.004)	4,591(0.125)	4,417(0.048)
dwarfdump	4,739	4,586(0.004)	4,730(0.5)	4,683(0.111)	4,826(0.111)	3,749(0.004)	4,556(0.004)	**4,775**(0.075)
tcpdump	**12,216**	10,503(0.004)	12,648(0.075)	9,764(0.004)	11,147(0.016)	10,404(0.028)	11,719(0.111)	11,992(0.155)
7za	5,158	3,233(0.004)	4,122(0.075)	2,943(0.004)	2,978(0.006)	3,752(0.004)	**5,164**(0.21)	5,135(0.79)
psicc	1,368	1,357(0.274)	**1,483**(0.004)	1,396(0.004)	1,539(0.004)	1,233(0.004)	1,273(0.004)	1,417(0.004)
total	**97,648**	86,361(13.07%)[b]	89,705(8.13%)	84,947(14.95%)	87,728(11.31%)	79,053(23.52%)	91,833(6.33%)	95,577(2.17%)

[a] The p-value in parentheses comes from a Mann-Whitney U-Test.
[b] The improvement ratio of HBFuzz compared to other fuzzers

The final code coverage data is listed in Table 5. The results in Table 5 show that HBFuzz consistently achieves superior code coverage compared to other fuzzing techniques across all 7 fuzzers and 16 tested programs, including AFL, AFL++, REDQUEEN, MOPT, HAVOCMAB, FAIRFUZZ, and SEAMFUZZ. With a total edge coverage of 97,648, HBFuzz outperforms all other techniques, demonstrating a 13.07% improvement over AFL, 8.13% over REDQUEEN, 14.95% over MOPT, 11.31% over AFL++, 23.52% over FAIRFUZZ, 6.33% over HAVOCMAB, and 2.17% over SEAMFUZZ. These results highlight HBFuzz's ability to explore more execution paths by leveraging runtime I/O information and focusing mutations on the parts of the input file actually accessed by the program. Although SEAMFUZZ and HAVOCMAB perform well in certain scenarios, HBFuzz generally achieves higher overall coverage.

The table illustrating the improvements of HBFuzz for each program is provided in the appendix (see Table 9). As shown in the table, HBFuzz achieves notable code coverage improvements in most programs.

The p-values in parentheses further confirm the statistical significance of these differences in most cases. The p-values were calculated using the Mann-Whitney U-test [47], a non-parametric statistical test that assesses whether there is a significant difference between two independent samples. This method is particularly suitable for analyzing fuzzing results, as it does not assume a normal distribution of the data. Typically, p-values less than 0.05 indicate statistical significance, providing strong evidence that the observed differences are unlikely to be due to a random chance. By comparing the results of HBFuzz with those of other fuzzers, the Mann-Whitney U-test validates that the improvements in code coverage achieved by HBFuzz are statistically significant in most cases. Overall, the results demonstrate that HBFuzz significantly enhances fuzzing efficiency and code coverage, establishing it as a promising tool for advancing fuzz testing techniques.

4.3 RQ2: Efficiency and Stability

To assess the efficiency of edge discovery, we evaluate the fuzzers based on their ranks in edge discovery at 1, 6, 12, 18, and 24 h of fuzzing. A lower rank indicates better performance. Figure 3 shows the ranking distributions of HBFuzz and other fuzzers (AFL, AFL++, REDQUEEN, MOPT, HAVOCMAB, FAIRFUZZ, and SEAMFUZZ) across 5 independent trials at different time intervals (1h, 6h, 12h, 18h, and 24h). The lower the rank, the better the performance. From the results, it is evident that HBFuzz consistently demonstrates superior performance in edge discovery, maintaining a lower median rank than most other fuzzers across all time intervals. Its distribution is tightly clustered around the top ranks, reflecting both stability and efficiency, especially in early stages of fuzzing (1h and 6h), where it outperforms other fuzzers significantly. As the fuzzing process continues into the mid-range and later stages (12h, 18h, and 24h), HBFuzz maintains its competitive advantage with consistently strong rankings and narrower distributions, indicating its robustness over extended durations.

In contrast, other fuzzers such as HAVOCMAB and AFL++ show more variable performance. While they occasionally achieve competitive rankings at certain time points, their broader distributions suggest less stability across trials. Traditional fuzzers like AFL and AFL++ exhibit consistently higher rankings, highlighting their comparative inefficiency in edge discovery. Similarly, REDQUEEN and MOPT, while performing slightly better than AFL and AFL++, still fail to match the consistent rankings of HBFuzz.

Overall, the violin plot underscores the superiority of HBFuzz in edge discovery efficiency, combining early-stage effectiveness with sustained performance over time. Its consistently lower median rank and narrower ranking distribution reflect a stable and robust fuzzing process, reinforcing its value as a highly effective fuzzing tool. This performance advantage is evident not only in short-term fuzzing but also over prolonged durations, where HBFuzz continues to outperform other fuzzers in uncovering new edges.

Meanwhile, to evaluate the stability of HBFuzz, we also plotted boxplots of the five repeated experiments for each program. Due to space constraints, these plots are included in Fig. 4 of the appendix.

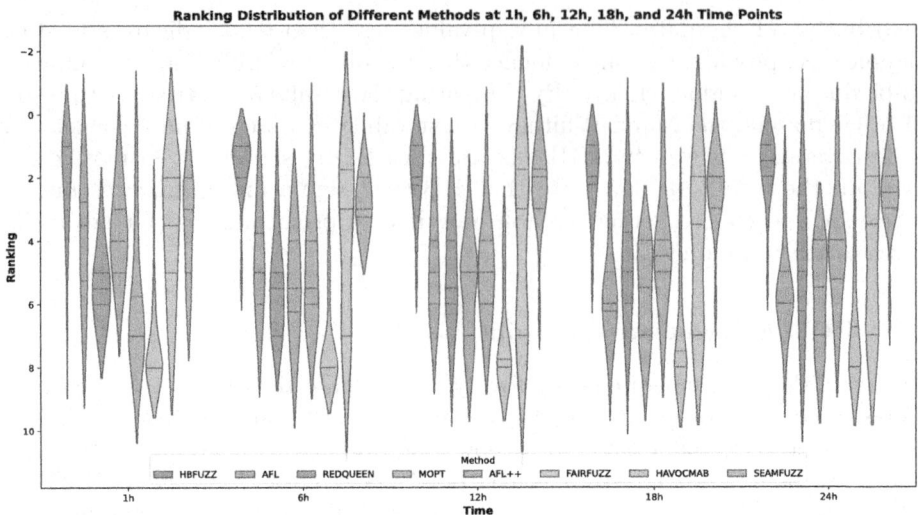

Fig. 3. The violin plot of edge ranks across 5 trials of different fuzzers after running for 1/6/12/18/24 h.

4.4 RQ3: Bug Discovery

This section compares the effectiveness of HBFuzz with other fuzzing tools in identifying vulnerabilities. We conduct five 24-hour testing rounds using the latest versions of real-world software programs (shown in Table 3). Due to continuous development and vulnerability fixes in these programs, some do not yield crashes within the testing period. The number of unique crashes discovered is summarized in Table 6. To identify unique crashes, we manually analyze the program's function call stacks at the time of the crashes to remove duplicates. As shown in the table, HBFuzz identifies more crashes than other fuzzers, demonstrating its superior effectiveness.

To further validate the capabilities of HBFuzz, we evaluate it using the MAGMA benchmark [23], a framework for fuzzing evaluation that includes real-world bugs and ensures consistent comparisons. We compare HBFuzz with widely-used fuzzers, including AFL, AFL++ (with the REDQUEEN method), MOPT, and FAIRFUZZ, all of which are provided as part of the MAGMA benchmark. Table 4 presents the programs used in the MAGMA dataset. By integrating HBFuzz into MAGMA, we assess its ability to discover bugs. Table 7 presents the total number of vulnerabilities discovered across three 12-hour testing trials for each fuzzer.

Table 7 demonstrates that HBFuzz outperforms all other fuzzers, identifying 38 unique bugs compared to AFL (16), AFL++ (32), MOPT (32), and FAIRFUZZ (18). Program-specific results show that HBFuzz leads in fuzzing critical programs such as libsndfile (7 bugs, tied with AFL++ and MOPT) and poppler (8 bugs, the highest among all fuzzers).

Table 6. Unique Crashes found by different fuzzers

Fuzzers	pdftotext	pdfinfo	pdfimage	pdftops	total
HBFuzz	2	3	3	2	10
AFL	1	2	2	4	9
REDQUEEN	0	2	3	1	6
MOPT	0	2	2	2	6
AFL++	0	1	2	1	5
FAIRFUZZ	0	1	3	1	5
HAVOCMAB	0	1	4	4	9
SEAMFUZZ	1	2	3	3	9

Table 7. The number of unique bugs found by different fuzzers (on MAGMA).

Programs	HBFuzz	AFL	AFL++	MOPT	FAIRFUZZ
libpng	2	1	2	2	2
soundfile	7	2	7	7	2
libxml2	4	1	4	4	1
lua	1	0	1	1	0
openssl	4	4	4	4	4
php	3	N/A[a]	1	N/A	N/A
poppler	8	2	5	5	2
sqlite3	4	1	3	3	2
libtiff	5	5	5	6	5
total	38	16	32	32	18

[a] AFL like fuzzer failed to compile php program.

Table 8. The Time to Bug (TTB) of fuzzers (on MAGMA). HBFuzz performs the best in discovering vulnerabilities.

Vulnerabilities	HBFuzz	AFL	AFL++	MOPT	FAIRFUZZ
CVE-2020-15945	2.01h	-	5.75m	2.63h	-
CVE-2017-9865	1.37h	-	3.23h	-	-
CVE-2019-10872	11.61h	-	-	-	-
Bug #106061	-	-	-	4.13h	-
Bug #101366	6.58m	2.92m	10.67m	2.75m	2.58m
CVE-2019-7310	4.34h	-	-	2.78h	-
CVE-2018-13988	45s	1.92m	1.17m	55s	1.67m
CVE-2018-10768	5.92m	-	2.09h	17.83m	-
CVE-2017-9776	10.04h	-	-	-	-
CVE-2017-14617	10.13h	-	2.26h	-	-
CVE-2019-11034	50s	-	-	-	-
CVE-2019-9638	1.17m	-	-	-	-
CVE-2018-14883	15s	-	5.08m	-	-
CVE-2015-8472	15s	15s	15s	15s	15s
CVE-2013-6954	12.75m	-	6.57h	28.25m	9.99h
CVE-2011-2696	3.58m	-	8.17m	6.58m	-
CVE-2017-6892	2.33m	16.58m	8.25m	1.00m	55s
CVE-2017-8361	15.25m	-	24.67m	8.92m	-
CVE-2017-8363	15.50m	-	17.42m	8.92m	-
Commit a8ab5b3	2.33m	59.50m	50s	25s	-
CVE-2017-8363	15.25m	-	19.08m	8.92m	-
CVE-2019-20218	4.92m	7.41h	23.67m	19.83m	3.16h
CVE-2019-19026	14.67m	-	7.15m	10.54m	-
CVE-2015-3414	14.67m	-	1.46h	2.02m	3.25h
CVE-2019-19880	3.02h	-	-	-	-
CVE-2016-2108	20.8m	-	1.35h	-	-
CVE-2016-6309	2.50m	3.33m	4.33m	2.75m	2.58m
CVE-2016-2109	10s	3.67m	3.08m	3.17m	3.17m
CVE-2017-3735	-	-	-	5.11h	11.11h
CVE-2016-6302	56m	9.89h	5.63h	9.18h	3.62h
CVE-2016-5314	-	-	-	10.48h	-
CVE-2016-10269	-	-	1.75m	-	-
CVE-2016-10269	5.78h	2.60h	1.75m	8.65h	-
CVE-2016-10270	10s	4.83m	25s	20s	1.83m
CVE-2015-8784	-	-	9.75h	-	7.61h
CVE-2019-7663	1.48h	9.47h	-	41.42m	7.62h
CVE-2016-3658	1.08m	2.31h	1.33m	6.75m	12.42m
CVE-2017-11613	1.92m	4.07m	25.75m	21.08m	5.99h
CVE-2017-9047	17.75m	-	28.42m	2.94h	-
CVE-2017-7375	36.17m	-	33.42m	-	-
CVE-2015-8317	8.67m	-	2.67m	5.75m	-
CVE-2016-1836	-	-	-	5.47h	-
CVE-2016-1762	30s	20s	30s	20s	20s
#The Fastest	23	2	5	11	5

Table 8 highlights the Time to Bug (TTB) performance of various fuzzers on MAGMA. The results show that HBFuzz is the fastest in discovering vulnerabilities for 23 out of the listed CVEs, significantly outperforming AFL (2), AFL++ (5), MOPT (11), and FAIRFUZZ (5). In particular, HBFuzz demonstrates a consistent ability to quickly uncover vulnerabilities such as CVE-2018-14883 (15 s), CVE-2016-10270 (10 s), and CVE-2019-20218 (4.92 m). Its superior TTB performance reflects the effectiveness of its runtime I/O-driven mutation strategy, which enables faster exploration of critical code paths.

Overall, HBFuzz not only excels in the total number of discovered vulnerabilities but also leads in minimizing the time required to uncover them, demonstrating its efficacy, efficiency, and reliability as a fuzzing tool.

5 Conclusion

In this paper, we introduced HBFuzz, a fuzzing framework that improves efficiency by leveraging runtime I/O information to focus mutations on relevant parts of input files, particularly for programs that read data incrementally.

Experimental results show that HBFuzz outperforms compared fuzzers in code coverage and vulnerability discovery, achieving these results in significantly less time. While HBFuzz already demonstrates strong potential as a reliable and efficient fuzzing tool, future work will focus on exploring advanced optimizations, such as memory monitoring after data reads and prioritizing critical intervals, to further enhance its performance and adaptability across a broader range of applications.

Acknowledgement. This work was supported by the Key Laboratory of Computing Power Network and Information Security, Ministry of Education (2023ZD034), the Major Key Project of PCL (PCL2023A06-4), the Natural Science Foundation of Guangdong Province (2025A1515011946).

A Box Plot of the Final Code Coverage After 5 Rounds of 24-Hour Fuzzing

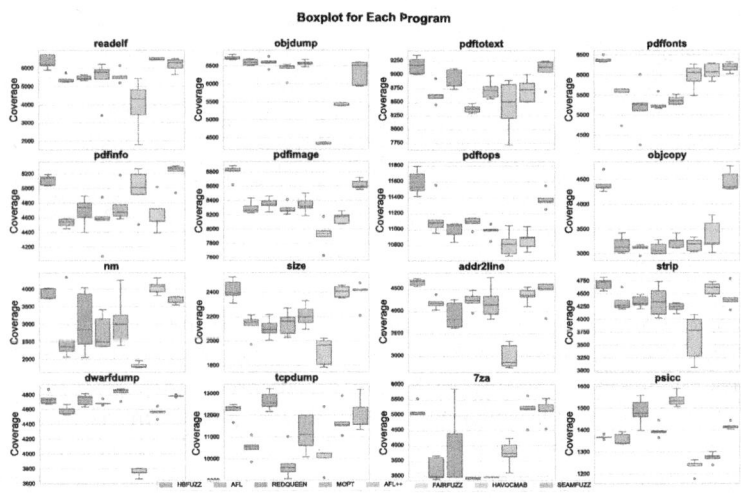

Fig. 4. Box plots showing the code coverage distributions achieved by HBFuzz and seven other fuzzers (AFL, REDQUEEN, MOPT, AFL++, FAIRFUZZ, HAVOCMAB, and SEAMFUZZ) across 16 programs. Each boxplot represents the coverage variability over 5 trials, with HBFuzz demonstrating superior and more consistent performance in most programs.

B Coverage Improvement per Program Compared to Other Fuzzers

Table 9. Coverage improvement for each program compared to other fuzzers

Programs	HBFuzz	AFL	REDQUEEN	MOPT	AFL++	FAIRFUZZ	HAVOCMAB	SEAMFUZZ
readelf	6,327	5,387(17.4%)[a]	5,456(16.0%)	5,332(18.6%)	5,547(14.1%)	3,949(60.2%)	**6,484**(−2.4%)	6,159(2.7%)
objdump	**6,722**	6,594(1.9%)	6,587(2.0%)	6,391(5.2%)	6,560(2.5%)	4,335(55.1%)	5,419(24.0%)	6,310(6.5%)
pdftotext	**9,173**	8,650(6.0%)	8,913(2.9%)	8,381 (9.4%)	8,732(5.1%)	8,432(8.8%)	8,722(5.2%)	9,069(1.1%)
pdffonts	**6,388**	5,449(17.2%)	5,186(23.2%)	5,280 (21.0%)	5,366(19.0%)	5,961(7.2%)	6,085(5.0%)	6,188(3.2%)
pdfinfo	5,112	4,574(11.8%)	4,683(9.2%)	4,763 (7.3%)	4,763(7.3%)	4,974(2.8%)	4,643(10.1%)	**5,202**(−1.7%)
pdfimage	**8,795**	8,293(6.1%)	8,349(5.3%)	8,281 (6.2%)	8,335(5.5%)	7,915(11.1%)	8,149(7.9%)	8,616(2.1%)
pdftops	**11,588**	11,151(3.9%)	10,995(5.4%)	11,089 (4.5%)	10,981(5.5%)	10,819(7.1%)	10,866(6.6%)	11,377(1.9%)
objcopy	4,403	3,227(36.4%)	3,157(39.5%)	3,165 (39.1%)	3,234(36.1%)	3,175(38.7%)	3,361(31.0%)	**4,465**(−1.4%)
nm	3,900	2,703(44.3%)	3,042(28.2%)	2,751 (41.8%)	3,085(26.4%)	1,817(114.6%)	**4,044**(−3.6%)	3,659(6.6%)
size	**2,416**	2,127(13.6%)	2,104(14.8%)	2,141 (12.8%)	2,205(9.6%)	1,914(26.2%)	2,402(0.6%)	2,386(1.3%)
addr2line	**4,653**	4,190(11.1%)	3,909(19.0%)	4,238 (9.8%)	4,201(10.8%)	2,989(55.7%)	4,357(6.8%)	4,409(5.6%)
strip	**4,690**	4,337(8.2%)	4,340(8.1%)	4,348 (7.9%)	4,230(10.9%)	3,637(28.9%)	4,591(2.2%)	4,417(6.2%)
dwarfdump	4,739	4,586(3.3%)	4,730(0.2%)	4,683 (1.2%)	4,826(−1.8%)	3,749(26.4%)	4,556(4.0%)	**4,775**(−0.7%)
tcpdump	12,216	10,503(16.3%)	**12,648**(−3.4%)	9,764 (25.1%)	11,147(9.6%)	10,404(17.4%)	11,719(4.2%)	11,992(1.9%)
7za	5,158	3,233(59.5%)	4,122(25.1%)	2,943 (75.3%)	2,978(73.2%)	3,752(37.5%)	**5,164**(−0.1%)	5,135(0.4%)
psicc	1368	1,357(0.8%)	**1,483**(−7.8%)	1,396 (−2.1%)	1,539(−11.1%)	1,233(10.9%)	1,273(7.5%)	1,417(−3.5%)
total	97,648	86,361(13.1%)	89,705(8.9%)	84,947 (15.0%)	87,728(11.3%)	79,053(23.5%)	91,833(6.3%)	95,577(2.2%)

[a] The improvement ratio of HBFuzz compared to other fuzzers

References

1. Chang, O., Metzman, J., Moroz, M., Barbella, M., Arya, A.: Continuous fuzzing for open source software, Oss-fuzz (2016)
2. Zalewski. American fuzzy lop. http://lcamtuf.coredump.cx/afl (2014)
3. Fioraldi, A., Maier, D., Eißfeldt, H., Heuse, M.: AFL++: combining incremental steps of fuzzing research. In: 14th USENIX Workshop on Offensive Technologies (WOOT). USENIX Association (2020)
4. Böhme, M., Pham, V.-T., Roychoudhury, A.: Coverage-based greybox fuzzing as markov chain. In: 2016 ACM SIGSAC Conference on Computer and Communications Security, pp. 1032–1043. ACM (2016)
5. Fioraldi, A., Maier, D.C., Zhang, D., Balzarotti, D.: LibAFL: a framework to build modular and reusable fuzzers. In: 2022 ACM SIGSAC Conference on Computer and Communications Security, pp. 1051–1065. ACM (2022)
6. Yue, T., et al.: EcoFuzz: adaptive energy-saving greybox fuzzing as a variant of the adversarial multi-armed bandit. In: 29th USENIX Security Symposium (USENIX Security), pp. 2307–2324. USENIX Association (2020)
7. Li, Y., Chen, B., Chandramohan, M., Lin, S.-W., Liu, Y., Tiu, A.: Steelix: program-state based binary fuzzing. In: 2017 11th Joint Meeting on Foundations of Software Engineering, pp. 627–637. ACM (2017)
8. Rawat, S., Jain, V., Kumar, A., Cojocar, L., Giuffrida, C., Bos, H.: VUzzer: application-aware evolutionary fuzzing. In: 24th Network and Distributed System Security Symposium (NDSS), vol. 17, pp. 1–14. The Internet Society (2017)
9. Zhu, X., et al.: CSI-Fuzz: full-speed edge tracing using coverage sensitive instrumentation. IEEE Trans. Dependable Secure Comput. **19**(2), 912–923 (2020)

10. Yue, T., Tang, Y., Bo, Yu., Wang, P., Wang, E.: LearnAFL: greybox fuzzing with knowledge enhancement. IEEE Access **7**, 117029–117043 (2019)
11. Gan, S., et al.: CollAFL: path sensitive fuzzing. In: 39th IEEE Symposium on Security and Privacy (SP), pp. 679–696. IEEE (2018)
12. Pham, V.-T., et al.: Smart greybox fuzzing. IEEE Transactions on Software Engineering (2019)
13. Miller, C.: Fuzz by number: More data about fuzzing than you ever wanted to know. CanSecWest (2008)
14. Herrera, A., et al.: Seed selection for successful fuzzing. In: 30th ACM SIGSOFT International Symposium on Software Testing and Analysis, pp. 230–243. ACM (2021)
15. She, D., Shah, A., Jana, S.: Effective seed scheduling for fuzzing with graph centrality analysis. In: 43rd IEEE Symposium on Security and Privacy (SP), pp. 2194–2211. IEEE (2022)
16. Böhme, M., Manès, V.J.M., Cha, S.K.: Boosting fuzzer efficiency: an information theoretic perspective. In: 28th ACM Joint Meeting on European Software Engineering Conference and Symposium on the Foundations of Software Engineering, pp. 678–689. ACM (2020)
17. Lyu, C., et al.: MOPT: optimized mutation scheduling for fuzzers. In: 28th USENIX Security Symposium (USENIX Security), pp. 1949–1966. USENIX Association (2019)
18. Lemieux, C., Sen, K.: FairFuzz: a targeted mutation strategy for increasing greybox fuzz testing coverage. In: 33rd ACM/IEEE International Conference on Automated Software Engineering, pp. 475–485. ACM (2018)
19. Lopez, J., Babun, L., Aksu, H., Uluagac, A.S.: A survey on function and system call hooking approaches. J. Hardw. Syst. Secur. **1**, 114–136 (2017)
20. Aschermann, C., Schumilo, S., Blazytko, T., Gawlik, R., Holz, T.: REDQUEEN: fuzzing with input-to-state correspondence. In: NDSS, vol. 19, pp. 1–15 (2019)
21. Wu, M., et al.: One fuzzing strategy to rule them all. In: 44th International Conference on Software Engineering. ACM (2022)
22. Lee, M., Cha, S., Oh, H.: Learning seed-adaptive mutation strategies for greybox fuzzing. In: IEEE/ACM 45th International Conference on Software Engineering (ICSE), pp. 384–396. IEEE (2023)
23. Hazimeh, A., Herrera, A., Payer, M.: Magma: a ground-truth fuzzing benchmark. ACM on Measur. Anal. Comput. Syst. **4**(3), 1–29 (2020)
24. Park, S., Xu, W., Yun, I., Jang, D., Kim, T.: Fuzzing JavaScript engines with aspect-preserving mutation. In: 41st IEEE Symposium on Security and Privacy (SP), pp. 1629–1642. IEEE (2020)
25. Groß, S.: FuzzIL: Coverage Guided Fuzzing for JavaScript Engines. Department of Informatics, Karlsruhe Institute of Technology (2018)
26. Han, H., Oh, D., Cha, S.K.: CodeAlchemist: semantics-aware code generation to find vulnerabilities in JavaScript engines. In: 26rd Network and Distributed System Security Symposium (NDSS). The Internet Society (2019)
27. Wang, J., Chen, B., Wei, L., Liu, Y.: Superion: grammar-aware greybox fuzzing. In: 2019 IEEE/ACM 41st International Conference on Software Engineering (ICSE), pp. 724–735. IEEE (2019)
28. Eisele, M., Maugeri, M., Shriwas, R., Huth, C., Bella, G.: Embedded fuzzing: a review of challenges, tools, and solutions. Cybersecurity **5**(1), 18 (2022)
29. Eisele, M., Ebert, D., Huth, C., Zeller, A.: Fuzzing embedded systems using debug interfaces. In: 32nd ACM SIGSOFT International Symposium on Software Testing and Analysis (ISSTA). ACM (2023)

30. Pham, V.-T., Böhme, M., Roychoudhury, A.: AFLNET: a greybox fuzzer for network protocols. In: 13th International Conference on Software Testing, Validation and Verification (ICST), pp. 460–465. IEEE (2020)
31. Schumilo, S., Aschermann, C., Jemmett, A., Abbasi, A., Holz, T.: Nyx-Net: network fuzzing with incremental snapshots. In: 17th European Conference on Computer Systems, pp. 166–180. ACM (2022)
32. Natella, R., Pham, V.-T.: ProFuzzBench: a benchmark for stateful protocol fuzzing. In: 30th ACM SIGSOFT International Symposium on Software Testing and Analysis (ISSTA), pp. 662–665. ACM, (2021)
33. Andronidis, A., Cadar, C.: SnapFuzz: high-throughput fuzzing of network applications. In: 31st ACM SIGSOFT International Symposium on Software Testing and Analysis, pp. 340–351. ACM (2022)
34. Meng, R., Duck, G.J., Roychoudhury, A.: Program environment fuzzing. In: 2024 on ACM SIGSAC Conference on Computer and Communications Security, pp. 720–734 (2024)
35. Clause, J., Li, W., Orso, A.: Dytan: a generic dynamic taint analysis framework. In: 2007 International Symposium on Software Testing and Analysis, pp. 196–206. ACM (2007)
36. Ganesh, V., Leek, T., Rinard, M.: Taint-based directed whitebox fuzzing. In: 31st IEEE International Conference on Software Engineering, pp. 474–484. IEEE (2009)
37. Enck, W., et al.: TaintDroid: an information-flow tracking system for realtime privacy monitoring on smartphones. In: ACM Transactions on Computer Systems (TOCS) (2014)
38. Haller, I., Slowinska, A., Neugschwandtner, M., Bos, H.: Dowsing for overflows: a guided fuzzer to find buffer boundary violations. In: 22nd USENIX Security Symposium (USENIX Security), pp. 49–64. USENIX Association (2013)
39. Portokalidis, G., Slowinska, A., Bos, H.: Argos: an emulator for fingerprinting zero-day attacks for advertised honeypots with automatic signature generation. ACM SIGOPS Oper. Syst. Rev. **40**(4) (2006)
40. You, W., et al.: ProFuzzer: on-the-fly input type probing for better zero-day vulnerability discovery. In: 40th IEEE Symposium on Security and Privacy (SP). IEEE (2019)
41. Gan, S., et al.: GREYONE: data flow sensitive fuzzing. In: 29th USENIX Security Symposium (USENIX Security), pp. 2577–2594. USENIX Association (2020)
42. Chen, P., Chen, H.: Angora: efficient fuzzing by principled search. In: 39th IEEE Symposium on Security and Privacy (SP), pp. 711–725. IEEE (2018)
43. Zhang, K., Xiao, X., Zhu, X., Sun, R., Xue, M., Wen, S.: Path transitions tell more: optimizing fuzzing schedules via runtime program states. In: 44th International Conference on Software Engineering, pp. 1658–1668. ACM (2022)
44. She, D., Pei, K., Epstein, D., Yang, J., Ray, B., Jana, S.: NEUZZ: efficient fuzzing with neural program smoothing. In: 40th IEEE Symposium on Security and Privacy (SP), pp. 803–817 IEEE
45. Li, Y., et al.: UNIFUZZ: a holistic and pragmatic Metrics-Driven platform for evaluating fuzzers. In: 30th USENIX Security Symposium (USENIX Security), pp. 2777–2794. USENIX Association (2021)
46. Zhang, K., Zhu, X., Xiao, X., Xue, M., Zhang, C., Wen, S.: ShapFuzz: efficient fuzzing via shapley-guided byte selection. arXiv preprint arXiv:2308.09239 (2023)
47. McKnight, P.E., Najab, J.: Mann-whitney U test. The Corsini encyclopedia of psychology, pp. 1–1 (2010)

VeriFLo: Verifiable Provenance with Fault Localization for Inter-domain Routing

Utku Tefek[1,2](✉), Ertem Esiner[1,2], Felix Kottmann[3], and Deming Chen[2]

[1] Illinois Advanced Research Center at Singapore, Singapore, Singapore
u.tefek@iarcs-create.edu.sg
[2] University of Illinois Urbana-Champaign, Champaign, USA
[3] Singapore-ETH Centre, Singapore, Singapore

Abstract. Modern digital infrastructure demands reliable data delivery across networks. While data plane provenance verification can attest to a packet's origin and path, it is susceptible to packet drops and malicious corruption of verification data, leaving the receiver unable to discern the cause of the fault. We propose a lightweight data plane provenance scheme with fault localization. By appending short, symmetric key marks at each hop and cumulatively reporting traffic counts, VeriFLo enables identification of links responsible for misbehavior in routing. Unlike existing fault localization schemes, the VeriFLo protocol does not require a path-aware network, and provides stronger security guarantees than BGPsec for inter-domain routing. We present security proofs for path unforgeability and fault localization, showing that either link of a misbehaving router can be identified with overwhelming probability even with a few bytes of marginal communication overhead per intermediary.

Keywords: BGP · DDoS · fault localization · Internet · provenance

1 Introduction

Critical infrastructure and performance-sensitive services require timely, reliable data delivery across multiple networks and administrative domains. Such operations depend on data flows across many services spanning independently managed entities. However, network faults, compromised entities, and network-layer distributed denial-of-service (DDoS) attacks jeopardize data delivery by causing packet drops, delays, malicious tampering, and injection. For instance, routers along the delivery path can indiscriminately drop packets while still responding to pings and traceroute probes. The routers gain impunity by shifting the blame to common network faults or other entities. Such actions are difficult to detect as most networks, including the Internet, lack security mechanisms to track the data delivery path and pinpoint misbehaving entities.

Today's Internet comprises around 80,000 Autonomous Systems (ASes) each operating independently within its domain but relying on the Border Gateway Protocol (BGP) for inter-domain routing. BGP provides a mechanism for ASes to exchange reachability information. The Resource Public Key Infrastructure (RPKI) forms the backbone of Internet's BGP security by cryptographically binding IP prefixes to the ASes authorized to originate them. This enables Route Origin Validation (ROV), ensuring that a BGP announcement is indeed from an AS that *owns* the prefix. However ROV only attests to the origin of the path, not the entire path. Therefore, a maliciously modified AS path will validate properly with ROV, as long as the authorized origin AS remains in the modified path announcement [19]. A security extension to the BGP, known as BGPsec, can provide integrity verification of the entire AS path using digital signatures. When an AS advertises a route to a neighbor AS, it signs the announcement, thereby adding the neighbor AS to the path. Each AS on the path in turn appends its own signature binding the next AS hop to the path, thus creating a chain of signatures. Upon receiving route advertisements with this chain of signatures, an AS uses the RPKI certificates to retrieve the public keys of the signers and verifies each signature in order.

Although ROV and BGPsec confirm the integrity of route announcements, they attest only to the reachability information of an AS, not to the forwarding of actual data packets. This means, while they largely prevent route (prefix) hijacking, they do not ensure that the traffic indeed follows the announced BGPsec paths. A malicious AS can still misroute, drop, modify, or inject packets undetected, all the while making valid route advertisements. Indeed, inconsistencies often arise between the advertised routes in BGP control plane and the actual traffic flows in the data plane, which often has limited visibility [15]. A malicious AS can exploit this discrepancy to manipulate data delivery while still appearing legitimate within the BGP framework.

Data plane provenance verification [8, 27] can mitigate path and traffic manipulations to some extent by providing cryptographic proof of a packet's integrity and routing history to the destination. For instance, (BGP gateway) routers would append a cryptographic mark to the packets, enabling the destination to verify the packet's path, and whether it has been tampered with. However, since intermediate routers typically do not verify provenance data to avoid processing overhead, a false mark or tampered packet introduced by a malicious AS can travel through the entire path. The destination eventually rejects the false mark, yet the networking and computing resources would have already been consumed in forwarding and verifying *bad* packets. This amplifies the impact of a potential DDoS attack due to additional cryptographic operations performed on the packets. Besides tampering and forging of provenance data, a malicious AS can arbitrarily drop legitimate packets while falsely claiming that other ASes along the path are responsible. Since redirecting blame and unintentional network faults grant impunity, fault localization is essential for reliable data delivery.

Fault localization identifies the link(s) responsible for packet losses, injections, and tampering. This information allows the network to isolate misbehaving routers or ASes. If performed reliably, fault localization may lead to filtering, blacklisting, or avoidance of malicious/faulty routers or ASes. For the Internet, it may further lead to the removal of misbehaving ASes from the Internet Routing Registry and revocation of their RPKI certificates in the BGPsec framework. Despite the benefits, fault localization mechanisms have not materialized for large networks as they either suffer from security or scalability challenges [2], are limited to the application layer [25], or require end systems to have awareness and control over the paths taken by network traffic, referred to as *path-awareness*. Numerous successful fault localization schemes have been proposed for path-aware networks: [5,9,12,14,26,27,29,30]. However, path-aware network architectures are difficult to achieve in today's ossified Internet structure often shaped by private policies and commercial relations.

1.1 Contributions

Without visibility or control over traffic paths, detecting faulty links is highly challenging for an Internet host – a challenge exacerbated by malicious corruption of provenance data and packet drops. In this paper, we address this unresolved problem by introducing VeriFLo, a lightweight protocol for verifiable provenance and fault localization. The main contributions and novelty of our work are summarized as follows.

- VeriFLo provides data plane provenance, offering stronger guarantees than control-plane integrity checks (as in ROV and BGPsec), since in the latter case, a malicious router can still manipulate data plane traffic.
- VeriFLo pinpoints the links causing packet drops, tampering, or forgery. Such fault localization is crucial against malicious intermediaries that deliberately manipulate traffic and falsely attribute faults to other network entities.
- We provide security proofs for path unforgeability and fault localization, showing that VeriFLo can identify misbehaving links while introducing minimal (a few bytes per node) communication overhead.
- VeriFLo is the first fault localization protocol suitable for inter-domain routing *without* reliance on path-aware networking. Our evaluation demonstrates that VeriFLo achieves performance comparable to path-aware schemes, while remaining compatible with the Internet protocol stack and infrastructure.

2 Problem Definition and Assumptions

2.1 System Model

We consider an inter-domain routing setting where packets traverse multiple Autonomous Systems (ASes), between the source and destination. We define traffic *path* as the ordered sequence of ASes traversed by a set of packets. For example, in Fig. 1, packets that traverse the ASes from the source AS to the verifier would have the path $\mathcal{P} = \{AS_0, AS_1, AS_2, AS_3, AS_4, AS_5\}$. The source AS, AS_0 refers to the first AS on the path participating in VeriFLo, not necessarily the origin AS of the traffic. The verifier V can be the destination host such as a web or cloud server, or destination AS that performs verification on host's behalf.

In line with the BGP, each AS knows its previous- and next-hop ASes but not necessarily the other ASes on the path. Not all ASes have to participate in VeriFLo but each participating AS must know its previous and next-hop ASes that participate in VeriFLo. For instance, if AS_0 and AS_2 do not participate, the traffic path for participating ASes would be $\{AS_1, AS_3, AS_4, AS_5\}$ and AS_1 would have to know that AS_3 is its next-hop participating AS. In line with packet switching, packets between the same source and destination can take different paths. We assume the verifier can establish a shared secret key K_i with any participating AS i. This can be done in many ways, such as using Diffie–Hellman key exchange on top of BGP announcements [13] if the verifier is an AS, TLS over RPKI, IPsec if the verifier is a web server, or using DRKeys [11] to derive keys on-the-fly from a single secret.

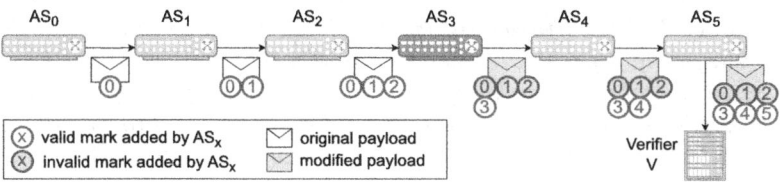

Fig. 1. Traffic path and marks from source AS AS_0 to verifier V.

2.2 Adversary Model

We consider a powerful adversary controlling multiple ASes. The adversary knows the cryptographic keys of the controlled ASes and can eavesdrop on the communication, drop, modify, and forge packets. The adversary is highly sophisticated with the ability to intelligently corrupt or spoof both the payload and headers of any packet, to evade detection. However, the adversary is probabilistic polynomial time (PPT) i.e., has polynomially bounded computational power and thus cannot break cryptographic schemes implemented with sufficient security.

The adversary's goal is to disrupt the traffic flow to any destination, for example by launching network-layer DoS or DDoS attacks coordinated across many adversary-controlled ASes. Dropping packets and forging packets can both be considered forms of DoS and modifying legitimate packets is simply a combination of dropping and forging. To evade detection, the adversary may attempt to incriminate honest on-path ASes by altering, removing, or forging verification data added to packets by these ASes. The adversary may also manipulate any control data sent by honest ASes.

While it is futile to predict attack strategies, a successful outcome for the adversary is path forgery which may cause the destination to misidentify paths. The adversary forges a false traffic path $\mathcal{P}'$ – meaning it attaches false path/provenance data to packets – aiming to deceive the verifier into accepting $\mathcal{P}'$ as a legitimate path. If performed over a large volume of traffic, this attack can mislead the destination into believing another path is responsible for a DoS flow, resulting in the blocking of a *good* path or exclusion of honest ASes from routing.

2.3 Desired Properties

Broadly, we desire the verifier to accurately identify the traffic paths, and examine these paths for packet drops and injections. Thus, reliable path identification is crucial for fault localization in a non-path-aware network. Since a DDoS attack requires considerable traffic volume to be effective, the verifier must only identify major traffic paths rather than every low-volume path. Consequently, our security goal is to ensure accurate identification of major traffic paths, and rejection of false paths with high probability, in the presence of malicious ASes as described above. We formalize this objective as path unforgeability below.

Definition 1. Path Unforgeability: *A scheme provides path unforgeability if the adversary cannot get the verifier to accept a false path that differs from the legitimate path in at least one honest AS. Concretely, suppose the verifier accepts a path only if it sees at least t packets with valid provenance proofs out of N total packets on that path. Then, the adversary should be unable to forge t or more packets with valid proofs for any false path, except with negligible probability.*

Security proof in Sect. 5, shows that the probability of path forgery in VeriFLo is a negligible function of the number of verified packets N, given fixed acceptance threshold t/N.

For interpretation, consider the path $\mathcal{P}$ in Fig. 1 where AS_3 is malicious. The honest AS subsequence is then $\mathcal{H}(\mathcal{P}) = \{AS_0, AS_1, AS_2, AS_4, AS_5\}$. Path unforgeability prevents forgeries that alter this honest subsequence, such as omitting, reordering, or inserting honest ASes. The definition permits the insertion of malicious ASes (for which the adversary can produce valid provenance data), as this does not alter $\mathcal{H}(\mathcal{P})$. However, such falsely inserted malicious ASes remain subject to scrutiny via security goal 2.

While path unforgeability ensures path integrity, it offers no visibility on the location of packet drops since provenance data of a dropped packet does not reach the verifier. Consequently, we require fault localization as follows.

Definition 2. Fault Localization: *A scheme provides* fault localization *if, given a path, the verifier can identify the malicious link(s) responsible for packet drops, tampering, and injections with high enough probability. Conversely, the probability that a malicious AS evades detection or that an honest link (of which both sides consist of honest ASes) is falsely accused is negligible.*

Upon fault localization, there are multiple ways to deal with faulty links, including, unauthorizing corresponding path advertisements, in-network filtering against malicious ASes, and path selection (in path-aware networks). These are orthogonal problems addressed for example in ROV [17], in-network filtering schemes [10], and as part of SCION [16].

3 VeriFLo Overview

This section introduces VeriFLo at a high level and positions it within the literature. In essence, the VeriFLo protocol identifies the paths of incoming traffic and localizes network faults along these paths.

3.1 Identifying Major Traffic Paths

Any AS participating in VeriFLo attaches a cryptographic *mark* to the packets, and the verifier checks these marks to validate the packets' provenance. VeriFLo's path identification can be viewed as a verifiable variant of traditional IP route record (RR) techniques [3,20]. While conventional RR or IP traceback schemes enable the destination to discover the path, they assume ASes are trustworthy. Since malicious ASes can insert false RRs, and modify or drop each others' RRs, these methods fail to guarantee path unforgeability in Definition 1.

Ensuring the provenance of every packet with sufficient bit security is costly in terms of communication and processing overheads. For example, having each on-path AS attach a Message Authentication Code (MAC) to a packet for verification would incur 256 bits per hop if SHA-256 is used in the MAC function. Our goal in path unforgeability is not for the verifier to identify the provenance of every single packet, but rather to identify the paths with substantial traffic. Thus, inspired by the ShortMAC approach [30] for source authentication and EPIC scheme [12] for hop authenticators, we require participating on-path ASes to attach n-bit MACs. n can be much smaller than a typical MAC tag of 160–256 bits. Unlike [12,30] which assume path-aware networking, VeriFLo does not require the source or intermediaries to have any control or visibility into the delivery path (except for the next-hop AS) to generate the marks, making VeriFLo suitable for BGP-based inter-domain routing in the Internet.

3.2 Path Unforgeability

We use a pseudorandom function (PRF) to construct n-bit MACs, such that the MAC tag is indistinguishable from any random string of n bits for a PPT adversary. While the adversary can correctly guess the MAC of an honest AS with a probability of 2^{-n} (plus a negligible function) without the secret key, it cannot do so consistently over a large number of packets. We provide a path unforgeability guarantee even for small n (e.g., $n = 4$) at the cost of verifying more packets as quantified in the proof of Lemma 1 in Sect. 5.

VeriFLo uses mark chaining to prevent path spoofing. Each AS generates its mark with a MAC computation using a secret key shared with the verifier, also incorporating the marks received from the previous ASes and the ID of the next AS on the path into this MAC computation. Chaining the marks this way binds all provenance information from the source to that AS. If an AS removes, corrupts, or changes the order of marks attached by a previous AS (e.g., AS_3 in Fig. 1 modifying the packet or AS_0's mark), all the marks from the modified AS to the malicious AS would fail verification, hence exposing the malicious AS.

3.3 Fault Localization

Packet drops are difficult to localize because the destination is often unaware of the dropped packets. VeriFLo performs fault localization to identify which link in the delivery path caused faults including packet drops. Other works used counters [1] or accumulators such as Bloom Filters [14] as traffic summaries. However, without authentication of packets, these methods cannot detect malicious tampering of packets. A malicious AS can modify the packet contents without affecting the total packet count or Bloom Filter image. If ASes authenticate the packet content as in [9,30], total packet count becomes a verifiable measure of packet content. However, this assumes a path-aware network architecture. Unlike in [9,30], VeriFLo does not require path-awareness, and no verification is needed at intermediary ASes.

In VeriFLo the verifier probes the identified paths, requesting packet counts as traffic summaries from participating ASes to localize the faulty link(s). Combined with provenance verification, each AS's claim on the number of packets forwarded along a path becomes a verifiable measure of packet integrity because any AS that under-reports or over-reports forwarded packets will cause a mismatch between its own and neighbors' reports. If an AS replaces the dropped packets with bogus packets without affecting the total packet count, the mark verification up to that AS will fail due to forged packet marks. In either case, the verifier pinpoints the misbehaving link.

4 VeriFLo Protocol and Algorithms

VeriFLo discretizes time into periods called epochs. In each epoch, the packets are ordered by a sequence number based on their time of generation at the source. The epoch and sequence number together uniquely identify a packet.

4.1 Mark Generation

In VeriFLo the participating ASes attach a small mark to the packets. These marks enable the verifier to identify the incoming traffic paths. Adding a mark to a packet involves only lightweight operations of message authentication code (MAC) computation and header assembly. We require the MAC function used in mark generation to exhibit pseudorandomness, i.e., the output looks like a uniformly distributed string to a PPT adversary. This can be obtained by hashing the input to a block size, then encrypting the digest using a secure block cipher, such as AES, known to be a pseudorandom permutation, and outputting only n bits of the ciphertext. To highlight the pseudorandomness of mark generation function constructed in this way, we refer to it as a PRF rather than MAC, as the latter does not necessarily imply pseudorandomness, but demands unforgeability.

To generate a mark, an AS inputs the constant packet bits (payload and headers of upper layers) along with epoch and sequence numbers, the path, and the mark it received from the previous AS (if any), into a PRF keyed with a secret shared with the verifier. The PRF outputs a truncated n-bit MAC tag called the mark.

Thus, the mark for each AS_i, $\forall\ i \in \{0, 1, \ldots, L\}$ is constructed as follows. We denote the source AS with the subscript 0 for continuity in the notation:

$$\begin{aligned}
\mathcal{M}_0 &\leftarrow \text{PRF}_{K_0}\big(\kappa(\sigma, \tau), \sigma, \tau, \mathcal{P}_0\big), \\
\mathcal{M}_1 &\leftarrow \text{PRF}_{K_1}\big(\kappa(\sigma, \tau), \sigma, \tau, \mathcal{P}_1, \mathcal{M}_0\big), \\
&\vdots \\
\mathcal{M}_L &\leftarrow \text{PRF}_{K_L}\big(\kappa(\sigma, \tau), \sigma, \tau, \mathcal{P}_L, (\mathcal{M}_0 \| \mathcal{M}_1 \| \cdots \| \mathcal{M}_{L-1})\big).
\end{aligned} \quad (1)$$

Here, $\mathcal{M}_i$ denotes the mark of AS_i, τ the epoch, σ the sequence number to be reset in every epoch, $\kappa(p, \tau)$ the constant part of the packet, and $\text{PRF}_{K_i}(\cdot)$ the pseudorandom function keyed with the symmetric key K_i shared between AS_i and the verifier. $\mathcal{P}_i$ represents the sequence of AS IDs from source AS to AS_{i+1}. For example, $\mathcal{P}_0 = \{AS_0, AS_1\}$, $\mathcal{P}_1 = \{AS_0, AS_1, AS_2\}$ and so forth, except for the last intermediary AS which includes the verifier ID as the next-hop AS.

Even if some on-path ASes do not participate, VeriFLo can still function and establish paths for the ASes that do participate. The construction requires an AS to append the ID of the next participating AS, such as its 16-bit AS number to the path sequence. The AS then computes the PRF based on the updated path sequence and previous marks, appends its mark to the packet, updates the path in the header field with its own ID, and forwards the packet to the next AS. The mark generation and packet marking algorithms of VeriFLo are presented in Algorithm 1 and Algorithm 2 respectively. In all algorithms, the packet **pkt** has attributes denoted as **pkt**.*attributeName*: constant packet fields (κ), sequence number (σ), epoch (τ), sequence of AS IDs (*path*), sequence of AS marks (*marks*). σ, τ, *path*, and *marks* are VeriFLo headers, and κ is the payload plus the headers from the Transport Layer and above, which remain unchanged as the packet traverses the path.

Algorithm 1. GenerateASMark

Input: packet pkt, current and next AS IDs: AS_i, AS_{i+1}
Output: mark for the current AS
1: $K_i \leftarrow \text{GetKey}(AS_i)$
2: $\mathcal{P} \leftarrow \text{pkt}.path \cup [AS_i, AS_{i+1}]$
3: **return** $\text{PRF}_{K_i}(\text{pkt}.\kappa \| \text{pkt}.\sigma \| \text{pkt}.\tau \| \mathcal{P} \| \text{pkt}.marks)$

Algorithm 2. MarkPacket

Input: packet pkt, current and next AS IDs: AS_i, AS_{i+1}
Output: packet pkt with updated marks and path
1: $\mathcal{M} \leftarrow \text{GenerateASMark}(\text{pkt}, AS_i, AS_{i+1})$
2: pkt.$marks$.append($\mathcal{M}$)
3: pkt.$path$.append(AS_i)
4: **return** pkt

If the PRF computation did not incorporate the entire path up to the next AS, a malicious AS could modify the path in the header for an earlier AS, causing its mark to be invalid. For instance, malicious AS_3 could alter AS_1 from the header field, resulting in an invalid $\mathcal{M}_1$. With PRF computation including the entire path, AS_3 could still modify AS_1, but this would invalidate all marks from $\mathcal{M}_1$ to $\mathcal{M}_2$ (or $\mathcal{M}_1$ to $\mathcal{M}_3$ if AS_3 uses the original path containing AS_1 to compute its own mark). This enables the verifier to pinpoint the malicious activity at either link of AS_3. The inclusion of all previous marks serves a similar purpose. If AS_3 modifies a previous mark, say $\mathcal{M}_0$ (or the packet as in Fig. 1), all the marks from $\mathcal{M}_0$ to $\mathcal{M}_2$ would be invalid, localizing the misbehavior.

Network Layer Headers	
epoch (τ)	sequence no (σ)
AS_0	$\mathcal{M}_0$
AS_1	$\mathcal{M}_1$
AS_2	$\mathcal{M}_2$
⋮	⋮
Transport Layer Headers	

Fig. 2. Headers of VeriFLo.

VeriFLo protocol can be implemented as a shim layer between Network and Transport Layers as shown in Fig. 2 which presents the header structure after the packet has passed through three ASes. At each AS hop, an AS ID and n-bit mark are appended to the header. The header size of VeriFLo is a function of the maximum path length and the length of marks. More than 75% of Internet paths involve less than eight ASes based on the CAIDA study [6] and seldom more than ten ASes [5]. Ten 8-bit marks, ten 16-bit AS numbers as IDs, a 32-bit epoch, and a 16-bit sequence number yields 36 bytes of VeriFLo headers.

4.2 Mark Verification

The VerifyMarks algorithm in Algorithm 3 is executed by the verifier to verify the marks in a received packet. The algorithm outputs a boolean array, where each entry represents the mark's validity corresponding to the respective AS ID in sequence. An entry with a 'False' indicates an invalid mark.

Algorithm 3. VerifyMarks

Input: packet pkt, verifier's ID: AS_V
Output: boolean array indicating validity of marks: isValid
1: $\mathcal{P} \leftarrow$ pkt.$path$
2: isValid $\leftarrow$ [False for i in 0 to $\mathcal{P}$.length -1]
3: **for** i in 0 to $\mathcal{P}.length - 1$ **do**
4: $\quad \mathcal{M} \leftarrow$ GenerateASMark(pkt, $\mathcal{P}[i], \mathcal{P}[i+1]$ **if** $i < \mathcal{P}.length - 1$ **else** AS_V)
5: $\quad$ isValid[i] $\leftarrow$ isEqual($\mathcal{M}$, pkt.$marks[i]$)
6: **end for**
7: **return** isValid

4.3 Traffic Reporting

Packet drops cannot be detected by packet marking alone, as marks from dropped packets never reach the verifier. A malicious AS could drop packets

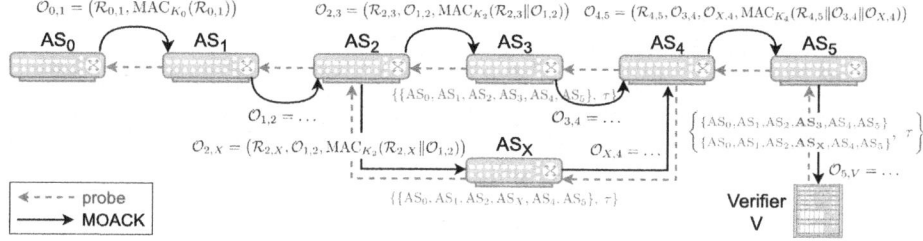

Fig. 3. Probing and traffic reporting with MOACKs

and claim that the packets never reached them or were dropped by subsequent ASes. To address this, VeriFLo employs a traffic reporting mechanism. When combined with packet marking, traffic reporting enables retrospective integrity verification of packets over an epoch, identifying links adjacent to the source of packet drop.

VeriFLo requires the participating ASes to track the number of packets during each epoch. Since packets may traverse multiple paths between the same source and destination, ASes maintain packet counts for every 3-tuple of (source, destination, next-hop AS ID). Figure 3 illustrates two paths for packets originating from AS_0 with a destination of V. For this flow, only AS_2 keeps two separate counts for packets forwarded to AS_3 and AS_X.

After an epoch, the verifier probes the identified paths to trigger traffic reporting, indicating the path(s) and epoch as shown in Fig. 3. Each AS (except source AS) forwards the probe to the subsequent AS(s) indicated in the probe using reliable link layer transmission and starts a timer set to the maximum round-trip time to the probe destination. Thus, except in cases of malicious dropping or tampering of the probe, the probe is received by all ASes participating in VeriFLo in the reverse order of traffic.

Traffic reporting adopts a multi-path variant of the *Onion report* approach used for fault localization in [28]. In Onion reporting, each intermediate node encapsulates the previous node's report in an onion-like fashion while incorporating its own report. However, since the Onion report and the subsequently proposed Onion ACK [30] were designed for path-aware Internet architectures where the source selects and monitors the forwarding path for packet-dropping activity, they are not applicable to packet-switched, multi-path settings. Therefore, we extend the Onion report scheme for multi-path routing. In our approach, the nodes at the traffic convergence points encapsulate all the received reports (Onion ACKs), resembling an onion with multiple bulbs wrapped by a tunic. For this reason, we refer to it as Multi-bulb Onion ACK (MOACK).

AS_j constructs the report on the number of packets $C_{j,k}$, forwards to AS_k,

$$\mathcal{R}_{j,k} = (\tau, \mathbf{P}, AS_j, AS_k, C_{j,k}) \tag{2}$$

where τ is the epoch, and $\mathbf{P}$ is the set of paths indicated in the probe. If an AS forwarded packets towards multiple next-hop ASes, then multiple traffic reports are constructed. E.g., AS_2 in Fig. 3 receives two probes and constructs separate reports for packets forwarded to AS_3 and AS_X.

Traffic reporting via MOACK starts from the source AS. Each AS combines its report with the report from the previous AS(s). In particular, AS_j receives a MOACK $\mathcal{O}_{i,j}$ from the previous hop AS_i, and combines it with own report $\mathcal{R}_{j,k}$, hence committing into a new MOACK,

$$\mathcal{O}_{j,k} = \big(\mathcal{R}_{j,k}, \mathcal{O}_{i,j}, \text{MAC}_{K_j}(\mathcal{R}_{j,k} \| \mathcal{O}_{i,j})\big). \tag{3}$$

Here MAC_{K_j} is the MAC keyed with the secret K_j shared with the verifier. If AS_j does not receive a MOACK before its timer expires, it initiates MOACK as,

$$\mathcal{O}_{j,k} = \big(\mathcal{R}_{j,k}, \text{MAC}_{K_j}(\mathcal{R}_{j,k})\big). \tag{4}$$

ASes handle divergence and convergence points when generating MOACKs, as illustrated in Fig. 3 and detailed in Algorithm 4 in the Appendix. The MOACK generation Algorithm is run by an AS upon receiving a probe.

4.4 MOACK and Traffic Report Verification

Upon receiving a MOACK, the verifier iteratively retrieves wrapped MOACKs in the reverse traffic order along each path. E.g., the verifier retrieves $\mathcal{O}_{5,V}$, $\mathcal{O}_{4,5}$, ..., $\mathcal{O}_{0,1}$ for path $\{AS_0, AS_1, AS_2, AS_3, AS_4, AS_5\}$. If retrieval fails at $\mathcal{O}_{j,k}$ the verifier immediately flags either AS_j or AS_k as malicious, given the reliable hop-by-hop transmission of probe and MOACKs.

The verifier then extracts and verifies the traffic reports contained in the MOACKs, using the MAC keys shared with each AS. If MAC verification fails for $\mathcal{O}_{j,k}$ the verifier identifies either AS_j or AS_k as malicious. After MAC verification, the verifier extracts and compares the packet counts $\{C_{j,k}\}$s from the corresponding traffic reports $\{\mathcal{R}_{j,k}\}$s. A drop in packet count at any link indicates a fault at that link. VeriFLo does not distinguish malicious packet drops from unintentional network faults such as buffer overflows. However, statistical methods, such as threshold comparisons can be employed to differentiate between the two [18,22,24]. The pseudocode and further details for MOACK verification is given in Algorithm 5 in the Appendix.

5 Security Analysis

5.1 Mark and Path Forgery

Packet marking ensures that an adversary cannot consistently forge valid marks for a false path. Mark validation on a single packet does not guarantee the legitimacy of the indicated path since marks can be *guessed* with a probability of 2^{-n}, where n is the output length of the PRF. Therefore, for small n, the verifier must set a threshold of packets with valid marks for accepting a path as a valid path. In particular, we let t be the minimum number of valid packet marks out of N required for the verifier to accept a path. The following Lemma establishes the adversary's probability of successfully forging t out of N packet marks on a path.

Lemma 1 (Path Unforgeability). *Let $\mathcal{P}$ be a legitimate traffic path, and let $\mathcal{H}(\mathcal{P}) \subseteq \mathcal{P}$ denote the ordered subsequence of all honest ASes along $\mathcal{P}$. Denote by $\mathbf{H}$ the set of all such subsequences $\mathcal{H}(\mathcal{P})$ for legitimate paths $\mathcal{P}$.*

Suppose an adversary $\mathcal{A}$ forges a new path $\mathcal{P}'$ for N distinct packets, where $\mathcal{H}(\mathcal{P}') \notin \mathbf{H}$. I.e., the subsequence differs from every legitimate path in at least one honest AS or its order.

If the verifier's acceptance of a path as legitimate requires a fixed threshold of t/N packets to contain valid marks, then for all PPT adversaries $\mathcal{A}$ and for each such $\mathcal{P}'$, there exists a negligible function $\mathbf{negl}$ and a constant $c > 0$, such that,

$$\Pr[\mathcal{A} \text{ gets } \mathcal{P}' \text{ accepted}] \leq \mathbf{negl}(\lambda) + \exp(-cN) \tag{5}$$

where λ is the security parameter for the underlying MAC function used as PRF.

Lemma 1 bounds the adversary's probability of success, defined as causing at least t distinct packets out of N to pass mark verification for a forged path $\mathcal{P}'$ where $\mathcal{H}(\mathcal{P}') \notin \mathbf{H}$. Thus the adversary's best strategy would be random guessing of each n-bit mark, which succeeds with a probability negligibly higher than 2^{-n}. Given a fixed n and acceptance ratio t/N, the proof below quantifies the adversary's success probability as an exponentially decaying function of N. This is in line with our DDoS setting and Definition 1, as the adversary needs many packets with valid marks to deceive the verifier into accepting a false path.

Proof. The proof follows the structure of first analyzing the security of the marking scheme using a truly random function. Then, we show that if there exists a PPT adversary $\mathcal{A}$ for which the inequality in Lemma 1 does not hold, then $\mathcal{A}$ distinguishes PRF from a truly random function that outputs bit-strings of the same length.

Recall from Sect. 4.1 that AS marks are generated by computing the PRF:

$$\mathcal{M}_i \leftarrow \text{PRF}_{K_i}\big(\kappa(\sigma, \tau), \sigma, \tau, \mathcal{P}_i, (\mathcal{M}_0 \| \mathcal{M}_1 \| \cdots \| \mathcal{M}_{i-1})\big).$$

Algorithm 3 follows the same mark generation function using the key shared between the verifier and AS i. We denote this marking scheme with Π.

Since the mark verification of Π sets the corresponding entry in isValid to True if the recomputed mark matches the packet's claimed mark, any forged packet must contain only correct marks for all ASes in the claimed path to pass verification. We consider a mark forgery experiment Mark-forge$_{\mathcal{A},\Pi}(n)$ where $\mathcal{A}$ wins if it correctly forges marks for a new path $\mathcal{P}'$ which differs in at least one honest AS from $\mathbf{H}$. If the forged path $\mathcal{P}'$ differs in more than one honest AS, $\mathcal{A}$ will have to *guess* all such AS marks, further decreasing the success probability. Successful path forgery requires $\mathcal{A}$ to win at least t many times in N such independent Mark-forge$_{\mathcal{A},\Pi}(n)$ experiments. We denote the probability of this event with $\varepsilon(\cdot)$ on the security parameter n and the tuple (N, t):

$$\Pr[\text{Path-forge}_{\mathcal{A},\Pi}(n; (N, t)) = 1] = \varepsilon(n; (N, t)). \tag{6}$$

Consider a marking scheme $\tilde{\Pi}$ which is the same as Π, except that a truly random function $f_n : \{0,1\}^* \to \{0,1\}^n$ that maps any finite-length strings to uniformly random n-bit strings is used instead of the PRF. Then,

$$\Pr[\text{Mark-forge}_{\mathcal{A},\tilde{\Pi}}(n) = 1] \leq 2^{-n} \tag{7}$$

because for any $\mathcal{P}'$ where $\mathcal{H}(\mathcal{P}') \notin \mathbf{H}$, $f_n(\kappa(\sigma,\tau),\sigma,\tau,\mathcal{P}',(\mathcal{M}_0\|\mathcal{M}_1\|\cdots))$ is uniformly distributed in $\{0,1\}^n$ from the viewpoint of $\mathcal{A}$. Successful path forgery in $\tilde{\Pi}$ requires $\mathcal{A}$ to win at least t times in N independent Bernoulli trials, which leads to the tail distribution $\Pr[X \geq t]$ where $X \sim \text{Binomial}(N, 2^{-n})$:

$$\Pr[\text{Path-forge}_{\mathcal{A},\tilde{\Pi}}(n; (N,t)) = 1] \leq \Pr[X \geq t]. \tag{8}$$

By the Chernoff-Hoeffding Theorem, Binomial tail $\Pr[X \geq t]$ is bounded by,

$$\Pr[\text{Path-forge}_{\mathcal{A},\tilde{\Pi}}(n; (N,t)) = 1] \leq \exp\left(-N\,\mathrm{D}\left(\tfrac{t}{N} \,\|\, 2^{-n}\right)\right), \tag{9}$$

where $\mathrm{D}(a\|b)$ is the Kullback–Leibler divergence between Bernoulli random variables with parameter a, b, and is given by

$$\mathrm{D}(a\|b) = a\ln\left(\tfrac{a}{b}\right) + (1-a)\ln\left(\tfrac{1-a}{1-b}\right).$$

If $t \geq N\,2^{-n}$, the bound in (9) is tighter with $\mathrm{D}(a\|b) \geq \frac{(a-b)^2}{2a}$. By the security assumption of PRFs, it follows that

$$\left|\Pr[\text{Path-forge}_{\mathcal{A},\Pi}(n;(N,t)) = 1] - \Pr[\text{Path-forge}_{\mathcal{A},\tilde{\Pi}}(n;(N,t)) = 1]\right| \leq \mathtt{negl}(\lambda). \tag{10}$$

Substituting (6) and (9) into (10) concludes the proof,

$$\left|\varepsilon(n;(N,t)) - \exp\left(-N\,\mathrm{D}\left(\tfrac{t}{N} \,\|\, 2^{-n}\right)\right)\right| \leq \mathtt{negl}(\lambda), \tag{11}$$

$$\varepsilon(n;(N,t)) \leq \mathtt{negl}(\lambda) + \exp\left(-N\,\mathrm{D}\left(\tfrac{t}{N} \,\|\, 2^{-n}\right)\right). \tag{12}$$

If a PRF with sufficient bit security is used, e.g., $n = 128$, a single packet with valid marks would be sufficient for verifier to accept a path as valid ($t = 1$), because the probability of a PPT adversary correctly *guessing* a PRF output would be negligibly higher than 2^{-n} by the security assumption of PRFs.

5.2 Fault Localization

Next, we show that either link of a malicious AS that drops a certain fraction of packets on a path is identified with high enough probability.

Lemma 2 (Fault Localization). *Let $\mathcal{P}$ be a traffic path carrying N packets over an epoch. An AS controlled by adversary $\mathcal{A}$ drops at least δN out of these N packets for $1 \geq \delta > 0$. Then, the probability that both links of malicious AS remain unidentified is a negligible function of δN.*

Proof Sketch. Recall from Sect. 4.3 that each AS maintains the count of packets forwarded towards next-hop ASes (e.g., $\mathcal{C}_{j,k}$ from AS_j to AS_k), and upon receiving the probe, sends this count towards the verifier via MOACK $\mathcal{O}_{j,k} = (\mathcal{R}_{j,k}, \mathcal{O}_{i,j}, \text{MAC}_{K_j}(\mathcal{R}_{j,k} \| \mathcal{O}_{i,j}))$ which encapsulates the previous MOACK $\mathcal{O}_{i,j}$, or MOACKs if the malicious AS is at a traffic convergence point. The malicious AS can either (i) drop the probe, (ii) drop the MOACK(s) from previous hop AS(s), (iii) modify MOACK(s) from previous-hop ASes, (iv) forge any MOACK (v) correctly follow the MOACK protocol, (vi) generate own MOACK but with false packet counts.

First, we show that actions (i) to (v) can be localized by the verifier. If the malicious AS AS_j drops either the probe (as in (i)) or MOACK(s) (as in (ii)), then the reporting starts from AS_j, allowing the victim to identify the malicious link as the one between AS_i and AS_j. Action in (iii) causes all the MOACKs from any modified MOACK to the malicious AS's MOACK to fail verification due to chaining of MOACKs, and given the unforgeability assumption of MAC function used in MOACK generation. This means the verifier identifies the malicious link as the first one that fails MOACK verification in reverse order of traffic, which would be the link between AS_i and AS_j. Action (iv) is also localized in the same manner because of the unforgeability assumption of the MAC function used in MOACK. It is straightforward to see that any combination of these actions also result in the identification of the malicious link pointing to the malicious AS. For instance if (iv) is combined with any of (i) to (iii), the verification of $\mathcal{O}_{j,k}$ will fail, localizing the malicious link as between AS_j and AS_k. Finally, if the AS correctly reports the counts and follows the MOACK traffic reporting protocol as in (v), then the link of packet drops is readily identified due to the drop in the packet count from AS_i to AS_j. This leaves us with only action where the malicious AS (vi) generates a valid own MOACK but with false packet counts.

If mark forgery probability is negligible (i.e., large n) the adversary cannot forge new packets and their marks to replace the dropped packets. Hence, if AS_j dropped any fraction $\delta > 0$ of packets, there has to be a drop in packet count from reports of AS_i to AS_j and/or AS_j to AS_k, thereby, identifying either link or both links of the malicious AS.

If mark forgery probability is non-negligible with 2^{-n}, the adversary may try to replace the dropped packets with forged packets (and marks) to conceal the packet drops or shift the mismatch in reported counts to another link. Concretely, malicious AS_j can attempt to forge n-bit marks on behalf of its previous-hop AS (or multiple previous-hop ASes albeit with a lower success probability) for the δN dropped packets so that the verifier observes no discrepancy in packet counts. The best strategy for malicious AS_j would be to forge δN marks for the previous-hop AS_i to replace the dropped packets. If AS_j can correctly guess all such δN marks, the verifier would observe (mostly) invalid marks up to AS_i, and valid marks from AS_i onwards, failing to pinpoint the malicious link. The probability of correctly guessing δN marks is negligibly higher than $2^{-n\delta N}$ (which is a negligible function of δN) by the security assumption of PRF.

6 Evaluation

Our implementation runs VeriFLo AS and verifier nodes as user-space processes on a 64-bit Windows desktop PC equipped with AMD Ryzen 7 7700X and 32 GB DDR5 RAM. We used C++ compiled with MSVC in 64-bit release mode, along with OpenSSL 3.4.0 for cryptographic primitives.

6.1 Computation Overhead

We abstracted the network-related processes by preloading packet contents and keys into local variables and recorded the CPU times for packet marking (Algorithms 1 and 2), and mark verification (Algorithm 3). We tested three PRF implementations, namely, HMAC (with SHA-1 and SHA-2) [7], AES-128-CMAC [23], and SipHash [4]. We used 128-bit symmetric keys for HMAC-SHA-1, AES-CMAC, and SipHash, and 256-bit symmetric keys for HMAC-SHA-2. Each reported data point is the average of 100,000 trials. We have not used parallelism, multi-threading, or operation-specific instruction sets. The PRF computations can be easily performed 10–100 times faster, for instance, via parallel execution of PRFs for different packets, using MACs such as UMAC that support multi-threading, hardware instruction sets, or ASIC/FPGA implementations [21].

Average processing times for VeriFLo's packet marking are shown in Fig. 4, and for mark verification in Fig. 5. Packet marking at an AS consists of a PRF call over the concatenated header fields, truncation of PRF output to mark length, and VeriFLo header assembly. Using SipHash as the keyed PRF yields the lowest packet marking time. Although HMAC with SHA256 as the hash function would provide better security for unforgeability and collision resistance purposes, for our purposes of path unforgeability (Lemma 1) SipHash with 128-bit output provides the necessary pseudorandomness property. Thus we use SipHash as the keyed PRF for the rest of our evaluation.

Packet marking and verification throughputs using a single CPU core are shown in Fig. 6. Packet marking throughput achieves several Gbps for packets over 500 bytes in size. Marking throughput decays very slightly over path length due to increasing VeriFLo header size for longer paths. For packets larger than 1000 bytes and an AS-level path length of less than 8, the verification achieves a throughput exceeding 1 Gbps on a single core.

Since probing and traffic reporting in VeriFLo is performed once per epoch, it does not meaningfully affect the throughput. For traffic reporting, each on-path AS performs a MAC computation per next-hop AS (line 16 in Algorithm 4), hence generating a MOACK. Unlike the truncated MACs used in packet marking, the MAC used in MOACKs must be unforgeable, such as HMAC with SHA256. Each MOACK generation with HMAC takes ~ 1 microsecond and is performed once for the entire epoch, therefore the performance impact is negligible. Likewise, the MOACK verification requires a MAC verification operation of ~ 1 microsecond for each on-path AS (line 15 in Algorithm 5).

6.2 Communication and Storage Overhead

VeriFLo header requires an AS ID and n-bit mark per AS in addition to a timestamp and sequence number set by the first AS. Using 16-bit AS numbers (ASNs), a 32-bit epoch, and a 16-bit sequence number, the header size of VeriFLo is $48 + l \times (n+16)$ bits, where l is the AS-level path length. With a small n, the largest contributor to the communication overhead is the ASN. It may be possible to compress ASNs by assigning a shorter VeriFLo specific ID for participating ASes, e.g., by excluding private ASes not responsible for interdomain routing. Control plane communication overhead is two packets (probe and MOACK) per epoch per flow which is negligibly small compared to the data plane overhead.

An AS can derive the PRF and MAC keys each of size 16 bytes from the long term secret on the fly. In case the AS wishes to preset the dynamic key for PRF, it stores 16 bytes per three tuple of (source, destination, next-hop AS). Additionally each router stores the packet count in an epoch for every three tuple. 4 bytes of a counter size would allow counting billions of packets per epoch per tuple, resulting in a storage overhead of 20 bytes per tuple.

6.3 Comparison with Path-Aware Fault Localization Schemes

Table 1 provides a rough quantitative comparison of overheads among fault localization schemes. VeriFLo exhibits comparable performance, but differs from existing fault localization schemes in that it does not rely on a path-aware network architecture. In contrast, others listed in Table 1 require path-awarene network, such as SCION-like [16] AS path selected by source in ShortMAC [30] and Faultprints [5], or source-driven control of routers in D3 [9]. This makes VeriFLo applicable to BGP-based Internet where path-control by source is uncommon.

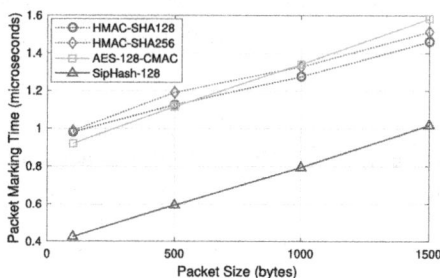

Fig. 4. AS latency in microseconds against packet size in bytes.

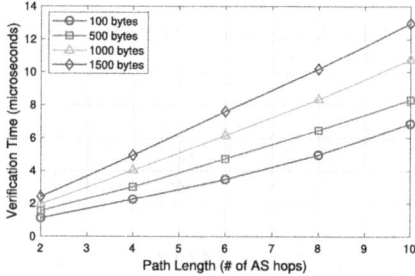

Fig. 5. Verifier latency in microseconds against AS-level path length.

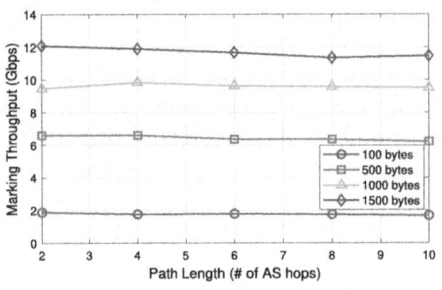 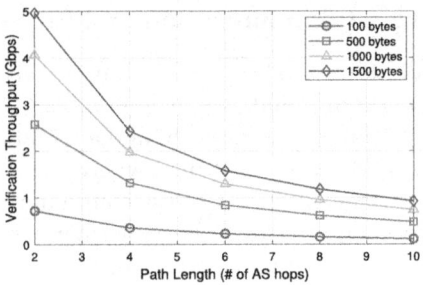

Fig. 6. Marking throughput (left) and verification throughput (right) on a single CPU core in Gbps versus AS-level path length for various payload sizes.

Table 1. Performance comparison among fault-localization schemes. l: # of AS hops, n: PRF/MAC length, pp: per packet, B: bytes.

Scheme	MAC (pp)	Data-plane overhead (B/pp)	Control packet (per epoch)	Storage overhead per AS	Path-awareness required
ShortMAC [30]	1	$l \times n \div 8$	2	21 B × # of flows	yes
Faultprints [5]	2	$8 \times l + 56$	many	468 MB for 100 Gbps link	yes
D3 [9]	1	20	l	5.3 B × # of flows	yes
VeriFLo	1	$l \times (n \div 8 + 2) + 6$	2	20 B × # of flows	no

7 Conclusion

VeriFLo is the first fault localization scheme for a host to verify traffic provenance and localize faults in a non-path-aware network. Our security analysis and evaluation results show that VeriFLo scales to multi-Gbps throughput on a single CPU core, adds minimal communication and manageable storage overhead. Potential optimizations may include probabilistic packet sampling to reduce overheads and implementation of VeriFLo on specialized hardware to achieve terabits per second throughputs. VeriFLo offers a practical solution for DDoS resilient inter-domain routing.

Acknowledgments. This research is supported by the National Research Foundation, Prime Minister's Office, Singapore, under its Campus for Research Excellence and Technological Enterprise (CREATE) Programme.

Appendix – MOACK Algorithms

The ASes run Algorithm 4 to generate a MOACK, and the verifier runs Algorithm 5 to verify a MOACK and traffic reports contained in it.

An AS initiates Algorithm 4 upon receiving (and forwarding unless it is the source AS) a probe. If the AS sits on a traffic convergence point, such as AS_4 in Fig. 3, it forwards the probe to all converging paths while starting a timer set to the maximum round-trip time from the farthest probe destination to itself. The AS then commits its report into a single MOACK combining all received

MOACKs before the timer expires via the for loop starting on line 9. If the AS is located at a traffic divergence point, such as AS_2 in Fig. 3, it generates multiple MOACKs via the loop starting on line 15. Each MOACK commits the counts of packets forwarded to a different next-hop AS.

As the accidental loss of either the probe or MOACK packets will prevent the verifier from obtaining the packet counts, hop-by-hop reliable transmission, e.g., via per-hop acknowledgment or negative acknowledgments, is needed for both probe and MOACKs. Thus, any inaction on the part of an AS upon receiving a probe or MOACK, or intentional dropping or modification of either immediately points to the malicious link. For example, if AS_3 in Fig. 3 drops the probe, AS_0, AS_1, and AS_2, will not be prompted to send MOACKs over this path. Alternatively, AS_3 may forward the probe, but drop the MOACK $\mathcal{O}_{2,3}$ by AS_2. In both cases, if AS_3 initiates the MOACK the verifier will identify either AS_2 or AS_3 as malicious, and if AS_3 does not initiate the MOACK, AS_4 will do so, and the verifier will identify either AS_3 or AS_4 as malicious.

Algorithm 4. GenerateMOACK

Input: Set of paths in probe P, probe epoch τ, Current AS ID: AS_j, Timer T_{max}
Output: List of Multi-bulb Onion ACKs: $\mathcal{O}_{j,k}$ for each next-hop AS AS_k

1: **Initialize:** $\mathcal{O} \leftarrow \emptyset$
2: $K_j \leftarrow$ GetKey(AS_j)
3: StartTimer(T_{max})
4: **for** $AS_k \in$ P.$nextHopAS$ **do**
5:     Retrieve packet count $C_{j,k}$
6:     $\mathcal{R}_{j,k} \leftarrow (\tau, P, AS_j, AS_k, C_{j,k})$
7: **end for**
8: **while** TimerNotExpired() $\land$ pendingMOACKS $\neq \emptyset$ **do**
9:     **for** $AS_i \in$ P.$prevHopAS$ **do**
10:        **if** ReceivedOnionACK(AS_i) **then**
11:            $\mathcal{O} \leftarrow \mathcal{O} \|$ GetOnionACK(AS_i)
12:        **end if**
13:    **end for**
14: **end while**
15: **for** $AS_k \in$ P.$nextHopAS$ **do**
16:    $\mathcal{O}_{j,k} \leftarrow (\mathcal{R}_{j,k}, \mathcal{O}, \text{MAC}_{K_j}(\mathcal{R}_{j,k} \| \mathcal{O}))$
17:    SendMOACK($AS_k, \mathcal{O}_{j,k}$)
18: **end for**

In Algorithm 5 the network topology is represented as a directed acyclic graph (DAG) in the direction of reverse traffic starting from the verifier. The verifier AS builds the DAG based on the probed paths before the algorithm is run. The DAG $\mathcal{G} = (N, E)$ has the set of probed ASes as its nodes, and links between those ASes as its edges. The algorithm uses Breadth-First Search starting from AS_V and traverses the ASes in reverse traffic direction. For each edge $v \rightarrow u$, the verifier AS extracts from the MOACK the local report $\mathcal{R}_{u,v}$, the aggregated upstream MOACKs $\mathcal{O}$ (i.e., the onion bulbs), and the corresponding MAC tag $\text{MAC}_{u,v}$ on line 14, then verifies the MAC using shared key K_u on line 15. If MAC verification fails, the link $u \rightarrow v$ is immediately returned. If Breadth-First Search completes without any MAC verification failures, the algorithm calls CheckPacketCounts on line 27. This method extracts and analyzes packet counts from reports ($\{\mathcal{R}_{u,v}\}$'s) for each DAG edge to identify faults. Finally, either these suspected links or VALID is returned.

Algorithm 5. VerifyMOACK

Input: DAG: $\mathcal{G} = (N, E)$, with nodes: $N =$ set of probed ASes, edges: $E =$ reverse links ($v \to u$), verifier AS ID where DAG traversal begins: $AS_V \in N$
Output: Either VALID or suspected link(s): ($u \to v$)
 — Step 1: Initialization
1: for all $AS_j \in N$ do
2: $\quad K_j \leftarrow \text{GetKey}(AS_j)$
3: end for
4: queue $\leftarrow [AS_V]$
5: verifiedEdge $\leftarrow \emptyset$
6: visitedNodes $\leftarrow \{\}$
 — Step 2: Verify MACs using Breadth First Search
7: while queue is not empty do
8: $\quad v \leftarrow$ queue.dequeue()
9: $\quad$ if $v \notin$ visitedNodes then
10: $\quad\quad$ visitedNodes $\leftarrow$ visitedNodes $\cup \{v\}$
11: $\quad$ end if
12: $\quad$ for all $(v \to u) \in E$ do $\quad\quad\quad\quad\quad\quad\quad\quad\quad\quad\quad\quad$ ▷ in reverse traffic direction
13: $\quad\quad$ if $(v \to u) \notin$ verifiedEdge then
14: $\quad\quad\quad (\mathcal{R}_{u,v}, \mathcal{O}, \text{MAC}_{u,v}) \leftarrow \mathcal{G}.\text{edgeData}(v \to u)$
15: $\quad\quad\quad$ if not VerifyMAC$_{K_u}$(MAC$_{u,v}$, $\mathcal{O}$, $\mathcal{R}_{u,v}$) then
16: $\quad\quad\quad\quad$ return ($u \to v$) $\quad\quad$ ▷ immediately identify faulty link if MAC verification fails
17: $\quad\quad\quad$ end if
18: $\quad\quad\quad$ verifiedEdge $\leftarrow$ verifiedEdge $\cup \{(v \to u)\}$
19: $\quad\quad\quad$ StoreMOACK($u, v, \mathcal{O}$)
20: $\quad\quad\quad$ StoreTrafficReport($\mathcal{R}_{u,v}$)
21: $\quad\quad$ end if
22: $\quad\quad$ if $u \notin$ visitedNodes then
23: $\quad\quad\quad$ queue.enqueue(u)
24: $\quad\quad$ end if
25: $\quad$ end for
26: end while
 — Step 3: Verify traffic reports
27: suspectLink $\leftarrow$ CheckPacketCounts($\mathcal{G}$) $\quad\quad\quad\quad\quad$ ▷ Compare packet counts in $\{\mathcal{R}_{u,v}\}$s
28: return suspectLink or VALID

References

1. Argyraki, K., Maniatis, P., Irzak, O., Ashish, S., Shenker, S.: Loss and delay accountability for the Internet. In: IEEE International Conference on Network Protocols, pp. 194–205. IEEE (2007)
2. Argyraki, K., Maniatis, P., Singla, A.: Verifiable network-performance measurements. In: Proceedings of the 6th International Conference, pp. 1–12 (2010)
3. Argyraki, K.J., Cheriton, D.R.: Active Internet traffic filtering: real-time response to denial-of-service attacks. In: USENIX Annual Technical Conference, General Track, vol. 38 (2005)
4. Aumasson, J.P., Bernstein, D.J.: SipHash: a fast short-input PRF. In: International Conference on Cryptology in India, pp. 489–508. Springer (2012)
5. Basescu, C., Lin, Y.H., Zhang, H., Perrig, A.: High-speed inter-domain fault localization. In: IEEE Symposium on Security and Privacy (SP), pp. 859–877. IEEE (2016)

6. Center for applied internet data analysis (CAIDA): all active monitors - archipelago measurement infrastructure. https://www.caida.org/projects/ark/statistics/all_monitors/#H2690, Accessed 20 Apr 2025
7. Eastlake 3rd, D., Hansen, T.: RFC 4634: US secure hash algorithms (SHA and HMAC-SHA) (2006)
8. Esiner, E., Tefek, U., Mashima, D., Chen, B., Kalbarczyk, Z., Nicol, D.M.: Message authentication and provenance verification for industrial control systems. ACM Trans. Cyber-Phys. Syst. **7**(4), 1–28 (2023)
9. Fu, S., et al.: Secure fault localization in path-aware networking. IEEE Trans. Dependable Secure Comput. (2024)
10. Gong, D., et al.: Practical verifiable in-network filtering for DDoS defense. In: IEEE 39th International Conference on Distributed Computing Systems (ICDCS), pp. 1161–1174. IEEE (2019)
11. Kim, T.H.J., Basescu, C., Jia, L., Lee, S.B., Hu, Y.C., Perrig, A.: Lightweight source authentication and path validation. In: Proceedings of the ACM Conference on SIGCOMM, pp. 271–282 (2014)
12. Legner, M., Klenze, T., Wyss, M., Sprenger, C., Perrig, A.: $\{EPIC\}$: every packet is checked in the data plane of a $\{Path-Aware\}$ Internet. In: 29th USENIX Security Symposium (USENIX Security), pp. 541–558 (2020)
13. Liu, X., Li, A., Yang, X., Wetherall, D.: Passport: secure and adoptable source authentication. In: Nsdi, vol. 8, pp. 365–378 (2008)
14. Mizrak, A.T., Cheng, Y.C., Marzullo, K., Savage, S.: Fatih: detecting and isolating malicious routers. In: International Conference on Dependable Systems and Networks (DSN'05), pp. 538–547. IEEE (2005)
15. Morillo, R., Furuness, J., Morris, C., Breslin, J., Herzberg, A., Wang, B.: ROV++: improved deployable defense against BGP hijacking. In: Network and Distributed System Security (NDSS) Symposium (2021)
16. Perrig, A., Szalachowski, P., Reischuk, R.M., Chuat, L.: SCION: a secure Internet architecture. Springer (2017)
17. Reuter, A., Bush, R., Cunha, I., Katz-Bassett, E., Schmidt, T.C., Wählisch, M.: Towards a rigorous methodology for measuring adoption of RPKI route validation and filtering. ACM SIGCOMM Comput. Commun. Rev. **48**(1), 19–27 (2018)
18. Rmayti, M., Khatoun, R., Begriche, Y., Khoukhi, L., Gaiti, D.: A stochastic approach for packet-dropping attacks detection in mobile ad hoc networks. Comput. Netw. **121**, 53–64 (2017)
19. Rodday, N.M.: Improving Internet routing security: from origin validation to path validation (2024)
20. Savage, S., Wetherall, D., Karlin, A., Anderson, T.: Practical network support for IP traceback. In: Proceedings of the Conference on Applications, Technologies, Architectures, and Protocols for Computer Communication, pp. 295–306 (2000)
21. Shahbazi, K., Ko, S.B.: High-throughput and area-efficient FPGA implementation of AES for high-traffic applications. IET Comput. Digit. Tech. **14**(6), 344–352 (2020)
22. Shu, T., Krunz, M.: Privacy-preserving and truthful detection of packet-dropping attacks in wireless ad hoc networks. IEEE Trans. Mob. Comput. **14**(4), 813–828 (2014)
23. Song, J., Poovendran, R., Lee, J., Iwata, T.: The AES-CMAC algorithm. Technical Report (2006)
24. Sultana, S., Bertino, E., Shehab, M.: A provenance-based mechanism to identify malicious packet-dropping adversaries in sensor networks. In: 31st International

Conference on Distributed Computing Systems Workshops, pp. 332–338 (2011). https://doi.org/10.1109/ICDCSW.2011.54
25. Sussman, W., et al.: The case for an Internet primitive for fault localization. In: Proceedings of the 21st ACM Workshop on Hot Topics in Networks, pp. 160–166 (2022)
26. Wu, B., et al.: RFL: robust fault localization on unreliable communication channels. Comput. Netw. **158**, 158–174 (2019)
27. Wu, B., et al.: Enabling efficient source and path verification via probabilistic packet marking. In: IEEE/ACM 26th International Symposium on Quality of Service (IWQoS), pp. 1–10. IEEE (2018)
28. Zhang, X., Jain, A., Perrig, A.: Packet-dropping adversary identification for data plane security. In: Proceedings of the 2008 ACM CoNEXT Conference, pp. 1–12 (2008)
29. Zhang, X., Lan, C., Perrig, A.: Secure and scalable fault localization under dynamic traffic patterns. In: 2012 IEEE Symposium on Security and Privacy, pp. 317–331. IEEE (2012)
30. Zhang, X., et al.: ShortMAC: efficient data-plane fault localization. In: Network and Distributed System Security (NDSS) Symposium (2012)

The Polymorphism Maze: Understanding Diversities and Similarities in Malware Families

Antonino Vitale[1]([✉]), Simone Aonzo[1], Savino Dambra[2], Nanda Rani[3], Lorenzo Ippolito[1,5], Platon Kotzias[4], Juan Caballero[5], and Davide Balzarotti[1]

[1] EURECOM, Biot, France
{Antonino.Vitale,Simone.Aonzo,Davide.Balzarotti}@eurecom.fr
[2] GenDigital, Paris, France
savino.dambra@gendigital.com
[3] Indian Institute of Technology Kanpur, Kanpur, India
nandarani@cse.iitk.ac.in
[4] BforeAI, New York, USA
platon@bfore.ai
[5] IMDEA Software Institute, Madrid, Spain
juan.caballero@imdea.org

Abstract. In this work, we explore the complexities introduced by polymorphism in malware families, a tactic used by malware authors to alter the appearance of their code and evade detection mechanisms, resulting in a growing volume of unique malware samples. We examine 66,160 malicious Portable Executable (PE) files grouped into 743 families from three popular malware datasets. Our research addresses three key questions: measuring structural component-level differences between PE files, identifying prevalent polymorphic techniques affecting multiple components, and pinpointing component-level causes of polymorphism.

We introduce a methodology for component-level structural comparison of PE files and apply it to investigate the diversity and similarity of samples within a family, considering factors such as packing and truncation.

Our study reveals that polymorphism in malware is driven by multiple overlapping factors, extending beyond just the use of packing tools. These findings highlight the complex nature of malware families and inform future research, improving our understanding of malware variations and their implications.

Keywords: Malware Polymorphism · Static Analysis · Malware Similarity

1 Introduction

What is a *malware family*? Despite decades of research and thousands of papers on malware, the scientific community lacks a precise definition. One possible definition is that a malware family consists of different malicious samples (i.e., different by file hash) derived from the same code base, analogous to how a *program* is defined in the benign case. Samples within a family are expected to share common characteristics, behaviors, and attribution to the same authors [1].

However, malware authors often adopt a wealth of techniques to introduce *polymorphism* (e.g., by re-packing samples) so that the same malware family version produces a large number of *variants* that are derived from the same source code but differ in their representation, i.e., have a different file hash. Polymorphism can also be introduced in other ways. For example, file infectors inject their code into other benign executables. Because of this, polymorphism is often cited as the main reason behind the large number of new malware samples routinely collected and analyzed by the security industry [16].

In summary, many reasons can be behind the differences (namely, polymorphism) between samples within the same family. What is more important is that these differences are not just a curiosity, but they also impose severe consequences for the analysis, detection, and classification of malware. For instance, we expect AntiVirus (AV) signatures to capture not a single sample but an entire family (or a part of it). Similarly, we expect ML models trained to recognize a given family to succeed when tested on new samples that belong to the same family. But this ability to generalize largely depends on **why** samples differ in the first place. Small differences in the PE header do not have the same impact as re-packing the code with a different protector.

This paper aims to provide the first comprehensive exploration of the reasons behind the polymorphism in the samples belonging to the same malware family. For this, we leverage three malware family datasets (the recently-proposed dataset by Dambra et al. [15], the MOTIF dataset [3], and the Malicia dataset [33]), building a superset composed of 66,160 samples split into 743 families. Our analysis involves a static examination of malware samples to understand the syntactic variations within samples belonging to the same malware family. Static analysis is preferred for examining such syntactic characteristics, whereas dynamic analysis is necessary for assessing behaviors. However, in our dataset, the behavioral similarities among the samples are already captured by the family labels assigned to the samples. More specifically, our work is organized to answer the following three Research Questions:

RQ1: *How can we measure the structural differences among multiple samples from the same family?* At first, in Sect. 3, we break down the PE file format in a number of disjoint *components*, that fully cover the whole PE file format structure and content. Then, given two executables, we design a structural comparison approach to precisely locate their differences and similarities at the component level. We implement our approach in an open-source tool we named *PEdiff* [4].

RQ2: *What are the polymorphic techniques that affect multiple components, and what is their prevalence?* In Sect. 4, we examine two main reasons for cross-component differences: file truncation and packing. *Truncation* occurs when the expected size of a sample is larger than the real size of the file on disk. Truncation occurs due to errors during sample collection (e.g. samples extracted from network traffic where packets were missing). *Packing* is a technique that compresses or encrypts code on disk and then recovers it at runtime. We measure packing in two ways: by using state-of-the-art signature-based tools to reliably detect known off-the-shelf packers and by implementing a machine learning (ML) classifier proposed by Aghakhani et al. [6] to also identify custom packers.

RQ3: *What are the many reasons of polymorphism at the component granularity?* In Sect. 5, we examine polymorphism in one or multiple components. Our results show that two-thirds of the families have no common components among their samples, meaning that all the PE components are at least slightly different. On the other hand, for 12.8% of the families, we were able to pinpoint the single reason behind the polymorphic variants.

In summary, we first developed a novel methodology for the structural comparison of PE files. Then, we highlighted the importance of two common elements (packing, truncation) which are crucial for the construction of malware datasets. We advocate for the community to conscientiously consider the elements they wish to exclude or include in their studies, given the potential bias these decisions may introduce. Lastly, we conducted a comprehensive measurement of polymorphism across 743 malware families. This analysis provides valuable insights for future research, enabling a targeted focus on the most prevalent trends and the timely development of appropriate solutions.

Finally, the scientific significance of this work is particularly relevant in the context of the design and evaluation of robust ML classifiers: we believe that their (in)ability to generalize to different samples needs to be always corroborated by an analysis of the variability of samples within the families in the dataset.

2 Dataset

We use three datasets of malware samples, each consisting of Windows PE executables labeled with the family to which the sample belongs.

Dambra et al. [15]. We use their balanced dataset which contains 67,000 hashes of 32-bit PE files that appeared in the VirusTotal (VT) feed between August 2021 and March 2022. The samples are equally divided among 670 malware families, i.e., 100 samples per family. The family labels were obtained by processing the VT reports using AVClass [42]. We download the hashes and family labels from their repository [2] and then download the samples and their reports from VT.

MOTIF [25]. This dataset contains 3,095 PE malware samples from 454 families. Samples and family labels come from threat reports published by 14 major cybersecurity organizations between January 2016 and December 2020. We obtained the list of sample hashes and family names from the MOTIF repository [3] and then downloaded the samples from VT. MOTIF is largely imbalanced. Of the 454 families, 131 (29%) have only one sample, while only 91 (20%) have at least 10 samples.

Malicia [33]. The Malicia dataset contains 9,908 Windows PE malware samples collected from drive-by downloads between March 2012 and February 2013 [33].

Table 1. Components of a PE executable and their type. The dagger † indicates an optional component.

Type	Components
Metadata	DOS Header, DOS Stub, Rich Header †, COFF Header, Optional Header, Data Directories †, Section Table
Sections	Entry Point Section, Resource Section †, Other Sections †
Extra	Certificate Table †, Overlay †

Labels for the samples were generated by clustering the samples using network features and screenshots obtained during the sample's execution, and the embedded icon. We obtained the samples and family labels from the dataset authors. Malicia is also largely imbalanced with 23 (43%) families having only one sample, while only 13 (25%) have at least 10 samples.

Final Dataset. We start with the Dambra et al. dataset and add families from MOTIF and Malicia with at least 10 samples, which we consider the minimum to analyze differences within a family. We exclude families already present in the balanced dataset. For families with over 100 samples we randomly selected 100 samples. This procedure outputs 68,683 samples split into 746 families.

As we elaborate in Sect. 4.1, we identified truncated samples in the datasets. We removed the truncated samples and also families with less than 10 non-truncated samples. In the end, the final dataset used in this study comprises of **66,160** samples distributed in **743** families.

3 Structural Comparison

While samples in a family differ in file hash, they may exhibit similarities, while their differences may be concentrated on specific parts. To examine similarities and differences within a malware family, we have designed a methodology for structural comparison of executables. It first divides each executable into 12 disjoint *components*, described in Sect. 3.1, that fully represent the PE executable format [30]. Next, it performs pairwise comparisons of all executables in a family at the component level, categorizing components as unchanged, similar, or different, as detailed in Sect. 3.2 We have implemented our methodology into *PEdiff* [4], an open-source tool comprising 1K lines of Python code.

3.1 PE Components

We split each executable into 12 disjoint (i.e., non-overlapping) components that capture its structure, depicted in Table 1. We grouped them into three parts: the *Metadata* contains the first seven components, which do not carry the actual content of the executable but define its structure and properties, the *Sections* which contain the code and data of the executable, and the *Extra*, which consists of components that are appended at the end of the file. Of the 12 components, six are optional and may not exist.

Within the Metadata, the *DOS Header* and *DOS Stub* correspond to the legacy MS-DOS information that is still present for compatibility. The *COFF header* and *Optional Header* capture the homonymous PE headers. The *Rich Header* is an undocumented component containing information about the tool versions used to build the different object files in the executable [50]. The *Data Directories* is an array of 16 entries, where each entry contains the start offset and size of a data directory, including the export, import, resource, and certificate tables. The *Section Table* is an array that defines the name, start offset and the size of the sections that form the main body of the executable.

We identify three Sections components: The *Entry Point Section* is the section that contains the *AddressOfEntryPoint* field of the Optional Header. The *Resources Section* is a special section that contains a tree structure holding data items such as strings, images, and icons. Finally, the *Other Sections* component captures all other sections in the executable that do not contain the entry point or the resources. This is the only component that does not necessarily correspond to a contiguous sequence of bytes, since the order of the sections is defined in the Section Table and the entry point and resources sections may not be the first or last sections.

Executables may contain two optional Extra components. For signed executables, the *Certificate Table* contains a digital signature and a list of X.509 certificates for validating the file's integrity and the identity of the publisher. The *Overlay* component captures data appended at the end of an executable. This data is not described in the PE header, thus it is ignored by the loader. However, it is accessible by reading it directly from the file on disk. The presence of an overlay can be identified because the file's expected size (i.e., the sum of the start offset and size of the last section) is smaller than the real size of the file on disk. Some tools consider the certificate table to be an overlay. However, we consider it a separate component because its start offset and size are defined in the Data Directories and thus its existence is known to the loader. For signed samples, we consider that an overlay exists if and only if there is additional data after the end of the certificate table.

3.2 Family Component Analysis

Given the samples in a family, our goal is to identify which components are similar and different in the family. For this, we compare the contents of a component across all pairs of samples in the family. For each component in each pair of samples, we apply a pairwise similarity function to determine whether the contents of the component across the two samples are similar or not, and accumulate results across all pairs of samples.

Pairwise Similarity. We experiment with three Boolean similarity functions that given the content of a component in two samples determine whether the component is similar. The first function computes the SHA256 hash of the sequence of raw bytes of the component[1] and checks if both hashes are the same. This is the strictest similarity function requiring both samples to have identical content in the component. The second function computes instead the TLSH [34] fuzzy hash over the components' raw bytes. Fuzzy hashes output similar digests when the inputs are similar. Among all the fuzzy hashes available in the wild, we chose TLSH because it is the one that can produce a hash for the smallest stream of bytes, given that the minimum size is 50 bytes. Thus, it can handle most of the smallest components that are usually headers. Other fuzzy hashes could require very large minimum sizes (e.g. SSDEEP requires at least 4KB to compute the hash). TLSH returns a distance in the $x \in [0, \infty)$ range, which we normalize ($y = max\{\frac{300-x}{3}, 0\}$) to a similarity in the $y \in [0, 100]$ range as suggested by other works [36,47]. The component values are considered similar if the TLSH similarity was $\geq$90, as proposed by Oliver et al. [34]. This function is more lax because it considers the component values to be similar even if they are not identical, as long as the raw byte differences are small. Pagani et al. [36] showed that TLSH can remain robust when small modifications are introduced in the code; however, they also observed that compiling the exact same source with seemingly minor tweaks (such as slightly different compiler flags) can result in anything from negligible differences to extensive ripple effects in the final executable. Therefore, we compute the code similarity using the popular BinDiff [18] tool, which disassembles both executables (using IDA Pro 8.1 in our setup) and uses graph isomorphism and heuristics to match their functions. It returns a similarity value in $[0, 1]$. The advantage of BinDiff is that it disassembles the code and thus can ignore differences in the data between code blocks and handle some code reordering. But, it only measures code similarity, so we only apply it to the Entry Point Section component. We determine that the Entry Point Section of two samples is similar if their BinDiff similarity is $>$0.85, as suggested by Egele et al. [17].

Family Components. To determine if a component is similar, different, or missing across a family we use Algorithm 1. It takes as input the $10 \leq n \leq 100$ samples that belong to a family, a similarity function, and a threshold t. For each component c, it initializes to zero two counters: C_d^c and C_p^c. The first captures the number of pairs a component differs and the other the number of pairs where the component is present. For each of the $n(n-1)/2$ pairs of samples in the family, it compares each of the 12 components. If a component c is present in both samples and is similar, it increments both counters for the component; if present in only one sample, the counters are not modified; and if the component is absent in both, it increments C_d^c. Once all pairs of samples have been analyzed, counters are normalized by dividing them by the number of pairs. For each component, if $C_p \geq t$ and $C_d \geq t$, the component is deemed *similar* (present and consistent in most samples), if $C_p < t$ and $C_d < t$, the component is present with varying

---

[1] For the Other Sections component, we sort the sections according to their offset, concatenate their raw bytes, and compute the SHA256 of the resulting buffer.

values and is classified as *different*, and if $C_p < t$ and $C_d \geq t$, the component is often *missing* and thus should be ignored as there is not enough information.

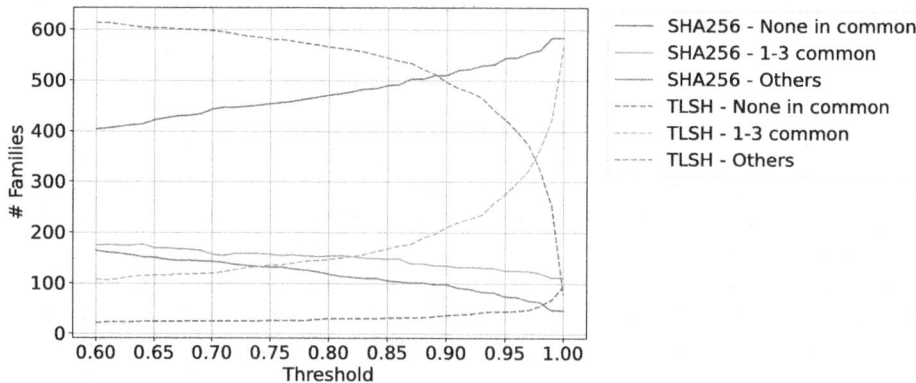

Fig. 1. Number of families with none, 1–3 or more than 3 common components by varying the threshold, and using SHA256 or TLSH.

Threshold Selection. Requiring a component to be similar across all pairs of samples (i.e., t = 1.0) is too strict, e.g., some samples could have wrong family labels. Instead, we evaluate lower threshold values that allow a fraction of pairs to differ. Figure 1 presents the number of families with none, few (1–3), or many (>3) common components while varying the threshold t for both SHA256 (solid lines) and TLSH (dashed lines). The results show clear differences between both pairwise similarity functions. Using SHA256, raising the threshold increases the number of families with no similar components gradually from 405 at t = 0.6 to 510 at 0.9, while the number of common components gradually decreases in opposite fashion. In contrast, using TLSH the number of families with no common components remains fairly constant around 20 and only starts to increase at high thresholds. Our manual analysis shows that using TLSH is problematic with small data components (i.e., PE headers in Metadata) where component similarity is determined even when important fields differ. Thus, we conclude that using the stricter crypto hash is more appropriate to analyze polymorphism. While changing the threshold of the crypto hash affects a relatively small subset of families, too low a threshold reduces confidence that components are truly shared, while too high a threshold increases the risk of discarding slightly different but essentially similar data. For the experiments in Sect. 5 we use the SHA256 pairwise similarity with a threshold of 0.75 which we have observed to strike a good balance by tolerating small differences without overlooking meaningful commonalities.

4 Cross-Component Analysis

Before proceeding to the analysis of individual components, we analyze different sources of variability that are not specific to a component but may instead affect the entire PE file structure: file truncation and packing.

4.1 Truncation

Millions of malware samples are collected and shared daily by various companies and services. Some are retrieved directly from filesystems by endpoint protection systems, while others come from emails, compressed archives, network traffic, or memory. Additionally, files may be pre-processed by tools like unpackers. During this collection and transformation process, a sample might become truncated, either intentionally or unintentionally. Truncated samples can be identified because their expected size (i.e., the sum of the start offset and size of the last section) is larger than the real size of the file on disk. One caveat is that if a sample has an overlay and the truncation only affects the overlay, then truncation cannot be detected as the overlay is not described in the PE headers. Among the 68,683 samples in the three datasets, 2,504 (3.6%) are truncated. Of those, the vast majority (2,486) belong to the Balanced dataset and 18 come from MOTIF, with Malicia having none. Truncated samples are distributed among 42.9% (320/746) of the families, showing that truncation is indeed a widespread phenomenon. We found 1.9% (14/746) families where more than half of the samples are truncated. The families with the majority of truncated samples are: *stone* (97%), *kuaizip* (92%), *ranumbot* (88%), *duote* (87%), and *spybot* (82%).

To measure the missing part, we define the *truncation ratio* as the quotient of the missing bytes (expected size minus real size) over the expected size. The mean truncation ratio is 50.2% (median 52.9%), indicating that, on average, more than half of the expected file size is missing in truncated files. Then, by analyzing which components are impacted by truncation, we found that the offset from which bytes begin to be missing always starts at least after the Section Table; thus, truncation affects sections, resources, certificates, and overlay.

Another aspect of the truncation is whether the truncated samples came from the same original sample (i.e., the only difference is the truncation size). Thus, for each family, we compared all the truncated samples by checking whether the smaller sample was once again a truncated version of the largest. This analysis revealed 77 (10.3%) families having at least 2 samples coming from the same original executable and truncated in different points. The extreme case is one family, *spybot*, where 80 truncated samples come from the same original file that has been truncated at different offsets.

While truncated files are rarely, if ever, mentioned in malware studies, their consequences are very important. For instance, truncated samples cannot be executed, and thus fail dynamic analysis. But also static signatures may not match, and even popular static analysis tools produce confusing results when run on truncated files. For example, the popular *pefile* [5] (a multi-platform Python module to parse PE files) erroneously reports an inexistent overlay on all truncated samples. Given that also VirusTotal uses pefile to parse PE executables, VT often reports truncated samples having a non-existent overlay.

We remove the truncated samples, as well as any families with less than 10 non-truncated samples, from the dataset. The dataset used in the remainder of this paper has **66,160** samples distributed in **743** families.

4.2 Packing

We adopt a broad definition of packing, encompassing all transformations applied to a PE file—such as encryption, compression, or encoding—that require a runtime component to recover the original data. While these transformations primarily aim to thwart static analysis, they can also generate vastly different executables by re-packing the same sample with different algorithms or encryption keys. Consequently, packing is often regarded as a key driver of polymorphism.

Accurately detecting packed samples is a challenging task and an active research area. To address this, we employ two state-of-the-art approaches. Signature-based tools are effective at detecting known off-the-shelf packers, offering low false positives (FPs). However, they suffer from false negatives (FNs) due to their inability to identify custom packers or all instances of off-the-shelf packers. To overcome these limitations, we incorporate an ML classifier capable of detecting both less common off-the-shelf packers and custom packing routines. However, the classifier may overestimate the number of packed samples. In summary, we use signature-based tools to establish a lower bound and the ML classifier to set an upper bound on packing presence in our dataset.

Signature-Based Tools. We use two publicly available signature-based packer detection tools: PackGenome [27] and Detect-it-Easy [20]. PackGenome generates YARA rules from dynamic traces of the unpacking routine collected during program execution. The authors released the code for generating YARA rules for 20 off-the-shelf "accessible" packers. These rules identify 24,134 (36.5%) samples as being packed. The most commonly reported packers are UPX (48.6% of detected samples), WinLicense (31.7%) and PECompact (9.8%). The popular open-source Detect It Easy (DiE) tool, whose output is included in the VT reports at the time of writing, identified 15,704 samples (23.7%) being packed. The top-3 packers identified are UPX (58.8% of detected samples), ASPack (12.3%) and VMProtect (9.5%).

ML Classifier. We implement a packer classifier by leveraging the datasets and the feature classes proposed by Aghakhani et al. [6]. On their datasets, we used the same nine static feature classes (56,485 individual features) they extracted to train a Random Forest classifier that predicts whether a sample is packed or not. We used 10-fold cross-validation to train and test the classifier and obtained an overall F1-score of 0.96. When applied to our dataset, the classifier predicted 55,773/66,160 (84.3%) samples as packed.

In summary, signature detection tools identify 23.7%–36.5% samples as packed, while the ML classifier identifies instead a much higher 84%, as summa-

Table 2. Component statistics. For each component, number of samples where the component is present, number of families where the component is present in none/half/all samples, number of families where the component differs, and number of families where the component is the only one with differences. A dash means zero in all columns. A dagger † indicates an optional component.

Component	Samples Present	Families Present(0%)	Present(≥50%)	Present(100%)	Differs	OnlyDifference
DOS Header	66,160 (100.0%)	-	743 (100.0%)	743 (100.0%)	524 (70.5%)	-
DOS Stub	65,059 (98.3%)	3 (0.4%)	734 (98.8%)	655 (88.2%)	484 (65.1%)	-
Rich Header †	42,577 (64.4%)	94 (12.7%)	497 (66.9%)	168 (22.6%)	494 (66.5%)	-
COFF Header	66,160 (100.0%)	-	743 (100.0%)	743 (100.0%)	622 (83.7%)	-
Optional Header	66,160 (100.0%)	-	743 (100.0%)	743 (100.0%)	652 (87.8%)	1 (0.1%)
Data Directories †	66,148 (99.9%)	-	743 (100.0%)	741 (99.7%)	638 (85.9%)	-
Section Table	66,160 (100.0%)	-	743 (100.0%)	743 (100.0%)	642 (86.4%)	-
Entry Point Section	66,155 (99.9%)	-	743 (100.0%)	739 (99.5%)	637 (85.7%)	2 (0.3%)
Resource Section †	57,230 (86.5%)	27 (3.6%)	661 (89.0%)	385 (51.8%)	625 (84.1%)	1 (0.1%)
Other Sections †	64,734 (97.8%)	3 (0.4%)	731 (98.4%)	583 (78.5%)	636 (85.6%)	7 (0.9%)
Certificate Table †	11,257 (17.0%)	344 (46.3%)	108 (14.5%)	19 (2.6%)	188 (25.3%)	1 (0.1%)
Overlay †	31,096 (47.0%)	87 (11.7%)	319 (42.9%)	87 (11.7%)	493 (66.4%)	37 (5.0%)

rized in Table 3 in Appendix. It is likely that the real fraction lies somewhere in between, so we use these numbers as lower and upper bounds, respectively. We illustrate the differences between both packer detection approaches using *privateexeprotector*, which has been mislabeled as a malware family but is rather a commercial protector. When the dataset by Dambra et al. [15] was created, AVClass taxonomy did not yet classify it as a packer, leading to its mislabeling. Executables labeled *privateexeprotector* may belong to different malware families using the same protector. Of 100 samples, 13 are tagged as "Private EXE Protector" by signature-based tools, 2 as UPX, and 87 remain undetected, showing high FNs. In contrast, the ML classifier detects 99 samples as packed, demonstrating minimal FNs, although potentially introducing FPs.

Finally, we noticed that many families use different off-the-shelf packers, a quick shortcut to achieve polymorphism. The most extreme cases are 8 families that use at least 15 different packers. In fact, we computed the Pearson correlation between the number of different components in each family and the total number of unique off-the-shelf packers in that family. We obtained a moderate relationship (0.42, p-value = 6.0e−34), namely, more packers, greater difference.

5 Component Analysis

We now use *PEdiff* to understand in which parts of a PE file the differences among samples of the same family are located. Section 5.1 first examines how frequently each component exists. Then, Sect. 5.2 identifies similar and different components in families. Section 5.3 examines where their polymorphism is being introduced in individual components.

5.1 Component Presence

Table 2 summarizes the presence of individual components in the dataset. Most required components are present in all samples (DOS Header, COFF Header, Optional Header, Section Table). Optional components vary significantly in presence. Three are common: Data Directories (present in 99.9% of samples), Other Sections (97.8%), and Resource Section (86.5%). Less common optional components include the Rich Header (64.4%), Overlay (47.0%), and Certificate Table (17.0%). The presence of an optional component is not consistent across all samples in a family. For example, while 399 (53.7%) families have some signed sample and 656 (88.3%) families have a sample with an overlay, only 19 (2.6%) families have all samples signed and only 87 (11.7%) have an overlay in all samples. Similarly, there are 94 families (12.7%) where no sample has the Rich Header, 168 (22.6%) where all samples have it, but in the majority of families some samples, but not all, have it (87.3%).

5.2 Similar and Different Components

This section examines how many similar and different components there are in each family. Roughly two-thirds of the dataset, specifically 454 families, contain samples with *no* components in common, i.e., where all parts of the PE files are, at least partially, different. Among the remaining 289 families, 95 families contain largely similar files, with only one, two, or three different components and 157 families contains instead files that are all different *except* for 1–3 components.

We examine these three family groups separately. In most families, differences among samples span all PE file components, not just localized parts. This suggests malware authors did not achieve polymorphism by altering a few bytes or simply re-compiling (which would preserve sections like data, resources, and the Rich Header). For the 42,498 samples in this group, 40.1% are packed according to the signature-based tools, 84.7% according to the ML classifier, and 90.4% when combining both methods. Of the samples in the remaining 289 families (23,662 samples), 38.4% are packed according to the signature-based tools, 83.6% according to the ML classifier, and 90.4% using both methods. Despite slightly higher percentages in the first group, the difference is too small to attribute polymorphism to packing alone.

We focus on families with files sharing few common components. The most consistent components are the DOS Header and Stub, in 95 and 131 families respectively, and the Rich Header, in 21 families. In highly similar families, the most variable component, is the overlay (78 families), appearing over three times more frequently than others like other sections (22), resource (17) and entry point (14) section. Rare differences include headers and, in three families, only the Certificate Table.

5.3 Individual Component Polymorphism

So far, our analysis has been binary—components were either identical or different. In this section, we explore differences and similarities in greater detail. For example, over 5% of the families in our dataset contain samples that differ only in their overlay. What do these overlays look like? Are they entirely different, or do they contain only a few unique bytes? To address these questions, we examine each component individually.

Rich Header. The Rich Header is an optional and undocumented component, which can be useful to detect if two executables may come from the same project. Among the 494 (66.5%) families where the Rich Header is different, in 12 families the entry IDs are similar, and in 4 family also its counts meaning that most objects used to build the samples are common.

Entry Point Section. This component contains the very first instruction of the program and thus can be considered a code section. The SHA256 pairwise similarity identifies 41 (5.5%) families where this component does not change at all and another 65 (8.7%) families where this component is similar. For the remaining 637 (85.7%) families, we use the BinDiff similarity to compare their code, identifying an additional 7 families with similar code. For 37/637 (5.81%) families BinDiff failed to properly disassemble all the samples, mainly because the entry point address points to invalid code. Such behavior is a common evasion technique in malware, where a custom loader, often implemented via TLS callbacks, dynamically reconstructs the correct code during runtime.

Resource Section. Among the 625 (84.1%) families where the resource section differs, there is one family (*dostre*) where this component is the only difference. The difference is in the resource values, in particular, there is one specific Bitmap resource whose value keeps changing. We manually reversed the code and discovered that the malicious code's payload (extracted and executed at runtime) was encoded within that image. We also identify four families (*moarider, winloadsda, axespec, sohana*) where their only difference lies in the order of the resource names, three families (*blackshades, umbra, virfire*) for which the resources are the same, but the padding of the section differs, ten families where the difference is in the Resource Table but not in the resources identifiers, and another (*lolbot*) has the only difference in a single string that changes for all the samples. The observed variations in the samples are likely introduced intentionally to achieve hash-bursting and, subsequently, polymorphism.

Other Sections. This component includes default sections with a pre-defined purpose (e.g., .idata, .bss, .rdata). But it is possible to create custom sections as well. This is the case of packers, which usually create one section for accommodating the unpacked payload. For one family (*ezsoftwareupdater*) the only difference in the whole executable is a single 32-byte string in the .rdata section, containing hexadecimal characters, likely a unique identifier, and in another family (*stormattack*) the difference was also in the .rdata section where a few hexadecimal strings were changing.

Overlay. To measure how much hidden data has been added to samples with an overlay, we define the *excess ratio* as the quotient of the size on disk over the expected size (i.e., without the overlay). The median excess ratio is 1.73x, an additional 73% content over the expected length. However, the mean is 130x, because some samples contain a vast amount of additional data. The extreme case is a sample with an expected size of 2.56 KB but an overlay of 454 MB.

We removed the overlays from all samples in the dataset and re-computed their SHA256 hash (which we will now refer to as "no-overlay hash"). About one-fourth (18,315/66,160) of the samples share the same no-overlay hash with at least another sample, indicating that the overlay was the only difference between them. In particular, 13 families only contain samples with the same no-overlay hash, and 46 families have at least 75% of their samples with the same no-overlay hash. Interestingly, 156 no-overlay hashes are shared across different families, with one matching samples in 12 families. This hash corresponds to 7zS.sfx, a template for 7-zip self-extracting archives. These archives are created by combining 7zS.sfx, a configuration file, and a compressed archive, with the overlay holding the latter two. Another hash matches 6 families and corresponds to Default.sfx, used by WinRAR for self-extracting files. These cases highlight the frequent use of self-extracting archives in malware for distributing multiple files, and likely also for obfuscation as analyzing them requires inspecting the overlay's compressed data.

Four families had overlay differences that stem solely from strings. In three cases, the overlay was entirely ASCII text, while the fourth had one meaningless differing string. However, examining the overlay revealed strings resembling CA names. Despite the Certificate Table fields being set to 0 in the Data Directory, treating the overlay as a Certificate Table revealed valid PKCS#7 signatures.

Finally, we analyzed overlay content using DiE. In 43.67% of cases (13,537/31,096), no file type was detected. Among the rest, 6.08% (1,890/31,096) were archives (RAR, ZIP, 7ZIP), 8.87% (2,750/31,096) were PE files, and 18.17% (5,650/31,096) contained ASCII text. Of these, 7.88% (445/5,650) were valid Base* encodings with no recognizable file types when decoded.

Certificate Table. For the 11,257 samples (17.0%) with a Certificate Table, we extracted the Authentihash and its hash algorithm. The Authentihash is computed from the file's content at signing, excluding the Checksum and Certificate Table Data Directory. We failed to extract a signature for 1,044 samples due to truncation or corruption (e.g., incorrect offset). For the remaining 10,213, a mismatched Authentihash indicated modification or unrelated signatures in 1,845 samples across 211 families. Thus, 8,368 samples (12.6%) had valid signatures when signed, though some may now be invalid (e.g., revoked). Among these, 1,098 samples had an overlay after the Certificate Table.

We computed the Authentihash for all samples using SHA256, resulting in 63,404 unique values, with 492 shared by multiple samples. Samples with identical Authentihash must belong to the same program (family and version), differing only in their Certificate Table and checksum. For instance, all the samples in the *amigo* family share the same Authentihash, checksum, and a chain of 5 certificates, indicating polymorphism in hidden parts of the Certificate Table.

Other Components. Of the remaining six components (DOS header, COFF and Optional Header, DOS Stub, Section Table, Data Directory), all except the DOS Stub have predefined structures in the PE format but can still be manipulated for polymorphism. For example, in *bebloh*, the only difference is the Optional Header's version values, while the code and data are identical. In *lebreat*, standard UPX section names (.upx0, .upx1, .rsrc) are replaced with random strings, though the content remains unchanged. We also analyzed the COFF Header's creation timestamp, which can be faked. It differs in 622 (83.7%) families, but 130 (11.3%) families share the same timestamp in over 75% of comparisons. Interestingly, *obit* has the same timestamp across all samples (Saturday, June 1, 2019 5:56:28 AM), likely fabricated, as the content differs.

5.4 File Infectors

File infectors, or viruses, infect benign executables with malicious code, creating samples with a combination of malicious and benign content. Furthermore, file infector families tend to be highly polymorphic since a single sample may infect many executables stored in the compromised host.

We investigated file infectors on our dataset using a combination of static and dynamic analysis. We first used AVClass [42] to obtain tags for all samples in the dataset. Using the tags, we identified 70 *likely-virus* families where the CLASS:virus tag appeared in more than half of the samples. For each of these families, we randomly selected 5 samples, dynamically executed them in a virtual machine (VM), and identified those that modified executables that already existed in the VM prior to the execution, i.e., the same filepath in the VM pointing to an executable file had different hashes before and after the execution. For those samples, we used *PEdiff* to examine the component differences between the original executable and the modified one produced during the execution.

Using this approach we identified 20 virus families. Of those, 16 are prepender viruses where the PE executable contains the malicious code and the infected (benign) executable is in the overlay: *lamer, induc, neshta, shodi, sinau, sivis, soulclose, xiaobaminer, memery, pidgeon, detroie, gogo, lmir, stihat, xolxo, xorer*. For all those 16 families, our analysis identifies the overlay as a component that changes. For two families (*gogo, soulclose*) the overlay is the only component that changes, i.e., the malicious executable has no polymorphism itself, but obtains it from the infected executable in the overlay. In the other 14 families, polymorphism is also added to other components. The remaining 4 families are appender viruses. Two of these (*expiro, wlksm*) extend one of the sections of the infected executable with the malicious code. The other two families (*triusor, wapomi*) add new sections at the end of the infected executable with malicious code. For all these four families, our analysis outputs that no component is similar across the family samples.

6 Related Work

Polymorphism. Malware achieves polymorphism by employing obfuscation techniques such as dead-code insertion, register reassignment, and instruction substitution [51]. This behavior renders static detection methods ineffective [7]. Therefore, prior works mainly focus on behavioral analysis to detect polymorphic malware: by using behavior-aware hidden Markov models [45], employing a mixed approach between static and dynamic analysis [35] or using an application-level emulator to perform flowgraph matching [13].

Code Similarity. Some approaches compare executable files by examining the similarity of the disassembled code [18,21,22,29]. These approaches may diff two versions of the same program [18,29], search for similar programs in a repository [21], or group similar executables [22]. We leverage BinDiff [18] as a representative of this class to identify code similarity within a family.

Fuzzy hashes (or similarity hashes) compare file similarity at the raw byte level by generating digests that remain close in distance space for similar inputs. Various fuzzy hashes exist, including *SSDEEP* [26], *TLSH* [34], *SDHASH* [40], and *MRSH-v2* [12]. Prior research applies fuzzy hashes to forensic analysis [41], malware detection [31,32,43], and clustering [8,9,44,48], while others evaluate their effectiveness [11,36]. Instead, we propose a fine-grained structural comparison across 12 PE file components to pinpoint byte-level differences. As part of our approach, we use TLSH to implement pairwise comparison of the values of a component across two executables. We observe high volatility when aggregating TLSH comparisons for family-wise similarity due to few, but significant, differences in small components such as PE headers.

Malware Clustering. A wealth of prior work has focused on grouping malware samples into families [10,23,37,39]. Each family cluster typically contains executables from the same malicious program, which may include different versions or polymorphic variants of a version. Malware clustering methods may use similarities in system calls [10], network traffic [37,39], raw bytes [23], or disassembled code [22]. We use three malware datasets where samples are labeled with their family and thus already clustered into families.

Malware Lineage. Lineage methods classify malware family samples, identifying polymorphic variants and tracing their evolution through phylogenetic trees [14,19,24,28,46]. Instead of detecting identical versions, our study examines tactics employed to create polymorphic variants.

7 Final Remarks

A Complex Picture. Our study aimed to identify the main causes of polymorphism and assess their prevalence across a large dataset of malware families. Through our experiments, we identified several causes, summarized in the following section. More importantly, we found that a single factor is rarely sufficient to explain the diversity of samples within a family. In fact, only 12.8% of the families (95 out of 743) exhibited polymorphism due to a single cause. For the remaining 87.2%, polymorphism arose from multiple overlapping factors. This is not a failure but a key finding, highlighting that attributing polymorphism solely to repacking is an oversimplification. It also suggests that no holistic solution exists to address the problem. For example, while removing or normalizing certain components may help in comparing samples, any approach addressing only one or a few causes will have limited success in explaining and mitigating the dissimilarities within a family.

Truncation. While truncated files are rarely, if ever, mentioned in malware studies, we observed that 3.6% of the files in the initial datasets are truncated, with 99.3% coming from the balanced dataset by Dambra et al. Since that dataset was collected from the VirusTotal file feed, a similar ratio of truncated PE executables might affect other studies using the VT feed [49]. Truncated samples are distributed among nearly half of the dataset families, indicating this is not an issue specific to some families but likely a common error that occurs during sample collection. Truncated samples pollute malware feeds and waste resources such as storage and sandbox time if they are queued for execution. Therefore, we suggest filtering out these samples, as we did, to avoid biasing the results.

Overlays. Similar to truncation, the impact and role of overlays are rarely mentioned in malware studies. However, our experiments show that they are extremely prevalent, affecting a stunning 47.0% of all samples in our dataset, being the most prevalent cause of polymorphism that we find. These overlays often contain a considerable amount of data, on average over a hundred times larger than the main executable alone. Despite this, previous works sometimes purposefully excluded overlays when extracting features for static analysis [38]. This is fine if the overlay contains useless data simply added to achieve polymorphism, but our analysis shows that this is not the case: 6.1% of the overlay data are compressed archives, and 8.9% are PE files.

Packing. Packing is a pervasive phenomenon in our dataset: while it is difficult to measure with precision, it might affect between 40% to 90% of our samples. This is not surprising since it is one of the most effective methods to counter static analysis. However, one would expect a significant difference in the components between the families where packing was most prevalent, but the distributions of packed samples and the negligible correlations we found did not confirm this expectation. We also discover that malware authors, in a trivial but effective way, achieve high polymorphism by using many different packers.

Other Polymorphism. Beyond packing, our study reveals that malware families introduce polymorphism into a variety of components. Among others, we observe families that modify PE headers to generate polymorphic variants such as *bebloh* that varies the version fields in the Optional Header. We also observe families that reorder resources without modifying them (e.g. *moarider, winloadsda*), introduce random bytes in the padding (*blackshades, umbra, virfire*), and introduce hidden data in the certificate table (*amigo*). There are also families whose differences are limited to some specific strings (e.g., *lolbot*). The range of techniques we observe shows that a structural analysis of the PE file format is a powerful tool for analyzing the reasons behind malware family polymorphism.

Dataset Limitations. Our analysis is limited by the datasets used. One issue is the quality of family labels. Despite dataset authors' efforts to refine labeling (e.g., identifying aliases and generic tokens), we found some errors such as *privateexeprotector* being considered a family. Also, the MOTIF and Malicia datasets are highly imbalanced, with few families having more than 10 samples. Still, our use of three datasets should help ameliorate selection bias.

Conclusions. Our large-scale analysis of 743 malware families offers a comprehensive understanding of the factors driving polymorphism in malware. The study reveals that in about 90% of cases, polymorphism results from multiple overlapping factors, rather than a single cause. This complexity underscores the inadequacy of simplistic solutions, such as attributing polymorphism solely to repacking, and highlights the need for multifaceted approaches.

Acknowledgements. This work was partially funded by two government grants managed by the French National Research Agency with references: "ANR-22-PECY-0007" and "ANR-23-IAS4-0001". Partial support was also provided by the Spanish Government MCIN/AEI/ 10.13039/501100011033/ through grants TED2021-132464B-I00 (PRODIGY) and PID2022-142290OB-I00 (ESPADA). The above grants are co-funded by European Union ESF, EIE, and NextGeneration funds.

A Appendix

Table 3. Packing prevalence in terms of packed samples and number of families with some/all packed samples.

Factor	Samples Present	Families Present(>0%)	Present(100%)
Packed (DiE)	15,704 (23.7%)	527 (70.9%)	20 (3.0%)
Packed (PackG)	24,134 (36.5%)	580 (78.1%)	45 (6.1%)
Packed (ML)	55,773 (84.3%)	726 (97.7%)	283 (38.1%)
Packed (All)	59,265 (89.6%)	731 (98.4%)	354 (47.6%)

Algorithm 1. Determine Component Status: Similar, Different, or Missing

Require: Array of samples S belonging to family F, Component c, Threshold t
1: Initialize $C_p \leftarrow 0$
2: Initialize $C_d \leftarrow 0$
3: $NS \leftarrow |S|$, number of samples in S
4: $P \leftarrow$ all combinations of S
5: $NP \leftarrow \frac{NS(NS-1)}{2}$, number of samples combinations and cardinality of P
6: **for all** $(S_x, S_y) \in P$ **do**
7:    **if** $c \in S_x$ and $c \in S_y$ and $S_x[c] = S_y[c]$ **then**
8:       $C_p \leftarrow C_p + 1$
9:       $C_d \leftarrow C_d + 1$
10:   **else if** $c \notin S_x$ and $c \notin S_y$ **then**
11:      $C_d \leftarrow C_d + 1$
12:   **end if**
13: **end for**
14: $C_p \leftarrow \frac{C_p}{NP}$
15: $C_d \leftarrow \frac{C_d}{NP}$
16: **if** $C_p \geq t$ and $C_d \geq t$ **then**
17:   **return** Similar
18: **else if** $C_p < t$ and $C_d < t$ **then**
19:   **return** Different
20: **else**
21:   **return** Missing
22: **end if**

References

1. Find malware detection names for Microsoft Defender for Endpoint. https://learn.microsoft.com/en-us/microsoft-365/security/intelligence/malware-naming. Accessed 17 Sept 2025
2. Hash and family of each sample. https://raw.githubusercontent.com/eurecom-s3/DecodingMLSecretsOfWindowsMalwareClassification/main/dataset/malware. Accessed 17 Sept 2025
3. MOTIF Dataset. https://github.com/boozallen/MOTIF. Accessed 17 Sept 2025
4. PEdiff. https://github.com/im-overlord04/PEDiff. Accessed 17 Sept 2025
5. PEfile. https://github.com/erocarrera/pefile. Accessed 17 Sept 2025
6. Aghakhani, H., et al.: When malware is Packin' Heat; limits of machine learning classifiers based on static analysis features. In: Network and Distributed Systems Security Symposium (2020)
7. Arfeen, A., Khan, Z.A., Uddin, R., Ahsan, U.: Toward accurate and intelligent detection of malware. Concurrency Comput. Pract. Experience **34**(4), e6652 (2022)
8. Azab, A., Layton, R., Alazab, M., Oliver, J.: Mining malware to detect variants. In: Cybercrime and Trustworthy Computing Conference (2014)
9. Bak, M., Papp, D., Tamás, C., Buttyán, L.: Clustering IoT malware based on binary similarity. In: IEEE/IFIP Network Operations and Management Symposium (2020)
10. Bayer, U., Comparetti, P.M., Hlauschek, C., Kruegel, C., Kirda, E.: Scalable, Behavior-Based Malware Clustering. In: Network and Distributed System Security Symposium (2009)

11. Botacin, M., Moia, V.H.G., Ceschin, F., Henriques, M.A.A., Grégio, A.: Understanding uses and misuses of similarity hashing functions for malware detection and family clustering in actual scenarios. Forensic Sci. Int. Digit. Invest. **38**, 301220 (2021)
12. Breitinger, F., Baier, H.: Similarity preserving hashing: eligible properties and a new algorithm MRSH-v2. In: International Conference on Digital Forensics and Cyber Crime (2013)
13. Cesare, S., Xiang, Y., Zhou, W.: Malwise–an effective and efficient classification system for packed and polymorphic malware. IEEE Trans. Comput. **62**(6), 1193–1206 (2012)
14. Cozzi, E., Vervier, P.A., Dell'Amico, M., Shen, Y., Bilge, L., Balzarotti, D.: The tangled genealogy of IoT malware. In: Annual Computer Security Applications Conference (2020)
15. Dambra, S., et al.: Decoding the secrets of machine learning in malware classification: a deep dive into datasets, feature extraction, and model performance. In: ACM Conference on Computer and Communications Security. ACM, November 2023
16. Drew, J., Moore, T., Hahsler, M.: Polymorphic malware detection using sequence classification methods. In: IEEE Security and Privacy Workshops (2016)
17. Egele, M., Woo, M., Chapman, P., Brumley, D.: Blanket execution: dynamic similarity testing for program binaries and components. In: USENIX Security Symposium (2014)
18. Google: BinDiff. https://github.com/google/bindiff. Accessed 17 Sept 2025
19. Haq, I.U., Chica, S., Caballero, J., Jha, S.: Malware lineage in the wild. Comput. Secur. **78**, 347–363 (2018)
20. horsicq: Detect It Easy. https://github.com/horsicq/Detect-It-Easy. 17 Sept 2025
21. Hu, X., Chiueh, T., Shin, K.G.: Large-scale malware indexing using function-call graphs. In: ACM Conference on Computer and Communications Security (2009)
22. Hu, X., Shin, K.G., Bhatkar, S., Griffin, K.: MutantX-S: scalable malware clustering based on static features. In: USENIX Annual Technical Conference (2013)
23. Jang, J., Brumley, D., Venkataraman, S.: BitShred: feature hashing malware for scalable triage and semantic analysis. In: ACM conference on Computer and Communications Security (2011)
24. Jang, J., Woo, M., Brumley, D.: Towards automatic software lineage inference. In: USENIX Security Symposium (2013)
25. Joyce, R.J., Amlani, D., Nicholas, C., Raff, E.: MOTIF: a large malware reference dataset with ground truth family labels. In: Workshop on Artificial Intelligence for Cyber Security (2022)
26. Kornblum, J.: Identifying almost identical files using context triggered piecewise hashing. Digit. Invest. **3** (2006)
27. Li, S., et al.: PackGenome: automatically generating robust YARA rules for accurate malware packer detection. In: ACM SIGSAC Conference on Computer and Communications Security (2023)
28. Lindorfer, M., Di Federico, A., Maggi, F., Comparetti, P.M., Zanero, S.: Lines of malicious code: insights into the malicious software industry. In: Annual Computer Security Applications Conference (2012)
29. Liu, B., et al.: αDiff: cross-version binary code similarity detection with DNN. In: ACM/IEEE International Conference on Automated Software Engineering (2018)
30. Microsoft: PE format (2023). https://learn.microsoft.com/en-us/windows/win32/debug/pe-format

31. Naik, N., Jenkins, P., Savage, N.: A ransomware detection method using fuzzy hashing for mitigating the risk of occlusion of information systems. In: International Symposium on Systems Engineering (2019)
32. Naik, N., et al.: Fuzzy hashing aided enhanced YARA rules for malware triaging. In: IEEE Symposium Series on Computational Intelligence (2020)
33. Nappa, A., Rafique, M.Z., Caballero, J.: The MALICIA dataset: identification and analysis of drive-by download operations. Int. J. Inf. Secur. **14**(1), 15–33 (2015)
34. Oliver, J., Cheng, C., Chen, Y.: TLSH–a locality sensitive hash. In: Cybercrime and Trustworthy Computing Workshop (2013)
35. Osorio, F.C.C., Qiu, H., Arrott, A.: Segmented sandboxing-a novel approach to malware polymorphism detection. In: International Conference on Malicious and Unwanted Software (2015)
36. Pagani, F., Dell'Amico, M., Balzarotti, D.: Beyond precision and recall: understanding uses (and misuses) of similarity hashes in binary analysis. In: ACM Conference on Data and Application Security and Privacy (2018)
37. Perdisci, R., Lee, W., Feamster, N.: Behavioral clustering of HTTP-based malware and signature generation using malicious network traces. In: USENIX Symposium on Networked Systems Design and Implementation (2010)
38. Quiring, E., Pirch, L., Reimsbach, M., Arp, D., Rieck, K.: Against all odds: winning the defense challenge in an evasion competition with diversification. Technical report (2020)
39. Rafique, M.Z., Caballero, J.: FIRMA: malware clustering and network signature generation with mixed network behaviors. In: Symposium on Research in Attacks, Intrusions and Defenses (2013)
40. Roussev, V.: Data fingerprinting with similarity digests. In: IFIP International Conference on Digital Forensics (2010)
41. Roussev, V., Quates, C.: Content triage with similarity digests: the M57 case study. Digit. Investig. **9**, S60–S68 (2012)
42. Sebastián, M., Rivera, R., Kotzias, P., Caballero, J.: AVClass: a tool for massive malware labeling. In: International Symposium on Research in Attacks, Intrusions, and Defenses (2016)
43. Seo, K., Lim, K., Choi, J., Chang, K., Lee, S.: Detecting similar files based on hash and statistical analysis for digital forensic investigation. In: International Conference on Computer Science and Its Applications (2009)
44. Shiel, I., O'Shaughnessy, S.: Improving file-level fuzzy hashes for malware variant classification. Digit. Investig. **28**, S88–S94 (2019)
45. Tajoddin, A., Jalili, S.: HM3alD: polymorphic malware detection using program behavior-aware hidden Markov model. Appl. Sci. **8**(7), 1044 (2018)
46. Tam, K., Feizollah, A., Anuar, N.B., Salleh, R., Cavallaro, L.: The evolution of android malware and android analysis techniques. ACM Comput. Surv. (CSUR) **49**(4), 1–41 (2017)
47. Upchurch, J., Zhou, X.: Variant: a malware similarity testing framework. In: International Conference on Malicious and Unwanted Software (2015)
48. Upchurch, J., Zhou, X.: Malware provenance: code reuse detection in malicious software at scale. In: International Conference on Malicious and Unwanted Software (2016)
49. van Liebergen, K., Caballero, J., Kotzias, P., Gates, C.: A deep dive into the VirusTotal file feed. In: Conference on Detection of Intrusions and Malware & Vulnerability Assessment (2023)

50. Webster, G.D., et al.: Finding the needle: a study of the PE32 rich header and respective malware triage. In: International Conference on Detection of Intrusions and Malware, and Vulnerability Assessment (2017)
51. You, I., Yim, K.: Malware obfuscation techniques: a brief survey. In: International Conference on Broadband, Wireless Computing, Communication and Applications (2010)

End-to-End Non-profiled Side-Channel Analysis on Long Raw Traces

Jintong Yu[1,4,5], Yuxuan Wang[1,4,5], Shipei Qu[1,4,5], Yubo Zhao[1,4,5], Yipeng Shi[1,4,5], Pei Cao[2], Xiangjun Lu[2], Chi Zhang[1,4,5(✉)], Dawu Gu[1,4,5(✉)], and Cheng Hong[3]

[1] Shanghai Jiaotong University, Shanghai, China
{zcsjtu,dwgu}@sjtu.edu.cn
[2] Viewsource (Shanghai) Technology Company, Shanghai, China
[3] Ant Group, Hangzhou, China
[4] State Key Laboratory of Cryptology, P.O. Box 5159, Beijing 100878, China
[5] Shanghai Pudong Institute of Cryptology, Shanghai, China

Abstract. With the advancement of deep learning techniques, Deep Learning-based Non-profiled Side-Channel Analysis (DL-NSCA) can automatically learn and combine features, making it a promising method that can skip the manual and precise selection of Points of Interest (PoIs). Existing DL-NSCA methods assume that the attacker can identify a short leakage interval (usually less than 5000 points) containing PoIs from raw traces (more than 100,000 points) and then feed the leakage interval into the neural network to recover the key. However, in practice, the attacker often faces a black-box scenario with unknown underlying implementations, making locating the short interval from raw traces challenging, especially when masking countermeasures exist. To address this issue, we propose a lightweight end-to-end DL-NSCA model called convWIN-MCR, which consists of a performance-optimizing component, convWIN, and an accelerator component, MCR. It can efficiently process raw traces without the need to manually identify the short leakage interval. On the public dataset ASCADv1, while the state-of-the-art model Multi-Output Regression (MOR) requires 28,000 traces and 24 min to recover the key from the leakage interval with 1,400 feature points, our framework only requires 6,000 traces in 13 min to directly analyze raw traces with 250,000 feature points. To further validate the practical applicability of our framework, we successfully crack a commercial USIM card by analyzing its raw traces and recovering its 128-bit AES key.

Keywords: Non-profiled side-channel analysis · End-to-end framework · Lightweight neural networks

1 Introduction

Side-Channel Analysis (SCA), first introduced in [10], recovers secrets of cryptographic algorithms by exploiting side-channel information leaked from real-world devices. Based on the attacker's capability, SCA methods can be categorized into two main types: profiled SCA and non-profiled SCA. Profiled SCA assumes the attacker has access to a profiling device identical to the target device. On the profiling device, the attacker characterizes the side-channel behaviors and then leverages them to recover the secret key from the target device. Under this condition, profiled SCA is regarded as one of the most powerful methods [14]. In practice, obtaining a fully controlled device that is the same as the target device is difficult, especially for closed devices (such as USIM cards). Non-profiled SCA releases this assumption, only requiring the collection of side-channel traces and corresponding plaintexts (or ciphertexts) from the target device. Therefore, it is more applicable in analyzing many practical scenarios [13,19].

Non-profiled SCA takes a divide-and-conquer strategy, splitting the key into multiple subkeys and analyzing them one by one. For AES-128, the 128-bit key is split into 16 bytes, and each is attacked individually. For each byte, the method tests all 256 key guesses by comparing correlations between side-channel traces and hypothetical leakages related to each key guess to identify the correct key guess by the highest correlation. Traditional non-profiled SCA methods utilize statistical tools to measure this correlation, such as Pearson correlation coefficients (i.e., Correlation Power Analysis, CPA) [3] and mutual information (i.e., Mutual Information Analysis, MIA) [22]. With more countermeasures proposed [1,9], traditional methods struggle to handle side-channel traces without known underlying implementation directly. In 2019, Timon proposed Differential Deep Learning Analysis (DDLA), first introducing deep learning techniques into non-profiled SCA [20]. Instead of statistical tools, DDLA exploits neural networks to learn the correlation between side-channel traces and hypothetical leakages. The advantage of neural networks lies in their ability to automatically learn the positions of Points of Interest (PoIs) and skip the feature selection process.

1.1 Motivations

Existing Deep Learning-based Non-profiled Side-Channel Analysis (DL-NSCA) models are all aimed at the **leakage interval**, which refers to a short interval (or the concatenation of several intervals) that contains PoIs. The leakage interval datasets in their experiments contain less than 5000 feature points. However, locating the leakage interval from raw traces directly without knowing the implementation details is the most challenging part of practical SCA. In real-world scenarios, the attacker can only locate a vague interval based on the type of algorithm, such as identifying the first round operation of AES based on empirical knowledge or trace segmentation techniques [23,24]. This often involves dealing with raw traces with more than 100,000 feature points, especially for software implementations, which we refer to as the **end-to-end** or **black-box** scenario. Processing raw traces is beneficial, especially against masking countermeasures, but the high dimensionality data often leads to poor performance or failed attacks for the following two reasons.

Firstly, existing DL-NSCA models perform low attack performance and have a long analysis time on the leakage interval, which hinders further expansion of the model's ability to process raw traces. Although DDLA performs better than traditional non-profiled SCA methods, the computational complexity and runtime are substantial. For instance, to recover a single-byte key, DDLA necessitates training 256 networks. To improve DDLA, Kwon et al. [11] proposed a parallel network and shared layers to reduce the attack time. Moreover, Do et al. [4] proposed the Multi-Output Regression (MOR) network, which outperforms DDLA and Kwon's method by predicting 256 outputs with a single regression model, reducing computation and easing the constraints of partition-based attacks [18,25]. However, on the leakage interval, MOR typically requires over 10,000 traces and more than 20 min for analysis, indicating room for improvement in attack performance and analysis time.

Secondly, existing end-to-end profiled SCA frameworks cannot be directly applied to end-to-end non-profiled SCA. Masure et al. designed a convolutional neural network to handle large-scale raw traces for polymorphic AES implementations [16]. Lu et al. proposed an end-to-end profiled deep learning framework using a deep Long Short-Term Memory (LSTM) network with an attention mechanism, which successfully breaks raw traces protected by first-order masking [2]. They comprise complex networks with multiple layers, and [2] takes three days to recover a 1-byte key. However, complex neural networks can lead to overfitting, as the model learns not only the mapping relationship between the hypothetical leakages related to correct key guess and traces but also the mapping relationship between hypothetical leakages of incorrect key guesses and traces, leading to failure analysis. In addition, its training cost is 256 times higher or more than the profiling setting because non-profiled SCA requires training 256 networks, making the required computational resources and analysis time unacceptable.

1.2 Contribution

In this paper, we propose a lightweight end-to-end model to address the above issues, and our contributions are as follows:

1. **Introducing an efficient neural component into DL-NSCA.** We introduce the convWIN layer, as the first layer of the network. We verify that adding convWIN to DDLA and MOR (State-Of-The-Art, SOTA) can recover keys with 76% fewer traces on average across multiple public datasets. It also enhances the robustness of the models against misalignment.
2. **A framework for lightweight end-to-end DL-NSCA:** We propose a lightweight end-to-end DL-NSCA framework, convWIN-MCR, containing a performance-optimizing component convWIN and an accelerator component MCR. It consists of four layers, enabling the attacker to recover the key in a short runtime in the end-to-end scenario. Our framework eliminates the need for the underlying implementation and manual identification of the leakage interval, requiring only the raw traces and corresponding plaintexts/ciphertexts.
3. **Satisfying results on public datasets and a real-world device:** Our model is capable of directly analyzing raw traces with over 100,000 feature

points, and the analysis target includes public datasets ASCADv1 and a USIM card from a mainstream operator. On a public dataset, MOR needs 28,000 traces and 24 min to recover the key from 1,400 selected points. In contrast, our framework only requires 6,000 traces in 13 min to analyze raw traces with 250,000 feature points. To demonstrate its real-world applicability, we also successfully crack a commercial USIM card by recovering its 128-bit AES key through direct analysis of raw traces.

1.3 Structure

The paper is organized as follows: Sect. 2 provides background information. In Sect. 3, we introduce our end-to-end framework, explaining the motivations behind its design and elucidating the effectiveness of our architecture. In Sect. 4, we validate the role of the convWIN layer in NSCA and experiment end-to-end analysis on public datasets and a USIM card. Finally, we conclude our work and discuss some potential research directions in Sect. 5.

2 Background

2.1 Notation

We use calligraphic letters to represent sets like $\mathcal{X}$, with bold upper-case letters (e.g., $\boldsymbol{X}$) denoting matrices, bold lowercase letters (e.g., $\boldsymbol{x}$) representing vectors, and lowercase letters (e.g., x) indicating the scalar value. We present functions using a sans serif font, such as f. We target recovering a 1-byte key of AES for each training in this paper, and there are 256 key guesses, i.e., the key space $\mathcal{X} = \{0, 1, \ldots, 255\}$. k_* represents the correct key (correct key guess).

2.2 Deep Learning Techniques.

Loss Function. The goal of a neural network is to learn the mapping relationship f between input set $\mathcal{X}$ and output set $\mathcal{Y}$, and we define the space $\mathcal{F}$ as the set of mapping relationships f: $\mathcal{F} = \{f | \mathcal{Y} = f(\mathcal{X})\}$. In this case, space $\mathcal{F}$ is usually a family of functions determined by a network's parameter vector $\boldsymbol{\Theta}$: $\mathcal{F} = \{f_{\boldsymbol{\Theta}} | \mathcal{Y} = f_{\boldsymbol{\Theta}}(\mathcal{X}), \boldsymbol{\Theta} \in \mathbb{R}^n\}$ The parameter vector $\boldsymbol{\Theta}$ takes values in the n-dimensional Euclidean space $\mathbb{R}^n$, which is called the parameter space. We set a training dataset of N samples $\mathcal{T} = \{(x_1, y_1), (x_2, y_2), \cdots, (x_N, y_N)\}$.

For a given input x_i, a loss function L is used to measure the difference between the output prediction value $f_{\boldsymbol{\Theta}}(x_i)$ and the label y_i, denoted as $L(y_i, f_{\boldsymbol{\Theta}}(x_i))$. According to the empirical risk minimization strategy, the problem of finding the optimal model in the model space $\mathcal{F}$ equivalent to solving the optimization problem: $\min_{\boldsymbol{\Theta}} \frac{1}{N} \sum_{i=1}^{N} L(y_i, f_{\boldsymbol{\Theta}}(x_i))$. Mean Squared Error (MSE) is a common loss function [7]. MSE measures the average squared difference between the predicted and actual values:

$$\text{MSE} = \frac{1}{N} \sum_{i=1}^{N} (y_i - \hat{y}_i)^2, \qquad (1)$$

where y_i denotes the label value, $\hat{y}_i$ denotes the predicted value.

Batch Matrix Multiplication. Batch matrix multiplication performs multiple matrix multiplications simultaneously. It is useful when numerous matrix multiplications with the same dimensions are needed. In computer vision, it helps apply transformations and projections to image features in parallel, speeding up processing for multiple images [5,21]. For time series tasks, it is commonly used to multiply hidden states with inputs efficiently [6,15].

Let $\boldsymbol{A}$ be a three-dimensional tensor of shape (N, M, K), and $\boldsymbol{B}$ be a three-dimensional tensor of shape (N, K, P), where N is the batch size. We define the batch matrix multiplication calculator as $\otimes$. We have

$$\boldsymbol{A} \otimes \boldsymbol{B} = (\boldsymbol{A}[0] \cdot \boldsymbol{B}[0], \boldsymbol{A}[1] \cdot \boldsymbol{B}[1], \cdots, \boldsymbol{A}[N-1] \cdot \boldsymbol{B}[N-1]),$$

where the dot product (matrix multiplication) is performed between $\boldsymbol{A}[i]$ and $\boldsymbol{B}[i]$, $i \in \{0, 1, \cdots, N-1\}$. The result of the batch matrix multiplication $\boldsymbol{A} \otimes \boldsymbol{B}$ is a three-dimensional tensor of shape (N, M, P).

2.3 DL-NSCA

Below we introduce the first DL-NSCA work DDLA and the SOTA work MOR.

Differential Deep Learning Analysis (DDLA). [20] Instead of calculating the correlation for every key guess $k \in \mathcal{K}$, Timon trains a neural network f_{Θ_k} for classification with side-channel traces $\mathcal{T} = \{x_1, x_2, \ldots, x_N\}$ as input and the hypothetical leakage $\mathcal{H}_k = \{h_{k,1}, h_{k,2}, \ldots, h_{k,N}\}$ as label. The author adopts the MSE loss mentioned in (1). Sort the loss values for each model to derive the correct key guess k_*:

$$k_* = \arg\min_{k \in \mathcal{K}} \frac{1}{N} \sum_{i=1}^{N} \mathsf{L}(h_{k,i}, \mathsf{f}_{\Theta_k}(x_i)) = \arg\min_{k \in \mathcal{K}} \frac{1}{N} \sum_{i=1}^{N} (h_{k,i} - \mathsf{f}_{\Theta_k}(x_i))^2.$$

Multi-output Regression (MOR). [4] MOR has made an improvement in the following three aspects:

1. MOR consists of a shared layer for common feature extraction, followed by 256 non-shared layers, each producing a separate output.
2. DDLA fails under the identity model, as partition-based DPA cannot handle injective target functions [18,25]. MOR addresses this by treating labels as continuous values and applying regression, making it the first effective DL-NSCA method in this context.
3. Unlike DDLA, which trains 256 separate networks, MOR uses a multi-output network with 256 continuous outputs. It maps side-channel traces $\mathcal{T} = \{x_1, \ldots, x_N\}$ to hypothetical leakages $\mathcal{H} = \{h_1, \ldots, h_N\}$, where each

$h_i = (h_{0,i}, \ldots, h_{255,i})$. The model is trained using MSE loss, and the correct key guess k_* is determined by minimizing the average loss:

$$k_* = \arg\min_{k \in \mathcal{K}} \frac{1}{N} \sum_{i=1}^{N} \mathsf{L}(h_i^k, \mathsf{f}_\Theta^k(x_i)) = \arg\min_{k \in \mathcal{K}} \frac{1}{N} \sum_{i=1}^{N} (h_i^k - \mathsf{f}_\Theta^k(x_i))^2$$

where $\mathsf{f}_\theta^k(x_i)$, h_i^k respectively represent the kth value of the model output $\mathsf{f}_\theta(x_i)$ and label h_i.

2.4 Hypothetical Power Model

Given the intermediate values, hypothetical power models are used to estimate the real power consumption. There are three commonly used models as follows:

- **Hamming Weight(HW) model:** For $a \in \mathbb{F}_2^n$, the HW is defined as $\mathsf{HW}(a) = \sum_{i=0}^{n-1} \mathsf{I}_{a[i]=1}$, where I is an indicator function and $a[i]$ denotes the i-th bit of a.
- **Least Significant Bit(LSB) model:** For $a \in \mathbb{F}_2^n$, the LSB model is defined as $\mathsf{LSB}(a) = a[0]$, where $a[0]$ represent the 0th bit of a. Different from the HW model, the LSB model only considers the least significant bit of the data.
- **Identity (ID) model:** For $a \in \mathbb{F}_2^n$, the ID model uses $\mathsf{ID}(a) = a$.

3 End-to-End Framework

3.1 Design Philosophy

Although there are no end-to-end works in non-profiled SCA, two works in profiled SCA use two types of neural network frameworks. The first category is the VGG-like architecture proposed by Masure et al. [16], which is also usually the optimal architecture in the leakage interval scenario [8,26,27]. The second category is the LSTM framework proposed by Lu et al. [14]. The commonality between the two frameworks is that they both utilize neural networks with a high number of layers.

The design suitable for the end-to-end non-profiled framework is significantly different from that of profiled SCA. Our design philosophy for DL-NSCA is to adopt a lightweight network. The complex networks mentioned above are difficult to implement in DL-NSCA for several reasons:

(1) In end-to-end non-profiled SCA, complex neural network architectures may lead to significant overfitting issues. The main reason lies in the network's dual behavior. While effectively extracting PoIs in raw traces and establishing correct label-to-trace mappings, it aggregates irrelevant noise points from raw traces simultaneously. These noise points form high-level representations through hierarchical feature composition, ultimately causing the network to erroneously establish spurious correlations between irrelevant features and labels of incorrect key guesses.

(2) For the same network architecture, the network parameters in profiled SCA will be amplified by a factor in non-profiled SCA. For example, training the profiling model in [14] to recover a 1-byte key can take three days. Therefore, it cannot perform well in DL-NSCA since training this framework for all key guesses (256 for 1-byte key) would require an unimaginable amount of time and computational resources (at least $3 \times 256 = 768\,\mathrm{d}$ on NVIDIA RTX 2080Ti GPU).

Therefore, the lightweight network should have the following features: (a) enhances performance by significantly improving the representation capability of high-noise raw traces without causing overfitting; (b) uses optimized operators to ensure acceptable analysis time.

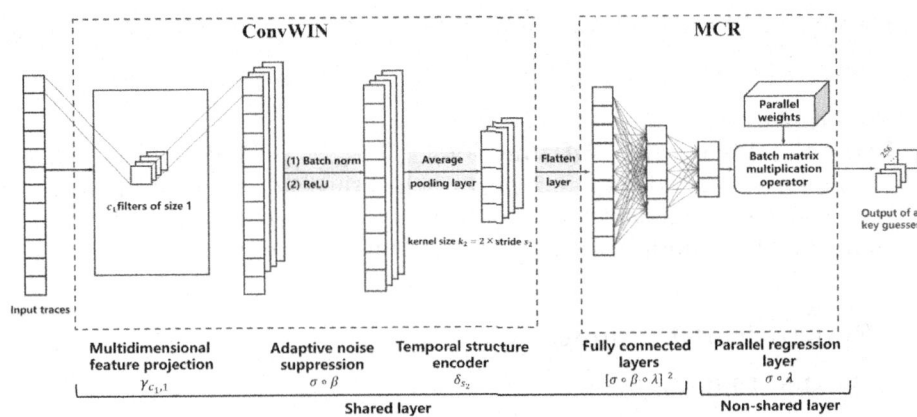

Fig. 1. End-to-end framework of convWIN-MCR.

We propose a lightweight end-to-end DL-NSCA framework, convWIN-MCR, as shown in Fig. 1. It comprises a performance-optimizing component, convWIN, and an accelerator component, MCR. We will introduce them in Sect. 3.2 and Sect. 3.3 respectively. We define this framework in Eq. (2), where $\gamma_{c_1,1}$ is a convolutional layer with c_1 filters of size 1, β denotes a batch normalization layer, σ represents an activation function ReLU, δ_{s_2} denotes an average pooling layer with kernel size that is twice of the stride size s_2, λ is the fully connected layer and $\boldsymbol{\lambda}$ denotes a parallel regression layer.

$$\underbrace{\sigma \circ \boldsymbol{\lambda}}_{non-shared\ layer} \circ \underbrace{[\sigma \circ \beta \circ \lambda]^2 \circ [\delta_{s_2} \circ \sigma \circ \beta \circ \gamma_{c_1,1}]}_{shared\ layer}, \qquad (2)$$

3.2 The Performance-Optimizing Component: ConvWIN Layer

To handle long raw traces, we aim to propose a structure that allows the existing model to enhance attack performance while reducing computational complexity.

We introduce a 'temporal feature distiller' called convWIN as the network's first layer. It consists of three parts:

(a) **The multidimensional feature projection** $\gamma_{c_1,1}$: We use a 1×1 convolutional layer, first introduced in the Network in Network (NiN) architecture by Lin et al. [12]. This layer helps learn independent leakage patterns like clock edges and bus inversions by using different kernels, providing multidimensional features for subsequent fully connected layers and enhancing feature interaction.

(b) **Adaptive noise suppression** $\sigma \circ \beta$: Batch normalization reduces noise and speeds up training, and the ReLU activation sparsify feature representations, adds non-linearity and increases sensitivity to important information.

(c) **Temporal structure encoder** δ_{s_2}: In machine learning, features are the measurable properties of a dataset. Those useful for the learning task are called relevant features, while the rest are irrelevant [28]. In SCA, relevant features typically refer to PoIs. In long raw traces, PoIs show three key patterns:
   - Few relevant features: Only a small portion of the trace contains useful information, often tied to specific operations like the SBox operation in AES.
   - Local concentration: Relevant features tend to cluster within specific time windows instead of being uniformly spread.
   - Coexistence of strongly and weakly relevant features: Strongly relevant features usually occur precisely when the intermediate value is directly involved in a computation or is actively being processed by a specific hardware unit. In addition, an intermediate value doesn't just appear; it moves through the chip's data path, with each gate or register flip consuming power. These propagated leakages, though less intensive than the strongly relevant features, still carry information and appear alongside the strong ones. We call them weakly relevant features.

We refer to these three characteristics as the sparsity of side-channel leakages. Based on the sparsity, using an average pooling layer as an encoder allows for maximizing the retention of leakage while filtering out noise and significantly reducing feature dimensions, thereby greatly decreasing the required number of parameters.

In addition, for misaligned traces, we demonstrate that applying the average pooling module can significantly improve the correlation of side-channel traces and hypothetical leakages corresponding to the correct key guess. Assume there is a main leakage point P_l at time l within the sequence of power consumptions $P_{-a}, P_{-a+1}, \ldots, P_a$, where l follows a uniform distribution in the set $\{-a, -a+1, \ldots, a\}$. Let the hypothetical leakages corresponding to the correct key guess as H_{ck}. Denote the Pearson correlation coefficient between P_i and P_j as $\beta_{i,j}$, where $\beta_{i,j} = \rho(P_i, P_j) = \frac{Cov(P_i,P_j)}{Var(P_i)Var(P_j)}, i,j \in \{-a, -a+1, \ldots, a\}$. $|\beta_{i,j}| \leq 1$, and the equality holds if and only if P_i is linearly related to P_j. Since the leakage occurs at P_l, there exists α_i, $\alpha_i \leq 1$, s.t. $\rho(H_{ck}, P_i) = \alpha_i \rho(H_{ck}, P_l), i \in \{-a, -a+1, \ldots, a\}$.

1. Without the average pooling layer: Denote C_0 as the correlation of misaligned traces and hypothetical leakages corresponding to the correct key guess, and the expectation of C_0 can be expressed as follows:

$$E[C_0] = E[\rho(H_{ck}, P_l)] = \frac{1}{2a+1} \sum_{i=-a}^{a} \rho(H_{ck}, P_i) = \frac{\sum_{i=-a}^{a} \alpha_i}{2a+1} \rho(H_{ck}, P_l).$$

2. Applying the average pooling layer: The output of the pooling layer is $\frac{1}{2a+1} \sum_{i=-a}^{a} P_i$. The correlation of misaligned traces and hypothetical leakages corresponding to the correct key guess C_1 is:

$$C_1 = \rho(H_{ck}, \frac{1}{2a+1} \sum_{i=-a}^{a} P_i) = \rho(H_{ck}, \sum_{i=-a}^{a} P_i) = \frac{Cov(H_{ck}, \sum_{i=-a}^{a} P_i)}{\sqrt{Var(H_{ck}) Var(\sum_{i=-a}^{a} P_i)}}$$

Assuming that the variance of $P_{-a}, P_{-a+1}, \ldots, P_a$ are all σ^2, we have

$$C_1 = \frac{\sigma \sum_{i=-a}^{a} \alpha_i}{\sqrt{Var(\sum_{i=-a}^{a} P_i)}} \rho(H_{ck}, P_l)$$

$$= \frac{\sum_{i=-a}^{a} \alpha_i}{\sqrt{(2a+1) + \sum_{i=-a, j=-a, i\neq j}^{a} \beta_{i,j}}} \rho(H_{ck}, P_l)$$

$$\geq \frac{\sum_{i=-a}^{a} \alpha_i}{\sqrt{(2a+1) + (2a+1)2a}} \rho(H_{ck}, P_l) = \frac{\sum_{i=-a}^{a} \alpha_i}{2a+1} \rho(H_{ck}, P_l)$$

$$= E[C_0]$$

We have $E[C_0] = C_1 \Leftrightarrow \beta_{i,j} = 1, i, j \in \{-a, -(a-1), \ldots, a\}$, where only when the power consumption corresponding to all $(2a+1)$ points are linearly correlated, it is unnecessary to adopt the average pooling strategy. However, this situation rarely occurs in practice. Therefore, adopting the average pooling strategy can improve the probability of distinguishing the correct key guess from incorrect key guesses, thereby enhancing the model's attack performance.

3.3 The Accelerator Component: MCR Layer

One of the main reasons existing DL-NSCA models have difficulty processing long raw traces is that low GPU utilization leads to long analysis time. Based on MOR, we propose an accelerator component, MCR, which improves GPU utilization by introducing batch matrix multiplication.

DDLA requires training a model for each key guess. The improvement of MOR is that only one network needs to be trained, but there are 256 non-shared layers trained in serial. MCR enables 256 non-shared layers to compute in parallel by merging several matrix multiplications into a single tensor operation.

From Serial to Parallel. Given the input $x \in \mathbb{R}^{N \times S_{k-1}}$ of the kth non-shared layer, there are 256 fully connected layer, each of which corresponds to one output. Set time stamp $\mathcal{T} = \{t_0, t_1, \ldots, t_{255}\}$. The existing serial network performs the following computation at time $t_j, t_j \in \mathcal{T}$:

$$z_k = x w_k^T + b_k$$

where $w_k^T \in \mathbb{R}^{S_{k-1} \times S_k}$, $b_k \in \mathbb{R}$ are the kth fully connected parameters and $z_k \in \mathbb{R}^{N \times S_k}$ is the kth output. We introduce batch matrix multiplication to merge 256 matrix multiplications into one single tensor operation. We refer to the newly added dimension as channels, where each channel represents the network training for each key guess. At one time stamp, there are the following computations:

$$Z^{parallel} = X^{parallel} \otimes W^T + b,$$

where $b = (b_0, b_1, \ldots, b_{255}) \in \mathbb{R}^{256}$, $W^T = (w_0^T, w_1^T, \ldots, w_{255}^T) \in \mathbb{R}^{256 \times S_{k-1} \times S_k}$ and $X^{parallel} = (x, x, \ldots, x) \in \mathbb{R}^{256 \times N \times S_{k-1}}$. $Z^{parallel} = (z_0, z_1, \ldots, z_{255})$ is the output. $\otimes$ represents batch multiplication calculator. The structure of the MCR model is shown in the right box of Fig. 1. In the parallel regression layer, each color corresponds to a different channel, i.e., one of the key guesses. The calculations in each channel are independent and are performed in parallel during the forward and backward passes of the neural network.

Remark. MOR and MCR are functionally equivalent, which means that given the same input and identical internal parameters, they should produce the same output and have the same computational complexity. MCR merges 256 matrix multiplications into a single tensor operation, which significantly reduces the analysis time.

4 Experimental Results

In this section, we first introduce public datasets ASCADv1 in Sect. 4.1 and validate the role of the convWIN layer in Sect. 4.2. Sections 4.3 and 4.4 are end-to-end experiments on public datasets and a real-world device, respectively. We set the maximum number of training epochs to 50 across all experiments and test the minimum number of traces required using steps of 500. Each model is trained independently 10 times to reduce randomness, such as weight initialization. We differentiate between correct and incorrect key guesses based on the loss value at the last epoch. In our results, there are two scenarios: (1) When the model successfully recovers the key, i.e., average key rank equals zero in ten times experiments, we find the minimum number of traces to evaluate attack performance. (2) When the model fails to break the target, the performance is measured by the average key rank given the maximum number of traces, denoted as GE. We follow the same pre-processing as in DDLA: normalize the input traces by subtracting the mean and scaling them to the range -1 and 1. All networks were implemented using the PyTorch framework with an AMD EPYC 7763 64-Core Processor, an NVIDIA GeForce RTX 4090 GPU card, and 1T RAM. The code for replicating the experiments can be found in our GitHub repository[1].

4.1 ASCADv1 Dataset

The ASCADv1 dataset is a public SCA dataset[2] It contains traces collected from an 8-bit ATmega8515 microcontroller running masked AES-128 encryption, using Boolean masking [1,17]. ASCADv1 is split into two versions: ASCAD_F (fixed key) and ASCAD_V (variable keys). Since non-profiled SCA targets a device under the same key, we use attack phase traces from ASCAD_V in our experiments (see Table 1). Each dataset provides traces for four types of scenarios. Taking the ASCAD_F dataset as an example, ASCAD_F, ASCAD_F_desyn, ASCAD_F_R and ASCAD_F_R_desyn represent aligned and misaligned traces in the leakage intervals scenario and aligned and misaligned raw traces respectively. For the misaligned traces, the datasets randomly shift the aligned traces within an interval range from the original dataset to simulate random delays.

Table 1. Settings of the ASCAD datasets

	Dataset	Traces	Feature points	Random delay
Leakage intervals	ASCAD_F	60,000	700	None
	ASCAD_V	100,000	1,400	None
	ASCAD_F_desyn	50,000	700	50
	ASCAD_V_desyn	100,000	1,400	50
Raw traces	ASCAD_F_R	60,000	100,000	None
	ASCAD_V_R	100,000	250,000	None
	ASCAD_F_R_desyn	60,000	100,000	128
	ASCAD_V_R_desyn	100,000	250,000	128

Table 2. Settings of Network Parameters

	DDLA [20]	convWIN-DDLA	MOR [4]	convWIN-MOR
convWIN layer	\	c_1, s_2	\	c_1, s_2
hidden layer 1	20	20	800	800
hidden layer 2	10	10	1000	1000
hidden layer 3	9/2	9/2	1	1
learning rate	0.001	0.001	0.001	0.001
batch size	1000	1000	50	50
loss function	MSE	MSE	MSE	MSE
optimizer	Adam	Adam	Adam	Adam

---

[1] https://github.com/jintongyucrypto/end2end_DL-NSCA.git.
[2] available on GitHub: https://github.com/ANSSI-FR/ASCAD.

4.2 The Role of the ConvWIN Layer in NSCA

In this section, we validate the role of the convWIN component in enhancing attack performance and improving robustness against misalignment in the leakage interval scenario. Additionally, the convWIN component has two hyperparameters, and we demonstrate how these internal hyperparameters influence model performance through experiments. Based on DDLA and MOR, we propose the convWIN-DDLA and convWIN-MOR models to explore the impacts of the convWIN component. It is acknowledged that fine-tunning the model can enhance performance for a given dataset; however, finding the optimal parameters for a specific scenario is not the main objective of this work. Therefore, we adopt the same model structure and parameters as the original papers, as shown in Table 2. DDLA consists of three fully connected layers, where the hidden size of the last layer depends on the hypothetical power model used (9 for HW, 2 for LSB). MOR comprises two fully connected layers in the shared part and one in the non-shared part. Since it is a regression model, the number of output neurons of the last layer is set to 1. Regarding the hidden size of the shared layers, the authors found that a larger hidden size leads to better model performance. Therefore, we set the hidden size of the shared layers uniformly to 800 and 1000, which will be used for experiments in this section on leakage intervals and in the next section on end-to-end scenarios.

Table 3. Attack performance on aligned and misaligned traces

Dataset	Hypothetical model	DDLA [20]	convWIN-DDLA	MOR [4]	convWIN-MOR
ASCAD_F	HW	GE57.5	**22,500**	8500	**6000**
	ID(LSB)	33,000	**16,500**	24,000	**19,500**
ASCAD_V	HW	GE100.6	**35,500**	28,000	**4,000**
	ID(LSB)	36,000	**9,000**	GE3.6	**34,000**
ASCAD_F_desyn	HW	GE75.1	**32,500**	GE21.2	**12,500**
	ID(LSB)	GE111.0	**4,500**	GE5.0	**46,500**
ASCAD_V_desyn	HW	GE112.8	**20,500**	GE18.6	**4,500**
	ID(LSB)	GE100.3	**3500**	GE16.8	**31,000**

Performance Improvement. We evaluate the attack performance of DDLA and MOR with and without the convWIN component, as shown in Table 3. We conduct experiments on the HW and ID models. Since DDLA cannot work in ID model [18], we use the LSB model as a replacement. We analyze ASCADv1 datasets using DDLA, convWIN-DDLA, MOR, and convWIN-MOR models, and the settings of network parameters are shown in Table 2. Here, we discuss the selection of the number of filters c_1. As mentioned in Sect. 3.2, c_1 represents the extraction of c_1 leakage patterns (linear transformations) for the subsequent network structure to learn. If we disregard computational complexity, a larger value of c_1 is better. We conduct experiments with $c_1 \in \{1, 2, 4, 8, 16\}$ and a fixed value of s_2, and the results are shown in Appendix A. As we can see, increasing the number of filters c_1 can improve the model's performance. The model performance with 1, 2, and 4 filters is significantly worse than that with 8 and 16 filters. Although the model performance corresponding to 16 filters may exceed or equal that of 8 filters in most situations, an increase in the number of filters corresponds to a substantial exponential growth in the number of parameters. Therefore, adopting eight filters represents a trade-off between performance and computational complexity, and we will also utilize $c_1 = 8$ in our subsequent experiments. As shown in Table 3, after adding convWIN to the first layer of DDLA and MOR, the minimum number of traces required by the model is reduced by an average of 73% and 56%, respectively.

Robustness Against Misalignment. We verify that the addition of the convWIN component can improve the model's robustness against misalignment, and the results on ASCAD_F_desyn and ASCAD_V_desyn are presented in the Table 3. The stride of the pooling layer s_2 determines the degree of feature dimensionality reduction. A large s_2 significantly reduces the number of network parameters but increases the level of information compression. We consider experimenting with $s_2 \in \{16, 32, 64, 128\}$ and obtain the optimal results. With the addition of the convWIN layer, the performance of DDLA and MOR is improved by an average of 85% and 89%, respectively.

The Accelerator Component MCR. The addition of the convWIN component to the DDLA and MOR models not only significantly reduces the minimum number of traces required for analysis but also decreases the analysis time. This is attributed to the enhanced power of models and the dimensionality reduction effect. Nonetheless, the analysis time for the aforementioned models remains long relative to the dimensionality of the processed traces. When the dimensionality of the input traces increases by a factor of 100, the analysis time becomes unmanageable. Therefore, we replaced the MOR model with our accelerator component MCR, and the experimental results are shown in Table 4. The convWIN-MCR model, while maintaining high performance, improves analysis speed by 95% on aligned traces and by 93% on misaligned traces compared to the convWIN-MOR model. Furthermore, the cost of parallelism, specifically the increased GPU memory consumption, is acceptable. Taking the ASCAD_F dataset as an example, the training process for convWIN-MOR consumes 0.94 GPU memory, and convWIN-MCR's training occupies 1.03 GB of GPU memory, representing an increase of only 9.6% in GPU memory usage. This allows efficient analysis of raw traces, as reflected in both performance and analysis time. Consequently, we will use the convWIN-MCR framework to analyze the raw traces in subsequent experiments.

4.3 End-To-End Experiments on Public Datasets

Settings for End-to-End Analysis. We will validate the effectiveness of our end-to-end framework, convWIN-MCR, on raw traces from ASCADv1. The network parameters are shown in Table 2. Since the appropriate stride s_2 depends on

Table 4. The role of the accelerator component MCR

Dataset	Model	Hypothetical Model	Minimum number of Traces	Analysis time(second)
ASCAD_F	DDLA [20]	HW/LSB	GE57.5/33000	fail/2581
	convWIN-DDLA	HW/LSB	22500/16500	2343/1569
	MOR [4]	HW/ID	8500/24000	404/1156
	convWIN-MOR	HW/ID	6000/19500	299/851
	convWIN-MCR	HW/ID	6000/19500	**15**/**42**
ASCAD_V	DDLA [20]	HW/LSB	GE100.6/36000	fail/5970
	convWIN-DDLA	HW/LSB	35500/9000	10119/2554
	MOR [4]	HW/ID	28000/GE3.6	1401/fail
	convWIN-MOR	HW/ID	4000/34000	199/1626
	convWIN-MCR	HW/ID	4000/34000	**10**/**84**
ASCAD_F_desyn	DDLA [20]	HW/LSB	GE75.1/GE111.0	fail/fail
	convWIN-DDLA	HW/LSB	32500/**4500**	8189/1228
	MOR [4]	HW/ID	GE21.2/GE5.0	fail/fail
	convWIN-MOR	HW/ID	12500/46500	918/2571
	convWIN-MCR	HW/ID	12500/46500	**62**/ **170**
ASCAD_V_desyn	DDLA [20]	HW/LSB	GE112.8/GE100.3	fail/fail
	convWIN-DDLA	HW/LSB	20500/**3500**	4510/893
	MOR [4]	HW/ID	GE18.6/GE16.8	fail/fail
	convWIN-MOR	HW/ID	4500/31000	245 / 1670
	convWIN-MCR	HW/ID	4500/31000	**15** / **101**

the feature dimensionality of the raw traces, we use grid search to find the optimal model. Experiments are conducted on aligned and misaligned raw traces, with the results presented in Table 5. In our experiments, we found that the MOR model fails to recover the key on all raw trace datasets listed in the table. Therefore, to better demonstrate the superiority of our model, we compare the results of MOR on the leakage interval with those of convWIN-MCR on the raw traces on the datasets.

Results on Aligned Raw Traces. On the ASCAD_F_R dataset, the experiment reveals that $s_2 = 200$ leads to the best performance, successfully recovering the key using only 10,000 traces in 3 min. Our model's analysis performance on raw traces approaches MOR's on the leakage interval with only 700 points, while the analysis time is also reduced by 59%. On the ASCAD_V_R dataset, which contains 250,000 feature points, the experiment shows that the best results are achieved when $s_2 = 1000$. On the leakage interval dataset containing 1400 points, MOR requires at least 28000 traces and 24 min to recover the key. Our framework analyzes the raw traces from the same dataset with 250,000 points, requiring only 6000 traces and completing the analysis within 13 min.

Results on Misaligned Raw Traces. On the ASCAD_F_R_desyn dataset, the convWIN-MCR model performs best when $s_2 = 1000$. It successfully recovers the key using 38500 traces in 10 min, while MOR fails to recover the key on the corresponding leakage interval dataset. On the ASCAD_V_R_desyn dataset, the experiments indicate that when $s_2 = 2000$, the optimal value is reached, successfully recovering the key using only 7000 traces in just 6 min. MOR fails to recover the key on the corresponding leakage interval dataset with 1400 points.

Table 5. Attack performance of convWIN-MCR on aligned and misaligned raw traces

Dataset	Number of feature points	Model	Hypothetical model	Minimum number of traces	Analysis time (second)
ASCAD_F	700	MOR	HW	8,500	404
			ID	24,000	1,156
ASCAD_F_R	100,000	convWIN-MCR	HW	**10,000**	167
			ID	42,500	632
ASCAD_V	1400	MOR	HW	28,000	1401
			ID	GE3.6	fail
ASCAD_V_R	250,000	convWIN-MCR	HW	**6,000**	744
			ID	50,000	1,588
ASCAD_F_desyn	700	MOR	HW	GE21.2	fail
			ID	GE5.0	fail
ASCAD_F_R_desyn	100,000	convWIN-MCR	HW	40,000	544
			ID	**38,500**	558
ASCAD_V_desyn	1400	MOR	HW	GE18.6	fail
			ID	GE16.8	fail
ASCAD_V_R_desyn	250,000	convWIN-MCR	HW	**7,000**	361
			ID	33,500	1,001

4.4 End-to-End Experiments on a USIM Card

Raw Traces Acquisition from a USIM Card. While deep learning-based SCA methods perform well on public datasets, few have been tested on real-world devices. We evaluate the practicality of our end-to-end framework in a realistic setting by targeting a 4G USIM card from a major mobile operator (referred to as Card A). $4G^3$ authentication uses the MILENAGE algorithm, based on the AES algorithm. To break a USIM card, an attacker must recover the master key K and random value OPc. Liu et al. achieved this by analyzing leakages of the SubByte operations in the first two rounds of AES using CPA [13]. Our replication shows that the success of the CPA is heavily dependent on the accurate selection of the leakage interval and alignment. In our experiment, we utilized an acquisition device, the PICO 3203D oscilloscope, and a PC to collect the power traces of the USIM card's authentication process, as shown in Fig. 5 of appendix B. As illustrated in Fig. 6, we collect 30,000 traces containing the first two rounds of operations without any additional preprocessing and create a dataset called TRACE_USIM[4], which includes 100,000 feature points for each round of operations in USIM_1rd and USIM_2rd.

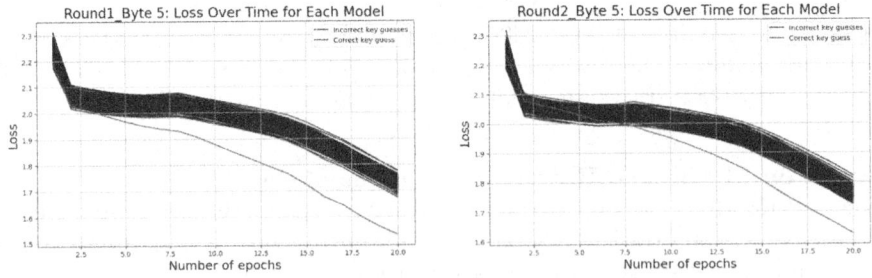

Fig. 2. Results of end-to-end analysis on the USIM card.

---
[3] https://www.3gpp.org/dynareport?code=33-series.html.
[4] https://github.com/jintongyucrypto/end2end_DL-NSCA.git.

Results of Analyzing Raw Traces Collected from USIM Card. We analyze the raw traces USIM_1rd containing the first round of AES encryption using Liu's method. We observe that it is impossible to distinguish between the correct key guess and incorrect key guesses. We use our end-to-end framework convWIN-MCR, taking raw traces as the input and the intermediate values $[HW[Sbox[p \oplus \texttt{0x00}]], HW[Sbox[p \oplus \texttt{0x01}]], \ldots, HW[Sbox[p \oplus \texttt{0xFF}]]]$ as labels, where p is the known plaintext. The model structure parameters are shown in the last column of Table 2. We perform a grid search on the parameter $s_2 \in \{100, 200, 500, 1000, 2000\}$ and consider that the output component corresponding to the fastest decrease of the loss function indicates the position of the correct key guess. Experimental results show that for all 16 bytes, we can successfully distinguish between the correct and the incorrect key guesses through the loss curve within 6 min, and Fig. 2 shows the loss curve for the 5th byte. Using the early stopping technique, we find that at 20 epochs, the model has already completed distinguishing between the correct and incorrect key guesses. Therefore, the value of $K \oplus OPc$ of this USIM card is recovered.

Next, we analyze raw traces USIM_2rd using the same model structure and the hyperparameter search to recover first round subkey. For all bytes, the loss curve shows strong distinguishability, and we recover the 128-bit round key in 7 min. We only show the loss curve of the 5th byte of the key in Fig. 2 considering space constraints. Based on the first round subkey, we can finally deduce the master key and OPc.

5 Conclusions

This paper proposes the first efficient end-to-end DL-NSCA framework, convWIN-MCR. This framework allows attackers to recover keys in a black-box scenario without owning a profiling device and knowing the implementation details. We get satisfying results on public datasets and a real-world device. On the public dataset, the number of feature points in the raw traces exceeds that of the leakage interval by more than two orders of magnitude. We demonstrate that convWIN-MCR achieves comparable or even superior performance in key recovery when analyzing the raw traces, compared to MOR which analyzes the leakage interval. Moreover, our framework significantly reduces analysis time. On a real-world device, we validate the practicality of convWIN-MCR in realistic black-box scenarios by successfully recovering the master key through direct analysis of raw traces from a USIM card.

Furthermore, our experiments utilize public datasets primarily employing first-order masking, as this masking scheme has minimal impact on algorithm performance and is the most widely used. However, higher-order masking implementations with higher security levels hold significant practical importance for future research.

Acknowledgments. This work was supported by the National Natural Science Foundation of China (Grant No.U2336210), the Ant Group, and the Startup Fund for Young Faculty at SJTU (SFYF at SJTU).

Appendix A Ablation study on the kernel size c_1

See Figs. 3 and 4.

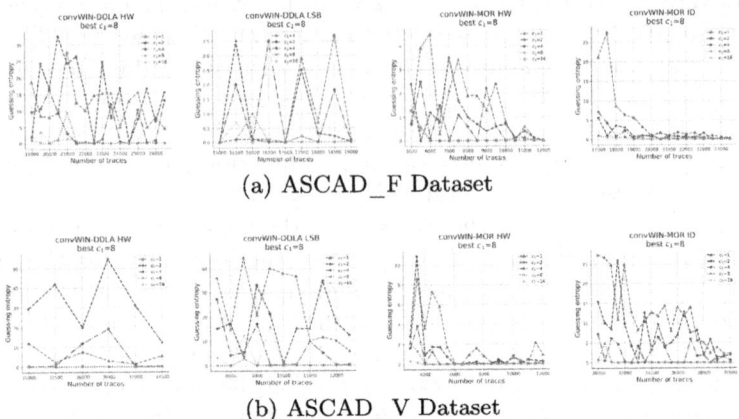

Fig. 3. Attack performance of convWIN-DDLA and convWIN-MOR given different settings of the kernel size c_1

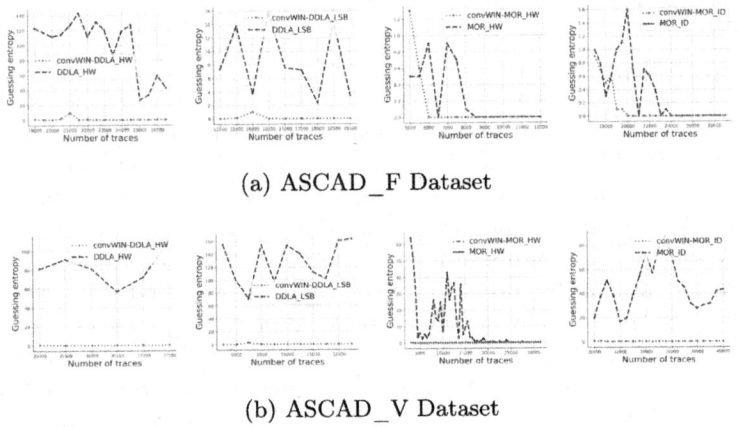

Fig. 4. Performance comparison between DDLA and convWIN-DDLA, MOR and convWIN-MOR

Appendix B The USIM Card Analysis

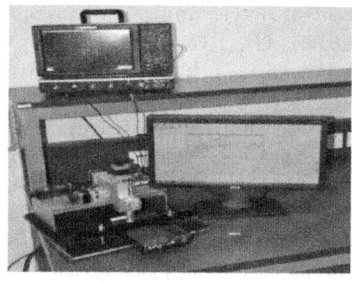
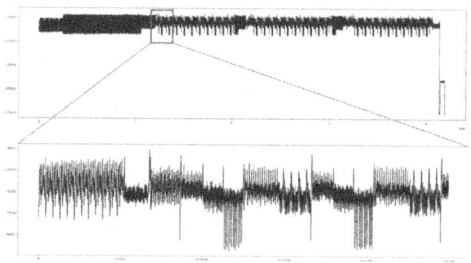

Fig. 5. The Acquisition settings for the USIM Card.

Fig. 6. Capturing traces from the first two round of AES encryption.

References

1. Akkar, M.-L., Giraud, C.: An implementation of DES and AES, secure against some attacks. In: Koç, Ç.K., Naccache, D., Paar, C. (eds.) CHES 2001. LNCS, vol. 2162, pp. 309–318. Springer, Heidelberg (2001). https://doi.org/10.1007/3-540-44709-1_26
2. Bengio, Y., Courville, A., Vincent, P.: Representation learning: a review and new perspectives. IEEE Trans. Pattern Anal. Mach. Intell. **35**(8), 1798–1828 (2013)
3. Brier, E., Clavier, C., Olivier, F.: Correlation power analysis with a leakage model. In: Joye, M., Quisquater, J.-J. (eds.) CHES 2004. LNCS, vol. 3156, pp. 16–29. Springer, Heidelberg (2004). https://doi.org/10.1007/978-3-540-28632-5_2
4. Do, N.T., Hoang, V.P., Doan, V.S.: A novel non-profiled side channel attack based on multi-output regression neural network. J. Cryptogr. Eng. **14**(3), 427–439 (2024)
5. Fu, J., et al.: Dual attention network for scene segmentation. In: Proceedings of the IEEE/CVF Conference on Computer Vision and Pattern Recognition, pp. 3146–3154 (2019)
6. Graves, A., Graves, A.: Long short-term memory. Supervised sequence labelling with recurrent neural networks, pp. 37–45 (2012)
7. Franklin, J.: The elements of statistical learning: data mining, inference and prediction. Math. Intell. **27**(2), 83–85 (2005). https://doi.org/10.1007/BF02985802
8. Kim, J., Picek, S., Heuser, A., Bhasin, S., Hanjalic, A.: Make some noise. unleashing the power of convolutional neural networks for profiled side-channel analysis. IACR Trans. Cryptographic Hardware Embedded Syst. 148–179 (2019)
9. Kocher, P., Jaffe, J., Jun, B.: Differential power analysis. In: Wiener, M. (ed.) CRYPTO 1999. LNCS, vol. 1666, pp. 388–397. Springer, Heidelberg (1999). https://doi.org/10.1007/3-540-48405-1_25
10. Kocher, P.C.: Timing attacks on implementations of Diffie-Hellman, RSA, DSS, and other systems. In: Koblitz, N. (ed.) CRYPTO 1996. LNCS, vol. 1109, pp. 104–113. Springer, Heidelberg (1996). https://doi.org/10.1007/3-540-68697-5_9

11. Kwon, D., Hong, S., Kim, H.: Optimizing implementations of non-profiled deep learning-based side-channel attacks. IEEE Access **10**, 5957–5967 (2022)
12. Lin, M., Chen, Q., Yan, S.: Network in network. arXiv preprint arXiv:1312.4400 (2013)
13. Liu, J., et al.: Small tweaks do not help: differential power analysis of milenage implementations in 3G/4G USIM cards. In: Pernul, G., Ryan, P.Y.A., Weippl, E. (eds.) ESORICS 2015. LNCS, vol. 9326, pp. 468–480. Springer, Cham (2015). https://doi.org/10.1007/978-3-319-24174-6_24
14. Lu, X., Zhang, C., Cao, P., Gu, D., Lu, H.: Pay attention to raw traces: a deep learning architecture for end-to-end profiling attacks. IACR Trans. Cryptographic Hardware Embedded Syst. 235–274 (2021)
15. Luong, M.T., Pham, H., Manning, C.D.: Effective approaches to attention-based neural machine translation. arXiv preprint arXiv:1508.04025 (2015)
16. Masure, L., et al.: Deep learning side-channel analysis on large-scale traces. In: Chen, L., Li, N., Liang, K., Schneider, S. (eds.) ESORICS 2020. LNCS, vol. 12308, pp. 440–460. Springer, Cham (2020). https://doi.org/10.1007/978-3-030-58951-6_22
17. Prouff, E., Rivain, M.: A generic method for secure SBox implementation. In: Kim, S., Yung, M., Lee, H.-W. (eds.) WISA 2007. LNCS, vol. 4867, pp. 227–244. Springer, Heidelberg (2007). https://doi.org/10.1007/978-3-540-77535-5_17
18. Standaert, F.-X., Gierlichs, B., Verbauwhede, I.: Partition *vs.* comparison side-channel distinguishers: an empirical evaluation of statistical tests for univariate side-channel attacks against two unprotected CMOS devices. In: Lee, P.J., Cheon, J.H. (eds.) ICISC 2008. LNCS, vol. 5461, pp. 253–267. Springer, Heidelberg (2009). https://doi.org/10.1007/978-3-642-00730-9_16
19. Tihmstar: Using a magic wand to break the iphone's last security barrier (2022). https://hardwear.io/netherlands-2022/speakers/tihmstar.php
20. Timon, B.: Non-profiled deep learning-based side-channel attacks with sensitivity analysis. IACR Trans. Cryptographic Hardware Embedded Syst., 107–131 (2019)
21. Vaswani, A., et al.: Attention is all you need. Adv. Neural Inform. Process. Syst. **30** (2017)
22. Veyrat-Charvillon, N., Standaert, F.-X.: Mutual information analysis: how, when and why? In: Clavier, C., Gaj, K. (eds.) CHES 2009. LNCS, vol. 5747, pp. 429–443. Springer, Heidelberg (2009). https://doi.org/10.1007/978-3-642-04138-9_30
23. Wang, A., He, S., Wei, C., Sun, S., Ding, Y., Wang, J.: Using convolutional neural network to redress outliers in clustering based side-channel analysis on cryptosystem. In: International Conference on Smart Computing and Communication, pp. 360–370. Springer (2022). https://doi.org/10.1007/978-3-031-28124-2_34
24. Wang, Z., et al.: Spa-gpt: general pulse tailor for simple power analysis based on reinforcement learning. IACR Trans. Cryptographic Hardware Embedded Syst. **2024**(4), 40–83 (2024)
25. Whitnall, C., Oswald, E., Standaert, F.-X.: The myth of generic DP... and the magic of learning. In: Benaloh, J. (ed.) CT-RSA 2014. LNCS, vol. 8366, pp. 183–205. Springer, Cham (2014). https://doi.org/10.1007/978-3-319-04852-9_10
26. Wouters, L., Arribas, V., Gierlichs, B., Preneel, B.: Revisiting a methodology for efficient cnn architectures in profiling attacks. IACR Trans. Cryptographic Hardware Embedded Syst., 147–168 (2020)
27. Zaid, G., Bossuet, L., Habrard, A., Venelli, A.: Methodology for efficient cnn architectures in profiling attacks. IACR Trans. Cryptographic Hardware Embedded Syst., 1–36 (2020)
28. Zhou, Z.H.: Machine learning. Springer nature (2021)

Author Index

A

Abdou, AbdelRahman 443
Adamsky, Florian 184, 204
Alcaraz, Cristina 423
Ang, Kian Kai 1
Aonzo, Simone 505
Austa, Cédrick 23

B

Balzarotti, Davide 505
Benzekri, Abdelmalek 43
Bethe, Timme 105
Billoir, Eddie 43

C

Caballero, Juan 505
Canavese, Daniele 43
Cao, Fei 263
Cao, Pei 526
Caubet, Juan 423
Chen, Chuan 464
Chen, Deming 484
Chen, Zhifeng 263
Cheng, Haibo 224
Cheng, Shaoyin 243
Choudhari, Amit 64
Chung, Minu 84
Conti, Mauro 382
Continella, Andrea 105

D

Dai, Hong-Ning 164
Dambra, Savino 505
Daniele, Cristian 105
Di Pietro, Roberto 382
Dricot, Jean-Michel 23

E

Esiner, Ertem 484

G

Geloczi, Emiliia 124
Gingupalli, Sarat Chandra Prasad 144
Gruss, Daniel 184, 204
Gu, Dawu 526
Guo, Hanyang 164
Guo, Li 342

H

He, Fengliang 164
Heckel, Martin 184, 204
Hong, Cheng 526
Hu, Guangwu 464
Huang, Fugeng 224
Huang, Hao 243
Hur, Junbeom 323

I

Ippolito, Lorenzo 505

J

Jahromi, Ali Sadeghi 443
Jang, Hyerean 283
Jarraya, Yosr 402
Jiao, Weihua 263
Juffinger, Jonas 184

K

Katzenbeisser, Stefan 124
Kermabon-Bobinnec, Hugo 402
Kim, Jinwoo 382
Kim, Taehun 283, 323
Kottmann, Felix 484
Kotzias, Platon 505
Kumar, Shorya 64

L

Laborde, Romain 43
Lamster, Lukas 303
Lee, Woomin 323

Li, Baiyang 342
Li, Qing 464
Li, Qingbao 263
Li, Wenting 224
Li, Xilong 263
Lin, Xingwei 361
Liu, Qingyun 342
Lopez, Javier 423
Lu, Xiangjun 526
Luo, Xiapu 164

M

Ma, Lin 361
Majumdar, Suryadipta 402
Mangard, Stefan 303
Marin, Eduard 382
Maugeri, Marcello 105
Mexis, Nico 124
Moghaddas Borhan, Alireza 402
Moon, Hyungon 84
Mühlberg, Jan Tobias 23

P

Parada, Javier 423
Pavoni, Alessio 382
Poll, Erik 105

Q

Qu, Shipei 526

R

Ranasinghe, Damith C. 1
Rani, Nanda 505
Rauscher, Fabian 184, 303
Román, Rodrigo 423
Rossow, Christian 64
Rütschlé, Yves 43

S

Shang, Xiuwei 243
Shi, Yipeng 526
Shin, Seunghee 323

Shin, Youngjoo 283, 323
Sun, Wenju 464

T

Tefek, Utku 484

U

Unterguggenberger, Martin 303

V

van Oorschot, Paul C. 443
Vitale, Antonino 505

W

Wang, Lingyu 402
Wang, Ping 224
Wang, Yuxuan 526
Wazan, Ahmad Samer 43
Weissteiner, Hannes 204

X

Xiao, Xi 464

Y

Yan, Qiben 464
Yang, Jiahong 224
Yao, Weiping 263
Yu, Jiadi 164
Yu, Jintong 526
Yu, Nenghai 243

Z

Zhang, Chi 526
Zhang, Guimin 263
Zhang, Junqi 243
Zhang, Weiming 243
Zhang, Yuedong 342
Zhang, Ziming 361
Zhao, Yubo 526
Zhou, Yajin 361
Zhu, Yujia 342

Made in the USA
Monee, IL
03 May 2026